T0323035

The Age of Agility

THE SIOP PROFESSIONAL PRACTICE SERIES

Series Editor
Nancy T. Tippins

The Age of Agility

Building Learning Agile Leaders and Organizations

Edited by

VERONICA SCHMIDT HARVEY

AND

KENNETH P. DE MEUSE

OXFORD

UNIVERSITY PRESS

OXFORD
UNIVERSITY PRESS

Oxford University Press is a department of the University of Oxford. It furthers the University's objective of excellence in research, scholarship, and education by publishing worldwide. Oxford is a registered trade mark of Oxford University Press in the UK and certain other countries.

Published in the United States of America by Oxford University Press
198 Madison Avenue, New York, NY 10016, United States of America.

© Oxford University Press 2021

Library of Congress Cataloging-in-Publication Data
Names: Harvey, Veronica Schmidt, editor. |
De Meuse, Kenneth P. (Kenneth Paul), editor.
Title: The age of agility : building learning agile leaders and organizations /
Veronica Schmidt Harvey, PhD, Kenneth P. De Meuse, PhD (Editors).
Description: New York, NY : Oxford University Press, 2021. |
Series: Siop professional practice series |
Includes bibliographical references and index.
Identifiers: LCCN 2020039428 (print) | LCCN 2020039429 (ebook) |
ISBN 9780190085353 (hardback) | ISBN 9780190085377 (epub) |
ISBN 9780197554951
Subjects: LCSH: Leadership. | Organizational change. | Management.
Classification: LCC HD57.7 .A347 2021 (print) |
LCC HD57.7 (ebook) | DDC 658.4/092—dc23
LC record available at https://lccn.loc.gov/2020039428
LC ebook record available at https://lccn.loc.gov/2020039429

DOI: 10.1093/oso/9780190085353.001.0001

3 5 7 9 8 6 4 2

Printed by Integrated Books International, United States of America

This book is dedicated . . .

. . . To my husband John who has challenged me to stretch my boundaries, helped me develop new mindsets, shared his own leadership experiences, supported me during stressful times and believed I was capable of achieving more than I dreamed.

VSH

. . . To my wife Barb whose unconditional love and unwavering support enabled me to chase my dreams, follow my passions, and experience the world. Learning agility has provided the language to understand the impetus for this portfolio career.

KPD

Contents

SECTION I: FOUNDATIONS OF LEARNING AGILITY AND ITS RELATIONSHIP TO LEADERSHIP

SECTION II: STRATEGIES AND HABITS THAT DEVELOP LEARNING AGILITY

SECTION III: ORGANIZATIONAL PRACTICES THAT SUPPORT AND ENHANCE LEARNING AGILITY

SECTION IV: LESSONS AND APPLICATIONS

Preface

The Professional Practice Series is an integral component of the strategy of the Society for Industrial-Organizational Psychology (SIOP) to achieve its goal of being the premier professional group advancing the science and practice of the psychology of work. Over the years, the editorial boards of the Professional Practice Series have tried to determine the needs of practitioners of industrial and organizational psychology, develop book ideas to meet them, and identify editors who can execute the ideas. In some cases, the goal has been to update industrial and organizational (I-O) psychologists on a "core" I-O topic; in others, the objective has been to present a new or rapidly evolving area of research and practice. A challenge is always to find experts in those areas who are well-grounded in both research and best practices.

During my tenure as editor of the Professional Practice Series, the editorial board realized that the topic of learning agility was one of increasing interest to the I-O community and, perhaps more importantly, recognized two outstanding I-O psychologists in this field, Veronica Schmidt Harvey, PhD, & Kenneth P. De Meuse, PhD. This volume, *The Age of Agility: Building Learning Agile Leaders and Organizations*, addresses a topic of great importance to organizations, particularly with respect to identifying high-potential employees and developing leaders who are capable of managing new business challenges in a rapidly changing context. The editors of this volume blend science and practice seamlessly and provide an engaging and highly readable book.

The Age of Agility is organized into four sections. In Section I, the book begins by defining learning agility and explaining its relationship to leadership. The first five chapters cover what the construct of learning agility is, what its theoretical underpinnings are, how it can be measured, how well it predicts leadership behaviors, and what the neuroscience of learning agility is. Seven chapters that focus on the development of learning agility comprise Section II. The first of these chapters offers a heuristic model. Then, four chapters in this section present different approaches for its development, such as mindfulness, getting out of one's comfort zone, feedback seeking, and reflection. Two more chapters discuss a developmental process for acquiring learning agility and the role of resilience in the face of failure. Section III explores the talent management practices that support the development of learning agile organizations. Various chapters provide a framework for building learning agility, evidence-based advice on becoming a learning agile organization, and creating a psychologically safe work environment to support learning agility. The two chapters that conclude this section focus on how the development of learning agility fits into the bigger picture of leadership development. The final portion of the book, Section IV, summarizes the key messages and lessons learned in the preceding chapters and highlights the research gaps that exist. The remainder of the book presents 10 real-world case studies. Written by practitioners, these case studies provide valuable lessons on how learning agility has been introduced and applied by various private and public organizations from around the globe.

A book of 20 chapters and 10 case studies is a significant undertaking for many people. The editorial board of the Professional Practice Series and I are grateful for the work of all involved. Veronica and Ken have done an outstanding job in structuring the book, identifying authors, and editing content. The authors of these chapters are clearly experts in various aspects of learning agility and have consolidated their experiences and research into highly readable and useful chapters. A particular word of gratitude goes to the authors of the cases studies, who have candidly shared their own experiences and lessons learned. Last but not least, the continued partnership of Oxford University Press has helped the Professional Practice Series inform a broad audience on timely topics.

I am confident this book will advance practice and science in the area of learning agility and help achieve SIOP's goal. I hope you will enjoy it and find it as useful as I have.

Nancy T. Tippins
Series Editor
2013–2019
May 2020

Backword

A Backward Glance From the Founders
of Learning Agility

The year was 1988, and we were trying to get a handle on this sort of "X factor," now called "learning agility." A group of us were conducting a research project with four corporate sponsors, including PepsiCo, where Bob was head of talent management at the time.* The question we posed seemed clear from our previous studies on male and female executives and summarized in the books, *The Lessons of Experience* (McCall, Lombardo, & Morrison, 1988) and *Breaking the Glass Ceiling* (Morrison, White, Van Velsor, & the Center for Creative Leadership, 1987). We knew that some executives gain skills and insights from experience and others, just as bright and just as accomplished, gain little. By then, we also knew about the dynamics of careers—what derails the promising, the role of luck, the power of first-time assignments, and all the other factors that can lead to derailment or success. What we couldn't understand was: "How do you learn what to do when you don't know what to do?"

The data were clear. Some people thrive in first time situations and many, most really, reach into their bag of tricks and pull out something that worked in the past. Mike remembers being captivated by a fascinating failed experiment. A simulation of a beer company was designed so that no matter what you did, nothing worked. The goal was to spur inventiveness. Unfortunately, the experiment was abandoned when no group came up with a new strategy, simply reaching into its bag of old tricks to pull out a past solution. And he thought, this experiment was filled with managers—bright, motivated people! Whatever inclination they must have possessed to tackle the new and

---

* Mike, Kerry Bunker, and Amy Webb were the leaders of learning from experience research at the Center for Creative Leadership (CCL) at that time.

different must have somehow been discouraged and eliminated in service to the tried and true.

Organizations emphasize "more of the same" jobs—a little more of this, a twist on that. The new and different is avoided until it cannot be. So, learn to skate and keep skating harder and better. This works great until you have to skate backward and jump some obstacles. We thought if we prompted high potentials to go beyond the obvious constrictions many organizations place on them, we could learn the nature of learning new behaviors, whether they be strategic, self-development, intellectual learning, or nuts-and-bolts skills.

And many did go beyond the constrictions. One memorable guy overcame his controlling nature sufficiently to have his kids plan the family vacation. Another went from pariah to friend with colleagues. But, there were others, including one who insisted on underlining known facts and telling us that forming buckets of thematically coherent but conflicting facts and assertions was, well, just wrong. Kerry Bunker (one of the CCL leaders), challenged high potentials and high performers one by one to pick an event in a mythical track meet he was hosting later that day. Not a person picked anything slightly different or slightly stretching. Most of them had learned to play it safe and not risk much.

We concluded that learning from first-time experiences is not much sought after, is tough, and, as one manager put it, "Let's see—I should pick something I don't know how to do with people who don't think I can do it and see if I can learn something from nothing. Can't wait." No wonder we called these challenges going-against-the-grain (GAG) assignments. But, this is the nature of growth. None of us comes out of school knowing how to manage older or balky employees, start units from scratch, fix the broken, successfully navigate wild periods of growth, and so on.

The development of those who lead well is the land of the first time and the risky. Success and failure will be obvious. In fact, they are the number 1 reason managers and executives cite an experience as developmental. That holds true for challenging jobs, courses ("I have got to know this right now to succeed at a project"), overcoming a failure, or learning from a bad boss. Adversity and diversity can lead to growth.

As our interest was and is in what might help someone on Monday, we (Bob and Mike) set out to capture what additional learning tactics helped when you didn't know what to do. We already had an initial list from the CCL male and female executive studies. In addition, we used the findings from the study previously mentioned with four corporate sponsors, as well as about 10 additional samples we collected while Mike was at CCL or that we conducted when we started our firm, Lominger. (For those of you whom might not know, Lominger is a combination of our two last names, "Lom"-bardo and Eich-"inger.")

We also looked at learning style research to find allied findings along with studies of resourcefulness, flexibility, resilience, openness, curiosity, grit, persistence, adaptiveness, accommodation, learning on the fly, fluid intelligence, and how learning new things creates new neural pathways. As few used the same terms and many of the learning tactics were vague, we decided we needed a new name and a new start. We picked the name *learning agility*. Since then, there has been robust academic debate both pro and con and much definitional enhancement and measurement. Now, the concept of learning agility, the 70–20–10 rule of development, and the 9-box talent management matrix are ubiquitous in most large companies.

From all of these sources, we came up with a list of about 150 behaviors we believed either characterized the behavior or were characteristics of those individuals who are willing to go against the grain. We measured these and reported them in a journal article published in *Human Resource Management* (Lombardo & Eichinger, 2000). Both of us felt that try as we had to get others to articulate how they learned these new behaviors and skills, very few people had any idea. What we usually heard was *what* people learned, not *how*. So, we were heartened that our results hung together in coherent factors and that those with higher learning agility are higher in potential and perform better once promoted.

More importantly, learning agility has turned out to be as egalitarian as we hoped it would be. Not gender, level, or age had an effect. An independent study showed that learning agility was not a surrogate for intelligence or personality factors (Connolly & Viswesvaran, 2002). Learning agility scores were essentially unrelated to IQ or personality variables and accounted for all the significant relationships with performance and potential. It was clearly, but not easily, developable. Certain personal characteristics, such as an interest and facility in abstraction and conceptualization, were necessary to complete the picture—so not just learning tactics, not just personal characteristics, but both.

The one regret we have is using the term *learning*. Learning agility is not highly correlated with cognitive horsepower or IQ. That has been difficult to explain. It is more related to conceptual complexity and pattern recognition. It is *closer to broad perspective, openness to change, and changing one's behavior without poisoning relationships with others.* In hindsight, maybe we should have called it "adaptiveness."

Regardless of terms, our idea turned out to be a thing unto itself, not something dragged along by intelligence or a Big Five personality factor. Of course, IQ and the Big 5 matter. We had just tapped into an additional source of variance that added to their ground-floor importance. Our view was and is that if IQ and a certain Big 5 profile get you in the game, learning agility is essential to stay in the game across time.

What we find most satisfying is that 62% of companies surveyed use the concept basically as we intended, as a measure of potential and of performance in first-time, high-stakes situations (*"Potential: Who's Doing What,"* 2015). Learning agility is indeed necessary for the long run.

Michael M. Lombardo, PhD

Cofounder of Lominger

Robert W. Eichinger, PhD

TeamTelligent, LLC and Cofounder of Lominger

References

Connolly, J. A., & Viswesvaran, C. (2002, April). *Assessing the construct validity of a measure of learning agility.* Paper presented at the Society for Industrial and Organizational Psychology Conference, Toronto, Ontario, Canada.

Lombardo, M. M., & Eichinger, R. W. (2000). High potentials as high learners. *Human Resource Management, 39,* 321–330.

McCall, M. W., Jr., Lombardo, M. M., & Morrison, A. M. (1988). *The lessons of experience: How successful executives develop on the job.* New York, NY: Free Press.

Morrison, A. M., White, R. P., Van Velsor, E., & the Center for Creative Leadership. (1987). *Breaking the glass ceiling: Can women reach the top of America's largest corporations?* Reading, MA: Addison-Wesley.

"Potential: Who's doing what to identify their best?" (2015). New York, NY: New Talent Management Network.

Foreword

As you look around while reading this introduction, think about what is "new" in your life during the last 10 (or pick a number) years. What is new about the place (house, office, hotel, or airplane) where you are reading this? What is new about your work—the industry and who your customers, investors, and competitors are and what they expect? How and where you are working with technology and the digital age? What about the pace of change that determines what challenges you are working on and how long you have to solve them?

I am writing this Foreword in the middle of the coronavirus pandemic. During the last 30 days—not months, not weeks, but days!—My personal life and professional agenda have been completely upended. While there may not be sudden global shocks as dramatic as the coronavirus, there are ever-increasing and unpredictable changes that disrupt our personal and work lives. We have lived for decades in a world marked by volatility, uncertainty, complexity, and ambiguity (i.e., the legacy VUCA mantra from the 1980s describing how to define the context of work). Thirty years later, the VUCA model is operating on steroids as the intensity and time horizon for change increases (Peterson, Chapter 13). Yet in this hyper-VUCA world, making sense of the complex is increasingly important (Heaton, Chapter 17). The half-life of what we know and what we should do is changing dramatically. As a professor and advisor, I now need to have 25% to 30% new ideas every 12 to 18 months. (Oh! How I long for yesterday.) A few days ago, I was working with a group of college students and I asked them to "email me questions." Gasp! Guffaws! Snickers! How out of date can I be?!!

Context for Learning Agility

I have proposed that "content is king" but "context is the kingdom." The content (strategies and design of an organization and competencies of leaders and individuals) required by business leaders must adapt to the context in which the content occurs. And, the business context is surrounded by unparalleled velocity and intensity of change. In this face of change, so many respected companies are gone (Amoco, Arthur Andersen, Bear Sterns, Blockbuster, EF Hutton, Kodak, General Foods, Netscape, Sears, Toys-R-Us; De Meuse & Harvey, Chapter 1). Much of the fuel for this hyperchanged world is technology like artificial intelligence, cloud computing, machine learning, and robots, which creates digital information asymmetries that ever so rapidly change the work context.

So, how does a company respond to a context of hyperchange? The words describing this response are many: transform, innovate, adapt, flex, change, reinvent, re-engineer, shift, pivot, renew, and so forth. In this outstanding anthology, the term *learning agility* captures the essence of these divergent ideas.

Content: Definition and Relevance of Learning Agility

The two words—*learning* and *agility*—combine to be very relevant. Agility is the capacity to adapt and change. Some organizations can do so as they experiment, benchmark, and continuously improve. Learning turns those change events into sustainable patterns. Agility without learning is chaotic, unfocused, and seemingly random events and activities. Learning without change is running faster in place. Combined, learning agility is the ability to create a future, anticipate opportunity, quickly respond, and learn always (see the evolution of learning agility by Lombardo and Eichinger in the Backword).

Stakeholders for Learning Agility Application

The underlying principles of learning agility apply to strategy, organization, leaders, and individuals as each stakeholder creates a future, anticipates opportunity, reacts quickly, and learns always. Learning agility and adapting to changing external circumstances have spawned a tsunami of assessments and measurements (Boyce & Boyce, Chapter 4), tools, and interventions (De Meuse & Harvey, Chapter 1). And, it matters. Learning agile strategies aggressively shape market opportunities more than simple seek–to-grow market share. Learning agile organizations adapt quickly to new market conditions and inspire entire industries to change and evolve. Learning agile leaders make proactive choices that position their firms to win in the marketplace. Learning agile leaders progress in their personal careers by saying and doing things that create a future for their organizations, their employees, and themselves.

Strategic Learning Agility

Strategic learning agility differentiates winning business strategies as they pivot from

- industry expert to industry leader;
- market share to market opportunity;
- who we are to how customers respond to us;
- penetrating existing markets to creating new and uncontested markets;
- beating competition to redefining competition; and
- generating blueprints for action to crafting dynamic processes for agile choices.

Strategic learning agility is less about what an organization does to win now and more about how it builds capacity for continual strategic change. It means continually and rapidly updating choices about where to play and how to win. This means stepping into an unknown space rather than penetrating existing spaces (McCauley & Yost, Chapter 8). Strategic learning agility also requires understanding the business context and environment and anticipating future stakeholder wants and needs. For example, strategically seeking out customer-focused insights leads to co-created products and services.

Organization Learning Agility

Organizational learning agility enables the organization to anticipate and rapidly respond to dynamic market conditions. More agile organizations win in the customer and investor marketplaces (Ruyle, De Meuse, & Hughley, Chapter 14; Leisten & Donohue, Chapter 16). Organizations that cannot change as fast as their external demands quickly fall behind, never catching up. Rapid response to future customer opportunities and fast innovation of products, services, and business models differentiate organizations that win.

Organizational learning agility is enhanced when organizations (a) create autonomous, market-focused teams that can move rapidly to create and define new opportunities; (b) allow values to evolve to match the desired culture and firm identity; and (c) discipline themselves to make change happen fast. These organizations continually experiment, improve, remove boundaries between internal silos, and interact intimately with customers outside the four walls of the company. They create networks or ecosystems for improvement. We have called this new organizational species a *market-oriented ecosystem* (MOE) and identified six principles for its operation in our book, *Reinventing the Organization* (Yeung & Ulrich, 2019).

Leadership Agility

Leadership learning agility matters because leaders are often the bridge between the organization and individuals throughout the organization. How leaders think and act creates an organizational culture and models accepted individual behavior. Learning agility has been found to be one of the key indicators of effective leadership at every level (Dai & De Meuse, Chapter 2).

Nearly every chapter in this anthology identifies the importance and actions for leadership learning agility, which becomes a core differentiating competence of effective leaders at all levels and across industries (Dai & De Meuse, Chapter 2). High-potential leaders can be identified based on their learning agility (Church, Chapter 3), which can be defined, assessed, and improved to create a leadership pipeline. Learning agility applies to many leadership processes around people, change, cognition, and results (Heslin & Mellish, Chapter 11). Learning agile leaders seek opportunities to do more than rehash the past, create more than replicate, and inspire others to be their best selves.

Individual Agility

Individual learning agility is the ability and internal motivation of people to learn and grow. More agile individuals find personal well-being and deliver better business results. Individual learning agility is the competence of an employee to learn and grow as a leader—in formal positions of supervision or informal roles on a team. It becomes a basic element of talent management

(Church, Chapter 3). Individuals who cannot change as fast as their work demands have limited impact. Individual learning agility is a mindset and mindfulness (e.g., growth mindset, curiosity) and a set of skills (e.g., asking questions, taking appropriate risks). Individual learning agility applies not only in work settings, but also in most areas our lives—family, community, church, hobbies, and day-to-day living (McKenna & Minaker, Chapter 18).

Individual learning agility comes in part from predisposition (nature and DNA), which are part of an individual's neurology (Ruyle, Chapter 5). It implies hiring individuals who are naturally agile (learn, change, and act quickly). But individual learning agility also can be enhanced by learning how to ask questions; take risks; experiment with new ideas and actions; auditing what worked and what did not; observing others; being resilient (Yost, DeHaas, & Allison, Chapter 12); embarking on stretch assignments (McCauley & Yost, Chapter 8); receiving feedback (Adler & Neiman, Chapter 9); and so forth. Individual learning agility alters the employee–employer contract from predictability to learning (De Meuse & Harvey, Chapter 1).

Increasing and Sustaining Learning Agility

Learning agility is not just an inherited DNA or predisposition, but can be learned as a set of intentional behaviors (Harvey & Prager, Chapter 6). The best learning comes from structured experiences that offer new challenges where people are stretched to improve, then encouraged to practice reflection to learn (Anseel & Ong, Chapter 10). For example, it has been shown that mindfulness training and techniques enhance well-being and improve productivity through increasing learning (Lee, Chapter 7).

Institutionalizing learning agility for all four stakeholders (strategy, organization, leadership, and individual) often comes from wisely deploying human resource practices around people, performance, information, and work. People can be hired, promoted, and trained to signal and encourage organizational and personal agility (De Meuse & Harvey, Chapter 1). Learning agility can become a behavioral factor in talent choices (Church, Chapter 3). An executive told me once, "If I put the right person in the right place at the right time, I don't have to worry about strategy because it will happen." Putting learning agile employees and leaders into key roles fosters strategic, organization, and individual agility.

Performance management systems and rewards can be aligned to agility or the ability to change and adapt. Financial incentives can be predicated on agility skills like learning and change. Nonfinancial rewards can signal the importance of agility also. In one company, when it held the "Top 100" leaders meeting, they invited 10 employees into this leadership pool not by title but by recent contribution. As they introduced these employees to this important nonfinancial reward, they added that, "Five of these agile (or innovative or change or learning) employees are here because they succeeded in their initiatives; the other five failed but focused on the right priorities, and their lessons learned will be valuable going ahead." A performance management process focused on feedback can help employees recognize the learning that they can achieve (Adler & Neiman, Chapter 9).

Information can be shared about successful change efforts to illustrate both successful and unsuccessful learning. The "after action review" logic has become standard in many companies today, ensuring that lessons learned from one setting can be generalized across boundaries of time and space to other settings.

Finally, work can be organized to foster learning agility. As previously stated, learning agile firms are increasingly creating high-performing teams who focus on market opportunities. Such firms also allow those autonomous teams to act independently to accomplish their goals quickly. But agile organizations go further to make sure that the independent teams are connected to other teams. The connection of independent teams into interdependent ecosystems institutionalizes agility.

Conclusion

Each chapter in this incredible collection of essays is a masterpiece replete with theories and ideas, research and evidence, and numerous tools and action items. Each chapter couples academic rigor with real-world relevance. Megakudos to each author and to Veronica and Ken for their tireless work in organizing and editing this neoclassic compendium that captures the state of learning agility and moves it forward. Collectively, the science and practice of learning agility has evolved from some clever observations to elegant theory to rigorous science to shaping the world around us (Lombardo & Eichinger, Backword).

My attempt to capture this incredibly complex learning agility discipline is summarized in Figure 1, which captures many (though not all) of the themes

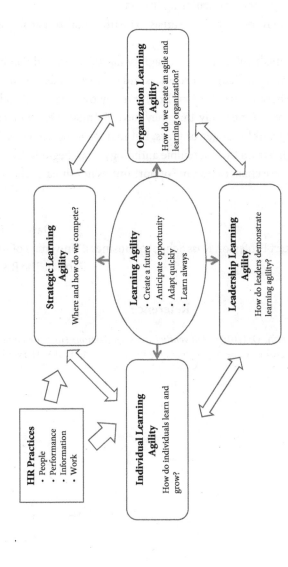

Figure 1 Overview of learning agility.

in this remarkable anthology. This taxonomic logic of learning agility can be captured as 3 fours:

- four definitions of learning agility;
- four stakeholders for learning agility; and
- four human resource practice areas to institutionalize learning agility.

Solving this Rubik's cube of learning agility has been, is, and will be an increasingly relevant challenge for scholars and business leaders alike.

To return where I started, when I observe my own personal and professional lives, I realize not only that they have dramatically changed in the last [fill in the blank] number of years, but that even more change is likely. With the insights from this incredible anthology I can begin to learn how to learn, so that these changes become opportunities not threats. The best is yet to come!

Dave Ulrich, PhD

Rensis Likert Professor, Ross School of Business, University of Michigan

Partner, The RBL Group

Reference

Yeung, A., & Ulrich, D. (2019). *Reinventing the organization: How companies can deliver radically greater value in fast-changing markets.* Boston, MA: Harvard Business Review Press.

Editors and Chapter Authors

Editors

Veronica Schmidt Harvey is founder and principal of Schmidt Harvey Consulting and supports organizations in building strong healthy leadership pipelines through assessment, coaching, and design of holistic leadership development processes. Over the course of her 30-year career she has worked with organizations across a wide range of industries implementing leadership best practices.

Early in her career, Veronica developed a passion for using science–based practices to accelerate the development of learning agility in leaders. As early as 1988, she conducted research on developing from the lessons of experience based on the data of 5,000 leaders. Since that time Veronica has been privileged to partner with over a hundred organizations and their leaders to help develop the mindsets and capabilities that will enable leaders at all levels not only to survive but also to thrive during the dynamic times we live and lead in.

Some of Veronica's most influential learning experiences have been growing up on a farm in Iowa, earning an MS in counseling psychology and PhD in industrial–organizational psychology from Iowa State University, creating a leadership development function at Pella Corporation, and successfully operating her own talent consulting business. She expanded her understanding of leadership during her 18 years serving as a partner with Aon Hewitt, a global consulting firm, assisting some of the most respected organizations in the world, such as FedEx, Bank of America, Nestle, Syngenta, Union Pacific, and many others. These experiences as well as interviewing contenders for Aon Hewitt's Top Companies for Leaders Research have provided her a unique window to some of the most learning agile leaders in the world.

Kenneth P. De Meuse (Ken) is founder and president of the De Meuse Leadership Group LLC, a global network of more than 250 coaches certified on the *TALENT×7° Assessment*. The firm specializes in leader identification, executive coaching, and research on high-potential talent. Ken is a global thought leader on the assessment and development of leadership and has presented his research on learning agility, leadership competencies, and succession planning at many professional conferences and meetings around the world. His 2010 journal article on learning agility is considered the first scholarly publication on the construct and laid the foundation for its scientific exploration.

Prior to establishing the De Meuse Leadership Group, he was executive vice president of Research and Product Development at Tercon Consulting, a global consulting firm headquartered in Washington, D.C. He also was vice president of global research at Korn Ferry International for 6 years. In addition, he was on the faculties of Iowa State University and the University of Wisconsin. He has published more than 50 peer-reviewed journal articles and authored 7 books.

Ken earned his PhD in industrial–organizational psychology from the University of Tennessee and his master's degree in psychology from the University of Nebraska. In acknowledgment for his contributions to the science and practice of talent management, he was elected Fellow in the American Psychological Association, the Society for Industrial and Organizational Psychology (SIOP), and the Society of Consulting Psychology.

Chapter Authors

Seymour Adler, PhD, industrial–organizational psychology, New York University, is partner and global leader of the Leadership Assessment and Development practice at Kincentric. For over 40 years, he has consulted for Fortune 500 companies and public agencies on issues of talent assessment and development and has contributed widely to the academic and professional literatures. He is the 2019 recipient of SIOP's Award for Distinguished Professional Contributions to the field.

Mackenzie Allison, MA, is a consultant with Avanade and a doctoral candidate in the industrial–organizational psychology program at Seattle Pacific University. She is passionate about studying resilience and resilience-building strategies. Research endeavors include leaders who are catalysts for the people they lead, how leader language affects the behavior of others, and investigating how leadership operates in complex adaptive systems.

Frederik Anseel is professor of management and associate dean of research at UNSW Business School Sydney. Previously, he held academic appointments at King's College London, Bocconi University, Essec Business School, and Ghent University. His research examines how people learn from experience and has been published in leading journals, such as *Journal of Applied Psychology* and *Psychological Science*. Frederik Anseel currently serves as the president of the European Association of Work and Organizational Psychology.

Anthony S. Boyce is a principal research scientist at Amazon.com, where he helps set and execute global talent assessment strategy. Previously, Tony was a partner in Aon's Assessment Solutions, where he directed development of assessment and leadership strategies, tools, and points of view to help organizations identify, develop, and retain top talent. He has been the recipient of several industry awards for his assessment research and has published several book chapters and journal articles.

Christine E. Boyce is vice president and principal consultant for Right Management and director of the ManpowerGroup Global Assessment and Analytics Center of Excellence. She has over 15 years of experience as a speaker, author, and talent assessment expert. She is ABD (all but dissertation) from the industrial–organizational psychology PhD program at SUNY Albany and was an award-winning instructor there before beginning her consulting career.

Allan H. Church is senior vice president of Global Talent Management at PepsiCo. His career has included 20 years with PepsiCo in various global talent management and organization development roles, 9 years as an external organization development consultant with Warner Burke Associates, and 3 years at IBM. He is also an adjunct professor at Teachers College, Columbia University. Allan received his PhD from Columbia University and is a SIOP, APA, APS, and SCP Fellow. In 2018, he received SIOP's Distinguished Professional Contributions award.

Guangrong Dai is senior director of research at Korn Ferry (USA). He was one of the key contributors to Korn Ferry's Leadership Architect competency library and learning agility suite of tools. These tools have been widely used in corporations around the globe. Dr. Dai received his doctoral degree in industrial–organizational psychology from Central Michigan University in 2006 and completed the executive coaching certification program at the University of St. Thomas in 2017.

CodieAnn DeHaas, MA, is a research scientist at the Center for Leadership and Strategic Thinking at the University of Washington. Her work focuses on leadership development and organizational change, with an emphasis on program assessment and evaluation. CodieAnn currently is a doctoral candidate in the industrial–organizational psychology program at Seattle Pacific University, researching resilience interventions in the workplace.

Jim Donohue is a partner in Kincentric's Leadership Assessment and Development practice and leads the Americas Consulting Group. For over 20 years, he has consulted with Fortune 500 companies and large privately held organizations on all aspects of human capital strategies, talent management practices, and executive coaching. Jim earned an MM (MBA) degree from Northwestern University and has completed additional graduate work toward a doctoral degree.

Robert W. Eichinger, PhD and SIOP Fellow. Bob has taught at several universities, been a practitioner at PepsiCo and Pillsbury, worked with the Lessons of Experience research team at CCL and cofounded and was CEO of Lominger Limited Inc. and vice chairman of the Korn Ferry Institute. He has co-created the 9-box performance potential matrix, Learning Agility, the 70–20–10 meme, assignmentology, and over 50 Leadership Architect* products and tools used in talent management globally. He is currently chief operating officer (COO) of TeamTelligent LLC.

Laura Heaton is vice president of talent development for Penske Transportation Solutions. Her work focuses on growth and development at the individual, group, function, and organization levels with an emphasis on applications of vertical development theory. She received a master's degree in organization development from Pepperdine University and completed the Advanced OD human resources management program at Columbia University Teachers College.

Peter A. Heslin is a professor of management at UNSW Business School. He is a psychologist who lives his passion for discovering and sharing useful ideas through his research, teaching, consulting, and speaking focused on the role of mindset dynamics in management, self-regulation, and career development. Since pioneering research on mindsets within organizations, Peter has developed the concept of being *in learning mode* in the service of leadership development and sustainable career success.

Charles (Chuck) W. Hughley is vice president of global human resources at Harsco Rail. Chuck has over 20 years of human capital management, strategic planning, and continuous improvement experience from both the public and private sectors. Chuck has extensive global human resources experience and has lived abroad in Hong Kong, where he led global talent management for Johnson Electric. Chuck has been an adjunct professor and was a contributing author to the *Handbook of Human Resource Management*, published by Springer International. Chuck holds two master's degrees and executive certifications from the University of Michigan and Columbia.

Kelly Jensen is the director for Walmart's Enterprise Leadership & Learning team. In her role, she provides data insights, analytics, frameworks, and strategy for building a robust talent pipeline. During her tenure with Walmart, Kelly has spent time in several strategy and talent development roles, where she focused on strategic initiatives and the upskilling of associate talent pools. She has her bachelor's degree from Olivet Nazarene University.

R. Andrew (Andy) Lee is the founder of Mindful Ethos and former chief mindfulness officer at Aetna. He is committed to enhancing individual well-being and organizational effectiveness through mindfulness and related practices. Previously, he held corporate and consulting roles in talent management, including leading enterprise-wide initiatives in talent development, career framework development, and competency modeling. Andy holds an MA in social–organizational psychology and is a certified mindfulness teacher and executive coach.

Jessie Leisten, MA, is a consultant, coach, and thought leader at Kincentric in Chicago. She is passionate about uncovering nuances that set leaders apart and driving positive impact for individuals and organizations. Her work on the Top Companies for Leaders research captures deep insights and extends her broad expertise across geographies, industries, and levels to promote tangible talent solutions for an ever-changing landscape.

Michael (Mike) M. Lombardo is cofounder of Lominger and has a long-term interest in learning agility, or learning in first-time situations, authoring an instrument with Bob Eichinger on the subject. He is also coauthor of *FYI, The Leadership Machine*, and while at the Center for Creative Leadership, *The Lessons of Experience, Benchmarks*, and *Looking Glass*.

Cynthia D. McCauley is a senior fellow at the Center for Creative Leadership, where she designs and manages R&D projects, coaches action learning teams, writes for multiple audiences, and is a frequent speaker at professional conferences. As a result of her research and applied work, she is an advocate for using on-the-job experiences as a key leader development strategy. Cynthia received a PhD in psychology from the University of Georgia.

Robert (Rob) B. McKenna was recently named among the Top 30 Most Influential I-O Psychologists and featured in *Forbes*. He is the founder and CEO of WiLD Leaders Inc., creator of the WiLD Toolkit, and previously served as chair of industrial–organizational psychology at Seattle Pacific University. Rob's research and publications all focus on intentionally preparing a generation of courageous and sacrificial leaders—whole leaders.

Leigh B. Mellish is a business psychologist and PhD candidate in management at UNSW Business School. He values the use of objective information to inform decision-making and behavior at work and enacts this value through conducting research, teaching, consulting, and speaking. His current research focuses on the careers of entrepreneurs and the interaction between personality and work environments.

Emily Minaker is a fourth-year doctoral student in industrial–organizational psychology at Seattle Pacific University. She is currently writing her dissertation on self-compassion and failure. Emily also holds a master's degree from the University of Denver in sport and performance psychology. Upon graduation, she plans to combine these two areas of study and make an impact in the field of sports.

Rachel F. Neiman holds an MS in industrial and organizational psychology and is the manager of a private charity foundation. As a consultant, Rachel has applied I-O principles to business, nonprofit, and educational environments, with a focus on employee and customer experience and well-being.

Madeline Ong is an assistant professor of management at the Hong Kong University of Science and Technology. She earned her PhD in business administration at the University of Michigan's Stephen M. Ross School of Business. Her current research interests include business ethics and leadership. Her research has been published in the *Journal of Applied Psychology* and *Organizational Behavior and Human Decision Processes*.

David B. Peterson is Chief Catalyst & Transformation Officer for 7 Paths Forward. From 2011 to 2020, he was senior director of executive coaching and leadership at Google. David has coached leaders in top organizations around the world and trained and mentored thousands of executive coaches. An innovative practitioner and thought leader for over 25 years, David is known for being on the cutting edge of the profession, challenging conventional wisdom, and exploring provocative new ideas to make development faster, better, and more rewarding for leaders and their organizations. His books include *Development FIRST* and *Leader as Coach*, with over a million copies sold.

Raphael (Rafi) Y. Prager is a senior director at Walmart. He is responsible for designing the organization's executive selection process and enterprise assessment strategy. Prior to Walmart, Rafi was a director at PepsiCo, leading efforts in external candidate selection, executive assessment and development, and competency model design. Previously Rafi held consulting roles in the talent practice within Aon's Talent Consulting organization. Rafi received his PhD in industrial–organizational psychology from the Graduate Center (CUNY).

Kim E. Ruyle, president of Inventive Talent Consulting, provides strategic talent management and organizational development consulting for leading global organizations. For more than 30 years, he has contributed to the field through frequent conference presentations, writing, and serving on numerous expert panels and editorial boards. Kim's academic credentials include three master's degrees, a PhD, and an Executive Certificate in Applied NeuroLeadership.

Lorraine Stomski is the senior vice president of enterprise leadership, learning, and performance at Walmart. She is responsible for driving the global strategy of learning, selection and assessment, succession, talent development, executive onboarding, and performance management for Walmart's 2.2 million associates. Prior to Walmart, Lorraine was the global practice leader for leadership and assessment at Aon. She has authored several articles and book chapters in the area of leadership. Lorraine received her PhD in industrial–organizational psychology from Stevens Institute of Technology.

Nancy T. Tippins, PhD is a Principal of the Nancy T. Tippins Group, LLC, where she brings more than 30 years of experience to the company where she manages teams that create strategies related to work force planning, talent acquisition, assessment, succession planning, and employee and leadership development. Active in professional affairs, she is a past president of SIOP and is also a fellow of SIOP, APA, APS, and Division 5 of APA. She also served as SIOP's Professional Practice Series Editor from 2013 to 2019.

Dave Ulrich is the Rensis Likert Professor of Business at the Ross School, University of Michigan, and a partner at the RBL Group, a consulting firm focused on helping organizations and leaders deliver value. He has published over 30 books and 200 articles/chapters that have shaped the fields of leadership to deliver results, of organizations to build capabilities, and of human resources to create value, where he is the known as the "Father of Modern HR." He has worked with over half of the Fortune 200; has numerous lifetime achievement awards for organization, leadership, and HR work; and is in the Thinkers 50 Hall of Fame.

Paul R. Yost is chair of industrial–organizational psychology at Seattle Pacific University. His research focuses on strategic talent management, leadership development, and change management. He is the coauthor of two books, *Real Time Leadership Development* and *Experience-Driven Leader Development*. Before teaching, Paul served as senior research specialist at Microsoft and manager of leadership research with the Boeing Company.

SECTION I

FOUNDATIONS OF LEARNING AGILITY AND ITS RELATIONSHIP TO LEADERSHIP

This section focuses on the importance of learning agility given the changing corporate landscape and VUCA (volatile, uncertain, complex, ambiguous) conditions of the twenty-first century. The theoretical foundation and conceptual evolution of learning agility are presented along with its relationship with other constructs. The role of learning agility in identifying future leaders is explored in-depth, including practical considerations for identifying and assessing high-potential leadership talent. A chapter critically evaluating various methods for assessing learning agility along with recommendations for future research is included. The section concludes with an exploration of the relationship between neurobiology and learning agility and how the brain's perceptions of threat directly impact learning agility.

1

Learning Agility

The DNA for Leaders and Organizations in the Twenty-First Century

Kenneth P. De Meuse and Veronica Schmidt Harvey

In a time of drastic change, it is the learners who inherit the future. The learned usually find themselves equipped to live in a world that no longer exists.

—Eric Hoffer (1898–1983), American philosopher and author

Standard Oil, General Foods, Arthur Andersen, Enron, Northwest Airlines, TWA, Pan Am, Compaq, MCI WorldCom, Woolworth's, Blockbuster, Tower Records, Borders, Paine Webber, Pets.com, Pullman Company, and the list goes on and on. Once mighty companies that dominated our landscape no longer exist today. Whether their demise was due to corporate scandal, changing technology, a merger or acquisition, financial mismanagement, or simply the survival of the fittest, these companies are gone. Clearly, "people don't listen" anymore when E.F. Hutton speaks since it is no longer talking. It will be interesting to discover if the corporate behemoths of today, such as Microsoft, Google, Amazon, Facebook, Apple, and Wal-Mart will survive during the next 50 years. Perhaps, the key lesson history has taught us is times change, and that size and dominance do not guarantee longevity. If so, dinosaurs still would be roaming Earth.

Companies—as well as animals and humans—need to adapt to prosper, which translates into leaders of those companies needing to learn, develop, and evolve. Leaders must become strategically focused, flexible, environmentally mindful, reflective, and responsive to feedback. The construct of "learning agility" is at the core of those behaviors. After all, companies are social systems at their essence (Katz & Kahn, 1978). Organizations are

Kenneth P. De Meuse and Veronica Schmidt Harvey, *Learning Agility* In: *The Age of Agility*. Edited by: Veronica Schmidt Harvey and Kenneth P. De Meuse, Oxford University Press (2021). © Oxford University Press.
DOI: 10.1093/oso/9780190085353.003.0001

composed of and led by people. If its leaders are not agile, other employees won't be agile, and the organization won't be able to adapt, thrive, or survive!

Practitioners and academicians alike agree that the proper identification and development of leaders is vital to the future success of any organization. Numerous articles and books have been written on the topic of leadership. A recent Google search of the word *leadership* yielded more than six billion (yes, billion, not million) entries. And yet, many organizations appear to be doing a poor job identifying and preparing its next generation of leaders. Every year, surveys of business leaders consistently report that having a strong leadership pipeline is one of the top problems organizations face (Bauer, 2011; Charan, 2005; Conaty & Charan, 2010; Gurdjian, Halbeisen, & Lane, 2014; Harvey, Oelbaum, & Prager, 2015; Petriglieri, 2014; Van Velsor & Leslie, 1995).

Over the years, scholars have observed that on average one half of all managers derail (Hogan, Hogan, & Kaiser, 2011), and nearly 40% of internal job moves involving high potentials end in failure (Martin & Schmidt, 2010). Researchers have found executives most often fail due to their inability to modify behaviors that were effective earlier in their careers but now cause problems—behaviors that once were nurtured, valued, and rewarded; behaviors that were shaped and molded over time and, ultimately, ingrained into their psyches. It appears that leaders who understand the necessity of behavioral change and possess the ability, willingness, and flexibility to lead based on the demands of the current situation are much more likely to be successful.

During the past two decades, a new concept has emerged to help organizations identify and develop such individuals. It is called "learning agility." Learning agility is the ability to learn quickly and then the willingness and flexibility to apply those lessons to perform well in new and challenging leadership roles (De Meuse, 2017; Lombardo & Eichinger, 2000). Perhaps, the underlying premise of learning agility was captured best in Marshall Goldsmith's advice to leaders when he cautioned them to realize that "what got you here won't get you there" (2007, p. 1). To continue down the path of success, leaders must change, adapt, grow, and develop. This capacity to learn from experience is what differentiates high potentials from other employees (De Meuse, Dai, & Hallenbeck, 2010; Eichinger & Lombardo, 2004).

The purpose of this chapter is to explore the need for "agility" at both the company level and the individual level. Initially, we investigate the changing corporate landscape. As an illustration, we track the Fortune 500 list during its 65 years of existence. When it first appeared in 1955, society was entering a period of unprecedented growth. World War II and the Korean War were over and prosperity reined. The advent of computers and the Internet during the 1980s and 1990s created landmark technological changes. Suddenly, the benefits of established supply chains, recognized production practices, loyal employees, brand-name products, and time-honored ways of doing business became an encumbrance to adjusting to the new laws of the marketplace and workplace. Disruptive forces in communication, transportation, and innovation caused a reshuffling of economies and countries. And our world grew smaller as we came to realize what it truly meant to be global. Certainly, those changes did not wane during the first two decades of the 2000s. It is interesting to view the impact on how companies appeared and disappeared from the annual Fortune 500 listings.

In the chapter, we also examine how the relationship of employees and employers has evolved and review how it has influenced the way we lead people. In addition, we investigate the emergence of learning agility as a psychological construct: a construct that is perfectly suited to capture the dynamic, evolving attributes needed to lead during these turbulent times. Finally, we identify key behaviors associated with highly learning agile leaders as well as highly agile organizations. Our goal is to set the stage for the following chapters in this book, which we called *The Age of Agility*. It is our hope that the contents of this book will assist both practitioners and academicians in their quest to understand and apply learning agility in order to identify, select, and develop leaders for the twenty-first century.

The Changing Corporate Landscape

In some ways, the era of 10-year strategic plans and 30-year work anniversary watches does not seem that long ago. Organizations were planful, proactive, and carefully mapped out their futures in great detail. Employees joined organizations, worked hard, climbed the corporate ladder, and often spent their entire careers in one company. Life was orderly, stable, and predictable. For better or worse, that world no longer exists (see Friedman, 2006).

Certainly, technology has played a huge role in altering how companies and employees work, interact, and operate. It is difficult to fathom that the Internet is less than a generation old, and the smartphone was invented roughly a decade ago. Both inventions have influenced nearly every fiber of our lives. However, many other factors have helped create this uncertain, dynamic, disorderly world we all work in today—both for organizations and for employees. The increasing role of big data and analytics, the growing number of employees who work virtually, the capability to conduct business globally, international and interdependent supply chains, the evolution of the human resources function and the emergence of talent management, the explosion of online assessments, and the proliferation of leadership coaching all have changed the global workspace in which we live.

Where once security, predictability, and order were valued, now chaos and flexibility rein. Where once jobs and the chain of command were clearly defined and fixed, now ambiguity, matrixed work environments, and constant role changes are commonplace. Where once full-time employment was the norm, it now is estimated that more than one fifth of all US workers—and even more globally—perform work under different arrangements (Cappelli & Keller, 2013). Many years ago, Kurt Lewin (1952) proposed a three-stage theory of change, involving the process of "unfreezing the old," "changing," and "refreezing the new." Today, it seems like we are in a constant state of "icy slush." By the time we freeze in the new behavior, it is time to unfreeze it, and then change anew. Consequently, the "age of stability" has given way to a new age—"the age of agility!"

The Changing Face of Companies

It is enlightening to look at the list of the Fortune 500 companies over time to understand just how volatile the workplace has become. *Fortune* magazine has measured the size of US public companies by the amount of their annual sales revenues for more than a half century. The first listing of Fortune 500 companies was published in 1955. The list was led by General Motors during that year, reporting a total revenue of $9.82 billion. In 2020, Walmart held the top position with more than $523 billion.

Most interesting is the extent to which the ranking of companies has changed over time. If we focus exclusively on the Top 10 companies on the inaugural list, none is on the 2020 list. In other words, the roster of the 20 largest companies in the United States changed completely during this 65-year period (Table 1.1). Some of this turnover is likely due to the changing methodology *Fortune* has used to track companies. From 1955 to 1994,

Table 1.1 Fortune 500 Companies

1955 (Inaugural Year)	2020 (Most Recent Year)
1. General Motors	1. Walmart
2. US Steel	2. Amazon
3. General Electric	3. ExxonMobil
4. Esmark	4. Apple
5. Chrysler	5. CVS Health
6. Armour	6. Berkshire Hathaway
7. Gulf Oil	7. UnitedHealth Group
8. Socony Mobil Oil	8. McKesson
9. DuPont	9. AT&T
10. Amoco	10. AmerisourceBergen

Note. Some listings of the 1955 Fortune 500 companies name ExxonMobil as Number 2. We did not include it on our list because the ExxonMobil merger did not occur until 1989.

only businesses in manufacturing, mining, and the energy sectors were included. Subsequently, companies in the service sector also were included. Nevertheless, a similar pattern is observed when we examine the entire list of Fortune 500 companies over time. Only 52 (10%) of the companies on the 1955 list likewise appeared on the most recent list of the Fortune 500 (Table 1.2).

A similar story unfolds across the world. The Fortune Global 500 first appeared in its current form in 1995. When we look exclusively at the Top 10 global companies, only one company (Royal Dutch Shell) continues to appear on the list in 2020 (the most recent listing). Whereas companies headquartered in Japan dominated the list in 1995, companies located in China and the United States led the list in 2020 (Table 1.3). Today, the listing of the Global 500 is much more worldwide in scope, with companies headquartered in seven different countries on it as opposed to only three countries 25 years ago.

The bottom line is it takes far more than sheer size, market share, brand recognition, and corporate muscle to remain a Fortune 500 company. It also requires more than quality products, low prices, and sound financial planning to be a great company today. What it does take is constant change, adaptation, and evolution to new environmental conditions. Technologies are fluid, consumer needs and wants change, governmental regulations come and go, competitors become more cutthroat or change completely, and employee

Table 1.2 Fortune 500 Companies Appearing on *Both* the 1955 and 2020 Listings ($N = 52$)

3M	DuPont	Merck
Abbott Laboratories	Eli Lilly	Navistar (International)
Alcoa	General Dynamics	NCR
Archer Daniels Midland	General Electric	Northrop Grumman
Boeing	General Mills	O-I Glass (Owens-Illinois)
Bristol-Myers Squibb	General Motors	Owens Corning
Campbell Soup	Goodyear Tire & Rubber	Paccar
Caterpillar	Hershey	PepsiCo
Celanese	Honeywell International	Pfizer
Chevron	Hormel Foods	Procter & Gamble
Coca-Cola	IBM	Raytheon (Technologies)
Colgate-Palmolive	International Paper	Rockwell Automation
ConocoPhillips	Johnson & Johnson	Textron
Crown Holdings	Kellogg	United States Steel
Cummins	Kimberly-Clark	Viacom (CBS)
Dana	Lear	Weyerhaeuser
Deere	Lockheed Martin	Whirlpool
		Marathon Petroleum

needs and expectations shift. Always remember that tomorrow someone will be quicker, faster, cheaper, and smarter. Size does not matter—agility does!

Several factors have contributed to the need for organizational agility during the past 65 years. Obviously, one of the primary reasons for the changes is the explosion of technology. Such companies as Google, Facebook, Apple, and Amazon are less than 50 years old. Uber, Lyft, Airbnb, Twitter, Instagram, and YouTube all are less than 15 years old. Even more impactful is the effect that technology has had on the operations of *every* company. Related to this increase of technology is the disappearance of the stable workplace. During much of the late 1980s and 1990s, organizational downsizing, corporate restructuring, and plant closings occurred (e.g., Sears, Boeing, Ford, IBM, Hewlett-Packard). No industry or employee level was immune (see De Meuse & Marks, 2003). And, obviously, when jobs disappear, employees disappear. Coworkers, mentors, and protégés go; colleagues and friends move on. Frequently, remaining employees are required to do more work, performing jobs that were accomplished by employees no longer there.

Table 1.3 Fortune Global 500 Companies

1995 (Inaugural Year)	2020 (Most Recent Year)
1. Mitsubishi: Japan	1. Walmart: USA
2. Mitsui: Japan	2. Sinopec Group: China
3. Itochu: Japan	3. State Grid: China
4. Sumitomo: Japan	4. China National Petroleum: China
5. General Motors: USA	5. Royal Dutch Shell: Netherlands
6. Marubeni: Japan	6. Saudi Aramco: Saudi Arabia
7. Ford: USA	7. Volkswagen: Germany
8. Exxon: USA	8. BP: Britain
9. Nissho Iwai: Japan	9. Amazon: USA
10. Royal Dutch Shell: Netherlands	10. Toyota: Japan

Note. Until 1989, the *Fortune Magazine* listed only non-US industrial corporations under the title "International 500," while the Fortune 500 contained and continues to contain exclusively US companies. In 1990, US companies were added to compile a truly global list of top industrial corporations as ranked by annual sales. Since its current form in 1995, the Global 500 listing also includes top financial corporations and service providers by revenue.

In addition, increases in part-time, contract, temporary, and virtual workers (which were enabled by the new technologies) added to instability in the workplace. The "traditional job" and "traditional employee" are becoming less and less prevalent. Many of our parents and grandparents followed a similar career path. They worked in the same organization, located in the same city, performing basically the same job their entire lives. Their jobs tended to be fragmented, limited in scope, relatively unskilled, and repetitive. They had regular hours of work and full employee benefits. In many ways, the workplace of today bears little resemblance to the one 30 or 40 years ago. Individuals—and organizations—who thrive in this new work world embrace those changes. Agility is becoming more and more important for success in contemporary society.

The Changing Face of the Employee–Employer Relationship

In 1956, only 1 year after the first list of the Fortune 500 companies, William H. Whyte wrote a fascinating book, *The Organization Man*. In it, he described a corporate America where an employee invested "himself" totally into "his" company, working 40–50 or more hours a week, traveling on the road whenever and wherever needed, and relocating on a moment's notice. In return, the employer provided a good job with good pay and benefits, gave annual wage increases, and offered ample opportunities for advancement. The employee gave unquestioned loyalty, and the employer granted continuous financial security. It was a so-called cradle-to-grave relationship (Rousseau, 1989).

The foundation of this type of relationship was based on mutual trust between employee and employer. Arrangements such as a "fair day's pay" for a "fair day's work" did not need to be spelled out. Each party knew and respected the other; they were in it for the long haul. Much has changed during the past six decades (De Meuse & Tornow, 1990). The former relationship of order, stability, and permanence has given way to one based largely on independence and self-reliance—in America and around the globe. Today, we live in a period of decreased job security, fewer employee benefits, and career lattices rather than ladders. We also live in an era of a greater focus on work–life balance, enhanced career mobility, and unparalleled job opportunities regardless of gender, race, or ethnicity. The work environment is weaving a new tapestry, one that is based on a fluid, diversity-oriented employment model rather than a fixed, homogeneous one. This evolving work arrangement not only requires new job roles and responsibilities but also offers fresh opportunities, for both employees and organizations (Table 1.4). However, this new work agreement likewise requires agility, for both employees and organizations.

The Changing Face of Leadership

Effective leaders, dating back to the Industrial Age, applied a directive, authoritarian—almost dictatorial—style of management. Individuals who were bestowed positions of power made all the important team and organizational decisions. For example, managers planned, organized, budgeted, directed, and evaluated all activities related to their workgroup. Employees were expected to comply with orders from the boss, not make waves, and show blind loyalty to their organization. The more fortunate employees had leaders who were paternalistic and viewed it as their role to protect those who reported to them. It was a militaristic style of supervision, rooted largely in

Table 1.4 The Old and New Employee–Employer Relationship

Employee's Responsibilities and Expectations	Employer's Responsibilities and Expectations
The Old Relationship	
• Fair day's work	• Fair day's pay
• Acceptable performance	• Continued employment
• Above-average performance	• Hierarchical advancement
• Organizational loyalty	• Job security
• Relatively stable job requirements	• Slow, modest change required
The New Relationship	
• Focus on personal needs and work–life balance	• Focus on company goals
• Responsible for own career	• Duty is corporate growth/survival
• Develop experience portfolios for advancement	• Create robust/flexible talent pools
• Seek legal protection if wronged	• Seek legal protection if wronged
• Self-reliance	• Self-reliance
• Continuous organizational changes expected	• Ongoing market/technological adjustments
• Agility	• Agility

people's experiences from World War II and the Korean and Vietnam Wars. Even the managerial nomenclature from this era suggested a relatively demeaning, controlling approach to leadership (e.g., hired hand, span of control, subordinate).

The face of leadership today is very different in most organizations (Table 1.5). Likewise, the expectations held by and for employees are equally different during the digital era. Organizations do not simply hire "hands," but brains and hearts too. Employees are expected to show initiative, accept responsibility, be flexible, communicate solutions as well as problems, and demonstrate an ability and willingness to change. The archaic militaristic paradigm fostered docile, compliant, and complacent employees. Leadership today must engage, empower, facilitate teamwork, and foster an environment of inclusion and diversity. Successful leaders have learned how to listen (as well as direct) and share decision-making. Most importantly, they must understand the appropriate skills to deploy in an ever-changing context. Once again, agility is required.

Table 1.5 The Changing Role of Leadership

Industrial Age	Digital Era
• Planning	• Delegating
• Organizing	• Facilitating
• Budgeting	• Involving
• Telling	• Listening
• Directing	• Coaching
• Judging	• Supporting
• Controlling	• Empowering
• Motivating	• Inspiring/engaging

This capacity to learn and adapt with agility is particularly critical for individuals in—and those aspiring to—leadership positions (Harvey & Donohue, 2013). As individuals traverse the leadership pipeline, new skills, competencies, and behaviors are required for success (Charan, Drotter, & Noel, 2001). Leaders must learn to abandon many former behaviors and competencies that contributed to their prior success. Simultaneously, they need to embrace and develop new ones that now are required to perform effectively. The term *learning agility* captures this ability and willingness to learn, grow, and evolve during one's career.

To help individuals develop, it should be recognized that the profession of leadership coaching likewise has changed greatly during the past couple of decades. At one time, leadership coaching was directed exclusively at managers who were derailing. It was deemed that such managers would benefit from "remedial" coaching. It often represented a last ditch effort by the organization to "save" a senior-level manager or executive before termination. Naturally, there was a stigma associated with being assigned a coach; it was a sign that the leader needed help or "fixing."

Much has changed during the past several years. Today, a majority of senior-level managers in large- and medium-size companies have a leadership coach (Zenger & Stinnett, 2006). In most cases, the services are viewed as "developmental" not "remedial." It has become a status symbol more than a stigma. The ability to talk with a specialist in the field of leadership represents a significant organizational investment in the development and growth of an important contributor to the success of the company. The concept of learning agility plays a significant role in an individual's journey into effective leadership. Indeed, learning agility not only increases survival, but also drives innovation.

The Emergence and Importance of Learning Agility

The concept of learning agility began to emerge in part as a result of the seminal book, appropriately titled, *The Lessons of Experience* by Morgan McCall, Michael Lombardo, and Ann Morrison (1988). These three researchers from the Center for Creative Leadership investigated why executives had succeeded or derailed in their careers and discovered all executives had much in common. Both groups of executives (a) were bright and ambitious, (b) had been identified as high potentials early in their careers, (c) had noteworthy records of achievement, and (d) willingly made personal and family sacrifices to advance their careers.

However, the researchers also discovered the group of executives who had derailed differed from the successful ones in three critical ways. First, the derailed executives tended to rely heavily on a narrow set of technical skills they had developed early in their careers and applied in current situations (even though it hampered their performance). Thus, their technical superiority—which was a source of success at lower levels of leadership— became a weakness as they ascended to higher levels, often resulting in overconfidence and arrogance. Second, derailed and successful executives differed in the way they dealt with mistakes. Leaders who derailed tended to be defensive about their failures, attempting to keep problems hidden while they tried to fix them, or they tended to blame others for their predicament. In contrast, those executives who were successful overwhelmingly handled failure with poise and grace. They admitted mistakes, accepted responsibility, and then attempted to correct the problems. And third, and most importantly, the derailed executives seemed unwilling or unable to change, adapt, and learn from their experiences. Frequently, they repeated the same behaviors that led to poor performance and/or previous mistakes. To the contrary, successful leaders willingly let go of old ways of doing things, experimented with new approaches and behaviors, and then latched onto the new ones that worked. It was their *willingness and ability to learn from experience* that appeared to be the major reason why those executives succeeded. Hence, the foundational elements of learning agility were identified.

Many other researchers also contributed to the origins of learning agility. For example, Beck, Cox, and Radcliff (1980) emphasized the importance of developing "learning to learn" skills as part of management education during this time. Likewise, Cynthia McCauley published a review of studies in 1986 that focused on life events in leadership development. Longitudinal studies conducted at AT&T dating back to the 1970s and 1980s reported that leaders who had been classified low on potential often were much more successful than expected when they had relevant developmental opportunities (Bray, Campbell, & Grant, 1974; Howard & Bray, 1988). Extensive research on the experiences, relationships, and practices that contribute to the development of leadership was also conducted at Honeywell during the 1980s (Schmidt, 1988).

Scholars in nearly every discipline (e.g., art, music, medicine, sports, and leadership) have observed that gaining expertise is largely the result of intentional experience and deliberate practice (Ericsson, Prietula, & Cokely, 2007)—not merely extensive practice, but mindful, intentional, and sustained effort. Skilled individuals reflect on their behaviors and then make appropriate modifications in future situations. Author Malcolm Gladwell (2008) estimated that it takes 10,000 hours of such practice before one becomes an "expert" in an area. Ironically, highly learning agile (i.e., high-potential) leaders seldom remain in a position long enough to master performance at the expert level before moving on to their next job. Organizational decision-makers should realize this is a natural outcome for leaders. Leaders do not need to become technical or functional experts (i.e., so-called high professionals). Rather, high potentials need to be exposed to new, varied situations and diverse experiences in order to develop their leadership skills. Equally important, organizational decision-makers should recognize the necessity of accelerating learning for their high-potential talent since they spend such limited time in specific roles.

The Construct of Learning Agility Takes Shape

Prior to the 1990s, most organizations classified high-potential leaders as possessing "the right stuff." This approach was popularized by the 1983 movie by the same name, which explored how test pilots were identified and the original seven astronauts were selected by NASA. The objective of most succession planning programs at the time was to look for early signs of those right stuff skills and competencies in professionals just beginning their careers.

Michael Lombardo and Robert Eichinger, the authors who coined the term *learning agility*, argued that when personal attributes are relatively stable over long periods of time (e.g., intelligence, certain personality traits), it makes sense to apply such an approach. However, they asked, "What evidence exists that a promising 25-year-old looks like a younger version of a 50-year-old successful executive?" (2000, p. 321). They surmised that if individuals learn, grow, and develop across time, comparing the leadership competencies of a 25-year-old with a 50-year-old is not very informative. From their perspective, "Identifying those who can learn to behave in new ways requires a different measurement strategy from those often employed, one that looks at the characteristics of the learning agile" (2000, p. 321). Consequently, they asserted that *learning from experience* plays a critical role with regard to how an individual demonstrates what is termed *high-potential leadership*. In a sequel to the *Lessons of Experience* book, Morgan McCall (1998) also emphasized the importance of learning from experience as the key distinction between those employees who are high potentials and those who are not.

Lombardo and Eichinger defined learning agility as "the willingness and ability to learn new competencies in order to perform under first-time, tough, or different conditions" (2000, p. 323). They posited a conceptual framework of learning agility consisting of the following four dimensions:

- **People Agility**—the degree to which people know themselves, learn from experience, treat others well, and are calm and resilient under pressure.
- **Change Agility**—the extent to which people are curious, like to experiment, are passionate about new ideas, and engage in skill-building activities.
- **Results Agility**—the level to which people achieve results, inspire others, and exhibit a personal presence that builds confidence in others.
- **Mental Agility**—the degree to which people are comfortable with complexity and ambiguity, think through problems from a unique point of view, and can explain their thinking to others.

In their 2000 study, Lombardo and Eichinger developed a multirater assessment to measure learning agility and administered it to 217 employees. They also collected supervisory ratings of "performance potential" for each of those employees and found a strong, statistically significant relationship between performance potential and each of those four dimensions of learning agility, ranging from a high of $r = 0.52$ (people agility) to a low of $r = 0.47$ (mental agility). Overall, the relationship between performance potential and the four scores of learning agility was $R^2 = 0.30$ ($p < .001$). These findings clearly reinforced the notion of an empirical linkage between learning agility and leadership potential.

Learning Agility Goes Mainstream

The number of dimensions thought to comprise learning agility, as well as the protocol used to measure it, have changed markedly during the past 20 years. Originally, learning agility was assessed by a multirater instrument called *Choices*™ (Lombardo & Eichinger, 2000). A fifth dimension—"Self-Awareness"—was added a decade later when the *viaEDGE*™ self-assessment was developed by Eichinger and his associates (see De Meuse et al., 2011). In the *Choices* multirater assessment, the concept of self-awareness was embedded in the people agility dimension.

Other conceptual frameworks and assessments have been devised during the past several years as well. For example, Ken De Meuse and his colleagues created the *TALENTx7*® *Assessment*, which postulates seven dimensions of learning agility as opposed to five (De Meuse, Lim, & Rao, 2019). The two additional dimensions of learning agility incorporated by those authors are "Environmental Mindfulness" and "Feedback Responsiveness." Warner Burke and his coauthors also developed an assessment. The *Burke Learning Agility Inventory*™ (or *BLAI*) measures nine dimensions of learning agility (Burke, Roloff, & Mitchinson, 2016). The newer assessments use different labels to identify the various dimensions due to the proprietary nature of *Choices* and *viaEDGE*. However, all of these measures appear to be capturing many of the same underlying components of the construct (Table 1.6).

During the past several years, the acceptance of learning agility as an indicator of leadership talent has increased dramatically throughout the business world. A recent survey found that learning agility was the most frequently used criterion to measure leadership potential, with 62% of the respondents citing it; cultural fit (28%), emotional intelligence (24%), personality (14%), and intelligence (13%) were identified much less often (*Potential: Who's Doing What*, 2015). Likewise, Church, Rotolo, Ginther, and Levine (2015)

Table 1.6 Dimensions of Learning Agility Measured by Three Different Assessments

viaEDGE™	TALENTx7°	BLAI
People agility	Interpersonal acumen	Collaborating Interpersonal risk-taking
Mental agility	Cognitive perspective	Flexibility
Results agility	Drive to excel	—
Change agility	Change alacrity	Experimenting Performance risk-taking
Self-awareness	Self-insight	Feedback seeking Reflecting
	Environmental mindfulness	—
	Feedback responsiveness	—
		Speed Information gathering

found that more than one half of the companies they sampled used learning agility/ability as an assessment for identifying high potentials (56%) and selecting senior executives (51%). Blog postings, media outlets, and consulting firms tout the virtues of learning agility on a daily basis. Business books likewise have extolled how vital it is to leadership performance.

Beyond the assessment of high potentials, learning agility increasingly has permeated the leadership development function. While it is not always referred to as learning agility, most leading organizations encourage leaders to expand their capacity to learn from experience. For example, the idea that leaders should develop their ability to learn from experiences (70%), others (20%), as well as through more formal processes (10%), is accepted widely in organizations (Kajewski & Madsen, 2012). Ironically, despite its common use, it remains unclear who originated the specific "70–20–10" formula or whether there is firm empirical evidence for those ratios (McCall, 2010).

Embedding the development of learning agility "habits" in leadership programs also has become common in many organizations today (e.g., Procter & Gamble, IBM, Nestle Purina, Brown-Forman, and Bank of America). For illustration, simulations and role plays have been used to help develop leaders' ability to learn more nimbly by experiencing the benefits of iterative experimentation, active feedback seeking, and purposeful reflection (Harvey & Donohue, 2013). Coaches can be also instrumental by supporting leaders in the development of specific leadership skills, such as delegation and time management, while at the same time helping them develop learning agile behaviors (e.g., strategic thinking, self-reflection, and environmental mindfulness).

The intriguing notion of possessing a "fixed" versus a "growth" mindset—and how it relates to how people learn and develop—also has contributed to the popularity of the learning agility construct during recent years. Carol Dweck observed that schoolchildren who had a fixed mindset tended to view their basic abilities such as intelligence as fixed traits (Dweck, 2006; Dweck & Leggett, 1988). Those children believed they were born with a specific (or fixed) amount, and that it is all they ever will possess. Therefore, Dweck found that performance mistakes lowered their self-confidence because they attributed the mistakes to a lack of ability (which they felt powerless to change). On the other hand, children with a growth mindset tended to view their intelligence as malleable and that it could be developed through education and hard work. Hence, those students believed mistakes stemmed from a lack of effort or acquirable skills, and that their mistakes could be corrected through perseverance. They perceived the brain (IQ) as a muscle that grows stronger with exercise. Ironically, those students perceived that failure causes learning more than success does. Dweck concluded that people with a growth mindset do not define mistakes as failure. Rather, they conceptualize them more like, "This didn't work. I'm a problem-solver. What else can I try?" (also see Dweck, 2019).

In a similar vein, Heslin, VandeWalle, and Latham (2006) found that managers who had a fixed mindset were less likely to seek or welcome feedback from their employees than were managers with a growth mindset. Those authors stated that managers with a growth mindset see themselves as works in progress and understand they need feedback to improve, whereas leaders with a fixed mindset are more likely to perceive feedback as criticism reflecting their underlying level of incompetence. Interestingly, the authors also observed executives with a fixed mindset were less likely to mentor their underlings, assuming that other people also were not capable of changing either (see also Heslin & Keating, 2017).

Defining Learning Agility

Despite this popularity, there is a lack of clarity about how learning agility relates to leadership development and leader success (De Meuse, Dai,

Swisher, Eichinger, & Lombardo, 2012; DeRue, Ashford, & Myers, 2012). There remains disagreement among scholars and practitioners alike with regard to its precise definition, how to measure it, how to develop it, and how it relates to other psychological constructs (see De Meuse, 2017). Nevertheless, the essence of the construct remains based on the foundational work of Michael Lombardo and Robert Eichinger. Most definitions of the construct assert—either explicitly or implicitly—that learning from experience is the crucial component (De Meuse, 2017; DeRue et al., 2012; Lombardo & Eichinger, 2000). Likewise, most definitions include both ability and willingness components (Burke et al., 2016; De Meuse et al., 2010; Lombardo & Eichinger, 2000). Finally, most definitions posit learning agility is most important for leadership roles.

Consequently, it seems prudent to define learning agility broadly to capture all of its complexity and nuances, recognizing there may be some loss of conceptual clarity and rigor. In addition, it is important to define learning agility in a way that it adds value to leadership selection and developmental efforts within organizations (Hezlett & Kuncel, 2012). Most scientists, as well as practitioners in consulting firms, agree on the following four points:

- Theorize learning agility as a multidimensional psychological construct;
- Conceptualize it in terms of learning from work and life experiences;
- Posit that it can be used as a key predictor of leadership potential; and
- Recommend that learning agility should be considered as an important component in leadership identification and development.

Thus, for parsimony and to capitalize on the construct's ongoing utility for leadership selection and development, we define learning agility as *the ability and willingness to learn from experience and then apply those lessons to perform well in new and challenging leadership situations* (see also De Meuse, 2017).

The Relationship of Learning Agility and Leader Success

Conceptually, the linkage between learning agility, effective adaption, and leader success is logical. However, it is important to examine what the empirical literature supports. One of the most definitive studies to examine the relationship between learning agility and high-potential leadership was conducted by Dries, Vantilborgh, and Pepermans (2012). Those researchers measured job performance and learning agility among employees in seven different organizations. They found that both performance and learning agility were statistically related to being classified as a high potential. More specifically, the authors observed high-performing employees were three times more likely to be identified as a high potential than employees with low performance. However, they found that being high in learning agility increased an employee's likelihood of being classified as a high potential by a factor of 18. They concluded that "learning agility is an overriding criterion for separating high potentials from non-high potentials" (Dries et al., 2012, p. 351).

Dai, De Meuse, and Tang (2013) conducted two separate field studies—one cross-sectional and one longitudinal—to explore the relationship between learning agility and leader success. In Study 1, the authors found learning agility was significantly related to the following two *objective* career outcomes at a large multinational consumer products corporation: (a) total compensation and (b) chief executive officer proximity. This study also observed a significant relationship between learning agility and ratings of leadership competence. In Study 2, the authors found learning agility was significantly correlated with career growth trajectory at a global pharmaceutical company. Highly learning agile individuals were promoted more often and received higher salary increases than their lower learning agile counterparts over a 10-year period. Dai and his colleagues concluded that "learning agility is crucial for leaders as they attempt to adapt to the constantly changing, complex business environment organizations face today" (2013, p. 128).

Recently, Ken De Meuse (2019) performed a meta-analysis to scientifically examine the relationship between learning agility and leadership. Meta-analysis is a statistical procedure researchers apply to combine data across multiple studies. It integrates the findings of many studies by computing a pooled estimate of the true "effect size." The statistical results of each individual study are weighted by the studies' respective sample size (see Hunter & Schmidt, 2004). In addition, statistical corrections are implemented to correct methodological errors in sampling and psychological measurement. The advantage of this approach is the aggregation of information, leading to higher statistical power and a more robust estimate than is possible from the findings derived from any one study. It enables one to scientifically derive an estimate of the actual or true relationship between learning agility and leadership in the population. The Greek lowercase letter rho (ρ) is used to depict the corrected "population" correlation coefficient.

In the meta-analysis, De Meuse (2019) investigated the empirical linkage between learning agility and both leader *performance* and leader *potential* in 20 field studies. Overall, data from a total of 4,897 employees were analyzed. The majority of participants were identified clearly as managers or executives ($n = 3,337$; 68%). Others were classified by the authors of the studies as a combination of both managers and nonmanagers ($n = 1,422$; 29%). A few participants appeared to be high-level professionals, with occupations such as engineer, law enforcement officer, and physician ($n = 138$; 3%). Twelve of the 20 studies (60%) used self-assessments of learning agility, whereas, 8 studies (40%) applied multirater approaches to evaluate learning agility. One study used a self-assessment, a multirater assessment, and an interview protocol to measure the construct. Leader success was assessed in a variety of ways. However, nearly all—18 of the 20 studies—used ratings of either current performance and/or potential as the criterion. In most cases, the immediate supervisor provided the ratings. Objective outcomes (e.g., number of promotions, average annual salary increases) were used in a few of the studies.

In total, 41 correlation coefficients were reported in the 20 field studies, ranging from a low of $r = 0.08$ to a high of $r = 0.91$. Of the 41 coefficients, 34 were statistically significant at the $p < .05$ level or higher. The overall mean correlation coefficient across all the studies was $\bar{r} = 0.47$ ($N = 10,402$, $p < .001$), indicating a very strong relationship between learning agility and the success of leaders. Thirty of the 41 correlations examined the specific link between learning agility and *leader performance*; the mean was $= 0.47$ ($n = 7,006$, $p < .001$). Eleven correlation coefficients explored the relationship between learning agility and *leader potential*; the mean coefficient was $= 0.48$ ($n = 3,396$, $p < .001$).

Subsequently, De Meuse (2019) corrected for sampling errors and unreliability of measurement in the 20 field studies to estimate the true relationship between learning agility and leader success. Once corrected, the population correlation coefficient between learning agility and leader *performance* increased to $\rho = 0.74$ and between learning agility and leader *potential* to $\rho = 0.75$. Interestingly, De Meuse (2019) also contrasted those findings with the extant literature investigating the relationship between job performance and IQ ($\rho = 0.65$) and job performance and EQ ($\rho = 0.32$ or 0.23, depending on whether EQ was measured as a series of personality traits or as a set of behaviors, respectively). Clearly, the results of this research indicated that the empirical relationship between learning agility and leader success is a very robust one.

Moving Leaders and Organizations into the Twenty-First Century

Perhaps no other factor is more important to organizational success than identifying, preparing, and developing the next generation of leaders. Similar to how DNA (deoxyribonucleic acid) carries the genetic instructions used in the functioning, growth, and reproduction of all living organisms, it can be argued that the selection and development of tomorrow's leaders is the DNA responsible for the financial performance and organizational health of a company's future.

This chapter highlights the importance of learning agility to accomplish it. Times change, and learning agility provides the genetic blueprint to enable leaders to understand those changes, embrace the new behaviors and competencies they require, and inspire others to perform in the new normal. We live in an era when stability and predictably have given way to disorder and agility. As Alvin Toffler, author of *Future Shock* (1970), had prognosticated, we have entered an age where, "The illiterate of the 21st Century will not be those who cannot read and write, but those who cannot learn, unlearn, and relearn." Effective leaders are effective learners. Successful organizations are agile ones.

While there is a rich history of learning research in psychology, dating back to the early experiments of Ivan Pavlov with salivating dogs and B. F. Skinner with maze-running rats, the construct of learning agility is more recent. It has much more to do with the application of learning and performance success than simply making a connection automatically between a stimulus and a response. Learning agility focuses on human behavior, high-level mental processing, and the transference of lessons learned in one setting and nimbly applying them in a different one. It includes experimentation, risk-taking, self-reflection, continuous improvement, mindfulness, resilience, and cognitively connecting experiences obtained in one situation to different challenges in another. During the past few years, there has been a renewed emphasis on the development of leadership and learning agility (see De Meuse, 2020; Harvey et al., 2017; Swisher, 2012).

Developing Learning Agility

Many, if not most, organizations today devote much time and effort to their succession planning efforts. Annual talent reviews, international assignments, 9-box models, mentorship programs, and executive coaching are commonplace. Yet, it is important to understand that being learning agile does not come naturally to everyone, particularly those individuals who were educated in technical disciplines (e.g., accounting, engineering, finance, law, the sciences). Employees who master expertise on a single set of skills easily can fall victim to honing those skills rather than continuing to grow and evolve in their careers.

As the term *learning agility* implies, individuals who are learning agile "learn" from their experiences and are able to apply that knowledge to future roles. Those employees possess the "agility" to alter their behaviors as situations and job role changes dictate, *letting go of old behaviors* no longer required (or that actually hamper performance) as well as *latching onto new behaviors* that now are necessary. Everyone has a certain amount of learning agility. Moreover, if one is willing and motivated, he or she can develop more of it. However, it is important for us to recognize that most behavioral changes are difficult. We have become the leaders we are due to many years of practice. Our organizations have rewarded us for this behavior. It is part of our identity. It is who we are!

We need to always remember that if behavioral changes were easy, diet books and smoking cessation programs would not be needed. Behavioral changes—both individually and organizationally—require courage, much effort, focus, discipline, determination, and perseverance. Changes make us feel awkward. We typically are not very good performing the new behaviors at first—our current behavioral patterns have become so natural, so automatic, so ingrained. Yet, unless we change such patterns, we will never grow, evolve, or develop as leaders. And, in turn, our organizations will stagnate, fall behind, and eventually die.

Unfortunately, there is no magic pill or secret formula. If changes were easy, all employees—as well as all organizations—would be dynamic, responsive, and successful. Succession plans always would identify winners and losers. There would be no such terms as "managerial derailment" or "executive derailment." The Fortune 500 lists of companies would have little turnover.

Organizational Support for Agility Learning

Organizational decision-makers have recognized the importance of learning and evolving for many years. Peter Senge introduced the concept of the "learning organization" in his 1990 classic book, *The Fifth Discipline*. He defined such organizations as those "where people continually expand their capacity to create results they truly desire, where new and expansive patterns of thinking are nurtured, where collective aspiration is set free, and where people continually learn how to learn together" (Senge, 1990, p. 3). Several other scholars have contributed to this work, which focuses more on the development of learning systems and dynamic corporate structures than on individual learning per se (e.g., Garvin, 1993; Pedler, Burgoyne, & Boydell, 1991).

There also is a long history of research on organizational change and development. Authors such as Richard Beckhard (1969), Edgar Huse (1980), and Wendell French and Cecil Bell (1973) have written textbooks, explaining how organizational strategies, structures, processes, and cultures influence employees' behaviors, attitudes, and performance levels. Change agents, OD interventions, and action learning were promoted by those authors as helping organizations adjust and grow. More recently, the OD field has expanded to focus on aligning organizations with their rapidly changing and complex business environments through organizational learning, knowledge management, and the transformation of organizational norms and values.

Learning agility and organizational change agility are highly interrelated. For example, in his book, *Leading Change*, John Kotter (1996) emphasized the importance of lifelong learning for leaders in order for them to successfully manage complex organizational changes. He described a study of 115 students from Harvard Business School's class of 1974 and how their competitive drive and strong willingness to learn helped their companies adapt to the rapidly shifting global economy.

The literature on learning organizations and organizational development highlights the importance of a number of organizational factors that influence an individual's learning agility and change. For example, bureaucratic structures, risk-averse cultures, unduly strict company policies, and micromanagement practices likely inhibit the development of learning agility. In contrast, a psychologically safe environment can foster inquiry and dialogue. It provides learning opportunities and managerial support, both keys for developing agile learners (Carmeli, Brueller, & Dutton, 2009; Edmondson,

2019; Garvin, 1993; Kerka, 1995). As leaders and organizations move into the twenty-first century, there has never been a more critical time to acknowledge the transformational power of learning agility in weathering (and embracing!) the waves of change.

The Purpose of This Book

Despite the popularity of learning agility during the past decade, there are numerous questions that still need to be answered. Some of them relate to such fundamental issues as (a) What specifically is learning agility? (b) How many facets or dimensions does it have? (c) How do we measure it? and (d) Can it be developed? Other questions are a little more nuanced. For example,

- Is learning agility genetic? If so, what aspects are fixed versus malleable?
- What are the theoretical underpinnings of the construct? How does it relate to the Big Five personality traits? Is learning agility related to intelligence? How so?
- If we assume learning agility can be developed, what specifically can individuals do to grow it? What can managers do to foster it? How can organizations encourage and support it? What do managers and organizations do to inadvertently stifle it?
- What strategies contribute the most to the velocity and flexibility of learning? Are certain strategies more or less effective for different leaders?
- Is a high amount of learning agility necessary for all jobs? If not, which ones? Why?
- Do all organizations require the same level of learning agility for their leaders? For their employees?
- Does the amount of learning agility required increase or decrease as leaders climb the organizational ladder?
- Is it true that the more learning agile your workforce is the better? Why not?
- Are older people more—or less—learning agile? Why?

Much of what we know about the construct of learning agility has been gleaned from its application by practitioners. While this knowledge is an extremely useful place to begin, our hope is to undergird this understanding with science.

Thus, the purpose of this book is to distill both the research and the practice of learning agility in three areas: (a) individual differences in learning agility, (b) leader behaviors that facilitate and inhibit the development of learning agility, and (c) organizational cultures and talent management practices that support or hamper the growth of learning agility (Figure 1.1).

Our goal is to help academicians, researchers, and all students of organizational behavior—as well as talent management professionals, managers, and executives—understand the psychological construct of learning agility and apply it effectively. Section I focuses on the construct of learning agility itself, its theoretical foundation, how to measure it, and how it can be applied as a predictor of leader performance and potential. The neuroscience of the construct and the changing nature of leadership over the years also are addressed in the chapters. Section II addresses the development of learning agility. The initial chapter of this section presents a heuristic model of the construct, followed by chapters reviewing various components of the model, such as mindfulness, getting out of one's comfort zone, feedback seeking, reflection, and resilience. A chapter examining how "being in a learning mode" (i.e., possessing a growth vs. fixed mindset) influences learning agility is presented. In Section III, organizational and talent management practices that support and enhance learning agility are reviewed. A framework for building a learning agile organization is posited as well as specific recommendations for building learning agile organizations (e.g., creating a

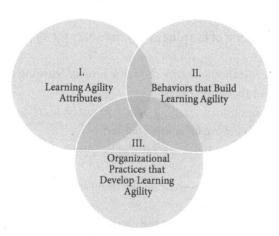

Figure 1.1　Overview of learning agility and its development.

psychological safe workplace, coaching the "whole person" as a leader) are discussed. One of the chapters reports specific characteristics of the top companies for developing learning agile leaders.

Finally, Section IV—Lessons and Applications—concludes the book with a chapter summarizing and integrating the key learnings from all the chapters. Specific implementation lessons for leaders and organizations are highlighted. Research gaps are explored. We also propose a nomonological network of variables and their interrelationships for the future study of the learning agility construct. In addition, we provide readers a series of 10 case studies examining how organizations have applied learning agility in their talent management and leadership practices. The cases are from a variety of organizations, ranging from school systems to healthcare organizations to Fortune 500 companies such as Procter & Gamble, IBM, and Johnson & Johnson. Organizations are based in the United States as well as in China and Australia. All of the case studies are written by practitioners. They identify how the concept of learning agility was introduced into their organizations, difficulties and pleasant surprises they experienced, and successes and drawbacks they observed. It is hoped those lessons will provide a roadmap of best practices for our readers.

Our overall objective of this book is to offer a status update on where learning agility is today, how to apply it successfully in business, and provide scientists future directions to research. We invite you to join us on our journey to more deeply understand—and practice—agile learning.

References

Bauer, T. N. (2011). *Onboarding new employees: Maximizing success.* Alexandria, VA: SHRM Foundation's Effective Practices Guidelines Series.

Beck, J., Cox, C., & Radcliff, P. (1980). Management education for the 1980s. In J. Beck & C. Cox (Eds.), *Advances in management education.* New York, NY: Wiley.

Beckhard, R. (1969). *Organization development: Strategies and models.* Reading, MA: Addison-Wesley.

Bray, D., Campbell, R., & Grant, D. (1974). *Formative years in business: A long-term AT&T study of managerial lives.* New York, NY: Wiley.

Burke, W. W., Roloff, K. S., & Mitchinson, A. (2016). *Learning agility: A new model and measure.* Working paper.

Cappelli, P., & Keller, J. R. (2013). Classifying work in the new economy. *Academy of Management Review, 38,* 575–596.

Carmeli, A., Brueller, D., & Dutton, J. E. (2009). Learning behaviours in the workplace: The role of high-quality interpersonal relationships and psychological safety. *Systems Research and Behavioral Science, 26*, 81–98.

Charan, R. (2005). Ending the CEO succession crisis. *Harvard Business Review, 83*(2), 72–81.

Charan, R., Drotter, S., & Noel, J. (2001). *The leadership pipeline: How to build the leadership powered company.* San Francisco, CA: Jossey-Bass.

Church, A. H., Rotolo, C. T., Ginther, N. M., & Levine, R. (2015). How are top companies designing and managing their high-potential programs? A follow-up talent management benchmark study. *Consulting Psychology Journal: Practice and Research, 67*, 17–47.

Conaty, B., & Charan, R. (2010). *The talent masters: Why smart leaders put people before numbers.* New York, NY: Crown Business.

Dai, G., De Meuse, K. P., & Tang, K. Y. (2013). The role of learning agility in executive career success: The results of two field studies. *Journal of Managerial Issues, 25*, 108–131.

De Meuse, K. P. (2017). Learning agility: Its evolution as a psychological construct and its empirical relationship to leader success. *Consulting Psychology Journal: Practice and Research, 69*, 267–295.

De Meuse, K. P. (2019). A meta-analysis of the relationship between learning agility and leader success. *Journal of Organizational Psychology, 19*, 25–34.

De Meuse, K. P. (2020). *Enhancing your learning agility: A guidebook to accompany the TALENTx7® Assessment* (2nd ed.). Minneapolis, MN: De Meuse Leadership Group.

De Meuse, K. P., Dai, G., & Hallenbeck, G. S. (2010). Learning agility: A construct whose time has come. *Consulting Psychology Journal: Practice and Research, 62*, 119–130.

De Meuse, K. P., Dai, G., Swisher, V. V., Eichinger, R. W., & Lombardo, M. M. (2012). Leadership development: Exploring, clarifying, and expanding our understanding of learning agility. *Industrial and Organizational Psychology: Perspectives on Science and Practice, 5*, 280–286.

De Meuse, K. P., Dai, G., Zewdie, S., Page, R. C., Clark, L., & Eichinger, R. W. (2011, April). *Development and validation of a self-assessment of learning agility.* Paper presented at the Society for Industrial and Organizational Psychology Conference, Chicago, IL.

De Meuse, K. P., Lim, J., & Rao, R. (2019). *The development and validation of the TALENTx7® Assessment: A psychological measure of learning agility* (3rd ed.). Shanghai, China: Leader's Gene Consulting.

De Meuse, K. P., & Marks, M. L. (2003). *Resizing the organization: Managing layoffs, divestitures, and closings.* San Francisco, CA: Jossey-Bass.

De Meuse, K. P., & Tornow, W. W. (1990). The tie that binds—Has become very, very frayed! *Human Resource Planning Journal, 13*, 203–213.

DeRue, D. S., Ashford, S. J., & Myers, C. G. (2012). Learning agility: In search of conceptual clarity and theoretical grounding. *Industrial and Organizational Psychology: Perspectives on Science and Practice, 5*, 258–279.

Dries, N., Vantilborgh, T., & Pepermans, R. (2012). The role of learning agility and career variety in the identification and development of high potential employees. *Personnel Review, 41*, 340–358.

Dweck, C. S. (2006). *Mindset: The new psychology of success.* New York, NY: Ballantine Books.

Dweck, C. S. (2019). What having a "growth mindset" actually means. *Harvard Business Review Special Issue*, Winter, pp. 26–27.

Dweck, C. S., & Leggett, E. L. (1988). A social-cognitive approach to motivation and personality. *Psychological Review, 95*, 256–273.

Edmondson, A. C. (2019). *The fearless organization: Creating psychological safety in the workplace for learning, innovation, and growth.* Hoboken, NJ: Wiley.

Eichinger, R. W., & Lombardo, M. M. (2004). Learning agility as a prime indicator of potential. *Human Resource Planning, 27*, 12–15.

Ericsson, K. A., Prietula, M. J., & Cokely, E. T. (2007). The making of an expert. *Harvard Business Review, 85*(7), 114–121.

French, W. L., & Bell, C. H. (1973). *Organization development: Behavioral science interventions for organization improvement.* Englewood Cliffs, NJ: Prentice-Hall.

Friedman, T. L. (2006). *The world is flat: A brief history of the twenty-first century.* New York, NY: Farrar, Straus, & Giroux.

Garvin, D. (1993). Building learning organizations. *Harvard Business Review, 71*(4), 78–91.

Gladwell, M. (2008). *Outliers: The story of success.* New York, NY: Little, Brown.

Goldsmith, M. (2007). *What got you here won't get you there: How successful people become even more successful.* New York, NY: Hyperion Books.

Gurdjian, P., Halbeisen, T., & Lane, K. (2014, January). Why leadership-development programs fail. *McKinsey Quarterly*, pp. 1–6.

Harvey, V. S., & Donohue, J. E. (2013). *Accelerating leadership growth: Teaching leaders how to learn* (White paper). Deerfield, IL: AonHewitt.

Harvey, V. S., Oelbaum, Y., & Prager, R. (2015). *Leadership assessment: The backbone of a strong leadership pipeline* (White paper). Deerfield, IL: AonHewitt.

Harvey, V. S., Weiss, R., Heaton, L., Lee, A., Peterson, D., & Yost, P. R. (2017, April). Innovations in leadership development: Up, down, and all around. Panel discussion at the Society for Industrial and Organizational Psychology Conference, Orlando, FL.

Heslin, P. A., & Keating, L. A. (2017). In learning mode? The role of mindsets in derailing and enabling experiential leadership development. *The Leadership Quarterly, 28*, 267–384.

Heslin, P. A., Vandewalle, D., & Latham, G. P. (2006). Keen to help? Managers' implicit person theories and their subsequent employee coaching. *Personnel Psychology, 59*, 871–902.

Hezlett, S. A., & Kuncel, N. R. (2012). Prioritizing the learning agility research agenda. *Industrial and Organizational Psychology: Perspectives on Science and Practice, 5*, 296–301.

Hogan, J., Hogan, R., & Kaiser, R. B. (2011). Management derailment. In S. Zedeck (Ed.), *American Psychological Association handbook of industrial and organizational psychology* (Vol. 3, pp. 555–575). Washington, DC: American Psychological Association.

Howard, A., & Bray, D. (1988). *Managerial lives in transition: Advancing age and changing times.* New York, NY: Guilford Press.

Hunter, J. E., & Schmidt, F. L. (2004). *Methods of meta-analysis: Correcting error and bias in research findings* (2nd ed.). Newbury Park, CA: Sage.

Huse, E. F. (1980). *Organization development and change.* St. Paul, MN: West.

Kajewski, K., & Madsen, V. (2012). *Demystifying 70:20:10* (White paper). Melbourne, Australia: Deakin University. Retrieved from https://www.deakinco.com/media-centre/white-papers/demystifying-70-20-10-1

Katz, D., & Kahn, R. L. (1978). *The social psychology of organizations* (2nd ed.). New York, NY: Wiley.

Kerka, S. (1995). The learning organization: Myths and realities. Retrieved from Eric Clearinghouse, https://files.eric.ed.gov/fulltext/ED388802.pdf

Kotter, J. P. (1996). *Leading change.* Boston, MA: Harvard Business School Press.

Lewin, K. (1952). *Field theory in social science: Selected theoretical papers by Kurt Lewin.* London, England: Tavistock.

Lombardo, M. M., & Eichinger, R. W. (2000). High potentials as high learners. *Human Resource Management, 39,* 321–330.

Martin, J., & Schmidt, C. (2010). How to keep your top talent. *Harvard Business Review, 88*(5), 2–8.

McCall, M. W., Jr. (1998). *High flyers: Developing the next generation of leaders.* Boston, MA: Harvard Business School Press.

McCall, M. W., Jr. (2010). Recasting leadership development. *Industrial and Organizational Psychology: Perspectives on Science and Practice, 3,* 3–19.

McCall, M. W., Jr., Lombardo, M, M., & Morrison, A. M. (1988). *The lessons of experience: How successful executives develop on the job.* New York, NY: Free Press.

McCauley, C. D. (1986). *Developmental experiences in managerial work.* Greensboro, NC: Center for Creative Leadership.

Pedler, M., Burgoyne, J., & Boydell, T. (1991). *The learning company: A strategy for sustainable development.* New York, NY: McGraw-Hill.

Petriglieri, G. (2014). There is no shortage of leaders. *Harvard Business Review Blog,* December. Retrieved from https://hbr.org/2014/12/there-is-no-shortage-of-leaders.

Potential: Who's doing what to identify their best? (2015). New York, NY: New Talent Management Network.

Rousseau, D. M. (1989). Psychological and implied contracts in organizations. *Employee Responsibilities and Rights Journal, 2,* 121–139.

Schmidt, V. J. (1988). An analysis of gender differences in experiences contributing to management development (Unpublished doctoral dissertation). Iowa State University, Ames, IA.

Senge, P. M. (1990). *The fifth discipline: The art & practice of the learning organization.* New York, NY: Random House.

Swisher, V. V. (2012). *Becoming an agile leader.* Los Angeles, CA: Korn Ferry International.

Toffler, A. (1970). *Future shock.* New York, NY: Random House.

Van Velsor, E., & Leslie, J. B. (1995). Why executives derail: Perspectives across time and culture. *Academy of Management Review, 9,* 62–72.

Whyte, W. H., Jr. (1956). *The organization man.* New York, NY: Simon & Schuster.

Zenger, J. H., & Stinnett, K. (2006). Leadership coaching: Developing effective executives. *Chief Learning Officer, 5*(7), 44–47.

2

Learning Agility and the Changing Nature of Leadership

Implications for Theory, Research, and Practice

Guangrong Dai and Kenneth P. De Meuse

> Leadership and learning are indispensable to each other.
> —John F. Kennedy (1917–1963), 35th US president

During the past several decades, the academic literature has experienced a significant shift in the approach to leadership issues in organizations. Most of the early leadership studies focused on the research question, What does good leadership look like? To answer this question, scholars investigated personal attributes that could define effective leaders. Those qualities included traits individuals possessed (also known as the trait theory of leadership; e.g., Kenny & Zaccaro, 1983) or behaviors leaders demonstrated (also known as the behavioral theories of leadership; e.g., Bass, 1985; Fleishman & Harris, 1962). These leadership models addressed the person–job fit issue. The premise was that the specification of leadership attributes and behaviors could assist organizations in their efforts to identify leaders who would perform successfully in their leadership roles.

Recent trends in the leadership literature reveal that greater attention is being directed toward a different research question, one that is much more practical for the times we are living in today. Increasingly, leadership scholars and practitioners alike recognize the dynamic nature of person–job fit. They now are asking, How can we help individuals become *and remain* effective leaders? This new approach to leadership recognizes that person–job fit is not static, that leadership effectiveness does not have a perfect end state. Rather, individuals have to develop continuously and evolve to be successful leaders.

Guangrong Dai and Kenneth P. De Meuse, *Learning Agility and the Changing Nature of Leadership* In: *The Age of Agility.* Edited by: Veronica Schmidt Harvey and Kenneth P. De Meuse, Oxford University Press (2021). © Oxford University Press. DOI: 10.1093/oso/9780190085353.003.0002

In an age of hyperchange (Genovese, 2016), leaders frequently find themselves in new and first-time situations on a near-daily basis and are asked to play at the edge of their competence. The goal is no longer simply *identifying* what good leadership looks like, but is much more focused on leadership *development*. Now, the challenge is to help leaders continuously learn, grow, and adapt (Petrie, 2014).

And, this current approach to leadership effectiveness is very different from the traditional "situational theories of leadership" from yesteryear. For example, in Fred Fiedler's contingency theory of leadership (1967), a leader's effectiveness is contingent on how his or her leadership style matches a situation. This theory assumes leaders have a fixed leadership style. Consequently, leadership training concentrates on helping leaders understand their styles and learn how to manipulate a situation so that the two match. In Victor Vroom and Phillip Yetton's contingency model (1973), a series of seven questions are answered by the leader to determine the degree to which direct reports should be involved in decision-making. The model assumes that leaders can transition seamlessly from "autocratic" to "consultative" to using "group-based decision-making," depending on the specific needs of the situation. Likewise, Paul Hersey and Ken Blanchard (1969) introduced a situational leadership model asserting there is no single "best" style of leadership. Effective leadership is task relevant; the most successful leaders are those who adapt their leadership style to the *performance readiness* (ability and willingness) of the individual or group they are leading. Effective leadership varies, according to Hersey and Blanchard, with not only the person or group that is being influenced but also the task, job, or function that needs to be accomplished.

In contrast, the new approach to leadership emphasizes the continuous growth of a repertoire of leadership behaviors and the development of the capability to vary those behaviors to different situations. Behavioral repertoire and behavioral differentiation are the two critical enablers of behavioral flexibility. *Behavioral repertoire* refers to the portfolio of leadership behaviors a managerial leader can perform. It is the range of skills and behaviors a leader is capable of executing. *Behavioral differentiation* refers to the ability of leaders to perform flexibly and appropriately the leadership roles that they have in their behavioral repertoire, depending on the needs of the business situation. Both of them are supported by a rich literature. For instance, the feasibility of the continuous expansion of behavioral repertoire—both cognitive and social facets—is supported by the research on the growth mindset

(Dweck, 2006) and neuroplasticity (Lillard & Erisir, 2011). Similarly, the psychological mechanisms underpinning the behavioral differentiation have been well studied in the literature on mindfulness (Brown, Ryan, & Creswell, 2007; Dane, 2011; Langer, 2016).

Recent surveys have shown the increasing adoption of the learning agility concept in the business world (cf. Church, Rotolo, Ginther, & Levine, 2015). Assessment of learning agility often is associated with the identification and development of high-potential leaders (Buckner & Marberry, 2018; Dries & Pepermans, 2008). Despite its growing applications, learning agility has received mixed reactions in the academic world. A special issue of the *Industrial and Organizational Psychology* journal was dedicated to the conceptual clarity of learning agility (DeRue, Ashford, & Myers, 2012). Nevertheless, scholarly publications on learning agility remain scarce. Many researchers continue to debate its definition, question its relationship with other constructs, and doubt its incremental predictive validity over other individual attributes. Above all these concerns is the lack of a theory-based conceptualization of learning agility.

This chapter attempts to address these very foundational issues. Initially, we review the inception of this construct and point out the limitation of relying solely on upward mobility as the outcome measure for leadership success. Implications for how to gauge the effectiveness of learning agility to predict leader effectiveness and potential are examined. Subsequently, we relate learning agility to a new dimension of leadership performance that has become important in today's volatile business environment. Within this context, a theory-driven conceptualization of learning agility is proposed. This conceptual model integrates recent studies from different disciplines regarding how people grow and adapt. Finally, future research opportunities and various application issues related to learning agility are discussed.

The Inception of Learning Agility and Leadership Potential

The origins of learning agility have been reviewed in several other publications (e.g., see De Meuse, 2017; De Meuse, Dai, & Hallenbeck, 2010) as well as summarized in Chapter 1 in this book. Perhaps the common thread across all definitions and conceptualizations of learning agility and its relationship with leadership is its close ties with learning from experience. Indeed, Morgan McCall (2010) identified seven what he referred to as "sure things" about leadership. Topping the list was learning from experience. He declared that, "To the extent it is learned, leadership is learned from experience" (McCall, 2010, p. 3). However, researchers have clearly demonstrated that *all* people do not benefit equally from *all* experiences (McCall, Lombardo, & Morrison, 1988). Individual differences influence greatly how much people are involved in and can capitalize on learning experiences—hence, the birth of the concept of learning agility.

The term *learning agility* has been attributed to Michael Lombardo and Robert Eichinger. In their 2000 *Human Resource Management* journal article, these authors identified learning agility as the primary indicator of leadership potential. A few years prior to this publication, however, scholars had been exploring the idea of separating early indicators from end-state competencies regarding the assessment and identification of high-potential leaders (e.g., Briscoe & Hall, 1999; McCall, 1998; Spreitzer, McCall, & Mahoney, 1997). End-state competencies refer to the knowledge and skills leaders have developed during the course of their careers. They are competencies that leaders currently possess. It is important to recognize that end-state competencies developed during the past may not be adequate to ensure a leader will master requisite competencies for the future, particularly in highly volatile business environments. Spreitzer and her colleagues asserted, "Given that future demands may include some skills that are different from the skills valued today, the ability to learn from experience may prove to be more important in the long-run than a high rating in a currently valued competency" (1997, p. 6).

An individual is said to have *leadership potential* when he or she has the qualities to effectively perform and contribute in broader or different roles at some point in the future (Silzer & Church, 2009). Early leadership researchers often associated leadership potential with upward mobility. For example, Spreitzer et al. (1997) measured potential in terms of "the likelihood to advance." In the Lombardo and Eichinger (2000) study, "promotability" was the key indicator separating high potentials from their counterparts. Dries and Pepermans (2008) conducted in-depth interviews to investigate how high-potential programs were practiced in organizations. They found that organizations viewed high potentials as being part of an elite workforce segment expected to "advance upwardly." Many of those who had been identified as high potentials possessed the same expectation. They explicitly stated in an interview that upward mobility was a priority in their careers, with some of them aspiring to be their organization's top executive one day. Silzer and Church (2009) came to a similar observation. They surveyed 20 major corporations and found that upward mobility was the most common definition of high potential. Fully 25% of the companies defined potential as moving and effectively performing two levels above the current role; another 35% defined it as moving into top or senior management roles.

The concept of the leadership pipeline reflects this upward mobility of leadership potential (Charan, Drotter, & Noel, 2011). Many employees begin their careers as individual contributors, perform very well, get promoted, and then continue to climb the various rungs of the corporate ladder (Figure 2.1). A key goal of talent management is to be able to predict which employees have the *potential* (i.e., ability, motivation, discipline, etc.) to perform successfully in future roles in the organizational hierarchy. Obviously, when mistakes are made, there are a number of adverse organizational outcomes, and careers often derail. The construct of learning agility was introduced to help forecast who had the potential to become leaders and grow their careers through the pyramidic lens of this structure.

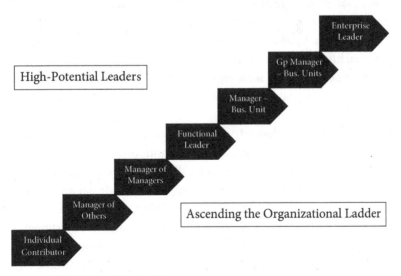

Figure 2.1 The leadership pipeline.
Adapted from Charan et al. (2011).

A New Definition of Leadership Potential in the Age of Agility

According to the Merriam-Webster online dictionary, potential means "existing in possibility." It refers to being "capable of development into actuality." Because of its future orientation, upward mobility or promotability was taken naturally as an operational definition of leadership potential. However, as the business environment becomes increasingly volatile and uncertain, promotion is not the only reason for a change in role responsibilities. Individuals often face new situations and are required to solve novel problems, even on the same job. In our current business world, change is the norm; stability is the exception. The necessity to learn and grow denotes more than simply preparing for the future, but is needed to be effective in *current* leadership roles. Therefore, in the era of hyperchange, the future is now—or, at least, closer than we think.

Consider the recent survey conducted by the World Economic Forum (2018). Survey responses from the top human resources executives in 313 global companies representing more than 15 million employees highlighted the huge demand for reskilling and upskilling. A significant shift on the frontier between humans and machines was reported. For example, the results revealed that an average of 71% of total task hours across the 12 industries covered in the survey were performed by humans during 2018, compared to 29% by machines. By 2022, the ratio was estimated to be 58% by humans and 42% by machines. Given the wave of new technologies and workplace trends disrupting businesses, the skills required to perform most jobs will shift significantly. The effect on those individuals who lead humans and machines will be dramatic.

Today, the tall, hierarchical structure of corporations with numerous levels of management and career stepping stone positions is part of a bygone era. Most companies are flatter, more decentralized, and less regimented with regard to line and staff positions. Many companies are virtual and matrixed. Many are entrepreneurial and relatively small but have a global reach. The Digital Era mandates speed, adaptability, and continuous adjustment and readjustment again. As depicted in Figure 2.2, careers have become more latticed than hierarchical for many employees (Benko & Anderson, 2010). Leadership roles are more fluid. During these times, the definition and measurement of leadership potential strictly in terms of hierarchical progression seems outdated.

Corporate Ladder
Progression

Multidimensional
Latticed Pathways

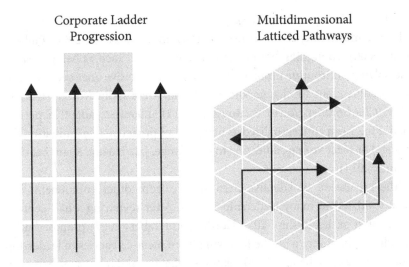

Figure 2.2 Hierarchical versus latticed career paths.
Adapted from Benko and Anderson (2010).

Leadership Potential and Adaptive Performance

Many scholars consider "adaptive performance" an important component of job performance and leadership effectiveness. More than 25 years ago, Borman and Motowidlo (1993) posited that performance was multidimensional. These authors distinguished between *task performance* and *contextual performance*. Task performance represents prescribed in-role behaviors relating to the accomplishment of tasks and activities that contribute directly to the attainment of organizational objectives. Contextual performance, in contrast, refers to behaviors that go above and beyond the prescribed role and contribute indirectly to organizational effectiveness by influencing the social environment in the workplace (e.g., altruism, volunteering). Allworth and Hesketh (1999) were among the first researchers who suggested there exists a third component of performance—*adaptive performance*—that reflects the changing nature of job requirements. The importance of separating adaptive performance from task and contextual performance also was endorsed by Campbell (1999).

Pulakos, Arad, Donovan, and Plamondon (2000) defined adaptive performance as the proficiency with which a person alters his or her behavior to meet the demands of a new task, event, situation, or environmental constraints. Many scholars have postulated that adaptive performance itself is a multidimensional construct (Griffin & Hesketh, 2003; Pulakos et al., 2000), containing both cognitive components such as being creative and solving nonroutine problems as well as noncognitive ones such as emotional adjustment to change and managing stress (Allworth & Hesketh, 1999; Charbonnier-Voirin & Roussel, 2012). Likewise, adaptive performance has been conceptualized as being either proactive (e.g., initiating the change) or reactive (e.g., adjusting to the change; J. L. Huang, Ryan, Zabel, & Palmer, 2014).

The separation of adaptive performance from other components has been validated in many leadership studies. After reviewing a half-century of research on leadership, Yukl, Gordon, and Taber (2002) proposed a hierarchical taxonomy with the following three meta-categories of leadership behaviors: (a) task behavior, (b) relations behavior, and (c) change behavior. They then created a survey and administered it to a sample of middle managers and a sample of students studying for their master's of business administration. The results from a series of confirmatory factor analyses supported their three-factor model of leadership effectiveness. Change-oriented leadership behavior clearly was distinguished from task-oriented and relationship-oriented behaviors.

One of us had access to a large ($N = 101,415$), global leadership assessment database. An exploratory factor analysis was conducted on the job characteristics measured, which yielded three factors. The first factor appears to be a proactive aspect of adaptive behavior. Sample items included the following: "Making significant change in the area for which I am responsible" and "Taking charge and implementing new initiatives." The second factor falls in the reactive category. Sample items included "Solving problems that have no obvious correct answers" and "Constantly meeting challenging time demands." And the third factor describes routine task performance. Sample items included "Relying on deep knowledge or expertise in one or a few areas to be successful" and "Following established processes for predictable outcomes." Figure 2.3 shows the mean scores across nine organizational position levels.

This figure illustrates clearly that across hierarchical levels—from individual contributors (Level 1) to top executives (Level 9)—all employees find their jobs demand more adaptive behavior than routine task performance. The difference widens as one climbs the leadership ladder, in that "routine task behaviors" decrease and "proactive adapt behaviors" increase.

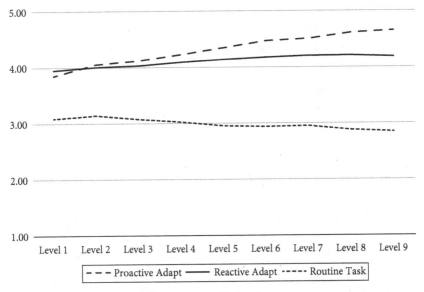

Figure 2.3 Demands on different types of behavior.

The findings suggest that potential in today's business environment appears less about upward mobility than about demonstrating adaptive leadership behavior to achieve success regardless of whether the formal positions are changed. This new view of leadership potential is consistent with today's leadership theories that emphasize empowerment, distributed power, partnership, sharing of responsibility, and collective leadership—all workplace characteristics that are needed for competing in the disruptive business environment of today (Yammarino, Salas, Serban, Shirreffs, & Shuffler, 2012).

Predicting "Adaptive" Leadership Potential

Several scholars have investigated various individual differences that allow employees to be effective under changing task conditions (e.g., Baard, Rench, & Kozlowski, 2014). The work by Pulakos and her colleagues represents one of the most systematic efforts. Their research identified eight dimensions of adaptive performance (Pulakos et al., 2000, 2002). For each of the eight dimensions, they developed the following three sets of measures: (a) past experience with a similar adaptive situation, (b) interest in working in this situation, and (c) adaptive self-efficacy. They found that the past experience with change predicted adaptive performance above and beyond cognitive ability and personality. However, the other two sets of individual differences they examined—interests and self-efficacy—failed to contribute beyond cognitive ability and personality.

The positive impact of past experience has been supported by other empirical studies as well. De Pater, Van Vianen, Bechtoldt, and Klehe (2009) found that individuals' challenging job experiences explained incremental variance in supervisory and organizational evaluations of promotability over and above current job performance and job tenure. Further, novel and challenging experiences have been observed to stimulate the development of a wide range of competencies, including business knowledge, visioning, strategic thinking, problem-solving, decision-making, change management, and interpersonal skill (DeRue & Wellman, 2009; Dragoni, Oh, Van Katwyk, & Tesluk, 2011; Dragoni, Tesluk, Russell, & Oh, 2009). In recruitment, job candidates with challenging experiences were rated by recruiters to be highly competent (Y. Huang, Chen, & Lai, 2013).

Nevertheless, it should be noted that the use of past experience to predict leadership potential has practical challenges. For one, experience is influenced by opportunity. It also relates to age and job tenure. How do we compare the experience of a recent college graduate against a middle-aged manager? How do we identify future executive leaders who are in their 20s when their experience is very limited? Using past experience to predict leadership potential also has theoretical challenges. Experience is retrospective. It reveals little about why some people have more experience with change than others. Scholars have criticized equating experience with learning (Tesluk & Jacobs, 1998). Learning and development do not automatically follow from experience; it requires reflection and a desire to learn from what has occurred (Seibert, 1996). Put simply, challenging experiences matter only to the extent individuals actually learn critical skills from those experiences. All individuals do not capitalize equally on the same challenging experience. Indeed, a challenging experience can be appraised as either developmental or hindering learning. For some people, the stress associated with the difficult experience can have a negative relationship with learning performance (LePine, LePine, & Jackson, 2004).

Several empirical studies have found that the relationship between developmental challenges and skill development was influenced by individual factors (DeRue & Wellman, 2009; Dong, Seo, & Bartol, 2014; Dragoni et al.,

2009). Learning agility is one of those factors. It can be argued that learning agility predisposes individuals toward challenging experiences (Dai & Hezlett, 2017). Likewise, it can be asserted that highly learning agile individuals are much more likely to learn from their experiences (Dai, De Meuse, & Tang, 2013). Regardless, learning agility appears important to the amount of learning and skill development that occurs.

A Theory-Based Model of Learning Agility

Although the construct of learning agility has been around for approximately 20 years and it continues to gain support in the business world, there remains confusion with regard to its scientific status. Some scholars remain skeptical about the unique nature of learning agility as a construct (cf. Wang & Beier, 2012). Others claim that there already are sufficient theoretical models of learning (e.g., double-loop learning, Argyris, 2005; four-stage experiential learning, Kolb, 1984). These scholars questioned whether adding another model actually makes a contribution to our understanding of learning and behavior. Yet, other academicians assert that learning agility suffers from conceptual ambiguity (DeRue et al., 2012). These authors declared that Lombardo and Eichinger's (2000) model of learning agility had evolved to become a "catch-all" phrase that included almost everything related to leadership effectiveness. DeRue and his colleagues (2012) recommended a much narrower conceptualization of learning agility that focused only on the cognitive aspect of leadership behavior, specifically mental processing speed and flexibility.

We agree with DeRue et al.'s concern that learning agility should not devolve into a catch-all term related to leadership effectiveness. We likewise agree with other scholars who have criticized the definitional clarity of learning agility. Nonetheless, we believe that the lack of a meaningful theoretical framework has led to this situation. It is important to understand that the early models of learning agility were empirically driven rather than theory based (e.g., Lombardo & Eichinger, 2000; Spreitzer et al., 1997). It appears that the original researchers began by writing assessment items reflecting individuals' experiential learning without going through a process of conceptualizing any theoretical framework. Consequently, those early models were derived primarily from empirical factor analyses. This approach was efficient from an instrument development perspective, but it was atheoretical.

The lack of a comprehensive theory explains the inconsistency among different researchers and practitioners in their operationalization of learning agility (see De Meuse, 2017). A theory-based conceptualization of learning agility will help reduce the operational inconsistency and allow for the accumulation and integration of research findings in the future. Further, the incorporation of the literature on adaptive leadership performance enables us to include other elements beyond those cognitive in nature (Allworth & Hesketh, 1999; Charbonnier-Voirin & Roussel, 2012). The conceptual bandwidth of learning agility should match the scope of adaptive leadership performance. While we share the concern that learning agility should not be all inclusive, we disagree with the suggestion for unjustified conceptual reduction.

Theoretical Framework of Learning Agility

Dai and De Meuse (in press) proposed a preliminary model of learning agility building on Lombardo and Eichinger's original research but grounded in theory. Lombardo and Eichinger (2000) posited that learning agility has three defining components: (a) ability to learn, (b) motivation to learn, and (c) the application of learning. The ability to learn is evidently critical to growth and development (Derry & Murphy, 1986), as is the importance of the motivation to learn. Challenging experiences can threaten our very sense of self-worth. Learning through challenging experiences demands an attitude that overcomes our natural compulsion for known and comfortable situations.

The "application of learning" is similarly an integral part of learning from experience. Saban, Killion, and Green (1994) identified "reflection-in-action" as a model of learning. Reflection-in-action occurs when we observe ourselves act out certain thoughts and behaviors in the moment, viewing what we are doing from a different perspective. The concept of reflection-in-action is similar to mindfulness in many ways. Mindfulness inhibits automaticity, allowing individuals to move from unconscious modes of information processing to more conscious ones (Brown et al., 2007). Due to this present-oriented awareness, individuals are able to respond to new and different situations in a more deliberate way rather than relying on routines or habits.

Likewise, the literature reveals that learning can occur in the following three contexts:

- cognitive (e.g., solving new problems);
- social (e.g., interacting with people from different cultural backgrounds); and
- self (e.g., understanding and renewing self-concept).

The cognitive and social aspects of learning are the most obvious. Indeed, many traditional leadership theories view leadership in terms of those two broad categories of activities—task oriented (i.e., concern for production, initiating structure) and people oriented (i.e., concern for people, consideration)—to facilitate goal accomplishment (cf. Blake & Mouton, 1964; Fleishman & Harris, 1962).

There has been a long history in the psychological literature delineating the *cognitive* and *social* aspects of learning. In fact, Hooijberg, Hunt, and Dodge (1997) postulated that leadership development is fundamentally about growing cognitive and social complexity. Cognitively complex individuals generally perform certain tasks more effectively than cognitively less complex individuals because they employ more categories to discriminate among stimuli and can perceive nuances and subtle differences. DeRue et al.'s (2012) processing speed and flexibility reinforce this cognitive aspect of learning from experience.

Leadership in many ways is a socially constructed and enacted process, involving bidirectional influences among two or more individuals (Day, Harrison, & Halpin, 2009). By default, leadership is a social interactive phenomenon, which cannot exist without a leader and one or more followers. The social embeddedness of leadership means leaders must learn to deal with growing social complexity as they assume new and different role responsibilities. Influencing without authority and overcoming social obstacles are simply some of the examples of challenging job experiences (McCauley, Ruderman, Ohlott, & Morrow, 1994). Developmental efforts that neglect the social aspects of learning represent one of the most common causes of leadership derailment (Bunker, Kram, & Ting, 2002; Hall, 2004).

The third context of learning pertains to the changing *self-concept*. We all have different mindsets to fit our roles in life, which shape how we see and interpret the world. Each mindset helps us organize our belief system and sets the foundation for our behaviors and actions. At its core, a leadership mindset is defined by how we perceive ourselves in our roles and the narratives we tell others about who we are as leaders. Today's business environment is characterized by rapidly changing strategies, business model innovations, and operational transformations. Leaders trapped in yesterday's mindset often struggle to find their place and voice in this new business world. To adapt to the disruptive landscape, leaders have to continuously reinvent themselves. Day and Harrison (2007) theorized an identity-based leadership development. According to this theory, an individual's identity evolves as a function of challenging environments. Depending on the developmental stage, one's self-concept can range from relatively simple and unsophisticated to complex and integrated. Cognitive and social complexity are grounded in and supported by self-complexity. Petrie (2014) called it "vertical development." He asserted, "At each higher level of development, adults 'make sense' of the world in more complex and inclusive ways—their minds grow 'bigger'" (p. 11).

The intersection between the three components of learning agility (i.e., motivation, ability, and application) and the three contexts of learning (i.e., cognitive, social, and self) generate nine different facets of learning agility (Figure 2.4). This approach has the advantage of more clearly defining individual attributes, which can be more precisely operationalized and measured. Further, this framework provides a clearer boundary for excluding nonessential elements from the construct of learning agility. Thus, it helps prevent learning agility from becoming a vague and "catch-all" term.

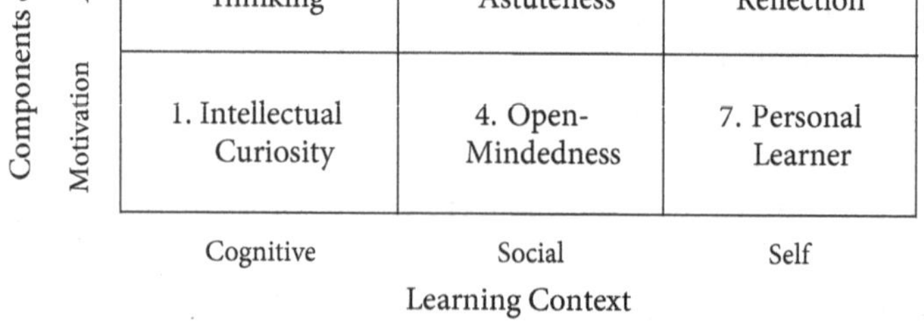

		Cognitive	Social	Self
Components of Learning Agility	Application	3. Cognitive Flexibility	6. Social Flexibility	9. Self-Regulation
	Ability	2. Unconventional Thinking	5. Social Astuteness	8. Self-Reflection
	Motivation	1. Intellectual Curiosity	4. Open-Mindedness	7. Personal Learner
		Cognitive	Social	Self
			Learning Context	

Figure 2.4 A theory-based model of learning agility.

Details of the nine facets can be found in the work of Dai and De Meuse (in press). Here are brief descriptions:

1. **Intellectual curiosity**: Intellectually adventuresome; stimulation seeking; demonstrates diverse and wide-ranging interests; eager to learn.
2. **Unconventional thinking**: Questions conventional wisdom; experiments with new ways of doing things.
3. **Cognitive flexibility**: Perceives events and situations from multiple perspectives; adjusts thinking to situations.
4. **Open-mindedness**: Accepts, supports, and embraces different points of views; suspends judgment.
5. **Social astuteness**: Socially sensitive; empathizes with others; instills confidence in others.
6. **Social flexibility**: Demonstrates role and interpersonal flexibility; picks up on social cues and quickly adjusts personal style accordingly.
7. **Personal learner**: Curious about self; demonstrates a desire to learn and understand personal purpose, values, beliefs, and motives .
8. **Self-reflection**: Open to feedback; comfortable admitting personal faults; exercises introspection.
9. **Self-regulation**: Mindful; inhibits automaticity; deliberate when thinking and behaving.

To understand the extent to which this theoretical framework captures the dimensions of learning agility measured by practitioners today, we analyzed the following four popular assessments of learning agility: (a) *viaEDGE*™, (b) *TALENTx7*®, (c) *Burke Learning Agility Inventory*™, and (d) Aon Hewett's (formerly part of Aon, now referred to as Kincentric) Accelerated Learning Model. These four instruments have been professionally designed by different talent management consulting firms and are used globally by companies to identify and develop leaders. We discovered that all four assessments measure multiple dimensions of learning agility. The three contexts of learning—cognitive, social, and self—all were reflected in the four assessments. Likewise, the three components of learning agility (motivation, ability, and application) were measured by the four instruments to various degrees (Table 2.1). Overall, we found these four existing assessments and models of learning agility mapped quite well to the proposed theoretical framework, providing initial evidence of its content validity. See Dai and De Meuse (in press) for details.

Table 2.1 Mapping the Theoretical Framework to Four Measures of Learning Agility

Facets of Learning Agility	viaEDGE Assessment	TALENTx7® Assessment	Burke Learning Agility Inventory	Accelerated Learning Model
1. Intellectual Curiosity	Mental agility	Change alacrity Drive to excel	Performance risk-taking	Seeks challenge and novelty
2. Unconventional Thinking		Cognitive perspective	Experimenting Information gathering	Lives to learn
3. Cognitive Flexibility	Change agility		Flexibility Speed	Flexibility
4. Open-Mindedness	People agility	Interpersonal acumen	Collaborating	Engages in communal learning
5. Social Astuteness			Interpersonal risk-taking	
6. Social Flexibility			Flexibility	Flexibility
7. Personal Learner	Self-awareness	Feedback responsiveness	Feedback seeking	Actively seeks feedback Takes advantage of learning opportunities
8. Self-Reflection		Self-insight	Reflecting	Takes time to reflect Gains insights from self and others
9. Self-Regulation	Results agility	Environmental mindfulness		Takes on challenge with resilience

Adapted from Dai & De Meuse, in press.

Incremental Validity of Learning Agility

In a recent meta-analysis of 20 field studies, De Meuse (2019) found a very strong relationship between learning agility and leader success. He reported that learning agility had a higher correlation with leadership performance than IQ, EQ (emotional intelligence), or job experience. However, an important question left unanswered was the degree to which learning agility predicts leadership outcomes *above and beyond* those individual attributes. If the impact of learning agility can be fully explained by other attributes frequently assessed in the employment setting, the measurement of learning agility would not be as beneficial as it initially may appear.

In an early study of 107 law enforcement employees, Connolly and Viswesvaran (2002) observed that learning agility had predicted supervisory ratings of promotability beyond what could be explained by cognitive ability and personality. This finding was replicated in a more recent study by Bedford (2011). He analyzed the data from 294 employees assessed by an executive search firm and found learning agility predicted advancement potential above cognitive ability and personality. The results from those two studies were particularly interesting since the authors employed different instruments to assess learning agility and applied different measures of leadership potential.

Likewise, in an unpublished study, Dai and De Meuse (2011) investigated the relationship between learning agility and EQ. They administered a self-assessment of learning agility, as well as a measure of EQ, to 83 district sales managers who had worked at a large pharmaceutical company for a minimum of 10 years. Subsequently, they tracked the number of promotions and salary increases each manager received during this period. Through a series of regression analyses, the authors found that learning agility accounted for a significant amount of additional variance beyond EQ when predicting promotion rate and salary increases.

The age-old cliché in psychology that "the best predictor of future behavior is past behavior" has been more and more challenged by situational volatility. For example, Bedford (2011) also found learning agility had incremental validity over job performance in predicting advancement potential. Even more persuasive evidence came from Dries, Vantilborgh, and Pepermans (2012). These authors investigated the relative importance of learning agility and past performance in high-potential identification. Their study found that *both* job performance and learning agility were highly related to high-potential classification. They observed that high performers were three times more likely to be categorized as high potentials when compared to low performers. However, the effect of learning agility was stronger. Being high in learning agility increased a person's likelihood of being recognized as a high potential 18-fold. This study also found that the positive impact of learning agility was mediated by on-the-job learning, validating the long-held belief that learning agility affects learning from experience, which in turn affects leadership success.

Overall, the extant research evidence clearly supports the incremental validity of learning agility.

Relationship With Other Individual Attributes

For the purpose of knowledge advancement and theory building, we need to understand how learning agility relates to other individual attributes. De Meuse (2017) proposed several hypotheses on the relationship between learning agility and the Big Five personality traits. This chapter proposed a new conceptual framework of learning agility. We expect that the Big Five personality traits will have differential relationships with the nine facets of learning agility in our theoretical model.

Among many personality traits, "conscientiousness" probably has received the most scholarly attention, likely due to previous research reporting its positive correlation with job performance (Barrick & Mount, 1991; Salgado, 1997). On the other hand, more recent research has provided mixed results. For instance, conscientiousness has been found to be *negatively* correlated with creativity (Reiter-Palmon, Illies, & Kobe-Cross, 2009); adaptive performance (LePine, Colquitt, & Erez, 2000). and leadership success (Boudreau, Boswell, & Judge, 2001). De Meuse (2017) hypothesized a negative correlation between conscientiousness and learning agility. Empirical data suggest this negative correlation may be due to the dependability aspect of conscientiousness. Using the same global leadership assessment database mentioned previously in this chapter, dependability was observed to be negatively correlated with learning agility ($r = -0.12$, $p < .001$) and involvement in challenging experiences ($r = -0.17, p < .001$).

Learning agility has been conceptualized as a multidimensional construct by several authors (e.g., De Meuse et al., 2010; Lombardo & Eichinger, 2000). Similar to how scholars have described adaptability as an individual difference (Baard et al., 2014), learning agility appears to be a compound construct comprising other individual attributes. But, the fundamental question is whether this compound construct is superficial or real?

Much research in personality supports the existence of compound psychological constructs. Since the establishment of the Big Five model of personality by Goldberg in 1992, the five factors (extraversion, agreeableness, conscientiousness, neuroticism, and open to experience) have been considered the most general or highest level of the hierarchy of personality traits.

Digman (1997) observed, however, a regular pattern of intercorrelations among the five factors. Through a series of factor analyses, he identified two *higher order factors* of the Big Five personality traits, provisionally labeled "Factor α" and "Factor β." Factor α was indicated primarily by the Big Five factors of agreeableness and emotional stability, as well as by some specific facets of conscientiousness (e.g., order and dependability). In contrast, Factor β was indicated by extraversion, open to experience, and achievement striving. DeYoung, Peterson, and Higgins (2002) renamed those two metatraits *stability* and *plasticity*. Stability and plasticity may reflect two fundamental human concerns: (a) the need to maintain a stable organization of psychosocial function and (b) the need to explore and incorporate novel information into that organization (DeYoung, Peterson, & Higgins, 2005).

Factor β appears to represent an individual's desire for personal growth, enlargement of self, and/or self-actualization by an adventuresome encounter with life and its attendant risks as well as by being open to all experiences, especially new ones (Digman, 1997; Mount, Barrick, Scullen, & Rounds, 2005). Research has found it to be negatively related to conformity, a tendency to comply with social expectations and the restraint of individual expression (DeYoung et al., 2002). Hirsh, DeYoung, and Peterson (2009) further observed that Factor β was positively related to engaging in a variety of behaviors associated with approach behavior and exploration. Overall, the metatraits—Factors α and β—predicated behavioral engagement beyond the Big Five traits. Thus, the findings strongly suggest that they represent substantive constructs rather than methodological or statistical artifacts.

We see a parallel between the two lines of research. Learning agility often is defined as a broad psychological construct, representing a constellation of individual attributes (De Meuse et al., 2010). In many ways, it is similar to the personality research that views Factor β or plasticity as a metatrait of a higher order than the Big Five factors in the personality hierarchal structure. Both constructs have been connected to an individual's tendency to challenge self for personal growth. The approach motivation or Factor β of personality may be the psychological mechanism underlines learning agility.

Moving Forward

It has been 20 years since Lombardo and Eichinger (2000) coined the term *learning agility*. During that period, the concept has been accepted widely in the business world. Many heads of talent management and leadership programs have grasped on to learning agility in an effort to apply science to the challenging process of forecasting leadership potential. The possibility of having an objective, quantifiable metric to make such decisions has been extremely appealing to them. Consulting firm promotions, blog postings, and anecdotal studies proclaiming the advantages of learning agility have fed into all the hype. It is easy to get captivated by headlines, such as "The Most In-Demand Business Skill of the 21st Century"; "One of the Most Important Factors in Great Leadership"; and "Learning Agility Equals Leadership Success."

The purpose of this chapter—indeed, this book—is to provide a more systematic, unbiased perspective of this construct. Certainly, several scholars have voiced their concerns previously regarding the clarity and value of learning agility. However, it is important to remember that the early researchers of the construct all were scientists in their own right (e.g., Lombardo & Eichinger, 2000; McCall et al., 1988; Spreitzer et al., 1997). Likewise, De Meuse and his colleagues who have actively promoted learning agility over the years are industrial/organizational psychologists with publication records in scholarly journals (De Meuse, 2017, 2019; De Meuse et al., 2010; De Meuse, Dai, Swisher, Eichinger, & Lombardo, 2012). Thus, the advent and progression of learning agility as a useful tool for leadership identification, selection, and development are recognized here. Nevertheless, it is time for the construct to be more clearly operationalized. A movement away from simply basing measures on dimensions emerging from factor analyses of empirical data to applying a more rigorous conceptual foundation will advance the field. Both academicians and practitioners will benefit from it.

To do this, we presented a framework of learning agility rooted in theory. It was based on the fundamental belief that learning agility is as its core "learning from experience." It was grounded in Lombardo and Eichinger's original definition, asserting that, "Learning agility is the ability and willingness to learn new competencies in order to perform under first-time, tough, or different conditions" (2000, p. 323). The three underlying components of this definition (ability, motivation, and application) were integrated into the three fundamental contexts of learning (cognitive, social, and self) to create a nine-cell theoretical model of learning agility. Those nine facets provide a conceptual foundation by which to measure the construct.

The definition and measurement of leadership potential also need to be revisited. In our complex and fast-moving world, viewing an individual's leadership potential solely in terms of climbing the rungs of the organizational ladder is myopic. Hierarchical progression is one approach for identifying potential. But, there are many other methods for one to advance his or her career in the latticed, matrixed, virtual, and global structures that characterize many organizations today. It would seem that leadership potential needs to be expanded to capture these nuances. In the following two sections, we explore some implications for both (a) the theory and research of learning agility and leadership and (b) various issues related to the application of learning agility. Our hope is to stimulate thought and move the field forward.

Implications for Theory and Research

Use Theory to Operationalize the Learning Agility Construct

Perhaps the Achilles heel of learning agility becoming an accepted construct in the psychological literature is its lack of a solid theoretical foundation. It largely is empirically derived, not theoretically grounded. This absence of theory to support the construct itself, as well as its various facets, has made learning agility vulnerable to definitional ambiguity, measurement messiness, and distinct as an important attribute of leadership success. Although the limitations have not appeared to impede its acceptance in the business world, it has greatly stifled it in the academic world.

The proposed nine-cell conceptual framework presented in this chapter may not be perfect, but it is a beginning. Future scholars should test it, then revise it as results dictate. Further, scholars can seek evidence in the literature that would reinforce the importance of adding or deleting facets in this model. For illustration, De Meuse et al. (2011) added "self-awareness" to the four-facet model proposed initially by Lombardo and Eichinger (2000). De Meuse and Feng (2015) incorporated the additional facets of "environmental mindfulness" and "feedback responsiveness" to their seven-facet model of learning agility. Those additions were based on their interpretation of the psychological literature and analysis of the data they had collected. It would be prudent for scholars to ascertain what the leadership and learning agility literature has found, then build theory as they refine the construct and develop instruments to assess it. Up to this point, the growth of the construct has been rather piecemeal. Systematic research and a theatrical foundation are required for learning agility to attain its next level of scientific acceptance.

Clearly Define the Dependent Variable

Historically, leadership potential has meant climbing the various levels in the organizational hierarchy. A common definition many companies employ is the ability to perform successfully two levels above one's current job (Silzer & Church, 2009). Today's world has made such a perspective obsolete—for several reasons. One, as organizations have become flatter, they naturally have fewer levels. Two, as organizations have become virtual and global, their fluid structure create new opportunities by which to exercise leadership (e.g., multisite project teams, virtual task forces, cross-functional committees, voluntary assignments, temporary engagements). Increasingly, leaders are placed in new situations to take on new responsibilities. It would appear that learning agility would be very relevant for identifying employees who would perform such roles effectively.

A third reason for clarifying the dependent variable of leadership potential pertains to the careers of so-called high professionals or technical experts. There is growing recognition, compensation, and organizational status for those roles in many companies—in particular, high-technology and scientific ones. Those technical and functional experts often do not manage any direct reports. The traditional career track of ascending from individual contributor to manager to C-suite executive is irrelevant to their potential value in a company. Is learning agility required for those types of jobs? Most likely not. In fact, many high professional and technical positions, such as engineer, accountant, bank teller, safety officer, mail carrier, welder, machine operator, assembly line worker, and scientist, probably perform more effectively when incumbents possess a relatively low level of learning agility. Those positions require very high attention to detail, diligently following established job procedures, strict adherence to company policies, and frequently repetitive work behaviors. Do employees performing those roles have potential? Maybe. However, it is unlikely that many of them have *leadership* potential. Do those employees need to bend and flex, learn new technologies, adapt, and grow over time to remain successful? Absolutely. However, their success may not be captured by the construct of learning agility.

In the workplace of today, defining and measuring leadership potential in terms of simply asking whether an individual has the ability to ascend the corporate ladder seems naïve. Individuals today can lead in a number of different organizational ways. Likewise, it is inappropriate to assume that all employees need learning agility because they must learn, grow, and be agile.

As scholars conduct studies trying to predict whether learning agility is related to leader success, more precision should be devoted to ascertaining the answer to, Potential for what? Learning agility pertains to leadership roles and the potential to perform successfully in those roles. Many of the roles may not appear as official management titles on an organizational chart. It also should be recognized that the roles of technical and functional expert require adapting and growing, but the learning agility construct does not seem to capture this type of learning from experience and the personal aspects required for it.

Investigate the Relationship Between Learning Agility and Other Individual Attributes

The following personal attributes come quickly to mind: (a) intelligence or IQ, (b) emotional intelligence or EQ, and (c) higher order personality factors. Preliminary evidence suggests the correlation between learning agility and IQ is quite small (Bedford, 2011; Connolly & Viswesvaran, 2002; De Meuse, Dai, & Marshall, 2012). If this is truly the case, a combination of those two employment assessments would be able to predict the success of a candidate to a very high degree (see De Meuse, 2019).

The present literature examining the relationship between learning agility and EQ is sparse. Nevertheless, the two attributes may be interrelated to a fairly high degree, given that both of them have "social" and "self" components as depicted in our theoretical model. Future researchers should continue to examine those relationships in more depth. In addition, scholars should explore the relationships between learning agility and other individual attributes, particularly the high-order personality Factors α and β described previously in this chapter. This research will help us better understand the nature of learning agility and the mechanism through which it affects leadership effectiveness.

Confirm the Development of Learning Agility

Today, leadership assessment often is used for dual purposes—selection and development (Church et al., 2015). To what extent can learning agility be developed relates to how it is defined and operationalized. If the construct is defined in terms of a meta-competency of leadership, there is much scientific evidence showing that competencies can be developed (e.g., London & Smither, 1995;

McCall & Hollenbeck, 2002). The entire practice of 360-degree assessment, feedback, and coaching is based on the premise that individuals can enhance their competencies and improve their leadership effectiveness.

The issue becomes more complex when learning agility is conceptualized as a trait-like construct because traits often are considered relatively stable. Yet, sufficient evidence has been accumulated to support the malleability of traits (Hudson & Roberts, 2014; Specht, Egloff, & Schmukle, 2011), even among people in old age (Jackson, Hill, Payne, Roberts, & Stine-Morrow, 2012; Kandler, Kornadt, Hagemeyer, & Neyer, 2014). In fact, goals to change personality traits are quite common. Tens of billions of dollars are spent each year by Americans on self-help books and programs promising to increase various personality traits (Hudson & Fraley, 2015). Direct research on the malleability of learning agility is scarce. Nevertheless, by breaking down the construct into narrowly defined dimensions, feedback and coaching on learning agility become more specific and concrete. As result, the development of learning agility seems more realistic under this new conceptualization.

Conduct Long-Term, Predictive Validation Studies

It is acknowledged that conducting longitudinal studies is difficult. Long-term studies do not fit into the short life cycle of academic tenure decisions, which require readily available research data generating ongoing publications. Neither does it mesh well with the business world, which operates on quarterly numbers. However, the results of multiyear studies are needed to capture whether learning agility actually *predicts* leader success. The extant research literature investigating the relationship between learning agility and leadership potential uses supervisory ratings to forecast potential (e.g., Bedford, 2011; Lombardo & Eichinger, 2000; Spreitzer et al., 1997). A more meaningful methodology would be to measure the learning agility of identified high-potential leaders, then track their progression as leaders in their careers 3, 5, and 10 years down the road. Such "predictive validation" studies would be of significant value to demonstrating the importance of learning agility to leader success.

Implications for Practice

Perhaps the number one lesson organizational decision-makers involved with the management of talent can glean from this chapter—and, indeed this entire book—pertains to the close linkage between learning agility and leadership. The importance of the proper identification and development of leaders has been recognized for centuries, dating back to electing popes in the Catholic Church and selecting officers in medieval armies. Corporations spend an inordinate amount of time on conducting annual talent reviews and generating multiyear succession plans, unfortunately often with limited success. The application of learning agility can help eliminate some of the guesswork, perceptual biases, and subjectivity. The addition of learning agility scores can move the conversation from hearsay, limited observations, and opinions to a discussion based on independently collected information and a quantifiable metric. In addition, scores on the various facets can provide bosses, executive coaches, and mentors new insights into an individual's leadership strengths and developmental needs.

However, the application of learning agility can expand beyond the identification and development of high potentials. In this chapter, we assert that defining leadership potential solely in terms of upward mobility is outdated. There are numerous ways individuals can exercise their leadership acumen during this era of environmental complexity and volatility. It would be prudent for heads of talent to view the identification of "leaders" well beyond promotability up the management ladder. Careers today seldom are strictly vertical, but more closely resemble a series of winding stepping stones in a long journey of job transitions. The use of learning agility can provide new insights into whom to select to lead a temporary task force or oversee a virtual committee.

The model of learning agility articulated in this chapter highlights the aspects of learning about self. This view resonates with the emergent thinking on mindset-based development (Petrie, 2014). Individuals make decisions and take actions based on their subjective interpretation of situations. The manner in which they interpret the environment is influenced by their beliefs and assumptions. Those beliefs and assumptions are shaped by their "lived" experiences. Although those beliefs and assumptions may have served them well in the past, they often become invalid or constraining in new circumstances. Therefore, continuously operating under an old belief system limits the ability and willingness to adapt. As individuals assume new roles and are exposed to new environments, they need to step back and take stock of their existing beliefs, question their self-imposed boundaries, and explore different alternatives. Most leadership programs focus on the development of new skills and behaviors. However, the most difficult challenges leaders face today frequently are associated with how to make sense of their fast-paced, ever-changing world. Mindset-based development activities can supplement existing leadership programs to prepare leaders for unpredictable business situations. The assessment of learning agility and providing leaders feedback can facilitate mindset transformation.

Concluding Remark

We began this chapter with John F. Kennedy's counsel that "leadership and learning are indispensable to each other." In other words, organizational leaders must continue to grow, adapt, and evolve. The same words of advice are appropriate for researchers and professionals in the field of leadership. The construct of learning agility has made a substantial impact in the business world despite some of its shortcomings. It is time for the academic community to reinforce or refute the apparent benefits of it. A theory-based foundation to the construct will enable researchers to test and revise it as needed. It will provide clarity of definition, consistency of measurement, and appropriateness of application. Those are outcomes both scholars and practitioners can support.

References

Allworth, E., & Hesketh, B. (1999). Construct-oriented biodata: Capturing change-related and contextually relevant future performance. *International Journal of Selection and Assessment, 7*, 97–111.

Argyris, C. (2005). Double-loop learning in organizations: A theory of action perspective. In K. G. Smith & M. A. Hitt (Eds.), *Great minds in management: The process of theory development* (pp. 261–279). Oxford, UK: Oxford University Press.

Baard, S. K., Rench, T. A., & Kozlowski, S. J. (2014). Performance adaptation: A theoretical integration and review. *Journal of Management, 40*, 48–99.

Barrick, M. R., & Mount, M. K. (1991). The big five personality dimensions and job performance: A meta-analysis. *Personnel Psychology, 44*, 1–26.

Bass, B. M. (1985). *Leadership and performance beyond expectations.* New York, NY: Free Press.

Bedford, C. L. (2011). *The role of learning agility in workplace performance and career advancement* (Unpublished doctoral dissertation). University of Minnesota, Minneapolis.

Benko, C., & Anderson, M. (2010). *The corporate lattice: Achieving high performance in the changing world of work.* Boston, MA: Harvard Business Review Press.

Blake, R., & Mouton, J. (1964). *The managerial grid: The key to leadership excellence.* Houston, TX: Gulf.

Borman, W. C., & Motowidlo, S. J. (1993). Expanding the criterion domain to include elements of contextual performance. In N. Schmitt, W. C. Borman, & Associates (Eds.), *Personnel selection in organizations* (pp.71–98). San Francisco, CA: Jossey-Bass.

Boudreau, J. W., Boswell, W. R., & Judge, T. A. (2001). Effects of personality on executive career success in the United States and Europe. *Journal of Vocational Behavior, 58,* 53–81.

Briscoe, J. P., & Hall, D. T. (1999). Grooming and picking leaders using competency frameworks: Does they work? An alternative approach and new guidelines for practice. *Organizational Dynamics, 28*(2), 37–52.

Brown, K., Ryan, R. M., & Creswell, J. D. (2007). Mindfulness: Theoretical foundations and evidence for its salutary effects. *Psychological Inquiry, 18,* 211–237.

Buckner, M., & Marberry, M. (2018). How to identify and grow high potentials: A CEO's perspective with proven results. *People & Strategy, 41*(1), 22–27.

Bunker, K. A., Kram, K. E., & Ting, S. (2002). The young and clueless. *Harvard Business Review, 80*(12), 80–87.

Campbell, J. P. (1999). The definition and measure of performance in the new age. In D. R. Ilgen & E. D. Pulakos (Eds.), *The changing nature of performance: Implications for staffing, motivation, and development* (pp. 399–429). San Francisco, CA: Jossey-Bass.

Charan, R., Drotter, S., & Noel, J. (2011). *The leadership pipeline: How to build a leadership powered company.* San Francisco, CA: Jossey-Bass.

Charbonnier-Voirin, A., & Roussel, P. (2012). Adaptive performance: A new scale to measure individual performance in organizations. *Canadian Journal of Administrative Sciences, 29,* 280–293.

Church, A. H., Rotolo, C. T., Ginther, N. M., & Levine, R. (2015). How are top companies designing and managing their high-potential programs? A follow-up talent management benchmark study. *Consulting Psychology Journal: Practice and Research, 67,* 17–47.

Connolly, J. A., & Viswesvaran, C. (2002, April). Assessing the construct validity of a measure of learning agility. Paper presented at the Society for Industrial and Organizational Psychology Conference, Toronto, Canada.

Dai, G., & De Meuse, K. P. (2011). *Criterion-related validity of viaEDGE™ Assessment: Findings from two recent field studies.* Minneapolis, MN: Lominger International.

Dai, G., & De Meuse, K. P. (in press). Learning agility: Definition and application in contemporary talent management. In I. Tarique (Ed.), *Companion to talent management.* London, UK: Routledge.

Dai, G., De Meuse, K. P., & Tang, K. Y. (2013). The role of learning agility in executive career success: The results of two field studies. *Journal of Managerial Issues, 25,* 108–131.

Dai, G., & Hezlett, S. A. (April, 2017). *Challenging experiences, learning agility, and extrinsic career success.* Paper presented at the Conference of the Society for Industrial and Organizational Psychology, Orlando, FL.

Dane, E. (2011). Paying attention to mindfulness and its effects on task performance in the workplace. *Journal of Management, 37,* 997–1018.

Day, D. V., & Harrison, M. M. (2007). A multilevel, identity-based approach to leadership development. *Human Resource Management Review, 17,* 360–373.

Day, D. V., Harrison, M. M., & Halpin, S. M. (2009). *An integrative approach to leader development: Connecting adult development, identity, and expertise.* New York, NY: Psychology Press.

De Meuse, K. P. (2017). Learning agility: Its evolution as a psychological construct and its empirical relationship to leader success. *Consulting Psychology Journal: Practice and Research, 69,* 267–295.

De Meuse, K. P. (2019). A meta-analysis of the relationship between learning agility and leader success. *Journal of Organizational Psychology, 19,* 25–34.

De Meuse, K. P., Dai, G., & Hallenbeck, G. S. (2010). Learning agility: A construct whose time has come. *Consulting Psychology Journal: Practice and Research, 62,* 119–130.

De Meuse, K. P., Dai, G., & Marshall, S. (2012). *The relationship between learning agility, critical thinking, and job performance: Engineers and project managers.* Minneapolis, MN: Lominger International.

De Meuse, K. P., Dai, G., Swisher, V. V., Eichinger, R. W., & Lombardo, M. M. (2012). Leadership development: Exploring, clarifying, and expanding our understanding of learning agility. *Industrial and Organizational Psychology: Perspectives on Science and Practice, 5,* 280–286.

De Meuse, K. P., Dai, G., Zewdie, S., Page, R. C., Clark, L. P., & Eichinger, R. W. (2011, April). *Development and validation of a self-assessment of learning agility.* Paper presented at the Society for Industrial and Organizational Psychology Conference, Chicago, IL.

De Meuse, K. P., & Feng, S. (2015). *The development and validation of the TALENTx7 Assessment™: A psychological measure of learning agility.* Shanghai, China: Leader's Gene Consulting.

De Pater, I. E., Van Vianen, A. E. M., Bechtoldt, M. N., & Klehe, U. C. (2009). Employees' challenging job experiences and supervisors' evaluations of promotability. *Personnel Psychology, 62,* 297–325.

Derry, S. J., & Murphy, D. A. (1986). Designing systems that train learning ability: From theory to practice. *Review of Educational Research, 56*(1), 1–39.

DeRue, D. S., Ashford, S. J., & Myers, C. G. (2012). Learning agility: In search of conceptual clarity and theoretical grounding. *Industrial and Organizational Psychology: Perspectives on Science and Practice, 5,* 258–279.

DeRue, D. S., & Wellman, N. (2009). Developing leaders via experience: The role of developmental challenge, learning orientation, and feedback availability. *Journal of Applied Psychology, 94,* 859–875.

DeYoung, C. G., Peterson, J. B., & Higgins, D. M. (2002). Higher-order factors of the big five predict conformity: Are there neuroses of health? *Personality and Individual Differences, 33,* 533–552.

DeYoung, C. G., Peterson, J. B., & Higgins, D. M. (2005). Sources of openness/intellect: Cognitive and neuropsychological correlates of the fifth factor of personality. *Journal of Personality, 73,* 825–858.

Digman, J. M. (1997). Higher-order factors of the big five. *Journal of Personality and Social Psychology, 73,* 1246–1256.

Dong, Y., Seo, M., & Bartol, K. M. (2014). No pain, no gain: An affect-based model of developmental job experience and the buffering effects of emotional intelligence. *Academy of Management Journal, 57,* 1056–1077.

Dragoni, L., Oh, I. S., Van Katwyk, P., & Tesluk, P. E. (2011). Developing executive leaders: The relative contribution of cognitive ability, personality, and the accumulation of work experience in predicting strategic thinking competency. *Personnel Psychology,* *64,* 829–864.

Dragoni, L., Tesluk, P. E., Russell, J. E. A., & Oh, I. (2009). Understanding managerial development: Integrating development assignments, learning orientation, and access to developmental opportunities in redesigning managerial competencies. *Academy of Management Journal, 52,* 731–743.

Dries, N., & Pepermans, R. (2008). Real high-potential careers: An empirical study into the perspectives of organizations and high potentials. *Personnel Review, 37,* 85–108.

Dries, N., Vantilborgh, T., & Pepermans, R. (2012). The role of learning agility and career variety in the identification and development of high potential employees. *Personnel Review, 41,* 340–358.

Dweck, C. S. (2006). *Mindset: The new psychology of success.* New York, NY: Ballantine Books.

Fiedler, F. E. (1967). *A theory of leadership effectiveness.* New York, NY: McGraw-Hill.

Fleishman, E. A., & Harris, E. F. (1962). Patterns of leadership behavior related to employee grievances and turnover. *Personnel Psychology, 15,* 43–56.

Genovese, M. A. (2016). *The future of leadership: Leveraging influence in an age of hyperchange.* New York, NY: Routledge.

Goldberg, L. R. (1992). The development of markers of the big five factor structure. *Psychological Assessment, 4,* 26–42.

Griffin, B., & Hesketh, B. (2003). Adaptable behaviors for successful work and career adjustment. *Australian Journal of Psychology, 55,* 65–73.

Hall, D. T. (2004). Self-awareness, identity, and leadership development. In D. V. Day, S. J. Zaccaro, & S. M. Halpin (Eds.), *Leadership development for transforming organizations* (pp. 153–176). Mahwah, NJ: Erlbaum.

Hersey, P., & Blanchard, K. H. (1969). *Management of organizational behavior—Utilizing human resources.* Upper Saddle River, NJ: Prentice Hall.

Hirsh, J. B., DeYoung, C. G., & Peterson, J. B. (2009). Metatraits of the big five differentially predicted engagement and restraint of behavior. *Journal of Personality, 77,* 1085–1102.

Hooijberg, R., Hunt, J. G., & Dodge, G. E. (1997). Leadership complexity and development of the leaderplex model. *Journal of Management, 23,* 375–408.

Huang, J. L., Ryan, A., Zabel, K. L., & Palmer, A. (2014). Personality and adaptive performance at work: A meta–analytic investigation. *Journal of Applied Psychology, 99,* 162–179.

Huang, Y., Chen, C., & Lai, S. (2013). Test of a multidimensional model linking applicant work experience and recruiters' inferences about applicant competencies. *The International Journal of Human Resource Management, 24,* 3613–3629.

Hudson, N. W., & Fraley, R. C. (2015). Volitional personality trait change: Can people choose to change their personality traits. *Journal of Personality and Social Psychology, 109,* 490–507.

Hudson, N. W., & Roberts, B. W. (2014). Goals to change personality traits: Concurrent links between personality traits, daily behavior, and goals to change oneself. *Journal of Research in Personality, 53,* 68–83.

Jackson, J. J., Hill, P. L., Payne, B. R., Roberts, B. W., & Stine-Morrow, E. A. (2012). Can an old dog learn (and want to experience) new tricks? Cognitive training increase openness to experience in older adults. *Psychology and Aging, 27,* 286–292.

Kandler, C., Kornadt, A. E., Hagemeyer, B., & Neyer, F. J. (2014). Patterns and sources of personality development in old age. *Journal of Personality and Social Psychology, 109,* 175–191.

Kenny, D. A., & Zaccaro, S. J. (1983). An estimate of variance due to traits in leadership. *Journal of Applied Psychology, 68,* 678–685.

Kolb, D. A. (1984). *Experiential learning: Experience as the source of learning and development.* Upper Saddle River, NJ: Prentice Hall.

Langer, E. J. (2016). *The power of mindful learning.* Boston, MA: Da Capo Press.

LePine, J. A., Colquitt, J. A., & Erez, A. (2000). Adaptability to changing task contexts: Effects of general cognitive ability, conscientiousness, and openness to experience. *Personnel Psychology, 53,* 563–593.

LePine, J. A., LePine, M. A., & Jackson, C. L. (2004). Challenge and hindrance stress: Relationships with exhaustion, motivation to learn, and learning performance. *Journal of Applied Psychology, 89,* 883–891.

Lillard, A. S., & Erisir, A. (2011). Old dogs learning new tricks: Neuroplasticity beyond the juvenile period. *Developmental Review, 31,* 207–239.

Lombardo, M. M., & Eichinger, R. W. (2000). High-potentials as high learners. *Human Resource Management, 39,* 321–329.

London, M., & Smither, J. W. (1995). Can multi-source feedback change perceptions of goal accomplishment, self-evaluations, and performance-related outcomes? Theory-based applications and directions for research. *Personnel Psychology, 48,* 803–839.

McCall, M. W., Jr. (1998). *High flyers: Developing the next generation of leaders.* Boston, MA: Harvard Business School Press.

McCall, M. W., Jr. (2010). Recasting leadership development. *Industrial and Organizational Psychology: Perspectives on Science and Practice, 3,* 3–19.

McCall, M. W., Jr., & Hollenbeck, G. P. (2002). *Developing global executives.* Boston, MA: Harvard Business School Press.

McCall, M. W., Jr., Lombardo, M, M., & Morrison, A. M. (1988). *The lessons of experience: How successful executives develop on the job.* New York, NY: Free Press.

McCauley, C. D., Ruderman, M. M., Ohlott, P. J., & Morrow, J. E. (1994). Assessing the developmental components of managerial jobs. *Journal of Applied Psychology, 79,* 544–560.

Mount, M. K., Barrick, M. R., Scullen, S. M., & Rounds, J. (2005). Higher-order dimensions of the big five personality traits and the big six vocational interest types. *Personnel Psychology, 58,* 447–478.

Petrie, N. (2014). *Future trends in leadership development.* Greensboro, NC: Center for Creative Leadership.

Pulakos, E. D., Arad, S., Donovan, M. A., & Plamondon, K. E. (2000). Adaptability in the workplace: Development of a taxonomy of adaptive performance. *Journal of Applied Psychology, 85,* 612–624.

Pulakos, E. D., Schmitt, N., Dorsey, D. W., Arad, S., Borman, W. C., & Hedge, J. W. (2002). Predicting adaptive performance: Further tests of a model of adaptability. *Human Performance, 15,* 299–323.

Reiter-Palmon, R., Illies, J. J., & Kobe-Cross, L. M. (2009). Conscientiousness is not always a good predictor of performance: The case of creativity. *The International Journal of Creativity & Problem Solving, 19,* 27–45.

Saban, J., Killion, J., & Green, C. (1994). The centric reflection model: A kaleidoscope for staff developers. *Journal of Staff Development, 15*(3), 16–20.

Salgado, J. F. (1997). The five factor model of personality and job performance in the European community. *Journal of Applied Psychology, 82*, 30–43.

Seibert, K. W. (1996). Experience is the best teacher, if you can learn from it. In D. T. Hall & Associates (Eds.), *The career is dead—Long live the career: A relational approach to careers* (pp. 246–264). San Francisco, CA: Jossey-Bass.

Silzer, R., & Church, A. H. (2009). The pearls and perils of identifying potential. *Industrial and Organizational Psychology: Perspectives on Science and Practice, 2*, 377–412.

Specht, J., Egloff, B., & Schmukle, S. C. (2011). Stability and change of personality across the life course: The impact of age and major life events on mean-level and rank-order stability of the big give. *Journal of Personality and Social Psychology, 101*, 862–882.

Spreitzer, G. M., McCall, M. W., Jr., & Mahoney, J. D. (1997). Early identification of international executive potential. *Journal of Applied Psychology, 82*, 6–29.

Tesluk, P. E., & Jacobs, R. R. (1998). Toward an integrated model of work experience. *Personnel Psychology, 51*, 321–355.

Vroom, V. H., & Yetton, P. W. (1973). *Leadership and decision making*. Pittsburg, PA: University of Pittsburg Press.

Wang, S., & Beier, M. E. (2012). Learning agility: Not much is new. *Industrial and Organizational Psychology: Perspectives on Science and Practice, 5*, 293–296.

World Economic Forum. (2018). *The future of jobs report*. Retrieved from https://www.weforum.org/reports/the-future-of-jobs-report-2018

Yammarino, F. J., Salas, E., Serban, A., Shirreffs, K., & Shuffler, M. L. (2012). Collectivistic leadership approaches: Putting the "we" in leadership science and practice. *Industrial and Organizational Psychology: Perspectives on Science and Practice, 5*, 382–402.

Yukl, G., Gordon, A., & Taber, T. (2002). A hierarchical taxonomy of leadership behavior: Integrating a half century of behavior research. *Journal of Leadership & Organizational Studies, 9*, 15–32.

3

The Role of Learning Agility in Identifying and Developing Future Leaders

Allan H. Church[*]

> Before you are a leader, success is all about growing yourself.
> When you become a leader, success is all about growing others.
> —Jack Welch (1935–2020), former chairman and chief executive
> officer of General Electric

When it comes to managing talent in organizations, one of the most fundamental questions among senior executives, middle managers, and human resource (HR) professionals concerns the definition, identification, and management of leadership potential. Questions such as, How do we define potential? and What should we be looking for in our future leaders? are commonplace even in organizations with the most sophisticated of talent management (TM) practices (Effron & Ort, 2010; Silzer & Church, 2009, 2010; Silzer & Dowell, 2010).

In fact, based on recent benchmarks, 91% of the top development companies (i.e., large organizations with a dedicated focus on development and robust TM systems) have formal leadership pipeline programs in place, 81% use formal assessments to identify high-potential talent, and 92% use their talent review process to place key talent into new critical experiences to accelerate their learning and development (Church & Rotolo, 2013; Church, Rotolo, Ginther, & Levine, 2015; McHenry & Church, 2018). Moreover, 80% of high potentials themselves have reported being given special assignments

[*] I would like to acknowledge the contribution of Jeff McHenry to the initial thinking regarding this chapter and Taylor Anne D'Ilio for her review and feedback regarding the contents.

Allan H. Church, *The Role of Learning Agility in Identifying and Developing Future Leaders* In: *The Age of Agility.*
Edited by: Veronica Schmidt Harvey and Kenneth P. De Meuse, Oxford University Press (2021). © Oxford University Press.
DOI: 10.1093/oso/9780190085353.003.0003

and opportunities (Campbell & Smith, 2014), and 59% of top development companies formally track the critical experiences that their leaders have obtained (McHenry & Church, 2018). Based on these data, it would appear that the classic concept of learning from experiences (Lombardo & Eichinger, 2000; McCall, 1998; McCall, Lombardo, & Morrison, 1988) as a means of both evaluating and developing future leaders is central to most strategic TM agendas.

Interestingly enough, however, when asked how these organizations define and conceptualize leadership (or high) potential, the most commonly cited indicator by far is current performance (75%), followed by those individuals who are viewed as having the capacity to be promoted two or more levels (64%) (Church et al., 2015). While these two approaches to identifying talent serve a purpose, what makes them challenging for executives focused on developing the future pipeline is that the first is a representation of the current state, not potential, and the second is typically based on a judgment call or planning factor. Neither of these indicators is based on an underlying conceptual framework regarding the skills and abilities required to perform in more senior positions and/or novel situations. Although many firms employ the nine-box framework using these factors (Effron & Ort, 2010), given that neither factor represents a theory- or data-based approach, their high-potential identification process is suspect (Church, 2018; Church & Waclawski, 2010).

From a TM lens, organizations that employ solely these methods with the absence of data reflecting other constructs are clearly limiting their ability to truly identify those individuals with the greatest leadership potential longer term. This is one of the primary benefits of using an integrated, data-based assessment and development approach for TM. It is also in part why the field has seen a dramatic increase over the past decade in the availability and use of individual assessment tools and measures like those focused on key facets of leadership, such as learning agility, resilience, judgment, strategic thinking, and emotional intelligence.

Despite the trend to leverage more assessment tools and techniques, there still remains a lack of clarity in many organizations (and among TM professionals) regarding the true underlying nature of potential (Church & Silzer, 2014; Finkelstein, Costanza, & Goodwin, 2018). This is somewhat surprising given significant work done over the past few years on conceptualizing potential, vis-à-vis models such as the Leadership Potential *BluePrint* and other related frameworks (e.g., Church & Silzer, 2014; Finkelstein et al., 2018; McRae & Furnham, 2014; Silzer & Church, 2009). It is further surprising when one considers that the now classic research on the impact of learning from critical experiences (McCall et al., 1988) has become a staple in most TM functions and remains a core model for development in general (McCauley & McCall, 2014).

Given the critical role that the ability and motivation to learn from experiences plays, as well as the inclusion of learning in most mainstream theoretical high-potential reviews and frameworks (e.g., Finkelstein et al., 2018; Silzer & Church, 2009; Thornton, Johnson, & Church, 2017), it is a seemingly obvious conclusion that the concept of learning agility is and/ or should be a core component of any successful TM system. Although a number of companies are using measures of learning agility for TM-related purposes (De Meuse, 2017; Hoff & Burke, 2017), many others struggle to find the right level of emphasis or the most useful application for their given context.

The purpose of this chapter is to focus on the connection between the construct of learning agility and our understanding of future leadership potential in an integrated TM system. For the purposes of this discussion, learning agility is defined as "The ability and willingness to learn from experience, and then apply those lessons to perform well in new and challenging leadership situations" (De Meuse & Harvey, Chapter 1, this volume). This chapter begins with a summary of the empirical and applied literature on the role of learning agility as an indicator of future leadership potential (and performance) over time. This is followed by a discussion of the application of learning agility in a TM context with a particular emphasis on practical applications of learning agility across the employee life cycle.

The four primary areas of TM that are a focus here include the use of learning agility as (a) an indicator of potential in selection systems; (b) development programs and interventions to enhance capabilities; (c) assessments for identifying high-potential talent; and (d) talent reviews and succession planning decisions. A short case study highlighting the use of the construct in an integrated assessment and development process at PepsiCo is also presented. The chapter concludes with a summary and areas of emphasis for future practice and research as it relates to the further study and utilization of learning agility in TM applications in particular.

Learning Agility as a Leading Indicator
of Leadership Potential

In general, a review of both the current academic (De Meuse, 2019; De Meuse, Dai, & Hallenbeck, 2010; DeRue, Ashford, & Myers 2012; Dries, Vantilborgh, & Pepermans, 2012; Finkelstein et al., 2018; Silzer & Church, 2009, 2010) and practitioner literature (e.g., Conger & Church, 2018a; Hoff & Burke, 2017; McCauley & McCall, 2014; Swisher et al., 2013) suggested there is considerable agreement intellectually that individuals who have and leverage the capacity to learn from their surroundings and experiences have the potential to become more successful in the long term. Whether this is called learning agility, learning ability (see Silzer & Church, 2009), learning capability, or catalytic learning (see Conger & Church, 2018a), the core belief from a TM and leadership development perspective remains the same. While perhaps not always articulated as part of their definition of the construct of learning agility (although some authors have suggested process models as well as content ones, e.g., DeRue et al., 2012; McCauley & McCall, 2014; McHenry & Church, 2018; Mitchinson, Gerard, Roloff, & Burke, 2012), the emphasis on placing individuals with higher levels of potential into stretch roles to enable, develop, or perhaps even test their capacity to learn is in fact a direct reflection of the original construct of learning agility (Eichinger & Lombardo, 2004) and learning from experiences research (McCall et al., 1988). PepsiCo, for example, uses the construct of "critical experiences" as both a key indicator of career growth and a placement factor when planning for high-potential talent (Church & Waclawski, 2010).

   In addition, recent reviews and theory regarding the underlying nature of leadership potential (e.g., Finkelstein et al., 2018; Silzer & Church, 2009) have identified the ability to learn from experiences (and the motivation and drive to do so) as one of the key components of potential. In the context of the Leadership Potential BluePrint (Church & Silzer, 2014), learning has been defined as a growth dimension, meaning it represents a stable characteristic building off the foundational principles of cognitive skills and personality characteristics yet is also an individual capability that can be developed throughout someone's career. Thus, learning as a construct seems to be integral to the determination of future potential even at a very basic level. Whether organizations are making talent slating and placement decisions (a) on the presence of the attribute, (b) with the intent of assessing whether a high potential is in fact learning agile, or (c) in the hopes of developing greater levels of learning agility in the spirit of Dweck's (2006) notion of growth mindset, needs to be further explored through research. This somewhat circular nature of the construct of learning agility as applied in organizations is arguably one of the primary reasons why the field of industrial and organizational (I-O) psychology has not yet landed on a common definition or set of measurement models.

Although the concept of learning agility is popular today in discussions among TM professionals and I-O psychologists alike, a review of the theoretical and empirical literature of the concept, while very promising in its link to identifying and developing future leadership potential and performance, highlights some significant and ongoing challenges as well. Both the strengths and opportunities with respect to learning agility as a measure of employee outcomes have been well documented in recent meta-analyses and review papers (e.g., De Meuse, 2017, 2019; DeRue et al., 2012), and there are some common themes that are worth noting particularly with respect to the construct's relationship to identifying leadership potential in TM systems. These are discussed next.

Core Theory and Research Findings

The origins of learning as an individual psychological variable used as a means to determine successful performance in organizational settings dates to assessments performed in the military and the assessment center work in the 1980s at AT&T (Bray & Grant, 1966; Jeanneret & Silzer, 1998; Scott & Reynolds, 2010). While originally measured as more of a personality trait, openness to experiences and the ability to learn and adapt in general have been core aspects of the assessment and development of leaders for decades. It was the applied research done in the 1980s, however, as a collaboration between scientists at the Center for Creative Leadership (CCL) and several key organizations that ushered in the current era of "lessons from experience" (McCall et al., 1988; McCauley & McCall, 2014).

In those studies, data collected from quantitative and qualitative sources on the careers of hundreds of managers resulted in a profile that identified experiential learning as the key driver of success (and a lack of willingness to adapt and change as a primary derailer). Their findings regarding the importance of challenging, stretch assignments for development (not just new experiences for the sake of moving people around) have been guiding HR and TM practices ever since. Case examples from organizations such as PepsiCo (Church & Waclawski, 2010) and others (e.g., McCauley & McCall, 2014; Silzer & Dowell, 2010) show the prominence that key experiences, or critical experiences as organizations refer to them today, play in the way they think about and move individuals as part of the talent processes.

Following the initial coining of the term *learning agility* by Lombardo and Eichinger (2000), two of the original researchers involved in the CCL research, the concept was initially defined using four different facets: people agility, mental agility, change agility, and results agility. These were then commercialized into various self-rating and multirater feedback tools (e.g., *viaEDGE*™ and *Choices*™) and used for leadership development and decision-making in organizational settings (De Meuse, 2017; Swisher et al., 2013). Over the years, this framework and the measurement tools associated with it have continued to evolve, and other overlapping and robust competitive models have emerged, such as the *TALENTx7*® (De Meuse, 2017) and the *Burke Learning Agility Inventory*™ (LAI) (Burke, Roloff, & Mitchinson; 2016; Hoff & Burke, 2017). However, the basic elements of learning agility share much in common across the different frameworks.

In particular, the ability and willingness to learn from experiences and their specific role in determining future leadership potential began with early research on the identification of future international executives (McCall, 1994; Spreitzer, McCall, & Mahoney, 1997), where it was operationalized as "the ability to take advantage of the experiences that will be offered" (McCall, 1994). Based on data collected from 838 managers across multiple levels from six different firms, results indicated that learning agility significantly predicted the likelihood of being classified as a high potential, and this was above and beyond the general competency ratings used for essentially control variables. Using a different measure of learning agility, Lombardo and Eichinger (2000) found similar results in their study of over 200 manager–employee pairs across six companies where learning agility was predictive of manager ratings of potential regardless of level, gender, age, or line versus staff functions. These authors all generally concluded that learning agility can be used as a means of assessing future potential.

Another facet of learning agility in some models concerns the role of self-awareness in ensuring a reflective process (De Meuse, 2017; Mitchinson & Morris, 2014). In fact, the benchmark study of top development companies reported that self-awareness was the second most common content domain when formally assessing either high potentials or senior executives

(Church et al., 2015). Those companies that assessed self-awareness were also more likely to assess learning agility ($r = 0.53$, $p < .05$), along with motivation ($r = 0.63$, $p < .001$), personality ($r = 0.39$, $p < .05$), and leadership skills overall ($r = 0.52$, $p < .05$).[†] These data support the multifaceted and possibly metacompetent nature of learning agility.

To this point, in a related stream of research, Church (1997) examined the role of "managerial self-awareness" (MSA) in the differentiation of 134 high-performing and 470 average-performing managers across multiple levels from four different organizations. In this study, MSA was defined as self–other agreement using 360-degree feedback ratings. The outcome variables included a variety of different measures such as performance ratings, awards, and—importantly in the context of learning agility—high-potential status as measured by both manager designations and objective assessments conducted by an external consulting firm. Results showed higher levels of self-awareness as differentiators of performance and potential. This is particularly meaningful given the potential ratings included external assessments versus solely manager ratings (which is a potential source of bias in much of the learning agility research available currently).

In sum, these early studies, although not conclusive, directly support the link between the learning agility, self-awareness, and reflective skills in managers and leaders perceived to have future leadership potential.

Contemporary Frameworks and Research

With the increase in focus on learning agility as a construct and the emergence of several competitive models and measurement tools, there has been an accompanying growth in empirical research regarding its relationship to both performance and potential. Two recent meta-analyses by De Meuse (2017, 2019) reviewed these findings in depth with relatively robust effects and highlighted the research challenges that remain as well. Next is a short summary of the highlights.

Based on 20 studies conducted using a variety of different instruments and data collected from almost 5,000 employees, De Meuse (2019) reported the overall relationship between learning agility and leader success (defined

---

[†] Correlations reported are based on source data and were not included in the original (Church et al., 2015) article.

largely by managerial ratings of performance or potential) as $r = 0.47$, $p <$ .001. Breaking the results down further, he reported a correlation of $r = 0.47$ across those studies measuring performance, and $r = 0.48$ for the studies that included leadership potential as an outcome variable (both significant at $p < .001$). Although the aggregate correlations suggest a strong set of relationships between learning agility and performance and potential, interestingly the range of findings in the individual studies was quite wide, from $r = 0.08$ to $r = .91$ (34 of the 41 total reported were statistically significant). While some of these effects were likely moderated by a host of other organizational factors, similar positive findings have been reported in technical reports by others as well (e.g., BLAI 3.3, 2018) with a number of different samples.

In short, the data collectively and across different instruments and models of learning agility would suggest that there is a strong relationship between the current measures of learning agility and managerial ratings of performance and potential. What is missing to date, of course, is robust research on the long-term impact of learning agility over time. The question remains, for example, regarding the directionality of the relationship between learning agility and potential. Does learning agility predict potential (an antecedent), or is learning agility reflective of having potential at a given point in time (an indicator)? Alternatively, perhaps learning agility is a process that emerges based on contextual variables as some have suggested (e.g., DeRue et al., 2012; Mitchinson et al., 2012). Or, perhaps it is a combination of all three facets inherent in the high-potential ecosystem.

In addition, from an assessment and development standpoint is learning agility a unique attribute or skill that is best measured on its own, or a metacompetency that can be derived from a combination of more standard core cognitive, personality, and motivational tests? While some research points to stronger relationships with outcomes using targeted learning agility tools versus other measures, these data are not conclusive and are an area for future research. From a practice perspective, the argument would be centered on the degree to which a company is focused on learning agility as a construct to be highlighted to employees and managers for development and decision-making processes, versus an underlying component of a broader predictive high-potential framework. In short, it may be an equal matter of measurement and emphasis.

Learning Agility as a Key Component
of Talent Management

Given the fundamental nature of the research describing how successful executives learn from their experiences and the increasing empirical evidence regarding the relationship between learning agility (however it is measured) and both performance and potential ratings, it is not surprising that leaders and HR professionals have embraced the concept. Benchmark research has shown that over half of top development companies (Church et al., 2015) include some aspect of learning agility in their assessment suites for both identifying potential (51%) and making talent-related decisions with their more senior executive populations (56%). Although current models of potential would suggest it is but one facet rather than the sole indicator, from an applied TM perspective, learning agility can be used in connection with a variety of other tools across the employee life cycle. Listed in the material that follows are four key areas where learning agility can be applied to improve the identification and development of future leaders.

Selecting the Best External Talent

In general, if learning agility is both an indicator of potential and a general capability required for success in many different types of roles (e.g., De Meuse, 2017; Hoff & Burke, 2017), it seems an obvious choice to include the concept as part of an external selection battery (Thornton et al., 2017). While little empirical research exists yet on the use of learning agility in this particular area of practice, it is nevertheless one of the primary applications that many consulting firms have suggested for the use of their tools. From a general employee base perspective, given the relationships noted with managerial ratings of performance, this makes perfect sense for raising the quality of talent in an organization overall.

New hires with the ability to learn from and adapt to their environment will be more likely to figure out the nuances of the organizational culture, its unique norms, and ways of operating. As Church and Conger (2018) have noted, those employees who figure out the culture quickly are more likely to survive in the long term. In a way, this application of learning agility may increase a new hire's chances of fitting in the organization; in addition, his or her scanning and adaptive behaviors are likely to be stronger than others. Including learning agility in a general selection process, however, should only be done if the tool in question, with or without a complementary battery measuring other dimensions, has been empirically validated within a given organizational setting. As selection experts know, the information included in detailed technical reports is not enough to legally defend the use of any tool in a broad-based selection context.

When it comes to selecting for leadership potential, however, the equation changes. At more senior levels in the organization, where strategic hiring has become the norm, the success of talent that has been brought in becomes even more critical. Employing a buy versus build mentality (Cappelli, 2008) at these levels has a significant cost associated with it, and each unique hire needs to be successful in both the short and long terms. Even when capabilities are purchased for a limited amount of time to fill a void (e.g., e-commerce or government regulatory knowledge), there is an expectation that these senior executives will hit the ground running and find their way quickly. In this context, learning agility is arguably even more critical for predicting success. While not all strategic hires are done for the leadership pipeline or succession planning purposes, expensive external hires need to demonstrate their value, often in a highly political and intensely competitive situation (Conger & Church, 2018a). Those individuals higher in learning agility are more likely to assess their surroundings and adjust their styles and behaviors accordingly.

Further, if the organization is hiring specifically for future succession purposes (e.g., a general manager of a business region with an expectation that if successful could take on a larger general manager role or even be considered for the position of corporate chief executive officer [CEO]), candidates with higher learning agility are more likely to be seen as high potentials by their managers (i.e., often the senior most leaders in the company). Thus, learning agility in this context should arguably be a critical aspect of any senior selection battery (Thornton et al., 2017). Given that cognitive skills and general personality orientation are highly stable over time (Church et al., 2016) and may be less important for diagnostic purposes at the most senior levels given the development of workaround skills (e.g., Church, 2014; Church & Ezama, 2019), the ability to learn, adapt, and read interpersonal cues remains paramount for success. This argument is consistent with the early research done by McCall (1994) and others. Once again, however, whatever tool or measure is used for selection purposes must be formally validated within the business context to ensure legal defensibility and mitigate risk for the organization down the road (Scott & Reynolds, 2010).

Developing Employee Capability

Similar to the external orientation, when applied to internal employee development practices and programs, the inclusion of learning agility as a concept seems highly compelling. Such an agenda would be directed at "the many" (versus "the few") and reflect more of an organization development (OD) rather than TM mindset (Church, 2013; Church, Shull, & Burke, 2018). Employees who can learn and adapt are more likely to be higher performers over time. Although there remains some debate about whether learning agility is an innate capability or a developable skill, decades of broader learning research and evaluation studies in the training literature (e.g., Kirkpatrick & Kirkpatrick, 2006) indicate that those employees who apply new knowledge and skills on the job are more likely to change behaviors and increase their performance. Given that learning agility can be thought of as a metacompetency, it is likely that certain elements are trait based (e.g., general cognitive and personality attributes), and others are behaviors and/or skills that can be enhanced over time (e.g., via environmental scanning, practice, and reflection). Thus, learning agility would likely be a useful component for any developmental agenda, particularly in light of the call for learning organizations, learning cultures, and the concept of lifelong learning (or catalytic learning as defined by Conger & Church, 2018a) in general.

Perhaps the best approach to incorporating learning agility into employee development efforts is through targeted feedback (e.g., a 360-degree feedback measure or self-assessment) followed by comprehensive development planning and coaching efforts. Of course, this is why there are several competing 360-feedback assessments available for measuring learning agility (Burke et al., 2016; De Meuse, 2017). These tools might be used in a stand-alone manner (e.g., an annual feedback program) or integrated with broader development and training efforts. The latter approach would also afford organizations the option of including learning modules on the concept of learning agility and encourage practice sessions with new behaviors. Given that 360-degree feedback measures can be used effectively under the right conditions for both development and talent decision-making processes

(Bracken, Rose, & Church, 2016; Church, Bracken, Fleenor, & Rose, 2019), it would seem a natural to use them to assess learning agility as well, at least at the behavioral level. The key is understanding exactly which behaviors (and based on what model) to measure.

Because the types of tools available to measure learning agility range in level of complexity, as well as expertise and expense required to deliver, broad-based development can be more difficult to do depending on the size and scale of the company. In addition, unless there is a cultural mandate to specifically enhance learning agility or learning capability, the focus may be lost to other more pressing cultural agendas (e.g., a broader set of leadership competencies or cultural indicators). For those organizations where the scale is beyond a TM or OD team's ability to manage feedback individually, surrogates and/or composite scores for learning agility via other assessments (e.g., standard personality measures with learning subcomponents, etc.) might be warranted. Many organizations take the approach of integrating key behaviors reflecting a host of different factors (which could easily include learning agility) into their existing broader feedback models (Bracken et al., 2016).

A third option, which has its own set of debates in practice, is to include learning efforts and outcomes as part of the formal performance management process (e.g., as suggested by Hoff & Burke, 2017). If individuals are required to include learning objectives in their annual or ongoing evaluations, they are more likely to execute those even when their own internal motivation to do so may be more limited. From this perspective, accountability becomes the primary driver of behavior. The potential downsides to this approach are many, however, including (a) the possibility of creating a negative perception of learning due to inadequate time or managerial support; (b) increased expectations of greater rewards or opportunities on the part of employees as a result of completing their learning objectives; or (c) the establishment of a check-the-box learning agenda without any meaningful outcomes. This is likely why only 13% of top development companies formally link learning progress to their performance management programs or hold managers accountable for the learning objectives of their staff (McHenry & Church, 2018).

Further, including a learning agility objective by itself could be even more challenging and difficult to measure without targeted tools before and after. Just because someone has learning objectives as part of their formal reviews does not ensure that they will learn how to learn from the process. Thus, leveraging learning agility for employee development efforts broadly, while likely very useful, has its challenges.

Identifying Future Potential

One of the more promising approaches based on the original lessons from experience research and the recent meta-analytic findings is to leverage the concept of learning agility as part of a suite of tools designed to identify future leadership potential in early to mid-career employees. Given the central role of learning agility in high-potential frameworks (e.g., Conger & Church, 2018a; Silzer & Church, 2009), integrating an assessment of this capability should help increase the predictive power of identifying those employees with greater capacity to learn and therefore be seen as high potential. While talent segmentation processes are probably best conducted via a multitrait, multimethod (MTMM) approach given the strengths and weaknesses of using any singular tool (Church & Rotolo, 2013), as Lombardo, Eichinger, and McCall all have noted collectively, the ability to learn from experience is indeed a critical indicator of future advancement potential. While more research needs to be done on the long-term impact of learning agility, not to mention a full consideration of the organizational and contextual factors that play a role in promotions over time (DeRue et al., 2012), the inclusion of some measure of learning agility as part of an early identification model seems highly valuable. This is likely why 51% of top companies leverage this concept in their high-potential assessment suites (Church et al., 2015).

As with the other uses of learning agility, however, it is important to recognize that the presence, absence, or degree of an employee's learning agility should not be the end state of the assessment but rather used as an indicator of future capability. In other words, having higher levels of learning agility might be an indicator of someone with greater potential, but this data point needs to be factored in with a number of other variables. As I-O psychologists, it is critical that we help TM and OD professionals understand the role that learning agility (and other dimensions of human behavior) plays in the process of career progression and success rather than use the concept itself as the sole differentiator. In addition, validation studies are again needed internally for any organization desiring to use learning agility as part of its talent identification suite. This is particularly important at lower levels in the organization (e.g., with early career professionals), where an assessment tool might be the only real source of objective information beyond the imme-diate manager's perception of potential. In contrast, at higher levels of man-agement, it is likely that multiple leaders in talent review meetings have had exposure to individuals being discussed for future roles. In these cases, the impact of manager bias in perceptions is somewhat moderated. Regardless of the level of employee being evaluated, however, the best approach is to create a validated predictive index or composite metric of future potential that is informed by behavioral measures of learning agility, rather than using any single assessment on its own.

Building Leadership Succession Bench

The fourth and final area where learning agility can play an important role in understanding potential in organizations is for building the leadership pipe-line for senior succession. In this context, as in the case of senior strategic external hires, learning agility could be a critical indicator of a leader with the ability to adapt to the most stressful and complex sets of roles in a corpo-ration (e.g., at the C-suite level). Given that the early research on executives demonstrated that the absence of learning agility led to derailing outcomes (McCall et al., 1988), and other models of potential emphasize learning skills (e.g., catalytic learning as described by Conger & Church, 2018a), as crit-ical at the highest levels of the organization, the inclusion of a measure of learning agility in some form could be instrumental in increasing the prob-ability of succession. For this application, the best approach would be to focus on those aspects of learning agility that are able to be developed rather than traits based on supporting enhanced coaching effectiveness (Church, 2014). At the senior-most levels, developing new workaround strategies for a limited ability to learn further might seem to be a waste of resources. What makes more sense is a deep dive into the learning agility–related skills and behaviors that can help a leader capitalize on existing inherent abilities. At this stage of one's career, however, there is also likely the need to understand the motivation levels as well, as many leaders either stop learning when they achieve a certain level of success or do not want to engage in the behaviors necessary to achieve the next level (Conger & Church, 2018b).

Another important facet of learning agility to consider as part of the talent review and succession pipeline process is the determination of whether a leader can and does actually learn from experiences and apply those to new ones. Once again, we are faced with the dilemma of whether learning agility is a predictor, a driver, a process, or an outcome of success, and research in this area lacks sufficient clarity and depth. The challenge with assessing learning agility as a predictor is that it is difficult to determine exactly what was learned from an assignment and how prior experiences might have been applied. Moreover, senior succession slates are often different from the final placement decision. While creating learning objectives when onboarding someone to a new role or embedding learning goals in performance management reviews can be useful, it is extremely difficult to assess with any accuracy whether someone learned new learning skills in these contexts. Although this might not be an issue if learning agility is defined purely as an individual trait, the difficulty is inherent in the use of critical experiences to test and/or build greater potential. Given that 72% of top development companies use experiences to develop new capabilities versus placing people in roles based on their existing skills and experiences (McHenry & Church, 2018), this raises important questions for research and practice about how we assess learning agility–related outcomes of new assignments.

While success in a new role can be defined in many ways (e.g., performance ratings, tenure in the assignment, or promotion out of the assignment), other political and organization cultural forces are present that can impede learning or the application of learnings which are often ignored or minimized from a TM perspective. Moreover, in organizations where ongoing potential is essentially assessed through success in successive roles, there may be little need for a formal learning agility metric in this context. Simply put, in the business environment, learning agility might be defined by those who demonstrate sustained high performance in roles of greater complexity over time (which is a partial argument for the nine-box TM methodology). One could argue that a leader who "thrives" is a high potential via this performance metric; someone who just "survives" with average performance over time may become a solid player (e.g., key contributor at PepsiCo; see Church & Waclawski, 2010); and someone who "fails" is likely to be managed out of the organization regardless of how the person scored on an assessment battery. Conger and Church (2018b) refer to these last types of individuals as "C players" (and once identified need to be exited).

Thus, in more senior talent planning and succession scenarios, it is critically important to understand how to leverage assessment tools in a given organizational culture and TM system. It is also important to consider what other indicators of learning outcomes need to be measured as part of a formal measure of the effectiveness of the new experience. This is extremely difficult to do and likely why only 13% of companies track outcomes of this nature (McHenry & Church, 2018). Yet this same benchmark study indicated that those that do track outcomes are significantly more likely to rate the effectiveness of their leadership development programs as more effective overall.

In the next section, a short case study is described where learning agility is fully integrated into the TM process using an MTMM design.

Case Study Application

In 2010, PepsiCo, a global consumer products company with $67 billion in sales, launched a new approach to identifying, developing, and moving talent across the enterprise, called the Leadership Assessment and Development (LeAD) program. The program was created in an effort to bring greater consistency and accuracy to the segmentation of high-potential talent across multiple levels of the organization from early career through to executives in preparation for C-suite roles (Church, 2019; Trudell & Church, 2016). Its design and execution was supported by the senior-most leaders in the organization, and it has been a fully operational model for many years. The organization has assessed over 10,000 individuals to date, from individual contributors new to the organization to middle managers to the senior-most leaders.

The program leverages an evidence-based MTMM framework and is tiered at four levels according to key transitions in the leadership pipeline (Charan, Drotter, & Noel, 2001) across an individual's careers. Underlying the program is the Leadership Potential BluePrint (Church & Silzer, 2014; Silzer & Church, 2009), which defines potential as based on foundational (cognitive abilities, personality characteristics); growth (learning and motivation); and career (leadership skills and functional capabilities) dimensions. Figure 3.1 provides an overview of the BluePrint expanded to include the contextual gatekeeper elements of sustained performance and culture fit, along with the guidelines for assessment and development focus areas. After several years of piloting and validation work with the BluePrint as the underlying model, the program was fully launched in 2013 across all four levels of key transitions.

The principles behind the LeAD framework are quite straightforward: (a) People differ in their inherent potential and capabilities, some of which are more easily developable (e.g., leadership behaviors, functional skills) than

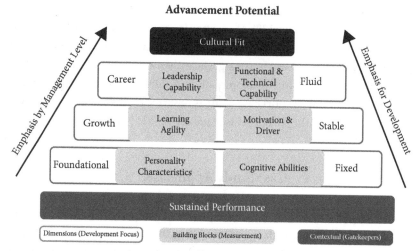

Figure 3.1 The Leadership Potential BluePrint Contextualized.
Adapted from Church and Silzer (2014) and Silzer and Church (2009).

others (e.g., personality, cognitive abilities); (b) the significance of these in-dividual factors in predicting future success differs depending on the stage of someone's career; (c) data-based insights on different competencies collected from multiple sources (using an MTMM approach) provide a more balanced picture of employees' strengths to leverage and opportunities to enhance than any single leadership trait or measurement tool; (d) enhanced self-awareness and learning drives behavior change and new skills, which in turn lead to growth and development for both the individual and the organization as a whole; and (e) these processes are only as good as the extent to which they are integrated with the overall TM infrastructure and championed by senior leadership.

While the mechanics and predictive outcomes of the LeAD program have been described elsewhere in depth (Church, 2019; Church, Del Giudice, & Margulies, 2017; Church & Rotolo, 2016; Silzer, Church, Rotolo, & Scott, 2016), it is useful here to discuss the role of learning agility as a key com-ponent of the assessment and development suite. As described in Figure 3.1, learning agility as a construct is part of the underlying model of poten-tial behind the program along with other factors based on the BluePrint.[‡]

[‡] Silzer and Church (2009) originally labeled this factor in the BluePrint as simply "Learning" and provided the examples of adaptability, learning orientation, and openness to feedback as supporting constructs. Learning agility is used in this version of the BluePrint to emphasize the connection in concepts.

In terms of measurement, rather than use an individual tool to directly assess learning agility, it was integrated into the suite of tools reflecting other domains. While some of these include core foundational measures of potential, such as cognitive and personality tests, additional measures that assess learning agility are a series of custom simulations and situational judgment tests and a multitier, 360-degree feedback tool. The 360 tool was based on a future-focused, PepsiCo-specific leadership competency model (the Leadership Effectiveness Framework or LEF), which includes learning and self-awareness as key constructs as well. Based on input and guidance from the CEO, the board of directors, key internal stakeholders, and external thought leaders, the LEF ensures a common language and profile of leadership success at different levels of career progression.

Rather than focus on feedback from each individual tool (though results are provided for participants from each measure), the assessment process and subsequent development efforts are delivered in the language of leadership competencies. These are developable by their nature and enable a focus on skills and behaviors that can be changed rather than absolute assessment scores. While the various components of different models of learning agility, such as learning, reflection, feedback seeking, adaptability, people skills, and self-awareness, are woven into the LEF (e.g., in 6 of the 10 competencies reflecting Smart Innovator, Embraces Challenges and Risks, and Champion Talent Developer, Demonstrates Global Acumen, Creator of an Inclusive Culture, and Collaborates Beyond Boundaries), the primary focus when presented to participants is on an integrated summary of the competencies. Some of the items in the competency Champion Talent Developer, for example, include "Demonstrates a passion for self-development and growth by seeking and acting on feedback from others about ways to improve" and "Pursues learning opportunities that enhance critical capabilities he/she needs to meet future challenges." Collectively, the construct of learning agility is woven throughout the model, yet the term itself is never used.

In terms of further integration with respect to the talent planning and review process, the LeAD results are included as part of the Employee "Data Card"—one of three profile pages generated by the TM system. This Data Card contains all elements available regarding employee performance and potential, including

- 5 years of dual-performance ratings (business results and people results);

- 5 years of potential ratings (each year an individual is assigned a talent call or high-potential/non–high-potential designation);
- strengths and opportunities from the manager's perspective;
- strengths and opportunities from the formal assessment suite;
- results of the upward feedback process (the Manager Quality Performance Index) reflecting basic managerial behaviors (see Bracken & Church, 2013; Church Dawson, et al., 2018, for more details);
- formal assessment results across all of the LEF competencies;
- 360-degree feedback results for all of the LEF competencies; and importantly the
- predictive assessment-based index of potential (based on a validated algorithm that predicts success at two levels up from the current level).

Using this card, the assessment index is the primary data-based measure of potential and is easily compared with the organization's talent call designation over the past 5 years along with performance during that same time period. This enables a more robust discussion and high degree of utility for true a nine-box facilitation, which limits the performance/paradox issue (Church, 2018; Church & Waclawski, 2010) common to most applications of this kind.

Space for contextual comments on both the ratings and the assessment results is also provided (completed by the TM professional, manager, or HR business partner). Development plans, slates, and career paths are included on a separate card (i.e., the Roadmap). While the 360-degree feedback results are also included at the competency level, the primary points of discussion are around the assessment outcome and the convergence between the different data sources. Combining all the relevant data in a single page for each employee enables a more robust and balanced discussion of his or her strengths and opportunities as a leader instead of focusing on unique traits, skills, or measurement results. It prevents the tendency to focus on single numbers.

While many of the current learning agility measures today also incorporate behavioral indicators, their use would have introduced a new language and model against just that construct, rather than ensuring focus on a unique set of integrated behaviors that reflect the organization's culture and senior leadership priorities. By integrating the BluePrint (reflecting the six dimensions of leadership potential, including learning agility) with the LEF (leadership competencies identified for the future of PepsiCo) in the context of the employee Data Card, the organization is leaning forward in ensuring a holistic platform. Learning agility is a key component of the assessment and development effort, but it is used as an underlying structure and not as a primary point of feedback.

Although results from this integrated talent agenda have been discussed in depth elsewhere (e.g., Church, 2019; Church et al., 2017; Church & Rotolo, 2016), overall the process has been extremely successful. It has been externally recognized with awards from the Society for Human Resource Management (SHRM), the Society for Industrial-Organizational Psychology (SIOP), the Association for Talent Development (ATD), and Brandon Hall. In terms of core organizational outcomes, these include (a) over 10,000 employees assessed, including the current C-suite leaders (prior to their ascension into those roles); (b) statistically significant relationships between LeAD results and performance, high-potential status and promotion rates over time; and (c) an increase in the fluidity and therefore accuracy (based on results and calibration discussions in talent reviews) of the future potential and succession bench. As noted by Church (2019), there has been a significant shift in the culture as well since the launch of the program and integration of results into talent reviews from a "gut"-driven mindset to one based on data-based feedback and more formal assessment results.

Future Directions for Practice and Research

In sum, the construct of learning agility has much to offer when it comes to understanding and predicting leadership potential and performance. Whether it is measured directly using one of the tools readily available or via an integrated assessment model as part of a broader leadership competency framework, it is clear that the ability to learn from experiences and apply those learnings to novel situations is a critical dimension for determining leader effectiveness. Although the construct is still relatively new in I-O psychology terms (De Meuse, 2017), significant progress has been made in demonstrating the relationships between learning agility and individual outcomes. There are a several areas, however, where the field could benefit from additional theory and research from a TM perspective. These are described briefly next.

Further Theoretical Expansion and Integration

Over the past 20 years, and as outlined previously, the construct of learning agility has been defined in a variety of ways with a host of different subdimensions and underlying facets. While many of these are consistent (in principle), there remains no singular unified or recognized definition of the construct or how best to measure it (DeRue et al., 2012; Silzer & Church, 2010), and some debate remains regarding whether it is a distinct construct from other factors (Thornton et al, 2017) (i.e., a meta-competency). A summary of the different labels and factors outlined by De Meuse (2017) showed the variety of terms and angles from which learning agility has been conceptualized. What is evident from this review is that the differences inherent in the models are more than just in name. Some focus more on learning speed and information processing, while others are centered on insights and interpersonal skills. All told, if one were to sum the total number of dimensions across the three models, there appear to be 21 different facets that someone might consider (recognizing there is considerable overlap). This is great fodder for theoretical debates but is difficult to swallow for practitioners and opens the door for anyone, including non–I-O psychologists, to play in the same space (Rotolo et al., 2018).

While the same can be said for a number of different domains in the I-O psychology literature, from a TM and practitioner perspective this is highly problematic. Essentially, the hype (rightly or wrongly) has continued to outpace the theoretical and measurement development associated with learning agility. This causes all sorts of complexities in organizations with an interest in leveraging the construct of learning agility for TM applications. Regardless of whether an organization is seeking a single solution for identifying potential or developing leaders more broadly, they can easily fall prey to the bright shiny objective syndrome (Rotolo et al., 2018). The fact that there are at least three major competitive frameworks and tools (De Meuse, 2017) for learning agility currently and a host of other minor ones does not help practitioners or HR professionals determine how best to use the construct internally. It has also not helped the research agenda when it comes to developing normative results for comparing leaders across organizations (which are much more robust with other foundational measures, e.g., cognitive and personality tools) or with respect to slotting learning agility in against an existing competency framework. While the competitive nature of these models and tools is understandable, it is not helping advance the field fast enough in this particular area.

Another key challenge from a theoretical perspective with practice implications reflects the question of whether learning agility is a trait, a process, or an outcome following a set of experiences (Mitchinson et al., 2012). Given the retrospective nature of some of the original research in this area, and the concurrent nature of most of the present studies, it is difficult to know where to focus from a TM perspective. Should senior leaders and HR practitioners emphasize identifying talent with learning agility, developing said skills (even in those that do not have them initially) by taking risks with new experiences (if so, then based on what criteria for selection?), or focusing on the processes that enable a more conducive learning environment (DeRue et al., 2012)? Perhaps it is all of these, but that would suggest that learning agility becomes the central facet of a TM program and that has other likely challenges.

For example, given senior business leader preferences for simplicity and clarity of frameworks used for TM discussions, having a construct that spans multiple facets of trait, state, and context is likely to be confusing. Although I-O psychologists may be comfortable with these conceptual distinctions coexisting, having talent discussions with line leaders about whether or not a dimension is developable or career limiting can be complex. It is arguably better to make a determination of how learning agility should be best treated from a TM context in a given organization and remain consistent in that application (whether for selection, leadership development, high-potential identification, or succession planning).

Related to this point, in the future, it would be ideal from a practice perspective to see a single unified model of learning agility that is linked to other critical constructs (e.g., personality, potential, leadership) with all of the various measures available (including perhaps new ones as well) that enable practitioners to choose the best one for their TM purposes. Highlighting the contextual variables in a manner more amenable to OD and culture change interventions to improve the broader system of support would be helpful as well. Such a unifying solution also could benefit theory in this area and quiet the debate regarding the inherent attributes and the developable components. The model presented by DeRue et al. (2012) is a compelling start, but even that is not presented or operationalized in a way that can be effectively used in an organizational context. A clear and consistent model would help to ensure learning agility becomes fully integrated in applied TM settings in the right way and for the right reasons (and not another bright shiny object).

New Directions in Measurement and Research

To date, the majority of tools measuring learning agility have been survey questionnaire based, either via self-assessments or 360-degree feedback-type measures (e.g., De Meuse, 2017; Hoff & Burke, 2017). While some organizations have experimented with structured interviews to assess learning outcomes and capabilities, there is an opportunity for researchers and consulting firms to expand their techniques and research to new models. It is well known that self-assessments are subject to a number of biases, including social desirability and faking behavior, and these concerns are only exacerbated from a TM perspective when employees know that their data will be used to inform talent decisions regarding future potential or placement on slates or into new roles. Although 360-degree feedback measures avoid these biases at the individual level, there remain a host of other measurement effects that can factor into any type of multirater data (Bracken et al., 2016), including overly positive or punitive tendencies, cultural biases, and more. Simulations and assessment center approaches largely avoid these issues, though they come with their own challenges in terms of time and resources (Scott & Reynolds, 2010). In the future, it would be helpful to see alternative forms of assessment emerge that can tap the nature of learning agility in empirically valid ways that organizations can use with confidence. While the emerging concept of talent signals (Chamorro-Premuzic, Winsborough, Sherman, & Hogan, 2016) is an intriguing place to start, considerably more thinking and research are required to identify the next level of assessment of the construct.

A second area of research that would also benefit practice applications and the theory behind learning agility in general is the pursuit of more longitudinal studies and those using more than simply manager ratings of performance. While a few studies in the past 20 years have included more hard metrics (e.g., promotions and performance at the next level), the literature is generally lacking in a long-term, data-based view. The outcomes used are often ratings of performance (or potential) by managers, which are likely to be highly correlated with manager ratings of learning agility due to same-source ratings bias. Other evaluation research based on 360-degree feedback and manager ratings has been prone to this criticism as well (Bracken et al., 2016; Church et al., 2019). Promotions and placement into new assignments are also useful, but those likewise are impacted by a host of other factors, and sustained success in those roles is often not included as part of the study design.

Although organizational performance metrics are notoriously difficult to come by and longitudinal studies take time, only until we see the true longer term impact of learning agility on employee careers from a predictive standpoint will we be in a better position to make definitive statements. Such quasidesign (or even controlled experimental) studies also need to include the administration of other measures of behaviors and attributes commonly deployed in TM systems as well to ensure the unique contribution of learning agility can be parsed out from other factors. Some early work has been done in this area (De Meuse, 2017; Hoff & Burke, 2017), but more is clearly needed.

Summary and Conclusion

In sum, it should be clear from the discussion that the concept of learning agility is indeed critical for understanding, identifying, and developing high-potential leaders in global TM systems. The concept of learning from experiences and being able to apply those learnings adaptively to new scenarios is a hallmark of the 70–20–10 model of development and has been shown to predict performance, potential, and promotions over time across a variety of applied settings. The construct in its various forms is central to other models of potential as well (e.g., the Leadership Potential BluePrint) and has found its way into the majority of formal assessment and development efforts for both early career and senior executives in top development companies per recent benchmark studies. While the field has yet to fully coalesce on a single definition and preferred method of measurement, and further research is still needed to determine the causal directionality of the construct, the utility of learning agility for a variety of TM programs and processes is clear. With appropriate validation in an organizational setting, learning agility reflects a powerful component for determining future leadership potential.

References

Bracken, D. W., & Church, A. H. (2013). The "new" performance management paradigm: Capitalizing on the unrealized potential of 360 degree feedback. *People & Strategy, 36*(2), 34–40.

Bracken, D. W., Rose, D. S., & Church, A. H. (2016). The evolution and devolution of 360 degree feedback. *Industrial and Organizational Psychology: Perspectives on Science and Practice, 9*(4), 761–794.

Bray, D. W., & Grant, D. L. (1966). The assessment center in the measurement of potential for business management. *Psychological Monographs, 80*(17), 1–27.

Burke Learning Agility Inventory: Technical report v3.3. (2018). Retrieved from https://easiconsult.com/wp-content/uploads/2018/10/burke-learning-agility-inventory-technical-report.pdf

Burke, W. W., Roloff, K. S., & Mitchinson, A. (2016). *Learning agility: A new model and measure.* Manuscript in preparation.

Campbell, M., & Smith, R. (2014). *High-potential talent: A view from inside the leadership pipeline.* Greensboro, NC: Center for Creative Leadership.

Cappelli, P. (2008). *Talent on demand: Managing talent in an age of uncertainty.* Boston, MA: Harvard Business Press.

Chamorro-Premuzic, T., Winsborough, D., Sherman, R. A., & Hogan, R. (2016). New talent signals: Shiny new objects or a brave new world? *Industrial and Organizational Psychology: Perspectives on Science and Practice, 9*(3), 621–640.

Charan, R., Drotter, S., & Noel, J. (2001). *The leadership pipeline: How to build the leadership powered company.* San Francisco, CA: Jossey-Bass.

Church, A. H. (1997b). Managerial self-awareness in high performing individuals in organizations. *Journal of Applied Psychology, 82*(2), 281–292.

Church, A. H. (2013). Engagement is in the eye of the beholder: Understanding differences in the OD vs. talent management mindset. *OD Practitioner, 45*(2), 42–48.

Church, A. H. (2014). What do we know about developing leadership potential? The role of OD in strategic talent management. *OD Practitioner, 46*(3), 52–61.

Church, A. H. (2018). Think outside the 9-box. *Talent Quarterly, 19,* 39–43.

Church, A. H. (2019). Building an integrated architecture for leadership assessment and development at PepsiCo. In R. G. Hamlin, A. D. Ellinger, & J. Jones (Eds.), *Evidence-based initiatives for organizational change and development (EBOCD)* (pp. 492–505). Hershey, PA: IGI Global.

Church, A. H., Bracken, D. W., Fleenor, J. W., & Rose, D. S. (Eds.). (2019). *The handbook of strategic 360 feedback.* New York, NY: Oxford University Press.

Church, A. H., & Conger, J. A. (2018, March 29). When you start a new job, pay attention to these 5 aspects of company culture. *Harvard Business Review,* online edition. Available at https://hbr.org/2018/03/when-you-start-a-new-job-pay-attention-to-these-5-aspects-of-company-culture.

Church, A. H., Dawson, L. M., Barden, K. L., Fleck, C. R., Rotolo, C. T., & Tuller, M. D. (2018). Enhancing 360 feedback for individual assessment and organization development: Methods and lessons from the field. In D. A. Noumair & A. B. Shani (Eds.), *Research in organizational change and development* (Vol. 26, pp. 47–97). Bingley, UK: Emerald Group.

Church, A. H., Del Giudice, M. J., & Margulies, A. (2017). All that glitters is not gold: Maximizing the impact of executive assessment and development efforts. *Leadership & Organization Development Journal, 38*(6), 765–779.

Church, A. H., & Ezama, S. (2019, November 14). Six truths about using personality data and talent decisions. *Talent Quarterly,* online edition. Available at https://www.talent-quarterly.com/6-truths-about-personality-data/.

Church, A. H., Fleck, C. R., Foster, G. C., Levine, R. C., Lopez, F. J., Rotolo, C. T. (2016). Does purpose matter? The stability of personality assessments in organization development and talent management applications over time. *The Journal of Applied Behavioral Science, 52*(4), 1–32.

Church, A. H., & Rotolo, C. T. (2013). How are top companies assessing their high-potentials and senior executives? A talent management benchmark study. *Consulting Psychology Journal: Practice and Research, 65*(3), 199–223.

Church, A. H., & Rotolo, C. T. (2016). Lifting the veil: What happens when you are transparent with people about their future potential? *People & Strategy, 39*(4), 36–40.

Church, A. H., Rotolo, C. T., Ginther, N. M., & Levine, R. (2015). How are top companies designing and managing their high-potential programs? A follow-up talent management benchmark study. *Consulting Psychology Journal: Practice and Research, 67*(1), 17–47.

Church, A. H., Shull, A. C., & Burke, W. W. (2018). Organization development and talent management: Divergent sides of the same values equation. In D. W. Jamieson, A. H. Church, & J. D. Vogelsang (Eds.), *Enacting values-based change: Organization development in action* (pp. 265–294). Cham, Switzerland: Palgrave Macmillan.

Church, A. H., & Silzer, R. (2014). Going behind the corporate curtain with a *Blueprint for Leadership Potential*: An integrated framework for identifying high-potential talent. *People & Strategy, 36*(4), 51–58.

Church, A. H., & Waclawski, J. (2010). Take the Pepsi challenge: Talent development at PepsiCo. In R. Silzer & B. E. Dowell (Eds.), *Strategy-driven talent management: A leadership imperative* (pp. 617–640). San Francisco, CA: Jossey-Bass.

Conger, J. A., & Church, A. H. (2018a). *The high potential's advantage: Get noticed, impress your bosses, and become a top leader.* Boston, MA: Harvard Business Review Press.

Conger, J. A., & Church, A. H. (2018b, February 8). The 3 types of C players and what to do about them. *Harvard Business Review,* online edition. Available at https://hbr.org/2018/02/the-3-types-of-c-players-and-what-to-do-about-them.

De Meuse, K. P. (2017). Learning agility: Its evolution as a psychological construct and its empirical relationship to leader success. *Consulting Psychology Journal: Practice and Research, 69*(4), 267–295.

De Meuse, K. P. (2019). A meta-analysis of the relationship between learning agility and leader success. *Journal of Organizational Psychology, 19*(1), 25–34.

De Meuse, K. P., Dai, G., & Hallenbeck, G. S. (2010). Learning agility: A construct whose time has come. *Consulting Psychology Journal: Practice and Research, 62*(2), 119–130.

DeRue, D. S., Ashford, S. J., & Myers, C. G. (2012). Learning agility: In search of conceptual clarity and theoretical grounding. *Industrial and Organizational Psychology: Perspectives on Science and Practice, 5*(3), 258–279.

Dries, N., Vantilborgh, T., & Pepermans, R. (2012). The role of learning agility and career variety in the identification and development of high potential employees. *Personnel Review, 41*(3), 340–358.

Dweck, C. S. (2006). *Mindset: The new psychology of success.* New York, NY: Ballantine Books.

Effron, M., & Ort, M. (2010). *One-page talent management: Eliminating complexity, adding value.* Boston, MA: Harvard Business School.

Eichinger, R. W., & Lombardo, M. M. (2004). Learning agility as a prime indicator of potential. *Human Resource Planning, 27*(4), 12–15.

Finkelstein, L., Costanza, D., & Goodwin, G. (2018). Do your HiPos have potential? The impact of individual differences and designation on leader success. *Personnel Psychology, 71*(1), 3–22.

Hoff, D. F., & Burke, W. W. (2017). *Learning agility: The key to leader potential.* Tulsa, OK: Hogan Press.

Jeanneret, R., & Silzer, R. (Eds.). (1998). *Individual psychological assessment: Predicting behavior in organizational settings.* San Francisco, CA: Jossey-Bass.

Kirkpatrick, D., & Kirkpatrick, P. (2006). *Evaluating training programs* (3rd ed). San Francisco, CA: Berrett-Koehler.

Lombardo, M. M., & Eichinger, R. W. (2000). High potentials as high learners. *Human Resource Management, 39*(4), 321–329.

McCall, M. W., Jr. (1998). *High flyers: Developing the next generation of leaders.* Boston, MA: Harvard Business School Press.

McCall, M. W., Jr. (1994). Identifying leadership potential in future international executives: Developing a concept. *Consulting Psychology Journal, 46*(1), 49–63.

McCall, M. W., Jr., Lombardo, M. M., & Morrison, A. M. (1988). *The lessons of experience: How successful executives develop on the job.* New York, NY: Free Press.

McCauley, C. D., & McCall, M. W., Jr. (Eds.). (2014). *Using experience to develop leadership talent: How organizations leverage on-the-job development.* San Francisco, CA: Jossey-Bass.

McHenry, J. J., & Church, A. H. (2018, April 18). *Leadership development programs: Current state and state-of-the-art.* Pre-Conference Workshop delivered at the 33nd Annual Meeting of the Society for Industrial and Organizational Psychology (SIOP), Chicago, IL.

McRae, I., & Furnham, A. (2014). *High potential: How to spot, manage and develop talent people at work.* London, UK: Bloomsbury.

Mitchinson, A., Gerard, N. M., Roloff, K. S., & Burke, W. W. (2012). Learning agility: Spanning the rigor-relevance divide. *Industrial and Organizational Psychology, 5*(3), 287–290.

Mitchinson, A., & Morris, R. (2014). *Learning about learning agility.* Greensboro, NC: Center for Creative Leadership. Retrieved from https://www.ccl.org/wpcontent/uploads/2015/04/LearningAgility.pdf

Rotolo, C. T., Church, A. H., Adler, S., Smither, J. W., Colquitt, A. L., Shull, . . . A Foster, G. (2018). Putting an end to bad talent management: A call to action for the field of industrial and organizational psychology. *Industrial and Organizational Psychology: Perspectives on Science and Practice, 11*(2), 176–219.

Scott, J. C., & Reynolds, D. H. (Eds.). (2010). *The handbook of workplace assessment: Evidenced based practices for selecting and developing organizational talent.* San Francisco, CA: Jossey-Bass.

Silzer, R., & Church, A. H. (2009). The pearls and perils of identifying potential. *Industrial and Organizational Psychology: Perspectives on Science and Practice, 2*(4), 377–412.

Silzer, R., & Church, A. H. (2010). Identifying and assessing high-potential talent: Current organizational practices. In R. Silzer & B. E. Dowell (Eds.), *Strategy-driven talent management: A leadership imperative* (pp. 213–279). San Francisco, CA: Jossey-Bass.

Silzer, R., Church, A. H., Rotolo, C. T., & Scott, J. C. (2016). I-O practice in action: Solving the leadership potential identification challenge in organizations. *Industrial and Organizational Psychology: Perspectives on Science and Practice, 9*(4), 814–830.

Silzer, R., & Dowell, B. E. (Eds.). (2010). *Strategy-driven talent management: A leadership imperative.* San Francisco, CA: Jossey-Bass.

Spreitzer, G. M., McCall, M. W., Jr., & Mahoney, J. D. (1997). Early identification of international executive potential. *Journal of Applied Psychology, 82*(1), 6–29.

Swisher, V. V., Hallenbeck, G. S., Orr, J. E., Eichinger, R. W., Lombardo, M. M., & Capretta, C. C. (2013). *FYI for learning agility—A must have resource for high potential development (2nd ed.).* Los Angeles, CA: Korn Ferry.

Thornton, G. C., Johnson, S. K., & Church, A. H. (2017). Selecting leaders: High potentials and executives. In N. Tippins & J. Farr (Eds.), *Handbook of employee selection* (Rev. ed., pp. 833–852). London, UK: Routledge.

Trudell, C. M., & Church, A. H. (2016). *Bringing it to life: Global talent scout, convener & coach: PepsiCo's LeADing talent management into the future.* CHREATE Advancing the HR Profession Forward Faster organization profile (best practices profile). http://docplayer.net/27368606-Leading-talent-management-into-the-future.html

4

Measures of Learning Agility

Christine E. Boyce and Anthony S. Boyce

If you cannot measure it, you cannot improve it.
—Lord Kelvin (1824–1907), mathematician

Those involved in talent management and human resource functions are increasingly looking for ways to measure learning agility in the hopes of achieving many desirable outcomes: earlier and more accurate identification of high-potential talent, improved ways to develop learning agility in individuals, and the creation of more agile organizations with learning cultures. This has prompted assessment developers to create a variety of options for practitioners to consider. The purpose of this chapter is to critically evaluate existing, publicly available learning agility assessments so that interested readers can more readily select the tool or tools most relevant to their needs. We begin by reviewing the different methods for assessing learning agility and their relative strengths and weaknesses, specifically self-report measures, multirater surveys, interviews, and simulations. Next, we turn our attention to specific measures of learning agility and the properties of these tools. We conclude with a discussion of the limitations of existing measures and some recommendations for future research.

Identifying Existing Measures of Learning Agility

To identify measures of learning agility, we outlined our criteria for inclusion and then took several steps to ensure we were as comprehensive as possible. To be considered for evaluation, the existing measure had to be publicly available at scale, that is, something developed for use by multiple clients. We

Christine E. Boyce and Anthony S. Boyce, *Measures of Learning Agility* In: *The Age of Agility*. Edited by: Veronica Schmidt Harvey and Kenneth P. De Meuse, Oxford University Press (2021). © Oxford University Press.
DOI: 10.1093/oso/9780190085353.003.0004

did not include scales from academic publications, dissertation theses, and the like.

Second, the measure had to make some claim of measuring learning agility. For example, measures of general personality that are not marketed as leaning agility assessments but that practitioners may have mapped to learning agility dimensions (e.g., the Hogan Assessment Suite, SHL's Occupational Personality Questionnaire [OPQ], Aon's ADEPT-15°) were not included. However, we do address this approach more generally in a subsequent section. This also meant that some tools with similar-sounding names were included and others were not; for example, Korn Ferry's Learning From Experience™ interview was included because it is explicitly marketed as a measure of learning agility, but the Center for Creative Leadership's (CCL's) Learning Tactics Inventory, which purports to measure an individual's preferred learning behavior (but not learning agility explicitly), was not. For similar reasons, we also did not include Development Decisions International's (DDI's) Leadership Potential Inventory or ChangeWise's Leadership Agility™ 360. The DDI tool is not intended for use as a measure of learning agility, and ChangeWise positions their measure of *leadership* agility as a concept distinctly different from *learning* agility.

Third, we did not limit inclusion based on how learning agility was defined by the test publisher. In other words, if the term *learning agility* was used to help describe the tool, it was included, regardless of whether the specific definition of learning agility and/or its dimensions matched those provided elsewhere in this volume. There is one caveat to this final criterion, however. Our research identified two tools, HFMtalentindex's Learning Agility GO° and the Mettl Learning Agility Assessment, which are general measures of personality and/or cognitive ability that have simply been rebranded as measures of learning agility. For this reason, these tools were not considered to be measures of learning agility. However, to help the interested reader formulate a complete picture of the available options, they are discussed further in this chapter when we cover mapping learning agility to existing measures of personality and cognitive ability.

In an effort to uncover all of the tools that met these criteria, we first looked to the academic literature and drew in particular from the 2019 De Meuse meta-analysis. Next, we reached out to our professional networks and fellow assessment practitioners and asked about measures of learning agility with which they were familiar. We then searched the *Buros Mental Measurements Yearbook* (n.d.) for measures of learning agility (none were found). As a final check, we also conducted Google searches for "learning agility," "measures of learning agility," and "learning agility assessments." By using this process, we identified three multirater tools (the Burke Learning Agility Survey™ [Burke LAS™],[1] the CCL's Benchmarks° for Learning Agility™, and Korn Ferry's Choices Architect°); four self-report assessments (the Burke Learning Agility Inventory°, Leader's Gene Consulting's *TALENTx7*°, Korn Ferry's viaEDGE™, and Korn Ferry Assess–Potential Solution[2]), and one publicly available interview (Korn Ferry's Learning From Experience) to include. While no readily available simulations were identified, we address this format as a possible option to measure learning agility. In addition, it should be noted that all of the publicly available tools we were able to uncover are associated in one way or another with competing consulting firms that are motivated to differentiate themselves. As a result, they often use different models of learning agility and/or different names for the various facets of learning agility, making it difficult for a human resources professional without expertise in this space to critically evaluate the substantive differences between the tools.

Administration Method

When selecting any assessment, one of the first features to consider is its administration method, that is, whether it is self-report, multirater, interview, or simulation based. Measures of learning agility are no different as they also exist in various forms, and the same questions should be asked of a measure of learning agility as you would an assessment of any other construct:

- Is this something for which an accurate self-report measure can be developed?
- Are the behaviors to be measured easily observed by other individuals who can then report what they have experienced in response to a multirater survey?
- Is there additional value provided by an interview format that allows for the exploration of context and the ability to probe for more details?
- Can a simulation with sufficient validity and fidelity be created and administered in a way that is not time or resource prohibitive?

---

[1] Includes both a 180- and a 360-degree option.
[2] Includes both the Leadership Potential Report and the Four Dimensional Enterprise Assessment.

- Are the available reporting options for the tool useful to individual test takers and to their organizations? Do they require certified coaches to interpret?

As the choice of format impacts all assessment types, a full treatment of this decision point is beyond the scope of this chapter. Nevertheless, when we consider learning agility in particular, there are a few points worthy of discussion here. These are organized by format type next.

Multirater Tools

While multirater tools were the earliest available in this space (e.g., Choices Architect), those we were able to identify generally had less detailed technical documentation behind them than did the self-report measures. For example, we were unable to find a singular source of technical documentation for Choices Architect and, instead, had to pull from a number of source documents speaking to different aspects of the tool. The technical report for the Benchmarks for Learning Agility (formerly also known as Prospector[*]) suffers from common method variance throughout; that is, when validating the tool, its publisher asked the same set of managers to provide ratings on the tool and also rate participant performance at the same time and then correlated the two sets of scores. While the technical report for the Burke Learning Agility Suite™ provides a relatively robust analysis of the self-report measure (i.e., the Burke Learning Agility Inventory™), additional analyses specific to the multirater (180 and 360) versions are not presented.

In addition, several of the multirater tools we identified did not always exhibit strong content validity with respect to their definitions of learning agility. For example, while Benchmarks for Learning Agility includes some dimensions that can be found across several measures of learning agility, such as flexibility/openness to change, it also includes a much more general set of leadership behaviors, like acting with integrity, being committed to making a difference, and understanding the financials of the business. Likewise, Choices Architect includes behaviors like delivering results, helping others succeed, and executive presence.

Finally, and no different from other multirater tools, multirater measures of learning agility are somewhat constrained relative to self-report measures as they often require more time to complete, involve collecting perspectives from multiple individuals, and are typically only appropriate for development (but not selection or promotion) purposes. However, when thinking about learning agility specifically, unlike other constructs that can be measured via multirater or self-report methods, organizations looking for measures of learning agility are often looking for ways of identifying those individuals in whom to invest more time and development; that is, they *want* to deploy the assessment for selection or decision-making purposes (e.g., to determine acceptance into a high-potential or emerging leader program).

Self-Report Assessments

Considering the constraints noted, more recently developed measures of learning agility come in the form of self-report. These tools typically require less time and fewer resources to administer than a multirater tool and are often created with an eye toward either the selection or development of individuals. All have their roots in one form or another in the original work done by Lombardo and Eichinger (2000) and Eichinger and Lombardo (2004) and then expanded on by De Meuse, Dai, and Hallenbeck (2010) and De Rue, Ashford, and Myers (2012). The technical documentation existing for these tools also tends to be more robust than that available for the multirater tools, and the dimensions they measure tend to be more tightly clustered around their respective definitions of learning agility, as opposed to taking a broader perspective on leadership in general. That said, self-report measures can be more prone to impression management and social desirability concerns than other approaches, the handling of which has been the subject of decades of research and debate (e.g., Griffith & Robie, 2013; McFarland & Ryan, 2000; Ones, Viswesvaran, & Reiss, 1996; Paulhus, 1984).

An important note with regard to self-report assessments is the fact that broader measures of general personality that were developed for use in the workplace (e.g., the Hogan Assessment Suite, SHL's OPQ, Aon's ADEPT-15) are, as previously noted, sometimes mapped by practitioners to the dimensions of learning agility, though some authors discount in large part the relationship between personality and learning agility (e.g., Connolly, 2001; Eichinger & Lombardo, 2004). This is a matter of some debate and is addressed further in a subsequent section.

Interviews

We were only able to identify one publicly available interview that purports to measure learning agility, so it may be difficult to generalize our findings as newer tools are developed. Given the experiential facets of learning agility (e.g., the ability to successfully deploy untested methods in novel settings), it follows that interview questions focusing on the demonstration of these behaviors would be appropriate. Like any interview, of course, there are limitations, including but not limited to, interviewer bias and candidate impression management (see Guion, 1998, for broader treatment of these factors). We were unable to identify any technical documentation for the one interview we identified, Learning From Experience, so we are unable to draw more specific conclusions and do not discuss the interview approach further.

Simulations

While we were unable to uncover any readily available simulation-based measures of learning agility, this format seems highly likely to yield positive measurement properties. Simulations provide a wide range of benefits, not the least of which is an opportunity for participants to behaviorally demonstrate their capabilities in a given area (Boyce, Corbet, & Adler, 2013). Because the very nature of the construct of learning agility requires an individual to demonstrate his or her ability to successfully learn from experiences and perform in new situations, it seems likely that a simulation-based assessment that exposed participants to new experiences where they were challenged to change their approach would be an ideal setting to measure their learning agility. Of course, these benefits must be balanced against the time and resource costs associated with developing, administering, and scoring such an assessment.

Taking a Closer Look at Specific Tools

Given the differences we observed in the existing technical documentation for multirater tools relative to the self-report assessments we identified, we address each of these administration methods in a separate section. For each, we begin with an overview of the properties of each tool, and then we conclude with an evaluation of the strengths and limitations of the measures as options for practitioners looking to assess learning agility in practice.

Multirater Assessments

We identified three publicly available multirater assessments that met our criteria for inclusion in our research: Choices Architect, Benchmarks for Learning Agility, and the Burke LAS. The Choices Architect tool has been officially retired by its publisher, but a description is included here to be comprehensive. It defines learning agility as "ability and willingness to learn from experience and subsequently apply that learning to perform successfully under new or first-time conditions" (Korn Ferry, 2016, p. 1). We agree with the sentiment expressed by De Rue et al. (2012) that defining learning agility in this way confounds the criterion with the predictor—that is, learning agility equates to successful performance (see De Meuse, Dai, Swisher, Eichinger, & Lombardo, 2012, for a contrary view). However, we leave the treatment of that topic to others in this volume and add that despite this concern, we believe there continues to be value in measuring the components of agility as described by Choices Architect:

- Mental Agility: The extent to which an individual embraces complexity, examines problems in unique and unusual ways, is inquisitive, and can make fresh connections between different concepts.
- People Agility: The degree to which one is open-minded toward others; enjoys interacting with a diversity of people; understands their unique strengths, interests, and limitations; and uses them effectively to accomplish organizational goals.
- Change Agility: The extent to which an individual likes change, continuously explores new options and solutions, and is interested in leading organizational change efforts.
- Results Agility: The degree to which an individual is motivated by challenge and can deliver results in first-time and/or tough situations through resourcefulness and by inspiring others.
- Self-Awareness: The degree to which an individual has personal insight, clearly understands his or her strengths and weaknesses, is free of blind spots, and uses this knowledge to perform effectively.

Choices Architect uses 81 Likert-type (5 points: not at all like this, does this less well or less often than most, about like most people, does this better or more often than most, one of the clearest examples of this) items to measure these five overarching dimensions and 27 subdimensions. A single study reporting the construct properties of the tool found very high intercorrelations among the items (average $r = 0.86$) and support for a single factor, as opposed to the multiple factors hypothesized (Connolly, 2001). This suggests that the measure is assessing a single unitary construct and limits interpretability of the separate dimensions. With the exception of openness to experience, Connolly also found no significant correlations between Choices Architect and personality or cognitive ability. Substantial criterion-related validity with ratings of job performance was found across several studies. However, some of the studies (e.g., Connolly, 2001) appear to have suffered from common method bias (see Podsakoff, MacKenzie, Lee, & Podsakoff, 2003, for an explanation of this issue) as the same supervisors contributed to ratings of learning agility and ratings of performance. Other studies (e.g., Eichinger & Lombardo, 2004; Lombardo & Eichinger, 2000) provided limited technical details on which to base an effective evaluation of the quality of the study.

The second multirater tool we identified was Benchmarks for Learning Agility. It contains 48 Likert-type (7 points: very strongly disagree, strongly disagree, disagree, neutral, agree, strongly agree, very strongly agree) items measuring 11 dimensions across two categories: learning to learn and learning to lead, as noted in Table 4.1 (Center for Creative Leadership, 2018).

Our view of Benchmarks is that (similar to Choices Architect) the technical documentation (Leslie & Braddy, 2015) is limited. Construct validity evidence is limited to reporting dimension intercorrelations (average

Table 4.1 Benchmarks for Learning Agility Dimensions

Learning to Learn	Learning to Lead
• Seeks opportunities to learn	• Committed to making a difference
• Seeks and uses feedback	• Insightful: sees things from new angles
• Learns from mistakes	• Has the courage to take risks
• Open to criticism	• Brings out the best in people
	• Acts with integrity
	• Seeks broad business knowledge
	• Adapts to cultural differences

Adapted from Center for Creative Leadership. (2018). *Benchmarks˚ for Learning Agility˚: Measuring adaptive knowledge.* Retrieved from https://www.ccl.org/wp-content/uploads/2016/08/benchmarks-for-learning-agility-brochure-center-for-creative-leadership.pdf

$r = 0.53$), and a correlation of $r = 0.35$ between supervisor ratings of learning agility and peer ratings on a separate measure of learning from experience. One criterion-related validity study is reported, but it suffers from common method bias as supervisors provided learning agility and performance ratings at the same time.

The third multirater tool, the Burke LAS, is available as either a 180-degree feedback tool (self-ratings, plus those from one other rater/rater group) or a 360-degree feedback tool (self-ratings, plus those from up to four other groups or individuals). It is based on the same model and contains the same 38 Likert-type (7 points: never, once in a while, sometimes, fairly often, often, constantly, always) items as the self-report measure described in the following material. The available technical report does not provide a review of the psychometric properties of the tool(s) that is specific to the multirater versions; the interested reader is directed to the self-report measures discussion that follows for further details on its development and rigor. From a reporting perspective, the 180 and 360 reports are similar in that both contain the following elements: spider web diagrams (self vs. others), dimension-level scores, highest and lowest scored items, unrecognized strengths/blind spots, item-level data by rater perspective, and responses to open-ended questions.[3]

Also consistent with our view of Choices Architect, we do believe there is value in measuring the behaviors included in the Benchmarks tool. In fact, the experienced reader will notice that many of the dimensions it covers can also be found in other multirater measures of general leadership (e.g., 3D Group's Leadership Navigator® also measures acting with integrity and building strong teams, and the Management Research Group's Leadership Effectiveness Analysis™ also measures willingness to take risks and bringing out the best in others). The feedback report for Benchmarks contains both importance for success and average scores for each competency (including self vs. other breakouts); norm group comparisons overall and by rater group; item-level feedback, including highest and lowest rated items; qualitative comments; and items with the greatest differences between all raters and self scores.

---

[3] When reviewing our comments regarding the reporting options available for any of the tools listed, it should be noted that one of the most frequently updated components of any vendor-developed assessment is the report itself. Statements made in this chapter pertaining to the content and use of each report constitute a point-in-time evaluation that is subject to change as tools and/or reports are updated by their publishers.

For practitioners interested in adopting one of the multirater measures of learning agility mentioned, we recommend the following:

- Ensuring the tools are used only for development and not in high-stakes (i.e., decision-making) settings.
- Carefully evaluating the dimensions being measured to be certain those are the (only) dimensions on which you would like to gather input.
- Ensuring those using the tool (participants, their coaches, their managers, human resources) clearly understand the purpose of the tool, how it should be used, and what it measures.
- Applying all other best practices associated with the use of multirater assessments (see Church, Bracken, Fleenor, & Rose, 2019, for broader coverage of this topic).

Self-Report Measures

Four self-report measures met our criteria for inclusion (note that three of these were also reviewed by De Meuse, 2017). We begin by presenting each in Table 4.2, which includes the test publisher's definition of learning agility, the dimensions being assessed, and a list of important test properties like reliability, validity, and features, such as length and whether or not certification is available. Based on a content analysis of the dimension definitions, we also mapped each tool's dimensions to those of the other tools to help the interested reader more readily identify similarities and differences across the measures. We follow this information with a discussion of the specific strengths and vulnerabilities of each tool.

Burke Learning Agility Inventory

Overall, the Burke Learning Agility Inventory™ demonstrates several strengths. First, it has a strong conceptual framework and avoids the issues noted concerning confounding performance and outcomes with predictors. Second, the three criterion-related validity studies included in the technical report used strong research designs, had sufficient sample sizes (from $n = 74$ to $n = 229$), and showed positive, uncorrected correlations with job performance ranging from $r = 0.13$ to $r = 0.42$ (Burke, 2019). Third, there is good construct validity evidence as established by confirmatory factor analysis

Table 4.2 Self-Report Measures of Learning Agility: Summary of Psychometric Characteristics

	Burke Learning Agility Inventory™	TALENTx7®	viaEDGE	Korn Ferry Assess–Potential Solution[a]
Definition	The engagement in learning behaviors to enhance the capacity to reconfigure activities quickly to meet the changing demands in the task environment.	Ability to learn quickly and then the willingness to apply those lessons to perform successfully in new and challenging leadership situations.	Ability and willingness to learn from experience and subsequently apply that learning to perform successfully under new or first-time conditions.	Ability and willingness to learn from experience and subsequently apply that learning to perform successfully under new or first-time conditions.
Dimensions	Flexibility: Being open to new ideas and proposing new solutions.	Cognitive Perspective: The degree to which individuals think critically and strategically to solve complex problems; embrace difficult, multifaceted organizational issues; approach situations from a broad, high-level perspective; and focus on multiple inputs rather than from only one or two functional/technical perspectives.	Mental Agility: The extent to which an individual embraces complexity, examines problems in unique and unusual ways, is inquisitive, and can make fresh connections between different concepts.	Mental Agility: Tendency to be inquisitive and approach problems in novel ways.
	Collaborating: Finding ways to work with others that generate unique opportunities for learning.	Interpersonal Acumen: The extent to which individuals interact effectively with a diversity of people; understand others' unique motives, values, and goals as well as their strengths and limitations; instill confidence in them; and leverage them to perform successfully on their jobs.	People Agility: The degree to which one is open-minded toward others; enjoys interacting with a diversity of people; understands their unique strengths, interests, and limitations; and uses them effectively to accomplish organizational goals.	People Agility: Skill in reading others and applying the insights gained when working with others.

Experimenting: Trying out new behaviors (i.e., approaches, ideas) to determine what is effective.	Change Alacrity: The level to which individuals are curious and eager to learn new ideas and ways of behaving; open-minded to new situations; relish change; and continuously seek innovative (and at times risky) approaches to perform their jobs.	Change Agility: The extent to which an individual likes change, continuously explores new options and solutions, and is interested in leading organizational change efforts.	Change Agility: Embracing change and taking well-reasoned risks in the face of that change to promote new possibilities and to take ideas from vision to reality.
—	Drive to Excel: The extent to which individuals are motivated by difficult assignments, set challenging personal and organizational goals, are resourceful, and can be counted on to deliver results in new and untested situations.	Results Agility: The degree to which an individual is motivated by challenge and can deliver results in first-time and/or tough situations through resourcefulness and by inspiring others.	Results Agility: Motivation to deliver outstanding results in new and tough situations.
Reflecting: Slowing down to evaluate one's own performance in order to be more effective.	Self-Insight: The degree to which individuals accurately understand themselves, their capabilities, weaknesses, beliefs, values, feelings, and personal goals as it relates to the workplace.	Self-Awareness: The degree to which an individual has personal insight, clearly understands his or her strengths and weaknesses, is free of blind spots, and uses this knowledge to perform effectively.	Situational Self-Awareness: Ability to regulate emotions, accept circumstances, live in the moment, and reserve judgment.

(continued)

Table 4.2 *Continued*

Burke Learning Agility Inventory™	TALENTx7®	viaEDGE	Korn Ferry Assess– Potential Solution[a]
—	Environmental Mindfulness: The level to which individuals are fully observant of their external surroundings, attentive to the changing job duties and requirements of new organizational roles, approach environmental changes in a nonjudgmental manner, and regulate their emotions effectively.	—	
Feedback Seeking: Asking others for feedback on one's ideas and overall performance.	Feedback Responsiveness: The extent to which individuals solicit, listen to, and accept personal feedback from others; carefully consider its merits; and subsequently take corrective action for performance improvement.	—	
Speed: Acting on ideas quickly so that those not working are discarded and other possibilities are accelerated.	—	—	

	Information Gathering: Using various methods to remain current in one's area of expertise.	—		—
Development Approach	Literature review and preliminary testing.	Eight subject matter experts developed and q-sorted items, followed by empirical refinements focused on reliability, construct validity, and minimizing subgroup differences.	Multiple phases of pilot studies to refine item pool over 2 years.	Not addressed.[b]
Number of Items	38	70 items measuring learning agility; 78 items measuring response validity.	53 items measuring learning agility; 63 items measuring response validity.	240–280; number of items specifically comprising learning agility scales not addressed.
Test Time	Not addressed	20–30 minutes.	30 minutes.	35 minutes.
Response Format	Likert (7 point: never, once in a while, sometimes, fairly often, often, constantly, always).	Likert (5 point: strongly disagree, disagree, neither disagree nor agree—neutral, agree, strongly agree) for learning agility; Likert and forced-choice for response validity scales).	Likert (5 point: anchors not specified); biographical data, situational judgment.	Forced-choice ranking (most to least preferred) with four-item blocks.
Measurement Model	Classical test theory.	Classical test theory.	Classical test theory.	Item response theory.

(continued)

Table 4.2 Continued

	Burke Learning Agility Inventory™	TALENTx7®	viaEDGE	Korn Ferry Assess– Potential Solution[a]
Reliability				
Internal Consistency (α)	>0.75 dimension scales.	0.92 overall; >0.70 dimension scales, except Environmental Mindfulness = 0.61.	0.88 overall; >0.70 for dimension scales.	>0.80 dimension scales, except Situational Self-Awareness = 0.65.
Test–Retest	Not addressed.	0.82 overall, 40-day period.	0.90 overall, 45-day period.	Not addressed.
Construct Validity				
Factor Structure	CFA support, average dimension intercorrelation 0.45 to 0.63 across three samples.	CFA support, average dimension intercorrelation 0.48.	CFA support, average dimension intercorrelation 0.34.	Not addressed.
Convergent and Discriminant (correlations with overall learning agility)	$r = 0.42$ with tolerance for ambiguity; $r = 0.42$ with generalized self-efficacy; $r = -0.27$ with locus of control; correlations ranged from -0.36 (neuroticism) to 0.44 (openness to experience) with measures of the Big Five ($n = 193$); correlations ranged from 0.53 ($n = 279$) to 0.75 ($n = 194$) with learning goal orientation; $r = -0.14$ with reactance ($n = 209$) and $r = -0.21$ with risk aversion ($n = 193$).	$r = 0.78$ with viaEDGE measure of learning agility ($n = 18$).	$r = 0.42$ with learning agility-focused structured interview ($n = 39$); $r = 0.73$ with learning agility-focused multirater ($n = 32$); correlations ranged from -0.12 (prudence) to 0.48 (inquisitive) with Hogan Personality Inventory ($n = 119$); correlations ranging from -0.16 (excitable) to 0.44 (colorful) with Hogan Development Survey ($n = 114$); $r = -0.03$ with undergrad GPA ($n = 375$ MBA students).	Correlations with overall learning agility not reported. Dimension score correlations ranged from $r = -0.26$ (between mental agility and attention to detail) to $r = 0.50$ (between change agility and adaptability) with the Global Personality Inventory[c] ($n = 481$).

Criterion Validity

No. of Studies	3	2	3	2
Coefficients	Study 1: $r = 0.42$ with executive recruitment firm ratings of executive-level success for wealth management executives (uncorrected, $n = 130$); Study 2: $r = 0.13$ with supervisor ratings of overall performance for high-potential mid- and senior-level leaders (uncorrected, $n = 74$); Study 3: $r = 0.14$ (judgment) to 0.34 (inspirational leadership) with supervisor ratings of performance for potential leaders (uncorrected, $n = 229$).	Study 1: $r = 0.31$ with supervisor ratings of performance for high-potential leadership program participants (uncorrected; $n = 32$); Study 2: $r = 0.62$ with supervisor ratings of overall leadership competence for supervisors and managers (corrected for unreliability and range restriction; $n = 43$).	Study 1: $r = 0.44$ and $r = 0.35$ with promotion rate and salary growth over 10-year period for district sales managers (uncorrected, $n = 83$); Study 2: $r = 0.29$, $r = 0.25$, and $r = 0.38$ with supervisor ratings of leadership competence, chief executive officer proximity, and compensation for managers and executives (uncorrected, $n = 101$); Study 3: $r = 0.12$ with supervisor ratings of overall job performance for engineers (uncorrected, $n = 30$) and $r = 0.35$ for project managers (uncorrected, $n = 27$).	Study 1: Learning agility dimension scores significantly higher for various leadership level vs. individual contributor roles, Cohen's d between role effect sizes varied from 0.10 to 0.73 (n varies from 551 to 4,915 depending on role); Study 2: $r = 0.08$ (Situational Self-Awareness) to $r = 0.37$ (Results Agility) with work engagement (uncorrected; $n = 54,048$).
Incremental Validity	Not addressed.	Not addressed.	Not addressed.	Learning agility measure demonstrated significant incremental validity over education (Study 1 and 2) and emotional intelligence (Study 1).

(continued)

Table 4.2 *Continued*

	Burke Learning Agility Inventory™	TALENTx7®	viaEDGE	Korn Ferry Assess–Potential Solution[a]
Response Validity				
Approach	Behaviorally based questions and frequency rating scale to mitigate response distortion concerns that are present with other types of self-report.	Selective wording used to avoid social desirability; pilot tests conducted to remove items with high mean scores, and specific measurement via scales.	Careful wording to avoid social desirability; pilot test to remove items with high mean scores, and measurement via scales.	Forced choice to mitigate response distortion concerns present with Likert-type self-report.
Social Desirability	—	One scale measuring overly positive or humble self-presentation; two scales measuring endorsement of socially desirable, but non–agility-related items that tend to be negatively correlated with learning agility (e.g., detail oriented, planful, methodical).	One scale measuring overly positive or humble self-presentation; two scales measuring endorsement of socially desirable, but non–agility-related items that tend to be negatively correlated with learning agility (e.g., detail oriented, planful, methodical); one scale measuring consistency of within-person ranking of scales relative to the norms for high and low learning agility individuals.	—
Inattentive Responding	—	Response consistency scale.	Response consistency scale.	—

Additional Considerations	—	Reported scores adjusted for systematic distortion due to self-presentation and flagged on the basis of other response validity scales and a combined overall accuracy index.	Reported scores adjusted for systematic distortion due to self-presentation and flagged on the basis of other response validity scales and a combined overall accuracy index.	—
Subgroup Differences				
Age	Not addressed.	$r = -0.04$.	$r = -0.03$.	Not addressed.
Race		Slightly higher means for African Americans and Hispanics than Caucasians.	$d = 0.05$ favoring Caucasians over African Americans and $d = -0.11$ favoring Hispanics over Caucasians.	$d = 0.01$ favoring African Americans over Caucasians, $d = 0.02$ favoring Hispanics over Caucasians, and $d = -0.12$ favoring Caucasians over Asians.
Gender	Not addressed.	$d = 0.00$.	$d = 0.04$ favoring men.	$d = 0.07$ favoring men.
Global Applicability				

(continued)

Table 4.2 *Continued*

	Burke Learning Agility Inventory™	TALENTx7®	viaEDGE	Korn Ferry Assess–Potential Solution[a]
Cross-cultural Measurement	Not addressed.	Not addressed.	Not addressed.	Not addressed.
Translations	Not addressed.	English, Chinese (Simplified), German, Indonesian, Japanese, Portuguese, Spanish, Turkish, French, Dutch (forthcoming).	English, Chinese (Simplified) French, Italian, German, Spanish (International), Portuguese (Brazil), Japanese.	Not addressed.
Reported Norms				
Sample Characteristics	Working population, 16% outside United States, $n = 445$.	Working population, 85% outside United States, $n = 3,550$.	Working population, 57% outside United States, $n = 3,000$.	Working population, global representation and characteristics depend on norm variant.
Variants	Not addressed.	Not addressed.	Not addressed.	Norms provided for six leadership levels: first-level leader, midlevel leader, functional leader, business or organizational unit/division leader, senior/top functional executive, top business or organizational group executive.

Reporting & Certification	Normed report provides overall learning agility score as well as score by dimension; the "original report" includes descriptions of strengths and development needs at the dimension level, and the "expanded report" provides this information at the item level. Reports require certification to interpret.	Three reporting options: (a) individual feedback report, (b) professional coach's report, and (c) organizational report. Both (a) and (b) require certification to interpret. The organizational report provides scores for each individual in a group. All scores are percentile based, and reports include an overall learning agility score as well as scores for each of the seven facets. At the facet level, both positive behaviors and potential derailers are identified.	Four options available: The optional individual summary report provides results on each scale but no specific scores. Scale names are replaced with descriptions of each learning agility factor. The feedback report provides percentile-based data for each learning agility factor; requires certification to interpret. The coaching report includes feedback report components plus additional psychometric details; only available to certified coaches. Group reports provide details for each individual, including overall and factor scores, group means, and score distributions.	Both in-depth reports that require certification to interpret and those that can be self-interpreted (no additional training required) are available, as are options to customize/configure the reports for a specific organization's needs.

(*continued*)

Table 4.2 Continued

	Burke Learning Agility Inventory™	TALENTx7®	viaEDGE	Korn Ferry Assess–Potential Solution[a]
Technical Report				
Version	3.5	Third edition	12.1b–05/16	19.1a–07/2019
Year	2019	2019	2016	2019
URL	https://easi.egnyte.com/dl/qzSLVOm9Ap/	https://thetalentx7.com/2016/07/development-validation-talentx7-assessment-psychological-measure-learning-agility/	https://easi.egnyte.com/dl/qzSLVOm9Ap	https://www.kornferry.com/content/dam/kornferry/docs/article-migration//KF4D_Executive_Manual_FINAL.pdf[d]

[a] While either the Korn Ferry Assess–Potential Solution (Leadership Potential Report) or the Korn Ferry Four Dimensional Enterprise Assessment can be used to measure learning agility, using what appear to be identical administration methodologies, the "Potential Solution" technical report was published more recently and was therefore used as the basis of this review.

[b] Indicates this item was not addressed in the technical documentation available to the authors at the time of writing.

[c] Additional information on the Global Personality Inventory can be found in Schmit, Kihm, and Robie, 2002.

[d] URL no longer available; must be requested from Korn Ferry directly.

CFA, confirmatory factor analysis.

and correlations in the expected directions with both related (e.g., tolerance for ambiguity, openness to experience) and unrelated (e.g., reactance, risk aversion) constructs. Finally, the test is less than half the length of the other self-report instruments. There are, however, some limitations in that the technical report provides no examination of subgroup differences and no evidence of test–retest reliability.

TALENTx7®

The *TALENTx7®* tool has several strengths of note as well. First, it is based on a strong conceptual framework, though its definition of agility does face the circular issue described previously by defining agility as successful performance. Second, virtually no subgroup differences were found in the studies presented in the technical report (De Meuse, Lim, & Rao, 2019). Third, the technical report lists nine available languages with one additional forthcoming. In terms of opportunities, however, limited construct validity evidence was provided (only one study with a sample of 18 people in which *TALENTx7®* scores were correlated with scores on viaEDGE), and the criterion-related validity studies that were completed had relatively small sample sizes (two studies with $n = 32$ and $n = 43$), although the uncorrected correlations with performance were significant ($r = 0.31$ and $r = 0.62$, respectively). Further, the test publisher uses social desirability scales to identify and correct for social desirability, a practice that may be of negligible utility, especially in selection contexts (Griffith & Robie, 2013).

viaEDGE

Like its counterparts, we observed several positive features of the viaEDGE tool as well. First, it presents thorough construct validity evidence via confirmatory factor analysis and correlations in the expected directions with both related (e.g., learning agility–focused interview, inquisitive) and unrelated (e.g., the Excitable dimension on the Hogan Development Survey) constructs (Korn Ferry, 2016). Second, criterion-related validity evidence was demonstrated across three studies with sample sizes ranging from $n = 27$ to $n = 101$ and showing uncorrected correlations with job performance ranging from $r = 0.12$ to $r = 0.44$. Third, virtually no subgroup differences were found. Fourth, the technical report lists eight available languages. However, the tool uses a similar approach to the use of social desirability scales as *TALENTx7®*, which may not be effective.

Korn Ferry—Assess–Potential Solution (and the Korn Ferry Four Dimensional Enterprise Assessment)

Learning agility scores can be computed from either the Korn Ferry Assess– Potential or the Korn Ferry Four Dimensional Enterprise Assessment in- strument using identical methodologies. The item response theory (IRT) measurement approach they utilize is a strength. In addition, the forced choice item format helps ensure response validity by mitigating item dis- tortion due to socially desirable responding. Further, the sample sizes used in the reported validity studies were sufficiently large, ranging from $n = 515$ to $n = 54,048$. However, given the similarity of scales, the test publisher has missed an opportunity to tie the factors measured by this tool back to those of its predecessor, viaEDGE, as a way of supporting construct and criterion- related validity.

Limitations of All the Self-Assessments Examined

Looking across all four self-assessments of learning agility, they share some common opportunities for future research. First, and most importantly, it remains an open question regarding whether learning agility provides incre- mental validity above and beyond the combination of personality and cog- nitive ability. While some research has made claims that this is the case (e.g., Bedford, 2011; Connolly, 2001), we were unable to find a well-designed study to clearly answer this specific question.

Second, none of the tools we reviewed reported having different norms for selection versus development use. This is important, given that test takers tend to perform differently in high-stakes (i.e., selection) versus lower stakes (i.e., development) settings (Ellingson, Sackett, & Connolly, 2007). This lim- itation persists even when corrections to learning agility scores are made based on the inclusion of social desirability scales designed to identify re- sponse distortion, as these scales have been shown to be ineffective in iden- tifying socially desirable responders (Griffith & Peterson, 2008; Griffith & Robie, 2013). Further, using social desirability scales to correct self-report assessment scores, especially in high-stakes settings, is not supported by research (Burns & Christiansen, 2006; Reader & Ryan, 2012).

Finally, while some of the technical reports showed no mean difference across racial backgrounds (e.g., *TALENTx7®*, viaEDGE), none of the tools reviewed provided evidence of true global equivalence (i.e., moving beyond racial descriptors to cross-cultural ones and utilizing the more robust approach of examining these relationships via multiple groups confirmatory factory analysis) or cross-cultural norms, despite some being translated into multiple languages.

Using Personality and Cognitive Measures to Assess Learning Agility: A Closer Look

As noted, there are two distinct situations where personality measures have been used to measure learning agility: when an existing personality (sometimes combined with cognitive) measure is explicitly repackaged as a measure of learning agility, and when existing personality measures are simply mapped to the dimensions of learning agility. When considering either option, there are important caveats to consider.

Our review uncovered two tools in particular that are marketed as measures of learning agility, but, on closer inspection, are existing personality measures being sold as learning agility measures. These are the Mettl Learning Agility Assessment and Learning Agility GO. The Mettl Learning Agility Assessment is actually a combination of two other Mettl assessments: Mettl Personality Profiler and Mettl Test for Cognitive Abilities. These assessments have been combined to produce reporting along four dimensions: mental agility, people agility, change agility, and results agility. However, the items are the same as the original tools, which were not designed with learning agility in mind. Learning Agility GO offers several learning agility–related reports, but at its core is a personality assessment whose results have been reconfigured for reporting purposes. It provides reporting along the same four dimensions as Mettl, plus the additional dimension of self-awareness.

The challenge in evaluating tools of this type, as well as determining whether it is appropriate to map the dimensions of other personality assessments to learning agility, is that the literature has yet to come to a decisive conclusion regarding whether learning agility is even related to either personality or cognitive ability, despite clear conceptual linkages (De Rue et al., 2012; Hezlett & Kuncel, 2012). Several studies have reported that learning agility is not related to personality. For example, Connolly (2001) reported that Choices Architect is largely uncorrelated with the Big Five personality dimensions (i.e., openness, conscientiousness, extraversion, agreeableness, and neuroticism; Digman, 1997), with the exception of mental agility and change agility being correlated with openness ($r = 0.21$ and $r = 0.23$, respectively). Bedford (2011) also showed no relationship between learning agility and either the Hogan Development Survey (HDS) or the California Personality Inventory (CPI™). It is important to note, however, that both studies also showed no relationship between the Big Five and performance, contrary to more common findings (e.g., Schmidt & Hunter, 1998).

This last finding suggests that methodological limitations (e.g., unique operationalization of learning agility or personality, range restriction in personality) may be at least partly to blame for the observation of no relationships between personality and learning agility. Contrary to these studies, both the Burke Learning Agility Inventory™ and viaEDGE technical reports documented substantial correlations between learning agility and personality measured with several different instruments (e.g., Hogan Personality Inventory; Table 4.2).

As with personality, the question of a relationship between learning agility and cognitive ability has yet to be decided in the literature. To begin, it is clear that cognitive ability is related to ability to learn (Gottfredson, 1997; Kanfer & Ackerman, 1989), so how might it be possible to measure *learning* agility without including some sort of cognitive component?

However, some oft-cited research has shown no relationship between learning agility and cognitive ability. For example, Connolly (2001) showed not only no relationship between learning agility and cognitive ability, but also no relationship between cognitive ability and performance or promotability. Similar to the personality findings, this is contrary to established research (e.g., Schmidt & Hunter, 1998). Bedford (2011) showed a similar pattern of results, with no relationship between cognitive ability and either learning agility or performance. This calls into question the methodologies of both studies.

In addition, the viaEDGE technical report also showed no correlation between learning agility and performance as measured by undergraduate grade point average (GPA), but their sample of current master's of business administration (MBA) students came from a range of different universities across the globe, making it difficult to confirm that GPA was measured similarly across institutions. In addition, GPA as a criterion likely suffered from severe range restriction in that all of the students had the ability to be accepted into an MBA program. One potential explanation of these findings could be that self-report measures of learning agility are contaminated by Dunning–Kruger cognitive biases (Kruger & Dunning, 1999), whereby individuals who are lower in cognitive ability are self-assessing as more learning agile than they actually are. Future research should explore these questions further.

The Future of Measuring Learning Agility

In today's complex assessment market, there is a wide range of publicly available tools that purport to measure learning agility. However, they vary not only in terms of what they measure, but also in how well they measure it, making it difficult for even the savviest practitioner to sort through it all. As noted, many of the tools we uncovered have strong measurement properties, but each also comes with its own unique limitations in terms of its design or the evidence that supports its use. With this in mind, we make several recommendations for future research.

First, the question of the relationship between learning agility and personality and cognitive ability needs to be clearly addressed via a program of research with strong study design and repeatable findings. Second, the question of whether measures of learning agility demonstrate incremental validity beyond personality and cognitive ability needs further exploration. Third, additional research to conduct confirmatory factor analysis testing of competing models—a standard practice in measurement development research—would help provide clarity around the dimensional structure of learning agility and its relationship to other constructs. Fourth, we encourage practitioners and researchers to explore other, more behavioral measures of learning agility (e.g., the development of simulations) that can provide ways of eliciting learning agility, which by its very definition, requires learning and relearning over time. Such research is critical in refining the measurement of learning agility to solidify its place as an enduring and critical component of leadership development and effectiveness.

References

Bedford, C. L. (2011). *The role of learning agility in workplace performance and career advancement* (Unpublished doctoral dissertation). University of Minnesota, Minneapolis.

Boyce, A. S., Corbet, C. E., & Adler, S. (2013). Simulations in the selection context: Considerations, challenges, and opportunities. In M. Fetzer & K. Tuzinski (Eds.), *Simulations for personnel selection* (pp. 17–41). New York, NY: Springer.

Burke, W. (2019). *Technical report: Burke Learning Agility Inventory®, v3.5*. Retrieved from https://easi.egnyte.com/dl/qzSLVOm9Ap/

Burns, G. N., & Christiansen, N. D. (2006). Sensitive or senseless: On the use of social desirability measures in selection and assessment. In R. L. Griffith & M. H. Peterson (Eds.), *A closer examination of applicant faking behavior* (pp. 115–150). Greenwich, CT: Information Age.

Buros Mental Measurements Yearbook. (n.d.). Retrieved from https://buros.org/mental-measurements-yearbook

Center for Creative Leadership. (2018). *Benchmarks® for Learning Agility™: Measuring adaptive knowledge.* Retrieved from https://www.ccl.org/wp-content/uploads/2016/08/benchmarks-for-learning-agility-brochure-center-for-creative-leadership.pdf

Church, A. H., Bracken, D. W., Fleenor, J. W., & Rose, D. S. (Eds.). (2019). *The handbook of strategic 360 feedback.* New York, NY: Oxford University Press.

Connolly, J. (2001). *Assessing the construct validity of a measure of learning agility* (Unpublished doctoral dissertation). Florida International University, Miami.

De Meuse, K. P. (2017). Learning agility: Its evolution as a psychological construct and its empirical relationship to leader success. *Consulting Psychology Journal: Practice and Research, 69,* 267–295.

De Meuse, K. P. (2019). A meta-analysis of the relationship between learning agility and leader success. *Journal of Organizational Psychology, 19*(1), 25–34.

De Meuse, K. P., Dai, G., & Hallenbeck, G. S. (2010). Learning agility: A construct whose time has come. *Consulting Psychology Journal, 62,* 119–130.

De Meuse, K. P., Dai, G., Swisher, V. V., Eichinger, R. W., & Lombardo, M. M. (2012). Leadership development: Exploring, clarifying, and expanding our understanding of learning agility. *Industrial and Organizational Psychology: Perspectives on Science and Practice, 5,* 280–286.

De Meuse, K. P., Lim, J., & Rao, R. (2019). *The development and validation of the TALENTx7® Assessment: A psychological measure of learning agility, third edition.* Retrieved from https://thetalentx7.com/2016/07/development-validation-talentx7-assessment-psychological-measure-learning-agility/

De Rue, S. D., Ashford, S. J., & Myers, C. G. (2012). Learning agility: In search of conceptual clarity and theoretical grounding. *Industrial and Organizational Psychology: Perspectives on Science and Practice, 5,* 258–279.

Digman, J. M. (1997). Higher-order factors of the Big Five. *Journal of Personality and Social Psychology, 73,* 1246–1256.

Eichinger, R. W., & Lombardo, M. M. (2004). Learning agility as a prime indicator of potential. *Human Resource Planning, 27,* 12–15.

Ellingson, J. E., Sackett, P. R., & Connelly, B. S. (2007). Personality assessment across selection and development contexts: Insights into response distortion. *Journal of Applied Psychology, 92*(2), 386–395.

Gottfredson, L. S. (1997). Why g matters: The complexity of everyday life. *Intelligence, 24,* 79–132.

Griffith, R. L., & Peterson, M. H. (2008). The failure of social desirability measures to capture applicant faking behavior. *Industrial and Organizational Psychology: Perspectives on Science and Practice, 1,* 308–311.

Griffith, R. L., & Robie, C. (2013). Personality testing and the "F-word:" Revisiting seven questions about faking. In N. D. Christiansen & R. P. Tett (Eds.), *Handbook of personality at work* (pp. 253–280). New York, NY: Routledge.

Guion, R. M. (1998). *Assessment, measurement, and prediction for personnel decisions.* Mahwah, NJ: Erlbaum.

Hezlett, S. A., & Kuncel, N. R. (2012). Prioritizing the learning agility research agenda. *Industrial and Organizational Psychology: Perspectives on Science and Practice, 5,* 296–305.

Kanfer, R., & Ackerman, P. L. (1989). Motivation and cognitive abilities: An integrative/ aptitude-treatment interaction approach to skill acquisition [Monograph]. *Journal of Applied Psychology, 79,* 826–835.

Korn Ferry. (2016). *viaEDGE® technical manual, version 12.1b–05/16.*

Kruger, J., & Dunning, D. (1999). Unskilled and unaware of it: How difficulties in recognizing one's own incompetence lead to inflated self-assessments. *Journal of Personality and Social Psychology, 77*(6), 1121–1134.

Leslie, J. B., & Braddy, P. W. (2015). *Benchmarks for learning agility technical manual.* Greensboro, NC: Center for Creative Leadership.

Lombardo, M. M., & Eichinger, R. W. (2000). High potentials as high learners. *Human Resources Management, 39,* 321–330.

McFarland, L. A., & Ryan, A. M. (2000). Variance in faking across non-cognitive measures. *Journal of Applied Psychology, 85,* 812–821.

Ones, D. S., Viswesvaran, C., & Reiss, A. D. (1996). Role of social desirability in personality testing for personnel selection: The red herring. *Journal of Applied Psychology, 81,* 660–679.

Paulhus, D. L. (1984). Two-component models of socially desirable responding. *Journal of Personality and Social Psychology, 46,* 598–609.

Podsakoff, P. M., MacKenzie, S. B., Lee, J. Y., & Podsakoff, N. P. (2003). Common method biases in behavioral research: A critical review of the literature and recommended remedies. *Journal of Applied Psychology, 88,* 879–903.

Reader, M. C., & Ryan, A. M. (2012). Methods for correcting faking. In M. Ziegler, C. MacCann, & R. Roberts (Eds.), *New perspectives on faking in personality assessments* (pp. 131–150). Oxford, UK: Oxford University Press.

Schmidt, F. L., & Hunter, J. E. (1998). The validity and utility of selection methods in personnel psychology. *Psychological Bulletin, 124*(4), 262–274.

Schmit, M. J., Kihm, J. A., & Robie, C. (2002). The global personality inventory (GPI). In B. de Raad & M. Perugini (Eds.), *Big Five assessment* (pp. 195–236). Boston, MA: Hogrefe & Huber.

5

The Neuroscience of Learning Agility

Kim E. Ruyle

I am a brain, Watson. The rest of me is a mere appendix.
—*The Adventure of the Mazarin Stone*, Arthur Conan Doyle (1859–
1930), British writer

Considered superficially, learning agility seems a simple construct—the ability and willingness to learn lessons and apply those lessons in new and challenging situations (Eichinger & Lombardo, 2004; Lombardo & Eichinger, 2000). But in practice, learning agility is far from simple. It is a complex, multifaceted construct. There are a variety of behavioral preferences and skills that enable learning agility; they tend to exist in concentrated combinations in individuals who are learning agile. For example, the learning agile are likely to demonstrate many of the following behaviors:

- Be engaged and energized by complexity, show a high degree of curiosity, and risk failure in order to learn.
- Empathize, accurately read the emotional state of others, and adapt their demeanor to optimize relationships.
- Experiment, be an early adopter, and champion change.
- Demonstrate resilience and maintain optimism when faced with difficulties that may create paralysis or panic in others.
- Be proactive in seeking feedback, recognize their own weaknesses, and demonstrate confidence without being self-satisfied.
- Demonstrate a high tolerance for ambiguity and quickly adapt to new situations. (De Meuse, 2017; Swisher, 2012).

One's personality comprises behavioral preferences in a given context (Hogan, Curphy, & Hogan, 1994). It follows then that learning agility is

Kim E. Ruyle, *The Neuroscience of Learning Agility* In: *The Age of Agility*. Edited by: Veronica Schmidt Harvey and Kenneth P. De Meuse, Oxford University Press (2021). © Oxford University Press. DOI: 10.1093/oso/9780190085353.003.0005 determined, to a significant degree, by one's personality. In addition to deep-seated behavioral preferences, learning agility is enhanced by giving a high level of attention to the situations in which lessons are learned. The very act of learning involves working memory, consolidation of working memory in long-term memory, and retrieval of those memories. All these things are enabled by the nervous system and governed by the brain. This chapter introduces the nervous system, with a focus on brain functions that can provide insight into how learning agility is developed and practically applied.

Neuroscience Fundamentals

Neuroscience is the study of the structure and workings of the nervous system, the network of nerve cells that quicken our being, that animate our bodies. The nervous system is organized in two primary channels: (a) the central nervous system, comprising the brain and the spinal cord, and (b) the peripheral nervous system, which innervates and connects organs and muscles to the spinal cord and, thus, to the brain.

The brain, the primary director of the nervous system, is perhaps the most complex thing we know of in the universe. Our complex emotions and behaviors all originate in our complex brain. It enables us to make sense of our environment and to move and make adjustments in our environment to ensure our survival. Movement to ensure our survival is the very reason we have a brain (see TED, 2011), and movement is not only physical, bodily motion but also attitudinal in response to perceived opportunities and threats in the environment. Our survival, our physical movement, and our approach and avoidance behaviors—they all originate in the brain.

As an analogy, we might think of the brain as the command center of our body. The command center sends and receives electrochemical signals through a specialized type of cell called a neuron. Our brains have about 85 billion neurons (Herculano-Houzel, 2009), and some extend into or through the spinal cord, which plays the role of flexible conduit for the large bundle of wiring required to manage the body's systems.

Imagine if you could shrink the entire population of Earth, compress each of about 7.6 billion individuals, so they would all fit inside a human skull. You would still need to multiply that number by about 11 to represent the number of neurons in the brain. Now further stretch your imagination to consider that each of those individuals is directly connected with many others so that no two individuals have more than a few degrees of separation, much like a gigantic LinkedIn network. Ironically, this degree of complexity, the complexity of the human brain, is such that it is not fully comprehensible by the brain (see Carter, 2019; Sweeney, 2009).

Signals pass between neurons through an electrochemical process, and one neuron can activate many other neurons at once. And, it is those neurons that make you the person you are. The firing of neurons controls your autonomic body functions—respiration, digestion, circulation, and the like. The firing of neurons accounts for your movement, both conscious and unconscious. The firing of neurons accounts for our ability to experience life. We can see, hear, smell, taste, and touch because of neurons. We learn and remember and have intuition because of the firing of neurons. When our neurons stop firing, we cease to live.

The human brain, this amazingly intricate organ, is relatively small—it weighs 2 or 3 pounds, for most people about 2% of their body weight. But the brain is like a small power plant. It consumes about 20% of the energy burned by your body. It uses about 20% of your blood supply and oxygen. And, it fatigues easily.

Taken together, the brainstem and the cerebellum comprise the hind brain. The brainstem, at the base of the brain, joins the spinal cord to the brain. Sometimes referred to as the "reptile brain," the brainstem serves several important functions, including the regulation of basic body functions, such as breathing, blood pressure, contraction/dilation of the pupils, and many more. The cerebellum sits behind the brainstem and is critical for coordinating our movements. The cerebellum enables us to learn all manner of psychomotor skills, such as typing, welding, and riding a bicycle. In short, the hindbrain regulates many of our body functions and enables us to balance and make coordinated movement (see Carter, 2010, 2019; Sweeney, 2009).

The largest and uppermost region of the brain, the forebrain, sits above the hindbrain, and for discussion, we'll divide it into two major components, the limbic system and the cerebral cortex. The limbic system is very important for creating emotions, learning, and influencing decisions. Its location in the middle of the brain is appropriate given the central role it plays in many brain functions, chief among them is assessing opportunities and threats (especially threats), assigning an emotional value, and initiating a response, including the release of chemicals and hormones that fuel the sympathetic nervous system. An emotion is more than a "feeling." An emotion is a physical response to a perceived opportunity or threat. The emotions generated by the limbic system play a critical role in the formation of memories and learning (see Goldin, McRae, Ramel, & Gross, 2007; Lieberman, 2013; Phelps, 2006).

The cerebral cortex is the largest part of the human brain, about 80% of its volume, and almost completely wraps around the rest of the brain, including the limbic system. The cerebral cortex is divided into a left and right hemisphere and further divided into lobes, which serve various brain functions. There is some specialization of the brain hemispheres, but most brain functions are distributed across both hemispheres. The cortex enables consciousness and high-level mental processes—prioritization, formal logic, language, spatial processing, and much more. The cortex enables emotional control and defines our personality (Koechlin, 2016; Kosslyn & Mille, 2013). Conscious, long-term memories are stored in various cortical areas, and the persistence of episodic memories—those of personal experiences—is affected by the degree of emotion generated by the limbic system when the memory was formed (McDonald & Mott, 2017; Tyng, Amin, Saad, & Malik, 2017).

The leading edge of the frontal cortex, located immediately behind the forehead, is called the prefrontal cortex (PFC), and it is this cortical region, in particular, that gives us our personality and makes us uniquely human. Humans have a larger percentage of cortical real estate devoted to the PFC than do other animals, and one of its primary functions is to manage emotions and relationships (Amodia & Frith, 2006). In evidence of the PFC's importance to social relationships, there appears to be a relationship between the relative size of the PFC and the size of the typical social group for a particular species. Humans have an ability to cognitively manage a large number of social relationships and have a correspondingly large PFC (Dunbar & Shultz, 2007; Ochsner & Gross, 2005).

The PFC also enables abstract thought and executive function—many of the abilities we ascribe to leadership, such as strategic planning, judgment, and prioritizing (Ahmad & Tajasom, 2015). Executive functions, though, are not divorced from emotions. There is bidirectional communication between the PFC and the limbic system. The limbic system communicates our body's emotional state to the PFC, and the PFC creates consciousness of a "feeling." It also works the other way. Our conscious thoughts can send signals to the limbic system that excite or inhibit emotions, (see P. Brown, Swart, & Meyler, 2009; Lieberman, 2009, 2013).

In the brain, the limbic system and the PFC tend to operate in a kind of seesaw relationship: When one of these regions is very active, the other is likely inhibited and less active. For instance, when the limbic system is actively generating a strong emotional response to a threat, the PFC's ability to make sound judgments can be compromised (Schmeichel & Tang, 2015). Every individual brain represents a unique neuronal schema, and our individual differences in personality, leadership ability, and learning agility are largely determined by variations in the interaction of our cortical and subcortical brain regions.

The Neuroscience of Personality

Other people know us through our repertoire of behaviors and preferences for behaving in certain ways depending on the circumstances. Those behaviors that we prefer, that are normal for us, give us a reputation and comprise our personality. Given the role of personality in learning agility, it is enlightening to consider personality through the framework of the brain's threat and reward networks.

The limbic system initiates emotional responses to opportunities and threats, which lead to movement. We move physically toward that which ensures our survival and away from that which threatens our survival, but movement is not limited to physical movement. We also move in affect in response to perceived opportunities and threats. Attitudes move and are manifested in approach or avoidance behaviors. The individual emotional responses that people make when presented with opportunities and threats are a way to describe personality, and it follows then that variance seen in individual personalities is mirrored in individuals' differing tolerance for threats and sensitivity to rewards.

An inverted-U arousal curve (Figure 5.1) reflects the Yerkes–Dodson law (Broadhurst, 1957) and is commonly used in psychology to illustrate the relationship between arousal (stress) and performance. It indicates that a certain amount of stress or pressure to perform serves to elevate focus and performance up to an optimum level, at which point increased stress leads to a drop off in performance.

In general, stress increases with a sense of loss of control, and the brain perceives loss of control as a threat. Individuals have different tolerance levels

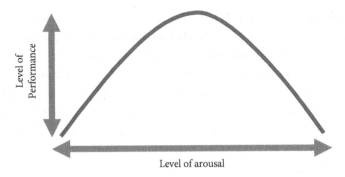

Figure 5.1 Arousal curve.

for stress—some people can juggle three balls, but add a fourth, and they are no longer in control. Others can barely manage to juggle two balls. The point is that each individual has their own arousal curve that will vary according to the context. What creates undue debilitating stress for one individual may be optimal performance-enhancing stress for another.

Physical threats to our well-being and survival will obviously generate a sympathetic nervous system response that causes us to move away from (or perhaps attack) the threat. But, even physical threats are perceived differently by different brains. Some people are frightened by heights or terrified of snakes. Others become tightrope walkers or herpetologists. Likewise, there is a wide variety of responses to psychological threats based on individual brain differences.

It is important to understand how the brain perceives opportunities as well as threats, but generally, threats create stronger and sometimes more unpredictable emotional responses. Physical threats are readily identified, and we rarely (it is hoped, never!) have to deal with them in the workplace. On the other hand, psychological threats are less easily identified but much more common. The workplace is teeming with potential psychological threats that can disengage employees and create all manner of unpredictable and undesired approach/avoidance behaviors.

Understanding the source and impact of psychological rewards and threats is key to analyzing and predicting individual and organizational performance. While there are countless possible psychological threats perceived by the brain, they generally fall into two broad categories: (a) threats to our sense of control and (b) threats that are social in nature. The *SCARF model* (Rock & Cox, 2012) is a slightly more granular way to classify psychological threats that includes two threats to our sense of control (*autonomy* and *certainty*) and three social threats (*status, relationships, and fairness*).

Our ability to survive depends on being able to accurately perceive our environment, make predictions with some degree of certainty, and confidently choose movements within our environment that enhance the odds of our survival. A stimulus that weakens our sense of control and interferes with our ability to predict will be deemed a psychological threat and elevate stress, perhaps even to crippling levels.

Any introduction of the new and different produces uncertainty. Each of us has a different point at which our brain perceives change to be a threat to our sense of control and ability to predict. The brain wants—needs—to be in control. We love being right and hate being wrong. In fact, we are more likely to remember the times we were proven right and, unless there were significant social consequences, less likely to remember the times we were wrong. Given the brain's need for certainty and control, it is no wonder that organizational change efforts are so difficult.

The second significant category of psychological threats is social in nature and comprises threats to our sense of belonging. Humans are social animals. We organize in groups in order to survive, and our brains are extremely sensitive to exclusion from our group. When our standing within our group is threatened, the brain perceives a threat. This can happen when we are socially rejected, embarrassed, bullied, ignored, or slighted in any way.

Social threats are very easy to introduce unconsciously by simply being dismissive of a coworker's idea, for instance. Raising our level of self-awareness and sensitivity to the reactions of others is key to reducing unnecessary and unintended behaviors that produce social threats. Our understanding and management of these behaviors is an indicator of our level of emotional intelligence.

When we are ignored, dismissed, or otherwise socially slighted, the sympathetic nervous system kicks in. We feel an emotion—embarrassment or anger, for instance. In addition to sensitivity to personal offenses, our brains are sensitive to social injustices imposed on others, especially if they are part of our in-group. Our brains are programmed to spot fairness violations, and we perceive these as a social threat.

A threat, whether physical or psychological, triggers an emotional response proportional to the perceived level of threat. As mentioned previously, emotions are not just "feelings." Emotions are physical responses. When the brain perceives a serious threat, the sympathetic nervous system is activated to initiate a fight or flight response. Keep in mind that the threat and resulting movement can be psychological (e.g., suppressing opinions after previously proffered suggestions were mocked or simply ignored by coworkers). A significant threat—physical or psychological—causes the release of cortisol, a relatively slow-acting hormone sometimes referred to as the "stress hormone" (Mayo Clinic, 2019) that increases blood sugar and suppresses the immune system so energy can be redirected to address the perceived threat. Other fast-acting hormones are also released, notably epinephrine (adrenaline), which increases heart rate, dilates the bronchial passages, and restricts blood vessels—all this to increase oxygen supply to the lungs and blood pressure to force blood to the brain and large muscles. When you are stressed and feel your mouth go dry and your palms become sweaty, you are likely experiencing the sympathetic nervous system at work.

The sympathetic nervous system has a counterpart, the parasympathetic nervous system, which is in control of autonomic processes and emotions in the absence of threat. This is sometimes referred to as a state of "resting and digesting" or "feeding and breeding" (Sarpolsky, 2004). Calm states also do create emotions and physical changes in brain chemistry and behavior, though they are generally less pronounced than those generated by the sympathetic nervous system. Whatever the case, our ability to recognize the source and intensity of our emotions and to modulate them is an indication of our emotional intelligence. Emotional intelligence contributes to leadership success, and even more so, lack of emotional intelligence may contribute to derailment (Goleman, 1995, 1998).

Every person's brain is uniquely "wired" to perceive and respond to opportunities and threats, and the differences directly define our behavioral preferences and define our personality. Individual differences in how we perceive and react to opportunities and threats, to a large extent, also explain our learning agility.

We can modify the shape of the arousal curve's inverted U to reflect the degree of comfort experienced in threat situations (Figure 5.2). Some version of this curve—we will call it the threat response curve—will apply to any particular threat perceived by an individual.

Comfort level and performance roughly track together and operate in a two-way causal loop. In one direction, comfort increases as one's performance improves. In the other direction, one's performance tends to degrade with a loss of comfort that can come from any number of psychological threats. When the perceived threat exceeds a threshold, the sympathetic

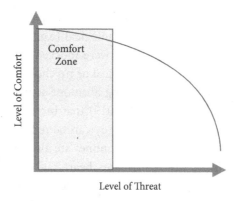

Figure 5.2 Threat–response curve.

nervous system kicks in, and the limbic system initiates emotional responses, which we experience as being "outside our comfort zone." When the threat is strong, the emotional result is correspondingly strong and can result in feelings of fear or panic accompanied by physical symptoms (e.g., increased respiration, heart rate, blood pressure, perspiration, suppression of digestion, and more). In such cases, the PFC is likely inhibited, which compromises executive function. A person experiencing this condition will certainly be aware of rising emotions but may be completely unaware of the impact on executive cognitive processes (Goldin et al., 2007).

This scenario may play out in many situations in the workforce when leaders must operate outside of their comfort zone. Normally, they are comfortable in their leadership position and highly effective, but when experiencing significant threat, their judgment may be compromised, most likely without their conscious awareness. Performance effectiveness generally tracks with comfort level. That is, we are normally comfortable when performing tasks that we do well.

The brain perceives threats and generates responses proportional to the level of threat, but individual brains and threat responses vary between individuals. Our typical emotional responses to threats and rewards determine our personality. Said in another way, our personality is based on the limits of our comfort zones for a wide range of threats and the brain-based emotional responses we have when those threats exceed our comfort level.

All this begs several questions: (a) Can personality change? (b) Can we change the boundaries of our comfort zones for various threats? And (c) to what extent is one's learning agility related to the breadth of comfort zones for particular contexts?

In answer to the first question, there is evidence that significant change in personality traits is unlikely. Personality is defined by stable traits that are unlikely to change significantly over time (see Conley, 1985; McCrae & Costa, 1994). We can debate the first question, but the second question is easier to answer. As we will see in the discussion of neuroscience and learning that follows, we can change the boundaries of our comfort zone. We can, in effect, change the boundaries and shape of the threat response curve by practicing outside the comfort zone. This is the essence of brain-based leadership development: (a) discovering what creates threats for us; (b) finding the limits of our comfort zones for various threats; and (c) intentionally placing ourselves outside of our comfort zones for practice so what was previously uncomfortable and threat inducing eventually becomes comfortable.

Learning agility is indeed defined by the way our brains perceive opportunities and threats, and the simple line of reasoning goes like this: (a) Personality is a significant determinant of learning agility, and (b) personality consists of preferred behaviors resulting from each brain's unique sensitivities to opportunities and threats. This conclusion is not particularly surprising, but it does suggest how learning agility might be studied at a deeper neurological level. Further, it yields insights into how learning agility might be effectively developed.

The Neuroscience of Attention

It has been proposed and widely accepted that the first step in instruction is to gain the attention of the learner (see Gagne, Briggs, & Wager, 1992), and this makes sense from both instructional design and neuroscience perspectives. The first step in creating a memory (learning) in the brain is attention to a stimulus. Attention intensifies our experience and causes neurons associated with the experience to fire repeatedly. There are three distinct attention networks in the brain, and understanding how and when these networks are engaged can enhance our ability to learn and be productive.

Default Mode Network

The default mode network is a system of interconnected neurons in several brain regions that are active during unfocused cognition as typically occurs when the mind is wandering and there is no intention to focus on anything in particular. Brain activity, as measured by the firing rate of neurons, is relatively low in this state. When you are awake but resting or daydreaming, you are in the default mode and likely having autobiographical thoughts, thinking about yourself, perhaps your interaction with others, or imagining yourself in some future scenario. Whatever the topic, it is not selected with any degree of focus or goal orientation. The default mode network allows your brain a time out, of sorts, and lets your brain recover from focused activity, to recharge during a period of relatively low metabolic activity. When cognition is in default mode, you will not be doing any focused problem-solving, but interestingly, it is in this mode that you may be most likely to have spontaneous insight and creative ideas (Jung-Beeman, Collier, & Kounios, 2008). Anecdotally, many people claim to have their most creative and spontaneous ideas just as they are falling asleep or soon after waking up in the morning when their brain activity is relatively low.

Dorsal Attention Network

In reference to the brain, dorsal refers to the direction toward the top of the head. Cortical structures that deal with reflective processes—conscious thought, decision-making, judgment, emotional control, and the like—are generally located in upper and forward portions of the brain (notably, the PFC). When conscious focus is brought to bear in thought processes, these areas of the brain are active and referred to as the dorsal attention network. The dorsal attention network is for intentional decisions and actions that require effort and span a wide range of cognitive tasks (e.g., when we make a grocery list, choose between two steaks at the meat counter, and decide to pay with cash rather than use a debit card at the checkout counter). These represent tasks at the simple end of the spectrum—They do not take much effort, but they do require a level of focus and conscious decision. Tasks at the other end of the spectrum can be much more difficult. We balance our checkbook, decide on purchasing a new car, write a letter to the editor of our local newspaper, and solve complex technical problems. These are examples of reflective cognitive processes that require a significant amount of focus and energy. And, the dorsal attention network does consume a lot of energy. If we are tired, lack motivation, or are feeling stressed, our ability to engage the dorsal attention network is compromised.

Learning and memory are inhibited or thwarted completely without a requisite level of attention and focus. However, note that the brain has limited stamina, and that the dorsal attention network consumes a lot of energy and fatigues quickly. Depending on how focus is defined and measured, studies identified varied estimates of human attention span, but 15 minutes is a likely upper limit (see Wilson & Korn, 2007). Even if you are highly motivated to pay close attention in a 1-hour lecture, you will likely lose focus at least four times during the lecture. Your mind will wander as the default mode network kicks in to give your brain a break. It is likely that your ventral attention network will activate at times to pull your attention away, when another participant in the lecture picks up his or her phone to check a text message, for instance.

Ventral Attention Network

In reference to the brain, ventral refers to the direction away from the top of the head. Ventral brain regions are more likely to deal with autonomic and reflexive processes, and the ventral attention network is also reflexive. It reflexively disrupts conscious focus to shift attention to whatever stimulus is intruding. Distracting stimuli often come from the external environment—the ding of a cell phone alert or conversation from the next cubicle, for instance. But the ventral attention network also can be activated by internal stimuli—low blood sugar or a sinus headache, for instance.

Multitasking

The dorsal attention network can only focus on one thing at a time. Tasks that require focused attention must be done serially, and that puts the lie to multitasking. Sure, you can walk and chew gum and carry on a conversation with a friend at the same time, but walking and chewing gum are habituated tasks that do not usually require attention—usually. But walking sometimes does require attention, and that explains the spate of accidents involving pedestrians talking on cell phones. While we may think we are skilled multitaskers, we are fooling ourselves. It is impossible for the brain to focus on two things at the same time. We may be able to rapidly switch our focus between tasks, but we cannot focus on them simultaneously. What people refer to as multitasking is, in fact, task switching, and there is a high price to pay for switching our focus from one task to another in an effort to juggle work. Likewise, every time the ventral attention network intrudes and pulls our attention from our intended task, we pay a price in lost productivity. Task switching takes time and energy and results in fatigue and mistakes (see Pashler, Johnston, & Ruthruff, 2004).

Mindfulness

There is evidence that the dorsal attention network can be strengthened, and the ability to focus can be increased. Mindfulness meditation seeks to do just that. As practiced by some, mindfulness is intended to achieve enhanced mental and spiritual health. In its simplest form, mindfulness involves quieting the mind and body and focusing on one thing, a fixed object or on one's breath, for instance, with the intention of maintaining focus. As thoughts intrude to distract attention, the mindfulness practitioner quietly and nonjudgmentally brings focus back to the intended target. With practice, it is possible to increase the attention span during meditation. Some research studies on mindfulness indicated that it may improve emotional regulation and reduce stress and associated levels of cortisol. The reduction of cortisol has definite health benefits; elevated cortisol levels are associated with numerous ailments, including digestive problems, weight gain, and sleeplessness (see Siegel & McCall, 2009).

The Neuroscience of Learning and Memory

Learning can be defined as internalizing the ability to do something new. The new behavior might be something simple, such as being able to confidently declare "Madison" when asked the state capital of Wisconsin. The new behavior might be a complex psychomotor task, such as flawlessly playing the Vivaldi violin concerto in G major or successfully welding an open-root pipe joint in the 6G position. Or, the new behavior might be a highly complex leadership task that requires both cognitive and affective learning, such as comfortably leading a large, complex team. In each case, the individual who has learned new behaviors will do them consistently when an appropriate cue is provided.

Learning largely consists of the acquisition and encoding of information through attention, rehearsal, and practice. The learned behavior cannot be demonstrated unless there is recall of the encoded information, and that ability to recall is attributed to memory. But, memory is not only retrieval, but encoding. The point is, memory is integral to learning, and it is valuable to understand how memory works and can be enhanced in order to accelerate learning and optimize performance.

Acquisition and encoding occur when a stimulus to the brain comes through one or more of several sensory channels—vision, auditory, tactile, and more. In general, a stimulus causes neurons to fire, and repeated firing of a group of neurons creates persistence, a degree of memory that reflects the level of conditioning that will cause the group of neurons to fire again with the right cue. Retrieval of a memory occurs when a cue, another stimulus, ignites the neural pattern that was formed when the memory was created.

Neuroplasticity

The ability of the brain to form, modify, and strengthen neural networks is called neuroplasticity. It is this ability that provides a biological basis for learning. Learning changes a person. Learners acquire new abilities, and those new abilities are accompanied by physical changes in the brain, in the strength of the connection between neurons. The connections between neurons are strengthened with repeated firing in a process called potentiation. Potentiation not only increases the likelihood that neurons will fire together but also can increase the speed at which signals travel between neurons. Long-term potentiation is described by Hebb's law, which can be stated as "neurons that fire together, wire together" (see R. E. Brown & Milner, 2003). Learning and memory, then, are based on conditioning a group of neurons to simultaneously fire in response to a cue.

Memory can be categorized in at least three different dimensions:

- consciousness—explicit memory versus tacit memory
- permanence—working memory versus long-term memory
- information type—semantic memory versus episodic memory

Explicit Memory

It is typical for us to have a degree of certainty about what we know. It is comfortable to believe that we know what we know, but in fact, we are only aware of our explicit memory. We are conscious of and can recall explicit memories when we decide to do so. Explicit memory is sometimes called declarative memory, and there are two types: semantic and episodic, which are described in the material that follows.

Tacit Memory

Not all memory is explicit. We have tacit memories that live under the surface of our consciousness. They are transparent to us but do exist nonetheless. A tacit memory may surface and be recalled with the right cue and surprise us with its unexpected appearance. Tacit memory, also called implicit memory, takes several forms. It can reveal itself through unconscious bias and intuition. Unfortunately, not all of our biases and intuition are correct, and they can cause trouble for us. A special type of tacit memory is kinesthetic, sometimes called muscle memory. Examples include knowing how to juggle or to throw a perfect spiral football pass or to ride a bike. You may or may not be able to articulate these things, but once learned, they can be done unconsciously, and tacit memory lives in the subconscious. Tacit memory guides many of our habits and everyday behaviors. And tacit memory is the driver of intuition for cognitive behaviors and is a foundational building block of expertise (Klein, 2013, 2015).

Working Memory

When a group of neurons fires in response to a stimulus, the connections made are fleeting unless there is conscious attention and rehearsal or there is a high degree of emotion wrapped up in the memory. Working memory is based on those short-lived neuronal connections that typically persist only a matter of seconds. Working memory serves as a mental scratch pad and allows us to hold symbols, patterns, and data long enough for it to be manipulated. When you memorize a phone number just long enough to dial and then immediately forget it, you are using working memory. If you multiply two 2-digit numbers in your head, you are relying on working memory. Unlike long-term memory, working memory is very limited and, for most people, degrades rapidly after five or six bits (or chunks) of information, and "7 plus or minus 2" is often used to describe its limitation (Miller, 1956). Neurological studies indicated a strong link between working memory and the ability to focus and learn. Working memory may even be a fair proxy for intelligence (see Constantinidis & Klingberg, 2016). Certainly, it is one of the most important enablers of generalized learning and problem-solving.

Long-Term Memory

Memory that is not reinforced degrades and is lost, perhaps within seconds or minutes, but certainly over days and weeks. But, with focus and rehearsal, memories are consolidated in neural networks in cerebral and cerebellar cortical areas and may persist for years, even a lifetime. Long-term memory refers to neural networks that are in the process of consolidation, and there is great variability in the level and integrity of those networks. If you look at a class picture from first grade, it is likely you do not remember the names of all your classmates, but you did know them when you were 6 years old. If you had pulled out the picture and rehearsed the names periodically during your grade school years, the names would likely have been consolidated in long-term memory.

Semantic Memory

Memories that are impersonal to you and comprise a record of stored facts are semantic memories. Names, dates, phone numbers, addresses, and formula that you are able to recall are some examples of semantic memories. If you recall the name of your first-grade teacher, that is a semantic memory that has been consolidated to a significant degree in long-term memory.

Episodic Memory

Some memories are personal and episodic in nature. They are based on a unique experience. When such a memory is retrieved, the effect is that we experience a simulated reliving of the original experience, but the memory is only a reasonable facsimile. Obviously, we do not actually relive an experience—even when memories are very vivid, we still recognize that it occurred in the past and the experience of the memory is different from the original event. Episodic memories are only approximations of the original, and over time memories morph so that what we remember may bear little resemblance to the original; regrettably, we are generally unable to identify which elements of the memory are inaccurate.

Episodic memory is a record of our personal experiences that have been stored. For instance, you may remember the name of your first-grade teacher (a semantic memory), but remembering how she greeted you with a hug on your first day of first grade is an episodic memory. An episodic memory is unique to you, a memory of an experience filtered through your unique lens and role in that experience.

The emotional content of memories largely determines how easily information will be encoded in long-term memory. If you recall your earliest episodic memories, they will be highly emotional experiences. They may be positive in nature—seeing a new bicycle under the Christmas tree. However, they could also be negative—being embarrassed and laughed at by your first-grade classmates when you struggled to read a passage aloud. Strong emotions stick to memories and help anchor them in long-term memory (McDonald & Mott, 2017).

Implications for Developing Learning Agility

Learning is acquiring the ability to do something new. From childhood, most of us learn to walk and talk and ride a bicycle. We learn to make friends and to tell a joke. We all learn these things and much more, but those who are highly learning agile range more widely in their learning and learn more quickly than others. The learning agile more readily identify patterns. They recognize similarities and anomalies in patterns that others miss. That recognition results in the capacity to transfer learning. Additionally, the learning agile have "wider comfort zones" and more readily push themselves beyond their comfort zone to where learning occurs. The unpleasant truth is that we do not learn much of anything when we are comfortable. The learning agile are less sensitive to psychological threat in a wide range of contexts related to characteristics we associate with learning agility (e.g., uncertainty, experimenting, interacting with diverse people, etc.).

Learning and intuition are possible because of neuroplasticity, the brain's ability to create new and change existing neuronal connections. This ever-evolving "wiring" of the brain constitutes our memory, our understanding, our personality, and our consciousness. It is not only the number and configuration of neuronal connections that can change, but also the strength of those connections and the speed at which electrochemical signals move between neurons. When neurons are fired simultaneously, the synaptic connections are strengthened in a process called long-term potentiation. When neurons are fired frequently, it stimulates the production of myelin, a coating that forms on the axons of some neurons and greatly increases the speed of the electrochemical signal passing between neurons.

Understanding the role of neuroscience can guide a brain-based strategy for developing learning agility that involves enhancing focus, improving memory, and changing our behavioral preferences to more closely align with characteristics associated with learning agility. A summary of neuroscience-based development tactics for learning agility follows.

Enhancing Focus

- **Schedule Short Work Periods.** To the extent possible, plan your day to accomplish meaningful tasks in 20-minute time periods. Begin each 20-minute slice of time by focusing on completing that task or set of tasks. At the end of 20 minutes, shift gears. Stand and stretch. Take a short mental break. The idea is to give your dorsal attention network a few minutes to recharge so you can reboot your focus and begin another 20-minute, highly productive work period.
- **Reward Yourself.** Accomplishing a goal activates reward networks in the brain. Attention is increased as the brain anticipates the reward. Identify a specific goal for each chunk of scheduled time and then provide yourself with some positive reinforcement when each goal is achieved. It does not have to be complicated or a big deal. Simply maintaining a list from which you can cross off completed action items can be quite rewarding—whatever you find rewarding and that does not work at cross purposes with your goal of being highly focused and productive.
- **Eliminate Environmental Distractions.** Consider all the irrelevant, distracting stimuli that are likely to engage your ventral attention network and pull your attention away. Turn off audible and visual email and phone alerts. If you have an email alert firing every few minutes throughout the day, you are losing productivity due to frequently switching your focus. Use just a few scheduled time slices during the day to check email rather than constantly and repeatedly checking your

inbox. Social media is a primary offender and thief of attention. Turn off all social media alerts if you are serious about boosting your focus.

- **Take Care of Your Mind.** Devote several minutes each day to mindfulness meditation. Sit quietly and give attention to your senses and state of mind. Without judging, explore your thoughts, your emotional state, and your physical condition. Relax, breathe, and just be present in the moment. You can complement mindfulness meditation with a few minutes of focused meditation in which you concentrate on a single point—it might be an object, a word, or your breath. As you sense your thoughts wandering, pull them back to the point of attention without judging. Meditation activates the parasympathetic nervous system (the "rest-and-digest" state) with many associated health benefits. Additionally, meditation can strengthen the dorsal attention network.
- **Take Care of Your Body.** Your brain's ability to focus is dependent on your general well-being. When something in your body is out of balance, it will likely engage the ventral attention network and rob you of desired attention and focus. Your brain and body are especially sensitive to levels of blood sugar. Adopt a diet that avoids wild swings in blood sugar. Keep hydrated. Get some exercise. And get enough sleep.

Improving Memory

The brain has a remarkable capacity for acquiring, managing, and retrieving information. Focus and rehearsal are primary enablers of memory, but there are many other tactics that will improve consolidation and recall.

- **Practice Memorization.** Develop discipline in focused practice and rehearsal. Memorization and rehearsal strengthen working memory and embed content in long-term memory, where it can be accessed at will and instantaneously. Easy access to information through search engines leads many to conclude that memorization has little value in the information age, but this belief is pernicious. Overreliance on technology and failure to practice memorization leads to atrophy of skills and neural networks that are essential to learning. Focus, discipline, attention, rehearsal, and memorization are critical skills for the motivated learner.

- **Chunk Content.** Chunking is a way to greatly increase working memory. Your brain does this naturally when you are reading. Right now, in fact, you are not interpreting each letter in each word on the page. Your brain encodes each word, perhaps groups of words, as one chunk of information. In the same manner, you can group content into chunks to overcome the 7 plus or minus 2 limitation of working memory.

- **Use Mnemonics.** Be inventive in applying mnemonics to provide cues for retrieval. How do you remember the colors of light dispersed by a prism? The notes on the lines of the treble clef? The firing order of a six-cylinder inline engine (if you are a mechanic)? Mnemonics that are amusing or bawdy will be easier to remember; if you have any doubt, ask a medical student how they memorized the cranial nerves or carpal bones.

- **Create Stories.** Information is also easier to encode if it is wrapped in context. Stories are useful for providing context, especially if it is personal, if you are part of the story. Context and story elements include cues that stimulate recall. Invent a story that includes the information you would like to memorize, cast yourself in a central role in the story, and give it an interesting, memorable plot. Emotional content largely determines how easily information will be encoded in long-term memory. Give your invented stories an emotional component that is truly meaningful to you, something that moves you.

- **Space Rehearsal.** Memory consolidation is more effective when there is repeated activation of neural networks with temporal spacing. Rather than cramming to try to remember, space your review and rehearsal of information over days and weeks. Repetition is important. Spaced repetition is most effective, and this applies to repetition of both acquisition and retrieval—the presentation and review of content and the demonstrated behavior of what is learned.

- **Create a Mental Model.** Organize information so that it fits a mental model that is known to you. Identify an analogy that simplifies content and enhances encoding and memory. There are endless sources of widely understood models from sports, entertainment, military, and science areas from which you can create analogies to enhance memory and serve the fundamental outcome of learning agility—transferring lessons learned to a new and challenging situation. A mental model is a pattern that gives meaning and coherence to content, and pattern recognition is a key indicator of the level of comprehension obtained by the learner.

- **Visualize.** Create a mental picture that combines elements to be remembered and associates them visually. Even better than a mental picture is an actual illustration, and this can be combined with chunking, analogies, and other tactics suggested previously. There is evidence that taking handwritten notes for study is more effective than typing study notes (Smoker, Murphy, & Rockwell, 2009), and drawing an illustration can further assist you in remembering concepts, processes, and principles.

Changing Behavioral Preferences

As discussed, the brain perceives psychological threats related to ambiguity (the loss of certainty) and related to relationships (our social status and sense of inclusion). Individual brains determine the threshold at which threats are perceived and the corresponding emotional response. This difference in our perception and emotional response to threats and rewards determines our personality and, to a large extent, explains our learning agility.

The essence of brain-based development is

1. Through feedback and reflection, to understand what creates threats for us;
2. Further, test and discover the limits of our comfort zones for various threats;
3. And then, intentionally place ourselves outside of our comfort zones so what was previously uncomfortable and threat inducing eventually becomes comfortable.

Conclusion

The "5 Whys" technique, popularized by Toyota, consists of repetitively asking why in order to drill down through underlying issues to find the root cause or answer to a complex question (Serrat, 2017). Why do some individuals exhibit more learning agility than others? Why is learning agility difficult to develop? How can one accelerate the development of learning agility?

If we recursively pose the right questions, the answers eventually will lead us to the brain.

As neuropsychologists, neurobiologists, and neuroscientists of all stripes continue their research, we will gain new insights into the interplay between the brain and the learning agility construct. In order to advance talent management practice, there are several questions that deserve attention, for example: (a) How can we better explain the relationship between the brain's reward and threat networks and learning agility? (b) How can we better explain the relationship between the brain's attention networks and learning agility? (c) How can we better explain the relationship between intuition and bias and learning agility? Science has come a long way in understanding the basic functions and functioning of the brain. As we reach toward the future, there is much more that we need to discover between how our brain relates to learning agility.

References

Ahmad, Z. A., & Tajasom, A. (2015). The neuroscience of decision making: A review. *NeuroLeadership Journal, 4*, 1–11.

Amodia, D. M., & Frith, C. D. (2006). Meeting of minds: The medial frontal cortex and social cognition. *Nature Reviews Neuroscience, 7*, 268–277.

Broadhurst, P. L. (1957). Emotionality and the Yerkes-Dodson law. *Journal of Experimental Psychology, 54*(5), 345–352.

Brown, P., Swart, T., & Meyler, J. (2009). Emotional intelligence. *NeuroLeadership Journal, 2*, 1–11.

Brown, R. E., & Milner, P. M. (2003). The legacy of Donald O. Hebb: More than the Hebb synapse. *Nature Reviews Neuroscience, 4*, 1013–1019.

Carter, R. (2010). *Mapping the mind*. Berkeley: University of California Press.

Carter, R. (2019). *The human brain book: An illustrated guide to its structure, function, and disorders*. London, UK: DK.

Conley, J. J. (1985). Longitudinal stability of personality traits: A multitrait–multimethod–multioccasion analysis. *Journal of Personality and Social Psychology, 49*(5), 1266–1282.

Constantinidis, C., & Klingberg, T. (2016). The neuroscience of working memory capacity and training. *Nature Reviews Neuroscience, 17*, 438–449.

Davachi, L., & Dobbins, I. G. (2008). *Declarative memory. Current Directions in Psychological Science, 2*, 112–118.

De Meuse, K. P. (2017). Learning agility: Its evolution as a psychological construct and its empirical relationship to leader success. *Consulting Psychology Journal: Practice and Research, 69*, 267–295.

Dunbar, R. I. M., & Shultz, S. (2007). Evolution in the social brain. *Science, 317*, 1344–1347.

Eichinger, R. W., & Lombardo, M. M. (2004). Learning agility as a prime indicator of potential. *Human Resource Planning, 27*, 12–15.

Gagne, R., Briggs, L., & Wager, W. (1992). *Principles of instructional design* (4th ed.). Fort Worth, TX: HBJ College Publishers.

Goldin, P. R., McRae, K., Ramel, W., & Gross, J. J. (2007). The neural bases of emotion regulation: Reappraisal and suppression of negative emotion. *Biological Psychiatry, 63*(6), 577–586.

Goleman, D. (1995). *Emotional intelligence: Why it can matter more than IQ.* New York, NY: Bantam.

Goleman, D. (1998). What makes a leader? *Harvard Business Review, 76*(6), 93–102.

Herculano-Houzel, S. (2009). The human brain in numbers: A linearly scaled-up primate brain. *Frontiers in Human Neuroscience, 3*, 31. doi:10.3389/neuro.09.031.2009

Hogan, R., Curphy, G. J., & Hogan, J. (1994). What we know about leadership: Effectiveness and personality. *American Psychologist, 49*(6), 493–504.

Jung-Beeman, M., Collier, A., & Kounios, J. (2008). How insight happens; learning from the brain. *NeuroLeadership Journal, 1*, 1–6.

Klein, G. A. (2013). *The power of intuition: How to use your gut feelings to make better decisions at work.* New York, NY: Crown Business.

Klein, G. A. (2015). *Seeing what others don't: The remarkable ways we gain insight.* New York, NY: Public Affairs.

Koechlin, E. (2016). Prefrontal executive function and adaptive behavior in complex environments. *Current Opinion in Neurobiology, 37*, 1–6.

Kosslyn, S., & Mille, G. W. (2013). *Top brain, bottom brain: Surprising insights into how you think.* New York, NY: Simon & Schuster.

Lieberman, M. D. (2009). The brain's braking system (and how to "use your words" to tap into it). *NeuroLeadership Journal, 2*, 1–6.

Lieberman, M. D. (2013). *Social: Why our brains are wired to connect.* New York, NY: Crown.

Lombardo, M. M., & Eichinger, R. W. (2000). High potentials as high learners. *Human Resource Management, 39*, 321–330.

Mayo Clinic. (2019). *Chronic stress puts your health at risk.* Retrieved from https://www.mayoclinic.org/healthy-lifestyle/stress-management/in-depth/stress/art-20046037

McCrae, R. R., & Costa, P. T. (1994). The stability of personality: Observations and evaluations. *Current Directions in Psychological Science, 3*(6), 173–175. https://doi.org/10.1111/1467-8721.ep10770693

McDonald, A. J., & Mott, D. D. (2017). Functional neuroanatomy of amygdalohippocampal interconnections and their role in learning and memory. *Journal of Neuroscience Research, 95*(3), 797–820.

Miller, G. A. (1956). The magical number seven, plus or minus two: Some limits on our capacity for processing information. *Psychological Review, 63*(2), 81–97.

Ochsner, K. N., & Gross, J. J. (2005). The cognitive control of emotion. *Trends in Cognitive Sciences, 9*(5), 242–249.

Pashler, H., Johnston, J. C., & Ruthruff, E. (2004). Attention and performance. *Annual Review of Psychology, 52*, 629–651.

Phelps, E. A. (2006). Emotion and cognition: Insights from studies of the human amygdala. *Annual Review of Psychology, 57*, 27–53.

Rock, D., & Cox, C. (2012). SCARF® in 2012: Updating the social neuroscience of collaborating with others. *NeuroLeadership Journal, 4*, 1–14.

Sarpolsky, R. M. (2004). *Why zebras don't get ulcers* (3rd ed.). New York, NY: Holt Paperbacks.

Schmeichel, B. J., & Tang, D. (2015). Individual differences in executive functioning and their relationship to emotional processes and responses. *Current Directions in Psychological Science, 24*(2), 93–98.

Serrat, O. (2017). The five whys technique. In O. Serrat (Ed.), *Knowledge solutions: Tools, methods, and approaches to drive organizational performance* (pp. 307–310). Singapore: Springer.

Siegel, D., & McCall, D. P. (2009). Mindsight at work: An interpersonal neurobiology lens on leadership. *NeuroLeadership Journal, 2*, 1–12.

Smoker, T. J., Murphy, C. E., & Rockwell, A. K. (2009). Comparing memory for handwriting versus typing. *Proceedings of the Human Factors and Ergonomics Society Annual Meeting, 53*(22), 1744–1747.

Sweeney, M. S. (2009). *Brain: The complete mind: How it develops, how it works, and how to keep it sharp.* Washington, DC: National Geographic.

Swisher, V. V. (2012). *Becoming an agile leader.* Los Angeles, CA: Korn Ferry International.

TED. (2011, July). *Daniel Wolpert: The real reason for brains* [Video file]. Retrieved from https://www.ted.com/talks/daniel_wolpert_the_real_reason_for_brains?language=en

Tyng, C. M., Amin, H. U., Saad, M. N. M., & Malik, A. S. (2017). The influences of emotion on learning and memory. *Frontiers in Psychology, 8*, 1–22.

Wilson, K., & Korn, J. H. (2007). Attention during lectures—Beyond ten minutes. *Teaching of Psychology, 34*(2), 85–89.

SECTION II

STRATEGIES AND HABITS THAT DEVELOP LEARNING AGILITY

In this section, attention is shifted to how learning agility can be developed. It begins with an overview of how the development of learning agility creates a competitive advantage for organizations and presents an integrated model of the learning agile process and learning agile behaviors. Subsequent chapters explore many of these behaviors and strategies in greater depth. The importance of mindfulness in cultivating learning agility is described, including research linking mindfulness and learning agility and recommendations for implementing mindfulness training to enhance learning agility. Next, the importance of pushing leaders to the edge of their comfort zone is explored, and the role learning agility plays as an antecedent, moderator, and outcome of stretch experiences. A chapter is devoted to the value of feedback and how it provides opportunities for experience-based learning to occur. Engaging in systematic reflection may be one of the most effective strategies for leaders to develop learning agility, and both research and practical reflection strategies are explored. A chapter on being in learning mode explains how leaders can foster their learning agility by deliberately priming a growth mindset. The section concludes with a discussion of how resilience and successful navigation of derailment allow a leader to grow from adversity.

6

Developing Learning Agile Behavior

A Model and Overview

Veronica Schmidt Harvey and Raphael Y. Prager

I am not afraid of storms for I am learning how to sail my ship.
—Louisa May Alcott (1832–1888), American author and activist

Over the past two decades organizational researchers and practitioners have paid increasing attention to identification of leaders who demonstrate learning agility (De Meuse, 2017; Lombardo & Eichinger, 2000, 2011; Silzer & Church, 2009). Discussions of learning agility sometimes imply that it is something binary—you either have it or you don't. While much research is still needed, undoubtedly there are individual differences that predispose a leader to be more or less learning agile, including, for example, personality characteristics such as openness to experience (Laxso, 2018), a growth mindset (Dweck & Leggett, 1988), or cognitive ability (DeRue, Ashford, & Myers, 2012).

However, we cannot lose sight of the *learnable* behaviors and organizational practices that enhance learning agility and accelerate learning. Just as a race car may have maximum horsepower and the best aerodynamics, the conditions of the track and the strategies deployed by the driver to adjust to them are also necessary for achieving maximum velocity. While identification and selection are certainly critical, it is equally important to consider processes that *develop* learning agility both for those who are and are not naturally predisposed to be agile learners. It is these learnable behaviors that are the focus of this chapter.

It is unrealistic for organizations to expect that leaders across all functions and business units will be inherently learning agile. Assuming that learning agility follows a normal distribution, by definition, only half of leaders have

Veronica Schmidt Harvey and Raphael Y. Prager, *Developing Learning Agile Behavior* In: *The Age of Agility*. Edited by: Veronica Schmidt Harvey and Kenneth P. De Meuse, Oxford University Press (2021). © Oxford University Press. DOI: 10.1093/oso/9780190085353.003.0006 above average learning agility, and just 16% of leaders could be described as highly learning agile. Focusing solely on leaders who are already learning agile severely restricts an organization's leadership pipeline. In the face of unprecedented change, leaders—and organizations—able to develop learning agility will have a significant advantage.

For leaders who are more naturally predisposed to be learning agile the development of Learning Agile Behaviors™ will allow them to take full advantage of these individual differences. As is the case with most natural gifts, a predisposition to be learning agile may be amplified through appropriate nurturing and practice. For example, research on constructs related to learning, such as growth mindset, goal orientation (Dweck & Leggett, 1988), and regulatory focus (Higgins, 1998), has shown that while individuals are inclined to behave consistently with their natural orientations, environmental factors and deliberate practice can impact mindsets and behavior. By extension, those organizations that assist leaders in developing their learning agility will have a competitive advantage keeping pace with rapidly changing business conditions. Knowing how to develop these important behaviors also creates a much more level playing field and can empower *all* leaders to become more learning agile.

Given the importance of understanding how learning agility can be developed, this chapter (a) defines what it means to *develop* behaviors that can enhance or supplement one's existing learning agility; (b) summarizes theories and models relevant to the development of learning agility; (c) presents a heuristic, integrated model of Learning Agile Behavior; and (d) provides an overview and practical examples of how behaviors that increase learning agility can be developed.

What Does It Mean to Develop Learning Agility?

There is much practical value in understanding the mechanisms that allow leaders to learn from experience quickly and efficiently. Becoming learning agile requires the development of behaviors associated with the ability to learn, adapt, and do both of these in a rapid and nimble manner within the crucible of dynamic leadership situations. In addition to learning from past experiences, keeping up with change will require forecasting and proactively developing the capabilities needed for the future. To guide our discussion, we propose the following definition:

Learning Agile Behaviors are the self-regulated behaviors, strategies, and habits that enable learning at an accelerated pace, facilitate more agile adaptation to dynamic conditions, and result in more effective leadership.

Learning Agile Behavior: Foundational Theories and Research

In developing a model of Learning Agile Behavior, it is important to build on theory and research on constructs both directly and indirectly related to learning agility, such as ability to learn, performance adaptation, and learning velocity. (a) *Learning ability*, while sometimes equated with general intelligence, also includes possessing knowledge and skill in applying different learning techniques and strategies. (b) *Adaptive performance* includes situation appraisal, strategy selection, self-regulation, and learning (Baard, Rench, & Kozlowski, 2014). (c) *Learning velocity*, the temporal dimension of learning, is also key given that learning agility requires being nimble in responding to changing conditions, quickly letting go of ingrained habits and picking up new ones (De Meuse, 2017; DeRue, Ashford, et al., 2012; Harvey, 2018). The theories and research listed in Table 6.1 were all considered when creating a model of Learning Agile Behavior.

These theories and historical research suggest a number of factors relevant to understanding Learning Agile Behavior. Describing each of these theories in detail is beyond the scope of this chapter; therefore, the key tenets of these theories are summarized in Box 6.1.

A Model of Learning Agile Behaviors for Leaders

Given the importance of developing learning agile leaders, a model integrating these diverse perspectives will be useful for both research and practice. In this section, we propose a heuristic model incorporating the learnable behaviors that contribute to learning agility. It is our hope it will provide a framework for furthering our understanding of Learning Agile Behaviors.

Table 6.1 Influential Theories From Literature Relevant to Developing Learning Agility

• Adult Learning Theory	Knowles, 1973, 1975
• Theory of Action and Double Loop Learning	Argyris, 1977, 1991; Argyris & Schon, 1974
• Social Learning Theory	Bandura, 1977
• Experiential Learning Theory	A. Kolb & Kolb, 2011; D. A. Kolb, 1984
• The Lessons of Experience	Center for Creative Leadership; Lombardo & Eichinger, 2011; McCall et al., 1988
• Growth Mindset	Dweck, 2008; Dweck & Leggett, 1988
• Transformative Learning Theory	Mezirow, 1991, 2000
• Constructive–Developmental Theory	Kegan, 1994; Kegan & Lahey, 2001, 2009
• Adaptive Performance and Adaptive Learning System	Bell & Kozlowski, 2010; Pulakos, Arad, Donovan, & Plamondon, 2000
• I-ADAPT Theory	Ployhart & Bliese, 2006
• The Construct of Learning Agility	De Meuse, 2017, 2019; De Meuse, Dai, & Hallenbeck, 2010

Agile Learning Process

Building on these influential theories and research, along with our own experiences assessing and coaching hundreds of leaders, a model is proposed based on the assumption that learning is an *ongoing process of personal change and adaptation*. We refer to it as the *Agile Learning Process*™. This process includes the following stages:

- *Identify Need for Change*—Detect internal and external indicators that signal a need for learning and the time and pace required for this adaptation.
- *Plan for Change*—Understand the set of Learning Agile Behaviors that will accelerate the learning process and identify the behaviors within this set most relevant within the context of dynamic leadership situations. Develop a learning plan, including clear goals, tactics, resources required and obstacle mitigation.
- *Implement Change*—Demonstrate mastery in implementing learning behaviors at the appropriate time and in the appropriate sequence,

Box 6.1 Factors That Influence the Development of Learning Agility

- Agile learning requires awareness of both internal and external experiences and interpretation of these experiences.
- Experiential learning can occur both directly through stretch experiences and vicariously through observation, media, dialogue, and storytelling.
- Increased self- or environmental awareness, crisis, or significant transitions can trigger learning by creating dissonance and discomfort.
- Critical reflection is essential to the process of converting concrete experience to abstract lessons that can be applied to future experiences.
- Learning requires breaking down self-defense mechanisms and openness to alternative views and approaches.
- Sustainable change requires self-insight, which may include uncovering unconscious assumptions, beliefs and values.
- Learning may be facilitated by guided discovery, dialogue, and various forms of "processing" with others to create self-awareness, trigger metacognition, or identify new frameworks.
- Self-regulatory processes such as resilience may be influenced by framing learning around mastery rather than performance goals and developing new ways of thinking about mistakes and failures.
- Being able to interact effectively with others facilitates learning from, with, and through others.
- Metacognition and the ability to "think about how we think" allows us to change our interpretation of the environment and our mental models.
- Appraisal of the situation and selection of the most effective learning strategy may contribute to adapting more quickly.
- Curiosity, openness to new experiences, and a willingness to take risks and try new approaches support learning agility.

resulting in learning at the velocity required given the rate of change in the environment.

- *Regulate and Monitor Change*—Regulate effort, discipline, and resilience in pursuing and modifying learning plans. Engage in monitoring of overall learning speed and effectiveness.

Based on a review of the literature and our experience working with organizational leaders across industries and contexts, we believe that increasing the quality and velocity of the Agile Learning Process will, in turn, increase a leader's ability to rapidly adapt to dynamic conditions. However, more empirical research is needed to support this assertion.

Learning Agile Behaviors

In addition, significant research exists to suggest the Agile Learning Process can be enabled or impeded by a wide range of behaviors, strategies, and habits. These are referred to here as *Learning Agile Behaviors* and have been grouped into the following five categories:

1. *Observing*: Includes mindful awareness of both internal and external experience as well as the ability to scan and forecast future conditions.
2. *Doing*: Involves demonstrating personal agency and internal locus of control by taking action on the environment, seeking new experiences, experimenting with new ways of responding, and actively seeking new information and frameworks.
3. *Connecting*: Focuses on connecting with and learning from others vicariously and directly by asking for help and feedback, learning with and from peers, mentors, role models, and coaches.
4. *Thinking*: Strategies that involve cognitively processing information, which include reflection, metacognition, questioning, and mindset shifting.
5. *Mobilizing*: Includes behaviors involved in harnessing emotions and motivation, such as self-control, goal setting, planning, demonstrating discipline, and developing resilience.

The proposed model is summarized in Figure 6.1.

In summary, understanding both the Agile Learning *Process* and Learning Agile *Behaviors*—the "building blocks" of agile learning—is important for

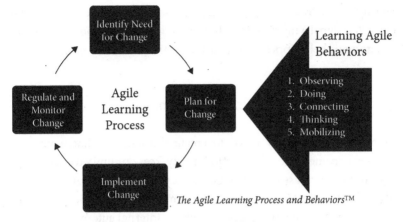

Figure 6.1 Model of agile learning process and behaviors.

developing learning agility. The proposed model assumes that mastery of the Learning Agile Behaviors and understanding when to deploy them will accelerate learning speed, flexibility, and overall effectiveness. The remainder of this chapter focuses on describing each of the Learning Agile Behaviors in greater detail, exploring how they contribute to learning agility and providing practical suggestions for how they can be developed.

An Overview of Learning Agile Behaviors and How They Can Be Developed

For each set of Learning Agile Behaviors, we briefly (a) define and describe the behaviors; (b) summarize key research supporting the importance of the behaviors in enhancing learning agility; and (c) discuss practical implications of how leaders can develop and implement these learning behaviors. The reader is also directed to Case Study F for an example of how development of Learning Agile Behavior was experienced by an early career leader.

1. Observing

Observing includes mindful awareness of both internal and external experiences as well as the ability to scan and forecast future conditions. Being skilled in observation allows leaders to accurately assess reality and potentially better predict the capabilities required for future success. Within the

Learning Agile Process, observing is especially important for detection of factors that signal a need for learning, and regulation of emotions, thoughts, and automatic behaviors that help or hinder the pace of learning.

Mindful Awareness

Our brains are naturally wired to create shortcuts so that many of our behaviors become "automatic." Automaticity frees our limited attentional capacity and (a) increases speed and efficiency; (b) allows parallel processing; and (c) reduces effort (Tversky & Kahneman, 1974). The challenge for leaders is to be intentional regarding when to rely on internal autopilot and when to take conscious control. Leaders can be more agile in their learning if they understand how to recognize and reduce automaticity when it chains them to habitual ways of thinking and behaving that are not productive.

Mindfulness is defined as the purposeful awareness and acceptance of present moment experiences, including internal (thoughts, bodily sensations) and external (physical and social environment) stimuli with an attitude of curiosity rather than judgment, minimizing automatic filters. Mindfulness is relevant to learning agility for the reasons summarized in Box 6.2.

Environmental Scanning and Future Forecasting

Scanning the environment and forecasting future events is typically associated with strategic planning at the organizational level. However, these learnable behaviors are also relevant to learning agility. Environmental scanning is the process of (a) detecting internal and external changes that are already underway; (b) attending to signals about potential changes; (c) using this information to identify threats and opportunities; and (d) determining a future direction (Le Pine, Colquitt, & Erez, 2000; Ployhart & Bliese, 2006). In the context of Learning Agile Behavior, this includes the ability to translate this information into a prediction of where and when different capabilities will be required for the future.

Environmental scanning is particularly important in uncertain and ambiguous environments and those where innovation is required. Given that leaders' work is constantly in flux, the skills required for success at a particular time or within a given context are also continuously changing. To respond with agility requires that leaders anticipate their learning needs and proactively take action to develop the new capabilities needed for the future and forecast the time required to develop them.

Box 6.2 Contributions of Mindfulness to Learning Agility

- **Increasing readiness for change** by surfacing implicit beliefs and altering allocation and stability of attention (e.g., Gondo, Patterson, & Palacios, 2013).
- **Disrupting automaticity and increasing cognitive flexibility** (e.g., Glomb, Duffy, Bono, & Yang, 2000).
- **Vigilance in scanning the environment** for both threats and opportunities given the volume of information leaders are regularly bombarded with (e.g., Shapiro, 2009).
- **Developing curiosity and openness to experience** (e.g., Good et al., 2016).
- **Increasing receptivity to feedback** (e.g., Lee, 2012).
- **Regulating emotions, behavior, and resilience** (e.g., Hülsheger, Alberts, Feinholdt, & Lang, 2013).

Practical Suggestions for Developing Learning Agile Behaviors: Observing

Increase Awareness of Personal Inclination for Mindfulness

Several assessments of mindfulness exist, such as the Mindfulness Attention Awareness Scale (K. W. Brown & Ryan, 2003); the Five Facet Mindfulness Questionnaire (Cortazar, Calvete, Fernández-González, & Orue, 2019); and the Langer Mindfulness Scale (Pirson, Langer, Bodner, & Zilcha-Mano, 2012). While not designed specifically for leaders, these instruments may be useful for increasing a leader's overall awareness of his or her level of mindfulness. In addition, one of the seven facets measured by the *TALENTx7*—an assessment specific to learning agility and leaders—is "environmental mindfulness" (see Chapter 4).

Engage in Meditative Mindfulness Practice

Research provides support that relevant training can increase mindfulness (Quaglia, Braun, Freeman, McDaniel, & Brown, 2016). An increasing number of organizations, such as Aetna, Google, and LinkedIn, offer mindfulness training in the workplace. In addition, technology has added more options through apps and tools such as Headspace and Calm. Readers are also directed to Yeganeh and Kolb (2009) for a practical set of mindful experiential learning practices. Given the wealth of resources, the challenge is knowing what type of training and practice will yield the desired results for particular leaders.

Monitor Internal and External Conditions for Changes That Translate to New Leadership Requirements

Many of the same techniques used in strategic planning can be deployed by leaders to identify learning needs, including regularly reviewing key business/industry publications, learning about industry changes from a network of contacts, and subscribing to important newsfeeds both internal and external to the organization. Translating these changes into leadership skill requirements is often relegated to the talent management function. However, leaders themselves can learn to analyze situations and determine the leadership capabilities required.

Regularly Seek Self-Assessment Information

Just as organizations conduct SWOT (strengths, weaknesses, opportunities, and threats) analyses, leaders also can learn to evaluate themselves using this framework. To do so effectively requires that leaders regularly seek informal feedback. Leaders can also increase self-awareness by taking advantage of formal feedback resources that are available to them, such as personality and learning agility assessments, 360 surveys, and behavioral simulations.

Prioritize the Leadership Capabilities to Be Learned and Let Go

Leaders who are learning agile must select the critical capabilities to be learned, and in some cases "unlearned" or used with less frequency. As leaders make each turn in the leadership pipeline, they must recognize that behaviors that led to success in the past may no longer be needed and could even be detrimental in new situations (Charan, Drotter, & Noel, 2001; De Meuse, 2017; Goldsmith & Reiter, 2007).

2. Doing

Doing involves taking action by proactively seeking new information, frameworks, and experiences; experimenting with new ways of responding; and practicing deliberately. These behaviors are central to the implementation stage of the Agile Learning Process.

Seeking Stretch Experiences

In *The Lessons of Experience*, McCall, Lombardo, and Morrison (1988) found that successful executives considered challenging job experiences to be the most critical driver of their development. The assumption is that learning occurs when there is a discrepancy between the leader's current skill set, past experiences, and the skills required to do the job. The leader must "stretch" to learn and try new behaviors or reframe previous ways of thinking in a new situation (McCauley, Ruderman, Ohlott, & Morrow, 1994). This gap in capability compared to role requirements can motivate leaders to be agile in learning what is needed, either to achieve a significant reward outcome or to avoid a negative outcome. Learning is accelerated when leaders feel compelled to employ tactics outside of their normal comfort zone and, as a result, acquire new skills and strategies.

Experimenting, Taking Risks, and Demonstrating Courage

Experimenting involves trying out different behaviors and strategies. Through testing new approaches, leaders are able to evaluate the effectiveness of various behaviors, develop new mental models, and get feedback on what worked and what should be done differently. This iterative process enables learning agility by increasing flexibility in readily drawing connections within and across experiences.

Experimenting with new behaviors inevitably requires taking risks and stepping to the very edge of one's comfort zone. Courage, "the intentional pursuit of a worthy goal despite the perception of personal threat and uncertain outcome" (Pury, 2008, p. 111), is a learnable behavior that facilitates the experimentation needed to try out new behaviors (e.g., Woodard & Pury, 2007). Multiple researchers have also emphasized the role of psychological safety in learning (e.g., Edmondson, 2019). In developing learning agility, we must help leaders develop the skills needed to overcome fears, take prudent risks, and create their *own* conditions of safety.

Sourcing Information and New Frameworks

New experiences require a leader to do things that he or she has never done before. Rather than simply trying out new behaviors in a trial-and-error fashion, systematically seeking new information can provide frameworks that empower leaders to be more targeted in their experimentation. Information sourcing behaviors include intentional actions taken to locate and access others' expertise, experiences, insights, and opinions. People use a variety of methods to access information; these are categorized in Table 6.2. Learning from experience can be accelerated by understanding the information sources available and the types of learning they best facilitate.

Practicing Deliberately

Deliberate practice involves practicing in an intentional and focused way, breaking down a skill into steps, attending to performance of those steps, and eventually reintegrating the steps into a new behavior pattern. Research on deliberate practice has shown it to be effective for developing expertise in a variety of domains. However, while the cliché "practice makes perfect" seems logical, repeatedly practicing a leadership behavior that is ineffective or no longer appropriate to the situation is a hallmark of leadership derailment. Deliberate practice may increase agility in changing from an ingrained behavioral pattern to a new, more productive approach and for developing the automaticity needed for routine leadership capabilities (Day, 2010).

Table 6.2 Information Sourcing Strategies

Strategy	Most Helpful for Learning
1. Dyadic: communicating directly with a single other expert	• Behaviors associated with adapting to the environment
2. Published knowledge: sourcing information through books, media, Internet, sources that are widely available	• Behaviors that reflect successful behavior of others, best practices, and commonly used steps for recurring problems
3. Group knowledge: intentional effort to locate and access others' expertise, experience, and insights and engage in public conversation	• Novel solutions to problems and radically different work practices and gaining a wider range of experiences and perspectives

Adapted from Gray, P. H., & Meister, D. B. (2006). Knowledge sourcing methods. *Information & Management, 43*(2), 142–156.

Practical Suggestions for Developing Learning Agile Behaviors: Doing

Identify the Right Stretch Opportunities and Explore How Assignments Are Made

Leaders can increase their learning agility by actively and intentionally seeking opportunities that will yield the greatest developmental returns. Some leading organizations (e.g., PepsiCo, Hershey, Kelly Services, IBM) hold detailed talent planning meetings to chart critical experiences for their leaders, pairing them with assignments that align with their existing skills and experiences, as well as those skills that can be developed through particular assignments. However, stretch assignments must be carefully designed to avoid negative consequences to both the leader and his or her organization. Nevertheless, all stakeholders should keep in mind that some failures are to be expected. In addition, it is important for both leaders and their organizations to avoid focusing solely on task achievement and place adequate emphasis on learning.

Engage in Action Learning Projects

Action learning is a process by which a community of learners works together on a real work problem, with the dual purpose of contributing to the business and learning (e.g., Marquardt & Banks, 2010). Learning occurs through concrete experiences, active questioning, and reflection. Action learning creates a safe environment for people to practice their leadership skills, obtain real-time feedback, and enhance the transfer of leadership skills to the job.

Apply Design Thinking

Even though design thinking was developed as an innovation process, it is highly relevant to helping leaders become more agile in experimentation. Design thinking is an iterative process in which the focus is on understanding stakeholders, challenging assumptions, redefining problems, and iteratively experimenting with solutions (T. Brown, 2008). It is considered most useful in addressing problems that are ill-defined, which is what leaders commonly face. A hallmark of the process is learning to "fail fast," which refers to experimenting quickly, seeking feedback, and embracing failure as a means of learning. For example, Johnson & Johnson encourages design thinking to support both innovation and learning agility (Cohen, 2019). As a result, the company has found participants have less fear of taking risks and understand that experimentation and iteration are key enablers of learning agility.

Bring Underlying Fears to the Surface, Calculate Risks, and Build Self-Efficacy

It can be helpful to surface the underlying fears that prevent leaders from stretching out of their normal comfort zone, allowing them to learn from experience. Articles, books, and TED Talks by authors such as Margie Warrell (*Find Your Courage*, 2009) and Brené Brown (*Daring Greatly*, 2012) can help leaders understand their fears, accept their vulnerabilities, and understand steps that will be helpful. Focusing on past successes and signs of success in the current situation can support self-efficacy. Gaining clarity about expectations and developing an action plan can also increase self-efficacy by creating a perceived pathway to success (Snyder, 2002).

The risks of experimentation can often seem greater than they really are, especially for high-achieving leaders who have rarely, if ever, failed. Pury (2008) noted that courage can be developed by learning cognitive techniques that reduce leaders' bias to have heightened sensitivity to risks. For example, reflecting on or talking with others about (a) how likely a feared outcome is and (b) how catastrophic it would be if the feared outcome occurred can result in a more realistic assessment of risk. In a *Harvard Business Review* article, Kathleen Reardon (2007) offered a practical "courage calculation" that includes questions such as, (a) What are my goals? (b) How important are they? (c) Do I have a supportive power network? (d) What are the risk/benefit trade-offs? (e) Is now the right time to act? and (f) Do I have a sufficient contingency plan?

Identify Appropriate Opportunities for Deliberate Practice

Leaders should consider which capabilities will benefit from repeated and deliberate practice (e.g., public speaking, facilitating meetings, conducting interviews). When planning their work, it is then possible to identify situations where deliberate practice will be possible. As previously noted, seeking real-time feedback from a trusted advisor and taking time to reflect on what to "start, stop, or continue" will likely result in the most benefit from deliberate practice.

The opportunity to practice leadership skills in a simulated environment is a safe way to learn from experience and to engage in situations that may not yet have been encountered or encountered with sufficient frequency to practice. Simulations can be technology enabled or high touch, involving interactions with skilled coaches or assessors. Simulations are a powerful way to develop learning agility by providing a microcosm of the experiential learning cycle, including preparation, practice, feedback, and reflection. (See Case Studies B and F for examples.)

3. Connecting

Learning rarely occurs in isolation from others and is often the outcome of interacting with peers, managers, direct reports, clients, customers, and other stakeholders. McCall and colleagues (1988) noted that a significant percentage of key learning events involved a specific person versus an assignment. Leaders can learn from others both vicariously and directly by observing role models, asking for help, seeking feedback, and learning with and from peers, mentors, role models, and coaches. Connecting with others is important across all stages of the Learning Agile Process.

Asking for Help

No one leader can possess all of the knowledge, skills, abilities, and capacity needed to achieve organizational goals. Proactively seeking help from peers, managers, or coaches can facilitate agile learning when leaders identify gaps in their knowledge or encounter problems. Initiating a request for help inherently involves some psychological risk, including perceived shame, embarrassment, and dependence. While it may seem intuitive for a leader to simply ask for help, it does not always happen! The development of Learning Agile Behavior may also be influenced by cultural and individual differences in the perceived risk of asking for help. For example, research suggested individuals from non-Western cultures, men, and those who are lower in achievement motivation and higher in self-esteem may be more likely to avoid seeking help (Lee, 2002; Tessler & Schwartz, 1972).

Seeking, Accepting, and Using Feedback

Feedback is essential to agile learning. Feedback helps leaders develop more accurate self-perceptions, clearly define expectations, gauge progress, and correct errors (e.g., Ashford, Blatt, & VandeWalle, 2003). Often, feedback is the only "mirror" available to leaders to help make course corrections when learning from experience. Feedback seeking is even more important for leaders compared to individual contributors because the amount of spontaneous feedback received from others becomes less frequent, skills are more complex, and success is not always self-evident. However, the decision to ask for feedback is influenced by whether the benefits of asking for feedback (e.g., reduced uncertainty) are perceived as greater than the costs (e.g., portraying oneself as uncertain or incompetent).

Becoming learning agile requires getting comfortable with actively seeking candid feedback, avoiding defensiveness, and asking specific, detailed questions from multiple sources. To result in learning, feedback must be accepted and integrated into existing belief and knowledge structures. Several studies have suggested that learning is especially strong when reflection is paired with feedback seeking, followed by action on the learned insights (Anseel, Lievens, & Schollaert, 2009).

Learning Vicariously From Role Models

It is well established that learning can occur vicariously through observation of role models to determine appropriate or effective behavior. We all learn from role models, whether consciously or not. Leaders can learn what to do and not do from both positive and negative role models, from direct experience with others as well as passive observation of media images (Kempster & Parry, 2014). Because of the practical limitations on how much direct experience any one leader can obtain, those who are learning agile are intentional about learning from role models. Leaders can round out their experience portfolio more quickly by proactively seeking vicarious experiences. As McCall et al. (1988) noted, "The lessons from other people are there for the taking, but more often than not, a person must go after them" (p. 73).

Leveraging Coaches and Mentors

The prevalence of using coaches and mentors has increased dramatically during the past decade (Frick, 2018). It is beyond the scope of this chapter to discuss what contributes to effective coaching or mentoring overall. However, most relevant to the development of learning agility is helping leaders know how to maximize their mentoring and/or coaching experiences. Participants are rarely clear on what to expect or how to "use" a coach or mentor. Some leaders enter coaching with fear, others may be defensive, and others assume that a coach or mentor will have all the "magic answers."

Learning agile leaders recognize that working with a coach or mentor is a two-way process and deploy actions to help them get the most from these interactions. Unfortunately, limited research exists on what does and does not work. An Amazon search resulted in over 4,000 books on how to *do* effective coaching but none on how to *receive* leadership coaching.

Practical Suggestions for Developing Learning Agile Behaviors: Connecting

Overcome the Psychological Barriers Associated With Asking for Help

A first step for leaders is to recognize the feelings of vulnerability associated with asking for help and focus on the rewards rather than the risks. Leaders can learn to (a) frame requests in ways that demonstrate asking for help as a strength and a willingness to learn; (b) remember that people are typically flattered to be asked to share their expertise; and (c) be realistic and specific in their requests for help (e.g., "I'm only looking for an hour of your time to learn how you handled this type of situation."). Learning to consistently express gratitude for the help received and describing the impact the help will have on self and others is also a learnable technique that increases the odds of receiving support.

Mindfully Observe and Reflect on the Behavior of Role Models

By being more mindful in their observation process, leaders can more deeply tune into (a) the nuances of the behavior being demonstrated; (b) the unique context; and (c) the outcomes that result from the role model's behavior. Just as reflection supports learning from direct experience, taking the time to reflect on observed experience can help in abstracting key lessons.

Seek Exposure to a Broad Range of Leaders

Relational proximity plays an important role in who we learn from, which can limit available leadership role models. Actively seeking opportunities to observe a broad range of role models increases exposure to different ways leadership behaviors are demonstrated. This allows leaders to pick and choose those most relevant to their own development and authentic to their personal style. It may be especially important for women and other groups who are underrepresented in the leadership ranks to seek additional role models similar to them, given that comparisons with others who share commonalities can be especially potent (Sealy & Singh, 2010).

Given accessibility to a wealth of media, leaders also have the opportunity to learn from the experiences of other leaders by reading biographies or watching videos, movies, and other media. For example, Accenture has supported leaders in learning from the experiences of others by capturing and digitally disseminating vignettes/stories that leaders are willing to share (C. Mirshokrai, Accenture, managing director of Global Leadership Development, phone interview, May 6, 2014).

Use Targeted Questions When Seeking Feedback

Seeking feedback by asking general questions like, "How did I do?" typically results in equally generic responses (e.g., "You did great"), especially when the feedback provider is not experienced or comfortable giving feedback. Leaders can learn to gain more useful feedback by asking more targeted questions, such as (a) What could I have done differently? (b) What did you think the impact was of [specific behavior] in that last meeting? (c) What do you think would happen if I tried [specific behavior]? or (d) How could I have done [specific behavior] even better?

Seek Feedback Often and From Multiple Perspectives

Feedback should not be a one-time process. Following up with feedback providers regularly enables leaders to track progress and identify further areas to refine, as long as it is not so frequent as to frustrate others! Seeking feedback from a variety of stakeholders ensures the leader gets a more complete and accurate picture of how new behaviors are working. Multisource surveys can help in obtaining robust and comprehensive feedback from multiple providers. However, it should not be an excuse for failing to seek feedback through the regular course of work. By demonstrating gratitude for feedback, leaders can subtly "train" those around them to be more comfortable providing it and help create a feedback-rich culture within their team and organization.

Seek a Coach With Expertise in Learning Agility

Seek out a coach who understands learning agility and can help in developing Learning Agile Behaviors. Coaches can certainly provide short-term help for developing a specific skill set, but their value will be even greater when they are able to simultaneously assist in developing a leader's learning agility for the long term. A coach versed in learning agility will help leaders understand the behaviors most helpful at certain stages in the Learning Agile Process and encourage the Learning Agile Behaviors described in this chapter.

Maximize Coaching or Mentoring Interactions

Informal surveys of coaches, nonempirical articles, and our own experience suggest several learnable steps that leaders can take to get the most from coaching and mentoring opportunities. Most important, leaders can participate in the coaching process with an open, growth-oriented mindset; share areas of vulnerability; and recognize that strong emotional reactions can be an important signal. Leaders can also be active in the process by (a) preparing for sessions (e.g., reflecting on progress, making notes on feedback received, considering examples of experiences to share, preparing a list of potential topics and questions); (b) taking responsibility for reflecting after discussions, owning what is within their control, following through on commitments; and (c) letting the coach know their personal needs. Last, realistic expectations about the process and tenacity are key. Change takes time and can often be uncomfortable!

Look for Micro-Mentors

A single mentor rarely has both depth and breadth across all the possible areas in which leaders must be skilled. "Micromentoring"—soliciting the help of known experts for shorter term interactions (e.g., coffee, lunch, or a phone call), focused on targeted subjects—is a useful alternative. In addition to the direct rewards, micromentoring often has the benefit of expanding a leader's network and exposing the leader to a variety of leadership role models.

4. Thinking

Until now, our discussion has primarily focused on *observable* behaviors leaders can develop to enhance learning agility. However, we cannot overlook the critical importance of *thinking*, the largely unseen cognitive aspect of actively processing and integrating information. Learnable thinking behaviors include reflection, metacognition, questioning, and mindset shifting. These behaviors are important in virtually all stages of the Learning Agile Process.

Reflecting

All leaders try to understand their experiences through their existing assumptions and frames of reference, which in turn shapes thoughts and feelings. Experiences serve as the catalyst, but it is critical reflection that cements learning and behavioral change. Learning how and when to reflect and then doing it consistently is an important learnable process that contributes significantly to agile learning.

Reflection involves integrating new information gained from experience, feedback, information seeking, and coaching in a meaningful manner—in short, "sense-making." Daudelin (1996) suggested that reflection includes the phases of (a) thinking about events, people, and actions as objectively as possible; (b) analyzing why things happened as they did; (c) developing hypotheses about how the event could have been handled differently; and (d) identifying insights for action. Multiple studies have demonstrated the value of reflection (e.g., Anseel et al., 2009; DeRue, Nahrgang, Hollenbeck, & Workman, 2012).

Engaging in Metacognition

While reflection involves thinking about our experiences, metacognition is the process of "thinking about our thinking" regarding those experiences. Developing the ability to actively monitor our cognitions is critical to becoming learning agile. Metacognition impacts self-regulation, seeking assistance, critical thinking, problem-solving, and reflection. It is a powerful overall predictor of learning (e.g., Bransford, Sherwood, Vye, & Rieser, 1986; Lai, 2011).

Research suggests that metacognitive skills *can* be learned (e.g., Zimmerman & Schunk, 2001). For example, the central premise of transformative learning theory is that learning requires metacognition and making changes to previously unquestioned frames of reference in order to integrate new experiences into one's worldview (Mezirow, 1991, 1997). Similarly, Argyris (1977, 1991) suggests that double-loop learning occurs when leaders uncover and change their underlying assumptions and mental models.

Questioning and Demonstrating Curiosity

Learning to ask effective questions is a potent Learning Agile Behavior in addition to being a powerful leadership skill. Questioning is the learnable behavior associated with curiosity. Questions can be internal (aiding in reflection and metacognition) or external (resulting in more meaningful dialogue with others). Marquardt (2011) suggested, "The capacity to ask fresh questions in conditions of ignorance, risk and confusion when nobody knows what to do next is at the heart of action learning" (Marquardt, 2011, p. 71). Questions can sometimes provide answers, but more importantly, they stimulate deeper thinking.

Learning from experience typically requires that leaders engage in solving complex problems where existing knowledge is often insufficient. By beginning with questions, a leader can determine if his or her existing knowledge is adequate and relevant. Being agile in questioning skills allows a leader to more quickly unpeel the layers of a situation, gather information, gain input from others, and explore new strategies. Questions direct attention, energy, and effort and have even been called "the ultimate empowerment tool for leaders" (Oakley & Krug, 1991).

Changing Mental Models

Everyone has mental models or implicit theories of how the world operates. A mental model is a cognitive representation that allows us to make sense of what is going on and act on our environment. Keating and Heslin (2015) defined a mindset as "a mental framework that guides how people think, feel, and act in achievement contexts" (p. 334). Mindsets can be adaptive or maladaptive in influencing leaders' (a) interpretation of situations, (b) self-talk, (c) emotional reactions, and (d) ultimate actions taken. Two mental models especially relevant to the development of learning agility are "growth mindset" and "error management mindset."

Carol Dweck (2008) has emphasized the value of having a growth versus fixed mindset. Those with a "fixed mindset" believe their capabilities are static. They are concerned with performance goals and being judged as competent. This mindset leads to setting goals that are easier, undervaluing the impact of effort, not asking for help, and less resilience when faced with challenges. In contrast, those with a "growth mindset" believe that growth is possible with effort, increasing the likelihood of trying different strategies, taking risks, and asking for help. Challenging goals and setbacks are viewed as opportunities to learn.

Error management is another relevant mindset that involves accepting errors as inevitable and framing failure as a learning opportunity. This mindset prevents negative emotions from consuming attention in a dysfunctional way (e.g., Keith & Frese, 2008). Those with an error management mindset may also be more likely to interpret negative emotions as motivational feedback regarding goal achievement (Frese & Keith, 2015).

While mental models can be difficult to change, the good news is that they *can* be shifted through coaching and other interventions. For example, significant research has demonstrated that cognitive therapy, based on changing underlying beliefs, is one of the most powerful interventions available for changing problematic emotions and behaviors (Butler, Chapman, Forman, & Beck, 2006). Similarly, mindset shifting may prove to be one of the most potent facilitators of learning agility.

Practical Suggestions for Developing Learning Agile Behaviors: Thinking

Learn to "Think About Thinking"

This may seem daunting, yet it is likely one of the capabilities most critical to the development of learning agility. A practical first step is simply to understand what metacognition is. This basic awareness can help leaders begin to "see" the frameworks that govern how they perceive the world. Another promising avenue is vertical learning (e.g., Petrie, 2015), which incorporates concepts from developmentalism (Kegan & Lahey, 2009), stages of consciousness (Rochat, 2003), and transformational learning (Mezirow, 1991). Vertical learning is about changing the way people view reality and make sense of their experiences. (See Chapter 17 for a more complete review of vertical learning.)

Develop a Reflection Routine

Leaders are typically biased for action, finding it difficult to shift into a reflection mode; they need to remind themselves reflection is value-added time. For many, a critical step is simply being disciplined about establishing a reflection routine, such as making an "appointment with self" on the calendar, consciously using commute time to reflect, or keeping a journal. For some, telling a friend, family member, or colleague about their experience can support reflective processing. Writing and talking appear to be especially beneficial when processing negative events to prevent rumination (Lyubomirsky, Sousa, & Dickerhoof, 2006). Keeping a digital or paper journal has the added benefit of recording the process, which can be a rich source for identifying patterns of thought, behavior, or emotional reactions over time.

Use Questions or Models to Guide Reflection

When leaders first begin a reflection routine, having some thought-provoking questions can be helpful. Table 6.3 provides some examples. Reflection using

Table 6.3 Example Reflection Questions

Reflecting on a Specific Situation	General Reflection
• What did I do well?	• What feedback did I receive during the past week?
• What should I consider doing differently the next time?	• Who should I be seeking additional feedback from?
• How might my perceptions be similar to or different from others who were involved?	• Are there any consistent themes in the feedback I have received?
• What were the assumptions that I made in choosing how to respond? What evidence do I have to support them?	• How have I done in staying focused on my key priorities? What helped or hindered me in doing so?
• What beliefs underlie the assumptions that I'm making, and could they be faulty?	• How am I progressing on my key development opportunities? Where did I do well or not so well?
• What are the filters or biases that may be influencing my interpretation of this situation?	• What information sources or other people could be resources?

models such as the "ladder of inference" can also be helpful in uncovering belief systems that are maladaptive but are being used without the leader's full awareness (see Senge, 1990).

Create Graphic Representations of Mental Models

The development of mental models may be necessary to think metacognitively about complex systems. Anecdotal evidence from working with leaders suggests that creating diagrams or storyboards of their mental models related to leadership concepts (e.g., teamwork) facilitates deeper questioning of underlying beliefs, assumptions, and how the pieces fit together. Leaders often find that creating a visual diagram to teach others about a topic compels them to clarify their own mental model.

Monitor Self-Talk

Through reflection and metacognition, leaders can monitor and intentionally focus on shifting toward a more growth-oriented mindset. For example, after reflecting on an experience perceived as a setback, leaders should monitor their self-talk for messages such as, "I'm just not smart enough", and intentionally replacing them with more productive messages, such as, "What strategy might work better the next time?" or "Who might be able to help me figure out a new approach?" Mindfulness may be useful for viewing the situation with curiosity rather than judgment. Initially, it may be helpful for a coach or trusted advisor to provide assistance in identifying maladaptive self-talk.

Seek Training on Growth and/or Error Management Mindsets

Leadership programs are beginning to promote the importance of having a growth mindset. For examples, see Cases B and D. While there is very little research specific to leaders, error management training is another promising approach for shifting mindsets, particularly given it has been shown to increase transfer of learning from one experience to different or novel experiences (Keith & Frese, 2008).

Focus on Asking Questions With a Learning Mindset

"Questioning our questions" is another form of metacognition. Asking questions focused on possibilities rather than on judgments is more conducive to learning agility. For example, What am I responsible for? or What can I learn? (learning mindset) versus Who is to blame? or How could I lose? (judging mindset). Michael Marquardt's book, *Leading With Questions* (2005), is useful for learning how to frame questions. Programs such as QuestionThinking and The Inquiring Mindset™ by Marilee Adams from the Inquiry Institute may also be useful (see also Adams, 2010). Action learning programs and appreciative inquiry are also vehicles for developing questioning skills useful to learning.

5. Mobilizing

Mobilizing behaviors are essential to the planning, regulating, and monitoring stages of the Learning Agile Process. These stages require harnessing emotions and motivation, self-control, setting goals, planning, and demonstrating discipline. Sustaining learning agility for the long term requires resilience and the ability to bounce back from challenges and even failure.

Setting Goals and Establishing Indicators of Success

Goal setting has been widely researched and is considered central in self-regulating processes (e.g., Locke & Latham, 1990). Agile learning is best supported by setting goals that are challenging and attainable but allow for iterative modifications during the learning process. Setting overly specific goals in environments that are complex or changing can inhibit learning by narrowing one's focus and preventing deeper information processing and experimentation (Ordóñez, Schweitzer, Galinsky, & Bazerman, 2009).

It is also essential for leaders not to confuse performance goals, which can lead to a fixed mindset, with learning goals, which encourage a growth mindset. For example, "To have superior influencing skills and be in the top 10% in achieving compliance among stakeholders in implementing key initiatives" is a performance goal. "To increase my understanding of influencing techniques and my capability in persuading key stakeholders to implement key initiatives" is a learning goal. Goals and indicators of success are also important for creating a motivating vision for future state against which progress can be evaluated. Identifying "success indicators" will help leaders recognize the signs to being on the right path and whether additional effort is required (e.g., "I will begin to find that my ideas are more quickly supported by key stakeholders").

Action Planning for Development

Evidence suggests that intentions are translated into action only about 50% of the time, which has been labeled the "intention–behavior gap" (Sheeran & Webb, 2016). Development action plans provide a way to bridge this gap and provide the structure needed to direct attention, focus effort, and self-regulate (Gollwitzer, 1999; Gollwitzer & Sheeran, 2006). Knowing how to create an effective development action plan and do so quickly and flexibly as needs arise supports agile learning.

Achieving a complex learning goal typically involves taking a variety of actions (e.g., reading an article, questioning a role model, practicing a new behavior). Effective development action plans break down these steps into manageable "bites" over which leaders perceive they have control—the expectation of being able to perform a given behavior, obtain needed resources, or overcome obstacles encountered (Ajzen, 2002). Perceived behavioral control accounts for a significant amount of variance in intention leading to actual changes in behavior (Armitage & Conner, 2010).

In addition, having a clear plan primes leaders to see and take advantage of learning opportunities in the flow of their work (Gollwitzer, 1999). When a development action plan includes situational cues for behavior, it reduces the amount of conscious cognitive effort and self-regulation needed to identify relevant opportunities. For instance, a development plan action, such as "Seek feedback from one person after each key stakeholder meeting," provides specific cues to where and when this action should be taken.

Demonstrating Self-Control and Resilience

In the process of pursuing their learning goals, leaders face a multitude of challenges in regulating their thoughts, behaviors, and emotions. As might be expected, self-control is a powerful predictor of learning outcomes (Duckworth & Seligman, 2005). Similarly, resilience in bouncing back from failure is equally important and learnable (Yost, 2016). A complete review of all possible interventions for strengthening self-control and resilience is beyond the scope of this chapter; however, the following are learnable behaviors that that support learning agility: (a) recognizing unproductive or competing thoughts and emotions; (b) breaking automatic habits; (c) implementing strategies to minimize procrastination; (d) anticipating obstacles; and (e) engaging in behaviors that support resilience. (see Chapter 12 for additional resources on resilience).

Practical Suggestions for Developing Learning Agile Behaviors: Mobilizing

Understand How to Create an Effective Development Action Plan

An effective action plan (a) provides a structure for goal setting focused on learning versus performance; (b) helps instill a belief that the leader has control over his or her behavior; (c) primes the leader to see cues for practice opportunities; and (d) supports mitigation of obstacles. It is often useful for leaders to think of development action plans as similar to a project plan, with which most are familiar. Research cited in the previous section and our experience suggest that development action plans are most effective when they include the elements listed in Table 6.4.

Create "If–Then" Statements

This technique involves considering potential obstacles (e.g., competing commitments, external influences) and then identifying effective ways to respond. Sheeran and Webb (2016) suggest using the following language: "*If* [opportunity/obstacle] arises, *then* I will [respond in this way]" (p. 13). For example, "*If* I hold back in meetings because I feel awkward, *then* I will remind myself that it is normal that doing something new will feel uncomfortable for a while" If–then plans are effective, because when an obstacle is encountered it is already mentally paired with a productive response.

Overcome Immunity to Change

Kegan and Lahey (2009) suggested most people have a powerful "immunity to change," a psychological protection mechanism that, paradoxically, prevents making changes that will often be beneficial. Immunity mapping is a metacognitive process that can help in self-regulating the underlying commitments and unproductive beliefs that prevent leaders from reaching their goals. Table 6.5 provides an example.

Monitor Progress

The inclusion of clear milestones and indicators of success in the development plan provides a means of monitoring one's progress. However, they should be adaptive to changing circumstances. Progress monitoring as part of reflection or conversation with a coach/mentor can be helpful. Many technology apps that exist for goal monitoring may also be useful. However, it is important for leaders to avoid simply "checking off the boxes." Emphasis should be placed on what was learned from each experience or action taken. Given the complexity of leadership challenges, mastery often requires extended, consistent focus; celebrating incremental progress toward goals helps sustain motivation. Coaches and accountability partners can help recognize successes along the journey.

Table 6.4 Development Plan Elements

Development Plan Element	Purpose
Clear goal statement	Clearly articulating goals is time well spent and makes the rest of the plan easier to create. Goals should be worded to reinforce a growth mindset and vivid enough to create a clear mental picture of the desired end state. Commitment is likely to be higher for goals where the outcome is perceived as important and with high relevance to personal identity. The number of goals should be limited (2–4) to be realistic in regard to time, resources, and focus.
Actions	Actions should include a mix of learning approaches (e.g., reading, learning from others, on-the-job practice, and experiences). For actions that will take place during naturally occurring work situations (e.g., providing or seeking more feedback), it is best to describe the types of situations so that the leader will be primed to "see" these opportunities when they arise. It's also important to think of the action items as a flexible, "living" idea list where additional actions may be added and others deleted as learning transpires.
Resources and time frames	When resources are required, such as support from trusted advisors, it can be helpful to list them as specifically as possible. A time frame for completing various actions provides an accountability mechanism; however, time frames may vary considerably depending on the nature of the action. For example, for reading the time frame may be "1 article per week," while for others it may be situation specific, such as "after each staff meeting."
Success indicators	Leaders often struggle with identifying success measures because they are accustomed to focusing on "hard data" types of metrics. It is useful to reflect on the question, What will I see, hear from others, and feel internally that will indicate to me that I am making progress?
Obstacle mitigation	Considering the potential obstacles that are anticipated can increase the odds of success. For each potential obstacle, create "if–then" statements as described in the text.

Enlist an Accountability Partner

Some leaders find it useful to identify a friend, family member, colleague, or coach to serve as an accountability partner—someone trusted to hold the leader to the standard he or she has set. This person should be someone (a) who can be trusted as a confidant, (b) who is willing to point out blind spots or excuses, (c) who asks about progress, and (d) who can serve as both a cheerleader and shoulder to cry on. This process works especially well when the relationship is reciprocal (e.g., when peers serve as accountability partners for each other).

Table 6.5 Immunity to Change Mapping

Elements of the Map	Example
1. Visible Commitment: The desired behavior or goal	Be more open to new ideas and flexible in responding.
2. Doing/Not Doing : The behaviors we are or not actually engaging in	Cutting off new ideas (doing), not asking questions to solicit others' views (not doing).
3. Hidden Competing Commitments: The reasons for doing something inconsistent with our visible commitment	To feel pride in ownership of new approaches.
4. Big Assumptions: The beliefs that fuel the inconsistency	I won't be valued if new ideas are not seen by others as mine.

Based on Kegan, R., & Lahey, L. (2009). *Immunity to Change: How to overcome it and unlock the potential in yourself and your organization.* Boston, MA: Harvard Business Review Press.

Summary and Conclusions

There is no question we live in a world where change is constant, and to thrive, learning must keep pace. As a result, learning agility is needed more than ever before and can—and must—be developed so leaders can maximize their potential and to ensure organizations sustain competitive advantage. The following are some of the lessons we have learned while writing this chapter and from our experiences as coaches and organizational practitioners.

Lessons Learned

An amazingly deep, rich body of both theory and research exists to help us better understand how Learning Agile Behavior can be developed. Our goal has been to heed the words attributed to Isaac Newton in 1675 that we can see much farther "by standing have provided the foundational building blocks for developing the Learning Agile Behavior needed to thrive in the decades ahead. In this chapter, we have integrated these building blocks into a simple model—being, doing, connecting, thinking, and mobilizing—that we hope will be practical and meaningful.

Far less is known about when to deploy various Learning Agile Behaviors within the stages of personal change and adaptation. Developing one's learning agility is itself a dynamic process within a dynamic context, which is likely more iterative than linear. Currently, the *process* of developing learning agility can be described better as an art than science. Table 6.6 provides a framework suggesting which Learning Agile Behaviors may be most relevant at various stages of the Learning Agile Process. However additional research is needed on the specific sequence, timing, and combination of Learning Agile Behaviors that optimize the development of learning agility.

Questions Yet to Be Answered

While there is much we know about the learnable behaviors that contribute to learning agility, there is even more we have yet to understand. The following are just a few of the questions yet unanswered:

Table 6.6 Learning Agile Behaviors Relevant to the Stages of the Agile Learning Process

Learning Agile Behaviors	Stage of Learning Agile Process for Which Learning Agile Behaviors Are Most Important
1. Observing • Mindful Awareness • Environmental Scanning • Future Forecasting	• Detection of need for change and identification of type of change required • Self-regulation of focus and energy
2. Doing • Seeking Out Stretch Experiences • Experimenting • Taking Risks • Demonstrating Courage • Sourcing Information and New Frameworks	• Implementation of Learning Agile Behaviors • Self-Regulation in Changing Thoughts, Emotions, and Behaviors
3. Connecting • Asking For Help • Seeking, Accepting, and Using Feedback • Learning Vicariously From Role Models • Leveraging Coaches and Mentors	• Implementation of Learning Agile Behaviors • Monitoring Effectiveness of Change
4. Thinking • Reflecting • Engaging in Metacognition • Questioning and Demonstrating Curiosity • Changing Mental Models	• Detection of Need for Change • Implementation of Learning Agile Behaviors
5. Mobilizing • Setting Goals and Establishing Indicators of Success • Action Planning for Development • Demonstrating Self-Control and Resilience	• Planning for Change • Self-Regulation in Changing Behavior

- Which Learning Agile Behaviors are most important in enhancing one's overall learning agility? Is this dependent on an individual's predisposition to be learning agile?
- Which dispositional personality, motivation, and cognitive characteristics are most likely to influence the effectiveness or adoption of Learning Agile Behaviors? How much of learning agility is learned versus genetic?
- What are the incremental and interaction effects of Learning Agile Behaviors used in combination? What is the best "formula" if not 70–20–10?
- Can it be empirically demonstrated that different Learning Agile Behaviors are more important at particular stages in the Learning Agile Process? Does the sequence matter?
- Where in the Learning Agile Process is the velocity of learning beneficial, and where can speed be detrimental? What contributes most to increasing velocity of learning? Is learning velocity more important in some contexts than others?
- Which of the Learning Agile Behaviors are more easily developed, and which are most challenging? Which are influenced most by the surrounding environment and organizational support?
- How do we best measure the acquisition and growth of Learning Agile Behaviors?
- What is the role of a leader's manager in supporting and encouraging Learning Agile Behavior? Are learning agile leaders more effective at developing learning agility in others?
- What organizational cultural attributes and practices best facilitate Learning Agile Behavior? How is reciprocal determinism at work?

Conclusion

We all have much to gain by encouraging partnerships among researchers and practitioners to answer these important questions. Doing so may require breaking down silos among disciplines such as industrial–organizational psychology; educational, social, clinical, and counseling psychology; and adult learning. Further, it will likely require greater integration of learning agility with related areas of study, such as learning ability and velocity, performance adaptation, and even wisdom. Clearly, it is essential that we accelerate our understanding of how to develop the learning agility of those we assess, coach, and guide in order to achieve the flourishing leadership pipeline needed to face the unknown leadership challenges of tomorrow.

References

Adams, M. (2010). The practical primacy of questions in action learning. In Y. Boshyk, & L. Dilworth (Eds.), *Action learning and its applications, present and future* (pp. 119–130). London, UK: Palgrave Macmillan.

Ajzen, I. (2002). Perceived behavioral control, self-efficacy, locus of control, and the theory of planned behavior 1. *Journal of Applied Social Psychology, 32*(4), 665–683.

Anseel, F., Lievens, F., & Schollaert, E. (2009). Reflection as a strategy to enhance task performance after feedback. *Organizational Behavior and Human Decision Processes, 110*(1), 23–35.

Argyris, C. (1977). Double loop learning in organizations. *Harvard Business Review, 55*(5), 115–125.

Argyris, C. (1991). Teaching smart people how to learn. *Harvard Business Review, 69*(3), 99–109.

Argyris, C., & Schon, D. (1974). *Theory in practice.* San Francisco, CA: Jossey-Bass.

Armitage, C. J., & Conner, M. (2001). Efficacy of the theory of planned behaviour: A meta-analytic review. *British Journal of Social Psychology, 40*(4), 471–499.

Ashford, S. J., Blatt, R., & VandeWalle, D. (2003). Reflections on the looking glass: A review of research on feedback-seeking behavior in organizations. *Journal of Management, 29*(6), 773–799.

Baard, S., Rench, T., & Kozlowski, S. W. J. (2014). Performance adaptation: A theoretical integration and review. *Journal of Management, 40*(1), 48–99.

Bandura, A. (1977). *Social learning theory.* New York, NY: General Learning Press.

Bell, B. S., & Kozlowski, S. (2010). Toward a theory of learning centered training design: An integrative framework of active learning. In S. W. J. Kozlowski & E. Salas (Eds.), *Learning, training, and development in organizations* (pp. 263–300). New York, NY: Routledge.

Bransford, J., Sherwood, R., Vye, N., & Rieser, J. (1986). Teaching thinking and problem solving: Research foundations. *American Psychologist, 41*(10), 1078.

Brown, B. (2012). *Daring greatly: How the courage to be vulnerable transforms the way we live, love, parent and lead.* New York, NY: Gotham Books.

Brown, K. W., & Ryan, R. M. (2003). The benefits of being present: Mindfulness and its role in psychological well-being. *Journal of Personality and Social Psychology, 84*, 822–848.

Brown, T. (2008). Design thinking. *Harvard Business Review, 86*(6), 84–92.

Butler, A., Chapman, J., Forman, E., & Beck, A. (2006). The empirical status of cognitive-behavioral therapy: A review of meta-analyses. *Clinical Psychology Review, 26*, 17–31.

Charan, R., Drotter, S. J., & Noel, J. L. (2001). The leadership pipeline: How to build the leadership-powered company. San Francisco, CA: Jossey-Bass.

Cohen, R. (2019). Johnson & Johnson case example. In V. Harvey (Chair), *Learning agility in action: How leading companies build agile leaders.* Panel conducted at the Society of Industrial Organizational Psychology Conference, Washington, DC.

Cortazar, N., Calvete, E., Fernández-González, L., & Orue, I. (2019). Development of a short form of the Five Facet Mindfulness Questionnaire—Adolescents for children and adolescents. *Journal of Personality Assessment, 101*, 1–12.

Daudelin, M. W. (1996). Learning from experience through reflection. *Organizational Dynamics, 24*(3), 36–48.

Day, D. V. (2010). The difficulties of learning from experience and the need for deliberate practice. *Industrial and Organizational Psychology: Perspectives on Science and Practice, 3*(1), 41–44.

De Meuse, K. P. (2017). Learning agility: Its evolution as a psychological construct and its empirical relationship to leader success. *Consulting Psychology Journal: Practice and Research, 69*, 267–295.

De Meuse, K. P. (2019). A meta-analysis of the relationship between learning agility and leader success. *Journal of Organizational Psychology, 19*, 25–34.

De Meuse, K. P., Dai, G., & Hallenbeck, G. S. (2010). Learning agility: A construct whose time has come. *Consulting Psychology Journal: Practice and Research, 62*, 119–130.

DeRue, D. S., Ashford, S. J., & Myers, C. G. (2012). Learning agility: In search of conceptual clarity and theoretical grounding. *Industrial and Organizational Psychology: Perspectives on Science and Practice, 5*, 258–279.

DeRue, D. S., Nahrgang, J. D., Hollenbeck, J. R., & Workman, K. (2012). A quasi-experimental study of after-event reviews and leadership development. *Journal of Applied Psychology, 97*(5), 997.

Duckworth, A. L., & Seligman, M. E. P. (2005). Self-discipline outdoes IQ in predicting academic performance of adolescents. *Psychological Science, 16*, 939–944.

Dweck, C. (2008). *Mindset: The new psychology of success.* New York, NY: Ballantine Books.

Dweck, C., & Leggett, E. (1988). A social-cognitive approach to motivation and personality. *Psychological Review, 95*(2) 256–273.

Edmondson, A. (2019). *The fearless organization: Creating psychological safety in the workplace for learning innovation and growth.* Hoboken, NJ: Wiley.

Frese, M., & Keith, N. (2015). Action errors, error management, and learning in organizations. *Annual Review of Psychology, 66*(1), 661–687.

Frick, S. A. (2018). *Why does coaching work? An examination of inputs and process variables in an employee coaching program* (Unpublished doctoral dissertation). University of South Florida, Tampa, FL.

Glomb, T. M., Duffy, M. K., Bono, J. E., & Yang, T. (2011). Mindfulness at work. In A. Joshi, Martocchio, & H. Liao (Eds.), *Research in personnel and human resources management* (Vol. 30, pp. 115–157). https://doi.org/10.1108/S0742-7301(2011)0000030005

Goldsmith, M., & Reiter, M. (2007). *What got you here won't get you there: How successful people become even more successful.* New York, NY: Hyperion.

Gollwitzer, P. M. (1999). Implementation intentions. Strong effects of simple plans. *American Psychologist, 54*, 493–503.

Gollwitzer, P. M., & Sheeran, P. (2006). Implementation intentions and goal achievement: A meta-analysis of effects and processes. *Advances in Experimental Social Psychology, 38*, 249–268.

Gondo, M., Patterson, K. D., & Palacios, S. T. (2013). Mindfulness and the development of a readiness for change. *Journal of Change Management, 13*(1), 36–51.

Good, D. J., Lyddy, C. J., Glomb, T. M., Bono, J. E., Brown, K. W., Duffy, M. K., & Lazar, S. W. (2016). Contemplating mindfulness at work: An integrative review. *Journal of Management, 42*(1), 114–142.

Gray, P. H., & Meister, D. B. (2006). Knowledge sourcing methods. *Information & Management, 43*(2), 142–156.

Harvey, V. (2018). Session introduction. In V. Harvey (Chair), *Going beyond the IDP: Measuring the velocity of leadership learning over time.* Panel conducted at the Society of Industrial Organizational Psychology Conference, Chicago, IL.

Higgins, E. T. (1998). Promotion and prevention: Regulatory focus as a motivational principle. In M. P. Zanna (Ed.), *Advances in Experimental Social Psychology* (Vol. 30, pp. 1–46). New York, NY: Academic Press.

Hülsheger, U. R., Alberts, H. J., Feinholdt, A., & Lang, J. W. B. (2013). Benefits of mindfulness at work: The role of mindfulness in emotion regulation, emotional exhaustion, and job satisfaction. *Journal Applied Psychology, 98,* 310–325.

Keating, L. A., & Heslin, P. A. (2015). The potential role of mindsets in unleashing employee engagement. *Human Resource Management Review, 25*(4), 329–341.

Kegan, R. (1994). *In over our heads.* Cambridge, MA: Harvard University Press.

Kegan, R., & Lahey, L. L. (2001). The real reason people won't change. *Harvard Business Review, 79*(10), 84–92.

Kegan, R., & Lahey, L. (2009). *Immunity to change: How to overcome it and unlock the potential in yourself and your organization.* Boston, MA: Harvard Business Review Press.

Keith, N., & Frese, M. (2008). Effectiveness of error management training: A meta-analysis. *Journal of Applied Psychology, 93*(1), 59–69.

Kempster, S., & Parry, K. (2014). Exploring observational learning in leadership development for managers. *Journal of Management Development, 33*(3), 164–181.

Knowles, M. (1973). *The adult learner: A neglected species.* Houston, TX: Gulf.

Knowles, M. (1975). *Self-directed learning.* New York, NY: Association Press.

Kolb, D. A. (1984). *Experiential learning: Experience as the source of learning and development.* Upper Saddle River, NJ: Prentice Hall.

Kolb, A., & Kolb, D. (2011). Experiential learning theory: A dynamic, holistic approach to management learning, education and development. In S. J. Armstrong & C. Fukami (Eds.), *The SAGE handbook of management learning, education and development* (pp. 42–68). London, UK: Sage. doi:10.4135/9780857021038.n3

Lai, E. R. (2011). *Metacognition: A literature review. Always learning: Pearson research report.* Retrieved from https://images.pearsonassessments.com/images/tmrs/Metacognition_Literature_Review_Final.pdf

Laxso, E. (2018). *Within and between person effects of learning agility: A longitudinal examination of how learning agility impacts future career success* (Unpublished doctoral dissertation). Colorado State University, Fort Collins.

Le Pine, J., Colquitt, J., & Erez, A. (2000). Adaptability to task contexts: Effects of general cognitive ability, conscientiousness and openness to experience. *Personnel Psychology, 53,* 563–593.

Lee, F. (2002). The social costs of seeking help. *The Journal of Applied Behavioral Science, 38*(1), 17–35.

Lee, R. (2012). Accelerating the development and mitigating derailment of high potentials through mindfulness training. *The Industrial-Organizational Psychologist, 49*(3), 23–34.

Locke, E. A., & Latham, G. P. (1990). *A theory of goal setting & task performance.* Englewood Cliffs, NJ: Prentice-Hall.

Lombardo, M., & Eichinger, R. (2000). High potentials as high learners. *Human Resource Management, 39*(4), 321–329.

Lombardo, M., & Eichinger, R. (2011). *The leadership machine*. Minneapolis, MN: Lominger International.

Lyubomirsky, S., Sousa, L., & Dickerhoof, R. (2006). The costs and benefits of writing, talking, and thinking about life's triumphs and defeats. *Journal of Personality and Social Psychology, 90*(4), 692.

Marquardt, M. (2005). *Leading with questions*. San Francisco, CA: Jossey-Bass.

Marquardt, M. (2011). *Optimizing the power of action learning: Solving problems and building leaders in real time*. Mountainview, CA: Davies-Black.

Marquardt, M., & Banks, S. (2010). Theory to practice: Action learning. *Advances in Developing Human Resources, 12*(2), 159–162.

McCall, M., Lombardo, M., & Morrison, A. (1988). *Lessons of experience: How successful executives develop on the job*. New York, NY: Lexington Books.

McCauley, C. D., Ruderman, M. N., Ohlott, P. J., & Morrow, J. E. (1994). Assessing the developmental components of managerial jobs. *Journal of Applied Psychology, 79*(4), 544.

Mezirow, J. (1991). *Transformative dimensions of adult learning*. San Francisco, CA: Jossey-Bass.

Mezirow, J. (1997). Transformative learning: Theory to practice. *New Directions for Adult and Continuing Education, 74*, 5–12.

Oakley, D., & Krug, D. (1991). *Enlightened leadership*. New York, NY: Simon & Schuster.

Ordóñez, L. D., Schweitzer, M. E., Galinsky, A. D., & Bazerman, M. H. (2009). Goals gone wild: The systematic side effects of overprescribing goal setting. *Academy of Management Perspectives, 23*(1), 6–16.

Petrie, N. (2015). *The how-to of vertical leadership development* (White paper). Greensboro, NC: Center for Creative Leadership.

Pirson, M., Langer, E. J., Bodner, T., & Zilcha-Mano, S. (2012). *The development and validation of the Langer mindfulness scale-enabling a socio-cognitive perspective of mindfulness in organizational contexts*. Fordham University Schools of Business Research Paper. doi:10.2139/ssrn.2158921

Ployhart, R. E., & Bliese, P. D. (2006). Individual adaptability (I-ADAPT) theory: Conceptualizing the antecedents, consequences, and measurement of individual differences in adaptability. In S. Burke, L. Pierce, & E. Salas (Eds.), *Understanding adaptability: A prerequisite for effective performance within complex environments* (pp. 3–39). St. Louis, MO: Elsevier Science.

Pulakos, E. D., Arad, S., Donovan, M. A., & Plamondon, K. E. (2000). Adaptability in the workplace: Development of a taxonomy of adaptive performance. *Journal of Applied Psychology, 85*, 612–624.

Pury, C. (2008). Can courage be learned? In S. Lopez (Ed.), *Positive psychology: Exploring the best in people* (Vol. 1, pp. 109–130). Westport, CT: Praeger.

Quaglia, J., Braun, S., Freeman, S., McDaniel, M., & Warren Brown, K. (2016). Meta-analytic evidence for effects of mindfulness training on vs. dimensions of self-reported dispositional mindfulness. *Psychological Assessment, 28*(7), 803–818.

Reardon, K. K. (2007). Courage as a skill. *Harvard Business Review, 85*(1), 58–64.

Rochat, P. (2003). Five levels of self-awareness as they unfold early in life. *Consciousness and Cognition, 12*, 717–731.

Sealy, R. H. V., & Singh, V. (2010). The importance of role models and demographic context for senior women's work identity development. *International Journal of Management Reviews, 12*(3), 284–300.

Senge, P. M. (1990). *The fifth discipline: The art and craft of the learning organization.* New York, NY: Random House.

Shapiro, S. L. (2009). The integration of mindfulness and psychology. *Journal of Clinical Psychology, 65*(6), 555–560.

Sheeran, P., & Webb, T. L. (2016). The intention–behavior gap. *Social and Personality Psychology Compass, 10,* 503–518.

Silzer, R., & Church, A. (2009). The pearls and perils of identifying potential. *Industrial and Organizational Psychology: Perspectives on Science and Practice, 2*(4), 377–412.

Snyder, C. R. (2002). Hope theory: Rainbows in the mind. *Psychological Inquiry, 13*(4), 249–275.

Tessler, R. C., & Schwartz, S. H. (1972). Help seeking, self-esteem, and achievement motivation: An attributional analysis. *Journal of Personality and Social Psychology, 21*(3), 318.

Tversky, A., & Kahneman, D. (1974). Judgment under uncertainty: Heuristics and biases. *Science, 185,* 1124–1131.

Warrell, M. (2009). *Find your courage: 12 acts for becoming fearless at work and in life.* New York, NY: McGraw Hill.

Woodard, C. R., & Pury, C. L. (2007). The construct of courage: Categorization and measurement. *Consulting Psychology Journal: Practice and Research, 59*(2), 135–147.

Yeganeh, B., & Kolb, D. (2009). Mindfulness and experiential learning. *OD Practitioner, 41*(3), 9–14.

Yost, P. (2016). Resilience practices. *Industrial and Organizational Psychology, 9*(2), 475–479.

Zimmerman, B. J., & Schunk, D. H. (2001). *Self-regulated learning and academic achievement* (2nd ed.). Mahwah, NJ: Erlbaum.

7

Cultivating Learning Agility
Through Mindfulness

A Framework and Recommendations

R. Andrew Lee

In the beginner's mind there are many possibilities,
in the expert's mind there are few.
— Shunryu Suzuki (1904–1971), Zen teacher

Mindfulness is generating a great deal of interest in the business community. A survey of large employers indicated that 52% of companies were offering mindfulness training or resources to their employees in 2018, and another 23% intended to begin doing so in 2019 (National Business Group on Health/Fidelity Investments, 2018). This interest is being driven mostly by a growing concern about the toll that stress is taking on employees. Workplace stress has been linked to reductions in employee engagement, increased absenteeism and turnover, decreased physical and mental well-being, and increased healthcare costs (Pfeffer, 2018). In fact, it is estimated that workplace stress may account for 5% to 8% of annual healthcare costs (Goh, Pfeffer, & Zenios, 2016).

Mindfulness is being recognized as an effective means to enhance well-being generally and to combat workplace stress in particular. Multi-week workplace mindfulness training programs can reduce stress by over 30% (Wolever et al., 2012). Even less rigorous interventions can have a positive impact. For example, using a mindfulness app for 10–15 minutes a day for 10 days can reduce stress by 14% according to Hartman, Bell, and Sanderson (2018).

More recently, the role of mindfulness in leadership development has also received increasing attention. Numerous books have been published on the topic of mindful leadership (e.g., Carroll 2007; Hougaard & Carter, 2018;

R. Andrew Lee, *Cultivating Learning Agility Through Mindfulness* In: *The Age of Agility.* Edited by: Veronica Schmidt Harvey and Kenneth P. De Meuse, Oxford University Press (2021). © Oxford University Press.
DOI: 10.1093/oso/9780190085353.003.0007

Marturano 2014) that explain to current and aspiring leaders how mindfulness can help them become more effective. Mindfulness has also been included as a dimension in emerging leadership theories, such as resonant leadership (Boyatzis & McKee, 2005) and authentic leadership (Baron, 2012).

Academic and field research on the direct impact of mindfulness on leadership effectiveness is nascent, but initial findings are promising. For example, leader mindfulness is linked to employee well-being and performance (Reb, Narayanan, & Chatruvedi, 2014) and to perceptions of procedural justice (Schuh, Zheng, Xin, & Fernandez, 2019).

There is also growing support for indirect, mediated relationships between mindfulness and leadership effectiveness. One such relationship operates through the construct of emotional intelligence (EI): The more effective a leader is at emotional self-management, the better he or she will be at influencing others (Rosete & Ciarrochi, 2005). In turn, mindfulness has been shown to enhance EI (Wang & Kong, 2014). Other examples of leadership qualities that are positively impacted by mindfulness include leaders' positive affect and self-efficacy (Carleton, Barling, & Trivisonno, 2018); managing ambiguity (Chesley & Wylson, 2016); psychological capital (Roche, Haar, & Luthans, 2014); and leadership flexibility (Baron, Rouleau, Gregoire, & Baron, 2017).

Yet, the leadership construct that may be most closely aligned to mindfulness is learning agility. Conceptually, learning agility reflects many of the core qualities of mindfulness. In addition, mindfulness has been linked to many of the qualities related to the development and application of learning agility.

The purpose of this chapter is to explore the role that mindfulness may play in the development of learning agility. First, both constructs are defined and described. Next, a model is introduced that organizes the many connections between mindfulness and learning agility. After this, the nature of these connections is described, and supporting research is presented. Finally, recommendations are provided for how leaders can cultivate mindfulness, as well as how to design mindfulness programs for leaders.

Mindfulness: What It Is and How It Works

Mindfulness is challenging to define because it refers to an internal state that has some inherently subtle qualities. A number of definitions have been offered in the literature, and while there are differences, many share the same core elements. While a full description of mindfulness is beyond the scope of this chapter (for a discussion, see Chiesa, 2012), the following definition of mindfulness is used for the purposes of this chapter: *Mindfulness is the quality of awareness that arises from paying full attention to one's present moment experience of internal states and external circumstances, with an attitude of receptiveness and curiosity.* This definition includes two foundational dimensions of mindfulness.

Paying Full Attention to One's Present Moment Experience

The mindful mind is not preoccupied by what happened in the past or what might happen in the future. Instead, the attention is focused on what is present right here and now. The word *preoccupied* is important here. There is nothing un-mindful about intentionally reflecting on events that have occurred in the past or taking the time to plan for the future. The issue arises when these thoughts arise spontaneously to interfere with present moment awareness. For example, an un-mindful moment may involve daydreaming about an upcoming vacation while participating in a conference call. In addition, paying *full* attention means that one's attention is not divided or fractured, but rather unified (though also flexible). For example, when a person is in conversation with someone else, the person's full attention is on the other person as opposed to toggling between the person and their phone.

The barriers to full present moment awareness in today's workplace are many. You may have noticed that your attention is constantly wandering to past and future events and jumping from one thought, emotion, or sensory input to another (Killingsworth & Gilbert, 2010). At other times—and perhaps even most of the time—we are only paying partial attention to what we are doing while "going through the motions" of a busy day, trying to expend a minimum of cognitive effort (Bargh & Chartrand, 1999). In contrast, mindfulness is the state of *not* being on autopilot, *not* multitasking, and *not* being lost in internal dialogue or mental rumination. Rather, mindfulness is the state of bringing full and conscious awareness to our internal states, our circumstances, and our actions (see Hanley & Garland, 2019).

Maintaining an Attitude of Receptiveness and Curiosity

The mindful mind focuses its attention on perceiving and investigating present moment experiences and events before jumping into judging, evaluating, and comparing what is being experienced. While initial emotional reactions are not suppressed, the link between initial perceptions and follow-on actions becomes less automatic and more intentional. Mindfulness is the act of pausing to take in a situation with an open and curious mindset before making interpretations and drawing conclusions (see Teper, Segal, & Inzlicht, 2013).

This quality of receptive attention has also been referred to as an attitude of nonjudgment and acceptance, which is sometimes misunderstood as taking a stance of moral passivity. It is better understood as a default sense of open-minded curiosity and interest that short-circuits reflexive judgments and reactions, and allows for less biased and more discerning evaluations. Mindfulness inclines us to strive to understand clearly and objectively what is present before deciding what it means, how we feel about it, and how we should respond to it.

Metacognition

Mindfulness also has a third quality that emerges with the practice of the two previously described elements: *Metacognition*, or thinking about one's thinking. Mindfulness cultivates an enhanced awareness of one's own patterns and habits of thought. The perspective shifts from simply enacting one's biases, preferences, and expectations to becoming aware of their operation and observing them from a relatively detached perspective (e.g., Solem, Thunes, Hjemdal, Hagen, & Wells, 2014). This perspective also affords one the insight to identify mental habits that do not serve us well. In addition, a metacognitive perspective reduces the power of ego-based reactions, such as defensiveness, because one becomes less personally identified with one's views and actions (Hölzel et al., 2011).

These three factors work together to change how experiences are processed. Mindfulness allows leaders to notice thoughts and emotions as they arise and recognize that they do not need to be *reacted* to automatically. Instead, it creates a space where these internal phenomena can be investigated with an open and curious mindset and then *responded* to in a conscious and intentional manner.

For example, imagine a scenario where a leader who does not practice mindfulness has come from a meeting with her manager where the leader's performance was scrutinized. Now, she is presenting an organizational change plan at her own departmental staff meeting. Due to the emotional impact of the previous meeting, the leader is still processing what was said and as a result is not fully engaged with her team. She presents her organizational change plan with little enthusiasm and becomes defensive in the face of questions. As a result, the presentation does not go well, issues are unaddressed, and the staff is left feeling disengaged and does not buy in.

If this same leader had the benefit of mindfulness, the situation might play out differently. When she arrives at her departmental staff meeting, the leader notices that her mind is still unfocused and preoccupied. As a result, she may make an extra effort to stay present. Or, she may decide to buy some time to recover by first discussing a less challenging topic. Then, when her staff offer feedback or resistance to her organizational change plan, she notices that it triggers the same defensiveness that she felt in her meeting with her manager, and she is careful not to overreact in the present situation. She stays open and present and explores and addresses issues as they arise. As a result, the presentation may still not have been her best, but mindfulness helped her to navigate a challenging situation more skilfully.

A Model of Learning Agility

Following Lombardo and Eichinger (2000), learning agility is defined here as the ability and willingness to learn from experience and then apply that learning to perform successfully under new situations. Learning agility has been generally described as a stable trait. Lombardo and Eichinger (2000) and others (e.g., De Meuse, 2017) have described and assessed it as an individual difference, or a "constellation of individual characteristics and attributes" (DeRue, Ashford, & Myers, 2012).

Different researchers have suggested varying components and structures of learning agility (see De Meuse, 2017). Among them, it is worth noting that several models of learning agility include factors that are closely related to mindfulness. They include *self-awareness* (De Meuse et al., 2011), *environmental mindfulness* and *self-insight* (De Meuse, Lim, & Rao, 2019), and *reflecting* (Burke & Smith, 2018).

Despite the prevalence of trait models of learning agility, the definition proposed by Lombardo and Eichinger (2000) is also wholly consistent with a process model. This process of agile learning would consist of (at least) the following steps: (a) taking some action, (b) learning from that action, and (c) applying the learnings successfully to another situation. Such an approach would also be consistent with the models of experiential learning proposed by Kolb (2015) and Ashford and DeRue (2012).

A process approach to learning agility has several advantages. From a research perspective, it can demonstrate how different aspects of learning agility, be they traits or behaviors, relate to different aspects of the construct, as well as to each other. From an applied perspective, a process model provides a way to explain to leaders what learning agility looks like in action and what they might do to enhance their own level of learning agility. For these reasons, this chapter adopts a process model to explore the connections between mindfulness and learning agility.

The model used here is based on Ashford and DeRue's (2012) mindful engagement model of experiential learning, which has been modified to bring it into greater alignment with a mindfulness-based approach. The proposed "Agile Learning Process™" includes five elements (Figure 7.1):

- **Mindset**—Maintaining a resilient and learning-oriented mindset
- **Awareness**—Recognizing and framing learning opportunities
- **Action**—Engaging in learning behaviors
- **Integration**—Reflecting on experience and extracting learnings
- **Application**—Applying learnings to different situations

Four of these factors are presented as stages that occur in a particular order for ease of understanding and application. However, the reality is that these stages may overlap, co-occur, and occur in a different order. Work is messy, and opportunities to learn, and to apply learnings, often arise unexpectedly. For example, many situations require learning "on the fly" instead of applying previous learnings to the current situation. In this scenario, a person may toggle between action and integration as a situation unfolds.

The next section reviews each of these stages of agile learning. The review begins by identifying qualities that support each stage and then describes the way in which mindfulness contributes to cultivating these qualities.

Learning Agility

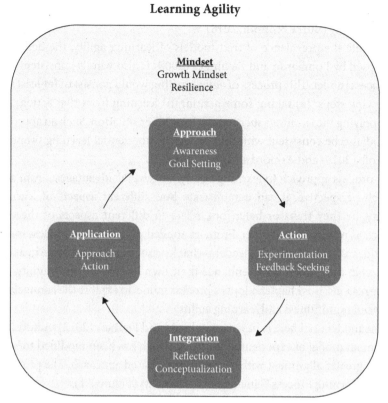

Figure 7.1   Agile learning process model.

Mindset

Mindset refers to qualities that have a generalized impact on learning. They are "table stakes" for agile learning to occur. The two qualities that are discussed in this section are growth mindset and stress resilience.

Growth Mindset

Growth mindset concerns the beliefs that people hold about the malleability of their basic qualities and abilities, including personality and intelligence as well as their innate talents. Dweck (2016) described two mindsets that make up ends of a continuum. People with a *growth mindset* assume that these qualities are malleable, and that they can improve their capabilities in almost any domain through learning and effort. As a result, these people are more focused on seeking opportunities to learn and on getting the most out of these experiences when they engage in them. In addition, people with a growth mindset are less concerned with failure because they see it as a natural part of the learning process (Heslin & Keating, 2017).

In contrast, people with a *fixed mindset* assume that their abilities are determined by an innate level of talent and cannot be significantly affected by learning and effort. Therefore, people with a fixed mindset are less interested in pursuing or exploiting learning opportunities. The fixed mindset is also related to a greater concern about failure since it is seen as diagnostic of their innate and stable abilities, rather than a temporary state that provides an opportunity to learn and grow.

Mindfulness is closely aligned with a growth mindset. Through mindfulness practice, one learns to set aside expectations and assumptions and investigate one's experience directly and objectively. All experiences are approached openly and as worthy of exploration and learning. Self-limiting assumptions about what can and cannot be done are set aside in favor of a "beginner's mind," in which our direct experience dictates what is possible.

While the connections between growth mindset and mindfulness seem inherent, there has been no research conducted on this relationship to date. However, similar outcomes have been associated with both qualities, including greater persistence (Raphiphatthana, Jose, & Salmon, 2018) and openness to critical feedback (Saunders, Barawi, & McHugh, 2013). Certainly, it is an opportunity for further investigation.

Stress Resilience

Stress resilience is the capacity to navigate stressful events without succumbing to chronic stress. Stress is a prevalent part of many leaders' day-to-day experience. In a recent survey, 88% of leaders identified their work as a primary source of stress, and 75% reported that their leadership roles have contributed to higher levels of personal stress (Campbell, Baltes, Martin, & Meddings, 2007). Unfortunately, stress is also a barrier to many aspects of the learning process. Stress affects how new information is encoded and retrieved, how it is integrated with existing information, and how it is recalled. For example, stress shifts the mind to encoding new information through a rigid and habitual system as opposed to a flexible and cognitively engaged system (Vogel & Schwabe, 2016).

In order to learn effectively on the job, it is critical that leaders maintain resilience by learning and employing practices to help them manage stress. Mindfulness practice has been shown to be an effective way to both reduce stress (Wolever et al., 2012) and increase resilience (Bajaj & Pande, 2016). Even the use of a mindfulness phone app has been shown to reduce stress significantly (Cavanagh et al., 2013). Mindfulness also helps people to recover more quickly from unpleasant experiences (Ortner, Kilner, & Zelazo, 2007) and protects cognitive processes from the negative effects of stress (Jha, Morrison, Parker, & Stanley, 2016).

Awareness

Awareness of learning opportunities is a prerequisite to learning from them. While this sounds self-evident, it is easier said than done. As discussed, our minds are predisposed to run on autopilot or ruminate about past or future events. Consequently, it is likely that potentially valuable learning experiences come and go during the regular course of business without even being noticed. In order to recognize such experiences, it is necessary to be fully present and attentive.

For example, imagine a scenario where a leader is asked to present at a colleague's staff meeting about one of his ongoing projects. To do so, he simply prepares and delivers the requested information as he has done many times before. While delivering the presentation, he is preoccupied with a looming deadline, and his main concern is to wrap up the meeting on time and get on with his day. To this leader, the presentation offered no new information or insights; it was like so many others, and it is quickly forgotten.

In contrast, another leader in the same situation may see the presentation as an opportunity to get helpful feedback on his work. As he presents, he observes the audience closely in order to assess their interest, and he encourages questions and discussion as he goes. He also probes for possible areas of collaboration for mutual benefit. As a result, this leader emerges from the meeting with a wealth of information and feedback that will inform his work going forward.

These types of situations occur all the time in organizations. But in order for leaders to benefit from them, it is necessary for them to recognize such situations as opportunities to learn and grow.

As discussed, paying attention is inherent to mindfulness. Mindfulness practice helps leaders to come out of distraction, rumination, and autopilot to be fully present and engaged with the present moment. Mindfulness also cultivates a sense of openness and curiosity about one's environment, which is conducive to recognizing and taking advantage of learning opportunities. Therefore, mindfulness practice enhances experiential learning by helping leaders to recognize and capitalize on learning opportunities.

This is supported by research that shows that mindfulness has a range of benefits for the regulation of attention. For example, mindfulness has been shown to improve attentional stability, control, and efficiency (Good et al., 2016), as well as improve the allocation of attentional resources (Malinowski, 2013). That said, most of the research in this area has been conducted in the laboratory using attention tasks, so the implications for workplace tasks have yet to be investigated.

In addition to recognizing learning opportunities, leaders can benefit from setting *learning goals* for their own work whenever appropriate. Learning goals are different from performance goals in that they prioritize knowledge acquisition and process improvement over outcomes. For example, a learning goal may be to develop the best way to produce a product, while a performance goal would set a goal for the number of products produced.

Research shows that setting learning goals not only increases the amount learned, but also leads to better performance if the task in question is novel, complex, or ambiguous (Seijts & Latham, 2005). For example, if the product being produced is new and different from previous products, setting a learning goal for its production would be indicated. This makes it a highly useful approach for leaders who are often faced with novel situations and a powerful approach to enhance learning agility.

While there has been no research conducted on the topic to date, the quality of open-minded curiosity that is inherent in mindfulness closely aligns with the setting and pursuit of learning goals. Mindfulness encourages one to focus on how things are progressing and how they might be improved in the present moment and to avoid becoming overly fixated on future outcomes. Therefore, it seems likely that mindfulness would lead to an increased propensity to set learning goals for one's work, and thus it would also enhance the learning that accrues along the way.

Action

Once a person is engaged in a learning experience, he or she needs to engage in the behaviors and strategies that generate learning beyond simply paying attention. There are several types of behaviors that are important in this process. The first is a *willingness to experiment* (Ashford & DeRue, 2012; Kolb, 2015). One needs to be open to doing things differently in order to learn from the outcome. This willingness to experiment is recognized in learning agility models by various names, including change agility (Lombardo & Eichinger, 2000); change alacrity (De Meuse et al., 2019); and experimenting (Burke & Smith, 2018).

Experimentation is a form of risk-taking that brings on a state of uncertainty. Therefore, it is likely to trigger uncomfortable emotional states. In order to be effective in this process, a leader needs to overcome the natural resistance to the unpleasant emotions that can accompany it. Mindfulness can be very helpful in managing the discomfort of experimentation, thereby making it both more likely to occur and more effective when it does.

One of the key capacities associated with mindfulness training is an ability to experience unpleasant sensations or emotions with the same qualities of curiosity and acceptance that are applied to other experiences. This creates greater tolerance for such states and greater willingness to pursue one's goals in the face of them. This is described as the willingness to "turn toward" uncomfortable experiences.

Research is supportive of the idea that mindfulness lowers psychological barriers to experimentation. For example, mindfulness enhances leaders' tolerance for ambiguity (Chesley & Wylson, 2016) and reduces resistance to change (Dunican & Keaster, 2015). Mindfulness is also hypothesized to enhance change readiness (Gärtner, 2013). Finally, mindfulness has been associated with greater perseverance or "grit" (Raphiphatthana et al., 2018), which is important when engaging in and following through on exploratory activities.

Another powerful learning strategy is *seeking feedback*. Feedback is an invaluable source of information and a catalyst for learning at all levels of leadership. Feedback-seeking behavior has been linked to the effectiveness of chief executive officers (CEOs) as well as the top management teams that report to them (Ashford, Wellman, de Luque, De Stobbeleir, & Wollan, 2018). In addition, the seeking of negative feedback in particular has been linked to managerial effectiveness (Ashford & Tsui, 1991). Conversely, defensiveness has the opposite effect, is detrimental to learning (Holmer, 2014), and has been proposed as a barrier to learning agility in particular (Mitchinson & Morris, 2014).

As with experimentation, seeking feedback requires a tolerance for ambiguity. But feedback seeking raises the stakes because it adds the potential for ego threat, which can intensify the unpleasantness of a negative assessment. Mindfulness mitigates the experience of ego threat through the cultivation of an attitude receptive curiosity. Mindfulness allows individuals to view negative feedback more objectively, instead of immediately engaging in self-criticism on one hand or defensiveness on the other. This makes ego-relevant negative feedback easier to receive, process, and learn from.

No research to date has linked mindfulness to actively seeking feedback. However, research suggests that mindfulness makes the experience of receiving ego-threatening feedback less unpleasant (Dandeneau, 2016). This suggests that mindfulness may make feedback-seeking behavior more likely, as it reduces the potential unpleasantness of the process. In addition, Saunders et al. (2013) found that mindfulness enhanced people's ability to recall self-threatening feedback, which suggests that it may also enhance how that feedback is processed. Overall, these results suggest that mindfulness has a salutary effect on leaders' openness to, and learning from, developmental feedback.

Integration

In this stage, the leaders process the lessons learned from paying attention, experimenting, and feedback seeking and integrate them into their broader knowledge base so they can be applied to future situations. Learning integration includes reflecting on one's experience to identify learnings and leveraging these learnings to develop new models, theories, or assumptions to guide future action. Both of these activities have long been associated with the experiential learning process (e.g., see Kolb, 2015).

Reflection

Reflection requires dedicating both time and open, unbiased attention to understanding one's experience. In order to engage in reflective observation, a leader must be both willing and able to reflect on the experience. Of all the aspects of agile learning, mindfulness may make its most unique and important contribution by enhancing the capacity for reflection.

Learning from experience is often portrayed as a purely rational process, akin to solving a business case. We may fail to solve a certain type of problem the first time, but through analysis and conceptualization, we learn how to adjust our approach in order to master similar problems in the future.

While rational problem-solving is certainly an important aspect of experiential learning, the richest learning experiences are often not cognitive challenges, but emotional ones. In their seminal book *The Lessons of Experience*, McCall, Lombardo, and Morrison (1988) referred to these learning experiences as "trial by fire." Often, the experiences that leaders learn the most from are those that might be considered humbling. Perhaps they are led to question their own competence, their judgment, or their priorities or values. They may need to ask themselves how they define success, what they stand for, or what is truly important to them. It is tempting to avoid reflecting honestly on such situations. Yet, this is exactly what is required in order to learn and grow from the most developmental of experiences.

Classic examples of developmental experiences include overseas and cross-functional assignments, where leaders are unable to lean on their expertise and past experience; turnaround assignments, where they may need to make difficult business and staffing decisions; and high-visibility roles, where both successes and failures are highly visible and scrutinized. Difficult setbacks in such roles are not uncommon, and leaders need not only persevere through them, but also learn and grow from them.

Mindfulness is a powerful practice for strengthening the constructive regulation of the difficult emotions that may arise in such situations (Hill & Updegraff, 2012; Teper et al., 2013). It enables the honest and constructive investigation of emotionally charged events. Mindfulness enables one to let go of (or reduce) self-judgment and defensiveness and to examine even difficult experiences in a way that facilitates exploration and learning.

The practice of mindfulness meditation in particular creates an internal environment that is supportive to investigating difficult experiences and emotions in a constructive way. During meditation, thoughts related to recent events and one's interpretations of them come up naturally. This is especially true if these events are emotionally laden. In fact, difficult thoughts and judgments often take center stage during meditation, providing a unique opportunity for processing difficult experiences. And when they do arise, there is no escaping them. But gradually, the discipline of maintaining an attitude of receptive curiosity begins to open up these experiences to exploration, learning, and meaningful growth.

As discussed, research supports the role of mindfulness in working with self-threatening information. Mindfulness reduces our natural tendency toward experiential avoidance (Hayes, Strosdahl, & Wilson, 2012), which limits the extent to which we are willing to acknowledge and process self-threatening information.

Conceptualization

Conceptualization is the process by which the insights gained from reflection are distilled into conclusions and implications that can be applied to future situations. When experiential learning is at its most impactful, this conceptualization can lead to a rethinking of one's values and priorities, as well as one's strengths and development areas. To do this effectively, leaders need to think clearly and creatively about the implications of their experience.

Mindfulness has two effects on cognitive processing that are relevant to conceptualization. The first is that it enhances cognitive flexibility, which is the ability to shift one's thinking between different concepts or perspectives. Mindfulness has been shown to enhance cognitive flexibility in several contexts: It improves the ability to discover and apply new approaches to solving problems (Greenberg, Reiner, & Meiran, 2012; it improves cognitive flexibility on computer-based tasks (Moore & Malinowsky, 2009); and certain mindfulness practices significantly improve divergent thinking skills, which are important for the generation of new ideas (Colzato, Szapora, Lippelt, & Hommel, 2017).

Second, mindfulness reduces the impact of biases and heuristics on our decisions. For example, mindfulness reduces the impact of the sunk cost bias on business decisions (Hafenbrack, Kinias, & Barsade, 2014). In addition, mindfulness leads to less race-based bias and discrimination in an online money-lending game (Lueke & Gibson, 2016). Taken together, these studies suggest that mindfulness may allow for a more flexible, creative, and unbiased processing of past experience and the enhanced development of new insights and paradigms to guide future action.

Application

The application of learnings to new situations is the final step in the learning agility process. In this stage, leaders take the insights that they have gleaned from past experience and apply them, appropriately and effectively, to new situations. To do this, leaders draw on many of the same skills and capabilities that have been applied during earlier stages. This includes from the approach stage, paying mindful attention to recognize opportunities to apply their learnings; from the action stage, managing the risk and uncertainty of trying something new; and from the integration stage, evaluating the results of their actions with an open, receptive, and curious mindset.

The application of learnings can also take the form of implementing organizational changes of some sort. Mindfulness has also been shown to help leaders manage the implementation of change more effectively. It does so by helping leaders maintain strong relationships with stakeholders and a balanced, big picture perspective on their work (Chesley & Wylson, 2016).

Research Opportunities

In summary, there is ample evidence to suggest that the cultivation of mindfulness enhances leader learning agility in numerous ways. At the same time, there are many opportunities for additional research. One initial means for investigating the link between mindfulness and the mediating constructs identified here is to conduct survey research that establishes correlations between them (e.g., between mindfulness and growth mindset or feedback-seeking). It could be followed up by controlled studies that use mindfulness training as an intervention.

Still, the biggest opportunity is for applied research with leaders. While the results cited here are promising, many of them come out of academic settings. There is much work to do in understanding how mindfulness impacts learning agility, and ultimately leadership development, in the complex and fast-moving environment in which today's leaders operate.

Recommendations for Practice

Based on the research presented, adding mindfulness training into a learning agility or leadership development curriculum could enhance and accelerate leaders' capacity to learn and grow. This could be done by offering a standalone mindfulness program, or by integrating the principles and practies of mindfulness into an existing program.

When taught separately, mindfulness training generally takes the form of a 6- to 8-week course. The curriculum includes defining and describing mindfulness, presenting supporting research, teaching a range of mindfulness practices (more on this follows here), and exploring how mindfulness can be applied to a variety of domains, depending on the goals and needs of the participants. Finally, resources are shared to support participants in their practice going forward, including access to guided mindfulness practiced that can be used daily.

Mindfulness training can also be integrated into an existing leadership development program. For example, it could be delivered in segments of 1 hour a day as part of a 1-week, full-time program—preferably as the first topic each day. Subsequently, brief mindfulness practices can be offered at different times of the day. This offers the added benefit of improving participants' capacity to learn and retain the other content that is being taught.

Finally, the principles of mindfulness can be embedded into an existing program. This can be done by limiting environmental distractions in order to facilitate present moment awareness; providing time for reflection and journaling; and including exercises that encourage participants to explore their deply held values, assumptions and beliefs.

During mindfulness training, participants are taught three types of practices that cultivate mindfulness both during and after the training: (a) formal practice, (b) informal practice, and (c) work practices.

Formal Practice

Formal practice is setting time aside to engage in the mental exercise that strengthens one's overall capacity for mindfulness much as lifting weights strengthens our capacity for physical activity. One common formal mindfulness practice is mindfulness meditation. In this exercise, one sits in an upright and relaxed posture, closes the eyes and places one's attention on the sensations of breathing. When the mind becomes distracted by thoughts, sounds, or other perceptions, one notices this shift in attention and then gently returns the attention back to the breath. This can be practiced for any period of time, from a few minutes to a half hour or longer. Formal practice can also use external stimuli as objects of awareness, such as sounds, and also incorporate movement, such as walking, meditation, where one's attention is focused on the sensations of walking.

Informal Practice

Informal practice involves using everyday activities as a means to intentionally bring our attention back into the present moment. The analogy to physical exercise would be taking the stairs instead of the elevator at work. One informal practice is to bring one's full attention to eating by noticing how our food looks, how it smells, and its texture and taste. Or closely attending to the act of driving by turning off the radio and taking careful note of the landscape, the weather, and the surrounding cars.

In fact almost any activity can become a mindfulness practice including walking the dog and doing the dishes, as long as it's practiced with full present moment awareness tempered by an open and curious mindset. One can also use micropractices, such as taking three conscious breaths and noticing one's own state of mind at the start of meetings.

Work Practices

Work practices are changes in how work is done that promote a greater sense of openness, self-awareness, and mental clarity. For example, leaders may request that no distracting technologies are brought into staff meetings. Or, they could create spaces where people who work in open floor plans can go to work undisturbed. Or, they could implement a minute of silence at the beginning of meetings at allow people to gather their thoughts. Or implement no-meeting blocks during the week. The range of work practices that promote mindful awareness at work is as diverse as our workplaces themselves.

If participants complete their training with both an understanding of and practical experience using each of these types of practices, they will be well prepared to maintain and strengthen their mindful awareness going forward. In addition in their role as leaders, they will be able to act as powerful role models for others for how to continually learn and grow on the job, even in the face of challenges and setbacks.

Building Acceptance of Mindfulness

Finally, it is important to acknowledge that some leaders may be skeptical about mindfulness due to a variety of misconceptions about what it actually is. For example, leaders may associate mindfulness with new age spirituality and assume that it is not supported by scientific research. These concerns are becoming less prevalent as mindfulness becomes more accepted by the mainstream culture, which is happening at a rapid rate. The number of people practicing mindfulness tripled between 2012 and 2017 and is now on par with yoga, and it is trending more quickly (Clarke, Barnes, Black, Stussman, & Nahin, 2018). Still, misconceptions persist. Here are some best practices that can help to win over skeptical leaders:

- **Engage a qualified teacher.** There is no widely recognized sanctioning body for mindfulness teachers, and the skills and qualifications of teachers vary greatly. Make sure that you partner with a teacher who has been practicing mindfulness for 10 years or longer and has attended multiday silent retreats. In addition, teachers should have experience teaching in the workplace and should be well versed in the relevant research.
- **Present research.** As we have seen, there is ample research available that supports the efficacy of mindfulness practice. Presenting this evidence to leaders is very helpful in building credibility and buy-in. In addition, many well-known business leaders practice mindfulness, including Marc Benioff, CEO of Salesforce; Mark Bertolini, former CEO of Aetna; Bill Ford, chairman of Ford Motor Company; and Jeff Weiner, CEO of LinkedIn, just to name a few.
- **Encourage ongoing practice.** Regular mindfulness practice is critical for leaders to experience the benefits described previously. This is why it is critical to strongly encourage leaders to practice regularly, especially during training and in the first weeks following it. Many times, the participants who do not see significant benefits from mindfulness are the ones who do not give it a fair chance by practicing regularly. Conversely, when leaders do experience the benefits of regular practice, it provides them with all the evidence they need to continue with the practice and often to become vocal advocates to others.

Summary and Conclusion

As the pace of change in the workplace continues to accelerate, it is becoming ever more critical that our leaders have the capacity to continually learn and grow in their roles. This is why learning agility is foundational to achieving sustainable success as a leader. Mindfulness can play an important role in helping leaders to develop and maximize this skill.

Mindfulness is not entirely new to leadership development, but it is a novel approach to understanding and developing learning agility. Furthermore, it is an approach that looks to be a very promising one. Based on the research presented in this chapter, leveraging mindfulness training to enhance learning agility could greatly enhance the ability of leaders to learn, grow, and thrive and to help their organizations meet the unknown challenges that will face them in the future.

References

Ashford, S. J., & DeRue, D. S. (2012). Developing as a leader: The power of mindful engagement. *Organizational Dynamics, 41*(2), 146–154.

Ashford, S. J., & Tsui, A. S. (1991). Self-regulation for managerial effectiveness: The role of active feedback seeking. *Academy of Management Journal, 34*(2), 251–280.

Ashford, S. J., Wellman, N., de Luque, M. S., De Stobbeleir, K. E. M., & Wollan, M. (2018). Two roads to effectiveness: CEO feedback seeking, vision articulation, and firm performance. *Journal of Organizational Behavior, 39*(1), 82–95.

Avolio, B. J., Gardner, W. L., Walumbwa, F. O., Luthans, F., & May, D. R. (2004). Unlocking the mask: A look at the process by which authentic leaders impact follower attitudes and behaviors. *The Leadership Quarterly, 15,* 801–823.

Bajaj, B., & Pande, N. (2016). Mediating role of resilience in the impact of mindfulness on life satisfaction and affect as indices of subjective well-being. *Personality and Individual Differences, 93*(2016), 63–67.

Bargh, J. A., & Chartrand, T. L. (1999). The unbearable automaticity of being. *American Psychologist, 54*(7), 462.

Baron, L. (2012, August). Developing authentic leadership through experiential training: An empirical study. Academy of Management Annual Meeting Proceedings.

Baron, L., Rouleau, V., Gregoire, S., & Baron, C. (2017). Mindfulness and leadership flexibility. *Journal of Management Development, 37*(2), 166–177.

Boyatzis, R., & McKee, A. (2005). *Resonant leadership.* Boston, MA: Harvard Business School.

Burke, W., & Smith, D. (2018). *Technical report v3.3: A guide for learning about learning agility.* Bridgeton, MO: Easi Consult.

Campbell, M., Baltes, J. I., Martin, A., & Meddings, K. (2007). *The stress of leadership.* Greenville, NC: Center for Creative Leadership.

Carleton, E. L., Barling, J., & Trivisonno, M. (2018). Leaders' trait mindfulness and transformational leadership: The mediating roles of leaders' positive affect and leadership self-efficacy. *Canadian Journal of Behavioural Science, 50*(3), 185.

Carroll, M. (2007). *The mindful leader: Ten principles for bringing out the best in ourselves and others.* Boston, MA: Trumpeter Books.

Cavanagh, K., Strauss, C., Cicconi, F., Griffiths, N., Wyper, A., & Jones, F. (2013). A randomised controlled trial of a brief online mindfulness-based intervention. *Behaviour Research and Therapy, 51*(2013), 573–578.

Chesley, J., & Wylson, A. (2016). Ambiguity: The emerging impact of mindfulness for change leaders. *Journal of Change Management, 16*(4), 317–336.

Chiesa, A., (2012). The difficulty of defining mindfulness: Current thought and critical issues. *Mindfulness, 4*(3), 255–268.

Clarke, T. C., Barnes, P. M., Black, L. I., Stussman, B. A., & Nahin, R. L. (2018). *Use of yoga, meditation, and chiropractors among US adults aged 18 and over* (NCHS Data Brief, no 325). Hyattsville, MD: National Center for Health Statistics.

Colzato, L. S., Szapora, A., Lippelt, D., & Hommel, B. (2017). Prior meditation practice modulates performance and strategy use in convergent- and divergent-thinking problems. *Mindfulness, 8*(1), 10–16.

Dandeneau, S. (2016). Implicitly activating mindfulness promotes positive responses following an ego threat. *Journal of Social and Clinical Psychology, 35*(7), 551–570.

De Meuse, K. P. (2017). Learning agility: Its evolution as a psychological construct and its empirical relationship to leader success. *Consulting Psychology Journal: Practice and Research, 69*, 267–295.

De Meuse, K. P., Dai, G., Zewdie, S., Page, R. C., Clark, L. P., & Eichinger, R. W. (2011). Development and validation of a self-assessment of learning agility. Paper presented at the Society for Industrial and Organizational Psychology Conference, Chicago, IL.

De Meuse, K. P., Lim, J., & Rao, R. (2019). *The development and validation of the TALENTx7® Assessment: A psychological measure of learning agility* (3rd ed.). Shanghai, China: Leader's Gene Consulting.

DeRue, D. S., Ashford, S. J., & Myers, C. G. (2012). Learning agility: In search of conceptual clarity and theoretical grounding. *Industrial & Organizational Psychology, 5*(3), 258–279.

DeRue, D. S., Nahrgang, J. R., Hollenbeck, J. R., & Workman, K (2012). A quasi-experimental study of after-event reviews and leadership development. Retrieved from the Cornell University, School of Hotel Administration website: http://scholarship.sha.cornell.edu/articles/759

Dunican, B., & Keaster, R. (2015). Acceptance of change: Exploring the relationship among psychometric constructs and employee resistance. *International Journal of the Academic Business World, 9*(2), 27–38.

Dweck, C. (2016). *Mindset: The new psychology of success.* New York, NY: Ballantine Books.

Gärtner, C. (2013). Enhancing readiness for change by enhancing mindfulness. *Journal of Change Management, 13*(1), 52–68.

Goh, J., Pfeffer, J., & Zenios, S. A. (2016). The relationship between workplace stressors and mortality and health costs in the United States. *Management Science, 62*(2), 608–628.

Good, D. J., Lyddy, C. J., Glomb, T. M., Bono, J. E., Brown, K. W., Duffy, M. K., . . . Lazar, S. W. (2016). Contemplating mindfulness at work: An integrative review. *Journal of Management, 42*(1), 114–142.

Greenberg, J., Reiner, K., & Meiran, N. (2012). "Mind the trap": Mindfulness practice reduces cognitive rigidity. *PLoS One, 7*(5), 1–8.

Hafenbrack, A. C., Kinias, Z., & Barsade, S. G. (2014). Debiasing the mind through meditation: Mindfulness and the sunk-cost bias. *Psychological Science, 25*(2), 369–376.

Hanley, A. W., & Garland, E. L. (2019). Mindfulness training disrupts Pavlovian conditioning. *Physiology and Behavior, 204*, 151–154.

Hartman, J., Bell, M. J., & Sanderson, B. (2018). Improvements in stress, affect, and irritability following brief use of a mindfulness-based smartphone app: A randomized controlled trial. *Mindfulness, 9*(5), 1584–1593.

Hayes, S. C., Strosdahl, D. S., & Wilson, K. G. (2012). *Acceptance and commitment therapy: The process and practice of mindful change.* New York, NY: Guildford Press.

Heslin, P. A., & Keating, L. A. (2017). In learning mode? The role of mindsets in derailing and enabling experiential leadership development. *Leadership Quarterly, 28*(3), 367–384.

Hill, C. M., & Updegraff, J. A. (2012). Mindfulness and its relationship to emotional regulation. *Emotion, 12*(1), 81–90.

Holmer, L. L. (2014). Understanding and reducing the impact of defensiveness on management learning: Some lessons from neuroscience. *Journal of Management Education, 38*(5), 618–641.

Hölzel, B., Lazar, S., Gard, T., Schuman-Olivier, Z., Vago, D., & Ott, U. (2011). How does mindfulness meditation work? Proposing mechanisms of action from a conceptual and neural perspective. *Perspectives on Psychological Science, 6*(6), 537–559.

Hougaard, R., & Carter, J. (2018). *The mind of the leader: How to lead yourself, your people, and your organization for extraordinary results.* Boston, MA: Harvard Business Review Press.

Jha, A., Morrison, A. B., Parker, S. C., & Stanley, E. (2016). Practice is protective: Mindfulness training promotes cognitive resilience in high-stress cohorts. *Mindfulness, 6*(6), 2015.

Killingsworth, M. A., & Gilbert, D. T. (2010). A wandering mind is an unhappy mind. *Science, 330*(6006), 932.

Kolb, D. A. (2015). *Experiential learning: Experience as the source of learning and development* (2nd ed.). Upper Saddle River, NJ: Person Education.

Lebuda, I., Zabelina, D. L., & Karwowski, M. (2016). Mind full of ideas: A meta-analysis of the mindfulness–creativity link. *Personality and Individual Differences, 93*, 22–26.

Lombardo, M. M., & Eichinger, R. W. (2000). High potentials as high learners. *Human Resource Management, 39*(4), 321.

Lueke, A., & Gibson, B. (2016). Brief mindfulness meditation reduces discrimination. *Psychology of Consciousness: Theory, Research, and Practice, 3*(1), 34–44.

Malinowski, P. (2013). Neural mechanisms of attentional control in mindfulness meditation. *Frontiers in Neuroscience, 7*, 1–11.

Marturano, J. (2014). *Finding the space to lead: A practical guide to mindful leadership.* New York, NY: Bloomsbury Press.

McCall, M. W., Jr., Lombardo, M. M., & Morrison, A. M. (1988). *The lessons of experience: How successful executives develop on the job.* New York, NY: Free Press.

Mitchinson, A., & Morris, R. (2014). *White paper: Learning about learning agility.* Greensboro, NC: Center for Creative Leadership.

Moore, A., & Malinowsky, P. (2009). Meditation, mindfulness and cognitive flexibility. *Consciousness and Cognition, 18*, 176–186.

National Business Group on Health/Fidelity Investments. (2018, May). *Ninth annual health and well-being survey.*

Ortner, N. M., Kilner, S. J., & Zelazo, P. D. (2007). Mindfulness meditation and reduced emotional interference on a cognitive task. *Motivation and Emotion, 31*, 271–283.

Pfeffer, J. (2018). *Dying for a paycheck: How modern management harms employee health and company performance—And what we can do about it.* New York, NY: Harper Collins.

Raphiphatthana, B., Jose, P., & Salmon, K. (2018). *Journal of Individual Differences, 39*(2), 76–87.

Reb, J., Narayanan, J., & Chatruvedi, S. (2014). Leading mindfully: Two studies of the influence of supervisor trait mindfulness on employee well-being and performance. *Mindfulness, 5*(1), 36–45.

Roche, M., Haar, J. M., & Luthans, F. (2014). The role of mindfulness and psychological capital on the well-being of leaders. *Journal of Occupational Health Psychology, 19*(4), 476–489.

Rosete, D., & Ciarrochi, J. (2005). Emotional intelligence and its relationship to workplace performance outcomes of leadership effectiveness. *Leadership & Organization Development Journal, 26*(5), 388–399.

Saunders, J., Barawi, K., & McHugh, L. (2013). Mindfulness increases recall of self-threatening information. *Consciousness & Cognition, 22*(2013), 1375–1383.

Schuh, S. C., Zheng, M. X., Xin, K. R., & Fernandez, J. A. (2019). The interpersonal benefits of leader mindfulness: A serial mediation model linking leader mindfulness, leader procedural justice enactment, and employee exhaustion and performance. *Journal of Business Ethics, 156,* 1007–1025.

Seijts, G. H., & Latham, G. P. (2005). Learning versus performance goals: When should each be used? *Academy of Management Executive, 19*(1), 124–131.

Solem, S., Thunes, S. S., Hjemdal, O., Hagen, R., & Wells, A. (2014). A metacognitive perspective on mindfulness: An empirical investigation. *BMC Psychology, 3*(24), 1–10.

Teper, R., Segal, Z. V., & Inzlicht, M. (2013). Inside the mindful mind: How mindfulness enhances emotion regulation through improvements in executive control. *Current Directions in Psychological Science, 22*(6), 449–454.

Vogel, S., & Schwabe, L. (2016). Learning and memory under stress: Implications for the classroom. *NPJ Science of Learning, 1,* 1–9.

Wang, Y., & Kong, F. (2014). The role of emotional intelligence in the impact of mindfulness on life satisfaction and mental distress. *Social Indicators Research, 116,* 843–852.

Wolever, R. Q., Bobinet, K. J., McCabe, K., Mackenzie, E. R., Fekete, E., Kusnick, C. A., & Baime, M. (2012). Effective and viable mind-body stress reduction in the workplace: A randomized controlled trial. *Journal of Occupational Health Psychology, 17*(2), 246–258.

8

Stepping to the Edge of One's
Comfort Zone

Cynthia D. McCauley and Paul R. Yost

A ship in harbor is safe, but that is not what ships are built for.
—John A. Shedd (1859–1928), American author and professor

Stretch experiences play a central role in the development of leaders. An experience is stretching to the degree that effective performance in the experience requires knowledge, skills, and perspectives beyond what the individual has currently developed. By taking individuals to the edge of their comfort zone, these experiences offer both the opportunity and the necessity to learn. Also referred to as job challenges or developmental assignments, stretch experiences come in all different sizes. They can range from major changes in a person's responsibilities or context (e.g., a first supervisory job, heading up a new strategic initiative, or an expatriate assignment in a culture very different from one's own) to everyday experiences that are unfamiliar, complex, or high stakes (e.g., organizing a fundraising event for the first time, giving difficult feedback to an employee, or presenting to an important stakeholder group).

The learning agility literature describes the relationship between stretch experiences and learning agility (i.e., an individual's ability and willingness to learn from experience) in multiple ways. Regularly stepping into stretch experiences with the intent to learn and grow is often portrayed as a hallmark of the learning agile individual (Hallenbeck, 2016; Lombardo & Eichinger, 2000); thus, learning agility can be an *antecedent* pointing to who is most likely to pursue stretch experiences. Facets of learning agility are also viewed as a *moderator* of the relationship between stretch experiences and development (Yost & McLellan, 2014). The greater an individual's learning agility,

Cynthia D. McCauley and Paul R. Yost, *Stepping to the Edge of One's Comfort Zone* In: *The Age of Agility*. Edited by: Veronica Schmidt Harvey and Kenneth P. De Meuse, Oxford University Press (2021). © Oxford University Press. DOI: 10.1093/oso/9780190085353.003.0008 the more likely he or she will learn from a stretch experience. Yet, learning agility is also regarded as an *outcome* of stretch experiences (Hallenbeck & Santana, 2019). Repeated encounters with stretch experiences can enhance efficacy and skill for learning at the edge of one's comfort zone.

This chapter focuses on how talent management and leadership development professionals encourage and support regularly stepping to the edge of one's comfort zone in ways that stimulate learning and development. We highlight three broad experience-based strategies for enhancing learning agility in organizations: (a) making stretch experiences more visible and valued, (b) getting people into the right stretch experiences for targeted development, and (c) increasing skill and confidence for continuous learning and development at the edge of one's comfort zone.

Our focus is on using stretch experiences for leadership development. However, we do not limit an organization's leader population to those individuals in managerial roles. In today's flatter, highly networked organizations, leadership is a capability needed at all levels throughout an organization. We highlight leadership development practices that can be incorporated into talent management processes, practices that managers can engage in with their direct reports, and scalable, self-reinforcing practices that everyone in an organization can adopt. We ground these strategies and practices in theories of adult learning and in research that looks more specifically at the role of stretch experiences in leadership development.

Stretch Experiences: Theory and Research

Numerous theories of adult learning and development point to experience—purposive interaction with one's environment—as the medium through which growth occurs. For example, experiential learning theory conceptualizes learning as an ongoing cyclical process of engaging in experiences, making observations and reflections on those experiences, forming concepts and generalizations, and testing those ideas in new situations (Kolb, 1984). A number of these theories emphasize experiences that are novel, challenging, or dissonance producing as the stimulus for development. Cognitive theories of learning (Kanfer & Ackerman, 1989) posit that people's knowledge structures grow and develop when they are challenged by novel information obtained via experience. Argyris and Schön (1974) added the concept of double-loop learning in which new information disrupts people's central assumptions, leading to the examination of those assumptions and the development of new meaning structures. From the perspective of constructive theories of adult development (Kegan, 1994), people develop more complex and adaptive ways of understanding self and the world as they work to make sense of disequilibrating experiences.

Research on developmental experiences in managerial careers also supports the role of stretch experiences in leader development. Across a series of studies, managers most frequently cited challenging assignments as a key driver of their own development (McCall, Lombardo, & Morrison, 1988; Van Velsor, Wilson, Criswell, & Chandrasekar, 2013). Subsequent research identified five major types of challenges that stretched individuals in these assignments: (a) unfamiliar responsibilities, (b) creating change, (c) high levels of responsibility, (d) managing across boundaries, and (e) dealing with diversity (Ohlott, 2004). Job incumbents who report these types of challenges are rated higher on leadership skill development, managerial competencies, and promotability by their supervisors (De Pater, Van Vianen, Bechtoldt, & Klehe, 2009; DeRue & Wellman, 2009; Dragoni, Tesluk, Russell, & Oh, 2009).

As noted, regularly stepping into these stretch experiences is considered a hallmark of the learning agile leader. Measures of learning agility often include items that assess the degree to which an individual seeks new opportunities, welcomes change, and is curious and willing to experiment (Burke, Roloff, & Mitchinson, 2016; De Meuse, Lim, & Rao, 2019; Lombardo & Eichinger, 2000). And, research examining antecedents of stretch assignments finds that individuals with a higher learning goal orientation are more likely than those with a lower learning goal orientation to report currently being in a job that provides challenge (Aryee & Chu, 2012; Preenen, Van Vianen, & De Pater, 2014).

An important caveat to note is that inequities often exist when it comes to who is given the opportunity to take on stretch assignments. Compared to men, women are less likely to be placed in challenging jobs critical for career advancement (e.g., mission-critical roles, international assignments) or be assigned challenging tasks as part of their jobs (King et al., 2012; Silva, Carter, & Beninger, 2012). When describing their developmental experiences, African American managers also do not report as many challenging assignments compared to their white counterparts (Douglas, 2003).

Facets of learning agility have also been studied as a moderator of the relationship between stretch experiences and both learning and performance outcomes. For example, Dragoni et al. (2009) found that learning goal orientation moderated the relationship between developmental impact of job assignments and supervisor ratings of competencies; the positive relationship was stronger for those with higher levels of learning goal orientation. Moderator studies have been particularly useful in understanding how learning agility decreases the potential negative consequences of stretch experiences. Although Dong, Seo, and Bartol (2014) found that stretch assignments can boost pleasant feelings, which in turn increase advancement potential, they also found that these experiences can increase unpleasant feelings, which are associated with turnover intentions. However, stretch assignments were positively related to turnover intentions only for those managers who were low on emotional regulation (i.e., the ability to detect, respond to, and manage emotions). The researchers argued that emotional regulation can serve as a buffer to prevent unpleasant feelings from developing into intentions to leave one's job. Courtright, Colbert, and Choi (2014) found that stretch assignments were associated with not only higher work engagement but also higher emotional exhaustion. Increased emotional exhaustion led in turn to higher incidents of laissez-faire leadership. This indirect relationship between stretch experiences and laissez-faire leadership held only for those managers with low leadership self-efficacy (i.e., perceptions of one's ability to effectively perform the functions of a leadership role). The researchers encourage organizations to enhance leaders' readiness for stretch assignments by building their self-efficacy through education, mentoring, and coaching.

Finally, learning agility has also been viewed as an outcome of stretch experiences, although little work has directly examined this relationship. Many of the competencies identified as facets of learning agility (e.g., self-insight, resilience, flexibility, and feedback seeking) are those that managers report learning from experience (McCall et al., 1988; Van Velsor et al., 2013). Researchers have also begun to examine the outcomes of stretch experiences from a social cognitive perspective, finding that the increased self-efficacy generated by stretch experiences mediates the relationship between challenging jobs and the incumbent's performance and promotability (Aryee & Chu, 2012; Seibert, Sargent, Kraimer, & Kiazad, 2017).

Research thus supports the view that learning agility is related to stretch assignments in multiple ways: as an antecedent, moderator, and outcome. In other words, learning agile leaders are more likely to seek stretch experiences,

Table 8.1 Facets of Learning Agility Related to Stretch Experiences

Antecedent: Predicts who pursues stretch experiences	Moderator: Moderates stretch-learning or stretch-performing relationship	Outcome: Enhanced by stretch experiences
Change readiness	Emotional regulation	Self-insight
Curious, experimental	Self-efficacy	Resilience
Learning goal orientation	Learning goal orientation	Flexibility
		Feedback seeking
		Self-efficacy

learn from them, and use those lessons to improve their performance, in the process enhancing their learning agility. Table 8.1 summarizes the emerging findings about this multifaceted relationship between stretch assignments and learning agility.

Encouraging and Supporting Learning at the Edge

Using learning theory and research-based knowledge on learning from stretch experiences, we now turn to strategies to encourage and support more leaders stepping to the edge of their comfort zone and, in so doing, demonstrate and enhance their learning agility. First, organizations can shine a brighter light on learning from stretch experiences, making this learning more visible and valued. Second, organizations can be more intentional in making the right stretch experiences available for all leaders. Finally, organizations can develop leaders' skill and confidence for continuous learning at the edge of their comfort zones.

Shine a Light on Learning From Stretch Experiences

To encourage stepping to the edge of one's comfort zone, stretch experiences need to be a bigger part of the learning and development conversation in organizations. And, to better leverage these experiences for their own development, leaders benefit from practicing learning from stretch experiences in supportive environments and from seeing the value that their organization places on this approach to development.

Table 8.2 Examples of Development-in-Place Stretch Assignments

Challenge	Reshape Your Job	Temporary Assignment
Unfamiliar Responsibilities	Ask your boss to delegate one of his or her job responsibilities to you.	Take on part of a colleague's job while he or she is on temporary leave.
New Directions	Be responsible for a new project or new process in your group.	Join a project team that is plowing new ground in your organization.
Inherited Problems	Be responsible for dealing with dissatisfied customers or difficult suppliers.	Redesign a flawed product or system.
Problems With Employees	Coach employees with performance problems in your group.	Resolve a conflict with a direct report.
High Stakes	Manage an annual organizational event with high visibility.	Do a tight-deadline assignment for your boss.
Scope and Scale	Serve on multiple project teams simultaneously.	Join a team managing a large-scale project.
External Pressure	Add external interface roles to your job.	Take calls on a customer hotline.
Influencing Without Authority	Manage projects that require coordination across the organization.	Represent concerns of employees to higher management.
Work Across Cultures	Serve as the liaison with a business partner in another country.	Work in a short-term assignment at an office in another country.
Work Group Diversity	Train regularly in your company's diversity program.	Lead a project team with a diverse group of members.

Adapted from McCauley (2006).

Build a Framework

One of the best ways to encourage the use of stretch experiences in leadership development is to make them more prominent. Leaders are often given a list of classes they can take for their development. They are less likely to receive a list of stretch experiences to consider pursuing. Any one of several challenging assignment frameworks can serve as a foundation for generating such lists (e.g., Kizilos, 2012; Lombardo & Eichinger, 2002; McCauley, 2006). Table 8.2 illustrates how such a framework can be used to generate examples of development-in-place opportunities in an organization.

Practitioners also emphasize the importance of stretch experiences by featuring them as a foundational element in the organization's leadership development strategy. For example, in Payless Holdings' leadership success profile, experiences needed for success are highlighted alongside the more common articulation of important leader attributes and competencies (Boyd, 2014). An experience-driven development strategy starts with the business strategy and the kinds of capabilities needed to realize that strategy, then identifies the experiences needed to develop the capabilities and the relationships needed to challenge and support learning from those experiences (Yost & Plunkett, 2009). The resulting "developmental map" can then be integrated into succession planning, training, and performance management processes so that leaders can pursue needed stretch experiences.

Highlight Stretch Experiences in Formal Development Programs

Formal development programs are an ideal setting to highlight and reinforce learning from stretch experiences. These programs are pervasive in organizations; those participating are already oriented toward learning and development; and perhaps most importantly, formal programs provide a space to practice learning from experience in a supportive environment.

The design of effective development programs has long emphasized the important role of experiential learning. Not only must participants be exposed to useful knowledge and perspectives, but they must also have the opportunity to apply the knowledge to real-life situations, practice skills, and generate their own insights from engaging in experiences. Thus, these programs feature elements such as using a new framework to diagnose and discover potential solutions to back-home challenges, practicing skills and receiving feedback via role plays and simulations, and engaging in and debriefing group exercises to generate new insights about oneself and working with others. What is critical from a learning agility perspective is emphasizing how the same learning tactics being utilized in the program—like experimenting with new approaches to a problem, practicing and getting feedback, and jumping into an experience then debriefing that experience with others—can be used for continuous learning from day-to-day experiences.

Formal programs designed to extend over time offer additional opportunities to access new stretch experiences and to emphasize learning from these experiences. For example, program participants can work in teams on action learning projects, accomplishing real work in the organization that stretches them to work in ways that are more strategic, cross functional, and innovative. At the same time, these teams are supported by coaches who interject and encourage learning in the midst of action via productive dialogue, reflection, and intentional experimentation (O'Neill & Marsick, 2007). Back-home learning projects can also be individualized. For example, in a program at Duke University for employees interested in moving into a management role, participants' supervisors agree to delegate one of their own job responsibilities to the participant during the course of the program (Allison & Green, 2014). And at Heineken, a program for first-time supervisors is structured as a continuous learning group where participants bring current challenges to gain insights from both facilitated discussion with others and modularized content most relevant to the challenge (Plunkett & Daubner, 2014).

Reinforce Learning From Experience as a Core Organizational Value

It is important to note that moving beyond practicing to regularly engaging in stretch experiences requires an organizational culture that values learning from experience and that tolerates the inevitable mistakes that leaders will make. How are such values communicated and reinforced? First, they are communicated through the actions of senior executives, for example, in the way they share their own experiences of learning from stretch experiences, who they tap for visible assignments, and how they react to missteps during these assignments. Second, valuing learning from experience is reinforced by what is recognized and rewarded in the organization. Are people rewarded for stepping to the edge of their comfort zone—even if their performance takes an initial dip as they are learning to deal with new challenges? Are they discouraged from pursuing a lateral move to broaden their perspective because such a move does not offer the same financial rewards as a promotion in their own function? Values are also communicated by what is measured and tracked in the organization. For example, if an organization evaluates the impact of its formal leadership development programs, but not the impact of its use of stretch assignments for development, it could be sending the message that it values and supports formal learning over learning from experience. Finally, values are reinforced by how the organization invests its

Table 8.3 Strategies for Making Stretch Experiences Happen in Organizations

Educate and Support Bosses	Staff for Development	Design New Stretch Experiences
• Recognize each direct reports' development needs • Use job moves, new responsibilities, and temporary assignments to create stretch experiences • Manage the risk of stretch assignments	• Identify stretch roles in succession management discussions • Highlight stretch experiences in formal development plans • Use rotational assignments beyond early career • Designate particular positions or team roles as developmental assignments • Create project marketplaces	• Create short-term assignments to equip more leaders with strategic competencies • Surround the experiences with learning resources: learning goals, coaching, formal training, and reflection

resources. Can a leader struggling in a stretch assignment readily access resources for a professional coach? To what degree is the organization willing to invest in attracting and retaining learning agile leaders?

Make Stretch Experiences Happen

Highly learning agile individuals will find ways to make stretch experiences happen on their own. However, the majority of people will benefit from organizational settings where stretch opportunities are readily available and where there is support for discerning which experiences are best for targeted development. Also, by making stretch experiences more readily available, organizations reduce the risk of losing talented leaders who might see greater opportunities with another employer. To make the right kind of stretch experiences happen for more people, organizations need to take a look at the role of bosses, the organization's staffing practices, and opportunities to create new stretch experiences (Table 8.3).

Equip Bosses to Use Stretch Experiences

In most organizations, a key managerial responsibility is developing direct reports in ways that enhance current and future performance. Yet, very few of these organizations actually teach bosses—the people who control access to many stretch experiences—how to use these experiences to develop leaders while accomplishing work. A little education can equip these managers with the basics to more proactively use job assignments to develop their direct reports (Box 8.1). These managers need to know how to identify an individual's strengths and weaknesses and recognize what kind of challenges will create stretch opportunities that target underdeveloped competencies. For example, serving on a cross-functional team is an opportunity to develop a broader framework for understanding organization issues and learn how to coordinate action across silos. Bosses also need to understand their role in applying common strategies for accessing stretch experiences: job moves, temporary assignments, reshaping current job responsibilities, and experiences outside the workplace in professional and community organizations. For example, does the manager keep an eye on open positions in the organization for individuals who are ready for their next big challenge, think about who will grow most from representing the function on a task force or making a presentation to higher management, consider shifting responsibilities among team members to develop more people with broader capabilities, and encourage direct reports to consider leadership roles in volunteer organizations?

Education for bosses should also generate discussion about the risks in inviting or pushing individuals to the edge of their comfort zone and strategies for mitigating those risks. Risks include poor performance, making mistakes, and endangering the success of critical work in the organization. The individual could become overly stressed, lose confidence in themselves, or derail their career. The bigger the stretch is, the greater the risks. Thus, for major stretch experiences, bosses need to consider what the individual will bring to the experience that can mitigate the risk: Has the individual regularly demonstrated an ability and willingness to learn from stretch experiences? Has the individual demonstrated potential for more complex work? Does the individual have a particular strength or expertise that will clearly contribute to success in the assignment? Contextual aspects of the experience can also mitigate risk: Will the individual be working with a talented team or have ready access to coaching and feedback from an experienced manager? The boss can directly mitigate risks by helping individuals set learning goals, ensuring that they have access to learning resources and feedback, being a sounding board, and asking questions to encourage reflection. Bosses need to guard against the sink-or-swim approach, that is, giving tough assignments as a

Box 8.1 Supporting Learning at the Edge: The Boss's Checklist

Take Responsibility for Developing Your Employees

- ❐ I make developing my employees a core part of my job.
- ❐ I look for ways to support employees in their efforts to learn and grow.
- ❐ I hold employees accountable for their development.

Use On-the-Job Experiences to Develop Employees

- ❐ I ensure that my employees' development plans go beyond formal programs to include on-the-job experiences.
- ❐ I make a point of identifying stretch assignments for each of my direct reports.
- ❐ I give direct reports assignments or experiences to help them develop specific competencies.
- ❐ I create new roles or job responsibilities to provide an employee with needed experience.
- ❐ I consider the development opportunities a particular assignment could provide when making decisions about how to staff key projects.
- ❐ I support employees who seek growth experiences outside the workplace (e.g., in community or professional organizations).
- ❐ I reserve certain types of assignments specifically for employee development.

Support Learning From Experience

- ❐ I help direct reports set goals for learning from stretch assignments, relationships, and formal coursework.
- ❐ I help direct reports assess progress toward learning goals.
- ❐ I give developmental feedback to direct reports.
- ❐ I have conversations with direct reports about what they are learning from their stretch experiences.
- ❐ I help direct reports connect with others who can support their learning and development (e.g., coaches, experts, peer mentors).

test and leaving individuals to fend for themselves. This approach not only discourages less courageous individuals from stepping to the edge of their comfort zone but also reinforces a message that demonstrating competence is more important than growing from the experience.

Staff for Development

Organizations typically approach the task of filling jobs and special assignments with the goal of finding the person who is most capable of high performance given the responsibilities of the job. Staffing for performance aims to maximize person–job fit. On the other hand, staffing for development requires some amount of person–job misfit to create a stretch experience. In the previous section, we noted how this type of misfit is what bosses need to strive for in making local staffing decisions with development in mind. This same approach can be used in formal talent management processes to make more stretch experiences happen.

Numerous talent management practices afford opportunities to staff for development. Decisions about job moves and special assignments, particularly for leaders who are recognized as high potentials, are often made as part of *succession management processes*. Typically, one or more stretch opportunities that target specific development needs are identified for each high potential. *Formal development planning* processes can highlight specific opportunities for stretch experiences in every leader's job and stimulate development conversations between managers and employees. *Rotational programs* typically move early career employees through a set of assignments designed to broaden their business knowledge and organizational networks, grow management skills, and develop a deeper understanding of organizational culture. Some organizations use rotational programs for more experienced leaders. These programs, like GE's Corporate Leadership Staff (Tisoczki & Bevier, 2014) and the US Intelligence Community's Joint Duty Program (Kolmstetter, 2014), customize the rotation experience to individual needs and often have the additional goal of enhancing collaboration across organizational boundaries. An advantage of using organization-wide talent management processes to leverage job experiences for development is the opportunity to monitor and enhance consistency in access to stretch experiences across social identity groups.

Special staffing policies can also support staffing for development. For example, organizations might designate particular roles as developmental assignments for high potentials. These are demanding jobs with clear performance expectations; however, labeling them as "developmental" sets the expectation that attention should also be given to learning, and designating them as "assignments" signals that they are flow-through positions that are more readily available as stretch experiences. Another example is regularly staffing certain types of core work in the organization that is accomplished by temporary teams, such as process improvement initiatives or new product launches, with development in mind. In other words, reserve at least one spot on the team for someone who can gain developmental benefits from the experience.

A common problem with staffing for development is that many potential stretch experiences can be missed because managers and their direct reports are only aware of the short-term, project-based opportunities in their immediate area of the organization. Intranet-based project marketplaces are a remedy for this dilemma (Davis, 2007). Projects looking for part-time help on certain tasks or in need of particular skills, short-term assignments, and jobs needed to be filled on an interim basis are posted; people from across the organization can learn about these opportunities and decide with their manager whether pursuing one of the posted assignments would have benefits.

Design New Stretch Experiences

What organizations quickly learn as they are working to leverage on-the-job experiences for development is that there are not enough of the right stretch experiences to develop certain competencies widely in the organization (e.g., a global perspective, strategic thinking, or cross-boundary collaboration). So, they find ways to create new stretch experiences where there were none. Let us take a look at some examples.

Born out of the need for a more globally savvy and responsible organization, IBM's Corporate Service Corps (CSC) uses international volunteering to develop leaders' business knowledge and global perspective while advancing business objectives (Flaherty & Osicki, 2014). At the core of the CSC experience is a 1-month assignment as part of a global team providing pro bono IBM expertise for organizations in disadvantaged, developing parts of the world. For 3 months prior to the on-the-ground experience, the team prepares together virtually—learning about their host country and consulting tactics, building the team, and identifying personal learning goals. After the experience, participants share their experience and insights with the company and in their local communities. Participants report that this demanding experience develops a number of capabilities, with collaborating globally, embracing challenge, and building mutual trust at the top of the list.

With emerging markets growing rapidly, Microsoft needed to grow in-country talent with a broad perspective on corporate business practices (Bhasin, Homer, & Rait, 2014). The organization designed an initiative that brought recognized local talent in emerging markets to corporate headquarters for a 3-month assignment on a project that both capitalized on their extensive knowledge of field operations and provided a tailored opportunity to fill a leadership gap. An opportunity profile clarified the assignment, identified a sponsor and day-to-day manager, and articulated the experience to be gained and competencies to be developed. Three elements supported a positive learning experience: intensive onboarding, an external coach, and an intentional reentry process that emphasized sharing lessons learned in the participants' local organization. Measuring the impact of the program found benefits not only for the participant but also for the corporate host organization (e.g., gaining a field perspective on major projects) and the home location (e.g., increasing knowledge of doing business at Microsoft).

In both of these examples, short-term assignments were created to give more leaders a stretch experience aimed at developing capabilities the organization needed to realize its strategic intents. The assignments also served purposes beyond individual development (e.g., corporate social responsibility, bringing field expertise to corporate projects). Perhaps most importantly, development was supported by surrounding the experience with learning resources, such as learning goals, coaching, formal training, and the opportunity to reflect on the experience and share insights gained with others.

Encourage the Practice of Daily Learning From Stretch Experiences

Developmental challenges can encompass the full job (e.g., turning a business around), but they can also be small, daily on-the-job challenges that promote continuous development (Sessa & London, 2015). Expertise in any field requires deliberate practice (Ericsson, Prietula, & Cokely, 2007). Learning to play the piano, for example, does not start with a Bach concerto, but instead begins with finger positions, scales, and learning to read musical notation. Why would something as complicated as working with others on ever-shifting challenges to accomplish the strategic aims of an organization be any less difficult?

But, development does not happen automatically, and leaders often miss the opportunity to extract learning from their daily work. People need to develop habits and practices that allow them to self-manage their learning; that is, they need to anticipate, adapt, and reflect on the developmental challenges they face (Ashford & DeRue, 2012). Considerable research suggests that people tend to rely on simple rules (heuristics) to make most decisions rather than engage in active cognitive processing, what Kahneman (2011) called System 1 versus System 2 thinking. He suggested that knowing the errors in one's thinking is not the magic solution—people still make the same mistakes. One potential way to sidestep the problem is to adopt better heuristics.

Consequently, the trick may be to provide leaders with a set of heuristics that promotes growth within developmental assignments. To have the maximum impact, the heuristic should be grounded in research, simple, habit forming, and self-reinforcing so that learning behaviors become self-sustaining (Duhigg, 2012; Yost, 2016). Eight heuristics that leaders can use to anticipate, adapt, and reflect on their daily development are discussed next and summarized in Figure 8.1.

Anticipating

One of the first tasks is to create the conditions that frame the stretch experience and cue the leader to see the developmental opportunities as they emerge.

Ask "What's My Story Today?" One anticipatory strategy is to frame the developmental challenge in a way that is motivating. People adopt a variety of narratives to understand their work experiences (Yost, Yoder, Chung, & Voetmann, 2015). An upcoming tough conversation can be seen as a potential tragedy, transformational moment, or just another existential moment in the meaninglessness of work. However, the stories that people tell themselves can have a powerful impact on the types of challenges they are willing to take on, the effort they will expend, and how long they are willing to persist (Ibarra & Barbulescu, 2010). One of the most powerful narratives is what Joseph Campbell (2008) called the hero's journey, a common type of story arc that crosses time and culture. In this narrative arc, the hero leaves the village, faces challenges and adversaries to overcome, ultimately requiring

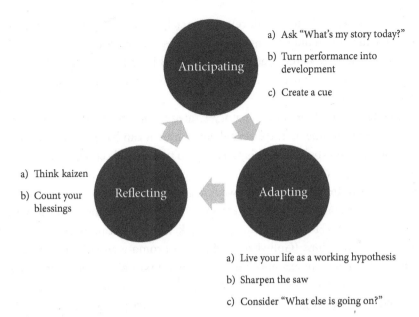

Figure 8.1 Strategies to encourage the practice of daily learning from stretch assignments.

conquering his or her own internal weaknesses to arrive at a new horizon. The power of this narrative is that it assumes challenges will come, they are a good thing, and they must be overcome to get to a better future. In this way, Carol Dweck's (2006) research on the power of a growth mindset builds on this and suggests that the framing of challenges is important. Developmental challenges should not be seen as evaluations of one's fixed abilities but as opportunities to grow. Developmental challenges inevitably come with successes and failure. In her TED Talk, Dweck (2014) suggested that in these moments of failure, it is important to adopt a heuristic that focuses on growth. The self-talk should not be, "I'm not good at this." Instead, the focus should be on the developmental journey, "Am I good at this? Not yet."

Turn Performance Into Development. A second anticipatory strategy is to bundle development with performance. Work is often seen through two lenses—performance versus development—that are considered to be in tension. They do not have to be. If the vast majority of a person's development happens on the job, then they can and do happen at the same time. The trick is to strategically place oneself in situations that are developmental and drive the business (Yost & Plunkett, 2009). For example, a person can volunteer to manage the team's budget to develop financial acumen. An emerging leader can take the lead in onboarding new employees to learn how to motivate and support others. A senior leader can enhance his or her strategic thinking by helping direct reports wrestle with the long-term implications of their decisions.

Create a Cue. A final anticipatory strategy is to create an environment that cues development. The external environment can have a profound impact on a person's behavior. This can result in two possible conclusions. First, the world around us controls us or we have control to craft an environment that guides us in the direction we want to go (Duckworth, Gendler, & Gross, 2016). The second is a lot more empowering. Cues are a powerful way to direct attention (Hofmann, Friese, & Strack, 2009) and can become implementation intentions (Gollwitzer, 1999) that promote growth and on-the-job development. For example, one leader might post his development goals above his computer. Another might paste a green dot on her computer to remind her that her goal in every email will be to delegate and equip people to do the work themselves. Another person might build in time at the beginning of a meeting for the team to reflect on "lessons learned" during the week. The possibilities are endless.

Adapting

The world seldom unfolds as predicted. Thus, it is equally important for organizations to help leaders navigate and capture learning in the moment. Several strategies are important during the experience to increase learning.

Live Your Life as a Working Hypothesis. The first adaptive strategy that leaders can adopt is to frame the experience as an experiment. In dynamic environments, a person needs to figure out what to do in the moment. Days will be filled with both wins and losses. It is important to develop the capacity to not simply react, but to actively learn in the moment, considering multiple futures and outcomes and testing them to create new insights about oneself and the world (Karoly, 1993). Dynamic environments require stepping into the unknown to learn what works and what does not. Rather than trying to execute a new leadership skill perfectly, leaders can break the skills they are trying to develop into smaller chunks. They can prototype smaller actions (e.g., contracting with smaller clients) in ways that succeed or fail in bigger projects (e.g., contracting with major clients). Like in design thinking, the development and risk are broken into smaller chunks (Brown, 2008; Rigby, Sutherland, & Takeuchi, 2016). Over time, development happens incrementally. People build on small wins to increase confidence and adapt their performance in complex, dynamic environments (Weick, 1984). In this way, organizations build cultures where people can learn to "fail fast" and iteratively build complex skill sets (Van Dyck, Frese, Baer, & Sonnentag, 2005). They develop agile learning capabilities and expertise that generalize to future challenges.

Sharpen the Saw. A second adaptive strategy is to ensure one takes the time to recharge. Daily challenges require energy, resilience, and persistence. In *Seven Habits of Highly Effective People* (1990), Stephen Covey's seventh habit is "sharpening the saw," suggesting that people will eventually become less and less effective, like an unsharpened saw, if they do not take time to rest and retool. Subsequent research has confirmed the importance of several habits in long-term well-being and effectiveness, including exercise, meditation or prayer, sleep, and social support (e.g., Tabibnia & Radecki, 2018). Setting aside time to recharge takes discipline, but it is a requirement for continuous development.

Ask "What Else Is Going On?" A final adaptive strategy is to step onto the balcony to assess the broader context. Challenging assignments happen in complex environments. In his book *Humble Inquiry*, Ed Schein (2013) suggested that a critical question that consultants should always ask is, "What else is going on?" There are always multiple dynamics at play. Asking the question allows people to see the system from multiple perspectives. They move from the dance floor to the balcony (Heifetz & Laurie, 2001) to develop more complex and adaptive ways of understanding themselves and the world (Kegan, 1994).

Reflecting

Lessons are not automatically captured when a challenge ends. The potential lessons need to be identified, remembered, and applied to future situations.

Think Kaizen. The first step of reflection in the moment is to remember that development is iterative and continuous. In the golden age of lean manufacturing and Six Sigma, the Japanese manufacturing concept of "kaizen" or continuous improvement was introduced (Imai, 1986). Because the development of complex behaviors is an iterative process, it is important to create daily opportunities to reflect on and lock in changes. Team huddles can be used at the beginning and end of a process to capture lessons and plan for the next day (Rigby et al., 2016). Daily on-the-job development opportunities can be enhanced with after-event reviews to explore what happened, why it happened, and what to do differently the next time (DeRue, Nahrgang, Hollenbeck, & Workman, 2012). In these reflection moments, the focus should be on learning, not blame. And, for heaven's sake, make sure people do not call them postmortems; no one wants to take time to revisit a dead project.

Count Your Blessings. The second important reflection strategy is to take the time to celebrate along the way. Small wins build confidence, which in turn improves future performance. Celebration might include reflecting at the end of the day about three things one is grateful for, celebrating milestone accomplishments, or expressing gratitude to colleagues with a quick thank you note (Lyubomirsky, Sheldon, & Schkade, 2005). Research suggests that these practices not only are good for the person, but also are infectious to the people around the person, who are more likely to engage in prosocial behavior themselves.

Encouraging Daily Learning Across the Organization

The anticipating, adapting, and reflecting heuristics that we have just reviewed are largely individual actions. However, the goal should be to introduce interventions that target individuals yet can spread across the organization to promote growth throughout the whole system. This should include building on-the-job development into human resource processes (Yost & Plunkett, 2010), such as emphasizing on-the-job development in the performance management process or training interventions and during job transitions when people are particularly open to learning new habits. Another way to increase the attention might include introducing a 30-day challenge with daily activities to increase on-the-job development (Preston-Dayne, 2014). Similarly, an organization might introduce a "development minute" that supervisors can discuss at the beginning of staff meetings (e.g., "This week's development minute is asking, 'Who's voice is missing?' so let's practice making sure no one dominates and everyone's voice can be heard."). Organizations will maximize development when they find ways to make daily learning an integral part of the culture.

Future Directions

When it comes to developing individuals in work settings, the last 30 years have brought increased attention to the importance of stretch experiences, yielded research-based insights about learning from these experience, and generated new practices in organizations aimed at leveraging experiences for development (McCauley & McCall, 2014). Moving forward, we see opportunities to expand the impact of this work and deepen our understanding of learning agility.

Perhaps the most progress from a practice perspective has been in those arenas where talent development professionals have direct influence, for example, the design of development programs, the facilitation of succession management discussions, and the creation of targeted development interventions to support the strategic needs of the organization. However, the fact that stretch experiences are woven into the ongoing work of the organization means that much of learning from stretch experiences is in the hands of leaders and their managers. Although tackling this dilemma from a cultural change perspective is possible (with enlightened senior executives and a powerful talent development function), we have been inspired by practitioners who have found ways to enhance experience-based learning in the organization from whatever role they happen to be in without waiting to be part of a large strategic initiative (Yost & Plunkett, 2010). Experimentation with tactics and tools for educating and encouraging leaders across the organization to seek out and learn from stretch experiences needs to continue, and insights gained from this work need to be more broadly shared in professional circles (McCauley, DeRue, Yost, & Taylor, 2014).

The emergence of the learning agility construct has in many ways energized the learning-from-experience movement in organizations, particularly in the context of leadership development. However, we do see a downside to the construct being too closely tied to the identification and advancement of high potentials. Although some facets of learning agility measures (see Chapter 1) are clearly related to the learning process (e.g., experimenting, feedback responsiveness), other facets appear more important for advancing to higher level management jobs in the organization (e.g., inspiring others, cognitive perspective). We would advocate for frameworks that better delineate the basics of learning agility—those competencies that help anyone step into and learn at the edge of their comfort zone—and the more advanced facets of learning agility for moving into more complex and strategic roles in organizations.

From a research perspective, we suggest that stretch experiences are a fruitful setting for discovering more about learning agility and how it impacts leadership development and performance. Following individuals over time during these experiences would yield more insights about the positive and negative dynamics of stretch experiences and the role of learning agility and contextual factors on any developmental gains. Experimental studies of interventions aimed to increase learning agility in the context of stretch experiences would also be beneficial.

Another promising area for additional research is identification of the facets of learning agility that are most important for maximizing learning from different stretch experiences. In the spirit of the original lessons of experience research that identified the unique pattern of lessons tied to each type of experience (McCall et al., 1988), research could identify the facets of learning agility that are most critical for learning from different experiences. For example, Lombardo and Eichinger (2002) identified experiences to develop a given competency. Similarly, McKenna, Boyd, and Yost (2007) used the original lessons of experience methodology to build a matrix of stretch assignments and learning agility dimensions for church clergy. Future research could more systematically assess which dimensions moderate the relationships between experiences and leadership growth for different types of stretch assignments or identify a subset of dimensions critical in all stretch assignments. Finally, significantly more work is needed to identify the daily incremental stretch moments that grow a leader and the critical role that learning agility plays in facilitating continuous growth.

In organizations today where change seems to be the rule and stability the exception, stretch experiences are plentiful. Organizations would be wise to equip leaders at all levels with the learning agility skills and capabilities that will allow them to thrive in a world of constant change.

References

Allison, S. A., & Green, M. (2014). Stretch assignments to develop first-time supervisors. In C. D. McCauley, D. S. DeRue, P. R. Yost, & S. Taylor (Eds.), *Experience-driven leader development* (pp. 113–117). San Francisco, CA: Wiley.

Argyris, C., & Schön, D. A. (1974). *Theory in practice: Increasing professional effectiveness.* San Francisco, CA: Jossey-Bass.

Aryee, S., & Chu, C. W. L. (2012). Antecedents and outcomes of challenging job experiences: A social cognitive perspective. *Human Performance, 25,* 215–234.

Ashford, S. J., & DeRue, D. S. (2012). Developing as a leader: The power of mindful engagement. *Organizational Dynamics, 41,* 146–154.

Bhasin, A., Homer, L., & Rait, E. (2014). Strategic corporate assignments to develop emerging market leaders. In C. D. McCauley, D. S. DeRue, P. R. Yost, & S. Taylor (Eds.), *Experience-driven leader development* (pp. 81–86). San Francisco, CA: Wiley.

Boyd, T. (2014). Profiles for success: Building a framework for internal transitions. In C. D. McCauley, D. S. DeRue, P. R. Yost, & S. Taylor (Eds.), *Experience-driven leader development* (pp. 459–462). San Francisco, CA: Jossey-Bass.

Brown, T. (2008). Design thinking. *Harvard Business Review, 86*(6), 84–92.

Burke, W. W., Roloff, K. S., & Mitchinson, A. (2016). *Learning agility: A new model and measure* (White paper). New York, NY: Teachers College, Columbia University.

Campbell, J. (2008). *The hero with a thousand faces* (3rd ed.). Novato, CA: New World Library.

Courtright, S. H., Colbert, A. E., & Choi, D. (2014). Fired up or burned out? How developmental challenge differentially impacts leader behavior. *Journal of Applied Psychology, 99,* 681–696.

Covey, S. R. (1990). *The 7 habits of highly effective people.* New York, NY: Fireside Books.

Davis, N. M. (2007, November). One-on-one training crosses continents. *HR Magazine,* pp. 55–56.

De Meuse, D. P., Lim, J., & Rao, R. (2019). *The development and validation of the TALENTx7® assessment: A psychological measure of learning agility* (3rd edition). Shanghai, China: Leader's Gene Consulting.

De Pater, I. E., Van Vianen, A. E. M., Bechtoldt, M. N., & Klehe, U. (2009). Employees' challenging job experiences and supervisors' evaluations of promotability. *Personnel Psychology, 62,* 297–325.

DeRue, D. S., Nahrgang, J. D., Hollenbeck, J. R., & Workman, K. (2012). A quasi-experimental study of after-event reviews and leadership development. *Journal of Applied Psychology, 97,* 997–1015.

DeRue, D. S., & Wellman, N. (2009). Developing leaders via experience: The role of developmental challenge, learning orientation, and feedback availability. *Journal of Applied Psychology, 94,* 859–875.

Dong, Y., Seo, M., & Bartol, K. M. (2014). No pain, no gain: An affect-based model of developmental job experience and the buffering effects of emotional intelligence. *Academy of Management Journal, 57,* 1056–1077.

Douglas, C. A. (2003). *Key events and lessons for managers in a diverse workforce.* Greensboro, NC: Center for Creative Leadership.

Dragoni, L., Tesluk, P. E., Russell, J. A., & Oh, I. (2009). Understanding managerial development: Integrating developmental assignments, learning orientation, and access to developmental opportunities in predicting managerial competencies. *Academy of Management Journal, 52,* 731–743.

Duckworth, A. L., Gendler, T. S., & Gross, J. J. (2016). Situational strategies for self-control. *Perspectives on Psychological Science, 11*(1), 35–55.

Duhigg, C. (2012). *The power of habits.* New York, NY: Random House.

Dweck, C. S. (2006). *Mindset: The new psychology of success.* New York, NY: Random House.

Dweck, C. S. (2014). *The power of believing that you can improve.* https://www.ted.com/talks/carol_dweck_the_power_of_believing_that_you_can_improve?language=en

Ericsson, K. A., Prietula, M. J., & Cokely, E. T. (2007). The making of an expert. *Harvard Business Review, 85*(7–8), 114–121.

Flaherty, V. L., & Osicki, M. (2014). Developing IBM leaders through socially responsible service projects. In C. D. McCauley & M. W. McCall Jr. (Eds.), *Using experience to develop leadership talent* (pp. 205–227). San Francisco, CA: Jossey-Bass.

Gollwitzer, P. M. (1999). Implementation intentions and effective goal pursuit: Strong effects of simple plans. *American Psychologist, 54,* 493–503.

Hallenbeck, G. (2016). *Learning agility: Unlock the lessons of experience.* Greensboro, NC: Center for Creative Leadership.

Hallenbeck, G., & Santana, L. (2019). *Great leaders are great learners: How to develop learning-agile high potentials.* Greensboro, NC: Center for Creative Leadership.

Heifetz, R. A., & Laurie, D. L. (2001). The work of leadership. *Harvard Business Review, 79*(11), 131–141.

Hofmann, W., Friese, M., & Strack, F. (2009). Impulse and self-control from a dual-systems perspective. *Perspectives on Psychological Science, 4,* 162–176.

Ibarra, H., & Barbulescu, R. (2010). Identity as narrative: Prevalence, effectiveness, and consequences of narrative identity work in macro work role transitions. *Academy of Management Review, 35,* 135–154.

Imai, M. (1986). *Kaizen: The key to Japan's competitive success.* New York, NY: McGraw-Hill/Irwin.

Kahneman, D. (2011). *Thinking, fast and slow.* New York, NY: Farrar, Straus and Giroux.

Kanfer, R., & Ackerman, P. L. (1989). Motivation and cognitive abilities: An integrative/aptitude-treatment interaction approach to skill acquisition. *Journal of Applied Psychology, 74,* 657–690.

Karoly, P. (1993). Mechanisms of self-regulation: A systems view. *Annual Review of Psychology, 44,* 23–52.

Kegan, R. (1994). *In over our heads: The mental demands of modern life.* Cambridge, MA: Harvard University Press.

King, E. B., Botsford, W., Hebl, M. R., Kazama, S., Dawson, J. F., & Perkins, A. (2012). Benevolent sexism at work: Gender differences in the distribution of challenging developmental experiences. *Journal of Management, 38,* 1835–1866.

Kizilos, M. A. (2012). *FrameBreaking leadership development.* Chanhassen, MN: Experienced-Based Development Associates.

Kolb, D. (1984). *Experiential learning: Experience as the source of learning and development.* Englewood Cliffs, NJ: Prentice-Hall.

Kolmstetter, E. B. (2014). Collaborative leadership in the intelligence community: Joint duty program. In C. D. McCauley & M. W. McCall Jr. (Eds.), *Using experience to develop leadership talent* (pp. 154–187), San Francisco, CA: Jossey-Bass.

Lombardo, M. M., & Eichinger, R. W. (2000). High potentials as high learners. *Human Resource Management, 39,* 321–330.

Lombardo, M. M., & Eichinger, R. W. (2002). *The leadership machine.* Minneapolis, MN: Lominger.

Lyubomirsky, S., Sheldon, K. M., & Schkade, D. (2005). Pursuing happiness: The architecture of sustainable change. *Review of General Psychology, 9,* 111–131.

McCall, M. W., Jr., Lombardo, M. M., & Morrison, A. M. (1988). *The lessons of experience: How successful executives develop on the job.* Lexington, MA: Lexington Press.

McCauley, C. D. (2006). *Developmental assignments: Creating learning experiences without changing jobs.* Greensboro, NC: Center for Creative Leadership.

McCauley, C. D., DeRue, D. S., Yost, P. R., & Taylor, S. (2014). *Experience-driven leader development: Models, tools, best practices, and advice for on-the-job development.* San Francisco, CA: Wiley.

McCauley, C. D., & McCall, M. W., Jr. (2014). *Using experience to develop leadership talent.* San Francisco, CA: Jossey-Bass.

McKenna, R. B., Boyd, T. N., & Yost, P. R. (2007). Learning agility in clergy: Understanding the strategies and situational factors that allow pastors to learn from experience. *Journal of Psychology & Theology, 35,* 190–201.

Ohlott, P. J. (2004). Job assignments. In C. D. McCauley & E. Van Velsor (Eds.). *The Center for Creative Leadership handbook of leadership development* (2nd ed., pp. 151–182). San Francisco, CA: Jossey-Bass.

O'Neill, J., & Marsick, V. J. (2007). *Understanding action learning.* New York, NY: AMACOM.

Plunkett, M. M., & Daubner, D. (2014). Experience-based first-line manager development at Heineken. In C. D. McCauley & M. W. McCall Jr. (Eds.), *Using experience to develop leadership talent* (pp. 331–354). San Francisco, CA: Jossey-Bass.

Preenen, P., Van Vianen, A., & De Pater, I. (2014). Challenging tasks: The role of employees' and supervisors' goal orientations. *European Journal of Work and Organizational Psychology, 23,* 48–61.

Preston-Dayne, L. A. (2014). Leadership fitness challenge: Daily exercise of the leadership muscle. In C. D. McCauley, D. S. DeRue, P. R. Yost, & S. Taylor. *Experience-driven leader development: Models, tools, best practices, and advice for on-the-job development* (pp. 123–128). San Francisco, CA: Wiley.

Rigby, D. K., Sutherland, J., & Takeuchi, H. (2016). Embracing agile. *Harvard Business Review, 94*(5), 40–50.

Schein, E. H. (2013). *Humble inquiry: The gentle art of asking instead of telling.* San Francisco, CA: Berrett-Koehler.

Seibert, S. E., Sargent, L. D., Kraimer, M. L., & Kiazad, K. (2017). Linking developmental experiences to leader effectiveness and promotability: The mediating role of leadership self-efficacy and mentor network. *Personnel Psychology, 70,* 357–397.

Sessa, V. I., & London, M. (2015). *Continuous learning in organizations: Individual, group, and organizational perspectives.* Boca Raton, FL: Psychology Press.

Silva, C., Carter, N. M., & Beninger, A. (2012). *Good intentions, imperfect execution? Women get fewer of the "hot jobs" needed to advance.* New York, NY: Catalyst.

Tabibnia, G., & Radecki, D. (2018). Resilience training that can change the brain. *Consulting Psychology Journal: Practice and Research, 70,* 59–88.

Tisoczki, B., & Bevier, L. (2014). A personalized rotation program to develop future leaders. In C. D. McCauley, D. S. DeRue, P. R. Yost, & S. Taylor (Eds.), *Experience-driven leader development* (pp. 93–98). San Francisco, CA: Wiley.

Van Dyck, C., Frese, M., Baer, M., & Sonnentag, S. (2005). Organizational error management culture and its impact on performance: A two-study replication. *Journal of Applied Psychology, 90,* 1228–1240.

Van Velsor, E., Wilson, M., Criswell, C., & Chandrasekar, N. A. (2013). Learning to lead: A comparison of developmental events and learning among managers in China, India, and the United States. *Asian Business & Management, 12,* 455–476.

Weick, K. E. (1984). Small wins: Redefining the scale of social problems. *American Psychologist, 39,* 40–49.

Yost, P. R. (2016). Resilience practices. *Industrial and Organizational Psychology, 9,* 475–479.

Yost, P. R., & McLellan, J. (2014). Identifying and assessing learning ability. In C. D. McCauley, D. S. DeRue, P. R. Yost, & S. Taylor (Eds.), *Experience-driven leader development* (pp. 309–316). San Francisco, CA: Wiley.

Yost, P. R., & Plunkett, M. M. (2009). *Real time leadership development.* London, UK: Wiley-Blackwell.

Yost, P. R., & Plunkett, M. M. (2010). Ten catalysts to spark on-the-job development in your organization. *Industrial and Organizational Psychology, 3,* 20–23.

Yost, P. R., Yoder, M. P., Chung, H. H., & Voetmann, K. R. (2015). Narratives at work: Story arcs, themes, voice, and lessons that shape organizational life. *Consulting Psychology Journal: Practice and Research, 67,* 163–188.

9

Seek and Ye Shall Learn

Exploring the Multiple Links of Learning Agility and Feedback Seeking

Seymour Adler and Rachel F. Neiman

—What got you here won't get you there.
　　　　—Marshall Goldsmith, leadership coach and consultant

For almost 100 years, our field has recognized the role of feedback in improving human performance (e.g., Blum & Naylor, 1968). Feedback is the mechanism through which leaders can learn the impact of their behaviors on performance-relevant outcomes. Through the experience of receiving feedback, leaders learn the relationship between the effort they invest in a task and the likelihood that task is performed effectively. They learn whether their decisions, and the reasoning applied to produce those decisions, resulted in desired outcomes. Simply put, feedback provides answers to the question, How am I doing? From which leaders can learn how to perform better in the future.

Feedback comes to leaders in many forms. Their own managers are expected to provide employees with timely and accurate feedback. Stakeholders of all sorts—peers, direct reports, customers—are potential sources of feedback. Leaders often generate their own feedback from observing and assessing their work. "My last team meeting did not go well; I did all the talking," and "I really like the tone of this email I wrote" are examples of self-reflections that leaders experience at work every day. Financial reporting, production records, engagement surveys, and sales numbers are all examples of potential feedback, increasingly provided in real time and at great frequency through modern reporting technologies.

Seymour Adler and Rachel F. Neiman, Seek and Ye Shall Learn In: *The Age of Agility.* Edited by: Veronica Schmidt Harvey and Kenneth P. De Meuse, Oxford University Press (2021). © Oxford University Press.
DOI: 10.1093/oso/9780190085353.003.0009

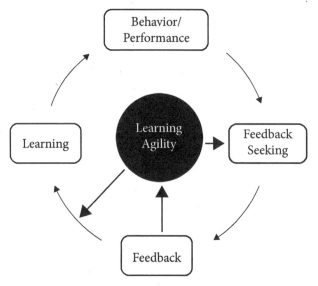

Figure 9.1 Multiple links of learning agility and feedback.

Structure of This Chapter

We begin our discussion of the linkages between learning agility and performance feedback by setting out three clear propositions:

- First, and as amply documented in this volume, learning agility reflects a capacity and motivation *to learn from experience.*
- Correspondingly, every feedback event provides an *opportunity* for experience-based learning to occur.
- And finally, feedback, from whatever the source, *conveys information* about performance in the widest sense—about performance-related behaviors or performance outcomes or both.

In this chapter, we explore the multiple roles that learning agility plays in feedback processes within the organizational context. Our chapter is explicitly focused on the learning agility of the feedback *recipient*, although through that lens, we also have observations and recommendations for feedback providers and for organizational practices.

In our view, there are at least three distinct pathways through which learning agility and feedback relate, as illustrated in Figure 9.1. Each of these pathways has different implications for individual learning and, ultimately, for organizational practices intended to foster learning from experience.

One pathway describes the impact of individual differences in learning agility on feedback *seeking*. The key question we explore here is, Under what circumstances are those high in learning agility more likely than those low in learning agility to actively *seek* performance feedback?

A second potential path in the learning agility–feedback relationship views learning agility as a *moderator* of the effect of feedback on subsequent learning. Here, the focus is on the influence of individual differences in learning agility on the degree to which feedback is subsequently internalized by the recipient and ultimately produces behavior change. The key question here is, Under what conditions are those high in learning agility more, or less, likely to actually *learn* from the feedback received, relative to those low in learning agility?

A third facet of the learning agility–feedback interplay pertains to the *content* of the feedback message itself. If, indeed, feedback is an opportunity to learn from experience, perhaps learning agility itself can be enhanced by encouraging employees through feedback to become more agile learners. Here, the focus of our discussion is on defining the agile mindsets and behaviors on which feedback messages can focus in order to promote a leader's learning agility.

Feedback Seeking

Feedback seeking in organizations has been a subject of research since Ashford and Cumming's (1983) early exploration of the topic. In this pioneering work, Ashford and Cummings identified the following two primary feedback-seeking strategies used by organizational members: (a) inquiring and (b) monitoring. Through inquiring, people directly elicit feedback from a source. Through monitoring, people infer feedback by intentionally observing potential sources of feedback in their social and physical environment. These two channels represent mechanisms through which people proactively obtain information from which they can potentially learn. Ashford and Cummings suggested that although inquiry is more direct and likely more informative, employees very often rely on monitoring because they perceive that directly inquiring may lead to social embarrassment. Yet, information inferred from monitoring—including trying to learn vicariously from observing when others are rewarded or punished (Weiss, 1977)—can lead to gross misinterpretations (Van Maanen & Schein, 1979). For instance, a leader may conclude it was the hours put in at the office, rather than the quality of work output, that led to a colleague's promotion. Organizations can and should encourage more transparent, accurate, inquiry-based feedback seeking. They can accomplish it (in part) by lowering the perceived risks and costs often associated with direct inquiry.

Since Ashford and Cumming's original work (1983), more nuanced taxonomies have emerged to describe the channels used by employees to seek feedback in organizations. In one such taxonomy, Miller and Jablin (1991) differentiated between direct and indirect inquiry. In the case of direct inquiry, the intent of the feedback seeker is clear to the provider (e.g., "So tell me, how do you think I'm doing?"). In the indirect case, the intent is more subtle (e.g., following a joint presentation given with a colleague, you turn to your boss and casually remark, "Looks like Maya did a great job, no?" as an attempt to actually elicit feedback on one's own performance). The indirect approach is often used to help mitigate loss-of-face risk compared to more direct inquiry.

Similarly, Miller and Jablin (1991) further distinguished two types of monitoring: (a) the overt approach (as when "shadowing" a colleague) and (b) a covert approach, such as what they refer to as "surveillance" (e.g., unobtrusively watching a colleague run a team meeting). Both of these monitoring strategies represent attempts to obtain information about how others perform as a basis of better evaluating one's own performance. Of course, how useful monitoring the performance of others will be as a basis for self-appraisal depends on how accurately leaders are interpreting their observations. Do they think the evident success of a colleague's board presentation was due to the expensive suit he wore, the joke he told to warm up the crowd, or the logical way he built a business case? Clearly, monitoring the performance of others in order to assess one's own performance risks misattribution and misinterpretation.

Feedback is more likely to be proactively sought if a leader expects the feedback to be delivered in ways that are positive and supportive. However, it does not necessarily mean that people will avoid seeking feedback if they expect that feedback will be negative, despite what some have claimed (Buckingham & Goodall, 2019). To the contrary, empirical results indicate that many leaders are motivated to seek feedback specifically when they anticipate the message to be unfavorable. This is especially true when the feedback source is perceived to be credible, the feedback is of high quality, and the feedback is delivered in a considerate manner (Steelman & Rutkowski, 2004). Hence, one of the core people management competencies required of feedback providers at all levels in an organization is skill at delivering negative feedback in credible, sensitive, and constructive ways.

Learning Agility and Feedback Seeking

Feedback Seeking and the Motivation to Learn

As we have seen throughout this volume, those high in learning agility are generally more motivated and open to learning from experience. Davis and Fedor (1998) identified four different motives driving those high in learning agility to actively seek opportunities to learn through feedback. First, feedback provides information that helps them determine the relative importance of different *performance goals* and the potential relative costs and rewards associated with achieving those goals. Second, information communicated through feedback reduces *uncertainty* about which behaviors are most likely to help achieve personal and organizational goals.

As a third driver, feedback makes it possible for leaders to experience a *sense of accomplishment* by having the effectiveness of their performance confirmed externally and acknowledged. Of course, it comes with the attendant risk that feedback will leave the leader with feelings of failure. Finally, Festinger's (1954) landmark social comparison theory highlighted the fundamental human need for *self-evaluation* to establish a sense of the level of one's own effectiveness. The need for self-evaluation can be met through direct feedback or absolute metrics of performance. But, in the absence of available feedback against an established metric, a sense of one's own effectiveness is often achieved through social comparison with relevant others in their environment.

Maximizing the Informational Value of Feedback

Active feedback seeking is likely to yield feedback with higher informational value in satisfying these motives (DeRue, Ashford, & Myers, 2012). Leaders who actively seek feedback, rather than passively waiting to receive feedback, are more likely to get feedback of higher quality and accuracy (Ashford & Tsui, 1991). Feedback that is actively sought is often more valuable to the recipient because it is likely to contain negative information—specific areas where performance fell short. Researchers have found that feedback providers are less inhibited about sharing the negative because the employee has actively "asked for it" (e.g., DeNisi & Sockbeson, 2018).

Due to these motivational forces, individuals high in learning agility are likely to perceive feedback opportunities to be especially valuable. Consequently, we expect there would be a meaningful correlation between learning agility and feedback-seeking activity. However, there is virtually no research that directly tests the causal relationship between individual differences in measures of learning agility and the intensity of feedback-seeking behavior.

Several scholars have looked at several individual difference attributes conceptually close to and, in some cases, empirically correlated with learning agility (see summary in DeRue et al., 2012). One such attribute, much discussed by talent management practitioners, is the *growth mindset* or *learning goal orientation* of the leader (Vandewalle, Nerstad, & Dysvik, 2019). Those with a strong growth mindset are oriented to focus on "learning goals" (e.g., What can I learn from this experience that will contribute to mastery?) rather than "performance goals" (i.e., Did I succeed or fail against my performance goal on this task?). Research by Carol Dweck (2016) and others has shown that individuals who believe their talents are malleable and can be developed by being open and attentive to input from others tend to achieve more than those who, in contrast, believe that their performance is determined by a fixed set of capabilities. When experiencing failure, those with a growth mindset reflect more on the experience and expend more effort determining why they failed than those with a fixed mindset. Further, they demonstrate strong resilience after failure. Simply put, those with a growth mindset put more energy into learning from their experiences. Their goals are less about using feedback to determine if they were successful or not and more about what they can learn from the feedback to be more effective in the future.

Consistent with what would be expected of those with high learning agility, in a longitudinal study of the relationship between type of goal orientation and feedback-seeking behavior, VandeWalle and Cummings (1997) found that learning goal orientation was positively related to the degree of feedback seeking, while performance goal orientation was negatively related to feedback seeking. These relationships were mediated by the perceived net value of seeking feedback. In other words, those with a learning goal orientation anticipated better informational return from feedback.

Similarly, in a study of sales professionals, VandeWalle, Ganesan, Challagalla, and Brown (2000) identified perception of net value as a mediator of the relationship between learning goal orientation and feedback seeking. They found that those high in learning goal orientation perceived the value of feedback more positively and the cost of seeking feedback less negatively than those low in learning goal orientation. Hence, the overall cost–benefit ratio of feedback-seeking effort is likely stronger and more positive for those high in learning agility. A meta-analysis conducted by Anseel, Beatty, Shen, Lievens, and Sackett (2015) found those with a learning orientation frequently seek feedback, particularly negative feedback. Similarly, Ashford, De Stobbeleir, and Nujella (2016) observed those high in learning agility were likely to place greater weight on the learning opportunity feedback provides and therefore often seek feedback, even in the face of the risk of receiving negative feedback.

The role of a growth mindset on feedback seeking is not limited to the search for feedback from managers (Heslin, VandeWalle, & Latham, 2006). In one study, managers with a growth mindset were more likely than those with a fixed mindset, or performance goal orientation, to actively seek performance feedback from their own direct reports.

On the other side of the feedback dyad, Heslin et al. (2006) also found that managers were more likely to *give* feedback to those they saw as having a growth mindset and less likely to provide feedback to those viewed as having a performance, or fixed, mindset. This is likely due to manager expectations about the greater efficacy of their feedback efforts based on implicit assumptions that those seen as having a learning goal orientation are likely to actually appreciate and apply the feedback provided. A concern here is that managers may be making inaccurate judgments about the mindset of their employees, which in turn may inappropriately influence the frequency and quality of feedback provided them.

One practical implication of this body of research—one that it seems leading organizations such as American Express and others have embraced—is that training in the characteristics of a growth mindset can stimulate all employees to be more open to learning through feedback and can stimulate managers to be more effective in stimulating more active feedback seeking. Performance management training today in these companies includes teaching managers how to frame feedback sessions as opportunities to explore lessons that might be extracted from examining past performance. Managers are taught how to encourage their employees to engage in deep self-reflection. They likewise are encouraged to project a belief in their direct reports' capacity to grow and improve during feedback sessions.

In their review of the feedback-seeking literature, Ashford et al. (2016) highlighted several attributes related to learning agility that impact feedback-seeking behavior, including innovative cognitive style (De Stobbeleir, Ashford, & Buyens, 2011) and feedback orientation (Dahling, Chau, & O'Malley, 2012; Linderbaum & Levy, 2010). Those individuals high in feedback orientation perceive feedback to have greater utility (Whitaker & Levy, 2012). Drawing on the five-factor model of personality, Krasman (2010) found that Openness to Experience was correlated with the use of observational approaches to feedback seeking. Further, those high in Openness to Experience were more likely to reflect on their observations of the social environment, including the way others react to them, in order to extract feedback information. In contrast, Openness to Experience in this study was unrelated to more direct, inquiry-based approaches for seeking feedback.

Learning Agility and Feedback Seeking: Some Open Questions

While growth mindset, openness to experience, and other similar constructs may be important correlates of learning agility, future research on learning agility and feedback seeking would benefit from the systematic use of measures intended to directly assess the learning agility construct. In addition, future research on the effect of learning agility on feedback-seeking behavior needs to more systematically examine factors that may moderate or mediate that relationship. The discussion that follows concerns some of the factors that future researchers might further explore.

Type of Feedback-Seeking Behavior

As noted, proactive inquiry in seeking feedback can be direct or indirect. It can involve paying more attention to available physical sources (e.g., metrics, gauges, monitors) or being mindful of social cues in the environment (e.g., What in a colleague's behavior is praised or criticized?). Consequently, the feedback seeking of those high in learning agility may be expressed in a wide range of behaviors, all with the same intent—to learn. The permutations of feedback type, source, frequency, timing, sign preference (positive or negative), environmental characteristics, and other factors need to be carefully teased out and individually examined empirically to better understand the factors governing *which* of the available feedback-seeking behaviors is most likely to be employed (VandeWalle, 2003). This in turn will have implications for organizations as they create alternate feedback channels that attempt to meet the needs of different employee segments.

Feedback Expectations

Those high in learning agility are likely to proactively solicit or more closely monitor sources of feedback information to the extent that they perceive there will be a valuable informational "yield" commensurate with their effort (VandeWalle et al., 2000). The pursuit of feedback often requires a significant investment of time and effort, whether it is scheduling more time with one's boss or expending more effort and time gathering details of production or sales reports. Beyond the expenditure of time and effort, the emotional investment of risking loss of face or an eroded sense of self-efficacy also must be weighed. Thus, it is important to consider how the expected value of feedback functions as a moderator of the relationship between learning agility and feedback seeking.

Early on, Ashford and Cummings (1983) pointed to the approach–avoidance conflict leaders may experience around seeking feedback. On the one hand, there is a desire to seek accurate and helpful feedback as a basis for improvement and ultimate success. In part, that means trying to leverage available opportunities for receiving accurate and helpful negative feedback. On the other hand, there is the natural desire for maintaining positive self-esteem and avoiding the negative. In addition, overtly expressed or concretely documented negative information on performance can damage the leader's brand within the organization. Leaders may well want to avoid the consequences of a tarnished brand on their long-term career prospects. We hypothesize that those low in learning agility will be likely to demonstrate behavioral defensiveness by avoiding feedback altogether or limit their search for feedback information, especially when negative feedback is anticipated.

Organizations need to experiment with ways of changing the calculus of feedback-seeking risk, particularly for those low in learning agility. One method for affecting this calculus is to ensure that feedback providers are skillful in conveying feedback in constructive—rather than in ego-threatening—ways. Indeed, many organizations incorporate role play feedback sessions as part of performance feedback training to hone these skills. They teach models like GROW (goal, reality, options, wrap-up), SBI (situation, behavior, impact), or Pause-To-Talk in performance management workshops as techniques for reducing defensiveness, as well as to encourage open reflection on the potential lessons to be learned from feedback conversations. Some organizations—too few in our view—actually build feedback role play exercises into promotional assessments to ensure that leaders possess these skills prior to being entrusted with responsibility for their teams.

Another potential approach for reframing this calculus is by providing choice in how leaders access feedback. For example, in many organizations 360 feedback or engagement survey reports are distributed simultaneously to leaders and their managers. This approach may be seen as a threat, provoking a defensive (rather than reflective) reaction to learning from the feedback among those low in learning agility. A better method might be to distribute such feedback reports only to the leaders themselves. Leaders then can be encouraged at their own discretion and timing to extract insights or selective individual results to share with their managers. Similarly, leaders can be given the choice of accessing or ignoring available normative performance information, using a "pull" rather than "push" approach. Giving leaders a measure of control over the feedback channels they access and how public their feedback becomes can help mitigate the risk of receiving negative performance information.

Finally, DeNisi and Sockbeson (2018) raised the interesting question of what happens when the feedback employees receive does not match the type or content of feedback they initially sought. Would those with high learning agility be more, or less, affected by that disappointment in guiding the channels and sources used in their subsequent feedback-seeking attempts?

Source

Whom do leaders turn to when seeking feedback? Research suggests that the answer is context specific (i.e., those high in learning agility are likely to turn to sources who have high yield, relative to effort, for producing accurate performance-relevant information). For example, De Stobbeleir and

Ashford (2014) found that leaders were more likely to seek feedback from a peer the more that leaders felt their own performance and that of the peer were mutually interdependent.

Do those high, rather than low, in learning agility apply different criteria to determine their target for feedback seeking? Are they more prepared to risk their reputation or blows to their ego for the sake of asking for feedback from a senior executive who has observed them delivering a high-stakes presentation? Will those lower in learning agility require a source that is perceived to provide a higher level of psychological safety to encourage more active feedback seeking (Edmondson & Lei, 2014)?

Competing Learning Channels

One of the primary drivers of feedback seeking in a given context is the degree to which employees feel they lack critical performance-related information, information they expect feedback to provide them. Carette and Anseel (2012) have termed this gap "epistemic motivation." Research generally shows the presence of such gaps enhances motivation to learn from experience. However, an open question is whether epistemic motivation will consistently lead to more active feedback seeking. After all, to satisfy their learning needs, agile learners have multiple learning channels to leverage in the organizational context beyond just feedback (e.g., training, new assignments, mentoring, and self-directed learning such as reading, TED Talks, and podcasts). Under what set of conditions will *feedback* be the learning channel of choice? And, how can feedback best be leveraged to support the learning experience of other channels?

Learning Agility and Responsiveness to Feedback

The Impact of Feedback on Subsequent Performance

In a now-classic meta-analysis of feedback interventions, Kluger and DeNisi (1996) showed feedback interventions typically—but not inevitably—improve performance. More specifically, they found that roughly a third of the effect sizes are actually negative, largely because feedback in those cases focused on the self rather than on the task itself. Based on an earlier narrative literature review by Ilgen, Fisher, and Taylor (1979), the positive impact of feedback is mediated by what is learned about task performance through the provision of performance feedback. Hence, it is reasonable to expect that the postfeedback performance of those with strong learning agility would be more strongly impacted than those low in learning agility by the receipt of feedback information concerning their task performance, both because they are more active feedback seekers and because they are more open to the learning opportunities provided by receiving feedback.

Consistent with those expectations, Braddy, Sturm, Atwater, Smither, and Fleenor (2013) found that individual differences in the degree to which people had a positive orientation to feedback predicted acceptance of feedback. In turn, the strength of an individual's positive orientation toward feedback correlated with the strength of his or her implicit beliefs that personal attributes are malleable rather than fixed (Levy, Stroessner, & Dweck, 1998). It seems reasonable to expect those with strong learning agility, insofar as they also ascribe to those implicit beliefs, will seize feedback opportunities when available and apply the lessons they can learn from feedback to enhance subsequent performance.

Research on the role of feedback seeking in postfeedback performance improvement provides a decidedly mixed pattern of results. Anseel et al.'s (2015) meta-analysis indicated that the relationship between seeking feedback and subsequent performance improvement was weak and inconsistent. The authors themselves noted that this finding is counter to both prevailing theory and prevailing practitioner assumptions. The rather surprisingly inconsistent findings have in turn stimulated a search for moderating and mediating factors that might provide a more granular understanding of the likely links between feedback seeking and subsequent performance improvement. That search has led to the emergence of a better, but still evolving, understanding of both individual and contextual factors that might interact with learning agility to moderate the relationship between feedback and postfeedback performance improvement.

Learning Agility and Feedback Responsiveness

Very explicitly, De Meuse, Lim, and Rao (2019), in their *TALENTx7®* *Assessment* of learning agility, introduced *feedback responsiveness* as one of seven factors comprising learning agility. DeMeuse and his colleagues defined feedback responsiveness as "the extent to which individuals solicit, listen to, and accept personal feedback from others, carefully consider its merits, and subsequently take corrective action for performance improvement" (De Meuse, Lim, & Rao, 2019, p. 12). Linderbaum and Levy (2010) identified a similar construct they termed "feedback receptivity," reflecting an openness to learning from feedback received. Their Feedback Orientation Scale measures individual differences in the degree to which employees view feedback as useful, are sensitive to how others perceive them, and feel effective and accountable for using the feedback they receive.

Again, there is virtually no empirical research directly examining measures of learning agility as moderators of the impact of feedback on subsequent behavioral change and performance improvement. However, here also, there are studies of constructs akin to learning agility that suggest a key moderating role for learning agility, indicating that those with stronger learning agility are more likely to be responsive to the feedback experience. For example, using their Feedback Orientation Scale, Linderbaum and Levy (2010) found a .40 correlation of positive feedback orientation with learning goal orientation in a sample of employed undergraduate students. Similarly, Gong, Wang, Huang, and Cheung (2017) found those with a stronger learning goal orientation more actively seek feedback generally and negative feedback specifically. In addition, they observed negative feedback about one's own performance had a stronger positive effect on subsequent performance improvement than positive feedback. Supporting this notion is a laboratory study by Moser, Schroder, Heeter, Moran, and Lee (2011). These researchers monitored the brain activity of those with a growth mindset or a performance mindset while performing a multistep learning task and found those with a growth mindset processed mistakes more deeply neurologically, which allowed them to take corrective action more quickly.

Longitudinal research by Cron, Slocum, VandeWalle, and Fu (2005) helps explicate the role of emotions, one of the key mediators of the feedback–learning relationship. In their study, participants received negative feedback on their initial performance. Those who had a weak learning goal orientation were more likely to have intensely negative emotional reactions as a result of the negative feedback and were more likely to lower their performance goals moving forward. In contrast, for those with a strong learning goal orientation, negative feedback was *un*correlated with the intensity of negative emotional reactions or with the level of self-set goals established for the next performance period. In other words, it would seem that negative feedback is less likely to impact the emotions and self-efficacy of those with stronger learning agility.

In another longitudinal study explicating some of the mediators of the feedback–performance linkage, VandeWalle, Cron, and Slocum (2001) found that after receiving feedback on their test performance, students with a stronger learning goal orientation subsequently demonstrated stronger self-efficacy, invested greater task effort, and set higher performance goals, all of which resulted in higher subsequent performance than for those with a lower learning goal orientation.

In their classic study entitled, "The Utility of Humility," Weiss and Knight (1980) showed how individuals lower in self-confidence were more quickly able to determine the right answer to complex problems. The authors observed it was a result of their being more open to helpful feedback than those higher in self-confidence. Similarly, in a series of studies Brockner (1988) identified situations where those lower in self-esteem were more responsive to feedback and more likely to apply feedback to improve subsequent performance. In the case of those low in self-esteem, it is hypothesized that self-doubt or felt uncertainty drives greater openness to the influence of externally provided information. Brockner (1983) termed this responsiveness to feedback—indeed to a wide range of social influences—"behavioral plasticity," rooted in the notion of epistemic motivation, the need to reduce uncertainty.

The Role of Cognitive Processes in Responsiveness to Feedback

Our field has long known of the powerful impact of general mental ability on learning. Here, also, we would expect those individuals with high learning aptitude—as reflected in strong general mental ability (g)—would more quickly learn from the full range of learning experiences to which they are exposed over time (Schmidt, Hunter, & Outerbridge, 1986), including the feedback experience. On the other hand, some attributes of those with strong mental ability—including a stronger sense of self-confidence in situations with complex intellectual challenges—may actually reduce their openness to learn from experience. Perhaps these offsetting attributes explain why the correlation between measures of g and of learning agility tends to be weak or inconsistent.

Beyond *g*, DeRue et al. (2012) suggested agile learners are capable of deploying a broad range of cognitive processes that may help them better leverage feedback. Correspondingly, managers should be taught how to communicate feedback in ways that best stimulate these cognitive processes in order to promote effective learning. For instance, those high in learning agility have a stronger ability to vividly conjure, and hence be more mentally prepared for, potential future work scenarios. Managers could take advantage of this ability by couching feedback in terms of rich and detailed descriptions of situations where the employee has struggled in the past, so the employee can start thinking of better strategies for dealing with those challenges in the future. DeRue et al. (2012) also cited research demonstrating the advantage of stimulating employees to engage in counterfactual thinking in order to enrich the impact of feedback. Managers should learn the technique of emphasizing the "what might have been" when providing feedback on a performance outcome as a way of stimulating employees to consider alternative courses of action they might have not considered in the past but might in the future.

Other cognitive attributes reflecting learning agility have been found to relate to responsiveness to feedback. As an example, Zmigrod, Zmigrod, Rentfrow, and Robbins (2019) recently found that a measure of intellectual humility correlated with cognitive flexibility. They described intellectual humility as an openness to revising one's viewpoints and demonstrating a respect for others' viewpoints. In turn, the authors found that the interaction of measures of cognitive flexibility and intelligence predicted scores on the intellectual humility measure.

The role of cognitive abilities may become even more critical in situations rich in feedback (DeRue et al., 2012). For example, some organizations have embraced a continuous feedback model in which mobile apps regularly collect and transmit to the employee evaluations and observations across multiple performance dimensions from a wide range of stakeholders (peers, direct reports, customers, etc.). In these settings, very frequent (weekly, or even more frequent) feedback discussions between employees and their managers are mandated. At the same time, other organizations use wearables or other electronic recording devices to provide a steady stream of input concerning employee activities, environmental conditions, and biometrics. Some organizations provide leaders with color-coded dashboards, dynamically tracking in real-time multiple "soft" (e.g., engagement scores of their teams) and "hard" (dropped calls, sales per product line) performance metrics. In such situations, the employee may receive much granular feedback from multiple sources across different channels with great frequency. This might well require strong cognitive skills just to sort through the complex information in order to grasp and apply the actionable messages to enhance their performance (DeRue & Wellman, 2009).

Learning Agility and Responsiveness to Feedback: Some Open Questions

Here as well, there are open questions that it is hoped will be addressed by future researchers. A few areas that might merit further investigation include the issues discussed next.

Mediating Mechanisms

While there is solid evidence that learning agility predicts leader performance (De Meuse, 2019; Hezlett & Kuncel, 2012), the mediating role of feedback in this process is largely unexplored. What are the dimensions and attributes of the feedback event that promote learning? Type, source, frequency, timing, sign, setting, and many other factors need to be individually examined empirically for their impact on learning (VandeWalle, 2003). As an illustration, feedback frequency is an especially important variable to explore as organizations increasingly embrace the "continuous listening" model. Perhaps, a key factor explaining the impact of feedback on performance is that agile learners simply provoke more frequent feedback because they engage more diligently in deliberate practice, creating more learning events.

Perception Versus Reality

As with so many other psychological phenomena, it is unknown whether it is the *objective content* of the feedback or the *perceived value* of the feedback experience that has the greater impact on subsequent performance. What is the role of perceptions about feedback? Exploring this question, Asumeng (2013) examined self-awareness as a potential mediating mechanism in the feedback–performance linkage. He hypothesized that the way feedback promotes performance improvement is by raising self-awareness. In a study of 142 Ghanaian managers across industries, he found that the impact on subsequent performance of upward feedback from subordinates on a multisource survey was not mediated by a manager's self-awareness. However, the manager's *perceptions* about the usefulness of subordinate feedback did influence subsequent performance through a significant mediating effect for self-awareness. The interplay of recipient perceptions of feedback versus the reality of the feedback information is an interesting one, especially if it turns out that those with stronger learning agility are more inclined to see every feedback event as potentially useful. This raises the question: What can feedback providers do to ensure their feedback messages are perceived as maximally useful?

Past Versus Future Focus

One key question discussed in the literature is whether feed*back* or feed*forward* has more impact. Traditionally, the focus of theory and research in this area has been on feed*back*, information on past performance-related behaviors or outcomes (e.g., Ilgen et al., 1979; Kluger & DeNisi, 1996). This line of research has focused on the relative impact of positive and negative feedback. However, Kluger in particular (e.g., Kluger & Lehmann, 2018) has emphasized the greater impact of feedforward, communication that focuses on what to do and what to avoid in the future (Gong et al., 2017).

Kluger argued that feedforward empowers employees to discover their own insights on performance and capability enhancement, under the guidance of appreciative inquiry from their managers. This discovery is more likely to lead to richer learning, changing how employees act in facing future challenges. Further, Kluger pointed out that patient and attentive listening by managers creates a safe space for employees and a strong level of attachment that increases receptivity to feedback. In general, Kluger suggests that using feedforward is very likely to generate behavioral change.

An open question is whether those individuals higher in learning agility are more motivated to internalize feedback or feedforward opportunities relative to their lower learning agility counterparts. We would hypothesize, based on the motivational forces driving feedback seeking outlined by Davis and Fedor (1998), that those high in learning agility would care less about past accomplishments. They would care more about understanding future-focused expectations and pathways to success moving forward. Therefore, they are likely to find feedforward more actionable than feedback. However, this hypothesis obviously needs empirical testing.

The Role of Feedback in Learning to Be an Agile Learner

Nurturing Learning Agility

Feedback itself creates an opportunity to learn to be more learning agile. As we have argued, feedback is a learning opportunity. To that end, we suggest that leaders should be provided with feedback on the behaviors that characterize high learning agility. In Chapter 1, De Meuse and Harvey point out that direct managers, as the prime source of feedback, have a particularly important role in building learning agility for all leaders irrespective of their current level of learning agility. Indeed the "upside potential" of concerted efforts to provide feedback on learning agile behaviors is likely larger for those who are not yet strongly learning oriented.

One approach to crafting feedback that builds learning agility is to apply the manipulations used by social psychologists in experimental studies of learning—versus performance—goal orientation. In a recent study, Yeager et al. (2016) experimentally tested a wide range of interventions intended to build a growth mindset in an educational setting where students were transitioning to high school. Adapted to the organizational context, feedback messages might include

- providing leaders with particular examples from the past where they themselves demonstrated strong learning agility;
- prompting leaders to reflect on their mindset that guided their past decisions—for instance, having concluded "I couldn't, because" rather than consider "I might have, if"; and
- comparing the leader's own behavior in various situations that had opportunities to learn from experience with that of others recognized as exemplary learners.

In the study by Yeager et al. (2016), interventions such as these had a significant effect on changing mindsets and enhancing subsequent student performance after their transition to high school.

Illustrative Agile Learning Behaviors

Kluger and DeNisi's meta-analysis (1996) demonstrated that the type of feedback most likely to induce positive performance improvement focuses on specific behaviors and not on the person. Therefore, feedback phrased as "you need to be more learning agile" is unlikely to promote behavior change. In contrast, feedback that specifies observable and actionable behaviors is far more likely to promote stronger learning agility. To that end, Box 9.1 presents observable behaviors reflective of agile learners on which employees at all levels should receive feedback. Several global organizations have deployed 360- or 180-feedback surveys incorporating these or similar lists of items to collect observations and provide structured, systematic feedback intended to promote learning agility as part of leadership development. Managers, coworkers, and others can be taught to incorporate them or a similar defined set of behaviors as elements in the performance feedback they provide.

It should be obvious that the key levers for employing feedback to develop learning agility are held by the manager. It is particularly important that manager training (and, perhaps, manager selection) ensures managers themselves are not locked into a fixed mindset. All individuals should deeply believe that each and every colleague has the *capacity* to learn, grow, change behavior, and enhance performance. To ensure that managers have the mindset that facilitates the provision of growth-oriented feedback, managers need exposure to the theory and practice of a learning goal mindset, and their mastery of that mindset needs to be systematically assessed through standardized tools.

Creating a Feedback-Rich Learning Culture

Design Imperatives

There is much talk about the importance of organizations nurturing a *culture* that is learning agile. This objective is seen as especially critical as organizations confront an increasingly VUCA (volatile, uncertain, complex, and ambiguous) environment. These environments require continuous learning at all levels to build a capacity for agile action. A core component of any learning culture is crafting a feedback-rich environment and providing an abundance of learning experiences from which leaders can grow (Batista, 2013; Schwartz, 2018). In this section, we turn our attention to factors that can help organizations and their leaders create such an environment. Based on what we have discussed previously, there are several levers that should be considered.

Box 9.1 Illustrative Learning Agility Behaviors

Seeks Challenge and Novelty

- Grasps opportunities to gain new knowledge and skills
- Takes on challenging assignments out of own comfort zone
- At own initiative, asks to take on novel work assignments, even where there is risk of failure
- Persists in solving problems by adjusting approaches or methods that are not working
- Experiments with novel approaches rather than only using established methods
- Regularly makes suggestions for improving products or processes

Gains Insights From Self and Others

- Regularly asks questions to gain insight from the experiences of others
- Takes time to reflect on own work behaviors
- Seeks feedback from others to understand areas for potential growth
- Initiates debrief sessions to identify "lessons learned" from projects or other work situations
- Actively seeks out support or advice from others when in challenging situations
- Consistently seeks feedback even if it is likely to be negative

Lives to Learn

- Voluntarily attends seminars, meetings, or conferences to increase knowledge and skills
- Frequently reads industry periodicals, journals, and publications
- Attends professional training or learning events even when not required

Availability

A feedback-rich culture is one in which feedback information is accessible across multiple channels and frequent opportunities (Steelman, Levy, & Snell, 2004). Laudably, many organizations have moved away from viewing performance feedback as a once-a-year formally mandated performance discussion between a manager and his or her direct reports. There is a recognition that effective manager feedback should be embedded in ongoing dialogue, with frequent—even weekly—scheduled touchpoints and informal "Pause-To-Talk" moments in between. In addition, as noted, some organizations have introduced mobile apps in which multiple stakeholders are prompted to submit observations and recommendations intended to provide feedback and feedforward to colleagues. An increasingly popular version of this approach at the leadership level is the use of short "pulse" surveys, which provide managers with frequent feedback on their team's current (and often oscillating) levels of engagement. Note that these initiatives may be more valuable for those initially low in learning agility than for those who, having strong learning agility, are more likely to proactively seek feedback even when it is not easily available.

Value

Organizations should ensure that feedback has strong personal and instrumental value to leaders, especially to those with lower learning agility who are less likely to proactively seek feedback. This means ensuring that recognition and rewards are tightly and visibly tied to performance improvement. Leaders should perceive a direct link between opportunities for accessing feedback and the likelihood of their receiving those rewards and that recognition by performing more effectively. The organization needs to emphasize that, especially in this VUCA environment, learning from the feedback experience is instrumental to career advancement. What organizations need to make abundantly clear is captured in the well-known quotation from Marshall Goldsmith in the epigraph: "What got you here, won't get you there!"

Credibility

Source credibility refers to the expertise and trustworthiness of the feedback source (Steelman et al., 2004). Source credibility has been shown to moderate the relationship between feedback and the motivation to implement the feedback (Steelman & Rutkowski, 2004). Not surprisingly, the perceived competence of the feedback source makes it more likely that feedback will be sought from a source and that the feedback received will be used (Fedor, Eder, & Buckley, 1989).

Organizations should invest in building the skills and mindsets necessary to prepare managers to more (a) consistently observe the performance of their direct reports, (b) objectively and insightfully analyze that performance against clear expectations and standards, and (c) credibly communicate that analysis to the leader in order to maximize learning. To enhance the credibility of multisource feedback, *all* sources require similar training. Especially when it comes to peer or subordinate feedback, perceived objectivity is key to perceived credibility (Campion, Campion, & Campion, 2019). Finally, organizations should consider the longer range consequences of feedback sources that lack credibility. The experience of receiving biased, incomplete, and/or erroneous feedback may undermine the credibility of that source and, by extension, the trustworthiness of the culture more generally as a source of performance-relevant information.

Delivery

To promote a learning culture, organizations also need to upgrade not only the quality of feedback—the accuracy, granularity, actionability—but also the manner in which that feedback is delivered. Feedback, whether positive or negative, is more likely to be internalized if it is delivered in a constructive, supportive manner. Many organizations have embraced SBI or similar models to structure feedback communication that is nonthreatening and leaves the recipient open to listening to, and acting on, the feedback message. We noted that Kluger (e.g., Kluger & Lehmann, 2018) has strongly advocated for a future-focused, feedforward approach to conducting performance discussions, with an emphasis on dialogue and open and appreciative inquiry. Supportive delivery is likely to be especially important in encouraging both seeking and learning for those *lower* in learning agility. In particular, the ability to deliver negative feedback supportively and sensitively appears key when communicating negative feedback to those low in learning agility. These leaders have a natural predisposition to avoid negative feedback and often fail to leverage the greater informational value of negative feedback to performance improvement (Carette & Anseel, 2012).

Is It Better to Be Positive?

Buckingham and Goodall (2019), Rock and Schwartz (2006), and others have argued that to promote a genuine learning culture, feedback should build on strengths and stay primarily positive. They claimed that feedback typically is "toxic," raises dysfunctional anxieties and fear on the part of employees, and fails to enhance performance. Evaluative feedback of any kind, they contended, triggers natural neurologically determined defensive reactivity that comes with being criticized. As we have seen throughout this chapter, the empirical research on feedback fails to support any of these claims at the aggregate level, although the effects these authors described are undoubtedly true for select populations and modes of feedback.

Naturally, feedback—especially when negative—that lacks credibility and quality and is communicated in an insensitive, blame-ridden manner is going to have harmful effects on recipients. Those with lower learning agility might indeed respond better to favorable feedback that encourages them to continue demonstrating successful behaviors, even if the informational value of that feedback would be enhanced by incorporating insights on areas requiring improvement. However, as we have seen, leaders high in learning agility are motivated to learn how to improve on past performance, whether it was good or bad.

While information on what one does well may be ego enhancing, learning what one needs to do better is typically more useful for enhancing performance (Finkelstein & Fishbach, 2012). Leaders who proactively seek feedback to figure out how to improve their performance take a less ego-involved orientation. Their response to feedback—especially negative feedback—is more productive than those who do not seek feedback (DeNisi & Sockbeson, 2018).

Inclusion

When attempting to foster a feedback-rich culture, it is critical to account for cultural backgrounds. People with different cultural backgrounds react differently to different types of feedback (e.g., Sully De Luque & Sommer, 2000). For example, leaders coming from collectivist cultures that emphasize the importance of social reputation may be less comfortable seeking feedback where there is a greater risk of public embarrassment and associated loss of face. For those from other cultural backgrounds, the type of feedback most likely to stimulate subsequent behavioral change might need to be very direct, detailed, and expressed in a forceful manner. But to leaders from different backgrounds, the same direct "no-holds-barred" approach to providing feedback might be viewed as microaggression. Blindness to these cultural differences can result in recipients avoiding, misinterpreting, or ignoring feedback, irrespective of their learning agility. An inclusive approach to feedback requires building the feedback-relevant cultural sensitivities of feedback providers, first and foremost, direct managers.

Taking a Multiprong Approach to Feedback-Rich Culture

Mandating a frequent cadence of feedback meetings, implementing state-of-the-art game-like feedback apps, rebranding performance management, and even enhanced people management training will, in our view, only have limited value transforming the organization's culture into one that is a genuine learning culture. The approach has to be more holistic in order to "move the needle." Organizations can create significantly more agile, feedback-rich learning cultures only by encouraging— indeed expecting and rewarding—leaders *at all levels* to proactively seek feedback to better equip themselves for future performance challenges. Organizations need to make a serious investment to upskill employees *at all levels* to provide each other high-quality, credible feedback through multiple channels in the spirit of collaboration, projecting an attitude that "we're all in this together." In that spirit, coworkers at all levels can feel psychologically safe as they share and receive objective, nuanced, actionable, task-focused performance feedback. At the individual level, all leaders need to take an inclusive orientation to feedback. They need to learn to adjust the feedback they provide to have positive impact for the particular recipient. Feedback for those initially low in learning agility, indeed, may need to focus at the start on the positive, on leveraging strengths. However, over time employees should learn to seek and accept negative feedback for its greater impact on learning from experience.

On a broader level, there is evidence that creating a culture of empowerment, participative decision-making, and trust engenders an environment that is richer in feedback and learning (Li & Qian, 2016). A genuine learning culture is built on an encompassing and empowering talent philosophy, a servant leadership style, low power distance, transparency, trust, and greater employee ownership of their own performance (e.g., Qian, Song, Jin, Wang, & Chen, 2018). Isolated and limited interventions intended to create an agile learning culture will have only limited value. But, as we have seen in this chapter, an environment that is feedback rich creates a dynamic learning flywheel that enhances the learning agility of all employees individually and of the organization collectively.

Conclusions

How can organizations best leverage feedback to accelerate learning from experience? We summarize this chapter with the following recommendations:

- Provide multiple channels and multiple opportunities for leaders to access feedback, recognizing people's diverse preferences and learning styles.
- Empower leaders to decide which channels to access and when, trusting them to be guided by the anticipated value of that channel.
- Build trust by auditing all channels of feedback rigorously to ensure validity and freedom from bias.
- Ensure—through assessment-based selection/promotion and training—that all feedback providers (managers, peers, other stakeholders) have effective feedback skill—the capacity to base feedback on insightful and acute observation of performance and to communicate that feedback in a constructive, sensitive, supportive manner.
- Ensure that feedback includes, where indicated, information about performance gaps.
- Transform the feedback conversation into active reflection on past performance as a basis for extracting learnings applicable to future performance.
- Frame feedback as an opportunity to engage in the active and continuous learning required to thrive in a dynamic environment with increasingly complex leadership challenges.

- Drive home the value of learning from feedback by explicitly linking rewards, recognition, and career advancement to improved performance.
- Target those who demonstrate lower levels of learning agility by incorporating feedback and programmatic developmental interventions with a specific focus on learning and internalizing the behaviors and mindsets that will build their learning agility.

In this VUCA world where "what got you here won't get you there," the role of feedback is critical. The capacity to foster a culture where feedback is perceived as valuable and easily accessible is a key enabler for leaders to learn from experience and enhance their individual, team's, and ultimately organizational performance.

References

Anseel, F., Beatty, A. S., Shen, W., Lievens, F., & Sackett, P. R. (2015). How are we doing after 30 years? A meta-analytic review of the antecedents and outcomes of feedback-seeking behavior. *Journal of Management, 41*(1), 318–348. https://doi.org/10.1177/0149206313484521

Ashford, S. J., & Cummings, L. L. (1983). Feedback as an individual resource: Personal strategies of creating information. *Organizational Behavior and Human Performance, 32*(3), 370–398. https://doi.org/10.1016/0030-5073(83)90156-3

Ashford, S. J., De Stobbeleir, K., & Nujella, M. (2016). To seek or not to seek: Is that the only question? Recent developments in feedback-seeking literature. *Annual Review of Organizational Psychology and Organizational Behavior, 3*(1), 213–239. https://doi.org/10.1146/annurev-orgpsych-041015-062314

Ashford, S. J., & Tsui, A. S. (1991). Self-regulation for managerial effectiveness: The role of active feedback seeking. *Academy of Management Journal, 34*(2), 251–280. https://psycnet.apa.org/doi/10.2307/256442

Asumeng, M. (2013). The effect of employee feedback-seeking on job performance: An empirical study. *International Journal of Management, 30*(1), 373–388.

Batista, E. (2013, December). Building a feedback-rich culture. *Harvard Business Review.* Retrieved from https://hbr.org/2013/12/building-a-feedback-rich-culture

Blum, M. L., & Naylor, J. C. (1968). *Industrial psychology.* New York, NY: Harper & Row.

Braddy, P. W., Sturm, R. E., Atwater, L. E., Smither, J. W., & Fleenor, J. W. (2013). Validating the feedback orientation scale in a leadership development context. *Group & Organization Management 38*(6), 690–716. https://doi.org/10.1177/1059601113508432

Brockner, J. (1983). Low self-esteem and behavioral plasticity: Some implications. In L. Wheeler & P. Shaver (Eds.), *Review of personality and social psychology* (Vol. 4, pp. 237–271). Beverly Hills, CA: Sage.

Brockner, J. (1988). *Self-esteem at work: Research, theory, and practice*. Lexington, MA: Lexington Books.

Buckingham, M., & Goodall, A. (2019, April). *The feedback fallacy*. *Harvard Business Review*. Retrieved from https://hbr.org/2019/03/the-feedback-fallacy

Campion, E. D. C., Campion, M. C., & Campion, M. A. (2019). Best practices when using 360 feedback for performance appraisal. In A. H. Church, D. W. Bracken, J. W. Fleenor, & D. Rose (Eds.), *The handbook of strategic 360 feedback* (pp. 19–60). Oxford, UK: Oxford University Press.

Carette, B., & Anseel, F. (2012). Epistemic motivation is what gets the learner started. *Industrial and Organizational Psychology, 5*(3), 306–309. https://doi.org/10.1111/j.1754-9434.2012.01451.x

Cron, W. L., Slocum, J. W., Jr., VandeWalle, D., & Fu, F. Q. (2005). The role of goal orientation on negative emotions and goal setting when initial performance falls short of one's performance goal. *Human Performance, 18*(1), 55–80. https://doi.org/10.1207/s15327043hup1801_3

Dahling, J. J., Chau, S. L., & O'Malley, A. (2012). Correlates and consequences of feedback orientation in organizations. *Journal of Management, 38*(2), 531–546. https://doi.org/10.1177/0149206310375467

Davis, W., & Fedor, D. B. (1998). *The role of self-esteem and self-efficacy in detecting responses to feedback*. 64 pp. US Department of Defense (DOD), Defense Technical Information Center (DTIC). https://doi.org/10.1037/e443592005-001

De Meuse, K. P. (2019). A meta-analysis of the relationship between learning agility and leader success. *Journal of Organizational Psychology, 19*(1), 25–34.

De Meuse, K. P., Lim, J., & Rao, R. (2019). *The development and validation of the TALENTx7° Assessment: A psychological measure of learning agility* (3rd Edition.). Shanghai, China: Leader's Gene Consulting.

DeNisi, A., & Sockbeson, C. E. S. (2018). Feedback sought vs. feedback given: A tale of two literatures. *Management Research: Journal of the Iberoamerican Academy of Management, 16*(4), 320–333. https://doi.org/10.1108/MRJIAM-09-2017-0778

DeRue, D. S., Ashford, S. J., & Myers, C. G. (2012). Learning agility: In search of conceptual clarity and theoretical grounding. *Industrial and Organizational Psychology, 5*(3), 258–279. https://doi.org/10.1111/j.1754-9434.2012.01444.x

DeRue, D. S., & Wellman, N. (2009). Developing leaders via experience: The role of developmental challenge, learning orientation, and feedback availability. *Journal of Applied Psychology, 94*(4), 859–875. https://doi.org/10.1037/a0015317

De Stobbeleir, K., & Ashford, S. J. (2014). The power of peers: Antecedents and outcomes of peer feedback seeking behavior. *Academy of Management Proceedings, 2014*, 37. https://doi.org/10.5465/ambpp.2014.37

De Stobbeleir, K. E. M., Ashford, S. J., & Buyens, D. (2011). Self-regulation of creativity at work: The role of feedback-seeking behavior in creative performance. *Academy of Management Journal, 54*(4), 811–831. https://doi.org/10.5465/amj.2011.64870144

Dweck, C. (2016). *Mindset*. New York, NY: Penguin Random House.

Edmondson, A. C., & Lei, Z. (2014). Psychological safety: The history, renaissance, and future of an interpersonal construct. *Annual Review of Organizational Psychology and Organizational Behavior, 1*(1), 23–43. https://doi.org/10.1146/annurev-orgpsych-031413-091305

Fedor, D. B., Eder, R. W., & Buckley, M. R. (1989). The contributory effects of supervisor intentions on subordinate feedback responses. *Organizational Behavior and Human Decision Processes, 44*(3), 396–414. https://doi.org/10.1016/0749-5978(89)90016-2

Festinger, L. (1954). A theory of social comparison processes. *Human Relations, 7*(2), 117–140. https://doi.org/10.1177/001872675400700202

Finkelstein, S. R., & Fishbach, A. (2012). Tell me what I did wrong: Experts seek and respond to negative feedback. *Journal of Consumer Research, 39*(1), 22–38. https://doi.org/10.1086/661934

Gong, Y., Wang, M., Huang, J.-C., & Cheung, S. Y. (2017). Toward a goal orientation-based feedback-seeking typology: Implications for employee performance outcomes. *Journal of Management, 43*(4), 1234–1260. https://doi.org/10.1177/0149206314551797

Heslin, P. A., VandeWalle, D., & Latham, G. P. (2006). Keen to help? Managers' implicit person theories and their subsequent employee coaching. *Personnel Psychology, 59*(4), 871–902. https://doi.org/10.1111/j.1744-6570.2006.00057.x

Hezlett, S. A., & Kuncel, N. R. (2012). Prioritizing the learning agility research agenda. *Industrial and Organizational Psychology, 5*(3), 296–301. https://doi.org/10.1111/j.1754-9434.2012.01449.x

Ilgen, D. R., Fisher, C. D., & Taylor, M. S. (1979). Consequences of individual feedback on behavior in organizations. *Journal of Applied Psychology, 64*(4), 349–371. https://doi.org/10.1037/0021-9010.64.4.349

Kluger, A. N., & DeNisi, A. (1996). The effects of feedback interventions on performance: A historical review, a meta-analysis, and a preliminary feedback intervention theory. *Psychological Bulletin, 119*(2), 254–284. https://doi.org/10.1037/0033-2909.119.2.254

Kluger, A. N., & Lehmann, M. (2018). Listening first, feedback later. *Management Research: Journal of the Iberoamerican Academy of Management, 16*(4), 343–352. https://doi.org/10.1108/MRJIAM-12-2017-0797

Krasman, J. (2010). The feedback-seeking personality: Big five and feedback-seeking behavior. *Journal of Leadership & Organizational Studies, 17*(1), 18–32. https://doi.org/10.1177/1548051809350895

Levy, S. R., Stroessner, S. J., and Dweck, C. S. (1998). Stereotype formation and endorsement: The role of implicit theories. *Journal of Personality and Social Psychology 74*(6), 1421–1436. https://doi.org/10.1037/0022-3514.74.6.1421

Li, X., & Qian, J. (2016). Stimulating employees' feedback-seeking behavior: The role of participative decision making. *Social Behavior and Personality: An International Journal, 44*(1), 1–8. https://doi.org/10.2224/sbp.2016.44.1.1

Linderbaum, B. A., & Levy, P. E. (2010). The development and validation of the feedback orientation scale (FOS). *Journal of Management, 36*(6), 1372–1405. https://doi.org/10.1177/0149206310373145

Miller, V. D., & Jablin, F. M. (1991). Information seeking during organizational entry: Influences, tactics, and a model of the process. *Academy of Management Review, 16*(1), 92–120. https://doi.org/10.5465/amr.1991.4278997

Moser, J. S., Schroder, H. S., Heeter, C., Moran, T. P., & Lee, Y. (2011). Mind your errors: Evidence for a neural mechanism linking growth mind-set to adaptive posterior adjustments. *Psychological Science 22*(12), 1484–1489. https://doi.org/10.1177/0956797611419520

Qian, J., Song, B., Jin, Z., Wang, B., & Chen, H. (2018). Linking empowering leadership to task performance, taking charge, and voice: The mediating role of feedback-seeking. *Frontiers in Psychology, 9*, 2025. https://doi.org/10.3389/fpsyg.2018.02025

Rock, D., & Schwartz, J. (2006, May 30). The neuroscience of leadership. *Strategy and Business*. Retrieved from https://www.strategy-business.com/article/06207

Schmidt, F. L., Hunter, J. E., & Outerbridge, A. N. (1986). Impact of job experience and ability on job knowledge, work sample performance, and supervisory ratings of job performance. *Journal of Applied Psychology, 71*, 432–439. https://doi.org/10.1037/0021-9010.71.3.432

Schwartz, T. (2018, March 7). Create a growth culture, not a performance-obsessed one. *Harvard Business Review*. Retrieved from https://hbr.org/2018/03/create-a-growth-culture-not-a-performance-obsessed-one

Steelman, L. A., Levy, P. E., & Snell, A. F. (2004). The feedback environment scale: Construct definition, measurement, and validation. *Educational and Psychological Measurement, 64*(1), 165–184. https://doi.org/10.1177/0013164403258440

Steelman, L. A., & Rutkowski, K. A. (2004). Moderators of employee reactions to negative feedback. *Journal of Managerial Psychology, 19*(1), 6–18. https://doi.org/10.1108/02683940410520637

Sully De Luque, M. F., & Sommer, S. M. (2000). The impact of culture on feedback-seeking behavior: An integrated model and propositions. *Academy of Management Review, 25*(4), 829–849. https://doi.org/10.5465/amr.2000.3707736

VandeWalle, D. (2003). A goal orientation model of feedback-seeking behavior. *Human Resource Management Review, 13*(4), 581–604. https://doi.org/10.1016/j.hrmr.2003.11.004

VandeWalle, D., Cron, W. L., & Slocum, J. W. (2001). The role of goal orientation following performance feedback. *Journal of Applied Psychology, 86*(4), 629–640. https://doi.org/10.1037/0021-9010.86.4.629

VandeWalle, D., & Cummings, L. L. (1997). A test of the influence of goal orientation on the feedback-seeking process. *Journal of Applied Psychology, 82*(3), 390–400. https://doi.org/10.1037/0021-9010.82.3.390

VandeWalle, D., Ganesan, S., Challagalla, G. N., & Brown, S. P. (2000). An integrated model of feedback-seeking behavior: Disposition, context, and cognition. *Journal of Applied Psychology, 85*(6), 996–1003. https://doi.org/10.1037/0021-9010.85.6.996

VandeWalle, D., Nerstad, C. G. L., & Dysvik, A. (2019). Goal orientation: A review of the miles traveled and the miles to go. *Annual Review of Organizational Psychology and Organizational Behavior, 6*(1), 115–144. https://doi.org/10.1146/annurev-orgpsych-041015-062547

Van Maanen, J., & Schein, E. H. (1979). Toward a theory of organizational socialization. In B. M. Staw (Ed.), *Research in organizational behavior* (Vol. 1, pp. 209–264). Greenwich, CT: JAI Press.

Weiss, H. M. (1977). Subordinate imitation of supervisor behavior: The role of modeling in organizational socialization. *Organizational Behavior and Human Performance, 19*(1), 89–105. https://doi.org/10.1016/0030-5073(77)90056-3

Weiss, H. M., & Knight, P. A. (1980). The utility of humility: Self-esteem, information search, and problem-solving efficiency. *Organizational Behavior and Human Performance, 25*(2), 216–223. https://doi.org/10.1016/0030-5073(80)90064-1

Whitaker, B. G., & Levy, P. (2012). Linking feedback quality and goal orientation to feed-back seeking and job performance. *Human Performance, 25*(2), 159–178. https://doi.org/10.1080/08959285.2012.658927

Yeager, D. S., Romero, C., Paunesku, D., Hulleman, C. S., Schneider, B., Hinojosa, C., & Dweck, C. S. (2016). Using design thinking to improve psychological interventions: The case of the growth mindset during the transition to high school. *Journal of Educational Psychology, 108*(3), 374–391. doi:10.1037/edu0000098

Zmigrod, L., Zmigrod, S., Rentfrow, P. J., & Robbins, T. W. (2019). The psychological roots of intellectual humility: The role of intelligence and cognitive flexibility. *Personality and Individual Differences, 141*, 200–208. https://doi.org/10.1016/j.paid.2019.01.016

10

Reflection

Behavioral Strategies to Structure and Accelerate Learning From Experience

Frederik Anseel and Madeline Ong

Experience is not what happens to a man; it is what a man does with what happens to him.
—Aldous Huxley (1894–1963), English writer and philosopher

In recent years, a learning routine of successful leaders has attracted the attention of business magazines and social media. Renowned chief executive officers (CEOs) such as Bill Gates and Mark Zuckerberg regularly take "think weeks." During these think weeks, they shield themselves from day-to-day business problems, not to go on a holiday but to reflect about where they have been and where they are going professionally. Often, they will take a deep dive into reading and writing to help structure their thinking, taking notes in reflection journals (Adler, 2016). Bill Gates, for instance, would share his think week notes with all Microsoft managers. Many business leaders have attributed their learning progress and new business ideas to such weeks of reflection. Other business leaders have gone even further and tried to make reflection pauses a daily or weekly routine. CEO Tim Armstrong, for instance, made his executives spend 10% of their day, or 4 hours per week, engaged in focused thinking about their jobs (Kellaway, 2014). Jeff Weiner, CEO of LinkedIn, schedules 2 hours of uninterrupted thinking time per day. Warren Buffet is famous for claiming to have spent, by his own estimate, 80% of his career just reading and thinking.

Clearly, some of the most successful leaders have discovered the value of reflection for structuring and accelerating how they learn from experience and plan for the future. These routines are backed up by empirical evidence,

Frederik Anseel and Madeline Ong, *Reflection* In: *The Age of Agility.* Edited by: Veronica Schmidt Harvey and Kenneth P. De Meuse, Oxford University Press (2021). © Oxford University Press. DOI: 10.1093/med/9780190085353.003.0010 as emerging research on reflection in the management literature points to the beneficial effects of reflection for learning and improving performance in organizations (Ellis, Carette, Anseel, & Lievens, 2014; Tannenbaum & Cerasoli, 2013). In fact, individual reflection has been identified as one of the key processes underlying learning agility (DeRue, Ashford, & Myers, 2012).

Although learning in organizations can encompass a wide range of developmental activities, such as online courses or on-the-job learning programs, much of what we call learning involves—at its core—drawing lessons from experience. This might be especially true for leaders. Leadership is not easily learned in the classroom; leaders develop their skills by directly engaging with their work environment. They interact with colleagues and employees to hear their opinions, observe the outcomes of their decisions, and experiment with new approaches. Learning then results from looking back on the accumulation of experiences and making sense of those actions to draw lessons from successful or failed outcomes (McCall, Lombardo, & Morrison, 1988).

Learning from experience, however, is often a slow and diffuse process as cause-and-effect chains are difficult to disentangle, and trial and error may initially lead learners in wrong directions. In a dynamic environment where disruptive events are unique and no two situations seem the same, learners often do not have the time and opportunity to let lessons from experience sink in slowly. Instead, a leader needs to "come up to speed quickly in one's understanding of a situation and move across ideas flexibly in service of learning both within and across experiences" (DeRue et al., 2012, p. 259), or in other words, contemporary leaders need to be agile learners. Engaging in and benefiting from systematic reflection may be one of the most effective strategies for leaders to foster and develop learning agility.

In this chapter, we first address the question, What do we know? by reviewing the existing empirical research on reflection processes and their outcomes. We not only elucidate the underlying processes that are assumed to accelerate learning, but also identify potential beneficial effects in addition to learning. In the next section, we delineate strategies for applying reflection knowledge in practice. In doing so, we distinguish between (a) targeted reflection interventions, often taking the form of after-event reviews (AERs; also referred to as after-action reviews and debriefs) or daily reflection practices and (b) day-to-day naturally occurring reflection processes. We also address the question, What don't we know? by describing areas where our existing knowledge about reflection is limited and more research is needed. Our review shows that we currently lack a solid basis to customize reflection

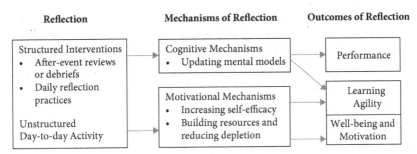

Figure 10.1 A research model summarizing reflection studies.

interventions for specific outcomes. We also discuss studies suggesting that individuals have a reluctance to reflect, which may be a barrier to enhancing learning agility. Finally, we explore situations where reflection may interfere with learning and might be disadvantageous for development. To guide our review of reflection research, we depict in Figure 10.1 the main relationships and mechanisms that have been examined so far.

What Do We Know?

Defining Reflection

The idea of reflection as a crucial learning mechanism has a long tradition in the organizational sciences, with probably the most influential learning models those of Argyris (1976) and Schon (1983), which suggest that reflection on action can help make tacit theories of how the world works more explicit to learners. Learners are assumed to constantly think while being in action (e.g., doing their jobs). At the same time, they consider their own actions (i.e., called the "double loop"); they critically examine their approach and decisions and design strategies to deal with future challenges. Although highly influential, these early learning theories did not clearly offer direct guidelines for the operationalization of reflection and its implementation in practice.

Building on these early theories, in recent years organizational scholars have developed ways to empirically study reflection processes in both laboratory conditions (e.g., Yang, Zhang, & Yang, 2018) and field settings (e.g., Lanaj, Foulk, & Erez, 2019). As a result, learning through reflection has now gained a substantial evidence base in settings as diverse as educational mentoring (Son, 2018); surgery (Vashdi, Bamberger, & Erez, 2013); firefighting (Allen, Baran, & Scott, 2010); armed forces (Ellis & Davidi, 2005); leadership development (DeRue, Nahrgang, Hollenbeck, & Workman, 2012); and aviation (Ron, Lipshitz, & Popper, 2006).

This recent line of research has strongly emphasized the cognitive process of reflection, a process "through which individuals attempt to increase their awareness of personal experiences and therefore their ability to learn from them" (Anseel, Lievens, & Schollaert, 2009, p. 23). In doing so, this approach has built on the notion of learning as a consequential change in knowledge through the accumulation of experience (e.g., Argote & Miron-Spektor, 2011; Fiol & Lyles, 1985). Reflection, however, goes beyond simply accumulating more experience. Reflection is an intentional cognitive effort to draw deeper lessons from these experiences by analyzing and codifying them in a systematic way. Ashford and DeRue (2012) depicted reflection as a cognitive process of probing cause and effect, questioning assumptions and analyzing the meaning of experiences, aimed toward gaining an understanding of why a particular situation was successful or not and how one's own behaviors and attributes contributed to that outcome. Simply put, leaders try to make sense of experiences by taking a step back from action and asking themselves questions aimed at systematically analyzing events: What did I do prior to, during, and after this experience? How effective was I in this situation? What has happened as a result of my actions and how could things have played out differently? and What have I learned from this experience that will improve my performance the next time?

Outcomes of Reflection

Given its grounding in cognitive learning theories, it is not surprising that a substantial number of studies have focused on knowledge and performance as outcomes of reflection. Studies adopting an experimental design with a nonreflection control group found that reflection increased information retention by 23% (as compared to simple practice) (Di Stefano, Gino, Pisano, & Staats, 2016) and resulted in richer and more elaborate cognitive maps of cause-and-effect relationships (Ellis & Davidi, 2005). Using a variety of task and work simulations, reflecting on past task performance was demonstrated to be successful in improving subsequent task performance (e.g.,

Anseel et al., 2009; Ellis & Davidi, 2005; Kray, Galinsky, & Markman, 2009; Vashdi et al., 2013). Interestingly, these positive outcomes were found not only in studies focusing on more cognitively oriented decision-making tasks, but also in studies focusing on complex tasks. Reflection was found to also result in improved interpersonal behavior, such as openness of communication and team cohesion (e.g., DeRue, Nahrgang et al., 2012; Grant & Dutton, 2012; Van Ginkel & Van Knippenberg, 2009; Villado & Arthur, 2013; Wong, Haselhuhn, & Kray, 2012).

In a comprehensive meta-analysis summarizing 30 empirical studies containing 46 independent samples, Tannenbaum and Cerasoli (2013, p. 240) quantitatively reviewed the effects of individual and team reflection interventions (which are labeled "debriefs" in their review paper) and concluded that "on average, debriefs improve performance by approximately 25%." Thus, this first meta-analysis bodes particularly well for using reflection as an intervention to boost performance. On average, reflection interventions yielded strong effect sizes of 20% to 26%, with similar results for both teams and individuals, in simulated and field settings, and for within- or between-group control designs.

A separate stream of reflection research has developed, in relative isolation from the previously discussed body of research, looking at well-being outcomes. These studies have used reflection measures and instructions that closely resemble the learning-from-experience reflection paradigm. However, their focus is not individual learning but how people cope with stress at work or capitalize on the beneficial effects of positive events at work. For instance, in a longitudinal experimental intervention in the field, Bono, Glomb, Shen, Kim, and Koch (2013, p. 1627) instructed their participants to reflect after work: "Every day for the next 8 days, you will be writing for 5–10 minutes about three things that went really well on that day and why they went well." This short positive reflection was found to decrease stress and lower blood pressure and physical complaints in the evenings through resource-building and depletion-reducing processes.

Lanaj et al. (2019) instructed leaders to reflect on and write about what makes them a good leader. This positive leader self-reflection intervention was conducted in the morning before leaders started their work. On days when leaders engaged in this morning reflection, they experienced less resource depletion and more work engagement. Fritz and Sonnentag (2006) did not give individuals specific reflection instructions, but simply measured positive work reflection occurring during vacations, which was found to result in greater well-being. Other studies found similar positive effects of work reflection on well-being and work–family enrichment (Fritz & Sonnentag, 2005; Meier, Cho, & Dumani, 2016). In sum, while these studies did not directly address reflection in relation to learning agility, they suggested that engaging in reflection might have other positive side effects that go beyond learning and performance outcomes.

How Does Reflection Enhance Learning Agility?

Two main routes have been identified that may explain the robust learning effects of reflection. A first route is based on cognitive theories of learning, which suggest that learning happens through expansion and reconfiguration of mental models. People at work engage in tasks to pursue specific goals. During such goal-striving activities, people work on the basis of a hypothetical knowledge base that helps them navigate the obstacles toward goal attainment; they have preexisting beliefs and assumptions about themselves, task strategies, and mental models of how they and the organizational environment work (Rouse & Morris, 1986). From time to time, they will receive feedback on their goal progress through success or failure or may simply receive direct external feedback from others. While positive feedback reinforces their existing mental models and encourages them to maintain their efforts and task strategies, negative feedback signals a lack of goal progress. Such a signal invalidates their current knowledge base (Chi, 2009). It means that some aspects of their existing mental model must be inaccurate or their task strategies were not in line with their mental model. Thus, (partial) failure or negative feedback challenges individuals to update and revise mental models or behavioral strategies.

However, revising behavioral strategies and mental models requires substantial cognitive effort. It implies a shift in information-processing modes from System 1 processing, which is automatic and fast and requires few cognitive resources, to System 2 processing, which is controlled, slow, and highly demanding of cognitive resources (Anseel et al., 2009; Di Stefano et al., 2016). This implies that as a prerequisite for learning from experience, cognitive resources need to be allocated to the task level. These resources are needed for reorganizing, updating, and integrating new experiential information in existing knowledge structures. Reflection is the mental activity that allows this shift to happen. By taking time to deeply analyze experiential information, learners slow down information processing to identify problems in their current thinking, come up with better task strategies, and implement the strategies. In the long term, reflection ensures that people work on the basis of accurate mental models, which paradoxically means that reflection might seem slow at first, but actually enhances the speed of learning over time.

The second route is a motivational one, suggesting that the learning effects of reflection depend on an individual's increased self-efficacy, i.e., "the belief in one's capabilities to organize and execute the course of action required to manage prospective situations" (Bandura, 1995, p. 2). Several studies have provided evidence that reflection increases self-efficacy (Ellis et al., 2014). By analyzing their successful experiences, learners become more aware of how their behavior contributed to success, which further increases their self-efficacy and motivation to put in even more effort and set higher goals, resulting in increased learning and ultimately performance improvement (Ellis, Ganzach, Castle, & Sekely, 2010). This raises the question of how the cognitive and motivational reflection routes work in concert.

In a series of laboratory studies and a field study, Di Stefano et al. (2016) found that reflection has an effect on both self-efficacy and task understanding (i.e., learner's mental model of the task), thus supporting both previous lines of research on reflection mechanisms. Results of mediation analyses further demonstrated that, when considered independently, both the cognitive and emotional mechanisms serve as mediators of the relationship between reflection and improved performance. However, when both mechanisms were considered together (i.e., entered in the same regression model), only task understanding significantly mediated the relationship, thus suggesting a more fundamental role for the cognitive route relative to the motivational route.

Designing Strategies for Reflection in Practice

Academic research on reflection activities at work has been characterized by two different approaches. One perspective has focused on using reflection as a structured intervention, either in the form of AERs or daily reflection practices. AERs are structured learning interventions promoting individual or team reflection following specific events, typically conducted with a group and a designated facilitator. Daily reflection practices involve individuals regularly spending a set amount of time on reflection at the start or at the end of each day or week, following a set of guiding instructions. A second, emerging approach on reflection focuses on how and when individuals also spontaneously engage in unstructured reflection in the course of their day-to-day work (Ong, Ashford, & Bindl, 2015). Here, we discuss a set of best practices when using and encouraging these approaches in practice.

Reflection as a Structured Intervention

When engaging in structured reflection, it is important to reflect on both one's successful and failed (or less successful) experiences. During an AER, individuals are typically instructed to analyze particular work events that were successful and/or unsuccessful and to draw lessons from them. Research has found that reflecting on *both* successful and unsuccessful events maximizes learning effectiveness and leads to the best performance, as opposed to reflecting only on unsuccessful events (Ellis & Davidi, 2005). Similar to reflecting on failures, reflecting on successes motivates learners not only to update their knowledge structures (e.g., by deliberating what they did that led to success) but also to set more challenging goals (e.g., through increased self-efficacy). Furthermore, focusing on both successes and failures elicits more complex mental models and richer cognitive structures. Even when an event has been largely successful, learners should not become complacent as it is important for them to reflect on any errors that have occurred or weaker aspects of their performance (Ellis, Mendel, & Nir, 2006). By focusing on their weaknesses, learners will continue to be motivated to test and update their knowledge and improve their performance. Furthermore, reflection helps tease out what specific behaviors were the key drivers of success relative to other behaviors.

Or, when the aim is to boost one's well-being rather than one's performance, research suggests that focusing on the positive is the way to go. There are various daily reflection practices available to individuals who wish to improve their overall well-being. Being a leader can be exhausting and depleting, and many leaders find it challenging to stay engaged. Just spending a few minutes each morning reflecting on three positive qualities that they possess as a leader can give them a much-needed boost in energy (Lanaj et al., 2019). Even for those who are not leaders, taking some time at the end of each day to reflect on three good things that had happened that day can help reduce stress and improve health (Bono et al., 2013). Managers and organizations concerned about employee well-being may benefit from giving positive events more prominence at work. For instance, positive organizational practices such as focusing on accomplishments, celebrating positive experiences, and communicating gratitude can give employees more material for positive reflection.

Although AERs have been generally found to be a useful learning procedure, they appear to be more beneficial for people with certain career experiences and personality profiles. Two people can go through the same developmental experiences, reflect in the same way, and emerge out of those experiences with different learning outcomes. Therefore, organizations need to pay attention to the personal characteristics of the employees engaging in structured reflection. People high in learning goal orientation are identified as those individuals with a desire to develop themselves by acquiring new skills, mastering new situations and improving their competence (VandeWalle, 1997). They have been found not only to benefit more from reflection but also to be more likely to reflect than those low in learning goal orientation, presumably because their mindsets toward processing information are more congruent with reflection activities (Anseel et al., 2009).

A similar pattern was found for individuals high in need for cognition, that is, individuals who engage in and enjoy effortful cognitive activity (Cacioppo & Petty, 1982). This suggests that highly learning agile individuals are more inclined to engage in reflection (e.g., reflect faster) and are also more effortful in engaging in reflection (e.g., reflect deeper). DeRue, Nahrgang and colleagues (2012) found that AERs are especially helpful for those who are conscientious, open to experience, and emotionally stable and have a rich base of prior developmental experiences. They explained that people who are conscientious are more methodical and deliberate in their reflection. Being open to experience helps as it allows the individual to consider a broader range of perspectives and explanations and thus realize more value from their reflection. Emotional stability is also important as reflection, especially when focused on new or challenging situations, can evoke stress and intense emotional reactions.

People who have a rich base of prior developmental experiences should be able to develop a more grounded and wise understanding of how they can improve their performance. Finally, DeRue, Ashford, et al. (2012) have also suggested that individuals with strong cognitive abilities should be more likely to benefit from reflection as they are able to store, process, and analyze more information in working memory and thus should reflect more efficiently. Understanding the individual differences related to reflection may open up avenues for identifying highly agile learners. When trait-like individual differences also include a state-like aspect (DeShon & Gillespie, 2005), situational cues may be offered to help people reflect. Table 10.1 summarizes individual difference related to reflection, tentatively indicating to what extent these individual differences may be affected by situational cues such as those provided in the work environment or by coaching.

Although a regular and consistent practice of reflection may be ideal (e.g., daily or other organizationally relevant time intervals), if one is time pressed, one can enjoy almost immediate positive benefits from just spending a few minutes engaging in reflection. Engaging in some reflection, no matter how

Table 10.1 A Summary of Individual Differences Related to the Value of Reflection

Individual Difference	Description	Influence of Situational Cues
Learning goal orientation	Desire to develop the self by acquiring new skills, mastering new situations, and improving one's competence	Sensitive to situational cues
Need for cognition	Tendency to engage in and enjoy effortful cognitive activity	Sensitive to situational cues
Conscientiousness	Tendency to display self-discipline, act dutifully, and strive for achievement	Limited (some long-term effects over career)
Openness to experience	General appreciation for unusual ideas, imagination, curiosity, and variety of experiences	Limited (some long-term effects over career)
Emotional stability	Ability to remain stable and balanced	Limited (some long-term effects over career)
Experience	Rich basis of prior developmental experiences	As experience grows
Self-efficacy	Belief in one's capabilities to organize and execute	Sensitive to situational cues
Cognitive ability	Individual's information-processing capacity	Limited

little, is better than none at all. While elaborate and time-consuming methods of reflection do exist, relatively short reflection interventions conducted in a temporary experimental setting have been found to have significant results (Ellis et al., 2010). If organizations are concerned about the amount of time and effort required to conduct the more complicated forms of structured reflection, they may consider conducting shorter and simpler forms of structured reflection. Even briefly reflecting on experiences of others, for instance in the form of case studies, has been found to improve performance (Bledow, Carette, Kühnel, & Bister, 2017).

Reflection as a Day-to-Day Activity

Apart from structured forms of reflection, organizations should also encourage employees to engage in spontaneous reflection as they go about their daily work. This type of spontaneous unstructured reflection can cover various domains of work, including the work goals being pursued, the methods used to attain those goals, how one's behavior and moods might be affecting one's work, and the quality of one's relationships with others (Ong et al., 2015). In contrast to those who engage in AERs or other reflection interventions, individuals who engage in unstructured reflection not only consider events as they occur, but also after they have occurred. This type of reflection may even occur in the absence of a particular work event.

Ong and colleagues (2015) argued that unstructured reflection is especially helpful in situations where norms are ambiguous, and there is uncertainty about the desirability and appropriateness of particular work behaviors. It gives individuals an opportunity to take a step back, gain a clearer understanding of their work situation and figure out how to adjust their own behavior accordingly. One advantage of unstructured reflection is that individuals can do it as and when required, and it can become a relatively habitual behavior. In contrast, structured reflection interventions are more episodic, and although they may have initial benefits, these benefits may not persist. Furthermore, individuals have the flexibility to engage in unstructured reflection on their own, deciding where, when, and how to reflect in the way most meaningful to them, whereas structured reflection in response to interventions can come at the wrong time or use a method that does not work well for particular individuals.

Given these potential benefits, the idea of individual work reflection as a day-to-day activity can be taught in leadership training programs. Many executives and leaders treasure the opportunity to attend leadership development or other executive education programs because they offer time away from their work organization to reflect on the people they are leading, how they are currently leading those people, and how they might adjust their leadership styles in the future. In such programs, on top of traditional leadership skill development, leaders should be taught about the value of adopting day-to-day reflection as a strategy to enhance their leadership. Those holding supervisory or managerial positions should also actively reinforce day-to-day reflection among their employees by engaging in such reflection themselves and articulating the value of reflection in their own work and by listening and asking questions that stimulate reflection (Garvin, Edmondson, & Gino, 2008). Over time, employees will learn from their supervisors about the practical value of reflection via a social learning process of observation, imitation, and modeling (Bandura, 1977).

In addition, organizations can deliberately create work conditions that facilitate leaders' engagement in unstructured reflection. When organizations reduce time pressure at work and provide leaders with more autonomy to determine their own work pace and schedule, they will have more time and flexibility to spontaneously engage in reflection. Furthermore, by including more task variety or dynamic performance standards in job design, organizations can activate deliberative (System 2) cognitive processing as opposed to automatic (System 1) processing in their leaders, which, in turn, encourages them to be more reflective on the job (Derfler-Rozin, Moore, & Staats, 2016; Sijbom, Anseel, Crommelinck, De Beuckelaer, & De Stobbeleir, 2018).

Organizations can also deliberately look for more reflective people in their new hires—that is, people with a stronger general tendency to engage in day-to-day reflection. For instance, hiring managers could focus on selecting individuals who have the capacity for introspection and the ability to accurately assess themselves (i.e., self-awareness; Church, 1997); who are motivated to set learning goals and improve themselves (i.e., learning goal orientation; VandeWalle, 1997); or who have a strong desire to engage in and enjoy cognitive activities (i.e., need for cognition; Cacioppo & Petty, 1982). Some combination of these individual characteristics indicates that the new hire is likely to be someone who habitually engages in unstructured reflection and thus is able to reap the benefits of such reflection.

Given the spontaneous nature of unstructured reflection, one natural question that comes up is, Does it matter when and where such reflection occurs? Must it happen at work and during work hours for it to benefit one's work? Current research suggests that unstructured reflection about work events does happen during nonwork or leisure time and can still have a positive impact on work outcomes. For example, positive reflection about work during the weekends has been found to reduce feelings of work-related burnout and increase motivation to learn something new at work (Fritz & Sonnentag, 2005). Reflection about work during one's vacations has also been found to impact well-being and work motivation (Fritz & Sonnentag, 2006). Therefore, managers and organizations do not necessarily need to expend time and effort administering structured reflections in the workplace. The simple act of allowing employees to take time off from work, whether in the form of weekends, holidays, or vacations, gives them the time and space to reflect spontaneously about events that have happened at work, with potential benefits for organizational outcomes. While this implies that people do not necessarily need to fully disconnect from all work thoughts in order to fully benefit from vacation time, there is a delicate balance to constructively reflecting on work issues without it turning into maladaptive rumination patterns (Takano & Tanno, 2009).

Finally, organizations can facilitate reflection through coaching. Coaching typically refers to a one-to-one developmental conversation or series of conversations, where an (executive) coach facilitates the learning process of a coachee (often a leader) through collaborative thinking and open discussions of key work experiences and challenges (Jones, Woods, & Guillaume, 2016). Coaching conversations provide a safe environment for leaders to reflect on experiences and work on improving areas of weakness. Especially for leaders that may not be naturally inclined to reflect, coaching may provide organizations with a structured approach to instigate reflection. However, also for those leaders who regularly take time to reflect, coaching may help structure and provide direction to their reflective thoughts. The mere act of verbalizing thoughts might provide new ways of understanding experiences. By voicing ideas out loud, leaders are trying to articulate what an experience means to them. These utterances often contain elaborations and specifications that may be hard to come by when reflecting in silence but help change behavior (Baumeister, Masicampo, & Vohs, 2011). Facilitating this type of reflection process, requires that coaches adopt an empathic and inquisitive attitude and engage in a behavioral process of exploration and discovery by asking questions, listening, and guiding the coachee to explore new ways of seeing (Castro, Anseel, Kluger, Lloyd & Turjeman-Levi, 2018; Van Quaquebeke & Felps, 2018).

What Don't We Know?

Disentangling Reflection Strategies

Despite the great progress made in recent years in terms of research on reflection, there remain many aspects of reflection that are not well understood. Theoretical progress in reflection research has been hindered by the holistic approach adopted in most reflection interventions. Most studies examining reflection have used comprehensive interventions, such as AERs, involving a long list of instructions intended to instigate individuals to broadly reflect on their experience (e.g., DeRue, Nahrgang, et al., 2012). Such a holistic focus is understandable because this is how interventions are often used in applied settings. Including multiple reflection instructions in a broad intervention likely results in stronger performance effects. However, such an approach provides little conceptual insight into the various factors contributing to the effectiveness of reflection. Research has mainly reported positive effects of reflection (Ellis et al., 2014). By disentangling the effects of different reflection strategies, we can go beyond the simple question of whether reflection is good or bad and offer a first step toward advancing reflection theory, research, and practice.

Most reflection research has considered reflection as a general practice, rather than a multifaceted practice comprising reflection on different dimensions. Ong and colleagues (2015) suggested that reflection comprises the following four dimensions, each representing an important domain of work on which individuals reflect: (a) goal-focused reflection, (b) methods-focused reflection, (c) self-focused reflection, and (d) relationships-focused reflection. It may be that these four dimensions of reflection have varied outcomes (e.g., goals- and methods-focused reflection may have greater relevance on task performance, and relationships-focused reflection may have greater relevance on relational outcomes). Furthermore, it is likely that each of the four dimensions of reflection are influenced by distinct individual difference and contextual factors (e.g., relationships-focused reflection is more likely to take place in interdependent work contexts and may be more beneficial for those who are less interpersonally sensitive). Future research should dig deeper into the antecedents and outcomes of different dimensions of reflection.

We encourage future research to delve deeper into various strategies or techniques that capture the full process of individual work reflection. For example, future studies might compare specific reflection strategies or techniques geared toward specific outcomes (e.g., cognitive, attitudinal, versus behavioral outcomes, or task versus interpersonal outcomes). They might also compare the impact of reflection undertaken in a variety of ways, for example, reflection involving factual versus counterfactual thinking, reflection that is written down (e.g., journaling) versus reflection that is verbally expressed, or reflection that occurs alone versus reflection that is conducted in a team setting or with a coach. In sum, learners can undertake numerous different forms and styles of reflection, and more research is needed to understand the implications of each type of reflection so that learners can pick the most appropriate type of reflection for their needs.

Reluctance to Reflect

Modern work is often characterized as nonreflective and overly action oriented (e.g., Porter, 2017; Seibert, 1999). In fact, as far back as 30 years ago, Mintzberg (1989) observed that in the workplace, many individuals "work at an unrelenting pace, that their activities are characterized by brevity, variety, and discontinuity, and that they are strongly oriented to action and dislike reflective activities" (p. 11). Today's workers are biased toward action and may not have much interest in engaging in reflection. More research is needed to understand both why people are disinterested in or avoid reflection and how organizations can encourage their employees to actively and enthusiastically engage in reflection.

As first observed by Anseel et al. (2009), a number of individuals do not reflect even when instructed to do so. It is unclear at this point to what extent previous reflection studies were able to ensure that all participants in the study actually reflected. There is a risk that some of the positive effects reported in the literature might be driven by a group of learners who were eager to follow reflection instructions, while a smaller group may not have reflected at all. People may also overreport the amount of reflection in which they actually engage because it is considered socially desirable. Recent studies have repeatedly shown that people generally prefer to avoid sitting quietly to reflect on their experiences, in so far that some actually prefer being administrated a painful electric shock instead of having to reflect (Wilson, Westgate, Buttrick, & Gilbert, 2019; Wilson et al., 2014). Thus, a particularly fruitful area of investigation should be to examine when people are more likely to reflect and in what type of reflection people naturally engage. New technologies such as social media and health tracker apps may open up new ways for studying the dynamics of reflection in real time (e.g., Gray et al., 2019).

Downsides of Reflection

To date, research has mainly reported the positive effects of reflection. This might lead to an uncritical adoption of reflection interventions for all types of outcomes. However, it is possible that some reflection strategies may have no beneficial effects or, under some conditions, may hinder rather than help some types of outcomes. In clinical psychology, for example, studies have found that rumination—a form of reflection in which individuals repeatedly focus on the causes, meanings, and consequences of their negative mood— predicts symptoms of depression and suicidal thinking (Miranda & Nolen-Hoeksema, 2007). Extending this to more general work settings, individuals who are in a negative mood or who are emotionally anxious and not able to regulate their feelings, may not necessarily reap the advantages of reflection that have been documented in previous research. Instead, they may get stuck in a negative downward spiral and become more stressed and overwhelmed, limiting their ability to work productively and efficiently. Future practice and research into reflection may therefore benefit from insights from cognitive psychology to develop techniques for learners to overcome this type of maladaptive reflection. For instance, research shows that helping people psychologically distance themselves from events facilitates adaptive self-reflection (Ayduk & Kross, 2010).

Another possible negative consequence of reflection is that it may lead to cognitive entrenchment and thus hinder creativity and innovation. Cognitive entrenchment occurs when one displays a high level of stability in one's domain schemas and has negative implications for one's flexibility in thought and behavior (Dane, 2010). As noted by Ibarra (2015), although reflection may be an excellent learning device, it may also anchor people in the past, amplify their blinders, and prevent them from harnessing their creative potential. Reflection that is excessively oriented on past events may limit people's ability to identify new solutions to problems and to generate creative ideas. One promising strategy to mitigate against this entrenchment effect is having people engage in imaginative reflection. Imaginative reflection is the process whereby people are challenged to think about what might have happened if another approach was chosen. Undoing the past and considering alternatives closely align with counterfactual thinking and hint at "a juxtaposition of an imagined versus factual state of affairs" (Epstude & Roese, 2008, p. 168). Imaginative reflection likely instigates a more flexible adaptation of mental models and has been found to enhance creativity (Rosseel & Anseel, in press). Summarizing what we currently know about reflection, Table 10.2 provides a series of best practices to facilitate learning through reflection, while Table 10.3 points to key research questions to be addressed in future research.

Table 10.2 Best Practices to Support Learning From Experience Through Reflection

Objective	Potential Stumbling Block	Best Practice
Engaging in reflection	Leaders may have a bias for action and do not take time enough to deliberately reflect on experience	- Teach reflection as a day-to-day activity in leadership development programs. - Encourage people to develop a reflection routine (e.g., reflect at a weekly fixed time, use a journal to help reflection through writing). - Create work conditions (e.g., reduce time pressure, increase task variety, use dynamic performance standards) that are conducive to reflective thinking.
	The organization seems to be missing reflective capacity to learn from previous experiences	- Include reflective capability as a desirable characteristic when hiring, for instance, by focusing on learning goal orientation, need for cognition, personality characteristics, or information-processing capacity. - Encourage leaders to actively reinforce reflection among their employees by engaging in reflection themselves and articulating the value of reflection in their own work.
	Some personality profiles may make leaders less inclined to reflect	- Help leaders reflect by assigning a coach trained in reflective inquiry and listening.

(Continued)

Table 10.2 *Continued*

Objective	Potential Stumbling Block	Best Practice
Engaging in more effective reflection	Risk of not consolidating key learnings for individuals and teams after crucial events	- Organize after-event reviews as a structured learning intervention. - During after-event reviews, reflect on both successful and failed experiences.
	Leaders are concerned about the amount of time and effort required to conduct complicated forms of structured reflection	- Use shorter and simple forms of structured reflection. Even briefly reflecting on others' experiences, for instance in the form of case studies, can improve performance.
	Leaders' reflection is not effective in accelerating learning from experience	- A coach can help provide structure, direction, and focus toward goals in reflection.
	Leaders work in situations where norms are ambiguous and there is uncertainty about the desirability and appropriateness of particular work behaviors	- Give people flexibility to engage in unstructured reflection on their own, deciding where, when, and how to reflect in the way most meaningful to them.
	Reflection turns into rumination, with leaders getting stuck in a negative downward thought spiral	- Learn techniques (e.g., from cognitive psychology) to overcome maladaptive reflection or involve a coach to help them reflect more constructively.
	Reflection leads to cognitive entrenchment, blocking creativity and innovation	- Encourage leaders to engage in imaginative reflection.
Improving well-being and motivation	Exhausted leaders with low levels of well-being and energy	- Regularly reflect on positive qualities and positive events.
	Leaders are at risk of burnout or suffer from low levels of motivation	- Encourage leaders to enough take time off, giving them time and space to constructively reflect on work issues.

Table 10.3 What Don't We Know? An Overview of Unresolved Questions for Future Reflection Research

Themes	Research Questions
Disentangling reflection strategies	What type of reflection techniques exist, and do they have different antecedents and outcomes? On which dimensions do people reflect, and do they have different antecedents and outcomes? How do different reflection modalities (e.g., alone vs. team, written down or verbally expressed, naturally occurring or coached) affect learning, well-being, and performance outcomes? How does reflection aimed at increasing well-being affect learning and vice versa? How do reflection dynamics and outcomes have higher level effects beyond the individual level, such as team and organizational learning?

Table 10.3 *Continued*

Themes	Research Questions
Reluctance to reflect	How can we encourage people to more regularly reflect at work?
	If people are reluctant to reflect, is this explained by motivation, ability, or opportunity to reflect?
	How do reflection processes naturally unfold in the work environment, and how are they shaped by situational influences (e.g., team climate, shocks, and events)?
	How might new technologies (e.g., social media, apps) facilitate reflection?
Downsides of reflection	Are there also downsides to reflection? If so, when, for whom, and for what outcomes?
	How can we counter potential downsides of reflection?
	What types of maladaptive reflection patterns occur, and how can they be overcome?

Conclusion

Theories of learning have long highlighted the crucial role that reflection plays in the learning process (Argyris, 1976; Schon, 1983). In more recent years, there has been a growing number of empirical studies documenting the benefits of reflection for learning, whether the reflection involves individuals following structured interventions or spontaneously reflecting without guidance. In this chapter, we discuss how engaging in reflection facilitates learning and performance and argue that it also helps foster learning agility. Although there has been significant progress in our theoretical understanding and practical application of reflection, there are many more new ideas and questions to explore. We hope that this chapter serves as a useful guide for those who hope to contribute to reflection research and practice.

References

Adler, N. J. (2016, January 13). Want to be an outstanding leader? Keep a journal. *Harvard Business Review*. Retrieved from https://hbr.org/2016/01/want-to-be-an-outstanding-leader-keep-a-journal.

Allen, J. A., Baran, B. E., & Scott, C. W. (2010). After-action reviews: Avenue for the promotion of safety climate. *Accident Analysis and Prevention, 42*, 750–757.

Anseel, F., Lievens, F., & Schollaert, E. (2009). Reflection as a strategy to enhance task performance after feedback. *Organizational Behavior and Human Decision Processes, 110*(1), 23–35.

Argote, L., & Miron-Spektor, E. (2011). Organizational learning: From experience to knowledge. *Organization Science, 22*(5), 1123–1137.

Argyris, C. (1976). Theories of action that inhibit individual learning. *American Psychologist, 31*(9), 638–654.

Ashford, S. J., & DeRue, D. S. (2012). Developing as a leader: The power of mindful engagement. *Organizational Dynamics, 41*(2), 146–154.

Ayduk, Ö., & Kross, E. (2010). From a distance: Implications of spontaneous self-distancing for adaptive self-reflection. *Journal of Personality and Social Psychology, 98*(5), 809.

Bandura, A. (1977). *Social learning theory.* Englewood Cliffs, NJ: Prentice Hall.

Bandura, A. (1995). *Self-efficacy in changing societies.* New York, NY: Cambridge University Press.

Baumeister, R. F., Masicampo, E. J., & Vohs, K. D. (2011). Do conscious thoughts cause behavior? *Annual Review of Psychology, 62*, 331–361.

Bledow, R., Carette, B., Kühnel, J., & Bister, D. (2017). Learning from others' failures: The effectiveness of failure stories for managerial learning. *Academy of Management Learning & Education, 16*(1), 39–53.

Bono, J. E., Glomb, T. M., Shen, W., Kim, E., & Koch, A. J. (2013). Building positive resources: Effects of positive events and positive reflection on work stress and health. *Academy of Management Journal, 56*(6), 1601–1627.

Cacioppo, J. T., & Petty, R. E. (1982). The need for cognition. *Journal of Personality and Social Psychology, 42*(1), 116–131.

Castro, D. R., Anseel, F., Kluger, A. N., Lloyd, K. J., & Turjeman-Levi, Y. (2018). Mere listening effect on creativity and the mediating role of psychological safety. *Psychology of Aesthetics, Creativity, and the Arts, 12*(4), 489.

Chi, M. T. H. (2009). Three types of conceptual change: Belief revision, mental model transformation, and categorical shift. In S. Vosniadou (Ed.), *Handbook of Research on Conceptual Change* (pp. 61–82). Hillsdale, NJ: Erlbaum.

Church, A. H. (1997). Managerial self-awareness in high-performing individuals in organizations. *Journal of Applied Psychology, 82*(2), 281–292.

Dane, E. (2010). Reconsidering the trade-off between expertise and flexibility: A cognitive entrenchment perspective. *Academy of Management Review, 35*(4), 579–603.

Derfler-Rozin, R., Moore, C., & Staats, B. R. (2016). Reducing organizational rule breaking through task variety: How task design supports deliberative thinking. *Organization Science, 27*(6), 1361–1379.

DeRue, D. S., Ashford, S. J., & Myers, C. G. (2012). Learning agility: In search of conceptual clarity and theoretical grounding. *Industrial and Organizational Psychology, 5*(3), 258–279.

DeRue, D. S., Nahrgang, J. D., Hollenbeck, J. R., & Workman, K. (2012). A quasi-experimental study of after-event reviews and leadership development. *Journal of Applied Psychology, 97*(5), 997–1015.

DeShon, R. P., & Gillespie, J. Z. (2005). A motivated action theory account of goal orientation. *Journal of Applied Psychology, 90*(6), 1096.

Di Stefano, G., Gino, F., Pisano, G. P., & Staats, B. R. (2016). *Making experience count: The role of reflection in individual learning* (Harvard Business School NOM Unit Working

Paper, 14-093). Retrieved from https://www.hbs.edu/faculty/Publication%20Files/14-093_defe8327-eeb6-40c3-aafe-26194181cfd2.pdf

Ellis, S., Carette, B., Anseel, F., & Lievens, F. (2014). Systematic reflection: Implications for learning from failures and successes. *Current Directions in Psychological Science, 23*(1), 67–72.

Ellis, S., & Davidi, I. (2005). After-event reviews: drawing lessons from successful and failed experience. *Journal of Applied Psychology, 90*(5), 857–871.

Ellis, S., Ganzach, Y., Castle, E., & Sekely, G. (2010). The effect of filmed versus personal after-event reviews on task performance: The mediating and moderating role of self-efficacy. *Journal of Applied Psychology, 95*(1), 122–131.

Ellis, S., Mendel, R., & Nir, M. (2006). Learning from successful and failed experience: The moderating role of kind of after-event review. *Journal of Applied Psychology, 91*(3), 669–680.

Garvin, D. A., Edmondson, A. C., & Gino, F. (2008). Is yours a learning organization? *Harvard Business Review, 86*(3), 109.

Fiol, C. M., & Lyles, M. A. (1985). Organizational learning. *Academy of Management Review, 10*(4), 803–813.

Fritz, C., & Sonnentag, S. (2005). Recovery, health, and job performance: Effects of weekend experiences. *Journal of Occupational Health Psychology, 10*(3), 187–199.

Fritz, C., & Sonnentag, S. (2006). Recovery, well-being, and performance-related outcomes: The role of workload and vacation experiences. *Journal of Applied Psychology, 91*(4), 936–945.

Grant, A., & Dutton, J. (2012). Beneficiary or benefactor: Are people more prosocial when they reflect on receiving or giving? *Psychological Science, 23*(9), 1033–1039.

Gray, K., Anderson, S., Chen, E. E., Kelly, J. M., Christian, M. S., Patrick, J., . . . Lewis, K. (2019). "Forward flow": A new measure to quantify free thought and predict creativity. *American Psychologist, 74*(5), 539–554.

Ibarra, H. (2015). *Act like a leader, think like a leader.* Boston, MA: Harvard Business Review Press.

Jones, R. J., Woods, S. A., & Guillaume, Y. R. (2016). The effectiveness of workplace coaching: A meta-analysis of learning and performance outcomes from coaching. *Journal of Occupational and Organizational Psychology, 89*(2), 249–277.

Kellaway, L. (2014, December 21). Scheduling time at work to "think" is a brainless idea. *Financial Times.* Retrieved from https://www.ft.com/content/eb7ebf76-85e9-11e4-b11b-00144feabdc0

Kray, L. J., Galinsky, A. D., & Markman, K. D. (2009). Counterfactual structure and learning from experience in negotiations. *Journal of Experimental Social Psychology, 45*(4), 979–982.

Lanaj, K., Foulk, T. A., & Erez, A. (2019). Energizing leaders via self-reflection: A within-person field experiment. *Journal of Applied Psychology, 104*(1), 1–18.

McCall, M. W., Lombardo, M. M., & Morrison, A. M. (1988). *Lessons of experience: How successful executives develop on the job.* New York, NY: Simon and Schuster.

Meier, L. L., Cho, E., & Dumani, S. (2016). The effect of positive work reflection during leisure time on affective well-being: Results from three diary studies. *Journal of Organizational Behavior, 37*(2), 255–278.

Mintzberg, H. (1989). *Mintzberg on management: Inside our strange world of organizations.* New York, NY: Simon and Schuster.

Miranda, R., & Nolen-Hoeksema, S. (2007). Brooding and reflection: Rumination predicts suicidal ideation at 1-year follow-up in a community sample. *Behaviour Research and Therapy, 45*(12), 3088–3095.

Ong, M., Ashford, S. J., & Bindl, U. (2015). Beyond navel-gazing: Exploring the concept and payoff of individual reflection at work. Annual Meeting of the Academy of Management, Vancouver, BC.

Porter, J. (2017). Why you should make time for self-reflection (even if you hate doing it). *Harvard Business Review.* Retrieved from https://hbr.org/2017/03/why-you-should-make-time-for-self-reflection-even-if-you-hate-doing-it

Ron, N., Lipshitz, R., & Popper, M. (2006). How organizations learn: Post-flight reviews in an F-16 fighter squadron. *Organization Studies, 27*(8), 1069–1089.

Rosseel, J., & Anseel, F. (in press). When reflection hinders creative problem solving: A test of alternative reflection strategies. *Journal of Business and Psychology.*

Rouse, W. B., & Morris, N. M. (1986). On looking into the black box: Prospects and limits in the search for mental models. *Psychological Bulletin, 100*(3), 349–363.

Schon, D. A. (1983). *The reflective practitioner.* New York, NY: Basic Books.

Seibert, K. W. (1999). Reflection-in-action: Tools for cultivating on-the-job learning conditions. *Organizational Dynamics, 27*(3), 54–65.

Sijbom, R. B., Anseel, F., Crommelinck, M., De Beuckelaer, A., & De Stobbeleir, K. E. (2018). Why seeking feedback from diverse sources may not be sufficient for stimulating creativity: The role of performance dynamism and creative time pressure. *Journal of Organizational Behavior, 39*(3), 355–368.

Son, S. (2018). The more reflective, the more career-adaptable: A two-wave mediation and moderation analysis. *Journal of Vocational Behavior, 109*, 44–53.

Takano, K., & Tanno, Y. (2009). Self-rumination, self-reflection, and depression: Self-rumination counteracts the adaptive effect of self-reflection. *Behavior Research and Therapy, 47*(3), 260–264.

Tannenbaum, S. I., & Cerasoli, C. P. (2013). Do team and individual debriefs enhance performance? A meta-analysis. *Human Factors, 55*(1), 231–245.

VandeWalle, D. (1997). Development and validation of a work domain goal orientation instrument. *Educational and Psychological Measurement, 57*(6), 995–1015.

Van Ginkel, W. P., & van Knippenberg, D. (2009). Knowledge about the distribution of information and group decision making: When and why does it work? *Organizational Behavior and Human Decision Processes, 108*(2), 218–229.

Van Quaquebeke, N., & Felps, W. (2018). Respectful inquiry: A motivational account of leading through asking questions and listening. *Academy of Management Review, 43*(1), 5–27.

Vashdi, D. R., Bamberger, P. A., & Erez, M. (2013). Can surgical teams ever learn? The role of coordination, complexity, and transitivity in action team learning. *Academy of Management Journal, 56*(4), 945–971.

Villado, A. J., & Arthur, W., Jr. (2013). The comparative effect of subjective and objective after-action reviews on team performance on a complex task. *Journal of Applied Psychology, 98*(3), 514–528.

Wilson, T. D., Reinhard, D. A., Westgate, E. C., Gilbert, D. T., Ellerbeck, N., Hahn, C., Brown, C. L., and Shaked, A. (2014). Just think: The challenges of the disengaged mind. *Science, 345*(6192), 75–77.

Wilson, T. D., Westgate, E. C., Buttrick, N. R., & Gilbert, D. T. (2019). The mind is its own place: The difficulties and benefits of thinking for pleasure. In J. M. Olson

(Ed.), *Advances in experimental social psychology* (Vol. 20, pp. 1–51). Cambridge, MA: Elsevier Academic Press.

Wong, E. M., Haselhuhn, M. P., & Kray, L. J. (2012). Improving the future by considering the past: The impact of upward counterfactual reflection and implicit beliefs on negotiation performance. *Journal of Experimental Social Psychology, 48*(1), 403–406.

Yang, M. M., Zhang, Y., & Yang, F. (2018). How a reflection intervention improves the effect of learning goals on performance outcomes in a complex decision-making task. *Journal of Business and Psychology, 33*(5), 579–593.

11

Being in Learning Mode

A Core Developmental Process for Learning Agility*

Peter A. Heslin and Leigh B. Mellish

> One must learn by doing the thing, for though you think you know
> it, you have no certainty until you try.
>
> —Aristotle (384–322 BC),

Leaders in our dynamic world need to swiftly acquire the knowledge, skills, and relationships required to achieve their objectives. Agile learners are those who are willing and able to learn from their experiences and apply those lessons in fresh contexts. Learning agility is thus a foundational leadership competence.

Learning agility can encompass learning relevant to many leadership realms. These realms include *people* (e.g., collaborating or negotiating effectively with others); *change* (e.g., readiness for change and experimentation); *cognition* (e.g., flexibility, mindfulness, information gathering, feedback engagement, and perspective taking); *self-awareness* (e.g., self-insight and reflecting); and *results* (i.e., drive and risk-taking; De Meuse, 2017). Learning agility has been associated with superior leadership performance, as indicated by multirater surveys, search firm evaluations, proximity to the chief executive officer (CEO), number of promotions, annual salary increases, and total compensation (De Meuse, 2019). Antecedents of learning agility include working in a culture that values learning and sharing information (Rebelo & Gomes, 2011); having a variety of work experiences across

* Acknowledgment: This research was supported by an ARC Linkage Seed Funding Grant from the School of Business, UNSW Sydney, and a UNSW Sydney Scientia Education Academy grant to the first author.

Peter A. Heslin and Leigh B. Mellish, *Being in Learning Mode* In: *The Age of Agility*. Edited by: Veronica Schmidt Harvey and Kenneth P. De Meuse, Oxford University Press (2021). © Oxford University Press.
DOI: 10.1093/oso/9780190085353.003.0011

one's career (Dries, Vantilborgh, & Pepermans, 2012); and being *promotion focused* (Wolfson, Tannenbaum, Mathieu, & Maynard, 2018) or high in *Openness to experience* (Connolly, 2001).

To supplement this literature on predictors of learning agility, in this chapter we introduce the concept of being *in learning mode* as a state that can be systematically deployed by leaders to prime their learning agility to master a required leadership competence. We explain how leaders can increase their learning agility by intentionally engaging in the developmental processes involved in being in learning mode. Doing so involves priming a growth mindset within themselves and those they lead before mindfully cycling through relevant *approach, action,* and *reflection* experiential learning processes. Being in learning mode is thus a leadership development metacompetency that facilitates experiential learning to cultivate required leadership competencies. We discuss implications for leaders and organizations concerned with fostering learning agility, as well as for scholars interested in conducting research on how being in learning mode enables leaders to be agile learners.

In Learning Mode

The notion of being in learning mode is rooted in Dweck's (1986) concept of *implicit theories of ability*, which Dweck (2006) relabeled as *mindsets*, as well as in Ashford and DeRue's (2012) model of *mindful engagement*.

Dweck (1986, 1999) observed that how people respond to setbacks depends substantially on their assumptions about how much they can cultivate the abilities required for the task at hand. A fixed mindset is the assumption that a particular ability cannot be developed much (e.g., "I'm too old to learn that"). This contrasts with the growth mindset assumption that a given ability is amenable to being nurtured via targeted initiatives to do so (e.g., through reading, coaching, role modeling, experimentation, and receiving feedback). Hundreds of studies have largely (though not entirely) converged in finding that people tend to set higher goals (Burnette, O'Boyle, VanEpps, Pollack, & Finkel, 2013); act more rigorously and persistently in striving to achieve them (Wood & Bandura, 1989); stay calmer (Burnette, Knouse, Vavra, O'Boyle, & Brooks, 2020); as well as learn and achieve more during moments when they hold a predominantly growth rather than a fixed mindset about the task at hand (Burnette et al., 2013; Costa & Faria, 2018).

An example of an exception is Burnette, Hoyt, Russell, Lawson, Dweck, and Finkel's (2020) finding that a growth mindset intervention increased interest in computer science but did not increase related academic performance.

Ashford and DeRue (2012) proposed that the extent to which leaders learn from their leadership endeavors is enhanced when they *mindfully engage* with those experiences. Being mindfully engaged involves active awareness of oneself and one's surroundings, openness to new information, and being willing and able to process experiences from multiple perspectives. Ashford and DeRue outlined a range of experiential learning steps whereby leaders can *approach, engage with,* and *reflect on* their experiences in ways that can enhance the lessons of those experiences.

Heslin and Keating (2017) discussed how each of the experiential learning processes identified by Ashford and DeRue (2012) might be framed and undertaken from the perspective of either a *fixed* or a *growth* mindset. For instance, when leaders hold a fixed mindset, they are inclined to construe feedback as liable to provide ego-threatening information. Doing so inclines them to seek feedback only from sources they believe will deliver relatively "good news." In contrast, a growth mindset primes leaders to anticipate that feedback may yield useful information about alternative and potentially more productive approaches. A growth mindset thus paves the way for courageously seeking ideas and feedback from sources that are likely to highlight possibilities for fundamental change and substantial improvement (Zingoni & Byron, 2017). Consequently, Heslin and Keating (2017) defined being *in learning mode* as pursuing each phase of the experiential learning process (Ashford & DeRue, 2012) while holding more of a *growth* than a *fixed* mindset.

Heslin, Keating, and Ashford (2020) critiqued, refined, and supplemented the work of Heslin and Keating (2017) by adding several critical experiential learning processes within the context of working to forge a sustainable career. The resulting depiction of what is involved in being in learning mode is presented in Figure 11.1 and discussed next in terms of how these experiential learning processes may foster leaders' learning agility.

Approach Phase: Create a Specific Learning Focus

Leaders are better equipped to learn from their experiences when they approach them as opportunities to develop (as well as exercise) particular

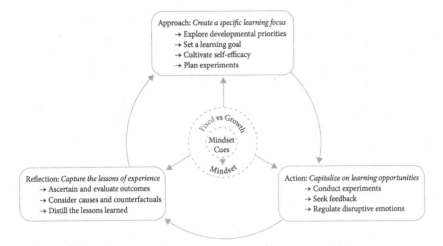

Figure 11.1 The role of mindsets and experiential learning processes when in learning mode.

From "How being in learning mode may enable a sustainable career across the lifespan," by Peter A. Heslin, Lauren A. Keating, and Susan J. Ashford, 2020. *Journal of Vocational Behavior, 117,* 103324. https://doi.org/10.1016/j.jvb.2019.103324. Copyright 2020 by Elsevier. Reprinted with permission.

leadership capabilities. Four tasks involved in the approach phase of being in learning mode are to explore developmental priorities, set a learning goal, cultivate self-efficacy, and plan experiments.

Explore Developmental Priorities

Crowded agendas and constant interruptions leave limited time and energy for leaders to focus on developing their leadership effectiveness. Prioritization is thus imperative. Leaders may glean insights about the most prudent focus of their leadership development efforts from observing other leaders, self-reflection (e.g., conducting a SWOT analysis), receiving 360-degree feedback, or working with a coach. To avoid being unfocused or becoming overwhelmed, leaders should identify and prioritize the most crucial skills to develop in order to meet their leadership challenges.

Holding a growth mindset emboldens leaders to consider working on potential developmental issues that they may feel sensitive about (e.g., how they listen, present, manage conflict, or their ethics). A fixed mindset inclines leaders to "play it safe" by focusing on polishing their strengths and avoiding ego-sensitive developmental areas they see as part of their identity and inherent leadership style. Such dynamics may be exacerbated by leadership development programs that focus on diagnosing personality types (e.g., with the Myers & Briggs Type Indicator˚) or character strengths. That is because doing so may reify fixed conceptions of who and what a person inherently is and is not. The resulting tunnel vision can limit learning agility in realms where development is needed for leaders to perform effectively or avoid career derailment.

Set a Learning Goal

After deciding which leadership competence or attribute to focus on mastering, leaders should crystallize this priority into a specific, challenging learning goal. Doing so facilitates learning through deeper information processing (Grant & Dweck, 2003), enabling focused and persistent effort in skill development (Latham, Seijts, & Crim, 2008), and fewer emotional disruptions when setbacks are encountered (Cron, Slocum, VandeWalle, & Fu, 2005). A learning goal can be written by stating: "I need to learn how to . . . " (Keating, Heslin, & Ashford, 2018, p. 46) followed by the specific leadership competence to be mastered (e.g., build stakeholder empathy, listen effectively to those with divergent ideas, speak effectively to the media, or express appreciation to my employees in an impactful manner).

When leaders have a clear focus, they glean more from whatever they read on the topic and whoever they observe exhibiting their targeted skill. They are also more determined to persist when their initial attempts to improve yield disappointing results. A fixed mindset dilutes the will to set specific, challenging learning goals that foster learning agility through these processes (Burnette et al., 2013).

Cultivate Self-Efficacy

Leaders' self-efficacy with reference to a particular learning goal is their belief about the extent to which they are capable of attaining that goal (Bandura, 1997). Self-efficacy is essential for leadership development because if leaders doubt they can learn to lead in a different, potentially more effective way, they are unlikely to experiment with promising alternative ways of leading.

Indeed, self-efficacy shapes facets of self-regulation, including the setting of specific goals, systematically developing plans to achieve them, seeking feedback that may not be flattering, and persisting when frustrations are encountered. Self-efficacy is thus a critical ingredient for capitalizing on learning opportunities (Sitzmann & Ely, 2011).

Social cognitive theory (Bandura, 1986, 1997) has established that self-efficacy to attain learning goals is largely a function of the mastery experiences, role modeling, and verbal persuasion that leaders encounter. Fortunately, leaders can proactively orchestrate these sources of self-efficacy to help convince themselves that they *have what it takes* to achieve their leadership development objectives.

Mastery experiences occur when leaders experience progress or success in attaining their goals. Leaders can increase the chance of having these experiences by breaking down their difficult learning goals into small, attainable subgoals, before taking progressively more challenging steps to enable rewarding success and avoid likely setbacks. They can also ensure that they have adequate resources (e.g., time, coaching, instructions) and that they recognize and appreciate the attainment of even modest milestones.

Role modeling involves observing others perform effectively in the realm targeted for development, affirming one's capability to lead similarly, and vividly imagining oneself doing so. Through role modeling, leaders can learn to refine their learning goals, as well as acquire strategies for attaining those goals and wise ways to respond to setbacks they encounter.

Finally, a leader's self-efficacy is built via *verbal persuasion* when they underscore to themselves their capability to learn, develop, persist, and achieve their learning goal, as well as when these kinds of optimistic messages are conveyed by others (e.g., a partner, boss, colleague, or coach). When inevitable setbacks are encountered, holding a growth mindset helps maintain high self-efficacy by priming leaders to construe those setbacks as challenges to be overcome, rather than as inherent deficiencies within themselves (Wood & Bandura, 1989) or those they lead (Heslin, 2009).

Plan Experiments

Once leaders have set a specific goal and developed strategies to maintain high self-efficacy, they can then plan to experiment with various approaches to master their targeted leadership skill. Planning to experiment is a process of deciding when, where, and how to initiate goal-directed behaviors, which significantly increases the likelihood of goal attainment (Bieleke, Legrand, Mignon, & Gollwitzer, 2018). The context of experimentation could be within and beyond formal leadership roles (e.g., within a community or family context). The nature of what leaders might plan to do differently could be generated through personal or group-based brainstorming, observing others either live or through media (e.g., in movies) or be suggested by a professional or peer coach.

Planning to experiment can enhance leaders' awareness of their often vast range of leadership development opportunities. Robust leadership development plans are contingent insofar as they identify backup options that may be deployed when constraints, setbacks, or surprises are encountered during a planned experiment with leading differently than usual. For instance, an attempt to experiment with using charismatic leadership techniques to increase executive presence (Antonakis, Fenley, & Liechti, 2012) may leave a leader feeling inauthentic or anxious. If this occurs, he or she might plan to be mindful that such feelings (a) often accompany attempts to alter long-standing behavioral routines and (b) tend to pass when we decide to steadfastly focus on our development goals (Seibert, Kraimer, & Heslin, 2016).

Action Phase: Capitalize on Learning Opportunities

The core of experiential leadership development is learning from the results of experimenting with doing things differently. The action phase of being in learning mode encompasses enacting experiments, seeking feedback, and regulating disruptive emotions.

Conduct Experiments

After planning experiments to undertake, the next step is for leaders to enact those experiments. Doing so often involves simultaneously engaging in routine leadership activities (e.g., giving presentations to sell a vision, negotiating, striving to motivate), while simultaneously experimenting with conducting at least portions of these tasks in a different way. Examples could include intentionally using gestures and metaphors while selling a vision (Antonakis et al., 2012), asking clarification questions to better understand a negotiating partner's interests (Emerson & Loehr, 2008), or striving to motivate by highlighting the positive impact that employees' work has had on other people's lives (Grant, 2011).

A hallmark of a good experiment is that there is a degree of uncertainty about the results. Experiments are best conducted in a relatively safe context and manner in order to safeguard self-efficacy by enabling mastery experiences. On the other hand, it is important to aim to think, feel, and act sufficiently differently so that the results of doing so can be observed and analyzed. Offline rehearsal and videorecording (where relevant), perhaps supplemented by self-, peer, or professional coaching, can provide a helpful way to prepare for live experimentation.

Seek Feedback

Feedback can reveal the results of experimentation. Such results can include not only the financial and other hard outcomes achieved, but also the impact on others while striving to achieve those results. For instance, even if employees literately "sign up" to a new organizational vision (i.e., publicly sign their name on a poster of a fresh vision and be photographed in front of it, as many employees at *YUM! Brands* did; Mike & Slocum, 2003), the extent to which they have heartfelt commitment to it may be another matter. Do they feel that the leader who presented the vision truly believes it? Are the anticipated benefits to themselves seen as realistic or oversold? Were the costs of the present modus operandi and the imperative to change overplayed? Are they truly willing to prioritize pursuit of the new vision over established ways of working? Given that authenticity and credibility are critical ingredients for effective leadership (Kouzes & Posner, 2017), organizing to receive feedback on such issues is invaluable for making sustained change.

Feedback can be sought by leaders asking others about their impact, either informally (e.g., asking others how they feel a meeting went) or more formally, such as via 360-degree feedback or by soliciting anonymous written comments. Such feedback is best arranged ahead of time so feedback providers know what to look for and are not taken by surprise when feedback is requested. Even timelier and perhaps valuable feedback may be gleaned from closely observing others' reactions (e.g., Are they actively or passively engaging in the interaction? How enthusiastically are they following through with what was discussed?). Holding a growth mindset fosters curiosity about one's overall impact as a leader, as opposed to a defensive reluctance to collect data about one's negative impacts (Heslin & Keating, 2017).

Regulate (Disruptive) Emotions

During each element of being in learning mode, though especially when setbacks are encountered or negative feedback is received, disruptive emotions may derail leadership development initiatives. Attempts at emotional regulation may have either a *hedonic* or an *instrumental* purpose.

Strategies adopted for a hedonic purpose aim to generally increase the experience of positive emotions (e.g., joy, gratitude, serenity), as well as minimize the experience of negative emotions (e.g., sadness, contempt, anxiety) via strategies such as noticing what is working well, counting one's blessings, and connecting with other people or nature (Fredrickson, 2013).

Broaden and build theory (Fredrickson, 2013) underscores how positive emotions also have instrumental value by serving to broaden a person's thinking and openness to consider and build on divergent possibilities, in contrast to the narrower and more myopic focus of attention associated with negative emotions. Given the substantial evidence that positive emotions increase mental agility, support recovery from negative emotional experiences, and improve the quality of interpersonal interactions (Fredrickson & Joiner 2018), they may be generally useful for keeping the implementation of planned experiments on track.

Another potential focus of instrumental emotional regulation is to elicit emotions relevant to attaining particular leadership goals. For instance, lowering emotional arousal (e.g., through deep breathing, yoga, and meditation) can support a learning goal such as to be more empathic with employees who are experiencing difficulties. Increasing emotional arousal (e.g., through upbeat music, or *power poses*; cf. Cuddy, Schultz, & Fosse, 2018) may foster greater impact when seeking to energize an audience to immediately take action (e.g., a sales blitz). Finally, feelings of anger or disappointment can support effectively conveying moral outrage about serious ethical violations or environmental destruction.

The more leaders believe that they can exercise control over their emotions, the more likely they are to apply such strategies and the more successful such strategies tend to be in eliciting the targeted emotions (Tamir, John, Srivastava, & Gross, 2007). Holding a growth rather than a fixed mindset about the malleability of one's emotions is thus a valuable resource for enabling effective emotional self-regulation (Burnette, Knouse, et al., 2020).

Reflection Phase: Capture the Lessons of Experience

Without thoughtful reflection on the results of experimentation, little learning is likely to occur. The reflection phase of being in learning mode involves ascertaining and evaluating outcomes: considering causes and counterfactuals and distilling the lessons learned so they can systematically guide next steps.

Ascertain and Evaluate Outcomes

An essential ingredient for learning from leadership experiences is to apprehend what happened during them. Leaders can fruitfully muse about a range of questions, such as the following: What did I observe in those around me as I enacted my experiment(s)? What have been their actions/reactions since? What do hard data (e.g., sales, signups, and mean satisfaction scores) indicate? What did I observe in myself, in terms of my thoughts, feelings, and behaviors? In what ways were my actions and reactions in line with my plans? What about the responses of those around me? How do I feel about what transpired in myself? How do I feel about my apparent impact on others?

Taking notes regarding answers to such questions may foster deeper engagement with them (Travers, Morisano, & Locke, 2015). A thorough accounting is also facilitated by scanning initial responses in terms of whether they include consideration of both *what worked well* as well as *what did not work out so well*. Doing so helps maintain self-efficacy (via mastery experiences; Bandura, 1997) and the positivity required to broaden and build motivation and the scope of analytical thinking (Fredrickson & Joiner, 2018) needed to effectively complete the next steps in mastering a learning goal.

Through conducting this reflection, leaders enhance their self-awareness and more deeply consolidate information into memory (Schlichting & Preston, 2014), making it easier to retrieve when needed in future challenges. When in learning mode, leaders are focused on ensuring they accurately ascertain and evaluate their impacts and outcomes, rather than focusing on the relative performance of others (Heslin, 2003), which undermines learning (Zingoni & Byron, 2017).

Consider Causes and Counterfactuals

Deriving lessons from prior experiences requires causal reasoning about why things unfolded as they did. This involves asking questions such as, What did I do (or refrain from doing) that contributed to positive outcomes? What else did I do (or fail to do) that fell flat—or worse? What role did others play? What factors undermined my results that I could have better controlled or better managed? What factors were beyond my control?

Holding a growth mindset helps leaders take responsibility for outcomes and make brave, internal causal attributions that support their proactive leadership development. This is because being growth oriented helps leaders avoid fixed-minded fatalism about themselves (e.g., "I've never been able to suffer fools gracefully, and that isn't going to change"); other people (e.g., "She's always had it in for me: Some CEOs are just like that"; Heslin, VandeWalle, & Latham, 2006); and the malleability of their context (e.g., "With virtually no hope of garnering support in our dog-eat-dog culture, I never stood a chance!"). When leaders hold a growth mindset, they instead place more focus on musing about the modifiable *situational* (e.g., resources, relationships, and support) or *personal* elements (e.g., preparation, focus of attention, and strategies developed; Levy & Dweck, 1998; Robins & Pals, 2002) that contributed to their outcomes. Doing so suggests potentially productive levers for change and alternatives for experimentation in striving for better outcomes.

Another sense-making technique is for leaders to engage in counterfactual thinking about their learning experience. This involves asking themselves, "What if?" followed by potential options not taken and their anticipated outcomes. Counterfactuals prompt leaders to assess their learning strategies and development outcomes against other approaches realized from hindsight (De Brigard & Parikh, 2019). Through these comparisons, leaders may glean further insights about promising paths forward.

Distill the Lessons Learned

Given how readily people tend to forget even their greatest insights (Ditta & Storm, 2017), leadership development is significantly enhanced by writing notes about what worked well and alternative strategies for experimentation next time. Leaders may vary their preference to record these notes via handwritten or typed journaling, voice recording, or summarizing key lessons with a coach or mentor.

A growth mindset grounds leaders in the realities that (a) their performance may both improve and decline (Heslin, Latham, & VandeWalle, 2005), and (b) substantial skill development is often the result of systematically striving to improve over time (Smith, 2005). These assumptions support adopting the potentially more arduous, though methodical, approach of swiftly and routinely making written notes about insights that can be being readily referenced to guide the testing of promising options and avoid approaches that have not worked well (Wood & Bandura, 1989).

Discussion

Effective leadership enhances organizational outcomes, including employee satisfaction with the leader, job satisfaction, motivation, as well as individual, group, and organizational performance (Antonakis & Day, 2017). Organizations thus have a vested interest in enabling leaders to be agile learners. We have proposed that being in learning mode is a learning meta-competency that enables agility in learning to master required leadership competencies.

Organizational Implications

Organizations often provide leaders with challenging leadership assignments to facilitate their skill development (McCall, 2004). Although leadership development does not necessarily flow from leading challenging projects, it is much more likely to occur when people mindfully engage and systematically work through their leadership experiences when holding a growth mindset and with a clear learning goal in mind (Ashford & DeRue, 2012; Heslin & Keating, 2017).

A range of avenues exists whereby organizations can foster leaders and those they lead being in learning mode. These include designing work roles and providing opportunities (e.g., training, projects) that facilitate learning and development (Parker, 2014). Staffing policies can also direct investments to developing the capabilities of emerging leaders within the organization, rather than primarily seeking to acquire leadership talent from the labor market (Murphy & Dweck, 2010).

Organizational cultures that value being in learning mode may be developed through written and verbal value statements that reiterate the importance of "leaders" throughout the organization (not just those in supervisory roles) engaging in continual development. These statements can be supported by celebrations of particular learning journeys that recount the kinds of learning mode initiatives undertaken (e.g., to build self-efficacy, engage in experimentation, regulate potentially disruptive emotions, etc.).

To ensure this culture is believed and supported by employees, organizations need to allow sufficient time, space, and resources required for skill development, as well as ensure that there is adequate *psychological safety*; that is, there is a climate where people feel it is safe to take interpersonal risks by speaking up and sharing divergent ideas, concerns, and questions (Edmondson, 2018). To enable psychological safety, leaders can underscore the imperative for issues and ideas being readily shared to enable organizational agility and sustainability. They can publicly acknowledge their own professional learning challenges, struggles, and current learning goals. Leaders can also reward those who share their struggles, mistakes, and what they have learned from them.

Finally, senior leaders can strive to consistently convey the message that we are all a *work in progress*, rather than a binary resource amenable to be characterized as either, for instance, *an asset* or *a liability*. One way of doing so is to frame performance in terms of behaviors or strategies adopted (e.g., "great approach," "nice moves," or "cool way to do it"), rather than labeling individuals by perceived inherent capacity (e.g., "star performer," "high potential (*hipo*)," or "legend"). The latter approaches induce fixed mindsets that prime people to avoid significant challenges/risks in case they yield subpar results that jeopardize their status as an elite performer (Heslin, 2009). Perhaps this helps explain why so many employees who are initially labeled as a hipo eventually disappoint or derail.

Personal Leadership Development Implications

For many leaders, just trying to keep afloat given multiple competing demands and deadlines may lead to pessimism about the viability of also simultaneously striving to engage in experiential learning projects. This concern is warranted given that being in learning mode requires greater cognitive, emotional, and behavioral effort than being focused solely on striving to accomplish one's immediate leadership objectives. When current approaches are working well, sometimes merely implementing them rather than striving to reinvent them is the most appropriate focus. On the other hand, leaders experiencing the pain and frustration of discouraging 360-degree feedback or having their career progression blocked by their perceived leadership shortcomings are compelling reasons to prioritize cultivating their leadership effectiveness via being in learning mode.

A first step in doing so is for leaders to audit and adjust their mindset-related self-talk, when needed. After a setback, for instance, leaders can strive to recognize their fixed-minded internal dialogue about themselves (e.g., "I'm too old for this") and others (e.g., "How can you soar with eagles when you're flying with turkeys?") before replacing it with more growth-minded alternatives (e.g., "I have some learning to do about this" and "I am surrounded by opportunities to develop and practice my employee coaching"). Examples of fixed- and growth-minded self-talk regarding each of the experiential learning tasks involved in being in learning mode are outlined in Table 11.1.

Leaders we have worked with have reported that they regularly slip into fixed mindsets and out of being in learning mode. This is understandable given all the time, energy, and self-discipline it involves. In light of this, it is probably prudent for leaders to strive to be *fully* in learning mode regarding only one or two learning goals at a time.

Research Implications

We derived our model of being in learning mode from decades of organizational, educational, and social psychological research (for details, see Heslin & Keating, 2017; Heslin et al., 2020). The role of leaders' learning mode in their learning agility is nonetheless ripe for direct empirical investigation. Two broad types of methodology that might be fruitfully deployed are (a) longitudinal correlational field research and (b) experimental field research. In the former, leaders' mindset and engagement in the learning mode behaviors identified in Figure 11.1 could be measured and then the extent to which they predict indicators of their learning agility some months later could be examined.

Table 11.1 Examples of Fixed- and Growth-Minded Self-Talk Related to Each Step of Being in Learning Mode

Learning Mode Steps	Fixed-Mindset Sample of Self-Talk	Growth Mindset Sample of Self-Talk
Approach		
Explore developmental priorities	Which of my strengths should I aim to showcase?	Which aspect of my leadership might I most fruitfully work to cultivate?
Set a learning goal	My development flows essentially from my innate talents.	My development flows essentially from whatever I methodically work on.
Cultivate self-efficacy	This failure signifies that I am just not good at this.	This failure signifies what I am not yet good at—so I need to work on it more.
Plan experiments	How could I show that I am right about this?	How could I test if I am right about this?
Action		
Conduct experiments	I do best when I focus on playing to my inherent strengths.	I enjoy cultivating my emerging strengths.
Seek feedback	Who will help me recognize my rate of progress?	Who will help me enhance my rate of progress?
Regulate disruptive emotions	I am being overtaken by those emotions that prevent me from being at my best.	I am going to discover ways to ensure my emotions do not prevent me being at my best.
Reflection		
Ascertain and evaluate outcomes	She just went silent when I asked how she would handle it: How ungrateful!	She just went silent when I asked how she would handle it: I wonder what she was thinking and feeling at that moment?
Consider causes and counterfactuals	She is obviously incapable of being empowered.	Perhaps she has low self-efficacy at offering suggestions; that's something I will explore and develop, if needed.
Distill lessons learned	There is little point in my writing plans for personal change that is unlikely to actually happen.	I am determined not to leave the site of an insight without a written note on how I can be more effective next time!

Adapted from Heslin and Keating (2017) and Heslin et al. (2020).

In the latter approach, leaders could be randomly assigned to receive either (a) a growth mindset intervention (e.g., Heslin et al., 2006; Heslin & Keating, 2016) within the context of experiential training and coaching in how to be in learning mode, based on the principles outlined by Heslin and colleagues (Heslin & Keating, 2017; Heslin et al., 2020), or (b) a placebo control training of similar length and intensity. Indicators of leaders' learning agility might then be assessed in the months after these interventions to provide a robust test of the fundamental premise of this chapter that being in learning mode fosters learning agility.

Related research questions include, What are the most critical steps of being in learning mode for learning agility? If leaders learn to take these steps in a growth-minded manner, is there incremental value in comprehensive instruction about mindsets before launching into learning about and practicing being in learning mode? What are the most efficient means of sustaining leaders being in learning mode? Does this depend on leaders' individual differences (e.g., conscientiousness) and context (e.g., psychological safety climate)? How does a leader's learning mode interact with other antecedents of learning agility (which are beyond the scope of this chapter) to shape how well leaders learn from their experiences and leverage those insights into enhanced leadership effectiveness?

Conclusion

Learning agility is a serious imperative and challenge for which there is no simple or singular remedy. We nonetheless hope to have conveyed that by diligently striving to be in learning mode, leaders may proactively work to cultivate their learning agility. Organizations can also foster learning agility via policies and practices that support leaders being in learning mode.

References

Antonakis, J., & Day, D. V. (Eds.). (2017). *The nature of leadership*. Thousand Oaks, CA: Sage.

Antonakis, J., Fenley, M., & Liechti, S. (2012). Learning charisma. Transform yourself into the person others want to follow. *Harvard Business Review, 90*(6), 127–130.

Ashford, S. J., & DeRue, D. S. (2012). Developing as a leader: The power of mindful engagement. *Organizational Dynamics, 41*, 146–154.

Bandura, A. (1986). *Social foundations of thought and action: A social cognitive theory*. Upper Saddle River, NJ: Prentice Hall.

Bandura, A. (1997). *Self-efficacy: The exercise of control*. London, UK: Freeman.

Bieleke, M., Legrand, E., Mignon, A., & Gollwitzer, P. M. (2018). More than planned: Implementation intention effects in non-planned situations. *Acta Psychologica, 184*, 64–74.

Burnette, J. L., Hoyt, C. L., Russell, V. M., Lawson, B., Dweck, C. S., & Finkel, E. (2020). A growth mind-set intervention improves interest but not academic performance in the field of computer science. *Social Psychological and Personality Science, 11*(1), 107–116.

Burnette, J. L., Knouse, L. E., Vavra, D. T., O'Boyle, E., & Brooks, M. A. (2020). Growth mindsets and psychological distress: A meta-analysis. *Clinical Psychology Review, 77*, 101816.

Burnette, J. L., O'Boyle, E. H., VanEpps, E. M., Pollack, J. M., & Finkel, E. J. (2013). Mind-sets matter: A meta-analytic review of implicit theories and self-regulation. *Psychological Bulletin, 139*, 655–701.

Connolly, J. A. (2001). *Assessing the construct validity of a measure of learning agility* (Doctoral dissertation). Florida International University. Retrieved from http://digitalcommons.fiu.edu/dissertations/AAI3013189

Costa, A., & Faria, L. (2018). Implicit theories of intelligence and academic achievement: A meta-analytic review. *Frontiers in Psychology, 9*, 829. doi:10.3389/fpsyg.2018.00829

Cron, W. L., Slocum, J. W., Jr., VandeWalle, D., & Fu, Q. (2005). The role of goal orientation on negative emotions and goal setting when initial performance falls short of one's performance goal. *Human Performance, 18*, 55–80.

Cuddy, A. J., Schultz, S. J., & Fosse, N. E. (2018). P-curving a more comprehensive body of research on postural feedback reveals clear evidential value for power-posing effects: Reply to Simmons and Simonsohn (2017). *Psychological Science, 29*, 656–666.

De Brigard, F., & Parikh, N. (2019). Episodic counterfactual thinking. *Current Directions in Psychological Science, 28*, 59–66.

De Meuse, K. P. (2017). Learning agility: Its evolution as a psychological construct and its empirical relationship to leader success. *Consulting Psychology Journal: Practice and Research, 69*, 267–295.

De Meuse, K. P. (2019). A meta-analysis of the relationship between learning agility and leader success. *Journal of Organizational Psychology, 19*, 25–34.

Ditta, A. S., & Storm, B. C. (2017). That's a good idea, but let's keep thinking! Can we prevent our initial ideas from being forgotten as a consequence of thinking of new ideas? *Psychological Research, 81*, 678–689.

Dries, N., Vantilborgh, T., & Pepermans, R. (2012). The role of learning agility and career variety in the identification and development of high potential employees. *Personnel Review, 41*, 340–358.

Dweck, C. S. (1986). Motivational processes affecting learning. *American Psychologist, 41*, 1040–1048.

Dweck, C. S. (1999). *Self-Theories: Their Role in Motivation, Personality, and Development*. Psychology Press.

Dweck, C. S. (2006). *Mindset: The new psychology of success*. New York, NY: Random House.

Edmondson, A. C. (2018). *The fearless organization: Creating psychological safety in the workplace for learning, innovation, and growth*. Hoboken, NJ: Wiley.

Emerson, B., & Loehr, A. (2008). *A manager's guide to coaching: Simple and effective ways to get the best from your people.* New York, NY: AMACOM.

Fredrickson, B. L. (2013). Positive emotions broaden and build. In P. Devine & A. Plant (Eds.), *Advances in experimental social psychology* (Vol. 47, pp. 1–54). New York, NY: Academic Press.

Fredrickson, B. L., & Joiner, T. (2018). Reflections on positive emotions and upward spirals. *Perspectives on Psychological Science, 13,* 194–199.

Grant, A. M. (2011). How customers can rally your troops. *Harvard Business Review, 89*(6), 96–103.

Grant, H., & Dweck, C. S. (2003). Clarifying achievement goals and their impact. *Journal of Personality and Social Psychology, 85,* 541–553.

Heslin, P. A. (2003). Self- and other-referent criteria of career success. *Journal of Career Assessment, 11,* 262–286.

Heslin, P. A. (2009). "Potential" in the eye of the beholder: The role of managers who spot rising stars. *Industrial and Organizational Psychology: Perspectives on Science and Practice, 2,* 420–424.

Heslin, P. A., & Keating, L. A. (2016). Stuck in the muck? The role of mindsets in self-regulation when stymied during the job search. *Journal of Employment Counseling, 53,* 146–161.

Heslin, P. A., & Keating, L. A. (2017). In learning mode? The role of mindsets in derailing and enabling experiential leadership development. *The Leadership Quarterly, 28,* 367–384.

Heslin, P. A., Keating, L. A., & Ashford, S. J. (2020). How being in learning mode may enable a sustainable career across the lifespan. *Journal of Vocational Behavior, 117,* 103324. https://doi.org/10.1016/j.jvb.2019.103324

Heslin, P. A., Latham, G. P., & VandeWalle, D. M. (2005). The effect of implicit person theory on performance appraisals. *Journal of Applied Psychology, 90,* 842–856.

Heslin, P. A., & VandeWalle, D. M. (2005, April). *Self-regulation derailed: Implicit person theories and feedback-seeking.* Paper presented at the annual meeting of the Society for Industrial and Organizational Psychology, Los Angeles, CA.

Heslin, P. A., VandeWalle, D., & Latham, G. P. (2006). Keen to help? Managers' implicit person theories and their subsequent employee coaching. *Personnel Psychology, 59,* 871–902.

Keating, L. A., Heslin, P. A., & Ashford, S. J. (2018). Good managers are good learners. *Harvard Business Review OnPoint, February,* 46–47. (See also https://hbr.org/2017/08/good-leaders-are-good-learners).

Kouzes, J. M., & Posner, B. Z. (2017). *The leadership challenge.* San Francisco, CA: Jossey-Bass.

Latham, G. P., Seijts, G., & Crim, D. (2008). The effects of learning goal difficulty level and cognitive ability on performance. *Canadian Journal of Behavioural Science/Revue Canadienne Des Sciences Du Comportement, 40,* 220–229.

Levy, S. R., & Dweck, C. S. (1998). Trait-versus process-focused social judgment. *Social Cognition, 16,* 151–172.

McCall, M. W., Jr. (2004). Leadership development through experience. *Academy of Management Perspectives, 18,* 127–130.

Mike, B., & Slocum, J. W., Jr. (2003). Slice of reality: Changing culture at Pizza Hut and Yum! Brands, Inc. *Organizational Dynamics, 32,* 319–330.

Murphy, M. C., & Dweck, C. S. (2010). A culture of genius: How an organization's lay theory shapes people's cognition, affect, and behavior. *Personality and Social Psychology Bulletin, 36,* 283–296.

Parker, S. K. (2014). Beyond motivation: Job and work design for development, health, ambidexterity, and more. *Annual Review of Psychology, 65,* 661–691.

Rebelo, T. M., & Duarte Gomes, A. (2011). Conditioning factors of an organizational learning culture. *Journal of Workplace Learning, 23,* 173–194.

Robins, R. W., & Pals, J. L. (2002). Implicit self-theories in the academic domain: Implications for goal orientation, attributions, affect, and self-esteem change. *Self and Identity, 1,* 313–336.

Schlichting, M. L., & Preston, A. R. (2014). Memory reactivation during rest supports upcoming learning of related content. *Proceedings of the National Academy of Sciences of the United States of America, 111,* 15845–15850.

Seibert, S. E., Kraimer, M. L., & Heslin, P. A. (2016). Developing career resilience and adaptability. *Organizational Dynamics, 45,* 245–257.

Sitzmann, T., & Ely, K. (2011). A meta-analysis of self-regulated learning in work-related training and educational attainment: What we know and where we need to go. *Psychological Bulletin, 137,* 421–442.

Smith, B. P. (2005). Goal orientation, implicit theory of ability, and collegiate instrumental music practice. *Psychology of Music, 33,* 36–57.

Tamir, M., John, O. P., Srivastava, S., & Gross, J. J. (2007). Implicit theories of emotion: Affective and social outcomes across a major life transition. *Journal of Personality and Social Psychology, 92,* 731–744.

Travers, C. J., Morisano, D., & Locke, E. A. (2015). Self-reflection, growth goals, and academic outcomes: A qualitative study. *British Journal of Educational Psychology, 85,* 224–241.

Wolfson, M. A., Tannenbaum, S. I., Mathieu, J. E., & Maynard, M. T. (2018). A cross-level investigation of informal field-based learning and performance improvements. *Journal of Applied Psychology, 103,* 14–36.

Wood, R. E., & Bandura, A. (1989). Impact of conceptions of ability on self-regulatory mechanisms and complex decision making. *Journal of Personality and Social Psychology, 56,* 407–415.

Zingoni, M., & Byron, K. (2017). How beliefs about the self influence perceptions of negative feedback and subsequent effort and learning. *Organizational Behavior and Human Decision Processes, 139,* 50–62.

12

Learning Agility, Resilience, and Successful Derailment

Paul R. Yost, CodieAnn DeHaas, and Mackenzie Allison

A life's work is not a series of stepping-stones onto which we calmly place our feet, but more like an ocean crossing where there is no path, only a heading, a direction, which, of itself, is in conversation with the elements.

—David Whyte, author and poet, *Crossing the Unknown Sea*

Organizations are increasingly complex and dynamic (Snowden & Boone, 2007; Uhl-Bien, Marion, & McKelvey, 2007). Change is the norm, and stability is the exception. In this environment, leaders and employees increasingly need to be agile and resilient. Other chapters in this book have explored the traits, behaviors, and organizational systems that promote learning agility. In this chapter, we shine a spotlight on times that are especially challenging: when leaders and organizations face crises, overwhelming odds, and failure. Our focus is on more than just survival. We follow other researchers in the movement to define resilience as the ability to move through challenges in a way that leads to increased positive adaptation to meet future challenges (Luthans, Youssef, & Avolio, 2007). Resilient leaders are able to navigate adverse situations with agility and bounce back, emerging stronger on the other side. Using Taleb's (2014) framework, leaders and organizations need to move beyond being fragile, fracturing under pressure (e.g., glass) and beyond displaying robust stability under pressure (e.g., rock) to a state of antifragility (e.g., muscle tissue), which actually is strengthened under pressure.

Paul R. Yost, CodieAnn DeHaas, and Mackenzie Allison, *Learning Agility, Resilience, and Successful Derailment* In: *The Age of Agility*. Edited by: Veronica Schmidt Harvey and Kenneth P. De Meuse, Oxford University Press (2021). © Oxford University Press. DOI: 10.1093/oso/9780190085353.003.0012

Learning Agility Versus Resilience Versus Derailment

Our understanding of learning agility can be significantly enhanced by examining the resilience and derailment literature. A metaphor may be helpful in thinking about how they relate. The leader's job for several decades now is best described as permanent white water (Vaill, 1989). The challenge is not to get to the next calm stretch, but to figure out how to keep moving forward in an environment of constant turbulence (Snowden & Boone, 2007). Learning agile leaders are likely not only to survive but also to thrive in these conditions. They see change as a natural part of the adventure; finding oneself off course is just another step of the journey (De Meuse, 2017; Lombardo & Eichinger, 2000). In this way, resilience and derailment can be considered the results, and learning agility represents the skills of the guide. Agile leaders are more likely to be and lead teams that are resilient, avoiding derailment. When off course, they are more likely to navigate through derailment successfully. Furthermore, one can look at the predictors of resilience and derailment to identify factors that support and/or enhance learning agility.

There is a vast research base on the elements that lead to increased resilience and derailment in organizations—too much to cover in one chapter. Rather than summarizing everything at a surface level, we focus on the *practices* that leaders can adopt to increase their resilience and ability to navigate through overwhelming challenges.

Deliberate Practice

The study of experts across professions suggests that expertise develops over time, typically requiring at least 10,000 hours and 10 or more years (Ericsson, Krampe, & Tesch-Roemer, 1993). It is not automatic but requires deliberate practice. Across a larger system, practices can be built into an organization's culture and climate to direct the behaviors and practices of its members (Schneider, Ehrhart, & Macey, 2013). However, not all practices are equal (Yost, 2016). The most powerful ones are characterized by the following four elements:

- *Research based*: Practices that will truly have an impact are based on theory and research; that is, there is strong evidence they actually will make a difference (Walton, 2014).

- *Learnable*: Practices should not depend on stable traits but should be behaviors that people can learn and develop (Ericsson et al., 1993). When adopted and practiced enough, they can become habits (Duhigg, 2012). In today's dynamic organizations, rather than relying solely on selecting people who are hired with the right traits, learnable practices allow an organization to build learning agility and resilience throughout the whole workforce.
- *Self-reinforcing*: Practices are most powerful when people experience positive emotions when they engage in them. They naturally build in a person over time. For example, expressing gratitude and encouragement toward others is reinforcing for the person who expresses it and can become self-sustaining (Fehr, Fulmer, Awtrey, & Miller, 2017).
- *Catalytic*: The most powerful practices go one step further. They not only increase over time but also are more likely to be "caught" by others. For example, in the case of gratitude, it is also reinforcing for the people who receive it and therefore likely to be passed on (Fehr et al., 2017). Catalytic practices can "go viral." In the language of organizational theory, they become microfoundations that reinforce and build within the organization, affecting and infecting the whole system (Ployhart & Moliterno, 2011; Teece, 2007).

Amazon provides an example of a practice that meets all of these criteria. The company has promoted the idea of "Day One." Employees are encouraged to think of their work every day as though it was a new start-up (Galetti, Golden, & Brozovich, 2019), and employees are encouraged not to settle for how things have always been done but reinvent their work every day. Amazon headquarters is named the Day One Building. The Day One idea relies on the four principles outlined, in that it encourages adaptive thinking, which research has shown is critical to organizational success (research based), can be developed (learned), sparks energy (self-reinforcing), and spurs fellow employees to engage in similar behavior (catalytic).

In the following sections, we explore in more depth a subset of practices that are related to three areas: (a) *short-term resilience,* allowing one to survive and navigate in the midst of a crisis; (b) *long-term resilience,* enabling individuals to thrive over time; and (c) *successful derailment,* navigating through failure and adversity to emerge better on the other side. Within each of these areas, we discuss individual actions and organizational systems. Throughout, we focus on leaders, but the principles apply to *all* employees within an organization. As organizations become flatter, more decentralized, and more dynamic, the practices should include not only senior leaders and managers, but also functional experts and front-line employees who increasingly are critical to an organization's long-term success.

Short-Term Resilience (Surviving)

Sometimes, the goal is simply to survive to fight another day. Although research suggests that stable traits such as emotional stability and hardiness predispose some people to be more resilient (Britt, Shen, Sinclair, Grossman, & Klieger, 2016), evidence also indicates that resilience can be learned (Luthans, Avey, Avolio, & Peterson, 2010; Yost, 2016). Individuals can develop resilience practices that aid in anticipating challenges and overcoming adversity. Practices that are particularly important for both individuals and organizations include (a) recognizing there is a problem; (b) building a fence to focus one's action; (c) managing emotions; (d) drawing on social support; and (e) investing in one's physical health.

Recognize There Is a Problem

When one is overwhelmed and the world feels chaotic, it is hard to know where to begin. Adversity can be paralyzing, making learning and action nearly impossible (Sweller, 1988). Identifying the heart of the problem is a good first step. However, recognizing that one has a problem is not always easy. For example, Prochaska, DiClemente, and Norcross (1992) noted that people trying to eliminate a negative habit such as smoking typically "quit" multiple times before they succeed. They have to progress through multiple stages (thinking about the problem, contemplating solutions, preparing for the change) before they are ready to take action. During the problem identification stage, there are a variety of practices that may be pursued. Individuals can write a comprehensive list of the things that must be done to identify the most important ones to free cognitive space and prevent rumination. Organizations can use balanced scorecards to identify potential problems (R. S. Kaplan & Norton, 2007). Change management tools can be used to create a sense of urgency (Kotter, 2007) and help leaders break problems down into actionable root causes (Hiatt & Creasey, 2012).

Build a Fence

Once problems have been identified, the next step is to take action. However, in crisis moments, problems can be overwhelming and paralyzing. To foster resilience, the leader needs to build a fence around the problem, identifying small, doable, next steps (Weick, 1984). Over time, the accumulation of small wins can build the self-efficacy needed to take on future challenges.

Agile team processes can be used to quickly break up complex problems into smaller more manageable pieces and then form solutions for each piece that will contribute to the overall whole (ClydeBank Business, 2016; Rigby, Sutherland, & Noble, 2018). Jared Diamond (2019) discussed how fence building can be used by leaders at the national level to build coalitions and consensus.

Manage Your Emotions

Emotional regulation can increase one's locus of control and resilience (Tabibnia & Radecki, 2018). Positive emotions and mindfulness are effective strategies for building resilience quickly (Tugade & Fredrickson, 2004). Beneficial mindfulness activities include activities such as deep breathing and breathing awareness (Jennings, Apsche, Blossom, & Bayles, 2013); meditation (S. Kaplan, 2001); and demonstrating self-compassion (Pidgeon, Ford, & Klaassen, 2014). Individuals can practice these through a variety of techniques to build objectivity (e.g., maintaining a gratitude journal, imagining a close friend or colleague in a similar situation). These all contribute to in-the-moment emotional regulation and coping strategies one can use when needed to quickly build resilience (S. Kaplan, 2001; Skinner, Edge, Altman, & Sherwood, 2003).

Williams, Guber, Sutcliffe, Shepherd, and Zhao (2017) identified several elements that increase the capacity of organizations to remain resilient and adaptive in adversity, especially as emotions increase. Resilient organizations are more likely to have (a) financial capacity to create slack in anticipation of future adversity; (b) cognitive capacity to provide purpose, vision, and expertise to manage challenges; (c) behavioral capacity to explore multiple alternatives; and (d) emotional regulatory capacity to promote hope, optimism, and ways to express emotions. In this last area, Druskat and Wolff (2001) suggested that organizational team norms may be particularly effective mechanisms to increase systemwide self-regulation. Norms can promote empathy (e.g., considering one's work from other people's perspectives); awareness (e.g., acknowledging emotions, thanking people); and emotional regulation (e.g., allowing team members to call a process check in the middle of stressful situations).

Draw on Social Networks

Social support is another important resource in the face of adversity (Tabibnia & Radecki, 2018; Williams et al., 2017). When experiencing an in-the-moment challenge, agile and resilient leaders are able to draw on a kaleidoscope of relationships for mentoring, feedback, emotional support, new ways of thinking, and how one is perceived by others (Bossen & Yost, 2014; Cohen, 2004). Mentors and role models who have faced similar challenges can provide insights and advice (Bandura, 1989).

Organizations can increase social networks by structuring work projects in ways that require leaders and employees to work across business units and functions. Organizations also can sponsor networking events, promote mentoring programs, organize affinity groups, and create external volunteering opportunities.

Promote Health and Well-Being

There is substantial research indicating that physical exercise, diet, and sleep habits have a significant effect on one's resilience (Tabibnia & Radecki, 2018). A meta-analysis of workplace exercise interventions found that they had positive effects on physical activity, fitness, work attendance, and stress (Conn, Hafdahl, Cooper, Brown, & Lusk, 2009). Exercise is especially important and does not have to be extensive. For example, the Mayo Clinic (2020) suggests that the average adult needs a minimum of 150 minutes of moderate aerobic activity or 75 minutes of vigorous aerobic exercise each week. It could include a run, fast-paced walk, or walking the stairs in one's building. At the organizational level, physical health promotion might include on-site exercise facilities and/or classes, gym memberships, health screenings, or organizational participation in a 5K for a local charity. Table 12.1 summarizes the practices that support to short-term resilience.

Table 12.1 Example Short-Term Strategies for Resilience

Dimensions	Individual Strategies	Organizational Strategies
Recognize there is a problem.	• Make a "to do" list and circle two items that are nonnegotiable today. • Share your struggles with others; listen to their advice.	• Create a balanced scorecard for your team. • Explore why the team is stuck (lack of awareness, desire, knowledge, ability, or rewards).
Build a fence.	• Break a big project down into small wins for the coming week. • Find and accomplish one thing you have been avoiding.	• Build a fence around the strategic initiative that will have the greatest impact on the organization's success.
Manage your emotions.	• Put a name to your emotions. Ask yourself what about today is making you happy, sad, hopeful, guilt, surprised, frustrated, and grateful. • Stop and take time to breathe throughout the day.	• Build team norms that promote emotional regulation: taking other's perspectives, encouraging others, calling a process check in the middle of stressful situations.
Draw on social networks.	• Make a list of the people in your life who provide mentoring, feedback, emotional support, new ways of thinking, and how one is perceived by others.	• Launch social networking groups: mentoring, affinity groups, lunch and learns, volunteer groups.
Promote health and well-being.	• Exercise for at least 20 minutes every day (the gym, a walking meeting, taking the stairs). • Bring a healthy lunch.	• Provide gym memberships, on-site exercise classes, health screenings.

Long-Term Resilience (Thriving)

Adopting short-term resilience strategies help a person weather the storm, but they do not necessarily build long-term sustainability. The resilience literature initially focused on the event and how people survived in the moment. More recent work has suggested that resilience is better conceptualized as a *process,* and that strategies deployed before, during, and after crisis moments are important to consider (Roux-Dufort, 2007). For example, crisis moments can be avoided or minimized if the right practices are adopted before the crisis occurs. Research recommends several behaviors that serve to sustain resilience and enhance growth as the result of successfully navigating adverse situations. The following five strategies are particularly important: (a) envision the future; (b) practice bricolage; (c) cue and reinforce learning and resilience; (d) build an environment of social support; and (e) reflect on the learning.

Envision the Future

Navigating uncertainty and complex environments requires a strong positive sense of self (Steele, Spencer, & Lynch, 1993) and a proactive focus (Lengnick-Hall & Beck, 2005). Individuals can practice this by envisioning potential future work selves, which in turn leads to greater proactive career behaviors (Strauss, Griffin, & Parker, 2012). The undiscovered is discovered (Chermack, Coons, O'barr, & Khatami, 2017). At the organizational level, scenario planning can be used to explore potential futures and how the organization should respond to them (Schwartz, 1996). Both future work selves and scenario planning provide a structured way to engage in the learning agility aspect of experimentation (De Meuse, 2017). Forecasting a potential future and exploring the strengths and weaknesses of the organization to address future challenges and opportunities (Britt et al., 2016) increases resilience.

Practice Bricolage

As with any expert performance, success is only possible with continual, deliberate practice (Ericsson, 2006). Intentional and continued experimentation are essential to persevere and build grit (Duckworth, 2016). Bricolage, the ability to create something out of the materials at hand (Mallak, 1998), represents one of these practices. For example, in the movie *Apollo 13*, the engineering leader dumps examples of the materials onboard the rocket and challenges the team to figure out how to help the astronauts build a CO_2 filter in space (Howard, 2005). Individuals can begin to practice bricolage in their day-to-day work by challenging each other to switch roles or challenging one another to use established tools and processes to build unique and creative solutions. Leaders can practice agile thinking simply by switching how they interact in meetings. Moving from being the expert to team questioner builds new skills and new perspectives.

Organizations can invest in regular on-the-job development and experimentation, encouraging leaders to engage in creative practice. Teams can adopt agile processes, such as team huddles, handoffs, check-backs, and debriefings that have been demonstrated to significantly improve emergency room team effectiveness (Agency for Healthcare Research and Quality, 2020). Practicing adaptive learning in lower pressure situations builds the skills needed to meet adaptive challenges when they emerge.

Cue and Reinforce Learning and Resilience

Leaders also can use situational cues to increase resilience in themselves and their teams. For an illustration, leaders who want to become better at empowering their teams might make tally marks to track how often they make statements versus how often they ask questions during team meetings. Leaders likewise can build reward systems that increase resilience (e.g., rewarding team members for small, iterative failures that improve project success). Checklists represent another tool (Gawande, 2009). Airline pilots and healthcare workers use checklists to institutionalize habits.

At an organizational level, feedback, recognition, and other reward systems all serve as powerful incentives to increase resilience (Mallak, 1998). Just as important, it is essential for organizations to remove organizational structures that are barriers to resilience practices. For example, an organization can remove communication boundaries between departments to allow for collaboration and publicly recognize and reinforce cross-organizational support when it occurs.

Build an Environment of Social Support

Building and maintaining strong social networks are essential for long-term resilience (Kuntz, Malinen, & Näswall, 2017). Social support and networks provide information, increase self-regulation, decrease stress, and promote well-being (Cohen, 2004; Fitzsimons & Finkel, 2010; Ghosh, Haynes, & Kram, 2013). Ibarra and Hunter (2007) identified the following three types of networks that are particularly important for leaders:

(a) operational, (b) developmental, and (c) strategic. Operational networks are used to get work done. Personal networks are used to enhance personal development and provide social support. Strategic networks are used to scan the environment and explore personal and business priorities. Leaders can be encouraged to identify the network they have in place and additional resources or support needed (Reivich, Seligman, & McBride, 2011).

From an organizational perspective, one can promote social support through cross-collaboration (Kuntz et al., 2017). Communities can promote feedback, gratitude, and prosocial behaviors in one another (Lyubomirsky, King, & Diener, 2005). To increase social support, teams can be encouraged to check in with one another; organizations can sponsor affinity groups and networking events or sponsor "lunch and learns" to explore emerging challenges facing the business.

Reflect on the Learning

As discussed in Chapter 10, the ability to reflect on one's experience and apply it to future situations is fundamental to learning individual and team adaptability. Similarly, reflection is a critical component in increasing team adaptability and resilience (Baird & Griffin, 2006). By exercising resilience-focused reflection, an individual is more likely to switch from reactive learning (This happened; what now?) to proactive learning (This happened; how will this help me in the future?). It increases the opportunities for an individual to take these lessons learned and apply them to future challenges (Hodges, Keeley, & Grier, 2005). Resilience is increased by optimistic reflection (Reivich et al., 2011) that is focused on capitalizing on strengths, rather than fear and failure. Individuals can practice optimistic reflection through journal activities with structured questions that focus on the meaning of their work and a long-term view of their actions (Hodges et al., 2005). Organizations can introduce structures that encourage and ask for regular reflection at meetings, workshops, and other points of discussion. For example, the use of "after-event reviews" can provide a structured way to explore successes, failures, and the reasons behind them (DeRue, Nahrgang, Hollenbeck, & Workman, 2012). Table 12.2 summarizes practices that support long-term resilience.

Table 12.2 Example Long-Term Strategies for Resilience

Dimensions	Individual Strategies	Organizational Strategies
Envision the future.	• Take 5 minutes each day and ask yourself: What does your future-self look like 5 years from now? What two actions can you do today to bring yourself closer to that future self?	• Lead your team or the organization in scenario planning. • Ask teams to consider what in this organization should *never* change? What should the organization *stop* doing? What should it *start* doing?
Practice bricolage.	• Switch your role in meetings: ask more questions, ask fewer questions, focus on strategy, focus on execution. Challenge team members to do the same.	• Institute agile team huddles at regular intervals of projects to report on what worked, what didn't, and why.
Cue and reinforce learning and resilience.	• Build checklists to routinize the things you don't want to worry about in your day-to-day work.	• Celebrate team members who have been persistent and resilient.
Build an environment of social support.	• Every day, list three things that you are grateful for. • Identify the people in your operational, personal, and strategic network.	• Make feedback a group norm. • Ask the question, Whose voice is missing? at each meeting to welcome every individual to the discussion.
Reflect on the learning.	• Start a work-focused journal: What does your job mean to you, to others? How does your work influence the future of your organization?	• Hold regular after-event reviews (AERs) postprojects: What practices/behaviors aided the group? What opportunities for change can be implemented in the future?

Derailment

In a world of constant change, even the most resilient and learning agile leaders fail occasionally. Business initiatives do not live up to their potential, projects go awry, and careers go off course. Research over the decades has identified several causes of derailment, strategies to avoid it, and ways to recover from it. This research has identified a variety of factors that can lead to derailment (see Hogan, Hogan, & Kaiser, 2011, for a comprehensive review). At the same time, research has consistently identified key experiences critical in a leader's development (McCall, 2010), and ironically several of them—business mistakes/failures, career setbacks, and personal trauma—are directly related to derailment! If true, then avoiding derailment is only half of the story; the other half is how to successfully navigate through it and emerge stronger on the other side. Furthermore, these negative events appear to teach lessons that are not likely to be taught anywhere else (McCall, Lombardo, & Morrison, 1988). Yet, in researching this chapter, only one article could be located that focused on what might be termed *successful derailment* (Kovach, 1989). The rest of this chapter therefore focuses on this underrepresented area, that is, how leaders can navigate failures and career setbacks in a way that allow the leaders to grow from the experience.

Causes of Derailment

Derailment has traditionally been defined as, "people who were very successful in their careers . . . but who, in the eyes of the organization, did not live up to their full potential" (McCall & Lombardo, 1983, pp. 1–2) and the setback is not voluntary or desired. Evidence suggests that derailment is common. Hogan et al. (2011) reported that leadership failure rates commonly range from 30% to 67%. Similarly, in *Onboarding New Employees,* Bauer cited research that "half of all senior outside hires fail within 18 months in a new position," and "half of all hourly workers leave new jobs within the first 120 days" (2010, p. 1). Kovach (1989) declared that simple mathematics indicate that senior management positions and senior technical roles are by nature limited at higher levels. The pyramid narrows to the point where only one in a thousand will reach the pinnacle. Thus, career stalls, setbacks, and derailment are natural outcomes for ambitious leaders, even those who are learning agile.

Derailment is triggered when external or role demands do not match an individual's capabilities. Mismatches are most likely to occur when individuals change roles (e.g., moving from supervisor to midlevel manager), requiring the acquisition of new skills, letting go of old behaviors, or exposing previously hidden weaknesses (De Meuse, Dai, & Wu, 2011; McCall & Lombardo, 1983). The causes of derailment fall into three general areas: external factors, leader traits, and leader behaviors.

External Factors

Several situational factors can trigger derailment (McCall, 1998). Leaders might be promoted to new roles and do not yet have the required skill set. They may fail to adjust and adapt to the new demands. Sometimes, derailment is simply bad luck (e.g., the leader gets caught in organizational politics, the external market for a product or service collapses, the leader has a team without the required skill sets and not enough time to replace or develop them). Some of the external causes are avoidable; some are not. Research suggests that certain personality traits can increase a leader's probability of derailing.

Traits

In a review of the literature, Hogan et al. (2011) summarized derailment characteristics across several studies (e.g., Moscosco & Salgado, 2004; Schmit, Kilm, & Robie, 2000). They noted that the traits related to leader derailment were consistent with Horney's (1950) three inclinations that hinder human growth: (a) moving away from others (e.g., being overly cautious, distrustful, passive-aggressive); (b) moving against others (e.g., being arrogant, malicious, melodramatic, manipulative); and (c) moving toward others (e.g., micromanaging, being overly submissive).

In parallel work, meta-analysis research suggested that a few traits are consistently related to greater effectiveness across industries and studies (DeRue, Nahrgang, Wellman, & Humphrey, 2011). This suggests that the opposite of these traits is related to less effective leaders who in turn are more likely to derail. The strongest predictors of effective leadership are cognitive ability, extroversion, openness to experience, and emotional stability. Agreeableness appears to be weakly or unrelated to most leadership outcomes. Thus, the opposites of these attributes (low cognitive ability, introversion, low openness to experience, and conscientiousness) are related to lower leader effectiveness. This is rather discouraging, suggesting, for example, that introverted leaders are more likely to perform poorly and potentially derail. But, there is another layer to the story.

Behaviors

In the meta-analysis by DeRue et al. (2011) cited previously, the researchers found that although traits were related to effectiveness, leadership behaviors predicted overall effectiveness above and beyond traits. That is good news because it indicates that traits may give a person an edge up, but leaders can adopt behaviors that compensate for these areas. For example, introverted leaders can learn to engage in extroverted behaviors.

Before moving to these compensatory behaviors, it is worthwhile to identify the behaviors that increase derailment. How leaders treat others is strongly related to derailment (Hogan et al., 2011), and many of these behaviors are the opposite of those associated with learning agility. Abusive behavior, overdependence on a small group of people, and isolation are particularly problematic. Other behaviors include problems with interpersonal relationships, failure to build and lead a team, failure to meet business challenges, and the inability to change or adapt during a transition (Van Velsor & Leslie, 1995). Leader behaviors associated with lower effectiveness (DeRue et al., 2011) include low task structure (e.g., failure to set goals, failure to hold people accountable); low consideration (e.g., failure to listen and support others); low transformational leadership (e.g., failure to cast a vision, inspire others, role model values and ethics, or stimulate innovation and creativity); and high laissez-faire leadership (e.g., a lack of leadership). Meta-analyses on emotional intelligence (EQ)—abilities that enable a person to understand their own emotions as well as those of others—indicated that EQ is related to employee performance across all jobs (O'Boyle, Humphrey, Pollack, Hawver, & Story, 2011), and the lack of it leads to lower effectiveness.

Leaders can decrease derailment by engaging in behaviors that either prevent derailing or support self-correction when they start to veer in the wrong direction. Learning agility can help them sense what is happening, experiment with new ideas, adapt their behavior to situational demands, capture the lessons, and apply them to new challenges (De Meuse, 2017). Leaders and organizations can build in "early warning systems" to identify potential problems and correct them before they become too severe (Yost & Plunkett, 2009).

Unfortunately, even when a leader engages in all the right actions, derailment can still occur. The question is no longer how to avoid it, but how to navigate through the experience and emerge as a better leader and person on the other side (Marks, Mirvis, & Ashkenas, 2014).

Successful Derailment

Learning agility and "bouncing back" (Luthans et al., 2007) sound pretty good when external factors can be blamed. What about when a leader knows he or she is partially or mostly responsible? Three strategies can increase the probability that derailment is successful in these situations: (a) reframe derailment, (b) draw on others, and (c) capture the lessons to be learned.

Reframe Derailment

Derailment isn't fun. No one enters a new role wanting to fail. However, there are better and worse ways to frame difficult times. Two elements are particularly important during times of derailment: the metanarrative that is adopted and the extent to which the leader adopts a growth versus a fixed mindset. To begin, the metanarrative is important because it locates the leader within a bigger story arc that can be adaptive or maladaptive to the person's continued growth (Jill & Combs, 1996; Yost, Yoder, Chung, & Voetmann, 2015). Is the derailment framed as a tragedy (failure is inevitable and meaningless), a cycle (here I go again), transformational (I will emerge a different and wiser person), or redemptive (I learned important lessons about myself and life that I can pass on to others)?

Organizational cultures can reinforce a survival-of-the-fittest mindset with winners and losers, or they can focus on the unique value and contribution of all employees and the ability of people to grow and change (Yost & Chang, 2009). In this way, leaders can adopt either a "fixed" or "growth" mindset (Dweck, 2006). Leaders who adopt a fixed mindset assume that talent is stable and primarily innate. In contrast, leaders who adopt a growth mindset view talent as largely under a person's control and perceive failure as an opportunity to learn. They believe their abilities can be developed through hard work. Microsoft has adopted the growth mindset as a foundational element of its culture (Ibarra & Rattan, 2018).

Derailment and failures are more likely to result in effective adaptation when they are framed as an iterative process—as a natural part of change, growth, and development (Keith & Frese, 2008). For example, several current approaches to change management, such as design thinking, are built on the concept that successes and failures are expected and instructive (Brown, 2009). Both "failures" and "successes" are a natural part of the adaptive process. At Amazon, for example, workers are encouraged to "fail fast." That is, they are encouraged to break their work down into shorter tasks so ideas can be tested along the way.

Draw on Others

As noted several times in this chapter, the role of other people is critical in learning agility and personal development (Ghosh et al., 2013). A support network can help pick a person up and point him or her in a new direction. However, the outcomes of derailment are not limited to what other people can do to help the person who has stumbled. Even when the derailment sometimes feels like the demotivational poster of a sinking ship with the caption, "It could be that the purpose of your life is only to serve as a warning to others" (Despair Inc., 2020), leaders who have experienced a setback are often in the best position to empathize and support others going through similar experiences. They can offer insights and reassurance in a way that someone who has not faced a similar setback can never do.

Several organizational systems can be leveraged to create this social capital. Simple activities such as regular one-on-one meetings between supervisors and employees can be used to discuss expectations, project deliverables, and provide ongoing development (London, 2003). Formal or informal mentoring programs can be adopted (Kendall, 2014). People can be encouraged to build their developmental networks (Bossen & Yost, 2014). And, people can be encouraged to meet regularly with key stakeholders in their network (Conger & Fishel, 2007; Watkins, 2013).

Capture the Lessons

In the original lessons of experience research (McCall et al., 1988), the following three key experiences related to derailment were identified: (a) failures/mistakes, (b) career setbacks, and (c) personal trauma. These three experiences shared two common lessons: learning about personal limits and blind spots and understanding how to cope with situations beyond one's control. An additional lesson, organizational politics, was shared by two of the experiences. These represent lessons that leaders should pay particularly close attention to as they navigate derailment in their careers.

Personal Limits and Blind Spots. Leaders reported that derailment experiences often taught them lessons about their personal limits, such as areas where they lacked leadership skills (e.g., strategic thinking). Leaders were likely to discover interpersonal weaknesses, including overconfidence, abrasiveness, and lack of delegation. They learned important lessons about how to treat other people more respectfully as well as strategies to work in partnership with other people in ways that supplement and complement their own weaknesses. For instance, a leader who is good at strategy might find people to partner with who are strong in planning and execution. Coming to terms with one's personal weaknesses and blind spots can also cause individuals to reassess what they value (Kovach, 1989). Several organizational systems can highlight potential gaps and equip leaders to improve in these areas. For example, 360-feedback processes and derailment assessments can identify potential problems (Conger & Fishel, 2007; Morgeson, Mumford, & Campion, 2005). Organizations can implement processes that reduce immunity to change (Kegan & Lahey, 2009). Senior leaders can be encouraged to share their derailment stories and what was learned from them (McCauley & Taylor, 2014). Learning agility assessments can be administered to identify behavioral areas, which could lead to overuse and potential derailment (e.g., De Meuse, Lim, & Rao, 2019).

Coping With Situations Beyond One's Control. Sometimes, situations are simply beyond one's control. Leaders need to choose the battles they are going to fight. As organizations become more dynamic, decisions move from simple cause–effect relationships with clear decision rules to emergent environments requiring leaders to act, assess the outcomes, and adapt for the next move (Snowden & Boone, 2007). Leaders who live through these experiences can capture insights about how to navigate into the unknown when so much isn't within their control. Derailed leaders can emerge better able to engage in real-time reflection, asking: What happened? Why did it happen? and What should I do the next time? (Hill, 2014).

Organizational Politics. By definition, organizations are collectives of people—multiple stakeholder groups vying for influence (Mintzberg, 1983). Tensions and conflict within these collectives are natural and can be healthy. Different groups bring different perspectives, potentially making the whole greater than the sum of the parts. In most instances, organizational politics are simply different groups with different priorities acting rationally from their location in the system. For example, sales departments commonly push for new features, while in contrast manufacturing departments want to minimize costly variability. What looks like politics is simply a clash of goals. In other situations, organizational politics can be people or groups trying to maximize their position over others. Other times, the behavior is unethical or degrading. Derailed leaders have the opportunity to learn the distinctions between these situations and how to manage them better the next time.

Organizational systems can be put in place to help leaders deal with such challenging situations. Creating a strong ethics culture is an important step (Treviño, Den Nieuwenboer, & Kish-Gephart, 2014). Introducing organizational development processes that bring diverse groups together to tackle problems also can be helpful. Finally, training people on ways to manage organizational politics can be a powerful tool to help leaders make sense of their environments during and after derailment episodes.

Derailment and failures provide key developmental experiences in a leader's journey. Learning agile leaders are focused on capturing the lessons that these events provide, applying them to future challenges, and passing them on to others.

Conclusion

In this chapter, we have taken on a rather daunting task of summarizing the resilience and derailment literatures, comparing them to learning agility theory and research, and distilling practical actions that individuals and organizations can take. We have attempted to limit this vast territory by focusing on the practices leaders and organizations can adopt to navigate through difficult times. Ironically, the "short" list we have created (five crisis practices, five long-term resilience practices, and three derailment practices) is rather overwhelming. It risks making readers even less resilient (e.g., Now I *really* don't know where to begin!)

Therefore, we would like to end the chapter by drawing on one of the practices—"build a fence"—to help leaders identify a way to get started. First, leaders should identify the broad challenges they are facing today. Are they in crisis? Are they attempting to build long-term resilience? Are they navigating through derailment? Next, they should look over the resilience-building practices associated with this area to identify the practice that triggers the most passion. For example, if a leader finds herself or himself in crisis, maybe the felt need is for social support for oneself or others.

As noted at the beginning, the practices highlighted in this chapter were selected because they are research based, learnable, self-reinforcing, and catalytic. Once instituted, they have the capacity to "go viral" in the larger system. For example, seeking social support is satisfying (self-reinforcing) and requires interacting with others in ways that are likely to also increase their social support.

One could argue the same catalytic processes should apply to most aspects of learning agility discussed throughout this book. Leaders who seek feedback will engage others and model the behavior they want to promote in the larger organization. The potential catalytic properties of learning agility represent an important area for future research. How can organizations teach and deploy learning agility practices in a way that increases the learning capacity of the whole organization? For instance, error management training (i.e., actively encouraging learners to look for and make errors so they can learn from them) can lead to better individual performance and an increased capacity to solve future problems (Keith & Frese, 2008). Furthermore, there is evidence that organizations can create error management cultures, which in turn lead to higher organizational performance (Van Dyck, Frese, Baer, & Sonnetag, 2005).

A second suggested area for future research is exploring how the resilience and derailment literature can enhance learning agility theory and research. What precursors of resilience are underrepresented in the learning agility literature? For example, well-being practices such as mindfulness and exercise clearly increase a leader's ability to remain learning agile. Similarly, the derailment research highlights the importance of ethics and values. However, this topic currently receives limited attention in the learning agility literature, but evidence suggests that morale resilience can be developed (May, Chan, Hodges, & Avolio, 2003).

Conversely, the learning agility literature has much to offer the resilience and derailment literatures especially in the area of capturing the lessons of experience and applying them in novel, challenging situations. It would be interesting to know whether individuals who are highly learning agile recover more quickly and effectively from derailment. Likewise, it would be intriguing to understand whether highly learning agile leaders tend to avoid derailment in the first place. The interplay among derailment, resilience, and learning agility is just beginning to attract the attention of researchers and points to exciting future directions to explore.

References

Agency for Healthcare Research and Quality. (2020). *Pocket guide: TeamSTEPPS. Team strategies & tools to enhance performance and patient safety.* Retrieved from https://www.ahrq.gov/teamstepps/instructor/essentials/pocketguide.html

Baird, L., & Griffin, D. (2006). Adaptability and responsiveness: The case for dynamic learning. *Organizational Dynamics, 4*(35), 372–383.

Bandura, A. (1989). Human agency in social cognitive theory. *American Psychologist, 44*(9), 1175–1184.

Bauer, T. N. (2010). *Onboarding new employees: Maximizing success (White paper).* SHRM Foundation. Retrieved from https://www.researchgate.net/profile/Talya_Bauer/publication/286447344_Onboarding_The_power_of_connection/links/5669965808ae430ab4f72b4f.pdf

Bossen, M., & Yost, P. (2014). Building a board of learning advisors. In C. D. McCauley, D. S. DeRue, P. R. Yost, & S. Taylor (Eds.), Experience-driven leader development (pp. 259–264). San Francisco, CA: Wiley.

Britt, T. W., Shen, W., Sinclair, R. R., Grossman, M. R., & Klieger, D. M. (2016). How much do we really know about employee resilience? *Industrial and Organizational Psychology, 9*(2), 378–404.

Brown, T. (2009). *Change by design.* New York, NY: HarperCollins.

Chermack, T. J., Coons, L. M., O'barr, G., & Khatami, S. (2017). The effects of scenario planning on participant reports of resilience. *European Journal of Training and Development, 41*(4), 306–326.

ClydeBank Business. (2016). *Agile project management quick start guide: The simplified beginner's guide to agile project management.* Albany, NY: ClydeBank Media.

Cohen, S. (2004). Social relationships and health. *American Psychologist, 59*(8), 676–684.

Conger, J. A., & Fishel, B. (2007). Accelerating leadership performance at the top: Lessons from the Bank of America's executive on-boarding process. *Human Resource Management Review, 17*(4), 442–454.

Conn, V. S., Hafdahl, A. R., Cooper, P. S., Brown, L. M., & Lusk, S. L. (2009). Meta-analysis of workplace physical activity interventions. *American Journal of Preventive Medicine, 37*(4), 330–339.

De Meuse, K. P. (2017). Learning agility: Its evolution as a psychological construct and its empirical relationship to leader success. *Consulting Psychology Journal: Practice and Research, 69*(4), 267–295.

De Meuse, K. P., Dai, G., & Wu, J. (2011). Leadership skills across organizational levels: A closer examination. *The Psychologist-Manager Journal, 14,* 120–139.

De Meuse, K. P., Lim, J., & Rao, R. (2019). *The development and validation of the TALENTx7˚ Assessment: A psychological measure of learning agility* (3rd ed.). Shanghai, China: Leader's Gene Consulting.

DeRue, D. S., Nahrgang, J. D., Hollenbeck, J. R., & Workman, K. (2012). A quasi-experimental study of after-event reviews and leadership development. *Journal of Applied Psychology, 97*(5), 997–1015.

DeRue, D. S., Nahrgang, J. D., Wellman, N., & Humphrey, S. E. (2011). Trait and behavioral theories of leadership: An integration and meta-analytic test of their relative validity. *Personnel Psychology, 64*(1), 7–52.

Despair Inc. (2020, February 28). Mistakes. https://despair.com/products/mistakes?variant=2457302467

Diamond, J. (2019). *Upheaval: Turning points for nations in crisis.* New York, NY: Little, Brown.

Druskat, V. U., & Wolff, S. B. (2001). Building the emotional intelligence of groups. *Harvard Business Review, 79*(3), 80–90.

Duckworth, A. (2016). *Grit: The power of passion and perseverance.* New York, NY: Scribner/Simon & Schuster.

Duhigg, C. (2012). *The power of habit: Why we do what we do in life and business.* New York, NY: Random House.

Dweck, C. S. (2006). *Mindset: The new psychology of success.* New York, NY: Random House.

Ericsson, K. A. (2006). The influence of experience and deliberate practice on the development of superior expert performance. In K. A. Ericsson, N. Charness, P. J. Feltovich, & R. R. Hoffman (Eds.), *The Cambridge handbook of expertise and expert performance* (pp. 683–703). Cambridge, UK: Cambridge University Press.

Ericsson, K. A., Krampe, R. T., & Tesch-Roemer, C. (1993). The role of deliberate practice in the acquisition of expert performance. *Psychological Review, 100*(3), 363–406.

Fehr, R., Fulmer, A., Awtrey, E., & Miller, J. A. (2017). The grateful workplace: A multilevel model of gratitude in organizations. *Academy of Management Review, 42*(2), 361–381.

Fitzsimons, G. M., & Finkel, E. J. (2010). Interpersonal influences on self-regulation. *Current Directions in Psychological Science, 19*(2), 101–105.

Galetti, B., Golden, J., & Brozovich, S. (2019). Inside day 1: How Amazon uses agile team structures and adaptive practices to innovate on behalf of customers. *People & Strategy, 42*(2), 36–41.

Gawande, A. (2009). *The checklist manifesto: How to get things right.* Gurgaon, India: Metropolitan Books.

Ghosh, R., Haynes, R. K., & Kram, K. E. (2013). Developmental networks at work: Holding environments for leader development. *Career Development International, 18*(3), 232–256.

Hiatt, J. M., & Creasey, T. J. (2012). *Change management: The people side of change* (2nd ed.). Loveland, CO: Prosci Learning Center.

Hill, C. (2014). Scaffolding reflection: What, so what, now what? In C. D. McCauley, D. S. DeRue, P. R. Yost, & S. Taylor (Eds.), *Experience-driven leader development* (pp. 229–234). San Francisco, CA: Wiley.

Hodges, H. E., Keeley, A. C., & Grier, E. C. (2005). Professional resilience, practice longevity, and Parse's theory for baccalaureate education. *Journal of Nursing Education, 44*(12), 548–554.

Hogan, J., Hogan, R., & Kaiser, R. B. (2011). Managerial derailment. In S. Zedeck (Ed.), *APA handbook of industrial and organizational psychology* (pp. 555–575). Washington, DC: American Psychological Association.

Horney, K. (1950). *Neurosis and human growth.* New York, NY: Norton.

Howard, R. (Director). (2005). *Apollo 13* [Film]. Universal City, CA: Universal Pictures.

Ibarra, H. & Hunter, M. (2007). How leaders create and use networks. *Harvard Business Review, 85*(1), 40–47.

Ibarra, H., & Rattan, A. (2018). Microsoft: Instilling a growth mindset. *London Business School Review, 29*(3), 50–53.

Jennings, J. L., Apsche, J. A., Blossom, P., & Bayles, C. (2013). Using mindfulness in the treatment of adolescent sexual abusers: Contributing common factor or a primary modality? *International Journal of Behavioral Consultation and Therapy, 8*(3–4), 17–22.

Jill, M. S. W., & Combs, G. (1996). *Narrative therapy: The social construction of preferred realities.* New York, NY: Norton.

Kaplan, R. S., & Norton, D. P. (2007). Using the balanced scorecard as a strategic management system. *Harvard Business Review, 85*(7), 8–13.

Kaplan, S. (2001). Meditation, restoration, and the management of mental fatigue. *Environment and Behavior, 33*(4), 480–506.

Kegan, R., & Lahey, L. L. (2009). *Immunity to change: How to overcome it and unlock potential in yourself and your organization.* Boston, MA: Harvard Business Press.

Keith, N., & Frese, M. (2008). Effectiveness of error management training: A meta-analysis. *Journal of Applied Psychology, 93*(1), 59–69.

Kendall, D. (2014). Building leaders in powerful developmental relationships. In C. D. McCauley, D. S. DeRue, P. R. Yost, & S. Taylor (Eds.), *Experience-driven leader development* (pp. 405–412). San Francisco, CA: Wiley.

Kotter, J. P. (2007). Leading change: Why transformation efforts fail. *Harvard Business Review, 85*(1), 96–103.

Kovach, B. E. (1989). Successful derailment: What fast-trackers can learn while they're off the track? *Organizational Dynamics, 18*(2), 33–48.

Kuntz, J. R., Malinen, S., & Näswall, K. (2017). Employee resilience: Directions for resilience development. *Consulting Psychology Journal: Practice and Research, 69*(3), 223–242.

Lengnick-Hall, C., & Beck, T. (2005). Adaptive fit versus robust transformation: How organizations respond to environmental change. *Journal of Management, 31*(5), 738–757.

Lombardo, M. M., & Eichinger, R. W. (2000). High potentials as high learners. *Human Resource Management, 39*, 321–330.

London, M. (2003). *Job feedback: Giving, seeking, and using feedback for performance improvement.* New York, NY: Psychology Press.

Luthans, F., Avey, J. B., Avolio, B. J., & Peterson, S. J. (2010). The development and resulting performance impact of positive psychological capital. *Human Resource Development Quarterly, 21*(1), 41–67.

Luthans, F., Youssef, C. M., & Avolio, B. J. (2007). *Psychological capital: Developing the human competitive edge.* Oxford, UK: Oxford University Press.

Lyubomirsky, S., King, L., & Diener, E. (2005). The benefits of frequent positive affect: Does happiness lead to success? *Psychological Bulletin, 131*(6), 803–855.

Mallak, L. A. (1998). Measuring resilience in health care provider organizations. *Health Manpower Management, 24*(4), 148–152.

Marks, M. L., Mirvis, P., & Ashkenas, R. (2014). Rebounding from career setbacks. *Harvard Business Review, 92*(10), 105–108.

May, D. R., Chan, A. Y., Hodges, T. D., & Avolio, B. J. (2003). Developing the moral component of authentic leadership. *Organizational Dynamics, 32*(3), 247–260.

Mayo Clinic. (2020, February 28). How much should the average adult exercise every day. Retrieved from https://www.mayoclinic.org/healthy-lifestyle/fitness/expert-answers/exercise/faq-20057916

McCall, M. W., Jr. (1998). *High flyers: Developing the next generation of leaders.* Boston, MA: Harvard Business School Press.

McCall, M. W., Jr. (2010). Recasting leadership development. *Industrial and Organizational Psychology: Perspectives on Science and Practice, 3*(1), 3–19.

McCall, M. W., Jr., & Lombardo, M. M. (1983). *Off the track: Why and how successful executives get derailed* (Technical report no. 21). Greensboro, NC: Center for Creative Leadership.

McCall, M. W., Jr., Lombardo, M. M., & Morrison, A. M. (1988). *Lessons of experience: How successful executives develop on the job.* New York, NY: Free Press.

McCauley, C., & Taylor, S. (2014). Teaching senior leaders the dynamics of derailment. In C. D. McCauley, D. S. DeRue, P. R. Yost, & S. Taylor (Eds.), *Experience-driven leader development* (pp. 529–534). San Francisco, CA: Wiley.

Mintzberg, H. (1983). *Power in and around organizations*. Englewood Cliffs, NJ: Prentice Hall.

Morgeson, F. P., Mumford, T. V., & Campion, M. A. (2005). Coming full circle: Using research and practice to address 27 questions about 360-degree feedback programs. *Consulting Psychology Journal: Practice and Research, 57*(3), 196–209.

Moscosco, S., & Salgado, J. F. (2004). "Dark side" personality styles as predictors of task, contextual, and job performance. *International Journal of Selection and Assessment, 12*(4), 356–362.

O'Boyle, E. H., Jr., Humphrey, R. H., Pollack, J. M., Hawver, T. H., & Story, P. A. (2011). The relation between emotional intelligence and job performance: A meta-analysis. *Journal of Organizational Behavior, 32*(5), 788–818.

Pidgeon, A. M., Ford, L., & Klaassen, F. (2014). Evaluating the effectiveness of enhancing resilience in human service professionals using a retreat-based Mindfulness with Meta Training Program: A randomised control trial. *Psychology, Health & Medicine, 19*(3), 355–364.

Ployhart, R. E., & Moliterno, T. P. (2011). Emergence of the human capital resource: A multilevel model. *The Academy of Management Review, 36*(1), 127–150.

Prochaska, J. O., DiClemente, C. C., & Norcross, J. C. (1992). In search of how people change: Applications to addictive behaviors. *American Psychologist, 47*(9), 1102–1114.

Reivich, K. J., Seligman, M. E. P., & McBride, S. (2011). Master resilience training in the US Army. *American Psychologist, 66*(1), 25–34.

Rigby, D. K., Sutherland, J., & Noble, A. (2018). Agile at scale. *Harvard Business Review, 96*(3), 88–96.

Roux-Dufort, C. (2007). Is crisis management (only) a management of exceptions? *Journal of Contingencies and Crisis Management, 15*(2), 105–114.

Schmit, M. J., Kilm, J. A., & Robie, C. A. (2000). Development of a global measure of personality. *Personnel Psychology, 53*, 153–193.

Schneider, B., Ehrhart, M. G., & Macey, W. H. (2013). Organizational climate and culture. *Annual Review of Psychology, 64*, 361–388.

Schwartz, P. (1996). *The art of the long view: Planning for the future in an uncertain world*. New York, NY: Doubleday.

Skinner, E. A., Edge, K., Altman, J., & Sherwood, H. (2003). Searching for the structure of coping: A review and critique of category systems for classifying ways of coping. *Psychological Bulletin, 129*(2), 216–269.

Snowden, D. J., & Boone, M. E. (2007). A leader's framework for decision making. *Harvard Business Review, 85*(11), 68–76.

Steele, C. M., Spencer, S. J., & Lynch, M. (1993). Self-image resilience and dissonance: The role of affirmational resources. *Journal of Personality and Social Psychology, 64*(6), 885–896.

Strauss, K., Griffin, M. A., & Parker, S. K. (2012). Future work selves: How salient hoped-for identities motivate proactive career behaviors. *Journal of Applied Psychology, 97*(3), 580–598.

Sweller, J. (1988). Cognitive load during problem solving: Effects on learning. *Cognitive Science, 12*(2), 257–285.

Tabibnia, G., & Radecki, D. (2018). Resilience training that can change the brain. *Consulting Psychology Journal: Practice and Research, 70*(1), 59–88.

Taleb, N. N. (2014). *Antifragile: Things that gain from disorder.* New York, NY: Random House.

Teece, D. J. (2007). Explicating dynamic capabilities: The nature and microfoundations of (sustainable) enterprise performance. *Strategic Management Journal, 28*(13), 1319–1350.

Treviño, L. K., Den Nieuwenboer, N. A., & Kish-Gephart, J. J. (2014). (Un)ethical behavior in organizations. *Annual Review of Psychology, 65,* 635–660.

Tugade, M. M., & Fredrickson, B. L. (2004). Resilient individuals use positive emotions to bounce back from negative emotional experiences. *Journal of Personality and Social Psychology, 86*(2), 320–333.

Uhl-Bien, M., Marion, R., & McKelvey, B. (2007). Complexity leadership theory: Shifting leadership from the industrial age to the knowledge era. *The Leadership Quarterly, 18*(4), 298–318.

Vaill, P. B. (1989). *Managing as a performing art: New ideas for a world of chaotic change.* San Francisco, CA: Jossey-Bass.

Van Dyck, C., Frese, M., Baer, M., & Sonnetag, S. (2005). Organizational error management culture and its impact on performance: A two-study replication. *Journal of Applied Psychology, 90*(6), 1228–1240.

Van Velsor, E., & Leslie, J. B. (1995). Why executives derail: Perspectives across time and cultures. *Academy of Management Review, 9*(4), 62–72.

Walton, G. M. (2014). The new science of wise psychological interventions. *Current Directions in Psychological Science, 23*(1), 73–82.

Watkins, M. (2013). *The first 90 days, updated and expanded: Proven strategies for getting up to speed faster and smarter.* Boston, MA: Harvard Business Review Press.

Weick, K. E. (1984). Small wins: Redefining the scale of social problems. *American Psychologist, 39*(1), 40–49.

Williams, T. A., Guber, D. A., Sutcliffe, K. M., Shepherd, D. A., & Zhao, E. Y. (2017). Organizational response to adversity: Fusing crisis management and resilience research streams. *Academy of Management Annals, 11*(2), 733–769.

Yost, P. R. (2016). Resilience practices. *Industrial and Organizational Psychology, 9*(2), 475–479.

Yost, P. R., & Chang, G. (2009). Everyone is equal, but some are more equal than others. *Industrial and Organizational Psychology: Perspectives on Science and Practice, 2*(4), 442–445.

Yost, P. R., & Plunkett, M. M. (2009). *Real time leadership development.* Chichester, UK: Wiley-Blackwell.

Yost, P. R., Yoder, M. P., Chung, H. H., & Voetmann, K. R. (2015). Narratives at work: Story arcs, themes, voice, and lessons that shape organizational life. *Consulting Psychology Journal: Practice and Research, 67*(3), 163–188.

SECTION III

ORGANIZATIONAL PRACTICES THAT SUPPORT AND ENHANCE LEARNING AGILITY

This section focuses on how organizational culture, practices, and processes can support learning agility. It begins with a practical framework for preparing leaders to thrive in VUCA times by increasing their exposure to diverse, novel, and adverse experiences (DNA). Next, the most prevalent attributes of learning agile organizations are shared along with recommendations for promoting organizational learning agility by optimizing talent management practices. This section also includes a deep dive into how a psychologically safe environment creates the conditions necessary for building and nurturing learning agility. Research from the longitudinal Top Companies for Leaders is shared, demonstrating the link between learning agile leaders and the organizational practices that support and drive this capability. A chapter is included highlighting the lessons learned in applying vertical development to improve learning agility with leaders in the context of an increasingly complex world along with key practices for facilitating vertical development in leaders. The section concludes with a discussion of how leaders must continually ask themselves the question "learning agility for the sake of what or whom?" in order to tap into their own unique inspirations to become learning agile.

13

The DNA of VUCA

A Framework for Building Learning Agility in an Accelerating World

David B. Peterson

A truly stable system expects the unexpected, is prepared
to be disrupted, and waits to be transformed.
—Tom Robbins (1932–), author

Around the world, the pace of change is accelerating (Diamandis & Kotler, 2020; Kurzweil, 2001; West, 2015, 2018). Not only are things changing faster and faster, but different kinds of things are changing, in different ways. Accelerating change and increasing complexity require leaders to anticipate new situations, to learn and adapt ever more quickly, and to help their organizations respond in new ways at ever-accelerating speeds. Disruption is on the horizon for virtually every industry and organization (Diamandis & Kotler, 2020). Learning agility—the ability to learn and adapt quickly to new situations—becomes a critical differentiator for long-term success.

Recently, the term *VUCA* has become the acronym of choice to describe these turbulent times (Bennett & Lemoine, 2014):

- **V**olatile: Rapid, sudden, repeated change
- **U**ncertain: Lack of clarity around what information is relevant and what actions are appropriate
- **C**omplex: Multiplicity of interconnected variables that often interact in unpredictable ways
- **A**mbiguous: Lack of clarity about the meaning of information and events

David B. Peterson, *The DNA of VUCA* In: *The Age of Agility*. Edited by: Veronica Schmidt Harvey and Kenneth P. De Meuse, Oxford University Press (2021). © Oxford University Press. DOI: 10.1093/oso/9780190085353.003.0013

When we unpack these four elements, we see that two aspects—*volatility* and *complexity*—are actually the driving forces: volatility because the pace of change and disruption is accelerating and complexity because there are so many interconnected pieces of the puzzle. As change happens in one part of the system, unanticipated consequences ripple through the rest of the system. Because it is hard to anticipate the impact of so many rapid changes, people experience *ambiguity* (What does this mean for me?) and *uncertainty* (How should I react? What should I do?).

Leaders who want to lead effectively in VUCA environments are encouraged to look at these issues from two perspectives. First, volatility (better defined as *accelerating* or *exponential change*) and complexity are best made sense of *rationally*, by trying to understand what is changing and how quickly, what the potential implications might be, and what risks and opportunities could be created. Useful approaches to make sense of exponential change and complexity include systems thinking, learning about complexity (Garvey-Berger & Johnston, 2015), exploring second- and third-order consequences (Dalio, 2017), trend analysis, exploring ways to make sense of and anticipate exponential change (Berman, Dorrier, & Hill, 2016), and studying what futurists are suggesting (Houle, 2020; Johansen, 2017).

Second, ambiguity and uncertainty are side effects of complexity and change, which generate significant *emotional* consequences. When people cannot make sense of what is happening and are unsure which way to turn, they often experience fear, anxiety, and confusion. They become more cautious, more reactive, and more self-protective. Leaders can best address this through an emotional lens, by listening with empathy and compassion to fears and concerns, building a sense of trust and psychological safety, acknowledging and welcoming diverse views and opinions, and fostering a sense of community and connection.

Most leaders today are underprepared to deal with, much less thrive and lead confidently, in VUCA conditions. And, most leadership development initiatives are not effective in preparing leaders for VUCA because they simply do not create the VUCA-style conditions that leaders need to get better at managing.

The ability to thrive in a VUCA world is enhanced by systematically increasing one's exposure to VUCA conditions in order to gain experience in acting decisively and leading with courage and confidence in the face of new, unexpected, and constantly shifting challenges. The more cycles of experience a leader has grappling with unexpected, difficult challenges, the more the leader develops the capability to handle them, as long as that leader is going through those experiences with the right mindset and organizational supports, which are outlined further in this chapter.

The DNA of VUCA

With that introduction to VUCA, let us turn to the DNA side of the equation. Just as DNA is the genetic code that contains the instruction set a living organism needs to develop and thrive (Binn, 2006), the *DNA of VUCA* is the instruction set humans need to develop and thrive in a VUCA world. This is built around seeking and making sense of experiences with increasing levels of the following:

- Diversity: Seeking new and different perspectives, ideas, people, and situations
- Novelty: Exploring and experimenting with new behaviors, actions, and ideas
- Adversity: Proactive exposure to difficult and challenging situations that stress and stretch people

Most people can appreciate the value of seeking novel experiences as a way to build the muscles needed for handling new and different challenges in the future. It is a bit more difficult to convince people to intentionally put themselves into awkward, stressful, and uncomfortable situations, but this is exactly what elite athletes do: They push themselves to the limit, stressing themselves and their muscles to ultimately gain strength and speed. This type of beneficial stress, or *eustress*, underlies many types of growth, including (a) physical growth in that muscles need to be stressed to get stronger and our immune system requires exposure to pathogens to become more resilient, (b) mental growth in that moderate amounts of stress improve alertness and cognitive performance, and (c) emotional growth in that the right amounts of emotional stress build resilience, well-being, and empathy (Lim & DeSteno, 2016). Taleb (2012) described this process as *antifragility*—where things benefit rather than break from stress and disorder.

It is a classic example of short-term pain for long-term gain: Developing a regular discipline of seeking DNA experiences helps prepare leaders and their teams for much greater challenges ahead. Investing in DNA experiences now will help prepare leaders for tomorrow's unexpected challenges.

The next section on triangulation—using different perspectives to solve a problem—explores how much and what type of exposure to DNA experiences might be required to actually produce meaningful improvements in learning agility.

Triangulation

Although there is significant research showing that DNA experiences increase agility and reduce the likelihood of derailment (De Meuse, 2019; Dotlich, Noel, & Walker, 2004; Hogan, Hogan, & Kaiser, 2010; Kizilos, 2012; Mitchinson & Morris, 2012; Sevy, Swisher, & Orr, 2014; Van Katwyk, Hazucha, & Goff, 2014), there is little research on how much diverse experience is optimal.

One approach is to use the analogy of *triangulation*, using three points in space to identify a specific location. Being able to see or experience something from at least three different perspectives may be a useful starting point for thinking about developing learning agility. A leader who has managed through at least three different types of leadership experiences (e.g., turning around a failing business; leading a large-scale, cross-functional initiative; leading the acquisition of another company) is likely to have a broader understanding of how to think about the next challenge. Avedon and Scholes (2010) have formalized something like this at Ingersoll-Rand, where senior leaders and general managers are expected to have experience in at least

- two regions of the world;
- two functions (e.g., operations, marketing, finance);
- two business sectors; and
- five key business experiences (e.g., those noted previously).

Since gaining the right level of experience in each of these—different geographies, functions, and businesses—might take years, aiming for two experiences in each domain rather than at least three—seems like a reasonable approach. However, if someone has only worked in the United States and China, as one example, they might tend to focus on only the dimensions that are different across the two of them. Should they spend time in Nigeria or

Brazil, they will encounter new and different dimensions by which cultures and traditions vary, expanding their palate of understanding.

Another analogy is multitrait, multimethod research (Campbell & Fiske, 1959), whereby deeper insight and accuracy are presumed to emerge from looking at a subject from diverse perspectives with different tools and methodologies and then triangulating.

In teams, diversity of perspectives and experiences has been shown to enhance team performance and innovation (Hong & Page, 2004; Reynolds & Lewis, 2017), summarized nicely in the title of Hong and Page's (2004) article, "Groups of Diverse Problem Solvers Can Outperform Groups of High-Ability Problem Solvers." Yet, there is additional evidence suggesting that *individuals* with the right background of diverse experiences can exceed diverse teams on measures of innovation. Taylor and Greve (2006) found that diverse teams (representing multiple domains of experience) outperformed individuals up to a point. But when an individual had significant experience in three or four domains, individual innovation exceeded team performance across the same number of diverse domains. The authors proposed that making meaning out of the diverse perspectives and experiences is easier for an individual than for a team, as there is less coordination and communication tax: the amount of effort that goes into explaining an idea and getting buy-in from people with different backgrounds and assumptions.

Collectively, this suggests that individuals' ability to triangulate and make sense across diverse experiences and perspectives enhances their agility and ability to make new, novel connections.

The Psychological Challenge

On the one hand, if a leader is facing conditions that are stable or predictable, it makes sense to build the exact capabilities required to perform optimally in those conditions. On the other hand, if conditions are unpredictable or constantly evolving, it makes the most sense to invest in *learning agility*, so one can adapt quickly as circumstances change. In essence, leaders are investing in building capabilities they can use in the future in unanticipated ways to address as yet unforeseen events.

As an investment in future performance, building learning agility requires devoting time and energy to learning, exploration, experimentation, and reflection, all of which are likely to *suboptimize* current performance. This commitment to learning requires people to put themselves in situations that we often avoid—new, unfamiliar, with the possibility of failure—in order to build the muscle and mindsets needed to handle them effectively. Ironically, perhaps, highly learning agile leaders are rarely the top performers in any given quarter or year since their focus is on long-term learning rather than short-term execution. Learning agility enhances resilience and adaptability, which decreases the likelihood of derailment and increases the likelihood of long-term success, especially in the face of change or disruption.

This dynamic choice—optimizing for current versus future performance—creates a dilemma for leaders. With the intense pressure to do everything possible to succeed with current priorities, the easy default is to invest in optimizing *current* performance. It requires discipline to consciously choose to seek DNA situations where there is inevitably no immediate payoff. Plus they face the additional stress of operating at the edge of their comfort zone.

It may help to view the trade-offs of optimizing for short-term versus long-term performance by analogy to making financial investments, where people choose the percentage of their resources that go toward conservative, low-risk options versus more aggressive, higher risk options. Making those decisions depends on one's personal goals, risk tolerance, time horizon, and the current economic dynamics. For example, if inflation is growing quickly, the conservative investment may not even keep pace with inflation and in the long run may have even higher risk.

The same is true for investing time and attention to learning agility. If conditions are changing slowly, leaders can be more conservative in their investments and experimentation. If conditions are changing rapidly, being too conservative means capabilities are becoming obsolete faster than leaders are developing new ones to replace them.

At an organizational level, McGregor and Doshi (2017) used similar language to describe two types of organizational performance:

- *tactical performance*, which focuses on rules, checklists, consistency, and standard operating procedures to optimize current performance; and
- *adaptive performance*, which is the manifestation of creativity, problem-solving, and innovation to find ways to improve future performance.

They pointed out that both are important, but most organizations focus on tactical performance and underemphasize adaptive performance. In a world where the value of future performance is often discounted and current performance is overweighted, it is incumbent on senior leaders to counterbalance people's natural instincts and find ways to reward and incentivize investments in adaptability and agility.

At an individual level, Epstein's *Range* (2019) makes a strong case that people who have more diverse experiences early in their lives and careers tend to get off to slower starts, but later surpass the performance of those with narrower specializations because they can draw on more diverse examples of how to approach new challenges. He noted that specialization—optimizing for high performance in a chosen field—only succeeds when the rules are clear, all the information is available, and feedback is immediate and accurate. Examples include chess and golf. He referred to Hogarth's (2001) depiction of these conditions as "kind environments," in contrast to "wicked environments" where people have to solve problems they have never encountered before, the rules are not clear, and feedback is slow or ambiguous, which seems to characterize circumstances in our VUCA world. Agility, built from repeatedly learning to solve new, diverse challenges, is key to success in those environments.

Mitchinson and Morris (2012) identified five factors that characterized the most learning agile leaders[*]:

- Innovating: Willingness to challenge the status quo;
- Performing: Remaining calm in the face of difficulty;
- Reflecting: Taking time to reflect on experiences;
- Risking: Purposefully putting oneself into challenging situations; and
- [Not] defending: Being open to learning and resisting the temptation to become defensive in the face of adversity.

Of these five facets of learning agility, the leaders in their study consistently reported that risk-taking—such as intentionally putting oneself into DNA of VUCA conditions—was the most difficult for them.

To close this section, a memorable phrase illustrates why seeking diverse, new, challenging experiences is essential: "No comfort in the learning zone; no learning in the comfort zone."

---

[*] See De Meuse (2017) for a discussion of different perspectives on the factors that may be critical to agile learning.

The Agility Cycle: Action, Reflection, Social Engagement

Although experiences with the DNA of VUCA are essential for developing learning agility for complex, changing times, they are not sufficient. Two other elements are also necessary: reflection and social engagement with others. *Reflection* is essential for leaders to make sense of what is happening, to see patterns, and to make intentional choices about courses of action. *Social engagement* provides the opportunity for emotional support, encouragement, and gathering other perspectives and insights, among other benefits. Each of these is explored further next.

These three functions—action, reflection, social engagement—operate in a cycle: The leader (a) seeks DNA experiences, (b) reflects on those experiences, and then (c) engages with colleagues to process their experiences, share in mutual support and encouragement, and discuss future courses of action, which leads to new DNA experiences.

Action

Building learning agility is a cyclical process that could begin anywhere. But at the very heart of agility is seeking new experiences and experimenting with new behaviors, so we start there. There are several ways to think about taking action. Moving from relatively simple steps to larger commitments, a leader might consider the following:

- Experimenting with *new behaviors* that stretch them in their current role, such as imposing artificial constraints on themselves to increase the level of challenge, for example, picking a routine task (writing a report, leading a meeting) and trying to do it in half the time.
- Taking on *new responsibilities* or assignments. Leaders might volunteer for a project outside their area of expertise or a cross-functional project that brings them into contact with people from different parts of the organization.
- Pursuing a *new hobby or activity* outside work, such as learning to play a musical instrument, participating in a new sport, or serving as a volunteer for a local arts organization.
- Making a big job or career move, such as moving to a *new country, new role,* or *new function.* These types of action are big investments, but in

the long run offer the types of development that senior leaders often describe as the most critical in their own development.

- In addition, participating in learning experiences is another way to take action, including reading widely, listening to podcasts, attending workshops, and so on, especially in areas outside the leader's usual experience to expand his or her perspective.

Several authors (De Meuse, 2020; Dotlich et al., 2004; Kizilos, 2012; Van Katwyk et al., 2014) have looked at different categories of experience that contribute to growth in learning agility, as well as resilience, versatility, and adaptability. Drawing from these books, Tables 13.1 and 13.2 provide a useful menu of DNA experiences that a leader might seek or, in the case of some of the more adverse situations, at least capitalize on when they occur. Dotlich et al. (2004) even used the diversity and adversity labels in their taxonomy. Two of Van Katwyk et al.'s (2014) categories—overcoming challenges and obstacles; risky and/or critical experiences—highlight the adversity side as well.

Table 13.1 Critical Learning Experiences for Leaders

	Career/Work	Life/Relationships
Adversity	Difficulty at work or in leading others • Responsibility for significant failure • Bad boss or competitive peers • Derailing, losing job, being passed over • Being acquired or merged	Personal turmoil, loss of meaning • End of a meaningful relationship • Debilitating illness or physical challenge • Losing faith in the system • Facing retirement or end of career
Diversity	Stimulating projects, assignments, roles • Stretch assignments • Moving to a new company or function • Moving into larger leadership role • Global exposure and international experience • Business unit responsibility	Breadth of life experiences • Living abroad or in different cultures • Taking up new languages or fields of study • Volunteering and social service • Building your legacy

Source: Adapted from Dotlich, Noel, and Walker (2004).

Table 13.2 Categories of Leadership Experience

General Management	• Developing organizational vision and strategy • Project management and implementation • Business development and marketing • Managing a growing business • Leading a start-up • Product development • Financial management • Operations • Human resources • External relations • Leading cross-functional teams or projects
Overcoming Challenges and Obstacles	• Inherited problems and challenges • Interpersonally challenging situations • Downturns and failures; turning around a failing business • Difficult financial situations • Difficult staffing situations; managing poor performers
Risky and/or Critical Experiences	• High-risk situations • Critical negotiations • Crisis management • Visible assignments or initiatives
Personal and Career-Related Experiences	• Self-development • Coaching, mentoring, and developing others • International and cross-cultural • Leading diverse/distributed teams • Extracurricular activities or hobbies

Source: Adapted from Van Katwyk, Hazucha, and Goff (2014).

Kizilos (2012) divided developmental experiences into two broad categories (Table 13.3). *High-intensity* experiences contribute to growth within a domain, ultimately leading to mastery under the right conditions. *Stretch* experiences, which push someone outside their area of expertise or preparation, contribute significantly to learning agility and versatility.

Although this chapter is focused on DNA experiences to increase learning agility and adaptability, leaders should also seek experiences aligned with their long-term career objectives. For example, a diversity of *stretch* experiences across different business challenges, functions, and regions is valuable preparation for general management and chief executive officer roles, where versatility and breadth of perspective are most useful. High-intensity experiences are well suited to leaders who want

Table 13.3 Two Types of Developmental Experiences

Intensity	Stretch
The degree to which an experience includes significantly higher expectations for performance, within an existing area of expertise or familiarity	The degree to which an experience pushes one outside their areas of expertise or preparation
Time pressure—Aggressive time constraints and deadlines	Relationships—Interacting with people who hold diverse perspectives or beliefs
Holistic responsibility—Overall responsibility for outcome(s)	Knowledge or skills—Requires gaining new expertise or capabilities
Risk—High financial, reputational, or other stakes, with at least moderate risk of failure	
Impact—Where results are critical for the business	Adaptability—Handling greater ambiguity or complexity than one is used to
Visibility—Work is visible at high levels of the organization, to key external stakeholders, and/or to large audience	Context—Working within a different function, department, region, or culture

Source: Adapted from Kizilos (2012).

to be senior functional or technical leaders—where domain expertise is critical.

Finally, leaders and organizations might consider business simulations, gaming, action learning, and other low-risk immersive situations as ways to expose leaders to DNA. Johansen (2017) made a strong case that realistic business simulations allow managers opportunities to rehearse for the future and are one of the best learning methods available to prepare leaders for VUCA leadership challenges.

Reflection

Whatever new experiences a leader has, reflection is essential to capture and integrate the right lessons to ensure development actually takes place (Mitchinson & Morris, 2012). Thomas Friedman, in his book *Thank You for Being Late* (2017), talked about the increased importance of slowing down, taking time to reflect, and accessing our deepest values in what he described as this "age of accelerations." It is a key skill for leaders who want to stay grounded in the midst of VUCA.

One simple way to cultivate a habit of reflection is to begin with 1 minute a day. In my executive coaching, I found that even leaders who did not see much value in reflection were willing to spend 1 minute a day reflecting on what they were doing to build new capabilities. From there, we would build to 2–3 minutes a week—looking back on the past week (What new things did you try? Where did you miss opportunities?) and looking forward to the coming week (Where are your best opportunities to try new things? What do you need to prepare in advance to be most effective in using your new skills?). We would progress through monthly, quarterly, and annual reflection, each time examining a longer time frame and taking a little extra time for deeper reflection. Table 13.4 presents the entire reflection calendar (Peterson, 2010, 2020), with scalable reflections from daily to 10-year time frames.

Reflection and action go hand in hand: Try something new, reflect on it and what you want to try next; rinse and repeat. The real key to building learning agility is increasing the number of reps (repetitions) a person has with new experiences and ideas. The more action–reflection cycles a leader completes, the faster the leader learns and the greater their learning agility grows. Similar to the reflection calendar, leaders can build *a portfolio of new experiences* across different time spans. Try one small thing every day, a slightly bigger experience once a week, some new experiment every month, and maybe a bigger move every 3–5 years. For example, a leader could get exposure to a different business by a big move—joining a new company or transferring to a new function—or by smaller steps, such as shadowing another executive for a couple of days. A regular habit of reflection, which supports stepping back to see the bigger picture and longer time frames, enables leaders to better see the underlying patterns in their behavior and in the system in which they operate.

For reflection to be most effective, leaders will want to approach it with genuine *curiosity*—trying to make sense of what has happened rather than trying to defend or explain away any failures, missteps, or awkward moments. *Humility* is equally important: accepting that it may be necessary to adapt or take another approach without letting ego or pride get in the way. They might also heed advice from Kahneman, Lovallo, and Sibony (2011) to be aware of and avoid confirmation bias and other potential distortions as they look back and try to make sense of their experiences.

Social Engagement: Community and Connection

Sustaining commitment to proactively seeking DNA experiences and regular reflection is difficult to do alone. Engaging with trusted colleagues, or a

Table 13.4 Reflection Calendar

Reflection Calendar
For each time frame—daily, weekly, monthly—reflect on the time period just past and just ahead for you. Add your own questions as desired to make it more useful for you.

Time Frame	Look Back Where were you most and least effective? What worked, what didn't, what have you learned?	Look Forward What are your most important priorities ahead? What actions do you want to take?
Daily 1 minute	• What new thing did I try today? • How did it go? What worked well, what didn't? • What's the most useful thing I learned today? • What opportunity did I miss? • What am I most grateful for?	• What one thing will I do tomorrow to stretch my comfort zone? • What will prompt me to do that?
Weekly 3–4 minutes	• What progress did I make last week? How satisfied am I with that?	• What do I need to focus on in the coming week? • Where are my key opportunities to further my learning and development?
Monthly 5–10 minutes	• How am I doing on my development objectives? • What has supported or enhanced my learning? • What is getting in the way of me making progress?	• Do I need to do anything differently to continue making progress? • What feedback do I want, who do I want it from, and how will I make sure I get it?
Quarterly 15–20 minutes	• What important lessons have I learned? • In the past 3 months, have I made the kind of impact on myself and my world that I want to make? • Where have I been making excuses for something I need to take personal responsibility for? • Have I been actively seeking new, diverse, and challenging experiences to foster my personal growth and development?	• What are my key priorities for this coming quarter, and what capabilities do I need to develop to achieve or fulfill them? • What do I need to do differently to manage my personal growth and professional development more effectively? • When do I need to make a big bet on doing something new or radically different? What are the signals that I should be looking for?

(Continued)

Table 13.4 *Continued*

Reflection Calendar
For each time frame—daily, weekly, monthly—reflect on the time period just past and just ahead for you. Add your own questions as desired to make it more useful for you.

Annually 1 hour	• How do I feel about the past year? What were my emotional highlights and lowlights? • What's most important in my life right now? What really matters to me? • How did I do on my most important priorities this past year? • What have I learned? • What do I need from myself and others to make an honest assessment of my life, my priorities, and what matters most to me and those I love? • How clearly do my actions and choices reflect those priorities?	• What kind of person am I becoming? Who do I want to be? What values will I live by? • Where do I want to be a year from now? What do I need to do or learn to get there? • Am I on the best path to become the person I want to be and live the life I want? • How can I be more intentional about living my values and fulfilling my mission in life? • What kind of support do I need from others and where will I find it? • What course corrections or changes in my life do I need to implement this year? • What am I doing to renew, reinvigorate, and reinvent myself and my life?
Triennially Deep reflection every 2–3 years "Disrupt or be disrupted"	• What are the most significant things I've learned? • Where have I been complacent or missed big opportunities? • Where am I at greatest risk? What am I holding on to that I need to let go of? • What trends or signals have I seen that might signal it's time to pivot, disrupt myself, or try something new?	• Given how fast things are changing around me, is it time to disrupt myself? How long do I have, realistically, before my life or career is disrupted by something else if I don't? • Given what I care about most deeply, what are the critical opportunities to capitalize on? • Where am I most afraid of taking decisive action? • What's the bold move I know in my heart I need to make?
By decade (or quinquennially) 1 day every 5–10 years	• How has my life story, my life's journey evolved? • What are the big choices I made in the last 10 years? • What kind of life am I living, and how does that compare to the life I want to live?	• Who do I want to be? What values do I want to guide my life? How do I connect to my deepest mission and purpose? • What do I need to invest in over the next 3–5 years to accomplish or fulfill what matters most? • What do I need to transform about myself or my life in order to accomplish my highest calling and purpose?

Table 13.4 *Continued*

Reflection Calendar For each time frame—daily, weekly, monthly—reflect on the time period just past and just ahead for you. Add your own questions as desired to make it more useful for you.		
Any Time Your personal reflections any time you're in a reflective mood	• What have I done lately to become a better person? • What have I done to bring joy to someone's life today?	• When is my next opportunity to act with compassion and love? • What else should I be asking myself or reflecting on?

Source: Adapted from Peterson (2010, 2020).

supportive community, has the potential to activate and expand the leader's learning by providing a safe place to share and make sense of new ideas and experiences, as well as the encouragement to continue.

Drawing from the notion of a learning community, or community of practice, a leader cultivates a set of relationships with people who can share ideas and insights. Unlike most definitions of a community of practice, these relationships are not organized around a shared domain of knowledge or practice, but of a shared interest in pursuing learning agility, or at least of supporting a particular leader on their journey toward agility. A potential paradox in this informal community is that diversity of perspectives, values, and experiences is an asset, yet it makes finding a shared sense of unity more difficult. As such, the leader may instead focus on cultivating a network of loose relationships rather than a tight-knit community of like-minded people. Loose networks are more likely to foster innovation because of the range and diversity of ideas to which one is exposed.

Once again, the idea of a *portfolio* of relationships may be especially appropriate to address the variety of needs a leader will experience as the leader invests in learning agility for VUCA times. The leader may cultivate different sets of people who can help gain access to new and different experiences, can provide unconditional support and encouragement, can coach and mentor them, or might provide very different perspectives. Following the notion of triangulation of experiences, leaders could seek reactions and input from three or four very different perspectives. Imagine a leader who seeks advice from the newest person in their organization, a former mentor, a friend who works in a completely different field, and someone who was raised in a different culture. Their diverse assumptions, experiences, and questions will provide a tapestry of different perspectives, which can expand how the leader is reflecting on and making sense of what they are going through. A loose community will also potentially provide opportunities for the leader to share what they are learning by teaching, mentoring, and coaching others. This type of two-way exchange of ideas and insights also reinforces and enhances learning.

Conclusion: Adapting at the Pace of Change

As the pace of change continues to accelerate (Diamandis & Kotler, 2020), we all face more volatility and complexity, along with increased ambiguity and uncertainty. Seeking DNA experiences *now* is one of the best ways to prepare for that VUCA future, by building resilience and learning agility so we can adapt to the pace of change. Although it will likely be difficult at times, and require an investment of time and energy, building learning agility will almost certainly pay off in the long run. And, the cost of doing nothing—of being complacent—is going to be much higher. The thing is, it does not get easier by waiting. Leaders can start right now with small steps, little experiments, rapid reflection, and build their agility muscles over time by gradually pushing more and more at the edge of their comfort zone. As author Karen Lamb (n.d.) noted, "A year from now you may wish you had started today."

References

Avedon, M. J., & Scholes, G. (2010). Building competitive advantage through integrated talent management. In R. F. Silzer & B. E. Dowell (Eds.), *Strategy-driven talent management: A leadership imperative*. San Francisco, CA: Jossey Bass.

Bennett, N., & Lemoine, G. J. (2014). What VUCA really means for you. *Harvard Business Review, 92*(1/2). Retrieved from https://hbr.org/2014/01/what-vuca-really-means-for-you

Berman, A. E., Dorrier, J., & Hill, D. J. (2016). How to think exponentially and better predict the future. *Singularity Hub*. Retrieved from singularityhub.com/2016/04/05/how-to-think-exponentially-and-better-predict-the-future/

Binn, C. (2006). Genes: The instruction manuals for life. *LiveScience.com*. Retrieved from https://www.livescience.com/10486-genes-instruction-manuals-life.html

Campbell, D. T., & Fiske, D. W. (1959). Convergent and discriminant validation by the multitrait-multimethod matrix. *Psychological Bulletin, 56*, 81–105.

Dalio, R. (2017). *Principles: Life and work.* New York, NY: Simon & Schuster.

De Meuse, K. P. (2017). Learning agility: Its evolution as a psychological construct and its empirical relationship to leader success. *Consulting Psychology Journal: Practice and Research, 69,* 267–295.

De Meuse, K. P. (2019). A meta-analysis of the relationship between learning agility and leader success. *Journal of Organizational Psychology, 19,* 25–34.

De Meuse, K. P. (2020). *Enhancing your learning agility: A guidebook to accompany the TALENTx7* Assessment* (2nd ed.). Minneapolis, MN: De Meuse Leadership Group.

Diamandis, P. H., & Kotler, S. (2020). *The future is faster than you think: How converging technologies are transforming business, industries, and our lives.* New York, NY: Simon & Schuster.

Dotlich, D. L., Noel, J. L., & Walker, N. (2004). *Leadership passages: The personal and professional transitions that make or break a leader.* San Francisco, CA: Jossey Bass.

Epstein, D. (2019). *Range: How generalists triumph in a specialized world.* New York, NY: Macmillan.

Friedman, D. (2017). *Thank you for being late: An optimist's guide to thriving in the age of acceleration* (2nd edn.). New York, NY: Picador.

Garvey-Berger, J., & Johnston, K. (2015). *Simple habits for complex times.* Palo Alto, CA: Stanford University.

Hogan, J., Hogan, R., & Kaiser, R. B. (2010). Management derailment: Personality assessment and mitigation. In S. Zedeck (Ed.), *American Psychological Association handbook of industrial and organizational psychology* (pp. 555–573). Washington, DC: American Psychological Association.

Hogarth, R. M. (2001). *Educating intuition.* Chicago, IL: University of Chicago Press.

Hong, L., & Page, S. E. (2004). Groups of diverse problem solvers can outperform groups of high-ability problem solvers. *Proceedings of the National Academy of Sciences of the United States of America 101*(46), 6385–16389.

Houle, D. (2020). 2020 forecasts [Web log post]. Evolution Shifts blog. Retrieved from https://davidhoule.com/2020s-forecasts/2020/01/20/2020-forecasts

Johansen, B. (2017). *The new leadership literacies.* Oakland, CA: Berrett-Koehler.

Kahneman, D., Lovallo, D., & Sibony, O. (2011, June). Before you make that big decision. *Harvard Business Review,* pp. 50–60.

Kizilos, M. (2012). *Framebreaking leadership development: Think differently about work experiences to achieve more, faster.* Experience-Based Development Associates.

Kurzweil, R. (2001). The law of accelerating returns. Retrieved from https://www.kurzweilai.net/the-law-of-accelerating-returns

Lamb, K. (n.d.). Karen Lamb quotes. Quotes.net. Retrieved March 21, 2020, from https://www.quotes.net/quote/14998

Lim, D., & DeSteno, D. (2016). Suffering and compassion: The links among adverse life experiences, empathy, compassion, and prosocial behavior. *Emotion, 16,* 175–182.

McGregor, L., & Doshi, N. (2017). There are two types of performance—but most organizations only focus on one. *Harvard Business Review, 95*(5). Retrieved from https://hbr.org/2017/10/there-are-two-types-of-performance-but-most-organizations-only-focus-on-one

Mitchinson, A., & Morris, R. (2012). *Learning about learning agility.* Columbia University and CCL. Retrieved from https://cclinnovation.org/wp-content/uploads/2020/02/learningagility.pdf

Peterson, D. B. (2010). Good to great coaching: Accelerating the journey. In G. Hernez-Broome & L. A. Boyce (Eds.), *Advancing executive coaching: Setting the course for successful leadership coaching* (pp. 83–102). San Francisco, CA: Jossey-Bass.

Peterson, D. B. (2020, June). The DNA of VUCA: Coaching leaders to deal with chaos, complexity, and exponential change. Presented at the Association of Coaching and Harvard Institute of Coaching Virtual Conference, Coaching in the Workplace: Performance, Culture, Mastery Presented online at https://coachingintheworkplace.org.

Reynolds, A., & Lewis, D. (2017, March). Teams solve problems faster when they're more cognitively diverse. *Harvard Business Review*. Retrieved from https://hbr.org/2017/03/teams-solve-problems-faster-when-theyre-more-cognitively-diverse

Sevy, B., Swisher, V., & Orr, J. E. (2014). *Seven signposts: The unmistakable markers that identify high-potential leaders*. Minneapolis, MN: Korn Ferry Institute.

Taleb, N. (2012). *Antifragile: Things that gain from disorder*. New York, NY: Random House.

Taylor, A., & Greve, H. R. (2006). Superman or the Fantastic Four? Knowledge combination and experience in innovative teams. *Academy of Management Journal, 49*, 723–740.

Van Katwyk, P., Hazucha, J., & Goff, M. (2014). A leadership experience framework. In C. D. McCauley, D. S. DeRue, P. R. Yost, & S. Taylor (Eds.), *Experience-driven leader development* (pp. 15–20). San Francisco, CA: Wiley.

West, G. B. (2015). Growth, innovation and the accelerating pace of life from cells and ecosystems to cities and economies; are they sustainable? Karlovitz Lecture at Georgia Tech. Retrieved from https://smartech.gatech.edu/handle/1853/53234

West, G. B. (2018). *Scale: The universal laws of life, growth, and death in organisms, cities, and companies*. New York, NY: Penguin.

14

Becoming a Learning Agile Organization

Kim E. Ruyle, Kenneth P. De Meuse, and Charles W. Hughley

> An organization's ability to learn, and translate that learning into action rapidly, is the ultimate competitive advantage.
>
> —Jack Welch (1935–2020),
> former CEO and chair of General Electric

Agility is defined as "the power of moving quickly and easily; nimbleness" (retrieved from https://www.dictionary.com). Agile organizations are characterized by their speed and flexibility when making and executing decisions. They adjust quickly and nimbly to changes in the competitive landscape by effectively leveraging technology, optimizing decision-making cycles, and implementing a structure comprising a network of highly effective teams (see Aghina, Handscomb, Ludolph, Rona, & West, 2020).

Agile organizations can transcend speedy and flexible reactivity to become *learning agile organizations,* which are highly proactive, innovative, and decisive. Learning agile organizations

- learn quickly from mistakes and failures (i.e., they quickly adopt new behaviors that demonstrate what has been learned);
- experiment by design and do so aggressively;
- creatively respond to changes in the global environment and market conditions;
- take appropriate risks; and
- are composed of highly learning agile leaders.

Kim E. Ruyle, Kenneth P. De Meuse, and Charles W. Hughley, *Becoming a Learning Agile Organization* In: *The Age of Agility.* Edited by: Veronica Schmidt Harvey and Kenneth P. De Meuse, Oxford University Press (2021). © Oxford University Press. DOI: 10.1093/oso/9780190085353.003.0014

These and other characteristics of learning agile organizations are fundamental enablers of innovation and execution, two of the primary drivers of success in business today.

In his landmark book, *The Fifth Discipline*, Peter Senge introduced the concept of the learning organization "where people are continually learning how to learn together" (1990, p. 1). Much has been written about the cultural attributes and supporting systems of learning organizations (e.g., Garvin, Edmondson, & Gino, 2008; Nonaka, 1991; Pedler, Burgoyne, & Boydell, 1991; Senge, 1994). For example, learning organizations can be described as those focused on (a) a systematic approach to recognizing patterns and solving problems, (b) learning from experience at the organizational level, and (c) the curation and sharing of knowledge.

This description sounds very much like learning agility at the organizational level. Overall, it would seem many of the same learning agile attributes on the individual level (e.g., quickly learning from experience; being strategically focused, willing to experiment and take risks; understanding one's personal strengths and limitations; and being responsive to feedback) transcend to organizations that are highly learning agile. Learning agile organizations create a culture of psychological safety that promotes experimentation, risk-taking, and constructive conflict. Learning agile organizations attract, engage, and deploy talent that has an optimum skill set and level of learning agility. And, perhaps most important, agile organizations have learning agile leaders! This chapter is divided into two major sections. The first section focuses on cultural attributes that foster a learning agile organization. The second section examines talent management practices that support current employees and establish a vibrant leadership pipeline that enables an organization to grow, develop, and evolve its agility.

Fostering a Culture of Learning Agility

Organizational culture is reflected in the collective habitual behaviors exhibited in the workplace. The way we do our jobs, solve problems, communicate, hire employees, terminate employees, celebrate, dress, and even park our vehicles all are a reflection of our culture. The effectiveness of an organization's culture is largely determined by the degree to which it supports the strategic intent of the organization. Irrespective of (and not necessarily related to) a culture's effectiveness, we can evaluate the strength of that culture. A strong culture has narrowly prescribed norms of behavior; a high degree of variance in habitual behavior indicates a weak culture.

Behaviors are a reflection of our values and assumptions about how the world works (Schein, 2010). Values are important and, when embraced, drive behaviors aligned with organizational strategy. It is a primary responsibility of senior leadership, especially the chief executive officer (CEO), to define the values important to the organization and that ultimately drive the desired strategy (Ruyle, 2014). Senior leaders aiming to creating a learning agile organization promote a culture that heightens a sense of urgency in the workforce, while simultaneously (and paradoxically) reduces the presence of threats in the workplace. Leaders in learning agile cultures do the following:

- **Clearly define values.** They express precisely and clearly what they truly care about, especially the things that set it apart from other businesses in the competitive landscape. Expounding values that are in vogue, politically correct, and simply expected has little impact. It takes courage to simplify and clarify the few values that provide a foundation for the desired culture.
- **Provide concrete, real-world examples.** The best leaders create stories that exemplify desired behaviors. They provide contextual lessons that guide employees to embrace constructive habits.
- **Consistently model the right behaviors.** Without fail, effective leaders of learning agile organizations are the exemplars of desired behaviors. They are unreservedly authentic. Hypocrisy is not in their repertoire.
- **Recognize and reinforce.** Effective leaders are on the lookout to catch individuals modeling actions aligned with core values. They take advantage of opportunities to recognize those individuals and provide them positive reinforcement and appropriate recognition. These opportunities may provide the basis for stories shared by leaders—stories that take on a life of their own and ripple through the workforce, illustrating what values look like in action.
- **Celebrate.** Effective leaders know when and how to celebrate. They recognize and celebrate teams that exemplify the desired cultural attributes.
- **Provide course correction.** Effective leaders also do not overlook counterproductive behaviors. They intervene to provide feedback and coaching for course corrections when contrary behaviors are demonstrated by employees.

Effective leaders who take these actions can shape a culture that supports the strategic intent. Furthermore, when those action are directed at promoting psychological safety, they are on their way to creating a culture in which organizational learning agility can flourish.

Psychological Safety

Psychological safety is a sense of trust in the environment that gives freedom for one to ask questions, show vulnerability when asking for help, reflect on errors, and proactively seek feedback (Edmondson, 2003). Intentional learning implies action—an attempt to do something new, to try a new behavior that carries the risk of failure. Learning agile organizations are safe places to experiment, try new approaches, and risk the possibility of failure when learning.

Psychological safety was identified in Google's Project Aristotle as the most important attribute of the organization's top teams (Duhigg, 2016). The teams that were most productive and innovative were characterized by a high degree of trust, a sense of camaraderie, and permission to incorporate flexible approaches to solve problems. Learning agile teams and learning agile organizations embrace this construct.

Effective leaders in learning agile organizations are able to promote the threat-free, psychologically safe environment and, paradoxically, at the same time instill a sense of urgency, focus, and energy. Specifically, effective leaders

- **Demonstrate empathy**. Empathy is listening while suspending judgment in order to understand. One of the most important aspects to understand is what generates threat for individuals. The learning agile leader asks lots of questions—good questions. The learning agile leader learns the boundaries of the comfort zones of team members and what they find motivating, so they can most successfully coach and avoid inadvertently introducing psychological threat.
- **Are approachable**. Learning agile organizations are relaxed, informal, and have leaders who are welcoming of all ideas and points of view regardless of organizational boundaries and position levels. They welcome challenge and eschew any hint of a punitive response to dissent.
- **Engender trust**. Psychological safety is not possible in the absence of trust. Learning agile leaders foster camaraderie and personal

relationships. They demonstrate trust by delegating, empowering, engaging, and supporting employee initiative.

- **Provide frequent feedback.** Feedback is a necessary component of learning, and a feedback-rich environment is a hallmark characteristic of learning agile organizations. Feedback in a threat-free environment tends to be specific, immediate, genuine, and more often positive (reinforcing) than negative (corrective).

- **Promote constructive conflict.** Learning agile organizations are trusting and respectful safe zones in which team members can disagree, even argue, without damaging interpersonal relationships. Employees can do this constructively because they respect each other and are united by their shared goals.

- **Organize with flexibility in mind.** Learning agile organizations are structured to serve their strategy and business model, but do not permit organizational structures to get in the way of nimbly responding to opportunities. They often make use of project teams, which readily morph to respond to perceived opportunities with bursts of energy.

- **Create a sense of urgency.** Learning agile leaders are more likely to appropriately ratchet up their own emotion to generate enthusiasm and excitement in others. They set clear targets and may define an adversary to be in the team's sights. The adversary may be a competitor or a metric (e.g., waste, cycle time, etc.). Having a common adversary generates team spirit and creates alignment. However, the adversary is never an internal entity. For example, it is obviously not productive for engineers to view the sales force as adversaries!

- **Tolerate reasonable risks and small failures.** Leaders in learning agile organizations teach the difference between smart, tolerable risks and stupid, unacceptable risks. They encourage smart risk-taking. They provide cover to allow experimentation and expect some—many— experiments will fail. Reasonable mistakes and failures are expected, but that does not mean they are celebrated. The focus is on learning in order to win.

Remember that leaders have an opportunity to hinder or facilitate the development of learning agility in others. How direct reports are managed plays an important role in their ability and willingness to learn from their experiences. Effective leaders challenge preexisting mindsets, are open to different ways of doing things, and—at all costs—avoid micromanaging.

Learning agility is imbued in a team by providing independence, autonomy, and the resources and support necessary to meet predetermined business goals. Learning agility is developed through encouragement and support for careful, planful risk-taking behavior. When mistakes are made, they are treated as "learning opportunities" to discuss rather than "performance failures" (Dweck, 2006).

Feedback-Rich Culture

Learning agile organizations are "feedback-rich" workplaces. Employees are provided continuous feedback on their job performance, leadership competencies, and various developmental behaviors. Whether it is obtained through 360-degree assessment and feedback programs, structured peer-to-peer interactions, after-event reviews, internal mentors, external coaches, or meaningful and regular supervisory feedback sessions, employees are constantly receiving information on how to improve and grow. The opportunity to obtain others' feedback helps identify lessons from experiences that otherwise would go unrecognized if individuals were left to process and interpret experiences on their own.

The crucial role feedback and reflection play in leadership development has been acknowledged for a long time. Feedback is especially important when situations are novel or ambiguous, such as after job promotions, temporary committees or project teams, developmental international assignments, and in new organizational settings and changing work roles (Brett, Feldman, & Weingart, 1990; Morrison, 1993). Those are the precise settings where high potentials and high learning agile talent are commonly placed. Feedback and reflection enable self-awareness and leadership behavioral corrections. It is a lack of self-awareness that is the single biggest factor in managerial derailment according to Hogan, Hogan, and Kaiser (2011).

Organizations that support learning agility create a culture where feedback is encouraged, time for reflection is provided, entrepreneurial risk and innovation are fostered, and developmental opportunities are widespread. Further, company structures are relatively flat, decentralized, nimble, and dynamic. Supervisors, managers, and executives are transparent, supportive, engaging, and team oriented. They serve as role models for future leaders. Abundant resources are devoted to employee development and are readily accessible (e.g., mentorship programs are established, internal and external

Table 14.1 Characteristics of Low Learning Agile and High Learning Agile Organizations

Low Learning Agile Organizations	High Learning Agile Organizations
• Focus on employee performance	• Focus on talent development
• Gain compliance through company policies	• Foster engagement and ownership through empowerment
• Use centralized decision-making	• Use decentralized decision-making
• Possess tall, bureaucratic structures	• Possess flat, nimble structures
• Engender risk-averse culture	• Stimulate experimentation and an entrepreneurial culture
• Focus on process execution	• Focus on process improvement
• Focus on others' best practices	• Focus on creating own best practices
• Limit feedback to annual reviews	• Nurture a feedback-rich culture
• Perpetuate systems that work	• Foster systems evaluation and change
• Focus on past	• Focus on future
• Create a need–to-know culture	• Create a transparent and open culture
• Have maximizing efficiency as its goal	• Have continuous improvement as its goal
• Rely on education and experienced-based selection approaches	• Incorporate learning agility as a key attribute for selection and development

Adapted from De Meuse (2020).

coaches are available, "lunch and learn" meetings are common). Overall, the decision-makers of the organization have made a deliberate effort to identify, groom, and promote the next generation of leaders. Systems, structures, policies, and practices promote learning agile behaviors and organizational flexibility (Table 14.1).

Talent Management Practices in High Learning Agile Organizations

There are several common characteristics among high learning agile organizations in the manner in which they manage talent. One of the primary areas is how they identify, select, develop, and manage employees. The temptation to treat all employees the same is purposefully discounted. Rather, the unique qualities and capabilities of each person are recognized as well as the business needs of the organization. Technical and functional specialists are valued differently from supervisors, general managers, and senior leaders. Distinct career paths are created. Different developmental opportunities are provided. In addition, learning agile organizations assess learning agility and use it as a key indicator of leadership potential. Talent identification and development are strategic imperatives and become a competitive advantage for those organizations. In the following sections, we examine how such organizations (a) differentiate talent, (b) apply learning agility to various work roles, and (c) implement succession planning to identify, select, and develop high-potential leaders.

Differentiating Talent

Learning agile organizations excel at differentiating talent to recruit and onboard the best talent and then apply differential treatment to develop and engage talent. Differential treatment allows development of talent in an intentional, focused way that best serves the needs of both the business and the employees. People are individuals and have unique needs, desires, and motivations. Unequal treatment does not imply unfair treatment. Differential treatment enables an individual's unique needs to be addressed while building organizational capabilities and learning agility.

There are multiple dimensions on which talent can be assessed and differentiated, including the following:

- **Performance**. In order to reward the contribution of individuals and promote a meritocracy, the net value of individual contributions is assessed. Performance is a function of the competence of the individual, the motivation of the individual, and the nature of the performance environment. Managers optimize performance by setting clear expectations, providing development, and creating a performance environment that provides the time, tools, feedback, and other required resources to support worthy accomplishments.
- **Career paths**. For employees who have potential to advance significantly beyond their current positions, two primary career paths are available: (a) a *specialist path* and (b) a *generalist path*. Most employees are hired as specialists of one type or another. They came to the job with a particular combination of skills, education, and experiences and began their career as a specialist of some sort (e.g., an accountant, a

programmer, a machinist, a teacher, an assembly line worker). At some point, as their career advances, they will reach a fork in the road. One direction continues down the specialist path, a narrow swim lane in which they continue to refine and develop in their discipline and contribute with their specialized skill set. The other direction leads them into new territory outside of their domain of specialization. They may switch to a different function or go into general management.

The career paths of specialists and generalists vary in several significant ways, including how individuals are engaged and developed. Specialists are most engaged by going deep and developing technical expertise. Generalists, on the other hand, are more likely engaged by breadth of perspective and task variety. They typically are deployed into projects or assignments and compensated differently. For example, specialists may spend more time in a given position because there are not as many available positions in their narrow swim lane to which they can move. Understanding the differences in career paths enables talent management professional to develop, brand, and market career options to employees, so they can make informed decisions about their careers. Likewise, it allows a company to make better decisions to satisfy workforce planning needs and develop organizational learning agility.

- **Employee potential.** Potential is the ability and willingness to learn and grow and enhance one's contribution to the organization. If we accept that definition, we will probably agree that almost everyone has at least some potential. What employee cannot or will not learn and grow? But, not everyone has *equal* potential. Some employees have limited potential and are essentially well placed in their current jobs. They are valuable in their current role but would falter or fail in other roles or if given much more responsibility. Others, authentic high potentials, can advance through their careers at a high velocity and ascend to senior leadership positions in the organization.

When we evaluate *performance*, we generally consider the present and look backward. In contrast, when we evaluate *potential*, we always look forward. Performance and potential are separate and distinct evaluations. Most high performers are *not* high potentials (Church & Silzer, 2010; Corporate Leadership Council, 2005). That is, if promoted beyond their current role, they would cease to be high performers. In contrast, virtually all high potentials are high performers and will continue to be as they take on new responsibilities. One way to think of it is like this: Potential is in the driver's seat and performance is along for the ride. Learning agility is a prerequisite of leadership potential.

Learning Agility as a Component of Potential

Several recent research studies have found that learning agility is a primary component of potential (e.g., De Meuse, 2017, 2019; Dries, Vantilborgh, & Pepermans, 2012). Indeed, all jobs require some level of learning agility, just as all jobs require some degree of intelligence. And just as some jobs require more intelligence than others, some jobs require a higher degree of learning agility. In general, the importance of learning agility increases as the role becomes less specialized and more generalized. Also, the value of learning agility increases as jobs become more complex, are more ambiguous, and are associated with the management of others (e.g., direct reports, task forces, temporary work teams, voluntary committees). Further, the importance of learning agility increases as we climb the organization's leadership hierarchy.

As illustrated in Figure 14.1, the benefits of learning agility are not just for general managers. Learning agility is an enabler for anyone serving in leadership roles in which they are under pressure and dealing with complexity, ambiguity, and the team goals, and this applies to both formal managerial positions and informal and/or temporary leadership roles.

If all the roles in an organization were simple, transactional, predictable, and never required dealing with complexity, ambiguity, or urgency, there would be little need for learning agility. The absurdity of that premise means that learning agility should play a prominent role for most organizations when it comes to assessing leadership potential and applying differential development for their workforce. Figure 14.1 depicts this relationship between role level/difficulty by position specialty.

Succession Planning and Talent Development

Succession planning and talent development should be integrated, coordinated processes. Organizations that divorce these processes are missing an

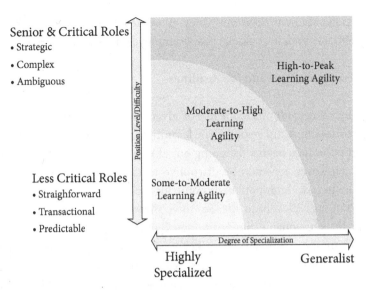

Figure 14.1 Application of learning agility by role.

opportunity to rigorously develop the talent pipeline and enhance organizational learning agility. Succession planning results in the strategic deployment of talent to ensure the business operates successfully now and in the future. The process considers the inventory of current talent and an inventory of key development and operational roles. Subsequently, deployment decisions attempt to match candidates with assignments based on their potential and developmental needs.

The commonly cited "70–20–10" rule of employee development asserts that we learn most of what we need for success by actually performing the job (Lombardo & Eichinger, 1996). And, this presents one of the great challenges of talent management. A job that is appropriately challenging and provides the opportunity to learn and master new skills is engaging and developmental. In contrast, a job which we have already mastered may provide little challenge and seldom offers an opportunity to develop.

That is the dilemma. If organizations deploy employees into jobs in which they currently lack capability, they put the business at risk, and if they deploy employees into jobs for which they are already fully capable, they do not have room to develop. Finding our way through this paradox is the crux of succession planning. Learning agile organizations are more sophisticated in the use of talent reviews to support succession planning and make more effective deployment decisions. They allow people to make mistakes and suffer setbacks and, in so doing, enable employees to learn and grow.

Rate of Advancement and Job Readiness

Naturally, there are limits to the rate of advancement even for high potentials who are moving at top velocity. The learning curve for most positions filled by high potentials begins flattening out after a year on the job, sometimes sooner. However, it would be disruptive to teams and be a management headache to have high potentials bouncing from job to job that frequently. Organizations will want to advance them through developmental positions as quickly as reasonable, but not so quickly that they are creating organizational turmoil or short-circuiting key lessons provided by the experience. Since some mistakes made in the first year are not revealed until the second year, it is usually a good idea to leave an employee in a role for at least 2 years before moving the employee on to the next assignment.

If individuals are moved too rapidly, they may be deprived of learning from their mistakes. On the other hand, if high-potential talent remains in a position for more than 3 or 4 years, they are likely wasting time. Many may become bored and leave the company for more enriching opportunities outside—often they go to a competitor. There is no hard and fast rule to determine the appropriate amount of time in a position. As a general rule of thumb, organizations might consider 2½ to 3 years for high potentials to be in a developmental role. Certainly, some jobs have a steep learning curve and require more time to wring the learning value from the experience. It is also possible for assignments to expand one's perspective by providing exposures to different customer segments, regions, or other aspects of the business. Frequently those perspectives can be gained in less than 2 years.

Very often, a candidate's readiness for a new assignment is inadvisably driven by the need to fill a job rather than the need to develop the candidate. Readiness should be just as much about—even more about—the readiness of the candidate to leave the existing role as it is readiness to enter a new role. Organizations must also be mindful that candidates who already possess all the skills required for success on a job will gain little once placed in that new role.

If development is a key consideration when deploying talent, it follows that competency assessment contributes to the determination of readiness. In this regard, a common approach is to contrast the individual's current level of competency with the level required in the targeted role. Intuitively, this makes sense, and indeed, consideration of the gap between current and targeted competency level is a relevant factor to consider. Just as importantly, however, organizations should consider readiness to leave the current role. For high-potential employees, in particular, it is a waste of development time to remain in a role beyond the point at which the required competencies have been mastered.

One of the differences between the *generalist* and *specialist* career paths is the typical rate of advancement. Generalists typically move through positions more rapidly and have a much greater variety in types of assignments compared to specialists. The roles of deep experts are narrower, and the positions are stickier, less prone to turnover. Usually, there simply are not enough different developmental roles within a narrow specialist career path to which high-potential specialists can be moved. Consequently, specialists tend to move between roles less frequently than do generalists. The high-potential generalist may move to a new position every 2 or 3 years, often making a lateral move. In contrast, high-potential specialists may remain in a position for 4 or 5 years. But, specialists still need to be aggressively developed in jobs just as generalists do, and this means we need to be especially creative about providing develop-in-place opportunities. When it is not possible or practical to move high-potential candidates to a new developmental role, we can provide them with special projects, opportunities to serve on cross-functional teams, temporary assignments, and other activities that are developmental (but do not require movement from their current position).

Developmental Stretch

A job is challenging and stretches according to the degree it (a) is unlike any other job performed previously, (b) has high organizational visibility, (c) has significant organizational consequences for failure, and (d) generally causes the individual to get out of his or her comfort zone of experiences. To optimize development, assignments with the optimum amount of stretch should be provided. It seems reasonable to assume that the level of stretch appropriate for any employee would be related to their learning agility. Highly learning agile employees can be stretched further. They have the capacity and the appetite for challenging assignments. Most employees will benefit from scaffolding, in which each subsequent job builds to some extent on the previous job. In this way, jobs are stepping stones in a natural career progression.

Each job builds on the previous job and prepares for the next. Highly learning agile individuals require less scaffolding. Their potential allows them to take giant steps that require more stretch than others can manage.

But how much stretch is enough? How much is too much? The ability to answer these questions hinges on the organization's ability to accurately assess potential in talent as well as to correctly evaluate the difficulty of jobs. Learning agility provides an excellent metric of an individual's likelihood of potential. However, other factors also should be considered such as IQ, EQ (emotional intelligence), character, values, and ambition. Likewise, various work experiences that have built leadership competencies are important to consider (Table 14.2). Note that the impact of learning agility is multiplicative. In other words, an employee can possess all "the right stuff" and various competency-building work experiences, but unless he or she is learning agile, leadership potential is limited.

An appropriate stretch assignment will require learning new skills and a high degree of focus and energy. If there is no chance of failure, there is insufficient stretch. If there is only a 50–50 chance of success, that is an excessive and unreasonable stretch. We want to push high potentials, to stretch them, to accelerate their development. However, we do not want to set them up for catastrophic career failures, and we cannot allow fiascos to unduly impact the business.

Deploying high potentials is not an exact science. Rather than precision, it requires good judgment and reasonable tolerance for risk. When filling a

Table 14.2 Learning Agility and the Identification and Development of High Potential Talent

Competency Building Leadership The Right Stuff	+ Work Experiences	x Learning Agility = Potential
• IQ	• Various jobs	• Ability to lead others
• EQ	• Stretch assignments	• Ability to take on broader roles
• Career ambition	• Hardships	• Ability to perform well two levels above job
• Willingness to lead	• Job feedback	
• Educational level	• Coaching	
• Character and values	• Workshops	
• Supportive family	• Readings	

critical position and given the choice between two candidates, one of whom has a track record suggesting a safe choice and the other a high potential who would need to stretch, organizations will almost always give the nod to the safer choice. In the short term, this approach reduces risk for the business. In the long run, however, it may increase the risk that leadership bench strength is compromised and fail to enhance the organization's future agility.

Preventing Catastrophic Failures

Development entails risk. Without a risk of failure, it is unlikely learners will experience much opportunity to develop. But, most businesses cannot tolerate serious failures, and we do not want to subject employees to derailing career missteps. Risk can be mitigated by assigning a more experienced, senior person to monitor the diciest stretch assignments and, figuratively speaking, play the role of lifeguard.

To illustrate, consider a talent review in which the next assignment for a high potential is being discussed. Emily is very highly regarded and on a fast track to a senior-level position. She is in her early 30s, and during her 10 years with the firm has excelled in a series of progressively more challenging jobs. Emily has made it look easy—as high potentials often do—to the extent that no one knows if she has really been seriously tested. The consensus is it is time to give her a stiff challenge. However, there is much resistance when the suggestion is made to assign her to lead an upcoming project with an important customer. The potential upside is that Emily will have a huge learning opportunity with significant potential to accelerate her career. The downside is that if she fails in this highly visible, critical assignment, the resulting business impact will be calamitous.

This uncertainty creates a threat that swirls among the talent review participants. To mitigate the risk and soften the threat, two actions are recommended. The first is to provide a safety net by assigning Nate as Emily's lifeguard. He is a senior leader who has successfully managed difficult projects with the customer and will monitor Emily's progress closely but discreetly. It is recognized Emily will be jumping into water over her head, but the idea is to give her a chance to figure out how to swim. Nate will intervene only as her lifeguard if she appears to be sinking.

The second action is for Emily's boss to discuss the assignment with her. The intention is to review the opportunity, emphasizing that it will stretch her like she's never been stretched previously. The message to her will include some suggestions for getting started on the right foot. Emily's manager also will express confidence in her ability without minimizing the difficulty to be faced. There will be no mention of Nate, her lifeguard. Part of Emily's development is to deal with the pressure of the assignment, all the while knowing the company is invested in her success and has confidence in her.

Talent Blockers

Some roles in the organization are highly developmental and comprise essential stepping stones on a particular career path. It is important that these roles are identified so organizations have an inventory of development roles to match to their inventory of talent. Key developmental roles are relatively few in number; they need to be filled by fast-track, high-potential employees who will stay in the role just long enough to climb the learning curve. When those roles are blocked by solid performers deemed to be well placed, it stifles succession and the use of select jobs as primary development vehicles. Talent blockers also frustrate and disengage high potentials who are chomping at the bit for increased challenge and advancement. Those employees often choose to leave the organization rather than mark time waiting for long-tenured employees to vacate a development role. Early career high potentials are especially sensitive to the "gray ceiling" in the organization and often jump ship to join a company that provides better development and career advancement opportunities.

Talent reviews provide a forum to educate organizational leaders on the importance of development roles and to set expectations about the periodic turnover expected in those roles as high potentials rotate through assignments. Expectations also need to be set for the solid, well-placed incumbents who are blocking developmental roles. Until expectations about development roles and high-potential assignments are widely understood, it can be very difficult to move blockers from their current position. They are usually solid, if not stellar, performers and comfortable in their jobs. The conversation about reassignment is threatening to both the incumbent and to the manager delivering the news; it is important for the organization to find suitable and rewarding roles for incumbents and to remove uncertainty and threat from reassignments. Messaging—to both the incumbent and others in the organization—should reinforce the value the incumbent provides to the firm and make clear that the reassignment is not being made because of a problem with the incumbent's performance.

Talent Hoarding

Talent belongs to the enterprise, not to the department, function, or manager. Some leaders wrestle with this concept. When a manager has a stellar employee, it is natural they want to retain the candidate. Therefore, often he or she hesitates to enthusiastically laud their achievements and potential in a talent review for fear of losing the employee. Such talent hoarding can occur *before* and *during* talent reviews when managers obscure a candidate's potential. Another variation of hoarding raises its head after the review when it is time to execute deployment decisions. Everyone in a talent review can nod in agreement about the intended next step, but when it comes time to assign the candidate to the next step position, a senior manager may try to intervene to negate the assignment to protect or promote a favored candidate.

If the senior leadership team does not take commitments made during talent reviews seriously and follow through on documented decisions, neither will other leaders. Lack of follow-through makes a mockery of all the preparation and effort expended in the talent review. However, when the senior leadership team sets a good example on follow-through, communicates clear expectations about executing talent decisions, and reinforces and recognizes managers who successfully cultivate talent, the firm's culture will change accordingly.

Transparency and Labeling

It is a good practice to be absolutely transparent about talent management guiding principles. Organizations should share the processes used for differentiating talent and the intention to treat people as individuals, providing job assignments that challenge and stretch people to the extent appropriate. However, it is also important to know when discretion is needed and when to avoid unnecessarily shining light where illumination is not constructive. Organizations need terminology to communicate clearly talent concepts and processes but avoid hanging (permanent) labels on employees. There are many good reasons to avoid branding anyone as a high potential:

- First of all, high potentials already know they are high potentials if you are applying differential treatment; the organization is treating them differently! They are getting more challenging assignments. They are exposed to additional training, mentoring, and coaching. They are being stretched more than others. And, over the long term, they will progress through their career at a higher velocity than the general employee population. Employees who are indeed high potentials certainly do not need anyone to tell them so. They already know it!

- There are no clear lines demarcating boundaries between low, medium, and high potential. Potential is a continuum, and everyone has some potential. Virtually every employee has the ability to learn, grow, and enhance their contribution to the organization. People are complex, and our methods of assessing lack precision. Couple this reality with the difficulty managers have distinguishing between *performance* and *potential*, and it is almost guaranteed some talent will be misclassified. A portion of those deemed to be high potential actually will be false positives. Moreover, there also will be false negatives—diamonds in the rough whose potential is not recognized. These factors are not lost on the employee population, who likely will feel they have been relegated to an inappropriate classification.

- Potential is not a right or permanent. There always is a high price to pay to be on the high-potential path, and some employees will make personal choices to abandon this path. Situations change (e.g., health, family dynamics, career aspirations). Also, success must be earned every step along the way. People sometimes disappoint us. It is possible that the employee who stood out during last year's talent review has hit a ceiling or derailed this year. It is hoped these are rare occurrences, but the point is there is no room for conferring high-potential status that may be perceived as permanent.

- The high-potential label can create a sense of entitlement, which may lead to undesired and dysfunctional behavior. Sometimes, the employee given the label of high potential can adopt prima donna behavior and expect favored treatment in terms of compensation and perks. Rather, high potentials should expect to receive assignments that are uncomfortable, severely challenging, and sometimes feel like a pressure cooker. They should expect to receive those assignments (and even feel honored by them) because it demonstrates the organization cares enough to put them into significant roles that accelerate their development.

Conclusion

What do 3M, Johnson & Johnson, Pfizer, Owens Corning, IBM, and Pepsi have in common? As pointed out in Chapter 1, they all have been listed on the Fortune 500 since its origin in 1955. Indeed, those companies continue to represent the top brands in their respective industries. Naturally, many different factors have contributed to their sustained success during the past 65 years. It should be noted, however, that those organizations aggressively manage the process of leadership identification and development. Talent assessment is part of their culture. Leadership potential is scrutinized carefully, and career plans are revisited annually.

Just as learning agility greatly enhances an individual's leadership potential, organizations that are able to learn and flex to the dynamic needs of the marketplace increase their competitive advantage. Learning agile organizations learn to let go of old technologies, outdated policies, and antiquated workforce practices that once were cutting edge but now hinder success. These organizations allow—indeed, encourage—dissent and foster a feedback rich culture where all stakeholders feel safe to experiment, make mistakes, and speak their minds. Executives and human resource professionals embrace talent management processes that create rewarding career paths for both technical specialists and managers to thrive. Learning agile organizations promote and systematically develop supervisors, managers, and executives who are able to lead in our VUCA world. They select and develop leaders who are learning agile and organizations that are consistently innovating and transforming. The twenty-first century will provide numerous opportunities for those individuals and companies sufficiently learning agile to see and capitalize on them.

References

Aghina, W., Handscomb, C., Ludolph, J, Rona, D., & West, D. (2020, March). Enterprise agility: Buzz or business impact. Retrieved from https://www.mckinsey.com/business-functions/organization/our-insights/enterprise-agility-buzz-or-business-impact

Brett, J. M., Feldman, D. C., & Weingart, L. R. (1990). Feedback-seeking behavior of new hires and job changers. *Journal of Management, 16*, 737–749.

Church, A. H., & Silzer, R. (2010). Identifying and assessing high-potential talent: Current organizational practices. In R. Silzer & B. E. Dowell (Eds.), *Strategic-driven talent management: A leadership imperative* (pp. 213–279). San Francisco, CA: Wiley.

Corporate Leadership Council. (2005). *Realizing the full potential of rising talent* (Vol. 1). Washington, DC: Corporate Executive Board.

De Meuse, K. P. (2017). Learning agility: Its evolution as a psychological construct and its empirical relationship to leader success. *Consulting Psychology Journal: Practice and Research, 69*, 267–295.

De Meuse, K. P. (2019). A meta-analysis of the relationship between learning agility and leader success. *Journal of Organizational Psychology, 19*, 25–34.

De Meuse, K. P. (2020). *Enhancing your learning agility: A guidebook to accompany the TALENTx7* *Assessment* (2nd ed.). Minneapolis, MN: De Meuse Leadership Group.

Dries, N., Vantilborgh, T., & Pepermans, R. (2012). The role of learning agility and career variety in the identification and development of high potential employees. *Personnel Review, 41*, 340–358.

Duhigg, C. (2016, February 28). What Google learned from its quest to build the perfect team? *New York Times*. Retrieved from https://www.nytimes.com/2016/02/28/magazine/what-google-learned-from-its-quest-to-build-the-perfect-team.html

Dweck, C. S. (2006). *Mindset: The new psychology of success*. New York, NY: Ballantine Books.

Edmondson, A. C. (2003). Managing the risk of learning: Psychological safety in work teams. In M. West, D. Tjosvold, & K. G. Smith. (Eds.), *International handbook of organizational teamwork and cooperative working* (pp. 255–275). West Sussex, England: Wiley.

Garvin, D. A., Edmondson, A. C., & Gino, F. (2008). Is yours a learning organization? *Harvard Business Review, 86*(3), 109.

Hogan, J., Hogan, R., & Kaiser, R. B. (2011). Management derailment. In S. Zedeck (Ed.), *American Psychological Association handbook of industrial and organizational psychology* (Vol. 3, pp. 555–575). Washington, DC: American Psychological Association.

Lombardo, M. M., & Eichinger, R. W. (1996). *The career architect development planner*. Minneapolis, MN: Lominger International.

Morrison, E. W. (1993). Newcomer information seeking: Exploring types, modes, sources, and outcomes. *Academy of Management Journal, 36*, 557–589.

Nonaka, I. (1991). The knowledge-creating company. *Harvard Business Review, 69*(6), 9–104.

Pedler, M., Burgoyne J., & Boydell, T. (1991). *The learning company: A strategy for sustainable development*. New York, NY: McGraw-Hill.

Ruyle, K. E. (2014). *Lessons from a CEO's journal: Leading talent and innovation*. Coral Gables, FL: Inventive Talent.

Schein, E. H. (2010). *Organizational culture and leadership* (4th ed.). Hoboken, NJ: Wiley.

Senge, P. M. (1990). *The fifth discipline*. New York, NY: Doubleday Business.

Senge, P. M. (1994). *The fifth discipline fieldbook: Strategies and tools for building a learning organization*. New York, NY: Currency.

15

Building Learning Agility Through Psychological Safety

Lorraine Stomski and Kelly Jensen

> If everybody is doing it one way, there's a good chance you can find your niche by going exactly in the opposite direction.
> —Sam Walton (1918–1992), businessman and entrepreneur

Sam Walton is known for many things, but mainly founding the largest retailer in the world in 1962—Walmart. He had a fervent passion to serve the customer first and foremost by providing everyday low prices and costs. In order to successfully propel the retailer forward, Sam understood he would need curious, high-performing, and avid learning "associates," as he called them, a term that was embedded in Walmart's culture. Sam founded his business on several core beliefs and values—service to the customer, respect for the individual, striving for excellence, and acting with integrity.

Respecting and valuing his associates' ideas, Sam placed the utmost value on those who took calculated risks and were always looking for new ways to learn, especially the store associates (Walton, 1972). He did this by creating a workplace environment that fostered a team mentality and eliminated hierarchical notions. In 1985, Sam wrote to his management team a memo, "Using First Names Throughout Our Company." In this memo, Sam went on to explain, "It is absolutely essential that we not in any way indicate that there are different classes of hourly and management associates at Wal-Mart. This philosophy of management just won't fly. There's no future for that approach in Wal-Mart" (Walton, 1972).[*] He emphasized that all leaders must be "servant leaders" and put the interests of the associate first, starting with

---

[*] Walmart utilized a hyphen in the company name until 2008.

Lorraine Stomski and Kelly Jensen, *Building Learning Agility Through Psychological Safety* In: *The Age of Agility.* Edited by: Veronica Schmidt Harvey and Kenneth P. De Meuse, Oxford University Press (2021). © Oxford University Press. DOI: 10.1093/oso/9780190085353.003.0015

addressing all associates within the company by their first name—a direction that went against typical workforce practices during that time. A key callout in the memo gave clear directions for leaders to implement this practice with their associates, by explaining why it was important to them and not simply a directive disseminated down from the chief executive officer (CEO). Sam was convinced this small act would help reinforce team unity and the concept that leaders earned respect based on how they treated their associates.

While a variety of leadership styles and approaches exists, Sam Walton knew the secret to success for his company. In letters to his associates, he frequently articulated how success in the company could not be achieved without the associates themselves. Each letter was filled with gratitude and appreciation, while still maintaining high expectations for the associates. In May 1972 he wrote, "I've been repeatedly asked by our Investment Banking friends and other retail people from other companies as to Wal-Mart's secret. Proudly, you're Wal-Mart's 'secret,' and we frankly admit to it" (Walton, 1972).

On multiple accounts, Sam emphasized the concept of the "open-door policy" and demanded leaders remove fear from their leadership style and approach (Walton, 1992). He knew if a leader led by fear associates would be afraid to voice opinions, often leaving problems to fester. Further, creativity and innovation would suffer, and associates would not take chances for fear of risking their leader's disapproval. When this occurs, the associates suffer, as does the company's success. Sam Walton didn't know it then, but he was working to build a "psychologically safe" environment that drove learning agility. His philosophy would lead to business outcomes and successes that were felt for decades to come within the retailer.

This chapter presents a look at psychological safety, a shared belief held by members of a team that the team is safe space for interpersonal risk-taking (Edmondson, 1999) and its positive impact on learning agility. Looking at the history of both psychological safety and that of learning agility, there is a shared belief that team psychological safety leads to desired team learning agility and success. We also consider the role of the leader in activating and accelerating team learning.

There are clear implications from various bodies of research and case studies that illustrate how the optimization of psychological safety and learning effectiveness occur through certain conditions and approaches. Results from a Walmart study of more than 370 leaders and teams of a validated *Psychological Safety Survey* highlighted the critical importance of a manager to direct report relationships that are built around trust and vulnerability. We also recommend further research on factors that lead to building psychologically safe team environments and foster learning agility.

Learning Agility and Psychological Safety

While there are many definitions of learning agility in the literature and popular press, De Meuse, in his comprehensive 2017 review on the topic, defined it as "the ability to learn from experience, and then the willingness to apply those lessons to perform successfully in new and challenging leadership roles" (p. 277). As he pointed out, learning agility is a relatively new construct, coined only 20 years ago by Michael Lombardo and Robert Eichinger (2000), who posited high-potential leaders are learning agile and outperform those who are not.

Now, more than ever, organizations are moving at rapid speed, quickly transforming their business models and how they serve their customers. The need for nimble and agile leaders has become not only important, but also essential for the future viability of organizations. In theory, the ability and willingness of leaders to adapt, respond to unanticipated challenges (e.g., Covid-19), build new skills, and pivot to new ways of working can be more easily accomplished by learning agile individuals. The construct of learning agility has quickly gained momentum in organizations (arguably outpacing the research) and spurred HR leaders to include it as an important component in the identification of talent, particularly those deemed to have high potential.

The debate also continues on whether a valid assessment tool can measure learning agility. Some of the more popular instruments that emerged during the past two decades include the multirater *Choices Architect*™ (Lombardo & Eichinger, 2000), along with various self-report measures, such as *viaEDGE*™ (De Meuse et al., 2011), the *TALENTx7® Assessment* (De Meuse, Lim, & Rao, 2019), the Center for Creative Leadership's *Prospector*, and the recently developed *Burke Learning Agility Inventory*™ (Hoff & Burke, 2017). While a deep dive into measurement is beyond the scope of this chapter (see Chapter 4 and De Meuse, 2017, for in-depth reviews), it is important to note some of the key individual characteristics that are measured across many of these assessments. Constructs such as self-awareness, risk-taking, and experimentation are included and have an explicit connection to fostering psychological safety. As we discuss further in this chapter, it is critical for leaders to embody these characteristics in order to create psychological safety in their teams.

Further, while learning agility theories primarily focus on the drivers and attributes that comprise an individual's propensity to *be* learning agile, there is less focus on the leader's role in growing or accelerating learning agility within others. Therefore, the focus of this chapter addresses the impact that leaders can have in the development of learning agile team members. We postulate that a major contributor to creating learning agile team members is through enabling a culture of risk taking, openness, and experimentation that accelerates the learning agility in others. This culture is achieved by fostering an environment of psychological safety, which is defined as the willingness to take interpersonal risk within the team (Edmondson & Lei, 2014).

More specifically, we postulate that beyond the intrinsic motivations and learning skills an individual embodies, leaders play an important role in creating a team environment and culture where employees feel empowered to learn by taking risks and trying new skills, practicing, failing fast, reflecting, and learning. We believe that a condition necessary for building and nurturing learning agility is psychological safety. In summary, can a leader build even more nimble, learning agile team members by creating an environment where people feel free to take interpersonal risks? We believe the answer is yes.

History of Psychological Safety

The origins of psychological safety date to the mid-1960s, when Schein and Bennis (1965) introduced the concept within the context of organizational change and learning. Their premise was that to enable change, one needs to feel "psychologically safe." More specifically, and tightly connected to learning, they postulated that for people to change their behavior in a new and rapidly evolving environment, people need to "feel secure and capable of changing their behavior." This secure and capable environment is what they defined as psychological safety. Schein further described the learner in a psychologically safe environment as feeling a new way of working is "possible and achievable, and the learning process itself will not be too anxiety provoking or demeaning" (Schein, 2010, p. 302).

Think about a time when you learned a new skill. Imagine it was snowboarding. You most certainly did not begin by strapping on the board and gliding smoothly down a black diamond run. You began slowly and likely made mistakes that caused some physical discomfort, like falling or even emotional pain by suffering a bit of humiliation as well. Perhaps, you fell in front of other experienced snowboarders, or you had to take your first runs on the beginner hill surrounded by kids under the age of 10 whizzing by you. Any of these scenarios required you to have a novice mindset, release the fear of failure, and experiment with new behaviors so you could learn. This mindset enabled you to focus all of your physical and cognitive functioning on the mastery of a new skill. You were fully engaged in learning how to snowboard!

However, imagine if making a mistake resulted in punishment, admonishment from your social group, or expulsion from the ski run entirely. In this case, you would likely not even bother to try, or if you did, the cognitive interference experienced would prevent you from fully focusing on the task at hand due to a fear of failure (i.e., the classic "fight–or–flight" response). In other words, it would stop you in your tracks from learning. It could lead you to avoid trying new things or experimenting with new behaviors in the future, instead leaving you to stick with the status quo, thus, remaining stagnant in your growth as a human (and as a snowboarder).

This tongue-in-cheek example illustrates the point Bennis and Schein (1965) made many decades ago. Learning is enabled, first, by having a psychologically safe environment—one that is free from fear, reprisals, and humiliation. As humans, we are hardwired to avoid situations fraught with these perils. Yet, with every new situation, it is natural to feel unsteady or anxious. To induce a "learner mindset," it requires a level of acceptance that some degree of anxiety will naturally come with any new experience. This is what Schein referred to as the paradox of learning. This role of anxiety was described by Schein in his 1992 speech at Davos as follows: "Anxiety prevents learning, but anxiety is necessary to start learning as well." Anxiety serves a purpose.

According to Schein (2010), there are three phases to learning. The first one is what Karl Lewin (1947) famously described as the "unfreezing" stage. In this stage, there needs to be a clear reason and motivation for change. This disequilibrium induces unfreezing, which creates the will to change and thus learn. For unfreezing to occur, Schein (1980, 2009, 2010) stated that the following three unique processes must occur: (a) enough disconfirming data to cause serious discomfort and disequilibrium; (b) the connection of the disconfirming data to important goals and ideals causing anxiety and/or guilt; and (c) enough psychological safety, in the sense of being able to see a possibility of solving the problem and learning something new without loss of identity or integrity.

Furthermore, core to transformational change is that individuals must also unlearn. To unlearn, a person needs to feel psychologically safe. When conditions of psychological safety are not in place, individuals likely will resist the change. While the current conditions may not be serving them well, they often provide other secondary positive features, like preserving the status quo and thereby reducing anxiety related to making the needed change. It is natural that individuals will often move to self-preservation methods such as disconfirming the evidence. This rationale frequently manifests in people saying, "It isn't so bad" or "Let's wait and see what happens when a new leader comes in." These tactics serve to preserve one's self-esteem and group membership (Schein, 2010).

The anxiety induced during transformation can manifest in many forms: (a) individuals fear the loss of power, (b) the feeling of incompetence and being punished for it, (c) a loss of identity because a new way of working is required, and finally, (d) the fear of being rejected or excluded from the group by moving forward and behaving in a new way (Schein, 2010). Schein further postulated that while this disconfirmation is prevalent throughout organizations, the most powerful way to eliminate this anxiety is by creating a psychologically safe culture that facilitates learning and encourages new behaviors. This theory has remained widely accepted throughout the years, but its focus was on psychological safety as an individual and/or an organizational construct. It wasn't until Amy Edmondson began studying teams during the mid-1990s that the power of psychological safety extended to teams.

Psychological Safety and Team Learning

Starting in the 1990s, the construct of psychological safety experienced renewed interest, in large part through the work of Amy Edmondson (1996). The focus during the past 20 years has been on the increased necessity for organizations and teams to continuously learn and drive innovation (Edmondson & Lei, 2014). In addition, the concept has moved beyond the traditional academic research. Recently, several books and business journals have focused on the importance of psychological safety as a mediator in driving performance, engagement, learning, productivity, and return on investment (Carmeli & Gittell, 2009; Delizonna, 2017; Edmondson, 2019).

Edmondson (1996) was the first to identify psychological safety as a group variable that lives within the team. This revelation emerged quite accidently when she was a first-year doctoral student. Her research was centered on investigating how teamwork influenced the effectiveness of performance outcomes, in this case medical errors. Logically, Edmondson hypothesized that the best performing teams would show the fewest human errors. Over the 6 months of the study, subject matter experts (i.e., nurses) collected error rates for each team. In addition, Edmondson administered a validated instrument called the *Team Diagnostic Survey* to understand how everyone felt about working together—from collaboration, socialization, to problem-solving. The instrument was administered to the doctors, nurses, and clerks within the teams (Edmondson, 1996).

At the end of the data collection, Edmondson (1996) observed a startling result. Unlike her hypothesis that the most effective teams would make the fewest errors, her results were the exact opposite. In fact, the most successful teams reported more errors, not less. Her insights following this study led her to conclude that psychological safety is not an organizational-level or individual-level variable, but in fact lives within the team. She proposed that because the best teams *reported* more errors, they likely had a climate enabling team members to be vulnerable and share openly about mistakes the team had made. Further, she suggested the better teams did not necessarily make *more* mistakes; they just felt more comfortable *reporting* their mistakes, given the climate of openness created within the team.

Years later, Tjosvold, Yu, and Hui (2004) examined 107 teams across various organizations in China. Their study specifically explored how these groups learned. Critical attributes of the team were assessed, and it is was found that the best teams had an open environment characterized by cooperation and discussion of mistakes. In sum, this openness enabled and nurtured a learning orientation within the team. The study also supported the notion that having a foundation of trust, openness, and absence of fear of reprisals around mistakes or failures enables a psychologically safe environment.

During the past several years, many outcomes have been studied around teams described as psychologically safe. For example, Choo, Linderman, and Schroeder (2007) investigated 951 team members across 206 projects and concluded psychologically safe environments enable divergent thinking, creativity, and risk–taking, which, in turn, leads to increased quality of learning behaviors and enhanced team performance. Given these findings, it only makes sense that leaders across organizations would strive to build a psychologically safe culture. However, it appears most organizations are unsuccessful.

A recent global study revealed only 47% of individuals across organizations believe they operate within a "psychologically safe and healthy environment" (Ipsos, 2012). This figure means more than one half of those participants reported they worked in an environment where they did not feel empowered to speak up, ask questions, or challenge the status quo. Given the exponential pace of change agile today, learners are needed to help drive transformation. The findings of this study are a sober reminder that many leaders are not leading teams in a way that enables learning or produces optimal outcomes. And, if we know having a psychologically safe environment serves as the catalyst for learning, we can infer a huge proportion of the workforce is operating in a suboptimal zone, producing suboptimal results. Most employees appear to be working in team cultures that stifle learning, growth, and innovation—precisely the things we need in this rapidly evolving world.

Project Aristotle

One of the most frequently cited research regarding teams and psychological safety was occurred at Google in 2012 (Duhigg, 2016). Google researchers were on a quest to find the secret ingredients for building the "perfect" team. In their study, multiple factors were examined, including social patterns such as how often people eat together. With no earth-shattering results uncovered, Google eventually honed in on team composition. They asked, "What were the elements of team composition that would actually produce the 'perfect team?'" Examining 180 teams within Google, researchers looked at the role of gender, hobbies, introversion/extraversion, educational backgrounds, and whether or not the team socialized outside of the office. Yet, despite looking at many different team composition variables, nothing seemed to differentiate the most from the least effective teams. In fact, in some cases, teams that had precisely the same composition varied greatly in their effectiveness. It left the researchers perplexed.

It was at this point that Google began looking at the emerging literature on social and group norms. By examining this research, the Google researchers dug deeper into the group norms that bind teams together and discovered while the norms could differ greatly between teams, the critical element was the *presence* of those norms that ultimately contributed to the success of the team. Further, the presence of the *right* norms elevated the "collective intelligence" of the team.

This finding was similar to that reached in an earlier study conducted at Carnegie Mellon (Woolley, Chabris, Pentland, Hashmi, & Malone, 2010). In this study, two elements emerged that differentiated good from poor teams: (a) the distribution of conversation within good teams was relatively equal among members and (b) the members within good teams exhibited high social sensitivity, meaning each team member could read the feelings, emotions, and energy in the room. In other words, the good teams demonstrated collective high emotional intelligence.

After the Google researchers began examining the historical research in the area of group norms and psychological safety, their findings suddenly made sense. After years of studying Google teams, it was concluded the underlying element critical to any successful team in an organization was the presence of psychological safety. The researchers concluded many factors were critical to team functioning, including

- Dependability—Can we count on each other to do high-quality work on time?
- Structure and Clarity—Are goals, roles, and execution plans on our team clear?
- Meaning of Work—Are we working on something that is personally important for each of us?
- Impact of Work—Do we fundamentally believe that the work we are doing matters?

However, it was the metafactor of psychological safety that served as the foundation for the team to work effectively together. It had to be present for the team to thrive—and learn.

This begs the next question: How do a team *and* the leader of that team create a psychologically safe environment? Vulnerability and empathy appear to be key factors in its creation. If members believe they can be their authentic selves within the team and show their vulnerabilities without fear, it is likely the team will experience psychological safety.

Activating and Accelerating Learning

As reviewed previously, there have been several studies supporting the relationship between learning and psychological safety (Carmeli & Gittell, 2009; Cataldo, Raelin, & Lambert, 2009; Edmondson, 1996; Huang & Jiang, 2012). The consistent theme across these studies is the notion that it is necessary to have psychological safety to enable team or group learning. Edmondson (2003, 2019) made the point that having psychological safety enables the conditions for learning. However, to truly accelerate the learning also requires high-performance standards and accountability. She described it in terms of a 2 × 2 matrix to illustrate the criticality of the two variables working together (Figure 15.1).

As the matrix illustrates, possessing a high degree of psychological safety is not the only requirement for achieving high performance and activating learning. A team may not be a high-performing team despite having a high degree of psychological safety. In the absence of performance standards and accountability, the environment becomes what Edmondson described as a "comfort zone," in which team members trust each other and are not afraid to speak up but are not necessarily challenged by the work. There is limited learning in this instance because no one is challenging the status quo despite

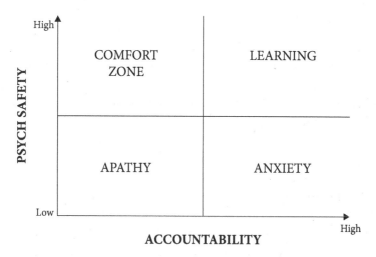

Figure 15.1 Conditions for learning and performance.
Adapted from Edmondson (2019).

the safe conditions that would encourage it. However, once accountability and performance standards are introduced within the team, it transforms into a "learning and high-performance Zone." This zone is characterized by collaboration, innovation, and learning. Team members challenge each other, they push against the status quo, and they lean into their learning anxiety because expectations and standards are high. Obviously, it is the zone we should strive to create as leaders.

Unfortunately, not all organizations and teams fall within the learning zone. In fact, as the following case study illustrates, many teams in highly transformative environments risk falling into the bottom right quadrant, the "anxiety zone." This zone is characterized by the fear of speaking up. By holding teams to high standards but not providing them the foundational environment that enables learning and the power to speak up, it becomes a fearful place. The consequence of working in this quadrant is suboptimal performance and a "heads down, mouth closed" culture. This type of fear-based culture impedes the ability to learn and shuts down cognitive functioning because the team members' focus is on survival.

This phenomenon can be partially explained through neuroscience and the "fight-or-flight" response to fear. On the opposite end (located in the lower left-hand quadrant of the matrix) is the "apathy zone." It is where neither accountability nor psychological safety is present. Consequently, team members focus on their own individual agendas, often engaging in unhealthy political behavior. Neither learning nor performance is a goal; little is accomplished as a team. Thus, if our goal is to create high-performance standards while concurrently having a psychologically safe environment, how do you develop it?

The Role of the Leader in Building a Psychologically Safe Culture

When organizations undergo transformation, numerous elements are out of a leader's control. Shifting cultures, organizational changes, and leadership movements all can produce chaos and uncertainty, preventing managers from leading effectively during times of change. That said, unlike many things out of a leader's control, psychological safety is something the leader *can* impact and create *within* his or her own team.

Walmart Case Study

In 2019, Walmart introduced the concept of psychological safety as part of the launch of a high-potential program for its leaders. The impetus came as a result of many discussions with leaders around their personal experiences going through large-scale transformations. Several themes emerged during those conversations, including challenges in driving change, ensuring the right talent, and working across functional silos. However, one theme seemed to strike a chord and resonate with many: How do we truly create an environment within our teams where people feel empowered to say no, disagree, take risks, or show vulnerability by saying "I don't know"? And how do we foster an environment where teams really embrace new ways of working?

In designing the session, we decided to "shock" the system by doing a simple "future-back" exercise. The exercise unfolded as follows:

- Participants were asked to imagine the following scenario:
  - It's 2030;
  - Big box formats have evolved into town centers;
  - The space becomes hyperfocused on the activities, businesses, and interests of the local communities it serves;
  - New amenities, new processes, new audiences/consumers, new ways of working, and new behaviors are required; and
  - We are surpassing financial expectations of the street and crushing our competitors.
- The question was posed, Who are the leaders that got us there? Instead of having participants name specific leaders, they were asked to describe those leaders. What leadership attributes and capabilities enabled them to lead the organization to this level of success?
- An hour-long session was then facilitated to take a deep dive into the descriptions of the leaders participants had identified, pulling out traits and capabilities and then analyzing them. For example, if someone said innovative, we asked the following questions: How is this any different from what we've always described as needing in our leaders? What behaviors look different? How does it show up in the individual? The team? How did we select for this? Can you select for this? Extensively facilitated, deep discussions enabled moving beyond just listing typical competencies. We began to delve into the

culture, conditions, and environments necessary to create and engage a high-performing team.

- From this discussion, we pivoted naturally to discussing the foundation that enables high performance—psychological safety, ultimately enabling the aforementioned capabilities around collaboration, innovation, and learning agility. Following the discussion around the concept of psychological safety and its components, we emphasized that discussion was only the beginning. The real work would begin once leaders got back home. The first step in that process was for leaders to assess how psychologically safe their team feel.

We utilized a validated assessment instrument derived from the work of Edmondson (1999) to assess a team's sense of psychological safety. Once back from the leadership program, the survey was administered to all of the leaders' teams. After the results were computed, we provided coaching for each leader to understand the results and helped leaders plan for debriefing sessions with their teams. Contrary to receiving the results and creating action plans on their own, leaders were coached to do a dedicated session *with* the team, reviewing and discussing the results along with identifying prioritized actions to improve the team's sense of psychological safety. We provided a recommended agenda, PowerPoint deck, templates, and discussion guides based on the results. However, we were very clear that the session needed to be led and delivered by the leader—not human resources.

This approach accomplished several things. It empowered the leader to "own the results" for his or her respective team and "lead" the debriefing session. It demonstrated the leader's vulnerability and willingness to acknowledge gaps in his or her leadership. It also put ownership and accountability on the team members. Outcomes were the creation of new rules of engagement (norms) for team members, holding each other accountable.

To date, close to 400 associates and leaders from around the globe have participated in the assessment and debriefing/action planning sessions. The strategy moving forward is to assess psychological safety annually or when the team composition changes significantly. The survey and its debriefing/action planning sessions (ultimately) begin a conversation between team members and their leadership to help further the connection between high psychological safety, innovation, collaboration, and learning agility.

Research Moving Forward

Despite the resurgence and interest in psychological safety, there continues to be unanswered questions. Potential cultural differences in the experience of psychological safety is one area that would benefit from additional study. While research has demonstrated countries with high-power distance relationships such as China and Japan (Hofstede, 2001) have lower psychological safety, it does not mean that psychological safety cannot be achieved in different cultures (Edmondson, 2019). More research is needed to identify the strategies and methods that will work *within* those unique cultural contexts.

In addition, as organizations increasingly use personality assessments as part of the selection process (Church, 2019), it would be useful to see how the personality attributes of the leader—and the various members of the team—impact psychological safety within the team. Likewise, it would be interesting to examine the extent to which various facets of learning agility of the team leader are related to a team's perceptions of psychological safety (see Chapter 2; De Meuse, 2017). Further, it would be interesting to understand how certain personality traits of the leader might enhance the team's learning agility while also creating an environment of psychological safety.

Finally, while we have a good understanding of what psychological safety looks like and some sense of how we enable an environment that supports learning, what are the factors that destroy it? How long lasting is it? What are the most critical elements and ways to turn declining psychological safety around? Is psychological safety in fact temporal and how delicate of a state is it? How can the introduction of a new team leader or new team member(s) impact that state? All of these issues deserve further insights and study. A summary of psychological safety conditions, outcomes, and hypothesized personality traits are illustrated in Table 15.1.

Conclusion

Since we began this chapter with the story of Sam Walton, it is only fitting that we end it with him. Sam Walton created a culture that continues to live on many years following his death in 1992. "Mr. Sam," as he was affectionately called, had 10 rules he wanted his associates to live by. Within these rules are the norms he created to build the Walmart culture. However, they likewise serve as a foundation for a psychologically safe culture.

Table 15.1 Psychological Safety, Behavioral Outcomes, and Personality Traits

Psychological Safety Conditions	Behavioral Outcomes	Supporting Leader Personality Traits
Address conflict in the open	Exposes new ways of thinking; increases problem-solving skills; reinforces inclusivity	High openness Extraversion
Show vulnerability by admitting mistakes	Encourages openness with group members; decreases fear of failure	High openness Low neuroticism
Encourage risk-taking	Enables test and learn	High openness
Presence of curiosity, questioning, and brainstorming	Diverse perspectives stimulate new ideas	High openness Agreeableness

Mr. Sam lived by the following credo: "I always prided myself of breaking everybody else's rules, and I always favored the mavericks who challenged my rules. I may have fought them all the way, but I respected them, and in the end, I listened to them a lot more closely than I did the pack who always agreed with everything I said. So pay special attention to Rule 10, and if you interpret it in the right spirit—as it applies to you—it could mean simply break all the rules" (Walton, 1992).

Rule 10: SWIM upstream. Go the other way. Ignore the conventional wisdom. If everyone else is doing it one way, there's a good chance you can find your niche by going in exactly the opposite direction. But be prepared for a lot of folks to wave you down and tell you you're headed the wrong way. I guess in all my years, what I heard more often than anything was that a town of less than 50,000 population cannot support a discount store for very long (Walton, 1992, p. 184).

Sam Walton knew, even then, that giving his associates the permission to "buck the system" was not only allowed, but also expected *and* respected. Through his actions, he began creating a culture of psychological safety that enabled continuous learning then and continues to do so today.

References

Carmeli, A., & Gittell, J. H. (2009). High-quality relationships, psychological safety, and learning from failures in work organizations. *Journal of Organizational Behavior, 30,* 709–729.

Cataldo, C. G., Raelin, J. D., & Lambert, M. (2009). Reinvigorating the struggling organization: The unification of Shein's oeuvre into a diagnostic model. *Journal of Applied Behavioral Science, 45*(1): 122–140.

Choo, A., Linderman, K., & Schroeder, R. G. (2007). Social and method effects on learning behaviors and knowledge creation in six sigma projects. *Management Science, 53*, 437–450.

Church, A. (2019, November 14). 6 truths around using personality data to make talent decisions. *Talent Quarterly.* Retrieved from https://www.talent-quarterly.com/6-truths-about-personality-data/

Delizonna, L. (2017, August 24). High-performing teams need psychological safety: Here's how to create it. *Harvard Business Review.* Retrieved from https://hbr.org/2017/08/high-performing-teams-need-psychological-safety-heres-how-to-create-it

De Meuse, K. P. (2017). Learning agility: Its evolution as a psychological construct and its empirical relationship to leader success. *Consulting Psychology Journal: Practice and Research, 69*, 267–295.

De Meuse, K. P., Dai, G., Zewdie, S., Page, R. C., Clark, L., & Eichinger, R. W. (2011, April). Development and validation of a self-assessment of learning agility. Paper presented at the Society for Industrial and Organizational Psychology Conference, Chicago, IL.

De Meuse, K. P., Lim, J., & Rao, R. (2019). *The development and validation of the TALENTx7® Assessment: A psychological measure of learning agility* (3rd ed.). Retrieved from https://thetalentx7.com/2016/07/development-validation-talentx7-assessment-psychological-measure-learning-agility/

Duhigg, C. (2008). What Google learned in its quest to build the perfect team. *New York Times Magazine*, February 25.

Edmondson, A. (1996). Learning from mistakes is easier said than done: Group and organizational influences on the detection and correction of human error. *Journal of Applied Behavioral Science, 32*, 5–32.

Edmondson, A. (1999). Psychological safety and learning behavior in work teams. *Administrative Science Quarterly, 44*, 350–383.

Edmondson, A. (2003). Psychological safety, trust, and learning in organizations: A group-level lens. In R. M. Kramer & K. S. Cook (Eds.), *Trust and distrust in organizations: Dilemmas and approaches* (pp. 239–272). New York, NY: Russell Sage Foundation.

Edmondson, A. (2019). *The fearless organization: Creating psychological safety in the workplace for learning, innovation and growth.* Hoboken, NJ: Wiley.

Edmondson, A., & Lei, Z. (2014). Psychological safety: The history, renaissance, and future of an interpersonal construct. *Annual Review of Organizational Psychology and Organizational Behavior, 1*, 23–43.

Hoff, D. F., & Burke, W. (2017). *Learning agility: The key to leader potential.* Tulsa, OK: Hogan.

Hofstede, G. (2001). *Culture's consequences: Comparing values, behaviors, institutions, and organizations across nations* (2nd ed.). Thousand Oaks, CA: Sage.

Huang C., & Jiang, P. (2012). Exploring the psychological safety of R&D teams: An empirical analysis in Taiwan. *Journal of Management and Organization, 18*, 175–192.

Ipsos (2012). Half (47%) of Global Employees Agree Their Workplace is Psychologically Safe and Healthy: Three in Ten (27%) Say Not. Retrieved from: https://www.ipsos.com/en-us/half-47-global-employees-agree-their-workplace-psychologically-safe-and-healthy-three-ten-27-say

Lewin, K. (1947). Group decision and social change. In T. N. Newcomb, & E. L. Hartley (Eds.), *Readings in social psychology* (pp. 197–211). New York, NY: Holt, Rinehart and Winston.

Lombardo, M. M., & Eichinger, R. W. (2000). High potentials as high learners. *Human Resource Management, 39*, 321–329.

Schein, E. (1980). *Organizational psychology* (3rd ed.). Englewood Cliffs, NJ: Prentice Hall.

Schein, E. (1992). How can organizations learn faster? The problem of entering the green room. Speech at Davos. Retrieved from https://dspace.mit.edu/bitstream/handle/1721.1/2399/SWP-3409-45882883.pdf

Schein, E., & Bennis, W. (1965). *Personal and organizational change through group methods: The laboratory approach.* New York, NY: Wiley.

Schein, E. (2009). *The corporate culture survival guide* (2nd ed.). New York, NY: Wiley.

Schein, E. (2010). *Organizational culture and leadership* (4th ed.). San Francisco, CA: Jossey-Bass.

Tjosvold, D., Yu, Z. Y., & Hui, C. (2004). Team learning from mistakes: The contribution of cooperative goals and problem-solving. *Journal of Management Studies. 41*(7), 1223–1245.

Walton, S. (1972, December). Sales up for October and first nine months of year! *Walmart World*, 1–2.

Walton, S. (1992). *Made in America.* New York, NY: Doubleday.

Woolley, A.W., Chabris, C.F., Pentland, A., Hashmi, N., & Malone, T.W. (2010). Evidence for a collective intelligence factor in the performance of human groups. *Science* 330, 686–688.

16

Developing Learning Agile Leaders

What We Can Learn From the Top Companies for Leaders

Jessie Leisten and Jim Donohue

Agility is the ability to adapt and respond to change
... agile organizations view change as an opportunity, not a threat.
—Jim Highsmith (1945–),

American software engineer and author

The current pace of change is unprecedented and continues to accelerate for most organizations. The economic, technological, regulatory, and social challenges across global boundaries have come together to form a "perfect storm." The concept of "VUCA" was first used in 1987 by the US military to describe and to reflect on the volatility, uncertainty, complexity, and ambiguity of general conditions and situations relating to the Cold War (Bennis & Nanus, 1985). This concept aptly describes the current environment we work in with its vast unknowns, ever-changing competitive landscape, and external forces on the economy that can often derail organizations. Yet, there are organizations that seem to address this storm with greater ease and success: organizations that intentionally dedicate the effort, resources, and support needed for their leaders to create a work environment that enables learning, discovery, growth, and resilience.

The construct of learning agility is defined as the ability to learn quickly with a willingness to apply those lessons to new and different circumstances (De Meuse, 2017; Lombardo & Eichinger, 2000). This construct applies to both individuals and the organizations that support them. The organizational cultures, programs, and infrastructure that foster decision-making

Jessie Leisten and Jim Donohue, *Developing Learning Agile Leaders* In: *The Age of Agility.* Edited by: Veronica Schmidt Harvey and Kenneth P. De Meuse, Oxford University Press (2021). © Oxford University Press.
DOI: 10.1093/oso/9780190085353.003.0016

speed, customer responsiveness, collaboration, inclusion, engagement, and the ability to mobilize across functions are markers of agile organizations.

Companies are realizing that in order to respond to the ever-changing needs of their customers and employees, they need to be learning agile at an enterprise level. They must continually seek opportunities, learn readily, adapt quickly, and expand their thinking to address VUCA circumstances and drive results. A recent study uncovered that companies with the greatest prevalence of executives with learning agility produced a 25% higher profit margin compared to peer companies (Knight & Wong, 2014).

As John Kotter (1996) explained in his book, *Leading Change*, lifelong learning allows leaders to successfully manage complex organizational changes by possessing an agility mindset that embraces change, acts thoughtfully and quickly, and establishes directional clarity for their teams. The concept of learning agility is similar to design thinking techniques used in the product development industry. Both require a process of design, trial, reflection, and iteration. There always will be new challenges ahead, and a learning agile leader views his or her circumstances as opportunities to improve, grow, and create greater value.

But what is it about certain leaders that creates the momentum, spirit, and buy-in that fosters an agile culture? How do these leaders engender the type of environment where growth, transparency, and purpose are primary markers of their legacy? How can organizations create the right practices and processes to properly identify leaders who will navigate uncharted territory? These questions are top of mind for executive leaders and human resource (HR) professionals as they seek to foster learning agile environments. Organizations need to be nimble, adaptive, and responsive to survive the complexities and dynamics at play. They need leaders who embrace and model the right behaviors.

The purpose of this chapter is to articulate the link between learning agile leaders and the organizational practices that support and drive this capability. First, key insights derived from nearly 20 years of practitioner research on tactics used by leading global organizations are reviewed (*Top Companies for Leaders*). We also examine how focusing on critical aspects of learning agility (e.g., resilience, engaging leadership, and self-awareness) can be a tipping point for creating talent programs and practices that nimbly address the changing corporate landscape. Our goal is to provide tangible examples of learning agility in practice to assist practitioners and academicians in the pursuit of unlocking the power of leaders and their teams.

Top Companies for Leaders Research Studies

Background and Methodology

In 2001, the Kincentric Advisory Solutions group (formerly part of Aon Corporation) began a longitudinal research journey to uncover the link between organizational leadership, talent practices, and financial results. Organizations competed for a spot on the coveted Top Companies for Leaders list by completing a rigorous selection methodology capturing objective and subjective data (Hewitt, Aon Hewitt, Aon Corporation, and Kincentric, 2001–2014). Any organization could participate, regardless of size, industry, geographic location, or institutional sector affiliation (e.g., privately held or publicly traded). Organizations were required to complete an in-depth survey (containing over 1,500 items) detailing the depth and breadth of their leadership and talent programs. Survey topics included the critical components of a holistic talent ecosystem (Table 16.1).

A comprehensive financial analysis was conducted for all finalist organizations using a variety of financial growth and return measures (e.g., compound annual growth rates [CAGRs] for sales and earnings, operating income, total shareholder return, return on asset, and return on equity). Privately held organizations were required to submit a financial performance history. Organizations were placed into quartiles determined by their average financial performance over a 5-year period compared to industry peers. Finally, research was conducted to uncover any incidents of negative publicity, litigation, scandal, or ethical violations within the prior 18 months of submission. This "bad press scan" was used in the selection process to highlight the issue and discover how the leaders of the organization addressed it.

The aforementioned inputs were summarized for each finalist organization and presented to an independent panel of judges of known leadership experts from top business schools (e.g., Harvard Business School, Institut Européen d'Administration des Affaires [INSEAD], Columbia University, Wharton School of the University of Pennsylvania, and India School of Business). Judging sessions were facilitated by a consulting team to ensure consistency across various regions, but the criteria used to identify and rank the winning organizations were determined by the local judges. Each region completed the judging process whereby all local winners were eligible to compete for placement on the *Global Top Companies for Leaders* list.

Table 16.1 Survey Section Descriptions

Survey Section	Description of Contents
About Your Organization	Details surrounding organizational structure, size, and leader demographics.
Leadership Strategy	Philosophy, business case, governance, and strategic alignment of core leadership practices. Evaluates organizational value for engagement, leaders/leadership development, time and effort spent by various leaders to review talent, plan for changes, participate in programs, and mentor/coach others.
Diversity and Inclusion	Efforts to recognize and execute on diversity strategies throughout the organization on a variety of demographics.
Attracting and Sourcing Talent	Details of employee value proposition and tactics to recruiting future leaders, sourcing, and turnover. Identifies onboarding process and tools used to identify and prepare candidates for assimilation to the organization or to their new role.
Leadership Capabilities and Performance Management	Components and use of competency models and mechanisms for managing performance through formal tools. Includes reward systems and accountability tied to compensation.
Succession Management	Prevalence and depth of succession planning, pipeline strength, and risk assessment techniques.
Assessment	Methods used to evaluate leaders using formalized assessment practices.
High Potential and Critical Talent	Prevalence, depth, and transparency of high-potential identification and development, formal high-potential education development. Includes prevalence of differentiated pay and development accountability tied to compensation.
Leadership Development	Formal education, development, and mobility opportunities provided to various leadership populations.

Winners were notified following the judging session and were announced via a global press release. Winners from 2001–2007 were featured in *Fortune Magazine*. Over the years, the Top Companies for Leaders research grew from a North American study to a global study (Hewitt Associates, 2007), with the implementation of the regional roll-up approach mentioned previously. Each iteration was a fresh start for organizations to compete for a rank on the list. Furthermore, organizations had benefits beyond just the bragging rights for a top placement; they also found the research to be essential for learning best-in-class practices for talent program design and implementation (Table 16.2 and Table 16.3).

Table 16.2 North American Top Companies for Leaders (2001–2014)

Rank	2001	2003	2005	2007	2009	2011	2014
1	IBM	IBM and J&J (*tie*)	3M Company	General Electric	IBM	IBM	IBM
2	Microsoft Corp.	General Electric	General Electric	Capital One	Procter & Gamble	General Mills	General Mills
3	General Electric	Colgate-Palmolive	Johnson & Johnson	Procter & Gamble	General Mills	Procter & Gamble	General Electric
4	Home Depot	Dell Computer	Dell Inc.	General Mills	McKinsey & Co.	Colgate-Palmolive	Procter & Gamble Co.
5	Dell Computer	UPS	Liz Claiborne	McKinsey & Co.	McDonald's Corp.	McDonald's Corp.	Colgate Palmolive
6	FedEx Corp.	Medtronic Inc.	IBM	IBM	General Electric	Whirlpool Corp.	3M
7	Pfizer Inc.	Procter & Gamble	Procter & Gamble	Medtronic Inc.	Colgate-Palmolive	PepsiCo Inc.	McDonald's Corp.
8	Colgate-Palmolive	PepsiCo Inc.	General Mills	Washington Group	Deere & Co.	General Electric	Intel Corp.
9	Philip Monis USA	Southwest Airlines	Medtronic Inc.	Eli Lilly & Co.	Whirlpool Corp.	Deere & Company	Whirlpool Corp.
10	Johnson Controls	Whirlpool Corp.	American Express Co.	Avery Dennison Corp.	3M Company	Target Corp.	Deere & Co.

Table 16.3 Global Top Companies for Leaders (2007–2014)

Rank	2001	2003	2005	2007	2009	2011	2014
1				General Electric	IBM	IBM	General Electric
2				Procter & Gamble	Procter & Gamble	General Mills	IBM
3				Nokia Corp.	General Mills	Procter & Gamble	Hindustan Unilever Limited
4				Hindustan Unilever Ltd.	McKinsey & Co.	Aditya Birla Group	General Mills Inc.
5				Capital One	ICICI Bank Ltd.	Colgate-Palmolive	ICICI Bank Ltd.
6				General Mills	McDonald's Corp.	Hindustan Unilever Ltd.	Procter & Gamble
7				McKinsey & Co.	General Electric	ICICI Bank Ltd.	Colgate-Palmolive Co.
8				IBM	Titan Cement Co.	McDonald's Corp.	3M
9				BBVA	China Mobile Communications Group Shanghai	Whirlpool Corp.	Novartis AG
10				Infosys Technologies Ltd.	Hindustan Unilever Ltd.	PepsiCo Inc.	Mahindra Group

Key Insights and Findings

The Need for Learning Agility Is Recognized

Each iteration of the study uncovered new, rich aspects of leadership as trends in the marketplace changed dramatically. The emergence of digitalization and the global economic recession were two major events that occurred during the study's life cycle, causing tremendous impact on how organizations viewed talent. For example, the 2011 study found that 92% of Global Top Companies reported that leadership investments were not impacted by the organization's financial performance (compared to only 62% of all other organizations). These organizations understood the importance of placing continued effort and focus on their talent pipeline and were better able to weather the storms of the tumultuous global recession.

Although the description of learning agility did not emerge until the 2011 study, Top Companies had been addressing elements of this topic for years. For example, Top Companies reported that business and leadership strategies were inescapably linked, and that the talent pipeline must evolve to address the changing dynamics of their customers and employees. They understood that concepts like growth mindset, resilience (learning from failure/setbacks and applying learnings), and flexibility were essential.

The 2014 study uncovered a resurgence of the term *VUCA* (volatile, uncertain, complex, and ambiguous). Executive leaders were using this concept in the finalist executive interviews we conducted to describe the complexities they and their organizations were facing in an ever-changing environment. These executives spoke about a critical need to think differently regarding the kind of capabilities they were trying to cultivate in their current and emerging leadership populations. When asked to identify the top three capabilities required for future success, Global Top Companies cited "supporting change" among their top three for senior, middle, and front-line leaders as well as "thinks strategically" for their senior and middle-level leaders (Aon Hewitt, 2014).

Companies were becoming more aware of the inevitable shift in the pace of change, the talent capabilities required, and the need to fill leadership positions with ready talent. It became clear that leaders needed to understand the impact of their unique strengths and development areas on achieving objectives, and the specific adjustments required to drive business forward. In the 2014 study, Global Top Companies indicated the top three talent challenges affecting their ability to achieve business objectives over the next 3 years as the following:

- insufficient number of ready-now leaders;
- change in demand for talent and skills required for success; and
- pace of talent development does not match the speed of growth initiatives.

Top Companies Embed Processes That Develop Learning Agility

Top Companies recognized that they needed to act fast. However, how could they change direction quickly? How could they implement new development programs that prepared leaders for unforeseen circumstances? They began to talk about the need to be agile as an organization and the need for leaders to be agile in learning, shifting, and responding to the changing dynamics. To do so, organizations needed to foster learning agility in their leadership populations and permeate this mindset throughout the company.

The executive interviews conducted as part of the 2014 study uncovered many examples of how learning agility was embedded into the fabric of their leadership programs. Top Companies for Leaders embraced the 80% rule, whereby tremendous success comes from a relatively few contributors. These leaders try new things and accept the notion of "failing fast." Top Companies also understood the importance of building resilience through stretching people in challenging assignments, encouraging adaptability to changing market demand, and cultivating a culture where appropriate risk-taking is valued and supported.

An executive from a major Indian conglomerate cited the following six pillars of leadership behavior their company wanted leaders to embody: (a) ability to make use of both left and right brain; (b) multipliers of passion, energy, and sense of ownership; (c) ability to manage fear and leverage failure; (d) mindfulness in the age of distractions; (e) global mindset, openness to changes; and (f) comfort with ambiguity and creating a culture of trust (Aon Hewitt, 2014).

How Top Companies Build Learning Agility

A distinct set of four interrelated disciplines has been identified that sets the Top Companies for Leaders apart and positions them for success (Figure 16.1). Tested and validated over the course of the longitudinal research, these four disciplines of leadership serve as the differentiating "truths" that

Leaders lead the way	Practical and aligned programs and practices
1 Senior leaders have a passionate and visible commitment to developing leaders	3 Leadership strategy clearly reflects the overall business strategy
2 An intense focus on talent permeates every level of the organization	4 The development of leaders is an institutionalized practice and mindset
Unrelenting focus on talent	When leadership becomes a way of life

Figure 16.1 How the Top Companies for Leaders differentiate.

distinguish exemplary practices and serve as a foundation for creating a culture of learning agility among leaders.

1. Leaders Lead the Way

At Top Companies, senior leaders model the behavior they expect all their leaders to display. Leaders set the tone for the cultural values, skills, strategy, and expectations of their organization. They actively demonstrate the learning agility behaviors they expect of all their leaders. In a recent *Harvard Business Review* article, Jim Whitehurst (2016) stated that establishing a culture always begins with the leaders' behaviors, and that if they are interested in changing the culture of an organization, leaders must ensure they are setting the right tone to serve as behavioral examples they want others to emulate.

2. Unrelenting Focus on Talent

Top Companies are serious about investing in top performers and ensure an intense focus on talent management permeates every level of the organization. Because Top Companies typically build from within, they understand success lies in developing a strong pipeline of learning agile leaders at all levels. They dedicate time, resources, and funds to ensure leaders receive individualized attention to their development and are supported throughout the process to track the efficacy of their investments. As one Top Company explained, their process for evaluating leadership attributes is much less concerned about the particular function leaders grew up in. Instead, they emphasize moving people based on where their attributes will make them successful (e.g., the president of US Operations started as a finance director). Taking a risk on people is essential to accelerating development, resting heavily on strategic experiences and feedback. The Top Companies research found that companies with a high degree of clarity and a strong business case for investing in leaders had 120% higher CAGRs for operating income compared to those in the low range.

3. Practical and Aligned Programs and Practices

Leadership strategies must clearly and comprehensively reflect the overall business strategy. At Top Companies, leadership programs and practices were aligned closely with overall business goals. Programs purposefully cultivated the capabilities needed to drive the business strategy. These companies recognized that as their business strategy shifts, so must their people strategy—that they go hand in hand. Therefore, Top Companies talent programs and practices must be scalable and reviewed with regular cadence to ensure they remain at the forefront of their market trends.

For example, given the importance of learning agility, one Top Company undergoing a strategic business transformation changed its definition of a successful leader by looking beyond the capabilities needed to lead *today* and focused more on the capabilities to lead *tomorrow*. They now relied less on previous work experiences and more on the required abilities to lead transformations, drive new business, operate with agility outside of silos, and have a broad perspective. Their new corporate leadership model evolved to place more emphasis on owning and driving change through innovation and transformation, recognizing cultural shifts, creating high-performance teams, having difficult conversations about building the right team, and possessing a global perspective. Another Top Company designed its talent programs to develop learning agility and strategic thinking, as well as the career aspirations of participants by putting them into "next-role situations," confronting them with "next-level discussions," and connecting them with talent communities beyond their usual network.

4. When Leadership Becomes a Way of Life

At Top Companies, learning agility and the development of leaders is an embedded mindset and set of practices. For leaders, it is a way of performing and behaving that is woven into every aspect of business (e.g., the culture, the way decisions are made, and the strategic initiatives that are implemented). Leaders in Top Companies are wired to think of agile learning as an essential part of their everyday professional lives. Agile learning becomes second nature; it is no longer simply an HR directive. At Top Companies leaders are expected to evolve, to continuously evaluate their environments and learn to adapt with agility. By design, the practices of the Global Top Companies are designed to encourage learning agility by consistently and quickly applying the lessons of experience to new and different circumstances. Overall, the lesson from the findings was when learning agility becomes a critical component of an organization's espoused, expected, and exemplified behaviors, it takes on a life of its own.

Lessons From the Top Companies for Leaders

Over the past 20 years, the workplace has changed dramatically. Disruptions in digitalization, market consolidations (through mergers and acquisitions), financial pressures, globalization, and the emergence of significant new players from the tech industry have radically changed the competitive landscape for many long-established organizations. As noted in Chapter 1, many once leading organizations no longer exist! Recent research shows that companies listed on the S&P 500 will continue to change, and that the average life span for organizations to stay on the listing will shrink to only 12 years (Anthony, Viguerie, Schwartz, & Van Landeghem, 2018).

However, there are key steps any organization can take to ensure its culture, leaders, and infrastructure support the agility needed to thrive within today's hypercomplexities. The four disciplines deployed by Top Companies described in the previous section provide a road map for developing an environment and culture that support learning agility. Further, the organization must be able to support leaders' desires to learn, provide opportunities to grow, and allow for the freedom to operate.

In addition, a robust and holistic talent management system must be in place geared to selecting, promoting, developing, and retaining leaders who demonstrate desired characteristics—including learning agility. In the latest Top Companies for Leaders study, we asked leaders to describe the essential leadership characteristics necessary to thrive in the VUCA environment. We uncovered three key themes that enable leaders to pivot and change during times of stress and uncertainty. The three attributes that emerged as foundational to learning agility were self-awareness, resilience, and engaging leadership. We discuss each one in the section that follows.

Leadership Attributes Foundational to Learning Agility

The Power of Self-Awareness

Best-in-class organizations know a leader's ability to recognize his or her own strengths and weaknesses is an integral component of learning agility and leading in the VUCA world. Self-aware leaders understand their personal strengths and weaknesses, and then use this information to become more successful leaders. As leaders enter the journey of self-discovery, they become aware of both the behavioral tendencies that help them succeed and potential derailers. Leaders must reflect on and iteratively adapt their approach to people and work, evaluate their progress, and make additional pivots as needed. This journey of self-discovery is continuous for agile leaders. Leaders who embrace this ongoing process of self-assessment are better positioned to make necessary adjustments to their approaches in response to the changing context around them.

Self-awareness surrounds countless practices championed by the Top Companies for Leaders. It is embedded in the infrastructure and culture, which permeates every aspect of those organizations' internal and external value propositions. As leaders mature in their style and scope of responsibility, they let go of behaviors that served them well previously to allow space to grow. In the classic work by Drotter and Charan (2001), leaders go through six stages in their development that represent major turning points during their leadership career. At each stage, it is critical for the leader to learn to let go of past behaviors to make room for new learning and experience.

The challenge for organizations lies in creating and supporting these transitions. Too often, organizations do not dedicate the proper focus needed to foster learning agility within their pipeline, which often creates a leadership culture of "those that do" rather than "those that inspire." Identifying and cultivating the skills needed at each turning point is essential as leaders evolve in their careers. Self-aware leaders are on a continuous journey of discovery, seeking clarity on their own behaviors and reflecting on how their actions impact peers, customers, and the bottom line. Effective leaders ask questions such as the following:

- How can I leverage my team to help fill my own developmental gaps?
- How am I leading through change?
- Why does this situation excite (or anger) me?
- Is this how I want others to perceive me?
- Am I celebrating others' success more than my own?
- When I fail or take a misstep, how open am I to my own faults?
- Is this an appropriate reaction?
- Am I really appreciating the power of inclusion and the importance of differences and diversity?
- Am I enabling great talent to flourish or am I holding others back to protect my own interests as a leader?

The Impact of Resilience

Leaders are expected to make decisions quickly but thoughtfully, to be curious and yet pragmatic, and to be structured and consistent while remaining flexible. These apparent contradictions can cause even the most capable leaders to struggle. To operate effectively in a changing environment and establish a culture of learning agility, leaders need to build resilience in themselves and their teams. One approach is through stretch experiences that encourage and support taking calculated risks, learning from failure and setbacks, and gaining exposure to multiple perspectives and ideas. A level of comfort with ambiguity is required to enter unknown territories, as well as a willingness to be vulnerable, accepting that one does not know everything.

Top Companies embrace the "80% right/100% fast rule," understanding that perfection is no longer a universal standard. They permit leaders to try new things and accept the notion of "failing fast." To build greater learning agility, they focus on creating an environment where open communication is essential—where leaders learn to let go of knowing everything and become comfortable with a journey of discovery. Many programs involve an element of storytelling that allow leaders to learn vicariously, share stories of success and failure, and avoid future missteps. Top Companies understand the importance of building resilience through (a) stretching people in challenging assignments throughout their talent pipeline, (b) encouraging adaptability to changing market demands by challenging the status quo, and (c) cultivating a culture where appropriate risk-taking is valued and supported.

Top Companies realize that as leaders build resilience, the organization overall becomes more agile in the face of change and adversity. Resilient leaders act with greater fluidity and confidence in new frontiers, recover quickly, and learn from missteps and setbacks. They are more apt to drive inclusive cultures where diverse perspectives are considered. Top Companies look for leaders who can recognize mistakes and learn from them. They dig into their surroundings to uncover what is driving the challenges and collaborate with diverse networks to build a sense of optimism.

The Value of Engaging Leadership

Engagement becomes particularly noteworthy for organizations during times of market disruption and organizational change. Engaging leaders help their employees navigate change more effectively and nurture others to have greater learning agility. Engaging leadership represents a leader's ability to leverage their guiding beliefs, to foster strong connections within the team, to build self-confidence, and to create followership (Oehler & Adler, 2019). Extensive interviews conducted in the best employers research (Oehler, Stomski, & Kustra-Olszewska, 2014) and in the Top Companies for Leaders research found that leaders who experienced and were shaped by stretch assignments early in their careers tended to have shared beliefs about the importance of leadership and agility. Engaging leaders seek and respond well to an ever-changing landscape of challenges and apply their learnings to new situations. They adapt as needed to the needs of their audience and pivot their communication style to maximize impact, influence, and results. Their ability to be learning agile and adapt to the needs of their stakeholders and the environment inspires others.

Building Ecosystems That Support Learning Agility

Focusing on the Future

Organizations that focus on learning agility are constantly reevaluating themselves, raising the bar, and preparing for the future with a focus on processes, programs, pipelines, and the right culture to support them all. Top Companies start with aligning their talent strategies with business strategies and focusing on processes to propel their leadership brand forward. By incorporating outcome-focused metrics, including fact-based assessments, organizations are better able to determine the impact of initiatives as well as to hold leaders accountable for learning the behaviors necessary to generate sustainable success. These companies create an ecosystem around learning agility that is scalable and tailored for specific populations. For example, alignment around an agility-focused competency model drives the culture of the organization.

The emergence of learning agility as a formal component of high-potential identification was first reported in the 2014 interviews. At the time, approximately 40% of the Top Companies mentioned it. Robust pipelines of leadership talent require early identification and a healthy churn of high-potential candidates, with movement in and out of the high-potential pool to ensure investments are made in the right way with the right people. Fully 76% of the 2014 Global Top Companies reported removing some high potentials from the pool once they had been selected, with an average change of approximately 14% (new or removed) each year. At Top Companies, the designation of "high potential" was not meant to be static, but rather a dynamic state of experiences, expectations, and opportunities that change depending on the individual's unique abilities, aspirations, and learning agility.

Changes in the high-potential populations enable the organization to invest strategically in talent and provide those exiting a rotation with the time and pace necessary to engrain their new skills. These organizations recognize that high potentials need time following an assignment to reflect, recharge, and reboot. Development programs for high potentials that focus on introspection, learning, trial and error, and leading others through change has tremendous impact on this critical population by actively incorporating characteristics of self-awareness, resilience, and engaging leadership into their assignments.

In summary, Top Companies for Leaders build cultures that embody a variety of comprehensive and consistent leadership practices needed to develop leaders today. Such practices include the following:

- Visible involvement of the board of directors, chief executive officer (CEO), and senior leadership who display a passion for agile learning and invest in development, coaching, and mentoring.

- HR and leadership learning practices are intentionally aligned to support the execution of the business strategy.
- Comprehensive leadership and talent programs across all levels that build in the active involvement of senior managers to support learning.
- Emphasize building agile leadership mindsets (e.g., self-aware, adaptable, innovative, resilient, entrepreneurial, people-centric) to address the VUCA demands.
- Leading with purpose by putting the team, organization, customers, and communities at the top of mind.

While some leaders may have natural tendencies to succeed in agile environments, these capabilities also can be developed using dedicated, multimodal techniques that, when consistently applied, offer an individualized approach to developing learning agile leaders.

Assessing Talent With Intention and Action

A disciplined fact-based approach to assessment is fundamental for identifying leaders who possess the attributes and motivators needed to support learning agility and resilience, as well as behaviors that reinforce the continuous development of others. Top Companies employ a full spectrum of assessments—from early career to executive level to inform developmental interventions (Table 16.4a and Table 16.4b).

While the specific assessment instruments vary depending on organizational preferences, traditions, and vendor agreements, the critical piece to get right is implementing a multimodal approach to evaluate the personality characteristics and behaviors that align to the strategic and cultural

Table 16.4a Global Top Companies' Utilization of Assessment by Type and Purpose

Purpose	Competency Based	Personality
Leadership development	84%	80%
High-potential development	88%	72%
Coaching	72%	64%

Source: Aon Hewitt (2014).

Table 16.4b Global Top Companies' Utilization of Assessment Type by Leadership Level

Type of Assessment	Senior	Middle	Front Line
Competency-based assessments	92%	96%	72%
Personality assessments	84%	84%	68%

Source: Aon Hewitt (2014).

objectives of the business. Characteristics that align with a propensity for resilience (e.g., optimism, courage, curiosity); self-awareness (e.g., openness to feedback and change); and engaging leadership also support learning agility.

Accelerating Talent Development Using Dynamic, Iterative Methods

The days of classroom-based development programs appears to be waning. Leaders no longer have the time or even desire to spend time attending lengthy development programs. They need to accelerate the pace at which they address their developmental needs. Top Companies are embracing a multimodal, digitally savvy, interpersonal approach to foster both leadership development and agile learning behavior. Approaches that foster the development of learning agility incorporate tactics such as (a) assessment-based coaching and feedback to enhance self-awareness, (b) partnership with line managers and mentors to learn from others, (c) peer networking opportunities to jointly reflect and learn from experiences, (d) experiential exercises designed to deliberately practice new techniques in safe learning environments, and (e) the encouragement of reflection. These elements, woven strategically together, result in a leadership journey where leaders feel free to authentically navigate new territory and practice learning agility.

One Top Company described how self-reflection and personal discovery inspired its leaders to bring their whole selves to their work. They used a "leaders teaching leaders" approach to design experiences—in and out of the classroom—that connected participants with each other and with a network of high-profile leaders. Their development was immersive and involved an innovative week-long off-site event that provided opportunities for continued growth for both the senior leaders and participants. Senior leaders were asked to step out of their regular jobs and conduct classes and coaching sessions with program participants, host networking dinners, round-table chats, and share leadership advice. Their goal was to build an adaptive leader capable of navigating uncertainty through a process of mindfulness and reflection. The deep insights and relationships they had developed endured much longer than traditionally engineered programs.

Experiential assignments and on-the-job opportunities help build learning agility by employing action learning and stretch or rotational assignments. The 2014 survey data uncovered how Top Company practices were more explicitly linked to learning from experience compared to their counterparts (Table 16.5).

Companies employing these methods take calculated risks with their people. They give them opportunities to stretch outside their comfort zone, moving talent across businesses and functions, and providing the experiences that will truly develop them. One high-tech executive told us his most transformational development experience involved opportunities at the right stage of his career to get in over his head, learn something new, and develop his skills (Aon Hewitt, 2014). Leaders who are hungry to learn and grow recognize they are better leaders even if they fail because of the experiential knowledge gained.

To develop learning agility organizations should consider incorporating a cross-functional, cross-geographic representation of participants. Leaders are often stuck in a familiar functional silo where their knowledge of the organization and the synergies across various geographical areas are limited.

Table 16.5 Development Opportunities Offered to All Leaders

Talent Management Practices	Global Top Companies			All Other Companies		
	Senior	Middle	Front Line	Senior	Middle	Front Line
Developmental assignments	80%	76%	64%	52%	51%	37%
Special projects/teams	68%	72%	64%	46%	57%	44%
Leaders serving as teachers	80%	76%	56%	40%	42%	34%
Corporate philanthropy exercises	68%	72%	72%	38%	40%	36%
Cross-cultural awareness training	72%	76%	68%	34%	38%	36%

Expanding their networks is a highly impactful way to break down these barriers, enhance their perspectives, and build new mindsets. In the safety of a learning environment, participants benefit from, and are often inspired by the diversity of thought they experience in group discussions and feedback exercises. Furthermore, including senior leaders and board members as teachers offers unique opportunities for leaders to interact and learn from role models they may not normally have access in their regular work lives. Coincidentally, it also gives those executives and board members the additional benefit of getting to know their future talent in new ways.

Summary and Conclusion

Crafting a culture that supports and develops learning agile leaders requires focus, investment, and a healthy dose of resolve. We know change is the new normal in organizations today. However, we should remember that this change environment presents opportunities at every turn. Those leaders who embrace an agile approach to their developmental journey are well suited to meet these future challenges with greater resilience. None of the executives we met over the last 20 years at Top Companies felt he or she had done it perfectly in their careers. None had checked off "developing leaders" from a priority list. It is yet another key differentiator for learning agile leaders. They are less cynical, less complacent, always uncomfortable, and focused on the learning needed for tomorrow.

As we look to the future of research on learning agility, we must challenge ourselves to find more direct links between the traits and behaviors of learning agile leaders with organizational agility indicators (e.g., financial performance, business renewal and survival). Organizations like Apple, Amazon, Microsoft, and others have dramatic stories of imagination and revival. What was it about these leaders, employees, and organizations that helped push them to new heights? We also lack research on segmentation by leadership level. Are different levels of learning agility required at different levels of leadership? An interesting area of study could be to evaluate how certain units within an organization with higher levels of learning agility perform differently from the rest of the organization.

We have only begun to scratch the surface on the power of learning agility. The need for agility is not expected to slow down. While we can learn a great deal from Top Companies, we must apply what we have learned to engage in new levels of research and continue to identify how organizations can support the learning agility needed to thrive in this VUCA world.

References

Anthony, S. D., Viguerie, S. P., Schwartz, E. I., & Van Landeghem, J. (2018). 2018 corporate longevity forecast: Creative destruction is accelerating. Innosight. Retrieved from https://www.innosight.com/insight/creative-destruction

Aon Hewitt. (2007). Top companies for leaders. Retrieved from https://aon.mediaroom.com/news-releases?item=78793

Aon Hewitt. (2011). Top companies for leaders. Retrieved from https://ir.aon.com/about-aon/investor-relations/investor-news/news-release-details/2011/Aon-Hewitt-The-RBL-Group-and-Fortune-Announce-the-Global-Top-Companies-for-Leaders/default.aspx?print=1

Aon Hewitt. (2014). Top companies for leaders. Retrieved from https://www.aon.com/attachments/human-capital-consulting/aon-hewitt-top-companies-for-leaders-highlights-report.pdf

Bennis, W., & Nanus, B. (1985). *Leaders: The strategies for taking charge.* New York, NY: Harper & Row.

De Meuse, K. P. (2017). Learning agility: Its evolution as a psychological construct and its empirical relationship to leader success. *Consulting Psychology Journal: Practice and Research, 69*(4), 267–295.

Drotter, S. J., & Charan, R. (2001). Building leaders at every level. *Ivey Business Journal, 65*(5), 21–21.

Hewitt Associates. (2001–2005). *Top companies for leaders.*

Knight, M., & Wong, N. (2018). The organizational x-factor: Learning agility. Korn Ferry Institute. Retrieved from https://focus.kornferry.com/leadership-and-talent/the-organisational-x-factor-learning-agility

Kotter, J. (1996). *Leading change.* Boston, MA: Harvard Business Review Press.

Lombardo, M. M., & Eichinger, R. W. (2000). High potentials as high learners. *Human Resource Management, 39*(4), 321–330.

Oehler, K., & Adler, S. (2019). The engaging leader. Kincentric. Retrieved from https://www.kincentric.com/-/media/kincentric/2019/december/engagingleaderupdatedec2019.pdf

Oehler, K., Stomski, L., & Kustra-Olszewska, M. (2014, November 7). What makes someone an engaging leader? Harvard Business Review Digital Articles. Retrieved from https://hbr.org/2014/11/what-makes-someone-an-engaging-leader

Whitehurst, J. (2016, October 13). Leaders can shape company culture through their behaviors. Harvard Business Review Digital Articles. Retrieved from https://hbr.org/2016/10/leaders-can-shape-company-culture-through-their-behaviors

US Army Heritage and Education Center. (2018, February 16). Who first originated the term VUCA (Volatility, Uncertainty, Complexity and Ambiguity)? USAHEC Ask Us a Question. Retrieved from http://usawc.libanswers.com/faq/84869

17

Sense-Making in a VUCA World

Applying Vertical Development to Enhance Learning Agility

Laura Heaton

We don't see things as they are. We see things as we are.

—Anaïs Nin (1903–1977), author

At its core, learning agility in action is about adapting and transforming ourselves to meet the demands of our environment. As the complexity of our business environment intensifies, such transformations are not only increasingly necessary but also more challenging. Now more than ever before, it is imperative to take multiple perspectives before responding to the challenges we face. To gain these multiple perspectives, we must expand our thinking. *Vertical development* describes the process of transforming the organizing structures we use to derive meaning from our experiences (Cook-Greuter, 2013). This can also be referred to as "sense-making," the process of changing from black and white, right and wrong thinking to more complex, dynamically interconnected, and systemic ways of knowing, doing, and being. The result is qualitatively meaningful advances in our learning, growth, and maturity (Kjellström & Stålne, 2017).

An experience analogous to vertical development can be found by perusing Istvan Banyai's (1998) *Zoom*, a wordless picture book that presents landscapes of pictures within pictures. "Zooming" from a farm to a ship to a city street to a desert island, each page progresses through a sequence of increasing perspectives. While each picture is complete in its own right, new realities and connections are revealed with each page turn, leading to a more expansive viewpoint and understanding.

Laura Heaton, *Sense-Making in a VUCA World* In: *The Age of Agility.* Edited by: Veronica Schmidt Harvey and Kenneth P. De Meuse, Oxford University Press (2021). © Oxford University Press. DOI: 10.1093/oso/9780190085353.003.0017

This progression in understanding is both transcendent (surpassing our previous awareness) and inclusive (attending to all available inputs). McGuire and Palus (2018) described this as *transclusion*, meaning "a primary pattern of growth, evolution and development in which a new, more complex perspective or logic emerges in a system which transcends and transforms logics and perspectives into a new dynamic structure" (p. 149). With increased self and system awareness, we begin to discern more choices and gain more agility in how we respond to our challenges.

Vertical development is critical in our VUCA (volatile, uncertain, complex, and ambiguous) world, which requires continual adaptations in how we make sense of our conditions, integrate new perspectives, and select and enact behaviors that serve our organization's needs (Garvey-Berger & Johnston, 2015). These demands for sense-making and adaptation in continually evolving conditions are central to learning agility (De Meuse, 2017; Lombardo & Eichinger, 2000). Successful leaders develop this capability both within themselves and within their workforces. Although Western educational systems were not designed for these aims, vertical development theories hold much promise for guiding this development. By increasing the breadth and depth of the perspective by which leaders can make sense of their experiences, they increase the choices available to them and, therefore, may enjoy more equanimity and effectiveness. These outcomes are critical for thriving in an increasingly connected and fast-paced world.

The purpose of this chapter is to highlight lessons learned in applying vertical development for improving learning agility within conditions of rapid growth and an increasingly complex marketplace. I begin by presenting a case that demonstrates the concept of vertical development. I then review the concept and theories of vertical development and consider the current contextual challenges and the needs for vertical development. Finally, I outline four key practices for facilitating vertical development in leaders and offer implications for practitioners.

Tale of Two Managers: An Examination of Vertical Development Needs

Frank is the director of a large and growing organization facing significant marketplace volatility, which requires ongoing agile organizational responses. It is essential that Frank's managers lead collaborative and engaged teams to think and act with the agility necessary to adapt the organization and its offerings to remain competitive. Two of these managers—Harriet and Vera—have teams that experience low engagement, feel underchallenged, and often feel micromanaged. Although Harriet and Vera are bright, knowledgeable, and committed to the organization's success, their teams are the least responsive and agile to ongoing organizational challenges.

Frank has determined the performance gap with both Harriet and Vera is attributable primarily to the fact they both struggle with delegating tasks effectively. He arranges for them to attend a leadership development course on delegation, where they will learn about delegation models and techniques and gain opportunities to practice. This course seems like an obvious choice. After all, it will fill the managers' perceived knowledge and skill gaps. Such training that expands one's skill and knowledge base without any corresponding shifts in how meaning is referred to as *horizontal* development.

After attending the delegation course, Harriet returns to his job energized by what he learned and eager to apply it. His team soon exhibited new energy, growth, and agility—and noticeably improved its performance—after implementing the newly acquired delegation skills. In contrast, Vera, despite attending the same course as Harriet, did not change her behavior, and her team's performance did not improve.

Vera's results reveal the limits of horizontal learning. Although she learned and even practiced various techniques and skills necessary for delegation in class, understands her boss' expectations that she must delegate, and genuinely *wants* to improve her performance, Vera still fails to delegate. What has become evident is that Vera is facing a vertical or adaptive development need (Heifetz, 1994). That is, her performance gaps were not wholly knowledge and skill based. Rather, the roots of her performance problem lurk outside her conscious awareness in the quiet forces constantly shaping her thoughts, feelings, and behaviors.

Vera grew up in a close-knit family of laborers with strong values and a shared sense of identity and belonging. She remains very close with her family and, to this day, shares an evening meal with them every Wednesday. One of her family's defining values is its identification with an ethic of hard work. This deeply held conviction often shows up as an "us versus them" dinner table narrative, whereby the heroes boldly accomplish Herculean tasks while the villains let others do the work.

Although she does not realize it, Vera's identity and sense of belonging are inextricably intertwined with doing work herself. It makes delegation an unrealistic objective. In order for Vera to internalize the behavior change, she would be well served by a development approach that involves deep self-reflection and discovery work focused on how what goes on within her connects to what goes on around her. Through reflection and inquiry, which progressively expand her perspective of self, her identity (or identities), and her family system, she can begin to see how her inner theater plays out on the larger work system stage. With this increased perspective, she will have greater ranges of choice when it comes to delegation. Consequently, she will demonstrate more agility to drive her team's performance. Without vertical development, however, the unconscious forces affecting her behavior will continue to tether her development, her performance, and her team's capacity to learn and change.

Overview of Vertical Development

The nature of our knowledge can be understood on two different dimensions: *what* we know (the horizontal dimension) and *how* we know it (the vertical dimension). Horizontal development refers to expanding what we know by acquiring content and information. Vertical development refers to simultaneously elevating and deepening our perspective to integrate what is going on within and around us, as well as cultivating an increasingly broad, systemic perspective of how everything is connected (Cook-Greuter, 2013). In some ways, horizontal development can be likened to crystalized intelligence, while vertical development may share properties with fluid intelligence (Cattell, 1967).

Theories and Constructs Foundational to Vertical Development

A number of researchers, primarily in educational and developmental psychology, have explored the nature of how we make sense of our world. Various hierarchical frameworks have been developed to examine different strands of experience. Table 17.1 highlights some of the constructs that can be considered part of the vertical development family.

Unlike theories of general intelligence, which assert that our level of intelligence is relatively fixed (e.g., Cattell, 1967), vertical development

Table 17.1 Constructs Related to Vertical Development

Construct	Researcher(s)
Ego Development	Cook-Greuter (2010); Loevinger (1979)
Subject Object / Forms of Mind	Garvey-Berger (2012); Kegan and La hey (2001)
Morals	Kohlberg (1981)
Defenses	Vaillant (1986)
Integral Theory	Wilber (1999)
Organization and Abstraction	Jaques and Clement (1991)

frameworks argue that during our lifetimes, we continually develop our capacity for sense-making and taking new perspectives. These perspectives proceed along a continuum of increasing emotional, cognitive, and behavioral complexity. Table 17.2 illustrates how this increasing complexity is exhibited according to three different vertical development frameworks. One, the *preconventional* level of sense-making, is the simplest expression of each construct. At this level, we experience the least amount of choice in our thinking due to limitations in our awareness. Second, the *conventional* sense-making is associated with mature adult expression—consistent with Piaget's (1954) view of development—as well as with greater choice. And third, the *postconventional* level represents the most complex level of expression. At this level, we experience the greatest amount of choice, agility, and efficacy in responding to our challenges.

Two frameworks particularly relevant to leadership development are constructive developmental theory (Kegan & Lahey, 2009) and ego development theory (Cook-Greuter, 2010; Loevinger, 1966; Torbert, 2004). These theories place our sense of identity and the ego—our conscious decision-making faculties—central to understanding our experience and focus on how the identity restructures itself as it develops from one stage to the next (Anderson & Adams, 2016). According to ego development theory, we progress from an undifferentiated sense of self to the apex of conventional development, at which point we operate with a strong, well-defined sense of self as part of an interrelated system of ideas and social constructions (Joiner & Josephs, 2007). As we develop beyond conventional levels, we start to question what we think and become increasingly curious about previously unexplored aspects of ourselves and others. At this point in the development journeys, the ego begins loosening its grip, and people start questioning and

Table 17.2 Sense-Making Stages and Their Expression

Sense-Making Stage	Morals (Kohlberg, 1981)	Ego (Loevinger, 1979)	Abstraction (Jaques & Clement, 1991)	Subject-Object (Kegan & Lahey, 2001)
Preconventional (simplest expression)	Heteronomous Morality *Maintains egocentric point of view. Doesn't consider other's interests*	Self-protective *Focus is on gaining control and advantage*	Concreteness *Works immediately on externally prescribed goals Sees considerable uncertainty*	Selfish *Focus is on what individual wants and on looking out for self Doesn't believe in what isn't clearly knowable*
Conventional (mature or adult expression)	Mutual interpersonal *Individual in relationships with others; aware of shared feelings and expectations*	Conscientious *Differentiated feelings; self-respect; achievements*	Serial conceptual *Linear scan for that which is conceptual Standards are internally set*	Achievement *Internalized self-governing rules Lives by their values and principles*
Postconventional (most complex expression)	Universal ethical principles *Moral point of view from which social arrangements are derived*	Integrated *Reconciling inner conflicts; cherish individuality; integration of the cognitive, emotional, and behavioral; self in social context*	Universal principles *Constructs and applies theory with concern for the overall nature of the enterprise*	Interindividual *Comfortable with paradox and ambiguity even within self Sees own shadow as a gift to explore*

redefining their worldviews and identities. Their attention shifts to interdependencies, and they begin to make sense of a world with many more shades of gray.

Development as a Dynamic, Multidimensional Process

Much of vertical development work involves exploring what lies below the surface of awareness and how those contents and processes affect our

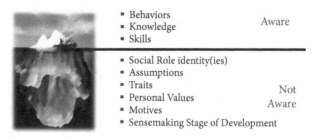

Figure 17.1 Iceberg metaphor of awareness.

behavior. The iceberg metaphor is often used to visually depict these dynamics (Figure 17.1).

Moreover, vertical development integrates concepts of cognitive, emotional, and behavioral maturation, although we do not evolve along these dimensions at the same pace or strength. Figure 17.2 visually depicts this interplay of maturation on these dimensions.

As shown, the development journey begins even before we are consciously aware of it. When something novel or "out of pattern" emerges, a quickening of awareness occurs, although the novel stimulus is often instinctively disregarded or ignored if it fails to match our worldview.

The novel stimulus may constitute a traumatic or disorienting dilemma that suddenly breaks through our awareness, shedding light on contents (e.g., beliefs, values, drives) that have been unconsciously affecting how we think, feel, or behave. Alternately, it may occur as a slow emergence of conscious experience over time. Either way, as this discussion implies, experience plays a central role in vertical development.

As our exposure to the new idea continues, the next evolution of development entails a cognitive response, such as a critique or justification of what is wrong with the idea, and therefore why it can be disregarded or argued against. With even more exposure to the novel stimulus, we begin considering its merits and generate some interest in it, especially if the idea is offered in a safe and supportive environment. Markers of development in the cognitive dimension include a shift from unawareness to awareness and interest.

With our interest piqued, our emotions follow suit and generate the energy we need to further explore the idea. Through this added exploration, the merits of the idea become even clearer and our receptivity even stronger. Gradually, it becomes a self-reinforcing cycle of exploration, exposure, and critical thinking wherein we begin favoring the new idea and start feeling

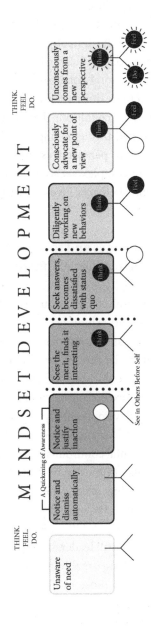

Figure 17.2 Development as a process.

emotional dissatisfaction with the status quo. Endorsing the new idea becomes progressively easier as this dynamic continues as the new idea becomes more and more compelling.

Subsequently, behavior begins to sync with the new perspective. This is often inconsistent at first, given the difficulty of establishing new habits. Even when we believe in the new idea and care about it, we still need discipline and time to develop the behavioral coherence and consistency that comes from an integrated perspective. Thus, vertical development is said to have occurred when we acquire new cognitions that are echoed emotionally and internalized and demonstrated through congruent behaviors. Disorienting experiences can catalyze new perspectives and restructure our way of knowing, resulting in more complex sense-making. Such experiences can also result in a developmental fallback (Livesay, 2015).

Contextual Challenges and the Need for Stratified Vertical Development

Given the current pace and complexity of business demands, organizations need leaders and followers who exhibit learning agility while being able to adapt to and lead the business of tomorrow—no matter what shape that future takes. However, many leaders report feeling "in over their heads" (Kegan, 1997). This feeling occurs when the conditions and developmental demands of our environment exceed our current level of development.

The importance of being developmentally aligned with our environment has been well established: As Darwin (2006) noted, a species' capability to adapt to changing environmental conditions is central to its survival. Within a business context, De Geus (1999) demonstrated in *The Living Company* that an organization's enduring effectiveness at adapting itself to changing environments is critical to its longevity. In a study of chief executive officers (CEOs), Rooke and Torbert (2005) found the stage of personal development was linked to successful leadership. Specifically, CEOs exhibiting "postconventional" sense-making capability were able to successfully transform their companies, whereas those exhibiting earlier stages of development were not.

Vertical development in practice aims to help people meet their environment and organizational demands with mindsets and skill sets equal to the complexity of their work. The mechanisms of cognitive, emotional, and behavioral maturation, endemic to vertical development, means that we can use these frameworks to help leaders develop the agility and competencies required to meet the challenges and complexity of our increasingly connected and fast-paced world.

As noted in *The Leadership Pipeline* (Charan, Drotter, & Noel, 2011) and *The Requisite Organization* (Jaques, 2017), leaders need a greater breadth and depth of perspective as they take on more responsibility and face significantly more dynamic and complex challenges. These two bodies of work provide useful insights into the differences in task complexity with different levels of leadership responsibility. Person and position fit are achieved when the sense-making capabilities of the individual are on par with the task complexity of the work. Table 17.3 provides a comparison of the varying roles, objectives, derailers, and levels of sense-making complexity needed at various leadership levels.

When woven systemically into leadership development systems, vertical development holds promise for helping grow leaders in new ways, resulting in greater collective agility and more effective organizational leadership—both of which are desperately needed in our increasingly interdependent business environment (Joiner, 2018).

These insights, when blended with vertical development frameworks, can be very useful for guiding capability development at the individual, leadership, and organizational level. At the individual level, the framework can inform position descriptions, coaching objectives, and development plans. At the leadership level, it can inform readiness for talent and succession planning, as well as content and pedagogy for level-specific leadership programs. At the organizational level, it can be integrated into performance management and inform enterprise leadership learning development systems that strengthen organization agility.

Key Practices for Facilitating Vertical Development

Vertical development theories were initially leveraged as a behind-the-curtain leadership development strategy. A confluence of theories informed the creation of a stratified leadership development framework. This framework honors the sense-making complexity required for qualitatively different levels of leadership responsibility and serves as a guide for individual and systemic leadership development. As leadership development practitioners

Table 17.3 General Framework for Increased Work and Sense-Making Fitness

Leadership-Level Task Complexity	Sense-Making Complexity	Roles	Horizontal Objectives	Vertical Objectives	Derailers
Lead Self TTH 1 day to 1 Year	Skill-Centric Expert	Individual Contributor	Technical Proficiency	Feedback Reputation	Not adapting to evolving standards
Lead Others TTH 3–24 Months	Self-Determining Achiever Achiever	Manager Supervisor	Assess Performance Delegate	Identity (Identities) Self-regulation	Not seeing more than one right way
Lead Leaders TTH 12 Months to 5 Years	Self-Questioning Redefining	Director	Systems Thinking Reframing	Deep Self-Aware Plurality of Perspectives	Defensive toward new ideas Micromanaging
Lead Business Unit TTH 5–10 Years	Late Stage Self-Questioning Redefining	Vice President	Polarity Management Strategic Frameworks	Triple-Loop Learning Meaning & Purpose	Not seeing interdependencies in decisions
Lead Enterprise Function TTH 10–20 Years	Self-Actualizing Transforming	Senior Vice President	CSR Vision Culture & Climate	Ambiguity & Paradox Letting Go Shadow	Hubris Complacency Impulsivity

Note. TTH denotes task time horizon.

gain comfort with the theories, literature, and practices of vertical development, it will emerge from behind the curtain and move into the spotlight for coaching sessions and leadership development programs. Based on a review of this literature, the following four practices are proposed as essential to facilitating leaders' vertical development.

Practice 1: Go First—Before You Can Guide Others, You Must Know the Path

You cannot be a Sherpa on a path you have not walked. Unlike the process of horizontal development, a person facilitating vertical development experiences should have personal experience with transformational development. This preparation extends far beyond learning about developmental theories. It entails long-term practices of reflection, inquiry, and exposure to others with later stage development (Cook-Greuter, 2004). When you experience the increase of perspective related to something meaningful and then dance with the existential tensions between what you think, feel, and do, you gain the capacity to help others pursue vertical development. When others feel your authentic support, your compassion rather than judgment about how they "should" act, think, and feel—and experience the connection to humanity inherent in the process—their prospects for growth dramatically improve. Moreover, having personally trod the path of vertical growth, you will be able to provide leaders with the elevated sense-making fundamental to vertical development experiences (Petrie, 2015).

It is additionally important to acknowledge the level of competence professionals need in order to work with individuals embarking on vertical development. Because this work engages leaders at deep levels of emotional development, the work can easily breach the boundaries of talent development and enter into a clinical domain. While it can be easily argued that emotionally transformative development work should be left to those with psychotherapeutic training, this would fail to capitalize on the abundant opportunities for development that naturally occur in daily work settings. To offer ethical, meaningful help that reflects the best of their ability, facilitators must accurately understand the edge of their competence, professional development, and experience. It often requires walking a very thin line.

Practice 2: Create a Developmental Container—Support Courageous Vulnerability

Learning happens best within a psychologically safe "container," meaning a learning environment where reflection, exploration of diverse perspectives, and courageous expressions of emotion are supported and defensiveness is minimized (see Edmondson, 1999). Such environments form when compassion for each other's humanity becomes the norm. This climate generally forms organically over time. It cannot be faked or mandated. One way to help create and nurture this type of learning environment is through a collaborative definition of the rules, which will be observed when working together. However, to truly support psychological safety, this exercise must go beyond words on a flip chart to understanding the emotional truth behind the leader-proposed rules. The insights gained then can be applied to create ongoing group norms that sustain a supportive developmental container.

Additionally, it is important to allow leaders to acknowledge when they are feeling limited psychological safety. For example, leaders embarking on vertical development may feel particularly sensitive to who is in the room, what roles others will play, and what judgments may be formed. Making these topics discussable and empowering the group with some control over who is in the room as well as what can and cannot happen therein are key to creating psychological safety (Argyris, 1993). For example, a group may not be comfortable if senior leaders want to sit in and observe their process. Enabling leaders to set boundaries goes a long way toward protecting the group's developmental container. It must take precedence over observers' desires to watch or engage in behaviors that risk damaging psychological safety.

Once established, it is imperative to be mindful that the developmental container remains quite fragile and must be carefully nurtured over the lengthy period it typically takes leaders to integrate and embody new perspectives. Yet, whether in a group or in a one-on-one coaching relationship, it is within this type of container that participants will feel emboldened to courageously engage in the vulnerable development work of deep self-reflection and growth in understanding.

Another central ingredient for creating a developmental container is for the facilitator or coach to strike an appropriate balance between supporting, challenging, and providing elevated perspectives to leaders. Doing so relies on attending to the dynamic relationship between what each person can see and do compared to the support he or she needs to grow. Petrie (2014) dubbed it as finding the "heat experience."

The concept of heat experience fits nicely with Vygotsky's "zone of proximal development theory" (Vygotsky & Kozulin, 1986). This theory states that individuals' strongest development gains occur when they are allowed to do as much as they can without assistance (referred to as "Zone 1," comfort and equilibrium), while receiving instruction and support to achieve those things that are just beyond their current competencies (referred to as "Zone 2," growth and container). It is especially important with vertical development to stay out of the regions a person cannot navigate even with assistance ("Zone 3," protection and defense). While the defense mechanisms triggered when encountering Zone 3 serve an important purpose in managing anxiety, it comes at the expense of learning. It ends up damaging the container and undermining the learning experience for all involved (Figure 17.3). Finding just the right amount of heat experience is as much art as it is science.

Figure 17.3 Developmental container.

Practice 3: Meet People Where They Are—Find the Developmental Edge

Vertical Development Assessments

Harriet David Thoreau advised, "Begin where you are and such as you are." Thus, an initial assessment can help leaders identify the stage at which individuals are currently making meaning and provide insights about other stages of sense-making. A variety of proprietary assessments are available. Although assessments can be costly and require certification to administer and debrief, there are benefits to integrating them into leadership development programs. They offer a standardized language and a framework for connecting vertical development theories to personal experience. There are several assessments and vertically oriented resources for facilitators to use. A few leading approaches include the following:

1. Semiprojective sentence stem assessments such as the Leadership Maturity Profile, Leadership Development Profile, and Global Leadership Profile, which all offer rigorous manual scoring protocols and accompanying reports that associate respondents' answers with their stage of ego development. Although rigorous, these assessments can be pricey and must be administered by an external certified provider.

2. Subject–object interviews assess the interviewee's sense-making structure according to Robert Kegan's (1997) constructive–developmental theory. The interview aims to discover how individuals construct their reality. More specifically (a) what they can take perspective of (hold as an object of conscious reflection) and (b) what they might be *subject to* but not yet able to see subconsciously *acting on* them. For example, in the case of Vera presented in this chapter, her deep commitment to hard work and resistance to delegating was a force to which she was *subject,* a force outside her conscious awareness that influenced her actions. Through vertical development, she may grow conscious of these influences, thus transforming them into *objects* of reflection. In subject–object interviews, the interviewer poses questions to elicit stories that showcase how the interviewee makes sense of his or her world. It is a difficult interviewing technique to learn to do well and

requires significant training to conduct (Lahey, Souvaine, Kegan, Goodman, & Felix, 2011).

3. Growth edge interviews (GEIs) are concerned with the range of sense-making demonstrated by an individual. The GEIs are an adaptation of the subject–object interview and yield a range of scores, a center of gravity, and developmental patterns (Berger, 2012).

4. Transformations™ is a two-deck set of cards created by the Center for Creative Leadership and designed to foster self-reflection and dialogue. If more expensive assessments are not an option, this tool can be an affordable way to foster reflection and gain insights about an individual's sense-making structures.

Connecting With Leaders Where They Are

Connecting with people where they are is perhaps the most important capability when coaching individuals or facilitating groups. Although vertical development models are undeniably hierarchical, it is critical for leaders to understand and embrace the gifts and liabilities of their own stage of development as it relates to their context. Facilitators can aid leaders' understanding of their stage through careful attention to the language they use, such as referring to more complex stages as *later* (vs. higher) and the simpler sense-making stages as *earlier* (vs. lower) stages. Likewise, it is important for facilitators to avoid the trap of thinking the most complex sense-making stage of development is always best.

It is important to make authentic and compassionate human connections with leaders as they embark on their journeys of development. It is best achieved when facilitators begin by accepting all of us as humans are perfectly imperfect. As facilitators and coaches, the more okay we are with our own imperfections, the easier time others have being in our presence. When we show up undefended, we gain far more developmental capacity for exploration. This is much easier said than done, given our egos are continually working hard to protect our idealized self-images and generally do not tolerate imperfections.

Connecting with leaders where they are requires cognitive capability to identify others' meaning-making structures, emotional capability to genuinely meet others with compassion, and vertical capability to invite perspectives that are slightly more complex than their present stage. Meeting leaders in this way helps us create an environment wherein they feel supported and psychologically safe as their imperfect selves begin stretching beyond their comfort zone.

Meeting people where they are also relies on discerning how they are making meaning moment by moment and what they can and cannot see in the way they are interacting with the world around them. Developing a *stage hypothesis* requires close attention to the language leaders uses when describing their perspectives and differentiating between what they say, the structure of how they tell their story, and what their words actually mean. It is critical to confirm inferences by asking what specific words or phrases mean. The subsequent dialogue gives leaders an opportunity to more fully process their experiences and develop a slightly more complex perspective about them.

For many reasons, cognitive complexity has been a focus of sense-making for a long time. However, our ability to know something intellectually is not the same as integrating or embodying that knowledge on an equally complex emotional and behavioral level. Vertical development occurs along cognitive, emotional, and behavioral dimensions, often at different rates for each. Paying close attention to the language used can reveal the degree of coherence between these dimensions and where the developmental edge is for a particular leader. Finally, always be cognizant that developmental conversations can happen anywhere, whether in a hallway, a leadership development program, a coaching session, a Little League game, or a C-suite meeting.

Practice 4: Elevate—Check Out the View From Here!

With practiced inquiry, discernment, intuition, and a solid working knowledge of vertical development frameworks, language can be adapted to navigate within the leader's current meaning-making structure. Once you have connected in a way a person feels heard, it is possible to provide elevated sense-making through inquiry or reframing experiences from a slightly more complex (a "one-click bigger") perspective. However, going too far by offering a perspective two or more stages more complex than the leader's current stage of making meaning creates the risk of becoming too abstract. Consequently, such attempts likely will fall flat. For example, if you inquire into the purpose of tasks with a leader who is highly task focused, you risk provoking their defensiveness, frustration, or insistence that the purpose of the tasks is to simply do them and get them done. In those instances, you miss the opportunity of providing an experience of increased perspective taking. Table 17.4 highlights how one could apply the one-click bigger technique.

Implications for Practice

Although the majority of this chapter has discussed the use of vertical development for leaders, the importance of practitioners cultivating their own vertical development cannot be overstated. Generally, this requires a love of and lifelong commitment to learning, growth, and doing deep development work on ourselves. These activities expand the edges of our own competence, which defines the territory of where and how we can serve as a developmental Sherpa for others.

This personal growth work generally rests on working with our own developmental tethers. Tethers show up as something rooted in an earlier stage of development—something outside our conscious awareness that creates a source of defensiveness. The work of releasing tethers is reminiscent to what Pat Williams (founder of Pepperdine's Master of Science in Organization Development program) referred to as the rubber band theory of change. That is, you cannot go too far without bringing everyone else along with you. Otherwise, like the rubber band, it will snap back and sting you. Vertical development asserts that progressing in our capabilities requires releasing these tethers and, in concert with that, developing the cognitive, emotional, and behavioral maturation to transcend the previous stage. Transcending and including ("transclusivity") is more powerful than simply transcending a perspective (McGuire & Palus, 2018; Wilber, 2017).

At the same time, pace and moderation are important: Whether facilitating our own or others' vertical development, we should be aware of the profound energy this type of learning takes. For this reason, it is helpful to blend horizontal and vertical learning experiences to manage individual and group energy. Moreover, keep in mind that development is the sovereign domain of every individual, and each person bears the ultimate responsibility for the extent of learning that will occur. Furthermore, just like Brussels sprouts, this kind of development is not for everyone. Some people may be too defensive, too stressed out, or too emotionally or physically burned out to engage in this work. We need to remember to cultivate genuine compassion for our own and others' psychological defenses because at one level they serve a protective purpose.

Table 17.4 Practicing the One-Click Bigger Perspective

Hypothesized Stage	Focus	Language Clue	1-Click Bigger Reframe	Inquiry Example
Self-centric	Gaining Advantage	Simple and dichotomous	Belonging	Conduct an appreciative inquiry (to minimize defensiveness) into the connection between their actions and results
Group-centric	Social Acceptance	Fitting in with norms	Differentiate self from group interests, more nuanced emotions	Help them see how their unique skills and perspectives add value to the group and others
Skill-centric	Task/ Efficiency	"Right" way	Goal and effectiveness	Inquire about how that makes other(s) feel and what is "good enough"
Self-determining	Goal	Effectiveness	Context/ impact	Explore assumptions and nuances of emotions
Self-questioning	Uniqueness Identity(ies)	Possibilities	Systems view meaning	Explore how perspective has changed Compare how perspectives differ Adopt a systems perspective
Self-actualizing	Meaning Wholeness	Universal principles Interdependence	Purpose Mystery	Rescript the story Explore defenses
Construct aware	Constructed nature of reality	Paradox	No boundaries Oneness	Embrace interconnectedness Accept what is

Finally, the line between vertical development and "clinical" work is very narrow. While the focus for most of us as practitioners is decidedly not clinical, the nature of the deeply reflective work often results in some therapeutic effects for participants. It is important to have a network of resources we can turn to if participants stumble and require a more specialized clinical setting.

At the end of the day, being agile in leadership development is about "human being development." Being able to walk alongside leaders on their developmental journeys and witnessing their transformation is a profound honor. For me, it creates an endless source of awe, humility, and hope for humanity in the face of our increasingly complex world.

References

Anderson, R. J., & Adams, W. A. (2016). *Mastering leadership: An integrated framework for breakthrough performance and extraordinary business results.* New York, NY: Conscious Leadership.

Argyris, C. (1993). *Knowledge for action: A guide to overcoming barriers to organizational change.* San Francisco, NY: Jossey-Bass.

Banyai, I. (1998). *Zoom.* New York, NY: Penguin.

Berger, J. G. (2012). *Changing on the job: Developing leaders for a complex world.* Palo Alto, CA: Stanford Business Books.

Cattell, R. B. (1967). The theory of fluid and crystallized general intelligence checked at the 5–6 year-old level. *British Journal of Educational Psychology, 37*(2), 209–224. doi:10.1111/j.2044-8279.1967.tb01930.x

Charan, R., Drotter, S. J., & Noel, J. L. (2011). *The leadership pipeline: How to build the leadership powered company* (2nd ed.). San Francisco, CA: Jossey-Bass.

Cook-Greuter, S.R. (2004), Making the case for a developmental perspective. *Industrial and Commercial Training, 36*(7), 275–281.

Cook-Greuter, S. R. (2010). *Postautonomous ego development: A study of its nature and measurement.* Berkeley, CA: Integral.

Cook-Greuter, S. R. (2013). Nine levels of increasing embrace in ego development: A full-spectrum theory of vertical growth and meaning making. Retrieved from https://www. semanticscholar.org/paper/Nine-Levels-Of-Increasing-Embrace-In-Ego-%3A-A-Theory-Cook-Greuter/cc0e81e8aaf82e6ec4faccbc3ed9889fe0cd2bb7

Darwin, C. (2006). *On the origin of species by means of natural selection, or, the preservation of favored races in the struggle for life* (Dover giant thrift ed.). Dover, England: Dover.

De Geus, A. (1999). *The living company: Growth, learning and longevity in business.* London, England: Brealey.

De Meuse, K. P. (2017). Learning agility: Its evolution as a psychological construct and its empirical relationship to leader success. *Consulting Psychology Journal: Practice and Research, 69,* 267–295.

Edmondson, A. (1999). Psychological safety and learning behavior in work teams. *Administrative Science Quarterly, 44*(2), 350–383. https://www.jstor.org/stable/2666999

Garvey-Berger, J. (2012). *Changing on the job: Developing leaders for a complex world.* Palo Alto, CA: Stanford University Press.

Garvey-Berger, J., & Johnston, K. (2015). *Simple habits for complex times.* Palo Alto, CA: Stanford University Press.

Heifetz, R. A. (1994). *Leadership without easy answers*. Cambridge, MA: Harvard University Press.

Jaques, E. (2017). *Requisite organization: A total system for effective managerial organization and managerial leadership for the 21st century*. London, England: Routledge.

Jaques, E., & Clement, S. D. (1991). *Executive leadership: A practical guide to managing complexity*. London, UK: Blackwell.

Joiner, B. (2018). Leadership agility for strategic agility. In C. Prange & L. Heracleous (Eds.), *Agility.X* (pp. 17–31). Cambridge, England: Cambridge University Press.

Joiner, B., & Josephs, S. (2007). *Leadership agility: Five levels of mastery for anticipating and initiating change*. San Francisco, CA: Jossey-Bass.

Kegan, R. (1997). *In over our heads: The mental demands of modern life*. Boston, MA: Harvard University Press.

Kegan, R., & Lahey, L. L. (2001). *How the way we talk can change the way we work: Seven languages for transformation*. San Francisco, CA: Jossey-Bass.

Kegan, R., & Lahey, L. L. (2009). *Immunity to change: How to overcome it and unlock potential in yourself and your organization*. Boston, MA: Harvard Business Press.

Kjellström, S., & Stålne, K. (2017). Adult development as a lens: Applications of adult development theories in research. *Behavioral Development Bulletin, 22*(2), 266–278. doi:10.1037/bdb0000053

Kohlberg, L. (1981). *The meaning and measurement of moral development*. Worcester, MA: Clark University Press.

Lahey, S., Souvaine, E., Kegan, R., Goodman, R., & Felix, S. (2011). *A guide to the subject-object interview: Its administration and interpretation*. Boston, MA: Minds at Work.

Livesay, V. (2015). One step back, two steps forward: Fallback in human and leadership development. *Journal of Leadership, Accountability and Ethics, 12*(4), 173–189.

Loevinger, J. (1966). The meaning and measurement of ego development. *American Psychologist, 21*(3), 195–206. https://doi.org/10.1037/h0023376

Loevinger, J. (1979). Construct validity of the sentence completion test of ego development. *Applied Psychological Measurement, 3*(3), 281–311. doi:10.1177/014662167900300301

Lombardo, M. M., & Eichinger, R. W. (2000). High potentials as high learners. *Human Resource Management, 39*, 321–330.

McGuire, J., & Palus, C. (2018). Vertical transformation of leadership culture. *Integral Review, 14*(1), 145–166.

Petrie, N. (2014). *Vertical leadership development—Part 1: Developing leaders for a complex world*. Greensboro, NC: Center for Creative Leadership.

Petrie, N. (2015). *The how-to of vertical leadership development—Part 2: 30 experts, 3 conditions, and 15 approaches*. Greensboro, NC: Center for Creative Leadership.

Piaget, J. (1954). *The construction of reality in the child*. (M. Cook, Trans.). New York, NY: Basic. doi:10.1037/11168-000

Rooke, D., & Torbert, W. (2005, April). Seven transformations of leadership. *Harvard Business Review*. Retrieved from https://hbr.org/2005/04/seven-transformations-of-leadership

Torbert, W. (1991). *The power of balance: Transforming self, society, and scientific inquiry*. Newbury Park, CA: Sage.

Torbert, W. (2004). *Action inquiry: The secret of timely and transforming leadership*. San Francisco, CA: Berett-Koehler.

Vaillant, G. E. (Ed.). (1986). *Empirical studies of ego mechanisms of defense*. New York, NY: American Psychiatric Press.

Vygotsky, L. S., & Kozulin, A. (1986). *Thought and language* (Translation newly rev. and edited). Boston, MA: MIT Press.

Wilber, K. (1999). *Integral psychology: Transformations of consciousness; selected essays.* Boston, MA: Shambhala.

Wilber, K. (2017). *Trump and a post-truth world.* Boulder, CO: Shambhala.

18

Learning Agility and Whole Leader Development

Robert B. McKenna and Emily Minaker

> I read a lot of different stuff, but I keep being open to inspiration.
> —Pete Carroll, NFL coach for Seattle Seahawks

If it is true that most of us would love to be more agile as learners, then why aren't we? Learning agility may be one of the most important emerging concepts of our time. It may make a difference not only for our organizations, but also for each of us and everyone around us. Discovering our unique inspirations to learn is key to unlocking our own potential and, maybe even more importantly, the potential of others. The purpose of this chapter is to expand our understanding of learning agility as one variable in the context of many other variables impacting the experience of a leader and to focus on our unique motivations to learn that play a fundamental role in our capacity to learn well. To that end, we hope to inspire each of us to explore our unique inspiration to learn and to grow, for our own sake and for the sake of those in our influence.

We recently had a conversation with a leader who was leaving his current job because, in his own words, "My manager only cares about results and I'm motivated by purpose." As we talked with this leader, we realized that his drive to leave was less about a difference in perspective and more about the reality that his manager was not willing to consider his unique motivations. Even more profound was the realization that his motivation to do his job was inseparable from his motivation to learn. While learning agility might be the goal, the path to becoming a more agile learner is about so much more than the goal. In fact, when we divorce learning agility from its interconnected parts, we piecemeal a solution that requires a more whole perspective on

Robert B. McKenna and Emily Minaker, *Learning Agility and Whole Leader Development* In: *The Age of Agility*. Edited by: Veronica Schmidt Harvey and Kenneth P. De Meuse, Oxford University Press (2021). © Oxford University Press. DOI: 10.1093/oso/9780190085353.003.0018 our experience as leaders—and as people. At the very least, being more agile includes a context and people around us who inspire us to learn in our own unique way and who help us prepare for what is ahead.

To integrate is, by definition, to make whole. With regard to learning agility, what would it mean to be more integrated? If, for the sake of simplicity, we narrow our perspective on learning agility to the simple outcome of developing an agile learner, we likely miss some of the most important questions that will advance our understanding. Simplicity is attractive because it just is, but integration is closer to our reality. While we may be drawn to quick one-off solutions or answers, our reality often includes a constellation of factors impacting every moment of our lives and learning. Other people play a role in our learning. Some of us are inspired to learn for different reasons and in different seasons. The context and culture around us (supporting or inhibiting learning) certainly matter.

In the spirit of integration, what are the questions we must ask regarding our own learning? Am I a natural learner, or can I learn to learn? Am I learning for the sake of learning, or am I learning for the sake of not failing? Does everyone enjoy learning, and do we still invest in those who don't? And maybe most profound, for the sake of what or whom am I learning? As you read these pages, keep that last question in mind because it is fundamental to our assumption regarding the purpose of learning agility. Like others (e.g., De Meuse, 2017; De Meuse, Dai, Swisher, Eichinger, & Lombardo, 2012), we would suggest that learning agility is about more than just going faster. If learning agility is all about learning faster and we never pause to ask, "For the sake of whom or what?" we will have missed the point. We are not minimizing the necessity for keeping up with the pace of change, but that learning well is just as critical.

Learning Agility—Learning to Learn Well

Agility is not only about moving but also about moving well. When we think of athletes, we naturally differentiate between speed and agility. If you were to pick players for your sports team, you would probably differentiate between the two, and the choice would depend on the context in which that player was going to play. That context might include the sport, the position, their biological attributes, their motivations, and the strengths and limitations you see in the rest of the players on the team. And, that is just for starters. Does the player's attitude make other people better? Is there a difference between the agility in the player's feet versus the agility in the player's hands? What has happened during the last 24 hours that makes him or her a different player than yesterday? Even more complex is how that player will respond when things either go as planned or not—a dropped ball indicating a failure or an opportunity to learn from it in the future. While it is normal for us to differentiate between the speed and agility of an athlete, we so often fail to differentiate the two when it comes to the development of a person. With some leaders, our focus may need to be on increasing the speed at which they learn, while others may need to improve how well they learn. Coming full circle, learning agility is not only about learning, but also about learning well. Consequently, would you rather have someone on your team who only learns fast or who also learns well?

Each of our answers probably depends on a variety of contextual factors. For our purpose, we suggest that responsible practices around increasing learning agility in leaders require a *whole* perspective on a person. And, speed, along with many other factors, including personality, motivation, purpose, other people, experience, and efficacy, plays a necessary role in what it means to be more learning agile. Moreover, each of those contributing variables should be considered less like good or bad factors in the agility of a person and more like a variety of gauges on a dashboard that give us an indication of where he or she is now. Speed or quickness of learning is certainly a part of what it means to be more learning agile (DeRue, Ashford, & Myers, 2012), but whether it is important to go faster or slower may depend on the context in which a leader finds him- or herself. Learning agility is as much about learning to move well as it is about learning to move faster.

For our purpose, we would add that the best forms of learning agility include the capacity to step into the unknown and maintain a sincere openness to becoming a better version of ourselves, for both our sake and for the sake of others. While the concept of learning in general could be developed or considered in a cloister, learning agility does not occur in a vacuum. And, by its very nature, learning well implies developing the capacity to move and perform well not only for our own sake but also for the betterment of others around us. Our proposed extension is that learning agility on its own is not enough. A more whole aspiration is to imagine developing leaders whose purpose for becoming more learning agile is connected to their performance, and to their performance for the sake of those within their influence. In other words, learning agility is as much about the process of how we learn, and for whose sake, as it is about the practice and performance on its surface. It is the difference between a professional football player learning to block and tackle more effectively to receive a higher paycheck on their next team or learning for the sake of making everyone else on the current team better.

Looking *With* Leaders Versus Looking *At* Leaders

For the average consumer of ideas regarding learning, learning agility probably is not on their radar. The way many think about learning is less often about becoming an agile learner and more likely about a lack of preparation or perceptions about the success or failure of the end product. It is easier to put ourselves in boxes or to evaluate our results than it is to answer the question of why we are in the box in the first place. With regard to learning agility, our preparation to move well, the process of learning to move well, and the act of performing well all play a role. Popular motivational speakers certainly graze the surface of the process of developing learning agility through tag lines like "be yourself," "fail fast," or "be bold," but that is only the beginning of what is important.

By its very nature, learning involves change, and change is hard for most of us. We would suggest that learning agility is less about our capacity or motivation to learn all the time and more about our willingness and ability to think or do something different (to change), even in the moments when it may be difficult to do (see Bardwick, 2000). Furthermore, until we attach value statements to what learning agility is all about, it is a neutral concept. Like any other topic, such as leadership, character, or motivation, it is not until we begin to ask the question for the sake of whom or what that we attach a purpose to our attempts to become more learning agile. There are quick and motivated learners all over our world probably doing horrible things right now. Our assumption is that any increase in learning agility should be done not only for the individual and the organization, but also for the sake of every person within their influence.

Most scholars would agree that learning agility includes some combination of willingness and ability to learn from our experiences, both good and bad (see Chapter 1). While there may be some disagreement about the relationship between the two, and the targeted outcomes of competence, performance, or speed, willingness and ability are certainly important factors. However, conceptualizing learning agility as some combination of willingness and ability reinforces our tendency to look *at* leaders, as opposed to looking *with* them. It is some combination of willingness and ability that likely is the recipe for motivating our learning. Even more, when we look at the motivation of an individual leader, we move away from sweeping statements about learning agility to more personal and unique inspirations to learn. As coaches and talent specialists, seeing through the eyes of a leader may change our language and help us understand the factors necessary for their improvement beyond the factors that we want to see them improve. Few leaders want to be told that they should learn faster, but most would want to be invited to acquire the capacity that they could. Maybe it is our job to simply invite them into their own learning, and how we talk to them may be just as important as any program we put in place.

One of our greatest challenges in helping people to move and perform more effectively is that the words they use are not the words we use. We call it learning agility, but until a leader reads our hypothetical bestselling book, *Learning Agility*, what do *they* call it? What is it that people talk about regarding their capacity to move and to shift well? In other words, why would a leader read our book? Here are some possibilities: "I'm bored and I need to do something different." "I just failed a test, and I know I shouldn't feel like a failure, but it's hard not to." "Why do I keep making the same mistakes over and over again?" "I don't have time to reflect." "Reflection and learning are exhausting; give me the Cliff notes." Many years of research have shown leaders do learn, grow, and develop. However, the way leaders speak about learning, growth, and development is not always the language we as academics, researchers, and talent management practitioners use. When we look through the lens of leaders' day-to-day experiences, we begin to form a more integrated perspective on their learning. While we might suggest leaders must be willing and able to learn, the leader is thinking, "Can I learn and how?"

We all have different motivational "keys" that unlock the door between our experiences and the learning on the other side—the catalyst that may change an experience to a learning experience. When we overemphasize structure and organizational needs over people, we miss the point that the greatest potential for leadership development lies with the individuals in the organization and the organization (Ashford & DeRue, 2012). Learning agility is less about the perfect system and more likely about providing a context within which individuals can thrive as learners. Our job is not simply to identify those high or low in learning agility, but rather to see those ready to learn and to help them identify their unique inspiration and motivation to learn.

The idea that inspiration and motivation are catalysts for behavioral change is not new (Thrash & Elliot, 2003). Learning agility is the beautiful collision between all that we know about the power of mindsets, developmental agency, motivation, purpose, and the impact of other people around us. How we see our world, who is around us, and our individual differences play a role in how we connect the dots between the ups and downs of life and the lessons available to us. Our intent is to go deeper into some of the keys that may be those catalysts that unlock the door between experience and learning and shift our paradigm about what it means to take a more whole perspective on learning to move and perform well.

Whole Leader Perspective on Learning Agility

A whole perspective on learning agility moves us from seeing it as our desired outcome (i.e., now I am looking at an agile learner) and more appropriately as an ongoing and repeating cycle of preparation, process, and performance. The challenge so many of us face with learning agility is that we have very little patience for preparation or process—we just want to get performing. If performing is the primary goal, the cycles of mindless repetitions and failures will likely continue. Is learning agility the goal, is it the process, or is it about the preparation? We are suggesting it is all of these. A whole leader approach to learning agility is not only about being complete or done, but also about embracing the reality that sometimes we are more or less ready to learn, that learning is an ongoing process, and that daily experiences are the practice fields for leaders (Figure 18.1). Preparation is the ongoing assessment of our readiness to move into situations that will require us to be agile as learners. Process is the ongoing integration of the interconnected variables impacting our capacity to learn well. Performance is the real-time laboratory.

The stakes are high for identifying and supporting agile leaders. Although it may be argued that organizations are different today than they were 50 years ago, our need for leaders who are willing to go first and enter into difficult circumstances in order to build a more sustainable future for so many is not (R. McKenna & Wenzel, 2016). The importance of looking at leaders is magnified when we recognize that the pressure of going first may be intensified when applying lessons to new and unfamiliar situations. We

Preparation ⟶ Process ⟶ Performance

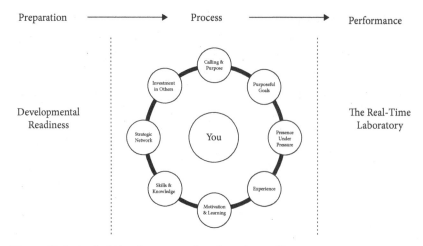

Developmental
Readiness

The Real-Time
Laboratory

Figure 18.1 A whole leader approach to learning agility.

cannot forget that leaders are people who made a choice to assume risk and pioneer change (R. McKenna & Wenzel, 2016). Learning agility is a critical and personal proposition for leaders because, by its very nature, learning is hard. While it may be wonderful at times, it would be wrong to assume learning to learn is always engaging, exciting, or comfortable. When we think of our own experiences of applying lessons learned to new and unfamiliar situations, alongside the heightened pressure to perform well, it is often anything but energizing and comfortable. And, we rarely learn or experience alone. Learning agility so often happens in the presence of others and in situations where we are forced to learn together and to learn through hardships (Thomas, 2008). A whole perspective expands our understanding. Imagine a world where learning agility is contagious.

What would change if more of us were inspiring others to learn well from the past—to become more agile? How would every moment of your day be different if part of your role as a leader was not only to increase your capacity to learn well, but also to inspire learning in every other person around you? We must increase our efforts to develop leaders who are learning agile, as well as leaders who are able to inspire learning agility in others. These are leaders who are willing to use their skills in ways they have seldom, if ever, used them before so that others may do the same. Leaders who are positive contagions of learning are composed and viral in a world that screams of volatility, uncertainty, complexity, and ambiguity. We want strong, long-lasting individuals who choose to learn in a world where so many of us will act out of compulsion and, at our worst, even blame.

What can we learn from the leaders who have gone before us regarding the real and gritty experiences of life and work and the keys to learning? Decades of research have revealed a troubling reality that is fundamental to our understanding of learning. Leaders learn the most in experiences that challenge them to the core (e.g., McCall, 1998; McCauley, Ruderman, Ohlott, & Morrow, 1994), where success or failure is a 50/50 proposition, and where the world will watch the outcome. While the troubling reality is that these are experiences they would never want to relive again, facing that reality is part of the fundamental solution to becoming more learning agile. If we think about what it was like for someone to learn from a difficult experience, certain levels of resilience, perseverance, and courage are necessary to withstand the storms that may come, and durability is built and sustained through a combination of complex variables in the life and experiences of a leader (see Chapter 12). Our whole leader perspective on learning agility acknowledges these complexities through understanding the different areas of a leader's life that may impact a leader's ability not only to show up at their best, but also to learn.

Whole and Intentional Leader Development

A whole leader perspective on the keys to unlocking the door between our experiences and the lessons available to us on the other side requires framing up at least some of the other factors in the day-to-day experiences of a leader. The challenge with designing a container consumable enough to house our understanding of learning agility is significant because learning is connected to everything (Figure 18.2). Before highlighting these keys (which we describe as personal motivational learning strategies), it may help to describe some of what we know about the whole experience of a leader.

The developmental opportunity of a leader is not only about learning agility, but also about a variety of factors in their preparation and process of learning that are interconnected. Why they lead, their motivation to lead, who they lead, who supports them, the experiences that have shaped them, the efficacy they feel in their competence, and how they show up when it matters most—all play a role. The hope is that learning will play a role in

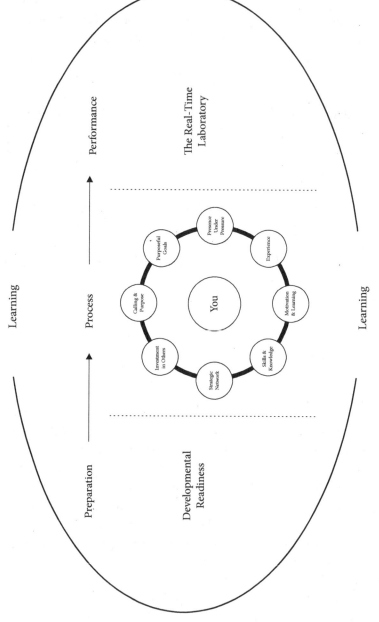

Figure 18.2 The cycle of a whole leader approach to learning agility.

every part of their experience, and every part of their experience plays a role in their future capacity to lead.

To bring what could be a fairly lofty framework back down to our more common experience, consider this: Do any of us look forward to the possibility that we will continue to make the same mistakes again? And, does our capacity to learn and to apply that learning more quickly, if at all, have anything to do with reducing the number of cycles it will take to get it right? Do we even get the opportunity to add to our list of skills and strengths without the refining fire of experience that could either shut down our confidence to learn or create a new universe of possibilities? So much in the leadership development literature focuses on the pieces of our developmental puzzle without asking the most basic question: What does my capacity to learn have to do with this and what are the personally challenging obstacles I could face or reveal that would bring my learning closer to my reality? And maybe in a more appreciative and approachable sense, what are the customized learning strategies that are so critically important for me and for others to understand about me that would have an accelerating impact on my learning potential—not for the sake of speed alone but for becoming a better version of myself for everyone?

Thinking about learning as a part of every aspect of a leader's work changes the talent game. It transitions our thinking about leaders as either competent or not to a focus that includes both their competence and their capacity to learn. It moves our focus from identifying the talented versus the untalented. The focus alters to their "readiness to learn." This is a significant paradigm shift because it changes the job of those invested in developing leaders and agile learners. Our first job becomes less about finding talent alone and now includes identifying people with the capacity to prepare well. The job of talent professionals becomes more like that of detectives than lie detectors—curiously figuring people out as opposed to sizing them up. The next question is how we more accurately understand the personal motivations of an individual to learn and the relationship between those motivations and the rest of their remarkable developmental puzzle.

Motivation to Learn and Whole Leaders

Learning agility is not one size fits all. Approaching learning agility as something you either have or do not have without thoughtfully considering how each of us learns would be like Amazon Prime having only one product available to order. While increasing or accelerating learning agility may be a good idea for most of us in principle, a whole focus on learning agility begs for a simple assessment of whether we are agile or not. What would change if the leaders around us knew what compels and inspires them personally to take the risk to learn—to change and to become better versions of themselves for their sake and for the sake of others? The idea that learning strategies, mindsets, and developmental efficacy influence a leader's capacity to draw the deepest marrow out of their experiences is not novel, but the idea that those learning strategies are both personal and motivational just might be. Research on learning strategies has shown that in a rapidly changing world, individuals who employ learning strategies throughout their life may be better able to adapt and evolve with changing demands (Weinstein, Acee, & Jung, 2011).

Like learning agility, there has not been an agreed-upon definition of learning strategies. However, researchers have generally agreed upon the notion that learning strategies involve the use of cognition, metacognition, motivation, affect, and behavior (Weinstein et al., 2011). Specifically, the interplay of motivation and cognition has been central to numerous researchers' work (Duncan & McKeachie, 2005; Pintrich, Smith, Garcia, & McKeachie, 1993). In research with college students, the students are thought to be active in the process of attaining knowledge, assuming their beliefs and cognitions are important mediators of the learning process (Pintrich et al., 1993). If we are to increase the capacity by which people can learn from their experiences, the strategies by which we do so may play an important role. It is important future researchers continue to investigate the relationship between learning strategies and learning agility and the way in which understanding the way an individual learns best may, in turn, increase his or her capacity to be learning agile.

Based on our research concerning nearly 10,000 leaders, we discovered that learning agility is not only something you can increase but also something you can motivate. We discovered that leaders were not perceiving learning from experience as simply a generalized approach to learning, but that their individualized motivations and the contextual factors around them were playing a role (R. B. McKenna, Yost, & Boyd, 2007). Motivational learning strategies are the personal keys to unlocking the inspiration to learn that opens up between and within our experiences and lessons learned. In that way, they are happening both while we are experiencing and when we are learning, as well as providing a connection between the two. In other words, a leader's capacity to learn is not simply about looking for lessons and intentional reflection; rather, it is also about their unique motivations and inspirations to learn. Think of the last time you learned something new. What is it that inspired you to learn that may be very different from another person's inspiration?

Referring to Figure 18.2, learning motivators are best understood as important in all stages of a person's developmental rhythm—including his or her preparation, process, and performance. For several years, individuals have been assessing their personal motivational learning strategies using a tool called the Motivational Learning Inventory™ as part of a whole leader development system known as the WiLD Toolkit™ (R. B. McKenna, 2019). Along with motivational learning strategies, this system provides insight into calling and purpose, goals, presence, experience, competence, support, and investment in others (Figures 18.1 and 18.2). In this way, learning agility not only leads to an end state but also plays an important role in every part of our developmental journey. And, increased awareness of our specific motivations to learn might open the door to more inspiration across all facets of our experience.

The Learning Motivators

There is always a temptation to generalize labels or profiles as either personality dimensions, character traits, or behavior styles. When referring to "learning motivators," our focus is on identifying each individual's personal inspirations to learn that likely increase the capacity to be more learning agile. This reinforces the possibility that learning agility is something leaders will be inspired to seek. The Motivational Learning Inventory provides insight into an individual's inspiration to learn in hopes of providing developmentally efficacious pathways to personal change.

Table 18.1 defines six learning motivators, their associated learning strategies, and the inspiration and context in which each of them thrives. The best way to understand these learning motivators as inspiration for others to learn is to examine them through your own learning lens. As you review these six learning motivators, consider the one or two that, when working well, create a deep level of motivation within you to learn. While people have a desire to use these labels as personality dimensions or traits, it is important

Table 18.1 Description of Learning Motivators and Their Corresponding Learning Strategies

Learning Motivators	Description
Seeker	You learn through your willingness to learn from past experience, to receive feedback, and to stretch yourself through new opportunities and challenges.
	Inspiration: Active reflection and development
	Environment: Encourages strategic pauses and the consideration of questions before compulsive execution
	Learning Strategies: • Seek feedback from others and take appropriate action as necessary • Look for opportunities to be challenged and take risks • Emulate role models (either good or bad) as examples of what and how to be or not to be.
Strategist	You learn through your ability to apply what you know as an expert at some things, and through your ability to think strategically about what should be done next, and in what order.
	Inspiration: Responsibility for others and some level of structured vision
	Environment: Leading process with or through others
	Learning Strategies: • Think systematically and see the bigger picture • Apply expert knowledge • Think strategically and prepare for future consequences/ decisions
Connector	You learn through your ability to relate well to others, build teams, manage conflict, and to work and lead through and with others.
	Inspiration: Leading together
	Environment: Direct, relational, supportive team
	Learning Strategies: • Network to build support communities • Take others' perspectives • Listen well to others
Influencer	You learn through your ability to stay true to your principles, the values that define you, your willingness to wait, and your desire to have a positive impact on others around you.
	Inspiration: Impacting others through things that matter to you
	Environment: Opportunities to speak and inspire others through their personal convictions
	Learning Strategies: • Act according to personal values and ideals even when faced with conflicting situations • Remain truthful and sincere during good and difficult times with others • Feel and demonstrate passion

Table 18.1 *Continued*

Learning Motivators	Description
Stabilizer	You learn through your willingness to take responsibility, to stay true to yourself, to laugh at yourself, and to remain flexible while staying on track.
	Inspiration: Opportunity to show up well and conscientiously complete tasks
	Environment: Responsive to the developmental needs of individuals along with a fair level of predictability
	Learning Strategies: • Remain flexible, adaptable, and okay with ambiguity • Look honestly at myself; assessing personal strengths and weaknesses • Remain optimistic and look for the bright side of a person or situation
Receptor	You learn through your willingness to be obedient to a greater calling on your life.
	Inspiration: A connection between a personal transcendent purpose and life or work activities
	Environment: Structure that, and others who, connect why and how.
	Learning Strategies: • Rely on spirituality to get through a situation • Remain open to being called to a higher purpose

to note that these are specific to the learning process and to an individual understanding the customized nature of what motivates his or her own learning agility.

The fundamental shift caused by a focus on personal learning motivators is that it moves our understanding of learning agility as an ability or willingness a leader either does or does not possess, to include the reality that ability and willingness are developmental processes in and of themselves. Learning agility is not only an end goal, but also a developmental process inside each of us that likely impacts everything. If we knew how we learn, what inspires us to learn, and the environments that support our particular motivations, we would increase our awareness of our need for more or less stretch in different seasons or circumstances where the stretch we are seeking is most inspired. While the general principle of more reflection might be good for all of us, it may be less important for some whose motivations to learn are less about seeking learning and more about structure, strategy, connections, influence, or a transcendent purpose.

For example, it is one thing to consider data across hundreds of athletes that inform us how well athletes in a certain category move or how quickly they run from one point to the next; it is another thing to understand the multiple factors within any one athlete contributing to his or her capacity to move well. Likewise, while it is important to understand the averages and general principles that apply to all leaders with high levels of learning agility, it is the story behind "why" for any individual leader that is equally, if not more, important.

If we achieve the goal of accelerating the learning agility of leaders and increasing their capacity and motivations to learn deeper and faster, it would be one of the most powerful and scary possibilities imaginable. It is powerful when considered in the context of the local and global challenges that could be solved by leaders like this. It is equally frightening to imagine the damage a leader could do more quickly when acting without consideration of the impact on others.

Our two-fold point is that learning agility is both generalizable and necessarily customizable to a person, and that we must continually ask ourselves the question, Learning agility for the sake of what or whom? Our hope is that as each of us step to the edge of the most transformational and difficult experiences ahead of us, we will see pathways to our unique inspirations to learn for our sake and, possibly more importantly, for the sake of others in our influence.

Implications for Research, Theory, and Practice

As we and others have suggested, learning agility is likely one of the most important concepts in the life and rhythm of a modern organization. And, developing and inspiring it in leaders and organizations likely requires more sophistication than simply telling leaders to be agile or setting up training programs that teach learning agility in a vacuum. Many related concepts have emerged during the past decade that tell us more about what it takes to become more agile as learners. In the following paragraphs, we propose several more integrated ideas on how to more effectively understand and grow as agile learners.

For Individuals

What would change if you knew what motivates you to learn? Our hope is that each of us might have not only a better understanding of learning agility but also increased curiosity about our unique motivations to learn and an understanding of how our motivations connect to the needs of others within our influence. Are you motivated to learn by the possibility of influencing others or more by systems and strategies? Are you motivated by moments of reflection or by learning itself? Or, are you motivated by your capacity to provide stability or by your capacity to connect others? Our suggestion is that understanding each of our unique motivations to learn is key, and it may be a primary ingredient in our learning going forward.

From a theoretical perspective, how powerful would it be if we could understand the connection between an individual's learning motivators and the individual's capacity to be more agile or even his or her capacity to remain agile over the long haul? We know that personal learning strategies and motivators matter. Future researchers could help us understand the key outcomes they impact. Here are two questions to consider:

1. What would change for you if you understood your unique motivations to learn?
2. How does understanding your own learning motivators increase your capacity to inspire learning agility in others?

For Those Who Support Leaders

For coaches, talent professionals, and leadership development specialists, there is an opportunity not only to teach leaders about the fundamentals of learning agility, but also to invite them into a deeper understanding of their motivations to learn. And, likely the best way to authentically invite them in is for each of us as professionals to understand our own motivations to learn. From a theoretical perspective, we know that intentional connections between our experiences and the lessons on the other side are directly impacted by both the situational factors and personal strategies at play (R. B. McKenna et al., 2007). While understanding the strategies that work for most people is certainly important, there is also a more personal story regarding motivations to learn that every leader with whom we work could understand (Molenaar, 2004).

There are three questions to consider:

1. How could you encourage leaders to identify the narrative that has defined their approach to learning?

2. How could you encourage leaders to think beyond simply being more agile, as well as to identify their unique motivations to learn?
3. How could you encourage leaders to reflect on the times when they were inspired to learn something new?

For Organizations

Moving large systems requires leaders who are willing to move. While it could be argued that many succeeding modern organizations are functioning at different levels of agility, it is important to separate agility (things like speed of communication, technological advances or changes, and simple cultural expectations) from learning agility. Whether or not people in our organizations are communicating more often or making decisions faster, learning agility will always be rooted in our capacity to learn and to change. Any organizational culture has the potential to produce habits, repeated behaviors, and perceptions of ourselves that may need to change at some point. Our suggestion is the best place for any organization to start building a learning agile culture is to encourage change with the full understanding that real change is always going to be difficult. And furthermore, it is important to understand trends and averages across our organization while remaining passionately committed to understanding the unique learning motivations of each individual. Here are two questions to consider:

1. As an organizational leader, what are you reluctant to change about yourself that may help others?
2. What system could you put in place that would encourage people to consider their unique motivations to learn in the context of your organization?

References

Ashford, S. J., & DeRue, D. S. (2012). Developing as a leader: The power of mindful engagement. *Organizational Dynamics, 41*, 146–154.

Bardwick, J. M. (2000). *Danger in the comfort zone: From boardroom to mailroom—How to break the entitlement habit that's killing American business* (2nd ed.). New York, NY: AMACOM.

De Meuse, K. P. (2017). Learning agility: Its evolution as a psychological construct and its empirical relationship to leader success. *Consulting Psychology Journal: Practice and Research, 69*, 267–295.

De Meuse, K. P., Dai, G., Swisher, V. V., Eichinger, R. W., & Lombardo, M. M. (2012). Leadership development: Exploring, clarifying and expanding our understanding of learning agility. *Industrial and Organizational Psychology, 5*, 280–286.

DeRue, D. S., Ashford, S. J., & Myers, C. G. (2012). Learning agility: In search of conceptual clarity and theoretical grounding. *Industrial and Organizational Psychology, 5*, 258–279.

Duncan, T. G., & McKeachie, W. J. (2005). The making of the motivated strategies for learning questionnaire. *Educational Psychologist, 40*(2), 117–128.

McCall, M. W., Jr. (1998). *High flyers: Developing the next generation of leaders.* Boston, MA: Harvard Business School.

McCauley, C. D., Ruderman, M. N., Ohlott, P. J., & Morrow, J. E. (1994). Assessing the developmental components of managerial jobs. *Journal of Applied Psychology, 79*, 544–560.

McKenna, R., & Wenzel, K. K. (2016). Developing whole leaders for the whole world. *The Journal of Values-Based Leadership, 9*(1), 1–16.

McKenna, R. B. (2019). *The whole leader guidebook: Whole and intentional leader development.* Seattle, WA: WiLD Leaders.

McKenna, R. B., Yost, P. R., & Boyd, T. N. (2007). Leadership development and clergy: Understanding the events and lessons that shape pastoral leaders. *Journal of Psychology and Theology, 35*(3), 179–189.

Molenaar, P. C. (2004). A manifesto on psychology as idiographic science: Bringing the person back into scientific psychology, this time forever. *Measurement: Interdisciplinary Research and Perspectives, 2*(4), 201–218.

Pintrich, P. R., Smith, D. A., Garcia, T., & McKeachie, W. J. (1993). Reliability and predictive validity of the Motivated Strategies for Learning Questionnaire (MSLQ). *Educational and Psychological Measurement, 53*, 801–813.

Thomas, R. J. (2008). *Crucibles of leadership: How to learn from experience to become a great leader.* Boston, MA: Harvard Business Press.

Thrash, T. M., & Elliot, A. J. (2003). Inspiration as a psychological construct. *Journal of Personality and Social Psychology, 84*, 871–889.

Weinstein, C. E., Acee, T. W., & Jung, J. (2011). Self-regulation and learning strategies. *New Directions for Teaching and Learning, 11*(126), 45–53.

SECTION IV
LESSONS AND APPLICATIONS

This—the final section—begins with a chapter summarizing the current state of both the science and practice of learning agility. This includes a synthesis of the foundational elements of learning agility as well as potential central mechanisms that may undergird these elements. Key implications for organizational culture, talent management practices, managers, and leadership coaches are identified, and a nomonological net of learning agility is presented along with several research questions that should be addressed by future scholars. This section also includes a series of ten case studies demonstrating how organizations have applied learning agility in their talent management and leadership practices. The cases are from a variety of organizations, ranging from school systems to healthcare organizations to Fortune 500 companies in the United States, China, and Australia. The lessons learned provide a roadmap of best practices for readers in their journeys to implement learning agility into their talent management practices and organizational cultures.

19

Learning Agility

What We Know, What We Need to Know, and Where Do We Go From Here?

Veronica Schmidt Harvey and Kenneth P. De Meuse

> The illiterate of the 21st Century will not be those who cannot read
> and write, but those who cannot learn, unlearn, and relearn.
> —Alvin Toffler (1928–2016), American author and futurist

As we wrote this chapter, the Covid-19 pandemic continued to spread across the globe. Two months before that, very few people outside of the medical profession had ever heard the word *coronavirus*. Now, it has completely turned the world upside down. Companies, schools, churches, shopping malls, and governmental offices have closed. Business owners are attempting to survive with little or no revenue coming in. Stock markets have plummeted. Parents are trying to cope with working from home, teaching their kids, and maintaining their sanity. Governments are spending trillions of dollars to stave off some of the negative outcomes a broken economy is creating. The question is, What will cause the next big disruption—a breakthrough technology, global integration, climate change, World War III, or another contagion? The term *learning agility* never seemed more relevant.

The acronym VUCA has been used frequently to describe our world today. Indeed, authors of two chapters in this book used it in their titles. While VUCA represents volatility, uncertainty, complexity, and ambiguity, the antidote can be characterized as follows:

- V—Vision
- U—Understanding

Veronica Schmidt Harvey and Kenneth P. De Meuse, *Learning Agility* In: *The Age of Agility*. Edited by: Veronica Schmidt Harvey and Kenneth P. De Meuse, Oxford University Press (2021). © Oxford University Press.
DOI: 10.1093/oso/9780190085353.003.0019

- C—Clarity
- A—Agility

In this book, we focus on *agility*, learning agility in particular. Our fundamental goal is to enhance our understanding of the construct of learning agility, synthesizing scientific knowledge and best practices from both research and application. We assembled a community of more than 50 highly respected scholars and professional talent management practitioners. We devoted over a year editing and writing this book, which itself was an exercise in learning agility! When the process first began, we did not fully anticipate just how deeply relevant the need for learning agility would be in 2020 and beyond. It is our sincere hope that the readers of *The Age of Agility* will learn as much as we did. And in the words of Sir Isaac Newton, this learning for us occurred by "standing on the shoulders of giants" (the authors of this book).

In our view, we have reached a critical pivot point in the evolution of learning agility. Learning agility can become simply another bright shiny object in the catalog of human resource trends. Or, it can become an effective, durable life raft for the turbulent times we face. In this chapter, we distill key elements from all the chapters and cases presented in this book. This summary chapter focuses on (a) what we know, (b) what is emerging in our understanding, (c) how we can better apply the lessons we have learned, and (d) key research needs.

What Do We Know?

In this section, we summarize those "truths" that we can articulate with a high degree of certainty based on existing scientific evidence.

Change Is Constant and Likely to Accelerate

The world around us is changing at a relentless and increasing pace. It is rare for a day to go by without news of another technological advance, scientific discovery, or black swan event (Taleb, 2007) that changes the way we live and work. The flood of information and choices we encounter can cause us to perpetually feel "in over our heads"—to use the term of Harvard Professor Robert Kegan (1994). Organizations are dynamic, and the future will be more fluid, not less. As noted in Chapter 1, society has transformed from an era of stability, predictability, and incremental change to a period of insecurity, uncertainty, and chaos, or, in the words of the title of this book, *The Age of Agility.*

It is abundantly clear that the ability to adapt is essential to survival. As defined by Merriam-Webster (2020), adaptation involves "modification of an organism or its parts that makes it more fit for existence under the conditions of its environment." However, most of us would likely prefer to do more than *just* survive! While adapting to circumstances is required for continued existence, it is learning agility that enables us to *thrive.* Learning agility shifts the focus from being "passive victims" of change to being "proactive creators" of our future. It switches the onus from being controlled by the environment to controlling it, from putting one's faith in others to show the way to placing trust in our own ability to adapt.

Leaders Will Need to Become More Learning Agile—*And* Lead the Way

We read in Chapter 1 that the "organization man" (and woman) of the 1950s and 1960s is long gone. And while we may have some good indications of what it takes to be successful as a leader today, we cannot predict with much accuracy what leadership capabilities will be needed next year, let alone 50 years from now. Leadership roles have changed dramatically and will continue to change. As aptly described by David Peterson (Chapter 13), leaders operate in "wicked" environments where they must solve problems never before encountered—perhaps by anyone—and without a rulebook. The importance of learning agility will increase, not decrease. As noted by Dai and De Meuse in Chapter 2, person–job fit is not static, and leaders need to continuously evolve as they find themselves in first-time situations.

But, we should not lose sight of another truth. Leaders have *always* been pioneers. The word *leader* is derived from an Old English word—lædan— which means "'to go before as a guide" (Macmillan Dictionary, 2020). As McKenna and Minaker point out in Chapter 18, we not only need learning agile leaders, but also need leaders who can inspire learning agility in others. Learning agility is likely required for other roles, perhaps many roles, but *it is leaders who must lead the way.*

Learning Agility Requires Courage

In the Backword to this book, the "fathers" of learning agility Michael Lombardo and Bob Eichinger wrote: "The development of those who lead well is the land of the first time and the risky." Virtually all of the contributors to this book recognize learning agility is not (at least initially) easy or comfortable. The essence of learning agility is performing under first-time, tough, and often difficult conditions (De Meuse, 2017). Frequently, learning something new or doing something for the first time is painful (Snell, 1992). However, much like riding a roller coaster, the journey is exhilarating as well as scary and challenging! As described by Kim Ruyle in Chapter 5, we are neurologically wired to feel threatened when changing requirements exceed our comfort level. While organizations can create conditions of psychological safety (Stomski & Jensen, Chapter 15), ultimately it is each individual leader who must choose between short-term comfort and development of learning muscle.

Highly learning agile leaders realize "courage is not the absence of fear, but rather the assessment that something else is more important than fear" (Franklin D. Roosevelt). Courageous people lead in the face of fear. Learning agility requires stepping to the edge of our comfort zone (Yost, DeHaas, & Allison, Chapter 12) and often moving intentionally *outside* our comfort zone to confront our fear until we can tolerate the discomfort. It is about our willingness and ability do something different, to change "even in the moments when it may be difficult to do so" (McKenna & Minaker, Chapter 18). It can require the leap of faith to suboptimize current performance as an investment in the future, something that feels quite risky (Peterson, Chapter 13). It is no wonder that Brené Brown's TED Talks on vulnerability and daring greatly are among the most viewed TED talks of all time! The paradox of leading in the age of agility is *getting comfortable with being uncomfortable.*

Learning Agility Can Be Empowering

One aspect of learning agility rarely discussed is its potential for empowerment, engagement, and inclusion. Increasing learning agility creates a pathway to change for anyone who has the minimum qualification of willingness. While there may be some foundational elements of learning agility that are relatively "fixed," this book has revealed there are many more that are malleable and can be developed. Consequently, the measurement of learning agility provides for a more level playing field in the identification of high-potential talent because it offers an objective, quantifiable metric when making such decisions. Research evidence indicated there are no group differences across race, gender, and age when learning agility is assessed properly (see De Meuse, Dai, Zewdie, et al., 2011; De Meuse, Lim, & Rao, 2019). As Lombardo and Eichinger note in their Backword, "Learning agility has turned out to be as egalitarian as we hoped it would be."

Many have forgotten about the transformative book *Breaking the Glass Ceiling,* by Ann Morrison, Randall White, and Ellen Van Velsor (1987). It was published about the same time as another classic book on leadership, *The Lessons of Experience,* by Morgan McCall, Michael Lombardo, and Ann Morrison (1988). At the time, both groups of authors participated in the Center for Creative Leadership research project to identify important executive experiences to develop leaders. However, Ann Morrison and her colleagues recognized a problem with the original research—it included very few women. With considerable effort, they identified and interviewed a sample of executive women, many of whom were "pioneers on the corporate prairie" (p. 9). Ultimately, these researchers concluded that the lessons most crucial to success were essentially the same for men *and* women (although the opportunities as well as the process of navigating through those experiences were indeed different).

As pointed out by Harvey and Prager in Chapter 6, we cannot afford to limit the development of learning agility to empower only the elite few. Furthermore, it would be shortsighted to place all our bets on those individuals we predict now will be the best leaders in the future because we *don't know* what those leadership requirements will be! It is a wise investment to build learning agility among the many versus the few. The scientific assessment of leadership talent and then providing opportunities for that talent to learn from experience and develop learning agility will surely contribute to greater diversity within the leadership ranks. Differential investment in talent is important, but at the same time we must strive to be inclusive to ensure appropriate access to the experiences and resources that build learning agility. We address the importance of fostering a culture where learning agility can flourish in a further section of this chapter.

Learning Agility Offers Organizations an Opportunity to Apply Science to Leadership

Executives continually report being dissatisfied with the current state of leadership development (Kotlyar & Karakowsky, 2014). And, it is no wonder, given we reportedly spend $366 billion each year on leadership development globally, with this figure regularly increasing (Westfall, 2019). Unfortunately, there appears to be no corresponding decline in the inadequacies of our leadership pipeline. As lamented by Kaiser and Curphy (2013), "we are spending more to develop leaders with whom we are less and less satisfied" (p. 295).

Learning agility presents a significant opportunity to reduce the gap between our investment and return in the identification and development of effective leadership. Empirical research continues to grow on the value of learning agility in predicting leader success (De Meuse, 2017, 2019). Although the mechanisms for *developing* learning agility are less clearly established, it is not for lack of trying on the part of practitioners! Certainly, research lags behind practice. Nevertheless, the chapters and cases in this book suggest there may be more evidence available than realized—albeit piecemeal and cross-disciplinary. Moving the development of learning agility from art to science may very well be one of the greatest opportunities facing industrial and organizational psychologists and talent management professionals today.

What Trends Are Emerging?

The chapters in this books suggest a number of trends that are surfacing but not yet fully confirmed. In the following section, we review the "emerging truths" about learning agility, which we hope will help illuminate pathways for research and guidance for practice.

Growing Interest in Agility Is Creating Confusion

Interest in the topic of agility continues to accelerate (Harsch & Festing, 2020; Joiner, 2019; Pulakos & Kantrowitz, 2020). Agility is increasingly viewed as vital given "the need for organizations to compete more successfully in today's hypercompetitive and rapidly changing work environment" (Pulakos, Kantrowitz, & Schneider, 2019, p. 305). The words *agility* and *agile* have become pervasive in the business nomenclature. For example, in a recent *Harvard Business Review* article, "The Agile C-Suite" is described as a new approach for top leadership (Rigby, Elk, & Berez, 2020). Further, AGILE is a set of principles and practices commonplace in the world of software development and project management (Benton & Radziwill, 2011; Denning, 2016). Some have even applied software terminology to agile learning (e.g., labeling a coach as "scrum master"; Longmuss, Höhne, Bräutigam, Oberländer, & Schindler, 2016; Overeem, 2015).

While this growing interest in agility is positive, using the terms *organizational agility, leadership agility,* and *learning agility* interchangeably creates confusion. Even among discussions with authors of this book, the lines between organizational agility and learning agility became blurred at times. While learning agility may *enable* both leadership agility and organizational agility, it is not synonymous with either concept.

Our perspective is that learning agility is an individual-level attribute that leaders of organizations possess in varying degrees. It is similar to other individual characteristics that are measured on a continuous scale—from low to high. It is also possible to be high on some dimensions of learning agility and low on others. For leaders, learning agility is typically a good attribute to have that will enable more effective leadership. The concept of "leadership at all levels" (Charan, 2008), which suggests that everyone is a leader in some capacity, implies that all roles require some degree of learning agility.

While undoubtedly some agility is required by everyone to deal with constant change, not all positions require high levels of agility. For positions that require strict attention to following rules and strict procedures, learning agility could be detrimental. It is also possible for a leader to possess too much learning agility for the position he or she occupies. It is analogous to "overuse" behaviors within the context of leadership (Kaiser & Overfield, 2011; McCall & Lombardo, 1983). If leaders are too learning agile for the role, they can be too change oriented and institute change for the sake of change. Or, they can take too many unnecessary risks or quickly become disengaged if insufficient learning opportunities exist. Perhaps, it can be construed as the "Goldilocks effect!" Possessing either too little or too much is not the ideal. Future studies are needed to confirm how much learning agility is needed for various roles and leadership levels.

Definitional Clarity Is Growing on the Construct of Learning Agility

As a construct, learning agility has suffered from a lack of consensus on what it does and does not include and how it differs from other related constructs. There is no doubt it is complex and multidimensional. The originators of the terminology focused on the *ability* and *willingness* to learn from experience (De Meuse, Dai, & Hallenbeck, 2010; Lombardo & Eichinger, 2000). A few authors (e.g., DeRue, Ashford, & Myers, 2012) have emphasized learning speed and flexibility. Likewise, other constructs, such as adaptability or versatility, appear closely related to learning agility. Wang and Beir (2012) asserted that learning agility has been researched under a host of aliases. Overall, it is suspected the typical talent management practitioner would have difficulty distinguishing among various related constructs.

Both scholars and practitioners have pointed out the commonality between the constructs of learning agility and adaptive performance. Performance adaptation has been defined as "behaviors demonstrating the ability to cope with change and to transfer learning from one task to another as job demands vary" (Baard, Rench, & Kozlowski, 2014, p. 49). Adaptive performance is viewed as "cognitive, affective, motivational, and behavioral modifications made in response to the demands of a new or changing environment or situational demands" (Baard et al., 2014, p. 52). It seems likely that this construct shares some common personality antecedents with learning agility (e.g., openness to experience, cognitive flexibility, self-efficacy). Mechanisms to develop both adaptive behavior and learning agility include increasing learning orientation, providing feedback, error management, and some of the same strategies suggested for the development of learning agility (see Harvey & Prager, Chapter 6).

In this book, learning agility has been described and defined in a number of ways (see Table 19.1 for examples). Despite the variations in definition, these conceptualizations have much more in common than not, including the following:

- learning agility includes *learning from all our experiences* (De Meuse & Harvey, Chapter 1; Dai & De Meuse, Chapter 2);
- it incorporates the intertwined components of *thoughts, emotions, behaviors, motivations, knowledge, and social interactions*

Table 19.1 Conceptualizations of Learning Agility

Conceptualization/Definition	Source
How you learn what to do when you don't know what to do	Lombardo & Eichinger, Backword
The ability to learn quickly and the willingness and flexibility to apply those lessons to perform well in new and challenging leadership roles	De Meuse & Harvey, Chapter 1
The willingness and ability to learn new competencies in order to perform under first-time, tough, or different conditions	De Meuse & Harvey, Chapter 1
Adapting and transforming oneself to meet the demands of one's environment	Heaton, Chapter 17
The ability to come up to speed quickly in one's understanding of a situation and move across ideas flexibly in service of learning both within and across experiences	Anseel & Ong, Chapter 10
The DNA of VUCA, the instruction set humans need to develop and thrive in a VUCA world; built around seeking and making sense of experiences with increasing levels of diversity, novelty, and adversity	Peterson, Chapter 13
A leadership metacompetency that facilitates agile experiential learning to cultivate required leadership competencies	Heslin & Mellish, Chapter 11
The self-regulated behaviors, strategies, and habits that enable learning at an accelerated pace, facilitate more agile adaptation to dynamic conditions and result in more effective leadership	Harvey & Prager, Chapter 6
The engagement in learning behaviors to enhance the capacity to reconfigure activities quickly to meet the changing demands in the task environment	Burke Learning Agility Inventory™ in Boyce & Boyce, Chapter 4

(Dai & De Meuse, Chapter 2; Harvey & Prager, Chapter 6; Peterson, Chapter 13; Heaton, Chapter 17);

- it is viewed as a *metacompetency*—an amalgamation of interrelated leadership competencies (De Meuse & Harvey, Chapter 1; Heslin & Mellish, Chapter 11);

- it includes the *temporal dimensions* of learning from the past, being mindful in the present, and taking action based on anticipated future needs (Harvey & Prager, Chapter 6; Lee, Chapter 7); and

- recognized as important for more quickly and *effectively adapting to future situations*, which are assumed to be even more dynamic than today.

At its core, learning agility is about adapting successfully, using various strategies to learn from all our experiences as the mechanism for change. The term *learning agility* is likely here to stay, but even those who coined it acknowledge the difficulty of capturing the construct in a single label: "The one regret we have is using the term *learning.* . . . It is more related to conceptual complexity and pattern recognition. It is closer to broad perspective, openness to change, and changing one's behavior without poisoning relationships with others. On hindsight, maybe we should have called it 'adaptiveness'" (Lombardo & Eichinger, "Foreword").

A Shared Understanding of the Elements of Learning Agility

It may be difficult to ever develop one standard definition of learning agility. Many of the instruments, tools, programs, and processes associated with learning agility are proprietary or customized to organizational needs. This situation creates a vested interest in retaining certain definitions and dimensions of the construct. While understandable, we must agree on the foundational elements of learning agility in order to facilitate useful empirical research.

In Chapter 2, Dai and De Meuse provide a comprehensive review of the elements of learning agility. Boyce and Boyce synthesize the dimensions most commonly assessed in proprietary measures of learning agility (Chapter 4). Elements of learning agility are also cataloged by De Meuse and Harvey (Chapter 1, Table 1.6) and Harvey and Prager (Chapter 6, Table 6.6). As would be expected, *every* chapter incorporates a subset of the elements of learning agility.

Despite a broad range of terminology used among authors, there is considerable consistency on the elements thought to comprise learning agility. A summary of these dimensions and behaviors/strategies is included in Table 19.2. These have significant overlap with the elements included in the framework provided by Dai and De Meuse in Chapter 2. Overall, there is a high level of consensus among the contributors to this book on what constitutes the foundational behaviors and strategies associated with learning agility.

While there are some aspects of learning agility that appear to be influenced by more stable factors (e.g., personality traits, cognitive ability, demographics, upbringing), far more are "learnable" strategies that can be developed by leaders. Nevertheless, it remains to be demonstrated

Table 19.2 Foundational Behaviors and Strategies for Learning Agility

Dimension	Behaviors/Strategies
Affective	• Aware of and able to regulate emotions
Behavioral	• Seeks opportunities to increase external awareness • Seeks information and actively listens • Seeks and responds to feedback • Applies structure to learning process • Behaviorally flexible • Willing to experiment and take risks
Cognitive	• Cognitively flexible, curious, and open-minded • Reflective and distills lessons from experiences
Knowledge	• Knows and implements learning strategies • Possesses and seeks insight on strengths and weaknesses
Motivation	• Learning and growth oriented • Demonstrates self-efficacy • Driven to seek challenges and excel • Willing and motivated to grow and evolve • Resilient and resourceful
Social	• Socially intelligent and flexible to others' needs • Able to leverage relationships and manage interpersonal conflict • Inclusive and appreciates diversity

empirically which are (a) most influenced by predisposition, (b) most readily changed through development, and (c) most critical overall.

Underlying Mechanisms of Learning Agility May Mediate Multiple Elements

Some aspects of learning agility are particularly prevalent across many chapters within this book, suggesting they may be of greater importance and/ or mediate multiple elements of learning agility. For example, mindfulness appears related to external awareness, cognitive flexibility, reflection, and emotional regulation. Growth mindset seems to influence virtually every learning strategy. Clearly, the elements of learning agility included in Table 19.2 are *not* orthogonal. It may be fruitful to determine the underlying *core mechanisms* of learning agility. Doing so may accelerate theory building and research, especially if we can leverage research that already exists on these core underlying mechanisms to build a nomological net around learning agility.

The following mechanisms seem particularly worthy of consideration: (a) a belief that personal change is possible, *learning mindset*; (b) the ability to control and shift our thinking, *cognitive control and flexibility*; (c) the capacity to regulate our emotions, *emotional regulation*; and (d) the willingness to let go of old behaviors and skill sets that are no longer useful and latch onto ones now required, *behavioral flexibility*. Interestingly, those align very closely with the mechanisms proposed by Bell and Kozlowski (2010) as those that moderate active learning.

Learning Mindset—A Belief That Personal Change Is Possible

One of the elements most frequently mentioned throughout this book is "growth mindset," also described at times as "learning orientation" and "goal orientation." In Chapter 11, Heslin and Mellish suggest that "learning mode" is a metacompetency for learning agility. In Chapter 7, Lee suggests that mindfulness is closely aligned with growth mindset due to its focus on approaching all experiences with openness and curiosity. The far-from-new concept of "self-efficacy" also seems related to growth mindset. According to Bandura's (1977) theory of behavior change, it is self-efficacy that determines whether coping behavior will be initiated, effort expended, and sustained in the face of obstacles and aversive experiences.

Central to all of these concepts is *the belief that change is possible and under our personal control.* Without this mechanism in place, the likely consequences are inaction, resistance, and/or feelings of being a victim. The last sounds remarkably similar to the "Po-Po syndrome," joked about by talent managers, whereby leaders not identified as hipos (high potentials) retreat to a state of being passed over and pissed off! Ironically, those individuals who choose to leave the organization are exercising some personal control.

Cognitive Control and Flexibility—The Ability to Control and Shift Thinking

A second underlying mechanism of learning agility that surfaces throughout the chapters is related to cognitive control and flexibility. Metacognition, mindfulness, and vertical learning have all been noted as important to learning agility, and all involve voluntary control of thinking processes. For example, Lee (Chapter 7) and McCauley and Yost (Chapter 8) describe how we must be able to "move from the dance floor to the balcony," so that we have a broader, more expansive perspective on our experience. Anseel and Ong (Chapter 10) likewise describe how reflection allows us to shift from System 1 (fast) to System 2 (slow) thinking and make sense of our accumulation of experiences and abstract lessons from them. Vertical learning is about gaining perspective on how we are making sense of the world at multiple levels to reduce our "tethers to invisible forces" (Heaton, Chapter 17). In other words, we must be able to consciously control and shift *how* we are thinking and *what* we are thinking about.

Leaders' daily experiences are often driven by automatic, unconscious mental processes. Learning agility is about breaking the chains of automaticity (Harvey & Prager, Chapter 6). Mindfulness, metacognition, and vertical development all provide methods for taking voluntary control of our thinking processes rather than allowing these thinking processes to automatically dictate feelings and attitudes. Researchers are beginning to build connections between mindfulness and metacognition (e.g., Jankowski & Holas, 2014), suggesting they may share common underlying processes—*cognitive control and flexibility*. In a study of the nomonological net of learning agility, Allen (2016) observed that the strongest predictor of two different measures of learning agility was cognitive flexibility.

Likewise, "fluid intelligence" has been cited by Lombardo and Eichinger as a variable they considered when first defining learning agility (see Backword). Fluid intelligence is the ability to solve novel and abstract problems that do not depend on task-specific knowledge. In contrast, "crystalized intelligence" refers to the accumulation of knowledge, concrete skills, and facts. Whereas *fluid intelligence* is inductive and synergistic because conclusions do not mechanically follow from their premises, *crystallized intelligence* is deductive and additive because conclusions mechanically follow from their premises. It is believed that one's overall IQ (what psychologist's often refer to as the "g" factor) comprises fluid and crystallized intelligence (Cattell, 1963; Sternberg, 1982).

Fluid intelligence likely plays a role in the constellation of cognitive control processes that support learning agility. Some scholars have hypothesized that aspects of cognitive ability may influence learning agility by enabling faster information processing and increasing the ability to see patterns (e.g., DeRue et al., 2012). Other researchers have found little relationship between IQ and learning agility (Connolly & Viswesvaran, 2002; De Meuse, Dai, & Marshall, 2012). Perhaps a more focused measure of fluid intelligence—rather than assessing overall IQ—would correlate with learning agility. It may also be more fruitful to look at the relationships between specific facets of learning agility (e.g., "mental agility," "cognitive perspective") to determine whether they have higher relationships to cognitive ability (e.g., cognitive control and flexibility).

Emotional Regulation—The Capacity to Moderate Emotions

In the process of learning from experience and adapting to new situations, emotional regulation is another starring player (both as a villain and hero). Emotion is central to our motivation to learn by creating dissatisfaction or discomfort with the status quo (Heaton, Chapter 17). Clearly, emotionally uncomfortable, disequilibrating experiences can be a stimulus for learning (McCauley & Yost, Chapter 8). Likewise, positive emotions resulting from a clear purpose for our learning or from experiencing desired outcomes creates inspiration (McKenna & Minaker, Chapter 18).

Emotional regulation is also central to the *resilience* needed to deal with tough, new leadership challenges (Yost et al., Chapter 12). In Chapter 13, Peterson points out that the "ambiguity" and "uncertainly" elements of VUCA cause the emotions of fear, anxiety, and confusion. Ruyle posits that moving forward despite the perception of threat is the essence of brain-based development (Chapter 5). In addition, regulation of emotion is central to many of the strategies thought to positively influence learning agility discussed in this book. Some examples include (a) a primary aspect of mindfulness is its role in strengthening regulation of emotions (Lee, Chapter 7), (b) receptivity to feedback is impacted by emotions (Adler & Neiman, Chapter 9), and (c) reflection can increase feelings of emotional well-being (Anseel & Ong, Chapter 10).

Behavioral Flexibility—Letting Go and Latching Onto

One of the key findings from *The Lessons of Experience* study was the willingness of successful executives to "let go" of old behaviors and "latch onto" new ones (McCall et al., 1988). Those researchers discovered executives who derailed during their careers tended to cling to behaviors and technical skills that had led to their previous success, either not recognizing or being unwilling to learn new behaviors and leadership competencies needed in their new roles. Thus, this unwillingness or inability to change prevented them from altering their leadership behaviors. Successful executives, on the other hand, transformed themselves by latching onto the leadership behaviors and skill sets required for their new roles.

There are several studies that have found the roles of leaders, and the competencies required to perform those roles, change as they advance up the organizational ladder (e.g., De Meuse, Dai, & Wu, 2011; Kaiser, Craig, Overfield, & Yarborough, 2011). In an expansive review of the literature, Hogan, Hogan, and Kaiser (2011) found that fully one half of all managers fail. Further, research has shown nearly 40% of internal job moves involving hipos end in failure (Martin & Schmidt, 2010). An underlying reason for much of this derailment likely can be traced to reliance on behaviors and competencies that once were needed but now hinder leader success. The need for the behavioral flexibility is captured in Charan, Drotter, and Noel's (2001) concept of the "leadership pipeline" as well as Lombardo and Eichinger's *The Leadership Machine* (2002). The title of Marshall Goldsmith's book, *What Got You Here Won't Get You There* (Goldsmith, 2007) also reinforces the need for behavioral flexibility in leaders. Overall, the behavioral transformation process of letting go and latching on as one assumes new leadership roles is central to learning agility.

Learning Agility Is a Dynamic Process

Many of the chapter authors propose process-oriented models to explicate learning agility or facets of learning agility. There appears to be a pull toward conceptualizing agile learning as something that happens in stages or phases that have some logical sequence. Table 19.3 provides a synthesis of various stages suggested by different authors. While there is little empirical evidence to support any one specific model at this time, a logical sequence of steps in practicing learning agility is likely to include (a) anticipating and identifying what needs to be learned, (b) developing a plan and strategies for achieving learning goals, (c) initiating action, (d) self-regulating and monitoring learning, and (e) fully integrating lessons learned.

Learning Agility Can Be Developed

A question sometimes asked: "Isn't the development of learning agility simply just leadership development?" Developing learning agility is certainly

Table 19.3 Learning Agility as a Process

Stage	Descriptors Used by Authors in the Book
Anticipating Needs	• Anticipate: McCauley & Yost, Chapter 8 • Approach: Lee, Chapter 7 • Identify need: Harvey & Prager, Chapter 6
Planning for Change	• Approach: Heslin & Mellish, Chapter 11 • Plan for change: Harvey & Prager, Chapter 6
Taking Action	• Adapting: McCauley & Yost, Chapter 8 • Initiate action: Lee, Chapter 7 • Action: Heslin & Mellish, Chapter 11 • Implement change: Harvey & Prager, Chapter 6
Self-Regulating	• Regulate and monitor: Harvey & Prager, Chapter 6
Integration of Learning	• Reflection: McCauley & Yost, Chapter 8; Heslin & Mellish, Chapter 11 • Integration, abstraction of lessons: Lee, Chapter 7

an important part of leadership development, but it has a narrower focus. Leadership development encompasses any of the myriad skills required to be effective as a leader, such as strategic thinking, time management, priority setting, or talent development.

In contrast, the development of learning agility involves understanding the learning agile process (Figure 6.1; Harvey & Prager, Chapter 6), as well as where, when, and how to deploy relevant learning behaviors and strategies to facilitate more nimble adaptation. As leaders increase their learning agility, they become more capable of regulating their own learning—regardless of the skill du jour that is required—and integrating learning it into their daily work. It can be considered a "meta-competency" that supports accelerated development in multiple areas of leadership.

There are likely factors that predispose individuals toward developing learning agility more readily (e.g., personality traits, cognitive ability, parenting practices, being exposed to an enriched and diverse environment as a child). However, learning agility requires actually implementing behaviors and strategies that can be learned and developed, as is the case with most talents. If someone is musically inclined, we cannot assume that he or she can play the piano without additional learning! While measures of learning agility reflect a leader's level of learning agility *at a particular point in time*, the level may increase or decrease over time. Unfortunately, limited research currently exists. Nevertheless, the development of learning agility can likely be accelerated through focus, effort, dedication, discipline, coaching, and a nurturing environment. As a starting point, leaders must be aware of learning agility, its importance to their success, and steps they can personally take to become more learning agile. The chapters in Section II offer a wealth of practical ideas for developing learning agility.

As described in Section III, the development of learning agility is likely supported or stunted by environmental conditions. Given the importance of learning agility to leadership success, organizations would be wise to invest in its development at all levels of leadership. While much more research is needed on organization-level impact, development of learning agility is likely to translate to greater organizational agility. We posit organizations that support learning agility and provide the conditions that nurture it will be more likely to thrive in the turbulent years ahead. Perhaps a silver lining of the pandemic will be increased awareness of the importance of leaders who can quickly learn and adapt.

Likewise, developing learning agility may result in higher levels of engagement and well-being. For example, Anseel and Ong in Chapter 10 cite evidence that reflection can reduce stress and lower blood pressure. In a recent *Harvard Business Review* article, Zao-Sanders and Schveninger asserted that we sometimes forget the joy sparked by learning: "There is an illumination of the unknown, as beams of light fall on hidden secrets and treasures. There's the awareness of a new capability and the freedom and independence that may bring—the power to deal better with the big uncertain world" (2020, p. 3).

Applying the Lessons Learned

As previously indicated, research tends to lag practice. Nevertheless, we were able to identify some key implications for the application of learning agility within organizations based on existing research and the experience of this volume's authors. They are divided into the following four categories:

- implications for fostering a learning agile organizational culture;
- implications for talent management professionals;
- implications for managers; and
- implications for leadership coaches.

Implications for Organizational Culture

It is clear from the chapters and case studies that organizational culture plays a significant role in supporting or suppressing learning agility. As defined by Schein, culture is "a pattern of shared basic assumptions that was learned by a group as it solved its problems of external adaptation and internal integration" (2004, p. 17). It includes shared beliefs, values, and assumptions about how things work in the organization. Those aspects of culture that appear most important to supporting learning agility include (a) creating psychological safety, (b) promoting a growth mindset, (c) encouraging experimentation, and (d) valuing learning agility.

Creating Psychological Safety

Psychological safety is especially important for learning agility. Many of the behaviors associated with learning agility (e.g., experimentation, risk-taking, asking for help, feedback seeking) require a psychologically safe work environment. When individuals feel safe, they are more likely to admit mistakes, ask questions, and demonstrate vulnerability. A growing number of studies support the importance of psychological safety for learning within organizations (see Edmondson, 2019). In Chapter 17, Heaton emphasizes the importance of providing a "psychologically safe container" where individuals can be vulnerable and explore perspectives and emotions. However, creating a psychologically safe environment should not be confused with "anything goes." It is important that organizations set clear boundaries; learning cannot be an excuse for inappropriate behavior or impulsive risk-taking. In Chapter 15, Stomski and Jensen provide a great example of how psychological safety has been embedded in Walmart's culture while maintaining accountability.

Promoting a Growth Mindset

Numerous organizations are beginning to promote the concept of "learning orientation" or "growth mindset." Some organizations have even connected a growth mindset culture with their business strategy (Harvard Business Review Staff, 2014). In a recent *Forbes* article, Childs (2019) advised, "A growth mindset environment can't merely be a branding campaign without engagement and substance. It also needs to be part of your organization's overall business strategy." Microsoft, for example, has deliberately created a growth mindset culture (Dweck & Hogan, 2016). Several case studies in this book emphasize a growth mindset as part of their learning agility initiatives (Ultimate Software, Case A; Procter & Gamble, Case B; IBM, Case D; and Fosun, Case G).

Encouraging Experimentation

Curiosity, experimentation, risk-taking, and learning agility go hand in hand. By creating a culture of experimentation, organizations not only enhance learning agility but also accelerate continuous improvement. Thomke (2020) suggested organizations should encourage the creation of hypotheses, provide resources for experimentation, and have leaders display intellectual humility when testing new ideas. Learning agility is likely to blossom in climates that encourage leaders to look at the world through the lens of a scientist and view daily experiences as opportunities to experiment, test hypotheses, and reflect on cause-and-effect relationships.

Valuing Learning Agility

Another primary way for organizations to build a culture focused on learning agility is by demonstrating that key executives value it. Chapter 16 (Leisten & Donohue) provides a good illustration of how companies best known for developing leaders emphasize learning agile behaviors such as self-awareness and resilience. They have built ecosystems promoted by senior leaders around learning agility. Virtually all the case studies demonstrate how learning agility was valued by employees throughout the organization and especially their senior leaders.

Table 19.4 provides examples of some of the norms, values, and beliefs likely to foster a culture supportive of learning agility.

Implications for Talent Management Practices

Learning agility can be integrated into virtually all essential talent management practices. As stated by Church in Chapter 3, "It is a seemingly obvious conclusion that the concept of learning agility is and/or should be a core component of any successful TM system." In Chapter 14, Ruyle, De Meuse,

Table 19.4 Factors That Support a Culture of Learning Agility

Norms	Beliefs	Values
• Openness to admitting mistakes • Acknowledgment that mistakes are an inevitable part of learning • Encouragement for experimentation and taking risks • Learning from others is promoted • Learning agile behaviors such as reflection mindfulness and resilience are supported • Leaders consistently promote learning from experience among their direct reports • Learning agile behavior is demonstrated by leaders at all levels	• Mistakes are an opportunity to learn • Candid, constructive feedback is a "gift" • Asking for help is a strength not a weakness • It is okay not to have all the answers and ask questions • Learning from experience is an integral part of work and life • Failures do not have to carry a stigma	• Learning is rewarded in addition to performance • Behaviors that support the learning of others are recognized • Learning from mistakes is considered an aspect of effective performance • Forecasting future capability needs is expected • Diverse perspectives are valued • Diversity of thought is considered a strength

and Hughley describe how learning agile organizations implement talent management practices that integrate learning agility. The following is a brief summary of some of the ways learning agility can be incorporated in talent management.

Job Analysis, Position Descriptions, and Job Design

The world is shifting, jobs are becoming increasingly complex, and technology growth and globalization are unprecedented. The pace of change requires that virtually all employees are adaptable, can reskill, and can learn new job competencies. Organizations today hire not only "hands" but also "brains" (see Chapter 1). However, as discussed previously in this chapter, not all roles require equal levels of learning agility. A more nuanced approach is to ask what degree and facets of learning agility are required for various positions and various managerial levels. Consequently, we may need to update our methods for analyzing jobs and determining the optimal level of learning agility based on the role, organization, and stage of organizational growth. For example, HumRRO (2020) suggested "Job Analysis 2.0" using artificial intelligence to profile jobs to more systematically track shifts in the importance of job requirements, identify emerging requirements, and automatically refresh job profiles.

It will also be useful for position descriptions to move beyond the typical knowledge, skills, and ability requirements and identify the competencies *learned* from the experiences encountered in particular roles (e.g., leading through crisis, turning around a failing business unit). As several contributors note, organizations should design roles specifically for the purpose of developing needed capabilities (e.g., Heslin & Mellish, Chapter 11). Many companies apply the 9-box model to evaluate talent and systematically provide developmental activities based on which box an employees is ascribed (Harvey & Prager, Chapter 6; McCauley & Yost, Chapter 8). Indeed, the purpose of "stretch assignments" is to develop employees on specific leadership competencies (e.g., international engagements to learn different cultural mores and business practices).

Assessment, Selection, and Succession Planning

Given the robust relationship between learning agility and leader success (De Meuse & Harvey, Chapter 1; Church, Chapter 3), it would seem prudent for virtually all organizations to assess learning agility for the selection and development of both internal and external leadership candidates. In Chapter 4, Boyce and Boyce provide a useful overview of commercially available measures and guidance for implementing the assessment of learning agility. Ruyle and his coauthors provide several valuable suggestions in Chapter 14. In addition, the application of multiple methods to measure learning agility (e.g., self-assessments, multirater surveys, interviews, simulations) can further enhance measurement accuracy. Many of the case studies provide examples of how assessments have been successfully used to support organizational needs.

We may also want to rethink the language used when describing leaders being groomed for higher level roles. As Heslin and Mellish point out in Chapter 11, labeling individuals as "hipos," "stars," or "legends" may inadvertently invoke a fixed rather than a growth mindset. These authors suggest using language that frames individuals in terms of the behaviors or strategies they use. For example, "consistently demonstrates learning agile behaviors" certainly conveys the message that learning agility is malleable and can be modified with attention and effort.

Onboarding, Organizational Development, and Learning

Naturally, the assessment of learning agility can be leveraged for the development of the leadership pipeline. As noted by Harvey and Prager in Chapter 6, organizations can ill afford to select only leaders who are highly learning agile. Scores on various facets of learning agility can serve as valuable feedback as part of an onboarding process. Church also suggests in Chapter 3 that incorporating learning agility more broadly into internal development processes can have compelling benefits. And, providing opportunities to learn mindfulness, feedback seeking, and reflection need not be complicated or expensive! It is hoped in the years ahead we will have a deeper understanding of how to implement such programs to develop learning agility, including strategies for tailoring them to accommodate individual differences.

While some organizations offer developmental assignments specifically for the purpose of creating more opportunities to learn from experience, it seems to be more the exception than the rule. Organizations will benefit from identifying developmental experiences big and small. Simulations can also provide experiences with low risk (e.g., see Case Studies B and F). Given that diverse and varied job experiences are key to enhancing agility (Peterson, Chapter 13), it is essential that assignment to those most potent stretch experiences be doled out fairly. Unfortunately, as McCauley and Yost note (Chapter 8), inequities still exist. The development of learning agility can be highly empowering and has the potential to increase the representation of those who are underrepresented in the leadership ranks.

Most organizations already make extensive use of mentors and coaches. The value of these relationships could potentially be amplified by ensuring that these "guides" are well versed in how to develop and encourage learning agile behaviors. In addition, the accessibility of media can facilitate more vicarious learning by leaders sharing their own learning journeys and experiences via videos and podcasts.

Performance Management, Rewards, and Recognition

Unfortunately, too many leaders and employees still associate feedback primarily with formal performance evaluations. Organizations will benefit from encouraging both *giving* and *seeking* feedback as a daily part of work to quell the notion feedback is only part of formal reviews (Ruyle et al., Chapter 14). Because many individuals find giving and receiving feedback uncomfortable at first, this learning agile behavior may require regular re-inforcement. Providing simple feedback models such as the situation, behavior, impact model can be helpful in supporting a feedback-rich culture (Adler & Neiman, Chapter 9).

Performance management is a means of holding leaders accountable for doing what the organization views as valuable. If learning agility is really valued, formal performance reviews should include evaluating leaders on how well they demonstrate learning agility and the extent to which they encourage it among members within their teams. However, it is essential for this to be conducted in a way that does not exacerbate fixed mindsets. This often requires leaders to be reminded that performance and learning are not two separate objectives. As McCauley and Yost note in Chapter 8, most development happens *through* work experiences. Thus, learning and performing are one and the same! Learning agility truly must become a way of life for leaders, with acumen in learning agility valued equally with other key leadership capabilities (Leisten & Donohue, Chapter 16).

Implications for Managers

Immediate managers are in an especially key position to promote and support learning agility among those who report to them. While by no means exhaustive, the list that follows provides several practical ways managers can incorporate learning into their daily work.

- Modeling learning agile behavior. One of the best ways for leaders to encourage learning agility is by walking the talk. It may involve being vulnerable about their own mistakes or opportunities for development.
- Encouraging a "community of learners" within their team and being mindful of the importance of social support in the learning process (Yost et al., Chapter 12).
- Developing a "feedback-rich" culture where everyone knows how to provide effective feedback and is encouraged and expected to both give and receive it (Adler & Neiman, Chapter 9; Ruyle et al., Chapter 14).

- Understanding what motivates and uniquely inspires learning for each leader (McKenna & Minaker, Chapter 18).
- Making after-event reviews part of normal operating procedures and emphasizing the value of mistakes as opportunities to learn. Encouraging the same kind of reflection on an individual basis and allowing time to do it (Anseel & Ong, Chapter 10).
- Consistently embedding messages and cues related to learning agility in the environment (McCauley & Yost, Chapter 8), for example, sharing an important lesson learned at each staff meeting or posting messages that encourage a learning mindset. Heslin and Mellish (Chapter 11) advise managers to convey the message that we all are a "work in progress."
- Giving adequate focus to "learning and adaptive performance" versus solely tactical performance (Peterson, Chapter 13). Hold direct reports accountable for learning as much as any other important performance goal. Encourage them to think about how learning can be embedded within everyday tasks (e.g., feedback seeking, deliberate practice, reflection).
- Consistently looking for opportunities to provide other leaders with stretch experiences large and small and providing the support and coaching needed to maximize learning from the experience (McCauley & Yost, Chapter 8). Be aware of how special assignments outside one's own department are made within the organization (Harvey & Prager, Chapter 6).
- Actively encouraging learning from others by pointing out role models or making connections with those who can provide mentoring or "micromentoring" (Harvey & Prager, Chapter 6).
- Promoting behaviors that support resilience, not only for physical well-being but also for their importance in becoming learning agile (Yost et al., Chapter 12).
- Guarding against fixed-mindset language in themselves first and then coaching team members to change their own "self-talk." For example, Childs (2019) suggested trying to transition members of the team from fixed-mindset languages such as "This is impossible," "I am terrible at . . .," or "I can't . . . ," to more growth-mindset messages like "It will be difficult, but it will get easier" or "I can't . . . *yet.*"

Clearly, there are many ways managers can develop learning agility within their teams. And, as described in the previous section, managers should be recognized and rewarded for doing so.

Implications for Leadership Coaches

Traditionally, leadership coaching has tended to focus on the development of managers in specific areas, either to prepare them for future roles or to prevent derailment in their current role. Coaching also can play a critical role in the development of learning agility (see Case Study F). In addition to supporting individuals in learning from current experiences, coaches can deliberately teach learning agile behaviors and habits along the way. For example, coaches typically encourage reflection. However, they likewise can emphasize it as a habit to be developed to support long-term learning agility. The development of questioning skills can be highlighted as a capability essential to both leadership *and* learning agility. There are significant opportunities to transform coaching to *learning agility* coaching.

When examining personality profiles and other assessment data to identify implications for leadership behavior, coaches can look simultaneously for factors that may help or hinder learning agility. For example, someone more introverted may require greater encouragement to pursue opportunities that involve learning from others. Someone naturally higher in anxiety may require more support when engaging in stretch experiences. Someone who is highly conscientious can leverage this strength within the learning agile process to overcome a lower degree of openness to new experiences. An achievement-oriented perfectionist may need more reminders to focus on learning and not only short-term performance.

Where Empirical Research Is Needed

While we have come a long way in our understanding of learning agility, many opportunities for research still exist. In this section, we outline the value of developing an agreed-upon nomonological net and highlight some of the most critical questions to be addressed by future researchers.

Learning Agility's Nomonological Net

One of the most vexing problems in learning agility science is the confounding circularity of how it has been investigated. As pointed out by Church in Chapter 3, learning agility has been applied as a predictor, a process, and an outcome in various studies. Similarly, McCauley and Yost (Chapter 8) describe how stretch experiences can be viewed as an antecedent, a moderator, or an outcome. Boyce and Boyce (Chapter 4) also note that research on learning agility often confounds the predictor and the criterion. For example, learning agility is commonly used as a predictor of leadership potential. In the adaptive performance literature, learning agility has been presented as a moderator of adaptive performance.

In addition, the manner by which learning agility has been measured varies among studies. Some studies have used multirater methods, some have used interviews, and some have used self-assessments. For those studies that have employed self-assessments, the specific instrument used to measure learning agility varied. Some researchers have used *viaEDGE*™, while others have used the *TALENTx7*, the *Burke Learning Agility Inventory*™, or created their own self-assessment. Each of those measures assess learning agility a little differently (e.g., some assess five, seven, or nine dimensions of the construct). The measurement of the criterion variable also varies across studies. Moreover, in a few multirater studies, the same supervisors who are evaluating the participants' learning agility also are rating the participants' leadership potential. De Meuse (2017) examined those issues in detail.

Perhaps the most important step we can take is to clarify the nomonological net surrounding the learning agility construct. Figure 19.1 provides an initial attempt to do just that. The model presents the following:

- Factors that may predispose leaders to be more or less learning agile such as personality, cognitive abilities, fluid intelligence, demographic variables and childhood experiences
- Central mechanisms such as learning mindset, cognitive control, emotional regulation and behavioral flexibility that potentially mediate predisposing factors and the effectiveness of various learning agile behaviors strategies
- The behaviors and strategies that accelerate the development of learning agility (e.g., asking for feedback, engaging in reflection)
- The role of environmental conditions for enhancing or suppressing learning agility (e.g., psychological safety)
- Both proximal outcomes (e.g., leader performance, leader potential) as well as possible distal outcomes (e.g., organizational agility)

It is our hope the model will stimulate more rigorous and systematic research examining the role that learning agility plays in the identification,

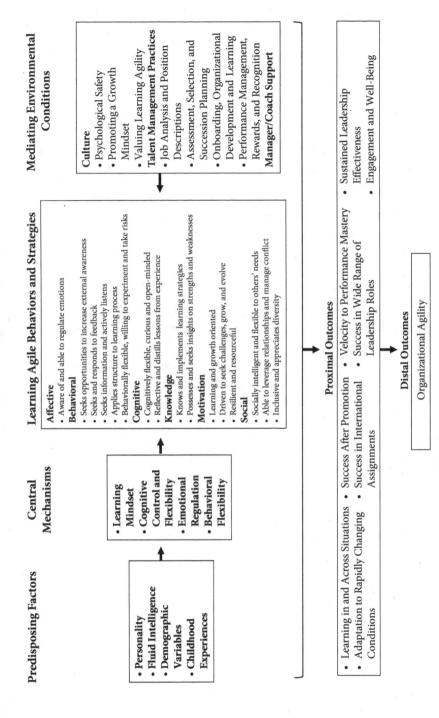

Figure 19.1 The nomonological net of learning agility.

selection, and development of leaders. The depiction of predisposing factors, central mechanisms, behaviors/strategies, mediating environmental conditions, and outcomes should offer a foundation of variables and relationships for future research to explore.

Critical Questions for Research

Dozens of rich opportunities for research are presented throughout the various chapters of this book. These can be approached most effectively through an organizing framework such as the nomonological net proposed in Figure 19.1. In Table 19.5, we summarize some of the most significant questions to examine. Greater consensus on definitions of variables will greatly enhance our ability to build the empirical evidence required to clarify the construct and test various relationships among variables. In addition, more research is needed similar to the study conducted by Lim, Yoo, Kim, and Brickell (2017), which explored the mediating role of learning agility with other related constructs, such as adaptive performance, transformative learning, and learning organization.

As can be seen from the case studies and examples shared in this book, there is a wealth of opportunities for collecting data. However, what may be needed is a better process for connecting scholars who possess the time and resources to conduct empirical data analysis with talent management professionals who have the data available to them in their organizations.

There appears to be a golden opportunity for those of us who are scientist–practitioners. Perhaps we can serve as a bridge. We can develop protocols for collecting data in ways to protect the confidentiality of individual participants as well as to protect the competitive edge of those companies investing in learning agility activities. We should work jointly with talent management functions and leadership development teams to study learning agility with a planned methodology to enable clearer causality links to be made.

Conclusion

To a cynic, learning agility is not a construct at all. It is simply, as the proverbial saying goes, "old wine in a new bottle." It is a confounded mixture

Table 19.5 Questions to Be Addressed by Future Researchers

Variables	Questions to Be Addressed
Predisposing Factors	• Which aspects of personality contribute most to learning agility overall? • How do various personality attributes and profiles of attributes help or hinder each type of learning agile behavior? • Do certain learning agile behaviors work more effectively for some personality types than others? • What aspects of learning agility are most helped or hindered by cognitive functioning and/or emotional intelligence? • Are there differences in learning agility for different demographic groups (e.g., age, gender, ethnic group, upbringing, and childhood experiences)?
Central Mechanisms	• What are the specific relationships between the central mechanisms of learning mindset, cognitive control, emotional regulation, and behavioral flexibility on each of the learning agile behaviors/strategies? • What are the interrelationships among these central mechanisms?
Learning Agile Behaviors and Strategies	• Which behaviors and strategies have the greatest impact on outcome measures? • Which contribute most to acceleration of learning? • What is the incremental value of particular learning agile behaviors used in combination or in a particular sequence? • How do we measure the acquisition and development of learning agile behavior? • Do learning strategies have a differential impact based on demographic factors? • What approaches are most effective in developing learning agile behavior (e.g., coaching, formal training?)
Mediating Environmental Conditions	• Which cultural attributes and talent management practices are most important to supporting learning ability? • Which leadership and coaching behaviors most encourage learning agility? • What is the incremental impact of various environmental conditions (e.g., culture, talent management practices, manager/coach support?)
Outcomes	• What outcome measures are most critical to focus on? • Does learning agility impact some outcome measures more than others? • For what roles or situations is learning agility detrimental? • What are the relationships among various outcome measures? • Are leadership agility and organizational agility distal outcomes of increased learning agility?

of independent and dependent variables. The construct lacks conceptual clarity. There are no theoretical underpinnings to support it. Instruments used to assess it lack consistency, reliability, and validity. There is no science supporting the presence or value of learning agility.

To the contrary, it is important for us to remember *the construct of learning agility is only 20 years old*. Contrast that timeline to the study of intelligence and personality. The measurement of intelligence can be traced back to the early 1900s when French psychologist Alfred Binet developed a test to evaluate a child's ability to succeed in school. General mental ability testing was used during World War I to select soldiers in the Army. The study of personality has a much longer history, dating back to Plato and Aristotle. Gordon Allport published his classic book on personality more than 80 years ago, sharing his vision for how personality should be systematically studied within the social sciences (Allport, 1937).

It was two practitioner psychologists by the names of Eichinger and Lombardo who asked the basic question, "How can organizations do a better job at predicting who will make successful leaders?" They argued, "Identifying those who can learn to behave in new ways requires a different measure strategy from those often used, one that looks at the characteristics of the learning agile" (Lombardo & Eichinger, 2000, p. 321). The measurement of learning agility remained largely in the business world for the first 10 years. A journal article by De Meuse, Dai, and Hallenbeck (2010) published 10 years later created some interest in the academic community. Two years later, a series of articles published in the journal of *Industrial and Organizational Psychology* spawned additional interest (e.g., De Meuse, Dai, Swisher, Eichinger, & Lombardo, 2012; DeRue et al., 2012). Nevertheless, scholars are just beginning to investigate the construct of learning agility in earnest.

In the Foreword of this book, Dave Ulrich asserts "the science and practice of learning agility has evolved from some clever observations to elegant theory to rigorous science to shaping the world around us." Dave was gracious and generous in his acclaim. However, there is so much opportunity still ahead. And at a time when agility is indispensable. It is our hope as editors that we have laid some groundwork to help learning agility achieve that lofty status of shaping—and healing—our world.

References

Allen, J. (2016). *Conceptualizing learning agility and investigating its nomonological network*. (Unpublished doctoral dissertation). Florida International University, Miami. doi:10.25148/etd.FIDC000747

Allport, G. W. (1937). *Personality: A psychological interpretation*. New York, NY: Holt.

Baard, S., Rench, T., & Kozlowski (2014). Performance adaptation: A theoretical integration and review. *Journal of Management, 40*(1), 48–99.

Bandura, A. (1977). Self-efficacy: Toward a unifying theory of behavioral change. *Psychological Review, 84*(2), 191–215. https://doi.org/10.1037/0033-295X.84.2.191

Bell, B. S., & Kozlowski, S. (2010). Toward a theory of learning centered training design: An integrative framework of active learning. In S. W. Kozlowski & E. Salas (Eds.), *Learning, training, and development in organizations* (pp. 261–298). New York, NY: Routledge.

Benton, M., & Radziwill, N. (2011, August 7–13). A path for exploring the agile organizing framework in technology education. Agile Conference (pp. 131–134). Salt Lake City, UT. Retrieved from https://ieeexplore.ieee.org/document/6005494

Cattell, R. B. (1963). Theory of fluid and crystallized intelligence: A critical experiment. *Journal of Educational Psychology, 54*, 1–22. doi:org/10.1037/h0046743

Charan, R. (2008). *Leaders at all levels: Deepening your talent pool to solve the succession crisis*. San Francisco, CA: Wiley.

Charan, R., Drotter, S. J., & Noel, J. L. (2001). *The leadership pipeline: How to build the leadership-powered company*. San Francisco, CA: Jossey-Bass.

Childs, S. (2019). Why a growth mindset should be a part of your overall business strategy. *Forbes*. Retrieved from https://www.forbes.com/sites/forbeshumanresourcescouncil/2019/09/16/why-a-growth-mindset-should-be-a-part-of-your-overall-business-strategy/#4ad252c66a8a

Connolly, J. A., & Viswesvaran, C. (2002, April). Assessing the construct validity of a measure of learning agility. Paper presented at the Society for Industrial and Organizational Psychology Conference, Toronto.

De Meuse, K. P. (2017). Learning agility: Its evolution as a psychological construct and its empirical relationship to leader success. *Consulting Psychology Journal: Practice and Research, 69*, 267–295.

De Meuse, K. P. (2019). A meta-analysis of the relationship between learning agility and leader success. *Journal of Organizational Psychology, 19*, 25–34.

De Meuse, K. P., Dai, G., & Hallenbeck, G. S. (2010). Learning agility: A construct whose time has come. *Consulting Psychology Journal: Practice and Research, 62*, 119–130.

De Meuse, K. P., Dai, G., & Marshall, S. (2012). *The relationship between learning agility, critical thinking, and job performance: Engineers and project managers*. Minneapolis, MN: Lominger International.

De Meuse, K. P., Dai, G., Swisher, V. V., Eichinger, R. W., & Lombardo, M. M. (2012). Leadership development: Exploring, clarifying, and expanding our understanding of learning agility. *Industrial and Organizational Psychology: Perspectives on Science and Practice, 5*, 280–286.

De Meuse, K. P., Dai, G., & Wu, J. (2011). Leadership skills across organizational levels: A closer examination. *The Psychologist-Manager Journal, 14*, 120–139.

De Meuse, K. P., Dai, G., Zewdie, S., Page, R. C., Clark, L., & Eichinger, R. W. (2011, April). Development and validation of a self-assessment of learning agility. Paper presented at the Society for Industrial and Organizational Psychology Conference, Chicago, IL.

De Meuse, K. P., Lim, J., & Rao, R. (2019). *The development and validation of the TALENTx7® Assessment: A psychological measure of learning agility* (3rd ed.). Shanghai, China: Leader's Gene Consulting.

Denning, S. (2016). What is agile? *Forbes*. Retrieved from https://www.forbes.com/sites/stevedenning/2016/08/13/what-is-agile/#30f4058426e3

DeRue, D. S., Ashford, S. J., & Myers, C. G. (2012). Learning agility: In search of conceptual clarity and theoretical grounding. *Industrial and Organizational Psychology: Perspectives on Science and Practice, 5,* 258–279.

Dweck, C., & Hogan, K. (2016). How Microsoft uses a growth mindset to develop leaders. *Harvard Business Review*. Retrieved from https://hbr.org/2016/10/how-microsoft-uses-a-growth-mindset-to-develop-leaders

Edmondson, A. (2019). *The fearless organization*. Hoboken NJ: Wiley.

Goldsmith, M. (2007). *What got you here won't get you there: How successful people become even more successful*. New York, NY: Hyperion Books.

Harsch, K., & Festing, M. (2020). Dynamic talent management capabilities and organizational agility—A qualitative exploration. *Human Resource Management, 59*(11), 43–61. https://doi.org/10.1002/hrm.21972

Harvard Business Review Staff. (2014). How companies can profit from a "growth mindset." *Harvard Business Review*. Retrieved from https://hbr.org/2014/11/how-companies-can-profit-from-a-growth-mindset

Hogan, J., Hogan, R., & Kaiser, R. B. (2011). Management derailment. *APA Handbook of Industrial and Organizational Psychology, Vol 3: Maintaining, Expanding, and Contracting the Organization*, 555–575. doi:10.1037/12171-015.

HumRRO. (2020). Job analysis 2.0: Mapping the pace of change. Retrieved from https://www.humrro.org/corpsite/article/job-analysis-mapping-the-pace-of-change/

Jankowski, T., & Holas, P. (2014). Metacognitive model of mindfulness. *Consciousness and Cognition, 28,* 64–80. doi:10.1016/j.concog.2014.06.005

Joiner, B. (2019). Leadership agility for organizational agility. *Journal of Creating Value, 5*(2), 139–149. https://doi.org/10.1177/2394964319868321

Kaiser, R. B., Craig, S. B., Overfield, D., & Yarborough, P. (2011). Differences in managerial jobs at the bottom, middle, and top: A review of empirical research. *The Psychologist-Manager Journal, 14*(20), 76–91. doi:10.1080/10887156.2011.570137

Kaiser, R. B., & Overfield, D. V. (2011). Strengths, strengths overused, and lopsided leadership. *Journal of Consulting Psychology: Practice and Research, 65,* 89–109.

Kaiser, R., & Curphy, G. (2013). Leadership development: The failure of an industry and an opportunity for consulting psychologists. *Consulting Psychology Journal: Practice and Research, 65*(4), 294–302.

Kegan, R. (1994). *In over our heads*. Cambridge, MA: Harvard University Press.

Kotlyar, I., & Karakowsky, L. (2014), Sources of satisfaction with high-potential employee programs: A survey of Canadian HR professionals. *Journal of Management Development, 33*(10), 1035–1056. https://doi.org/10.1108/JMD-08-2012-0113

Lim, D., Yoo, M., Kim, J., & Brickell, S. (2017, April). Learning agility: The nexus between learning organization, transformative learning, and adaptive performance.

Adult Education Research Conference, Norman, OK. Retrieved from https://newprairiepress.org/aerc/2017/papers/28

Lombardo, M. M., & Eichinger, R. W. (2000). High-potentials as high learners. *Human Resource Management, 39,* 321–329.

Lombardo, M. M., & Eichinger, R. W. (2002). *The leadership machine: Architecture to develop leaders for any future.* Minneapolis, MN: Lominger.

Longmuss, J., Höhne, B., Bräutigam, S., Oberländer, A., & Schindler, F. (2016, September). Agile learning—Bridging the gap between industry and university. Proceedings of the 44th SEFI Conference, Tampere, Finland. Retrieved from https://www.sustainum.de/wp-content/uploads/2016/11/SEFI_Agile-Learning_paper.pdf

Macmillan Dictionary. (2020). Leader [Web log post]. Retrieved from http://www.macmillandictionaryblog.com/leader

Martin, J., & Schmidt, C. (2010). How to keep your top talent. *Harvard Business Review, 88*(5), 2–8.

McCall, M. W., Jr., & Lombardo, M. M. (1983). *Off the track: Why and how successful executives get derailed.* Greensboro, NC: Center for Creative Leadership.

McCall, M. W., Jr., Lombardo, M. M., & Morrison, A. M. (1988). *The lessons of experience: How successful executives develop on the job.* New York, NY: Free Press.

Merriam-Webster.com. (2020). Adaptation. Retrieved from https://www. merriam-webster.com/dictionary/adaptation

Morrison, A., White, R., & Van Velsor, E. (1987). *Breaking the glass ceiling: Can women reach the top of America's largest corporations?* Reading, MA: Addison-Wesley.

Overeem, B. (2015). The scrum master as a coach. Retrieved from https://www.scrum.org/resources/blog/scrum-master-coach-0

Pulakos, E., & Kantrowitz, T. (2020). How performance management must change to drive organizational agility and high performance. In E. Pulakos & M. Battista (Eds.), *Performance management transformation: Lessons learned and next steps* (pp. 211–232). New York, NY: Oxford University Press.

Pulakos, E., Kantrowitz, T., & Schneider, B. (2019). What leads to organizational agility: It's not what you think. *Consulting of Psychology Journal: Practice and Research, 71*(4), 305–320.

Rigby, D., Elk, S., & Berez, S. (2020). The agile c-suite: A new approach to leadership for the team at the top. *Harvard Business Review.* Retrieved from https://hbr.org/2020/05/the-agile-c-suite?utm_medium=email&utm_source=newsletter_perissue&utm_campaign=bestofissue_activesubs_notdigital&deliveryName=DM76718

Schein, E. (2004). *Organizational culture and leadership.* San Francisco, CA: Jossey Bass.

Snell, R. (1992). Experiential learning at work: Why can't it be painless? *Personnel Review, 21,* 12–26. http://dx.doi.org/10.1108/EUM0000000000806

Sternberg, R. J. (1982). *Handbook of human intelligence.* New York, NY: Cambridge University Press.

Taleb, N. N. (2007). *The black swan: The impact of the highly improbable.* New York, NY: Random House.

Thomke, S. (2020). Building a culture of experimentation. *Harvard Business Review, 98*(2), 40–48.

Wang, S., & Beir, M. (2012). Learning agility: Not much is new. *Industrial and Organizational Psychology: Perspectives on Science and Practice, 5,* 293–296.

Westfall, C. (2019). Leadership development is a $366 billion industry: Here's why most programs don't work. *Forbes*. Retrieved from https://www.forbes.com/sites/chriswestfall/2019/06/20/leadership-development-why-most-programs-dont-work/#4ffd749f61de

Zao-Sanders, M., & Schveninger, C. (2020). The simple joy of learning on the job. *Harvard Business Review*. Retrieved from https://hbr.org/2020/03/the-simple-joy-of-learning-on-the-job

20

Learning Agility in Action

Case Studies

Case Authors

Tanya Castiglione Andrews is UKG's pioneer internal executive coach. She leads the practice of strategic leader assessment and development. For 25 years, her passion has been customizing individual development to drive the leadership pipeline and support business priorities.

Sarah Brock is global head of talent assessment, performance, and succession management at Johnson & Johnson. She holds a PhD in industrial and organizational psychology from the University of Tulsa and a bachelor's degree in psychology and Spanish from Wellesley College.

Marilyn Buckner has been a consultant for more than 20 years and owner of NTS Inc. She is a Master Trainer for several assessments, including *TALENTx7*®, *Hogan*, and *StyleView*. Formerly, she was head of succession planning at Coca-Cola and board chair of *HR People + Strategy*.

Joshua D. Bush leads Procter & Gamble's high-potential program. In P&G's Talent Management Center of Excellence, Josh also designs, measures, and experiments in areas like workforce planning, succession, career pathing, and diversity and inclusion.

Yolanda de Beer, a registered organizational psychologist, has a deep passion for psychometrics and all things new. As a partner at the Kaya Group, she supports the team with the tools and systems to make a difference in the lives of clients.

Daniel Hallak is the chief commercial officer for WiLD Leaders Inc. He is an expert in coaching and leader development who speaks at countless events and conferences. His work focuses on whole leader development and building authentic relationships.

Alison M. Hartmann is part of the global leadership assessment team at IBM. She is the portfolio lead for a number of internal assessment initiatives. She holds a master's degree in management, economics, and politics from the University of St. Andrews, Scotland, and has 20 years of experience living abroad.

Veronica Schmidt Harvey is founder and principal of Schmidt Harvey Consulting and supports organizations in building strong, healthy leadership pipelines through

Learning Agility in Action In: *The Age of Agility*. Edited by: Veronica Schmidt Harvey and Kenneth P. De Meuse, Oxford University Press (2021). © Oxford University Press. DOI: 10.1093/oso/9780190085353.003.0020

assessment, coaching, and design of holistic leadership development processes. She is also co-editor of *The Age of Agility*.

Kevin Hedman is an associate principal and comanager of the assessment writing team at Korn Ferry. He studied English literature at Drake University and lives in New York City.

David F. Hoff, MEd, principal EASI consult and president of Burke Learning Agility Products (2003–present). He is a former vice president of human resources, Dimension Data North America (2000–2003). Anheuser-Busch, positions in organization development, leadership development, talent management, and international human resources (1983–2000). McBer and Company (1977–1983).

Kent Ingle is the president of Southeastern University and has held leadership positions in higher education, ministry, and the nonprofit sector and is the founding member of the Presidents' Alliance on Higher Education and Immigration.

Jack Lim is the cofounder of Leader's Gene Consulting and former managing director for Korn Ferry and Mercer in China. He is one of the Top-Ten Most Insightful Authors by *Harvard Business Review China* and Fifteen People in Fifteen Years by *China Staff*.

Julie Maloney, MA, is the Director of Coaching for UKG. Her passion is shifting leader mindsets through coaching and development to drive learning cultures in a VUCA world. Her career spans leadership and executive coaching roles in professional services firms and Fortune 100 global companies.

A. Silke McCance leads executive development at Procter & Gamble. As part of P&G's Global Talent Center of Excellence, Silke manages the Global Executive Coaching Program and designed P&G's first-ever developmental assessment center for top talent senior leaders.

Robert B. McKenna is the CEO of WiLD Leaders Inc., a firm focused on whole and intentional leader development and creator of the WiLD Toolkit, a leader development system with 10 assessments designed to increase learning agility and developmental readiness.

Miriam Nelson is a senior partner in Korn Ferry's assessment and succession practice in North America. Her work with clients is currently focused on the consumer industry. Miriam earned her PhD in industrial and organizational Psychology from Stevens Institute of Technology.

Glen Prior serves as a leader in the not-for-profit sector, building leaders and sustainable financial structures. He currently leads an asset management group helping fund the mission of the Free Methodist Church, where he serves as a denominational executive.

Jeff Rogers is the chairman for OneAccord, a corporation providing senior leadership for private companies, and the Solomons Fund, which operates a portfolio of companies. He is founder of KIROS and is a board member at Revive Families, C3 Leaders, and Doingood Foundation.

Brian J. Ruggeberg is a partner in Kincentric's Leadership practice, with nearly 30 years of consulting experience. Brian earned his PhD in industrial and organizational psychology from Old Dominion University and has contributed widely to the profession through presentations, publications, and leadership roles.

Ann E. Schulte is the chief learning officer at Procter & Gamble. She has global responsibility to drive continuous learning as part of company's strategic agenda and accelerate the skill development of managers and leaders to impact key business requirements, now and in the future.

Lianne Sipsma has spent her 27+-year career, including 19 years as an organizational psychologist, within large corporate organizations, and in the last decade has managed her own business. Lianne has a master's degree in industrial psychology, cum laude, and is the global managing partner of the Kaya Group.

Sharon A. Stratton is an industrial and organizational psychologist, organization consultant, and ICF (International Coach Federation)-certified professional coach. She founded and leads Cincinnati-based NOW Coaching & Consulting LLC after a nearly 30-year career at the Procter & Gamble Company in human resources.

Sarah E. Thomas is a consultant in the leadership assessment and development practice at Kincentric. Her work focuses on helping leaders identify and leverage their strengths and develop their opportunity areas. Sarah holds a PhD and MA in industrial–organizational psychology.

Todd A. VanNest is founder and principal consultant for Next Summit Enterprises LLC (Chicago). An applied organizational psychologist and talent innovator, his specialties include change leadership, organization effectiveness, talent management, executive coaching, and succession management.

Case Study A

Ultimate Software

Nurturing a Growth Mindset in Our Leadership Pipeline[*]

Tanya Castiglione Andrews and Julie Maloney

Organizations exhibit increasingly high levels of complexity and constant change and transition. Mastery of relationships, mastery of the business, and mastery of the future are essential competencies for leader success. Therefore, being able to assess and develop these competencies is an imperative for building leadership capability at Ultimate Software.

The Situation

During the early 1990s, a start-up tech company was born in south Florida—as far as one can get from Silicon Valley and still be in the continental United States. The founders envisioned the "ultimate" company that put employees first, thus giving it the name *Ultimate Software*. The essence of this "people-first culture" was that if employees were put first, they would put customers first, and shareholders would benefit. The people-first culture truly resonated with employees, and the human capital management software company became wildly successful.

Within 25 years, Ultimate Software had grown to nearly 4,000 employees (i.e., "UltiPeeps"), which necessitated greater intentionality in the structure, processes, and programs of the People Team, including the human resources (HR), talent, and learning functions. The addition of an internal executive coaching practice supported the assessment and development of the organization's senior leaders. Eighteen months after the first executive coach (an industrial–organizational psychologist) initiated the coaching practice, a second executive coach (a sociologist) joined the team due to overwhelming client demand.

[*] Ultimate Software merged with Kronos in 2020. It's new name is Ultimate Kronos Group (UKG).

Context

At the time, Ultimate Software was—and continues to be—a high-growth company. However, the hypothesis that high-growth companies are inherently populated by leaders with strong growth mindsets was not consistently supported. As with any organization and any group of leaders, growth mindsets are not a given but need to be purposely cultivated. While some leaders begin with a greater capacity for growth mindset, the strength of growth mindset varies significantly across organizational and demographic categories. Hence, an effective leadership assessment and development strategy must move the needle not only with respect to Ultimate Software's current (at the time) leadership competency model, but also relative to a growth mindset. Intentionally cultivating a growth mindset was key to strengthening the organization's leadership pipeline and building leadership capability for the future.

Talent Assessment Review

At its inception, the purpose of Ultimate Software's Talent Assessment Review process was to validate a single manager's perspective on the next-level readiness (i.e., promotability) of his or her direct reports. Over time, the process grew to include a behavioral self-assessment and interviews with both talent and business leaders in order to provide objective and holistic feedback and recommendations. In partnership with the business, the coaches and their teams identified, assessed, and developed individuals who demonstrated high readiness for mobility through the leadership pipeline. Referring leaders along with their participating direct reports received both ratings of readiness and recommended development actions based on their strengths and development needs. It became the foundation for a 70–20–10 individual development plan.

The two executive coaches recognized the need for a more substantive assessment that was better connected to the overall talent strategy. As they led the strategic reimagining and realignment of the Talent Assessment Review process, the coaches sought a more reliable, objective, and scalable way to assess leadership competencies and growth mindset. Their goal was to measure both agility (essential for mastery of the future) and emotional intelligence (essential for mastery of relationships). It should be noted that a lack of emotional intelligence is a frequent derailer for strong technical/job knowledge leaders. During this time, the coaches realized that bringing in a more substantive assessment was a bit more complicated than connecting the assessment process to the overall talent strategy.

What Was Done

To assess talent, the executive coaches strongly advocated for measuring a new, more substantive and holistic construct—learning agility. However, a hurdle was how to internally sell the idea of measuring a new construct given an already existing socialized and familiar assessment. The coaches clearly and regularly communicated the key reasons for assessing learning agility, specifically the *TALENTx7®* Assessment. They emphasized this assessment was scalable, could be used globally, fit the culture, and reliably and validly measured how individuals might perform in new and different situations (in other words, if promoted). The ease of the online, self-service portal enabled scalability. The facets of the instrument had widespread face and statistical validity. Furthermore, the *TALENTx7®* had a dual focus on the well-established facets of learning agility and the essential facets of emotional intelligence—fitting both the organization's competency model and the people-first culture.

Although the coaches could not immediately sell the idea of replacing the current (at the time) behavioral assessment, the organization was ripe for change. As the company continued to grow at a high rate, the demand for the identification, assessment, and development of leadership talent through the pipeline also grew. The team came to several conclusions during this time. The thinking was that existing behavioral assessment may not (a) accurately distinguish between levels of performance, (b) holistically link to our competencies, or (c) intuitively connect to competency development.

Enter the vice president of talent: With her knowledge of and experience with the learning agility construct and measurement, she became the senior leader advocate. Sponsorship at the executive level was the proverbial icing on the cake that enabled pilot testing of learning agility via the *TALENTx7®* as part of the Talent Assessment Review process. Thus, the team now had a consistent, reliable way to "pressure test" for learning agility beyond the existing behavioral assessment and subjective competency-based interviews.

Pilot Testing

During a 3-month pilot, the *TALENTx7* was used by the coaches, who, along with the participants and their leaders, provided feedback about both the construct and the assessment. The *TALENTx7* framework was meaningful, intuitive, and integrated well with the existing competency model. The report visuals were clear and concise. Moreover, the dual percentile rank scales of technical and leadership orientation (as opposed to a single low-to-high scale) strongly resonated with our peeps, given the often technical nature of their work.

An inherent and important message emphasized during the process is that a technical orientation is as valuable in some roles as a strategic orientation is in others. In the context of a tech company in which many employees rose up through technical/subject matter expert career paths and were assessed and rewarded for a technical orientation, this learning agility assessment validated their journey. The *TALENTx7* also beautifully captures the fluidity of the middle of the dial—the "transitional zone"—suggesting that individuals are not limited by a technical orientation. The feedback enables productive career conversations, supporting movement toward a more strategic orientation regardless of level or role. With self-awareness and desire, our peeps can literally move the dial on desired facets.

Most importantly, the unique and value-added emphasis on the emotional intelligence facets made the *TALENTx7* a perfect and consistent fit with our culture.

The Outcomes

On reflection, the pilot of the assessment of learning agility was successful for the following reasons:

- The facets were meaningful at all levels of leadership and clearly linked to the leadership competency model. The balance of the learning agility and emotional intelligence facets fit well with our culture.
- The *TALENTx7* is benchmarked and has strong statistical support in terms of its relationship to leader competence, performance, and potential.

- The assessment report and accompanying development guide provide concise, manageable, and applicable feedback.
- The company's strong "promotion from within" culture necessitates assessment and development for next-level readiness. As part of the Talent Assessment Review process, the *TALENTx7* provides our internal peeps a readiness "advantage" over external applicants.
- The power of the *TALENTx7* is that it is a self-assessment. Participants cannot infer that subjective perceptions or rater bias negatively impacted their ratings. Their learning agility scores are based on their own responses. Furthermore, as an organization, we are protected from self-rating errors in that the accuracy scales prevent or cue the possible presence of deliberate perception management.

Both Sides of the Coin

For Ultimate Software's senior leaders, the talent assessment process includes follow-on 360-degree leadership assessment and executive coaching in addition to the *TALENTx7*. Particularly for these senior leaders, the *TALENTx7* validates both sides of the "readiness" coin. The assessment results confirm those who are "ready now" for a next-level leadership role and those who require additional leadership development.

In the case of one director—let's call her "Ann"—the assessment validated both her leader's perspective and key stakeholders' insights from the 360 that she was a strong, "ready now" candidate for a senior director role. The *objective TALENTx7* results confirmed the more *subjective* feedback from both her leader and key stakeholders. This strong evidence led not only to the identification of strengths to leverage and opportunities to enhance but also to Ann's next-level promotion—for which her leaders now have both quantitative and qualitative performance evidence that confirms her success.

For another director—let's call her "Lynn"—there was a different story. Although Lynn's leader referred her to the process because he believed she was ready now, the *TALENTx7* challenged his perspective. The learning agility assessment showed opportunities within key facets required for success at the senior leader level. These facets coincided with the feedback received from key stakeholder interviews. Identified as having potential, an individual development plan was crafted for Lynn with leader and coach support to grow her in these areas and increase her readiness for a next-level role in the future.

Implementation Organization-Wide: Some Challenges

From the initial idea phase to the pilot test, it took about 2 years to craft and sell the business case for the measurement of learning agility as part of the talent assessment process. Now, over a year into full implementation, there is some (typical) concern about *typing* leaders according to their learning agility ratings versus accepting the data as feedback for growth and development. For example, might those employees with more of a technical orientation be perceived as having a *low* or *bad* learning agility score and perhaps be presumed to lack the ability to succeed in leadership roles? Would those employees with more of a leadership orientation—a *high* or *good* score—be given a *pass* to a next-level role despite substantive opportunities?

Although the *TALENTx7®* is used in combination with other data to support talent assessment, leaders may seek more information or draw conclusions around levels of learning agility *needed* for success at different levels of leadership. Might this lead to a demand for cut scores? If seeking to promote an individual to a level of leadership, is there any underlying belief that a minimal level of learning agility is required? And, are there sufficient data to support this?

Outcomes for Individuals

One of the best things about the *TALENTx7®* is that it truly forces individuals to pause and reflect. The feedback is solely based on the self-report data provided by the individual; thus, it encourages individuals to be accountable to how he or she responded. The results are a mirror to enhance self- and other-awareness and more deeply understand the impact of words, behaviors, and how we may be perceived. In other words, a leaders' *brand*. Refreshingly, at Ultimate Software, most often the results align with peeps' self-perceptions as well as their leaders' perceptions of them.

Outcomes for the Business

In the context of Ultimate Software's Talent Assessment Review process, the *TALENTx7®* provides leaders with additional objective validation of other subjective data collected from human sources that may have potential for bias. As experience and familiarity with the assessment increase, so does the confidence the organization's leaders have in the learning agility data. It has supported and continues to effectively support the scalability of the talent assessment process and thus quality movement through our leadership pipeline.

Lessons Learned

Of the many things learned on the journey, the following three stand out:

1. As with any significant organization change, it is important to begin with strong executive sponsorship. This support will smooth the path forward and direct investments toward the greatest returns.
2. Take time to clarify the assessment strategy (i.e., the what, why, when, and how for all assessments). It is essential to be unwaveringly confident in the answers to these questions prior to communicating them broadly. Clarifying and connecting the assessment strategy to the business strategy is essential to successfully sell the assessment and relevant talent processes to the business.
3. Start small, pilot, and iterate. Testing enables business advocacy. Key leaders drive interest and reach by sharing their experiences, telling their own story, and referring the assessment and process as a solution to others.

Case Study B

P&G

Fostering Learning Agility in the Next Generation of Leaders

A. Silke McCance, Ann E. Schulte, Brian J. Ruggeberg, Joshua D. Bush, and Sharon A. Stratton

The Situation

For more than 180 years, Procter & Gamble (P&G) has found small but meaningful ways to improve the lives of consumers around the world, providing branded products and services of superior quality that have become household names. Our iconic brands are trusted in millions of living rooms, kitchens, laundry rooms, and bathrooms—and have been passed down from generation to generation. Today, P&G brands such as Tide, Pampers, Gillette, Swiffer, Febreze, and Bounty are sold in over 180 countries, serving nearly 5 billion consumers globally each day. With operations in nearly 70 countries, P&G employees represent over 145 nationalities. P&G consistently ranks among the top companies for reputation, leadership, and diversity according to *Forbes, Chief Executive Magazine, DiversityInc, Working Mother*, and Human Rights Campaign.

P&G has long understood that learning agility determines which businesses thrive in dynamic contexts and which businesses lose their competitive advantages to disruptive innovation. We have assessed learning agility in our leadership high-potential framework for more than a decade. However, identifying agile learners is not the same as embedding learning agility in P&G's culture. We needed to do more to foster agile learning and ensure P&G continues to deliver outstanding results amid an increasingly fast and complex business environment. To address this gap, we partnered with Kincentric to design a growth ecosystem for P&G's future leaders in which learning agility can thrive. We believe if our senior leaders champion learning agility, their organizations will, too.

What Was Done

The program is based on a competency model created by researching the behaviors of the most successful general managers at P&G and then combining this information within the context of a dynamic world. The model is aptly named *Leadership Differentiators* because it codifies the most effective leaders and describes (a) *who* they are (in terms of their personal mindset and traits), (b) *what* they do, and (c) *how* they lead. Learning agility is at the core of the model. Our internal research studies have shown that P&G's most effective leaders are deeply *curious* lifelong learners who ask questions, experiment, and create a culture in which employees are encouraged to challenge the status quo, try new approaches, and learn from mistakes. They are also *adaptive*: able to test and learn, accept feedback, and pivot in an agile manner. The model has been extremely well received and has helped create clarity, build engagement, and deliver meaningful results among program participants.

At the center of our growth ecosystem, we built the Leadership Development Center (LDC). The LDC is a developmental assessment center (Lievens & Thornton, 2005; Thornton, Rupp, & Hoffman, 2015) that assesses and develops program participants on the Leadership Differentiators. Participants go through a 3-day, fully immersive experience in which they engage in realistic scenarios, playing the role of a regional vice president and global brand franchise leader within a fictitious consumer goods company. The role and the company are closely modeled after the general manager role at P&G. Participants receive personalized feedback from Kincentric coaches, who role-play 1:1 with them, providing the psychological safety needed to experiment with their style and facilitate maximum development.

Participants are encouraged to be vulnerable, to try different approaches and possibly fail, using the skills and strategies presented in the Leadership Differentiators outline (which may be new or may not come naturally given existing ingrained leadership styles). Another way in which learning agility is fostered is via reflection and journaling. Participants receive a journal at the beginning of the program, along with an article emphasizing the importance and value of journaling as a method of reflection. They are encouraged to reflect after every simulation and learning circle and to document their key learnings, insights, and questions.

Learning circles themselves are built into the LDC as an opportunity for deeper learning and new skill application. Following every simulation exercise, one of P&G's senior leaders facilitates a debrief session. In these sessions, participants are asked to reflect on how they handled the scenario, why they acted the way they did, and how the simulation tied back to the differentiators. They are encouraged to share with their cohort and consider the various approaches that were taken to address the problem at hand. The senior leader then offers his or her own perspective and some real-life context and examples relevant to the simulation.

In Chapter 1, De Meuse and Harvey define learning agility as "the ability and willingness to learn from experience, and then apply those lessons to perform well in new and challenging leadership situations." The LDC brings this definition to life through an immersive 3-day experience. Specifically, participants are given a designated time period to review critical situational information, which they then need to leverage and incorporate into their performance in the role-play interactions. Following the role play, participants reflect on their performance, receive targeted feedback from the role-playing coach, and then apply the learning, insights, and feedback in a subsequent interaction (see Figure B.1). This design element is known as "spacing." Both learning and neuroscience research has found that repetitions of content with some time delay between them produces more effective learning and better long-term retention (Thalheimer, 2006).

The capstone event of the program is a learning session dedicated to a growth mindset—another intentional design choice to focus on the agility

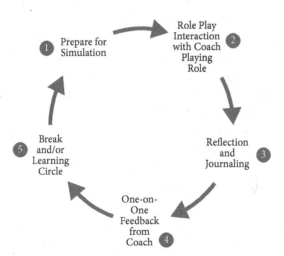

Figure B.1 Leadership Development Center process.

required to lead in a dynamic world. In this intimate session, participants are asked to reflect on leaders who they have worked with that had exhibited a growth versus fixed mindset and share the personal impact of working for these leaders.

Throughout the LDC, participants are assessed on the Leadership Differentiators and receive developmental feedback along those dimensions. At the end of the program, they each receive a personal developmental feedback report and co-create a development plan with their Kincentric coach, HR partner, and manager. Subsequently, they are paired with a certified internal coach from P&G's executive coaching cadre for ongoing development. The LDC is not a "one-and-done" event. Rather, it is only the beginning of a developmental journey to foster learning agility. Ongoing coaching is an integral part of the developmental ecosystem. Participants are also offered a curated menu of 70–20–10 learning experiences to support them in continuing to grow their leadership strengths and address any gaps and blind spots. Some examples are quarterly alumni sessions, the opportunity for a 3-month apprenticeship, and shadowing a senior leader.

The Outcomes

The development of this program was itself guided by the principles of learning agility. The team designed a minimally viable product, piloted it, collected feedback, and iteratively upgraded and improved the program over the course of two subsequent pilots. Initial feedback and results were overwhelmingly positive, with participants rating the program as exceeding expectations across a range of key success metrics (Table B.1). The following is one of our favorite participant quotations: "By far the BEST training I've ever had. The simulations give you an opportunity to understand who you are as a leader, and to construct a development plan that is actionable and based on your true needs. This program is a GIFT for me and my development."

Lessons Learned

The key challenges faced by the LDC are similar to those faced by all training and development offerings: Today's leaders are extremely time starved, with myriad issues and tasks that constantly tug at their attention. We found that

Table B.1 Leadership Development Center Pilots—Posttraining Survey Results

Survey Item	Result ($N = 101$)
How would you rate the overall LDC?	95% Favorable[a]
Would you recommend this program to fellow general manager potentials?	100% Agree
The situations encountered during the program were realistic and similar to those faced by actual leaders at P&G.	100% Agree
This program was worth the time away from my job.	99% Agree
This program helped me develop relevant skills.	99% Agree
Using these concepts, methods, and tools will give me a competitive advantage when I return to my job.	98% Agree
The LDC is "much better/better" than other training programs at P&G.	98% Agree

[a] Specific ratings were as follows: 69% "Excellent," 26% "Very Good," and 5% "Good."

the fast pace of the program is a wonderful antidote for this issue. Initially, we worried that the quick succession of activities—simulation preparation, simulation, coach feedback, learning circle—and then starting over again for the next simulation would be too exhausting for participants. Instead, we found it was a strength of the program design. In fact, 89% of participants agreed that the pace was "just about right" and told us that "the dynamic and speed kept me really engaged and kept the energy high." Participants also mentioned not even wanting to get into their email and really appreciated the opportunity to disconnect from their everyday work and focus on their own development.

Another common challenge is transfer of training: How can we ensure our future senior leaders will continue their development and make self-reflection a habit? This is why we designed the LDC as an ecosystem versus a one-and-done training event. Each cohort is added to a "Teams" group (a Microsoft networking tool for business) exclusive to LDC alumni. The Teams group enables participants to access materials used in the LDC and encourages continued networking after the event. As mentioned previously, participants receive a journal at the beginning of the program. We challenge them to continue journaling for at least 1 month after its completion. Quarterly interactive alumni learning sessions offer an opportunity to bring all cohorts back together to keep learning about new topics of relevance. Ongoing coaching allows participants to keep progressing along their own personal development journey. Finally, we are tracking participants in a longitudinal study to evaluate the long-term impact of the program on outcomes such as retention and promotion. This study also serves as a sporadic nudge to participants to remember to take the time to focus on their own development.

In summary, the LDC represents P&G's first holistic approach for developing top talent from across the organization to accelerate readiness for company leadership positions and to deliver outstanding results and competitive advantage for P&G both for today and in the future. This highly intentional and personalized program is centered on the concept of learning agility and aims to make it second nature for our future generation of senior leaders. Evaluation data show that participants consider this program to provide unparalleled value and impact with respect to the depth and quality of feedback received, knowledge acquired, developmental insights gained, self-awareness enhanced, and learning agility strengthened. It has clearly earned its reputation as the flagship program for assessing and developing future senior leaders at P&G.

References

Lievens, F., & Thornton, G. C., III. (2005). Assessment centers: Recent developments in practice and research. In A. Evers, N. Anderson, & O. Smit-Voskuijl (Eds.), *Handbook of selection* (pp. 243–264). Hoboken, NJ: Blackwell.

Thalheimer, W. (2006, February). Spacing learning events over time: What the research says. Retrieved September 23, 2019, from https://www.worklearning.com/wp-content/uploads/2017/10/Spacing_Learning_Over_Time__March2009v1_.pdf

Thornton, G. C., III, Rupp, D. E., & Hoffman, B. J. (2015). *Assessment center perspectives for talent management strategies* (2nd ed.). New York, NY: Routledge/Taylor & Francis Group.

Case Study C

Using the *TALENTx7®* to Identify High-Potential School and System Leaders

Lianne Sipsma and Yolanda de Beer

The Situation

In 2017, an education provider in Western Australia recognized their traditional approach for identifying and developing future school and system leaders was not meeting current leadership demands. It had become clear that individuals appointed through the traditional "hands-up" approach did not possess the required leadership attributes necessary to effectively lead school and school systems now and in the future.

Additional variables influencing the shortage of leadership talent for school and systems leaders included an aging population and a significantly limited pipeline of talented individuals. As it relates to the aging population, the Australian Institute for Teaching and School Leadership (AITSL) reported in 2014 that 71% of principals were over the age of 50, indicating an urgent need to ensure a pipeline of leaders ready to fill the vacancies left when this workforce reached retirement (AITSL, 2015). The report also noted that between 3% and 4% of school leaders viewed principal and deputy principal positions as "unattractive" or "very unattractive" to qualified applicants, suggesting the desirability of the role was perceived as negative, further threatening the capacity to fill these vacancies as they arise.

With only a third of deputy principals planning to apply for the role of principal during the following 3 years, it was evident urgent action had to be taken to ensure an adequate supply of qualified principals. A further contributing factor identified was that talented staff members often did not regard themselves as potential leaders. Consequently, they would choose not to apply for leadership positions (AITSL, 2015).

At the same time, the world of education has changed rapidly over the past several years. Traditional leadership approaches appear no longer adequate to navigate the cultural, social, economic, scientific, and technological changes found within the education environment. Research undertaken by Gallup suggested, "Leadership is second only to classroom instruction among school-related factors that contribute to what students learn at school" (Gordon, 2013, p. 3). Within education systems across the world, the identification of future talent has become an urgent priority and the development of a leadership pipeline an integral component of a sustainable workforce development program.

There is acknowledgment the pathway to becoming a school leader needs to be different from that in the past. School leaders feel well prepared for instructional leadership but underprepared for other leadership elements of the job (Pont, Nusche, & Moolman, 2008). Principals, for example, typically are required to set strategy and direction, design the school to deliver against its objectives, build a culture of high performance, and generally think differently about the way they undertake their work.

Creating a pipeline of high-performing instructional and organizational leaders who are innovative and able to lead within a distributed system requires a systematic process. Self-selection into leadership development programs and promotion by tenure will not unlock the full potential that exists within schools. The identification, development, and succession planning of future leaders is an important aspect of talent management within the education context. Succession planning requires a long-term strategic plan coupled with shorter term fast-tracking processes.

The Action Taken

Kaya Consulting approached the client in 2017 to share our views and approaches to leadership talent identification, including an introduction to the concept of learning agility. We were conscious of the client's need to identify talent in an evidence-based, scientific manner and deemed the *TALENTx7® Assessment* as a best practice solution. As a result, a client representative attended a *TALENTx7®* certification program with the goal of becoming a certified *TALENTx7®* coach. The representative's in-depth understanding of the construct and associated tool has ensured a collaborative working relationship and equipped the client to co-design the process along with the consultants.

Next, the client, in consultation with Kaya, designed a leadership identification and development program consisting of four phases. Phase 1

entailed a customized 360-degree leadership assessment tool, which identified specific attributes required to lead effectively in this specific educational
context.

For Phase 2, participants who met the predetermined minimum
requirements on the 360-degree tool were invited to complete the *TALENTx7®*
Assessment of learning agility. In addition, a facilitated session was conducted
in which participants were introduced to the construct of learning agility, received their reports, participated in coach-led feedback sessions, and had the
opportunity to engage with accredited psychologists for further exploration
and discussion. Candidates were selected for the next phase based on their
overall learning agility scores, as well as a select subset of facet scores identified
through a review of previous data and the profiles of successful candidates.

In Phase 3, successful candidates were invited to participate in structured
interviews designed to assess their ability to cope with work and role complexity. In the final phase, successful candidates participated in leadership
development opportunities specific to their individual leadership development needs for aspects of learning agility identified through the *TALENTx7®*
Assessment.

A group of 49 individuals participated in the first three phases of the pilot
program in 2017. On completion, several recommendations were made,
including the decision to implement a full rollout of the program (which
commenced in 2018).

The Outcomes

Prior to the implementation of this leadership identification and development program, the client facilitated focus groups drawn from the initial 2017 pilot study to solicit feedback on the process, including the use of
the *TALENTx7®* Assessment as a talent identification tool. The majority of
participants in the focus groups found that the *TALENTx7®* tool generated a
deeper level of personal reflection than they had experienced following other
tools they had completed. In many cases, the results confirmed behavioral
tendencies the participants were aware of already. For other participants, the
results were described as initially surprising but, on reflection, became development areas these individuals were consciously working on. Participants
reported the feedback on learning agility scores added value to the overall
program. See Table C.1 for a summary of the average results for all groups

Table C.1 Mean Results of *TALENTx7* Facets and Overall Learning Agility

Year	Number of Participants	Interpersonal Acumen	Cognitive Perspective	Environmental Mindfulness	Drive to Excel	Self-Insight	Change Alacrity	Feedback Responsiveness	Overall Learning Agility
					Mean Percentile Score				
2017	84	67	55	66	62	58	38	58	58
2018	148	69	54	72	63	64	55	63	66
2019	108	74	63	77	71	63	58	74	75
Total	**340**	**70**	**57**	**72**	**65**	**62**	**52**	**65**	**67**

over a period of 3 years on the learning agility facets and overall learning agility.

It is evident from the results in Table C.1 that participants in the program are predominantly learning agile. It is interesting to note Overall Learning Agility significantly increased from 2017 ($M = 58$) to 2018 ($M = 66$) to 2019 ($M = 75$). Further, the scores on all seven learning agility facets increased from 2017 to 2019, with the exception of the Self-Insight score, which decreased 1 percentile from 2018 but was up 5 percentiles from 2017. Based on this 3-year trend, it seems that the client substantially improved its selection process to identify potential leaders more effectively than was the case when the program began.

The Interpersonal Acumen scores and Environmental Mindfulness scores are relatively high in comparison to the other facet scores. Research indicates that interpersonal and communication skills of teachers have a significant role to play in the academic achievement of students (Khan, Khan, Zia-Ul-Islam, & Khan, 2017). Thus, this may explain why the Interpersonal Acumen scores were higher. Recently, there has also been growing awareness of the benefits of mindfulness in teaching (Gold, Smith, Herne, Tansey, & Hulland, 2010; Meiklejohn et al., 2012; Rocco, 2012), which may account for the high Environmental Mindfulness scores observed. However, further research is required to support these statements scientifically.

Based on our observations, the following recommendations were made to the client to maximize the likelihood of identifying high-potential candidates in a cost-effective manner: First, we recommended it continue the current process of using multiple assessments to generate complementary data, including the use of 360-degree feedback. Second, we encouraged the client to continue allowing unsuccessful candidates to reapply for the program at a future date in recognition of the potential for individuals to develop competencies over time.

Lessons Learned

In addition to being a scientifically validated instrument (see De Meuse, Lim, & Rao, 2019), the *TALENTx7*® Assessment was selected because of its alignment with the attributes of the 360-degree leadership tool and the clear linkage between learning agility facets and the identified leadership competencies. It was an important factor for ensuring the face validity of the tools and processes we applied.

Although the organization had access to an internal, accredited resource, the decision was made that Kaya Consulting would administer the assessment. Kaya consultants had extensive expertise with regard to the use and interpretation of the tools, and the client made the decision to outsource this phase of the talent identification process to further ensure participants perceived the process as fair.

Some participants revealed that the interpretive narrative in their individual reports did not appear to "match" other data they had received previously with regard to their leadership competencies. Their view was that psychometric tools are subject to error and should be complemented with face-to-face conversation to either confirm or modify what the numbers indicate. This perspective mirrors our practice at Kaya Consulting to reinforce assessment scores with other qualitative results and observations. Consequently, we were able to allay these individual concerns as they arose by addressing each individual's queries and explaining how the various data integrate and how psychometric assessment results should be interpreted and applied holistically.

The majority of participants were positive about their experience and were confident the processes and the tools being used were based on credible evidence regarding the attributes of effective leadership and how to best measure leadership potential. Nevertheless, some participants with lower learning agility profiles were less positive about the process. Consequently, steps were taken to address their concerns. Kaya consultants spent time with those candidates exploring the results of assessments to ensure they understood the benefit of self-awareness in future career planning. All participants reported the tools added significantly to their level of self-understanding and provided a strong basis for shaping their own development as future leaders.

Several participants felt strongly that the project represented a significant and welcome shift in the recruitment practices of the organization. Some even described the program as "the beginning of a new era" for the greater school system. The use of well-developed psychometric instruments to make better informed personnel decisions brought the organization closer to what they believed was already a common and best practice in both the private-sector and progressive public-sector agencies. They perceived the process would result in staff having a more equal opportunity to progress into leadership positions, especially for those staff whose current school context may limit opportunities to demonstrate their leadership potential.

Consistent feedback among the focus groups was that the success of the pilot also was attributable to the highly professional nature of the project leadership. Each stage was "managed expertly," feedback sessions were of a "high caliber," communication was "first class," and each individual was sensitively responded to. Without exception, focus group participants endorsed the commencement of the second, broader program of the talent identification component launched in 2018.

Finally, the client concluded that it is in the interest of all organizations—educational systems and private companies—to continually examine and refine their talent identification process. The selection and development of tomorrow's leaders are critical to the success of any organization. We believe the program that was designed and implemented was a cost-effective way to do it with our client.

References

Australian Institute for Teaching and School Leadership (AITSL). (2015). *Preparing future leaders—Effective preparation for aspiring school principals*. Melbourne, Australia: Author.

De Meuse, K. P., Lim, J., & Rao, R. (2019). *The development and validation of the TALENTx7® Assessment: A psychological measure of learning agility* (3rd Edition.). Shanghai, China: Leader's Gene Consulting.

Gold, E., Smith, A., Herne, D., Tansey, G., & Hulland, C. (2010, April). Mindfulness-based stress reduction (MBSR) for primary school teachers. *Journal of Child and Family Studies, 19*(2), 184–189. doi:https://doi.org/10.1007/s10826-009-9344-0

Gordon, G. (2013, July 15). School leadership linked to engagement and student achievement. Retrieved from Gallup website, https://www.gallup.com/services/176711/school-leadership-linked-engagement-student-achievement.aspx

Khan, A., Khan, S., Zia-Ul-Islam, S., & Khan, M. (2017). Communication skills of a teacher and its role in the development of the students' academic success. *Journal of Education and Practice, 8*(8), 18–21.

Meiklejohn, J., Phillips, C., Freedman, M. L., Griffin, M., Biegel, G., . . . Saltzman, A. (2012). Integrating mindfulness training into K–12 education: Fostering the resilience of teachers and students. *Mindfulness, 3*, 291–307. doi:https://doi.org/10.1007/s12671-012-0094-5

Pont, B., Nusche, D., & Moolman, H. (2008). Improving school leadership: Policy and practice. Retrieved November 27, 2019, from http://www.oecd.org/education/school/40545479.pdf.

Rocco, S. (2012). Mindfulness for well-being in schools—A brief survey of the field. *Redress, 21*(3), 14–18.

Case Study D

IBM

Incorporating Learning Agility Into First-Line Manager Selection

Alison M. Hartmann

The Situation

First-line managers represent about 10% of the entire employee population at IBM and play a critical role in the execution of IBM's operational object-ives since their teams are on the front line in interacting with IBM clients. First-line manager roles exist across a number of diverse IBM business units, such as hardware, software, services, research, enterprise functions, and sales. Consequently, the development of a profile that captures common characteristics for all first-line roles in all regions presented a unique chal-lenge because IBM does business in more than 170 countries.

In 2016, the IBM Leadership Development team was asked to review a recently launched Assessment and Development Center (ADC) for aspiring first-line managers being used in several regions across the company. The goal of the review was to determine whether the ADC was delivering on its promise of predicting performance in markets where the ADC was being used to identify and develop candidates for first-line manager positions.

The ADC used a multimethod, multirater approach, which included five different assessment instruments applying the following three distinct methodologies:

- an online assessment of cognitive ability, personality, and situational judgment customized to an IBM success profile;
- a behaviorally based structured interview; and
- three job simulations.

The assessment delivered two results: (a) one overall fit score divided into three bands and used for selection and (b) 16 attribute scores corresponding to each of the 16 attributes of the IBM Manager Success Profile (MSP) used for developmental purposes.

The MSP was designed to serve as a rigorous foundation globally, for not only aspiring manager selection but also enterprise-wide first-line manager development programs. It was created in 2013 through job analysis and was criterion validated the following year using the following two measures: (a) manager evaluations of the identified behaviors via a survey and (b) annual performance ratings (3-year average). The MSP was found to account for 30% of the variance ($r = 0.55$) in incumbent first-line manager performance globally at IBM. It also provided robust criteria against which we were able to map assessment instruments to build the ADC. Regional HR professionals and line managers served as observers and facilitators of the Center and delivered final evaluations.

A review of the regional ADC in the largest market deploying this methodology found the first-line managers selected had a significant difference in engagement scores compared to those not selected. Additionally, the introduction of a rigorous assessment elevated perceptions about the importance of the first-line manager role within that function of the organization. As a result, this approach attracted more candidates who were willing and aspiring to become first-line managers, increasing the quality of the potential pool of candidates. Finally, the use of a standard criterion (i.e., the MSP) helped management teams better articulate and differentiate the capabilities necessary to be effective in the role. This in turn drove higher quality coaching and development conversations, as well as more differentiated appraisals. The review was successful at proving the quantitative and qualitative value of the approach.

What Was Done

Subsequently, it was decided to deploy assessments more broadly for the selection of first-line managers based on the positive outcome of the review. However, there was one caveat. It would be necessary to offer an assessment center that was *scalable* to identify and develop aspiring managers if it were to expand globally. The existing ADC was not a viable enterprise-wide solution for the global volume of first-line manager appointments due to the time, cost, and resources required. The need to be scalable meant that the entire approach had to be achieved through an online experience.

The first action taken for creation of the online assessment center was a review of the existing, validated MSP to ensure that it remained current as well as relevant for the future state of work. Within the short time between the original validation of the success profile and the start of this initiative, global and digital influences were bringing about rapid change. As the team at IBM began our literature review, Petrie's 2014 *Future Trends in Leadership Development* strongly influenced our thinking on the evolution of the manager role. More specifically, Petri asserted that the future will intensify the need to address not only good leadership but also the process of adapting and changing at the right pace. The MSP had been extensively validated, and we believed the 16 attributes sufficiently captured "good leadership" in the first-line manager role across IBM. However, the process of adapting and changing at the right pace was not represented in the original model, although related attributes could be found in MSP attributes (e.g., leading change and embracing challenges). Identification of the theoretical underpinnings of this new component led us to explore research on learning agility.

A brief Google Scholar search revealed the number of journal articles published on learning agility had more than doubled between the years 2010 and 2016. Many of the authors stated it was a primary factor for defining high-potential talent, an early indicator of leadership competence and/or a distinguishing feature related to general leader success (De Meuse, Dai, & Hallenbeck, 2010; DeRue, Ashford, & Myers, 2012; Dweck, 2007; Kegan, 2001; McCall, Lombardo, & Morrison, 1988; Mitchinson & Morris, 2014; Silzer & Church, 2009; Swisher, 2013). The review further confirmed our view that this construct would become an increasingly important element of leadership success and should be incorporated into a refreshed model of our MSP. Incorporating the construct of learning agility also would enable us to use the assessment results for two purposes: (a) selection into the manager role and (b) early identification of those leaders with high potential in our management pipeline. Learning agility appeared similar in nature to two concepts already introduced into our organization—growth mindset and agile ways of work. These concepts supported organizational adaptability to the increasingly volatile, uncertain, complex, and ambiguous environment.

With the new attribute identified, the more challenging part began with the following questions: First, how would we integrate this concept into our MSP so that it made sense for aspiring managers and first-line managers? Second, how would we ensure the construct incorporated into our success profile is theoretically valid? Third, would the addition of learning agility provide incremental value in supporting decisions that matter to the business when selecting effective managers?

As we searched for common definitional clarity and a concrete criterion for test measurement, we discovered that multiple definitions of learning agility existed. It seemed that there was no one agreed-upon way to operationalize the construct (De Meuse, 2015). Although the lack of consensus in the research presented a challenge for us at the time, it strengthened our belief that this element was critical for the future state of leadership. The research simply seemed to be lagging behind the future needs of organizations.

Several credible assessments of learning agility were on the market at that time that we reviewed as part of this process. The thinking was as follows: If we started with concrete measurement, we could back into a definition of learning agility suited to our needs but grounded in some theory. Specifically, we looked at (a) Korn Ferry's *viaEDGE™*, (b) the Center for Creative Leadership's (CCL's) *Prospector*, and (c) a customized assessment of growth dimensions modeled on the work of Church and Silzer (2014). These instruments included similar facets, such as adaptability, achievement orientation, motivation to apply learning, risk-taking, and openness. Korn Ferry's viaEDGE appeared to be the most comprehensive measure and was well known to us. However, many of the learning agility dimensions it measured overlapped with our existing MSP attributes and the Kenexa online assessment of traits that was already being used. Integrating Korn Ferry's model with ours was not practical or easy to explain. Cost for the instrument also was a factor. Ultimately, we decided to eliminate viaEDGE from consideration.

The CCL assessment also was eliminated since it was a multirater survey and not viable to scale. Church and Silzer's (2014) Leadership Potential BluePrint not only had a definition of learning agility called "growth dimensions," but also offered a conceptual framework for integrating our two existing components (i.e., the MSP and the Kenexa online assessment). Therefore, we could add an assessment of learning agility while simultaneously integrating the other two necessary elements in a coherent, theoretically sound way. The growth dimensions consisted of two building blocks: (a) learning skills and (b) motivation skills. Both are considered "intervening variables" to individual learning that can either help or hinder further development (Church & Silzer, 2014). The foundational dimension in the Leadership Potential BluePrint also aligned well with our existing Kenexa online assessment measures of cognitive ability and personality. They represented the dimensions most stable and unlikely to change much over time. The career dimensions included leadership skills for specific contexts, which were aligned to the MSP attributes and easier to develop over time.

With the integrated model and specific measurement decided, we were able to complete a concurrent, criterion-related validation study for the two new scalable assessments—growth dimensions and a customized simulation. These would be added to the existing Kenexa assessment to create a fully on-line assessment battery for selecting first-line managers. The results of the validation study generally supported our refreshed MSP model of manager success. Specifically, the overall growth dimensions scales had a strong positive correlation with the mean work effectiveness ratings of incumbents ($r = 0.37, p < 0.01$) as well as with overall potential ratings ($r = 0.17, p < .01$). Additionally, the correlation between the overall scores on the first-line manager simulation and growth factors assessments was $r = 0.35$ ($p < 0.01$), suggesting the assessments were related but measuring different constructs.

The Outcomes

Incorporating learning agility into an existing, extensively validated success profile and assessment process required a great deal of effort from a variety of internal and external stakeholders. However, integrating learning agility in a manner that aligned to IBM's purpose of selecting successful first-line manager candidates has added tangible value to our selection approach and to the MSP. During our first year of deployment, we experienced 20% month-on-month growth in number of assessments taken. We also expanded into markets that had never previously used assessment centers for selection.

Specifically, this approach delivered the following benefits for aspiring manager selection:

- Provided a definition of learning agility that is integrated within the context of IBM's existing first-line manager success profile (i.e., the MSP).
- Showed incremental predictive capability as a result of adding a measurement of learning agility to the assessment of first-line manager.
- Added insight on leadership potential as well as performance, which increases the value of the assessment as an early indicator of high potential.

- Enabled data ownership allowing for further internal research and analysis on the effects of the learning agility variable on other variables of interest (e.g., cognitive ability, personality).
- Provided us the ability to work across the talent life cycle and use learning agility for a variety of purposes—prediction, development and diagnostics, measurement and monitoring of past as well as current performance.
- Gave us information that is easily understood by end-users and professionals alike, and also contributes value and insight above and beyond the other assessment components.
- Registered high user satisfaction with the overall experience of the assessment process as measured by the "Net Promotor Score" consistently staying above 60 (the excellent range) over a 2-year period.

Overall, successfully integrating the construct of learning agility into our existing MSP contributed to the strong overall outcome of our project. Further, the incorporation of learning agility was perceived as attractive to end users and positioned IBM strategically for the future.

Lessons Learned

Although our assessment is grounded in the current research on the topic of learning agility—and we are confident learning agility is measured by the assessments—we chose to name it Growth Mindset within our MSP. As there were already a number of leadership initiatives using the concept of growth mindset, it enabled us to leverage that momentum to be easily recognizable for the end users. The word *mindset* also gave us the opportunity to draw attention to attitude as a success factor in a management role. The promotion from individual contributor to first-line manager represents one of the more difficult shifts a person must make in their leadership career.

At the time we started the initiative, learning agility research provided little clarity on the construct and no agreed-upon definition. In addition, no assessment existed that met our specific needs related to first-line manager success as our company defined it. We therefore found it necessary to develop our own—in context—point of view on learning agility, grounded in the existing research and applied to our specific purpose. While this felt risky at the time, we are now in a strong position to evolve our point of view on the effects of learning agility based on our own data and analysis.

References

Church, A., & Silzer, R. (2014). Going behind the corporate curtain with a blueprint for leadership potential. *HR People & Strategy, 36*(4), 50–58.

De Meuse, K. P. (2015). *Using science to identify future leaders: Part I—Introducing the concept of learning agility*. Minneapolis, MN: Wisconsin Management Group.

De Meuse, K. P., Dai, G., & Hallenbeck, G. S. (2010). Learning agility: A construct whose time has come. *Consulting Psychology Journal: Practice and Research, 62*(2), 119–130.

DeRue, D. S., Ashford, S. J., & Myers, C. G. (2012). Learning agility: In search of conceptual clarity and theoretical grounding. *Industrial and Organizational Psychology, 5*(3), 258–279.

Dweck, C. (2007). *Mindset: The new psychology of success*. New York, NY: Random House.

Kegan, R. (2001). The real reason why people won't change. *Harvard Business Review, 79*(10), 84–92.

McCall, M. W., Lombardo, M. M., & Morrison, A. M. (1988). *The lessons of experience: How successful executives develop on the job*. New York, NY: Free Press.

Mitchinson, A., & Morris, R. (2014). *Learning about learning agility* (White paper). Greensboro, NC: Center for Creative Leadership.

Petrie, M. (2014). *Future trends in leadership development* (White paper). Greensboro, NC: Center for Creative Leadership.

Swisher, V. (2013). Learning agility: The "X" factor in identifying and developing future leaders. *Industrial & Commercial Training, 45*(3), 139–142.

Case Study E

J. M. Huber

Using Learning Agility for Succession Planning and Leadership Development

Marilyn Buckner

The Situation

The J. M. Huber Corporation is a global manufacturing company with multiple businesses. A few years ago, the organization faced the challenge of determining which high-potential leaders at a senior level were ready to enter a talent development program to prepare them to move into the roles of C-suite leadership, country manager, or president. There was a desire to use science in the decision-making process to ensure potential successors could transition effectively into roles they had never performed previously. Ultimately, a decision was made to assess learning agility because of its link to an organizational agility model and a formal process to develop future leaders.

What Was Done

Several validated measures were used by the organization to identify high potentials. The key measure, the *TALENTx7® Assessment*, was chosen to measure learning agility. The *TALENTx7®* is a comprehensive, easy-to-use instrument that identifies who is most likely qualified and ready for advancement. In addition, competency ratings and experience ratings by multiple raters were used to supplement and strengthen the accuracy of predicted ratings. An important consideration was the desire to prevent derailment of leaders through the self-awareness derived from the assessment, feedback, development, and coaching.

A Blueprint for High-Potential Identification

Initially, a "blueprint" was constructed to identify and evaluate high-potential leaders. The model was created by Dr. Kenneth P. De Meuse and his colleagues at Leader's Gene Consulting for defining high-potential leadership factors. The heart of the model was the measurement of the following seven facets of learning agility: (a) Change Alacrity, (b) Cognitive Perspective, (c) Drive to Excel, (d) Feedback Responsiveness, (e) Environmental Mindfulness, (f) Interpersonal Acumen and (g) Self-Insight. While other factors likely predict high potential (e.g., intellect, emotional intelligence, education, ambition, job experience), it was recognized that those factors alone—without learning agility—would not predict high-potential leadership. These additional success factors were measured with other assessments, which are described further in this case.

Key Steps for Using Learning Agility in Succession Planning and High-Potential Selection

Step 1: Identify Leadership Competencies and Map to Learning Agility Assessment

The J. M. Huber Corporation had identified a list of leadership competencies important for success in high-level positions. This list was initially developed by interviewing top management and the board of directors. An external consultant (NTS Inc.) strengthened the list by developing competency definitions and a list of specific behaviors for rating each competency, resulting in a set of customized competencies for success at high levels in the company. Subsequently, behavioral indicators of the competencies were also defined that could be rated easily by the supervising manager. The competencies were then linked to the learning agility facets by using an expert panel to confirm the mapping rationale. This step was important to lay a foundation for the high-potential selection and development model as well as to provide a framework for the talent reports.

Step 2: Rate Competencies Using Behavioral Indicators to Provide a Measure of High Potential

A competency rating sheet was developed to provide numerical ratings for each competency utilizing multiple behavioral items. Those ratings provided guidance on specific examples of performance and work experiences. The competency rating worksheet was completed by each prospective high-potential leader's supervisor and others familiar with the leader's performance. The information provided was important for supporting other learning agility data with examples of work experience.

Step 3: Map Learning Agility to Multiple Measures and Personality Traits

Relevant factors were identified across the various assessments to develop a comprehensive view of each high-potential leader. The seven learning agility facets from the *TALENTx7®* were mapped to both the leadership competency model and the following suite of Hogan assessments: *Hogan Personality Inventory; Hogan Development* (Derailer) *Survey; Hogan Motivation, Values, and Preferences Inventory*; and the *Hogan High Potential Talent Report*. This was to integrate multiple measures and strengthen the predictive power of the overall assessment process. The *Decision Styleview™* instrument also was administered to all leaders.

Step 4: Obtain Nominations to Generate a Candidate Pool

Next, a list of high-potential leaders was requested from top management, supervisors, and the HR leader to develop a pool of prospective high-potential candidates. Nominations were based on performance and other high-potential criteria (e.g., competencies, ratings on ability to move two levels or into a certain type of position, specific work experiences relevant to leadership in the company, and performance evaluations).

Step 5: Create Individual Snapshot Reports for Candidate Comparison

To facilitate talent and executive reviews, a one-page, color-coded dashboard summary report was prepared highlighting the data across all assessments for each participant. Additional data on work experience and emotional intelligence were also provided. Summary paragraphs highlighting job experiences and personality traits were included to provide further insight into the readiness or developmental needs of each of the participants. This simple dashboard format made it very easy to compare each candidate's strengths and developmental needs.

Step 6: Develop Targeted Questions for Talent Review to Validate Selection Results

Based on the leaders' assessment results, structured interview questions with behavioral indicators were created to validate results. These interview questions were developed to promote a meaningful talent review and to help calibrate real-life job examples and performance results. Questions were also selected to verify other assessment information, gain information on compensating factors that should be considered in the nomination decision, and to challenge and examine nominated candidates who did not seem to be ready for promotion at this time. In addition, this discussion helped identify certain development experiences that would benefit each candidate.

Step 7: Conduct Robust Talent Reviews Using Objective Data to Reduce Bias

The talent review team met to discuss and review the assessment results for each high-potential candidate. The goal was to reach consensus on those most ready to be developed for new opportunities. Having objective data from multiple assessments in a one-page, color-coded dashboard format helped support ratings of high-potential status and minimized the bias and ambiguity common in talent review meetings.

Step 8: Design an Accelerated Development Program

To create the development program, information was gathered from a variety of academic and consulting areas to identify high-impact content and tools for developing learning agility. Three programs were designed for each of the 1-week executive education programs and development coaching programs. Each program was designed to engage senior leaders by using complex simulations, action learning projects, and a variety of strategic thinking and planning tools. An organizational agility model—referred to as "SCORE"—provided a compass for developing the following five modules: (a) Strategically Agile, (b) Capability Building of Talent, (c) Organizational Design and Decisions, (d) Readiness of an Agile Culture, and (e) Execution.

- **Strategically Agile.** Leading-edge strategic tools such as "blue ocean strategy" for creating new market space and the traditional "Competitive Strategy" were used to identify potentially new innovation products for the company. Other methods such as "Design Thinking" and a change simulation were taught to enhance general management skills.
- **Capability Building of Talent.** A general manager high-performance simulation was used, with participants taking on different functional leader roles with cross-functional teams to make talent and other general management decisions.
- **Organizational Design and Decisions.** Scenario planning, using real product lines and custom cases and change implementation, was part of the program.
- **Readiness of an Agile Culture.** A comprehensive culture survey that predicts financial performance was used. It employed a multiyear growth metric with cascading action plans on organizational agility areas to reinforce culture and support the overall business strategy.
- **Execution of Strategy.** A strategic execution simulation and a custom new product strategic execution case and tools were used.

Implementation of the Accelerated Development Program

All of the high-potential leaders that were selected entered into a 3-year executive leadership program created by NTS Inc. The primary goal of this program was to develop learning agility and other leadership competencies. The first two sessions were separated by approximately 18 months. Near the end of this 3-year leadership program, participants were measured again on learning agility using the *TALENTx7®* Assessment. Results showed a significant increase in learning agility scores for leaders on five of the seven facets. As can be seen in Figure E.1, 88% of the leaders substantially increased their Interpersonal Acumen, 95% improved their Cognitive Perspective, 88% enhanced their Drive to Excel, 62% increased their Self-Insight, and 57% improved their Change Alacrity.

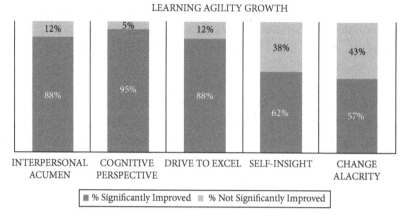

Figure E.1 Learning agility growth across time.

The Use of Certified Learning Agility Coaches

A team of coaches certified in the three primary assessments used in the program (i.e., *TALENTx7*®, the Hogan Suite, and Decision Styleview) provided one-on-one coaching and feedback to all of the high-potential leaders who attended the leadership development training. The coaching was intended to supplement the training, help the leaders grow in agility, develop in the factors identified as important for success in higher level positions, and prevent derailment. Particular emphasis was given by the coaches on those assessment scores identifying overuse behaviors to prevent potential derailment.

Because emotional maturity is a common cause of career derailment, coaches focused deeply on this topic for leaders with low scores in this area. For example, the *TALENTx7*® facet scores on Interpersonal Acumen, Self-Insight, Feedback Responsiveness, and Environmental Mindfulness were explored in detail. Likewise, the derailers identified by the Hogan Development Survey were examined. Common themes across the different assessments were especially powerful and helped leaders understanding the importance of changing their behaviors.

The Outcomes

The combination of selection and development programs resulted in an acceleration of the leaders' learning agility in a short period of time. The

TALENTx7® Assessment was a critical part of the high-potential development program. The assessment scores provided concrete, objective, and quantifiable data on each high-potential leader's ability and willingness to succeed in higher level positions. The client concluded that this program provided a strong return on investment for the organization due to the identification and significant accelerated growth of the high-potential leaders.

Many positive outcomes of the program were realized by J. M. Huber, including the following:

- Pre/post learning agility scores demonstrated significant growth, and were used to identify high potentials "most ready" to be promoted or given developmental assignments.
- Talent data, such as promotions, expanded job responsibilities, and accelerated "ready now" status were obtained with several leaders who were elevated to top management in a short period of time.
- Direct hands-on observations and support by presidents, board members, and CEOs for the growth and complex skill sets of the participants in the programs strengthened confidence in promotion decisions throughout the organization.
- The Denison Culture Survey was administered to those employees reporting to the leaders at the top of the organization and showed positive changes in culture between years, suggesting that learning agility was a contributor to these changes.
- Participant evaluations of the 3-year development program were very high, reinforcing that the agility content was useful and engaging.
- Pre-/post results on the *TALENTx7*® clearly demonstrated a significant increase in learning agility scores for those leaders (Figure E.1).

Lessons Learned

A key contributor to the success of the program was the hands-on involvement of the company CEO and leadership team, not only in the design but also in the implementation of the learning agility program. Their participation visibly demonstrated their support to the entire organization. Further, it enabled them to more effectively understand the high-potential selection and development process, preventing biases that often occur in a large organization when executives do not have frequent contact with high-potential individuals. Allowing the leadership team to see the full capabilities of each leader provided confidence in decisions regarding future assignments. In addition, a very useful practice was for the executive team to meet with the program designers at the conclusion of the program to debrief the experience. At that time, key stakeholders reviewed the performance of each participant and gained in-depth insight into leadership strengths and gaps for identifying developmental assignments.

Additional lessons learned pertained to the inclusion of high-involvement simulations in the training design. The simulations accelerated the development of learning agility through real-time feedback. It also enabled us to assess participants before and after training to fully understand the impact of the training. Overall, we found the measurement of learning agility put science and predictability into the talent decision-making process and instilled confidence in the development practices that we used.

Case Study F

Developing Learning Agility

Through the Lens of a Leader

Sarah E. Thomas and Veronica Schmidt Harvey

The purpose of this case study is to share the experience of developing increased learning agility from the perspective of an individual leader. Our intent is to describe (a) how a leadership development program can be structured to enable the development of agile learning behaviors and (b) illustrate how an individual leader was empowered as a result of the program's commitment to building learning agility.[†] In this case study, we cover the situation and context of the program as well as the process involved before, during, and after the program. Outcomes and lessons learned from the program are also be shared.

The Situation

The focus of this case study is an internal leadership development program facilitated at a large, multinational consumer packaged goods organization based in the United States. The organization has increased its emphasis on agility through multiple initiatives focused on operating with greater speed, skill, and flexibility in a constantly changing competitive landscape. The program was developed in partnership with Kincentric (formerly Aon) to cultivate leadership skills in high-potential individual contributors and managers. In addition, the program was developed around the organization's leadership competency model, and elements support the development of learning agility and the organization's commitment to enabling continuous learning.

---

† We would like to thank the focal program participant for contributing her experiences and lessons learned to this work. We would also like to acknowledge Joseph Gier, PhD, for his early work establishing the program and building the foundation for its success.

In this case study, the key elements of the program are described, along with how they contribute to the development of learning agile behavior. Table F.1 is a summary of program elements and their linkages to the development of the learning agile behaviors described in Chapter 6. These themes are illustrated from the perspective of a program participant who shared details about the experience with her coach. The quotations throughout this case study are from this participant and have been used with her permission.

Table F.1 Program Element and Corresponding Learning Agile Behaviors

Program Element	Learning Agile Behaviors Developed
• Preworkshop Assessment and Feedback	• Environmental scanning and future forecasting • Seeking, accepting, and using feedback
• Workshop—Simulation	• Experimenting • Practicing deliberately • Reflection • Seeking, accepting, and using feedback
• Workshop—Learning Circle	• Learning vicariously • Sourcing information and new frameworks
• Development Planning	• Setting goals and establishing indicators for success • Planning for development • Sourcing information and new frameworks
• Coaching	• Leveraging coaching and mentors • Asking for help
• Implementing the Development Plan	• Seeking out stretch assignments • Experimenting and taking risks • Learning vicariously • Practicing deliberately • Questioning and demonstrating curiosity • Seeking, accepting, and using feedback • Reflection • Demonstrating discipline, effort, and resilience

What Was Done

Employees are nominated to participate in this 8-month program, and multiple cohort groups are facilitated each year. Before the in-person workshop, participants engage in a 360-degree survey process and complete a personality assessment. The results of both tools are provided as feedback to the participant and discussed jointly with his or her coach, as well as shared with the participant's manager. Additionally, participants are assigned reading materials to review and are briefed on the value of feedback and coaching. This prework sets the stage for creating a psychologically safe environment for receiving feedback and considering the leadership capabilities that may be needed for success in the future.

Participants then attend a 2-day workshop, comprising multiple learning cycles consisting of the following: (a) role-play simulations based on commonly encountered leadership situations (e.g., coaching, communicating change); (b) reflection time focused on what was done effectively and what could have been done better; (c) feedback from coaches (who also serve as the role players); (d) group learning circles to share experiences with peers, offering the opportunity to learn vicariously through others; and (e) facilitated discussions of new frameworks based on readings and other materials that can then be applied in subsequent simulations.

These components create a microcosm of the experiential learning cycle in which the participant learns through considering new leadership approaches, preparing for the experience, experimenting with new behaviors, reflecting on performance, receiving immediate feedback, and discussing the situations and effective responses with others partaking in the learning process.

> **Participant Comment 1:**
> *"I learned so much from that iterative process of preparing, practicing, reflecting, and getting feedback, and so I tried to hold myself accountable to do this outside the [workshop] session."*

The aim is for participants to extrapolate this learning process from the workshop and apply it to their everyday work experiences. Understanding and participating in this experiential learning cycle can be a powerful step in the development of learning agility.

The workshop concludes with additional reflection on the feedback that has been received from all sources (i.e., 360, personality assessment, and simulations). Participants also meet with their respective coaches to discuss implications for achieving both short- and longer term career goals, with consideration of how their work environments may be changing. Time is spent formulating specific development plans that include elements such as those described in Chapter 6, Table 6.4.

Following the in-person workshop, participants engage in five 1-hour, phone-based coaching sessions over the course of approximately 5 to 6 months. These sessions focus on how the individual can leverage his or her strengths and actions that can be taken to make strides in areas identified as development needs. Participants are actively encouraged to engage in learning agile behaviors such as feedback seeking, reflection, asking for help, deliberate practice, and experimenting.

The Outcomes

In addition to the individual-level outcomes that are highlighted, the program has seen much success from an organizational perspective. At the end of each session, participants are asked to complete an evaluation survey to collect their perceptions and feedback on the program. Overall, participant responses have indicated the program is fulfilling its purpose and achieving its objectives of developing leaders and continuous learners. Due to the perceived value of this program, the organization has continued to invest in this program for more than *15 years*, involving *over 40 cohorts* of participants! Further, a key outcome of this process is the development of learning agile behaviors among participants. The words of the participant highlighted in this case put into context how she developed learning agile behaviors associated with observing, doing, connecting, thinking, and mobilizing (referenced in Chapter 6).

Observing

The development program is intended to increase participants' mindfulness of both their internal and external experiences. By becoming more aware of the nuances of what is going on around them, participants learn to pay closer attention to both their behavior and those of others. It is a key first step for replacing automatic behaviors with potentially more productive ones.

Participant Comment 2:
"It has been really interesting to take the broader view, focusing on the total and taking a more holistic view. By just observing, I found learning opportunities that I didn't consciously seek just by paying attention to things that were relevant."

Doing

The program is designed to assist participants to recognize the learning opportunities that exist in their *current* roles by participating in role-play simulations that mimic real-life scenarios. The coaches also work with the participants following the workshop to identify the work situations they can leverage as learning opportunities.

> **Participant Comment 3:**
> *"It's not just theoretical education. I see situations where I've been able to practice in the areas I'm trying to develop, and that's been really helpful and critical to my learning process."*

In addition, participants typically discover that courage—and sometimes discomfort—are necessary when trying new behaviors. Within the workshop, the role-play simulations enable the participants to try different behaviors and experiment in a safe environment. Additionally, these deliberate practice sessions allow the participants to take risks and move outside of their comfort zones, an important component in gaining confidence to engage in new behaviors.

> **Participant Comment 4:**
> *"In order to get there, I had to break out of what is comfortable, take the risks, and just try and see how it goes; learn from it and keep iterating. The first few times it's pretty uncomfortable, but then it becomes habit, and you realize nothing bad happens. Within this process, I found more confidence in myself."*

Connecting

Another powerful aspect of developing learning agility is demonstrating willingness and openness to learn from others and their experiences. During the workshop, participants benefit from opportunities to hear and learn from the experiences of others who are diverse in their professional backgrounds, knowledge, and expertise. At the encouragement of her coach, the focal participant applied this

> **Participant Comment 5:**
> *"Some of those who I went to for mentoring were peers; some were higher level leaders. I found myself surprised that I was learning even from interns that came to me for guidance. I think it was important to be open to learning from everyone I interact with, not just leaders."*

beyond the workshop, actively seeking role models and mentors, and in doing so, made an important discovery about the value of learning from others.

A critical component of this development program is the coaching the participants receive during and following the workshop. The benefits of a coach include having accountability built into the process. In addition, the coach also encourages the participant to actively develop learning agile behaviors and offers resources and support.

Throughout the development process, the participants are also encouraged to ask for feedback more regularly, ingraining the practice in their daily habits. One way to seek feedback is to curate a set of trusted advisors who can be turned to for advice and perspective on a regular basis.

> **Participant Comment 6:**
> *"My coach had really good tips and got me thinking about things I hadn't thought about before, helping me see progress I had made, but opening my eyes to other areas and considering this a continual learning process."*

> **Participant Comment 7:**
> *"People have been very open to giving feedback once when I share why I'm asking; they know what I'm working on, and they can then tailor their feedback. . . . The more I ask for feedback, the more holistic the feedback becomes."*

Thinking

Leaders seeking to increase their learning agility must reserve time and energy for reflection, a difficult task when put into practice. Reflection and mindful observation allow individuals to broaden their perspectives, recognize learning opportunities, and benefit from such opportunities.

> **Participant Comment 8:**
> *"After an event, I reflected on what the objective was we were trying to accomplish, and did we get there or not? If yes, I thought about what worked and how can I keep applying that? If not, what didn't work, and what could I try next time to get there? I did calendar blocking for reflection time, so I would focus not just on the daily things, but on my broader development. This helped me determine . . . am I making progress?"*

Another important component of the agile learning process is the shift to a growth mindset. When trying new behaviors and ways of working, failure is a possibility. When setbacks occur, an individual armed with a growth mindset is able to learn from the situation and apply the knowledge to subsequent scenarios.

> **Participant Comment 9:**
> "I try to focus on what worked or didn't work, what I can do differently next time, and just constantly keep trying, learn from it, and continue to build on my experiences."

Mobilizing

The agile learner whose words are quoted in this case was extremely motivated because she was intentional in setting goals and believed they would directly impact her long-term career success. She also understood how the program offered her opportunities to make progress against those goals.

> **Participant Comment 10:**
> "I was motivated to keep working on my development goals because I could see how they personally tied to what I wanted out of my career. I saw what I could get out of program and what the personal benefit would be."

Creating a detailed development plan with specific goals and timelines served as a valuable tool for holding herself accountable and monitoring progress, crucial elements in an iterative learning process.

> **Participant Comment 11:**
> "Holding myself accountable to those things that I learned and found helpful during the [workshop] and then applying those to daily work life helps me to think differently."

In our case example, the element of monitoring goes well beyond performance in the workshop, but pertains to tracking one's performance relative to

> **Participant Comment 12:**
> "The process allowed me to try new things and learn quickly. I know this is not done; development is never done. I need to keep checking in with myself on how I'm doing and stay active in seeking opportunities, exposure, and feedback."

development over time. At the end of the overall 8-month engagement, the coach, the participant, and the participant's manager close the program by discussing the participant's progress on the development plan, key learnings, and steps that will be taken to maintain learning momentum. At the close of this process, the aim is for the participant to recognize that becoming an agile learner is an ongoing process that requires a commitment to demonstrating learning agility throughout one's career.

Lessons Learned

Reflecting on especially successful participants of the program, a few themes highlight the significant amount of personal effort and commitment the development of learning agility requires. Individuals must be thoughtful when engaging in the following activities:

- Setting development goals that are clear and personally motivating.
- Identifying the inherent learning opportunities in work tasks and interactions.
- Demonstrating a willingness and openness to learn from others.
- Showing courage and discomfort when trying new behaviors.
- Reserving time and energy for reflection.
- Exhibiting a growth mindset.
- Actively engaging in the coaching process.
- Regularly seeking feedback from others.
- Holding oneself accountable and monitoring progress.
- Recognizing the ongoing nature of learning.

Overall, by developing the agile learning behaviors of observing, doing, connecting, thinking, and mobilizing, a road map is created that can sustain participants' success for both the short and long term.

Case Study G

Fosun International Limited

Learning on the March to Adapt to Rapid Growth

Jack Lim

Fosun International Limited, also known as Fosun, is a well-renowned Chinese privately owned enterprise with multiple business lines and a global footprint. The company was founded in 1992 solely as a market research firm. Later, Fosun successfully transformed and expanded its business into a global ecosystem covering three major business sectors: (a) health (pharmaceuticals, medical devices, etc.); (b) happiness (entertainment, tourism, fashion, etc.); and (c) wealth (insurance, asset management, etc.). The company's cofounder and now chairman Mr. Guangchang Guo is viewed as a business guru and, more importantly, a man with great learning agility who forged and cultivated an agile organizational culture.

In emerging markets like China, the business environment has evolved quickly during the last two decades. Fosun has been agile in adjusting its business strategies to quickly adapt to the dynamic business environment. When Fosun first started, it seized the opportunity presented by China's Market Economy Reform in 1992, quickly developing its businesses in healthcare and real estate, which have become cornerstones of its success. Then, during the early 2000s with the blossom of China's infrastructure and heavy machinery industry, Fosun accelerated its growth with proactive mergers and acquisitions, starting in the iron and mining field. By 2019, Fosun had become the holding corporation of four publicly listed companies, and a Top 10 shareholder for 16 publicly listed companies in China.

Beginning in 2007, the company kicked off its overseas expansion with the purchase of New York City's landmark building, One Chase Manhattan Plaza. Additional purchases followed with the acquisitions of vacation resort provider Club Med; Portuguese's largest insurance company Fidelidade; and Cirque Du Soleil in Canada. As a result, Fosun has been deemed one of China's most acquisitive enterprises. Most recently, in order to keep up with the digital era and to meet increasing customer demands, Fosun once again shifted its strategy from "industrial investment" to "industrial development" as it began to engage more deeply in a post-M&A management period.

Fosun's talent strategy likewise evolved along the way. At the merger and acquisition stage, talent with high intelligence, analytical skills, financial acumen, and strong negotiation skills were the most needed. With the recent industrial development strategy, Fosun shifted its expectations for talent, especially leadership talent. New and different leadership competencies were required to run a business (as opposed to buy a business). In addition to hiring from outside, it was necessary for existing managers also to evolve quickly.

According to the company's chief human resources officer Ms. Haining Mu, "This most recent shift implies new requirements for in-depth industrial knowledge, operational skills, and profit and loss management ability, which were not that critical for investment managers in the past. We desperately needed to quickly equip our managers with skills to operate business units, so learning agility has become one of the critical success factors for our managers to shift gears" (H. Mu, personal interview, October 22, 2019).

Fosun has hired many experienced managers from leading multinational companies. Most of them have accumulated rich operational experience in their domains. What set apart those who made a successful career transition is their growth mindset and ability to adapt to a new organization's culture. At Fosun, leaders have less legacy framework to follow compared to some organizations, but much more authority to act. They need to let go of previous ways of thinking and behaving. Behaviors that once led to their success in other roles and other companies now were either not useful or

---

Haining Mu, Fosun Chief Human Resources Officer

"*If you can create value and be recognized by the top management, you can work out your initiatives boldly at Fosun. Otherwise others may take your lunch. In this recent decade, Fosun has become not only larger but also nimbler—an agile organization—one with a flat organizational structure, horizontal reporting structure, and quite flat decision-making process. Front-line people facing customers in the market have more authority to make responsive decisions. We do make wrong decisions, but we are able to identify and correct the errors quickly*" (Personal interview, October 22, 2019).

an impediment to business success. Leaders had to adapt to the flexible and ever-changing Fosun organization, where there was a less clearly defined job scope and role limitations.

What Was Done

To cultivate and consolidate an agile learning environment, Fosun's CEO took the lead in quarterly talent meetings. Almost every other day, he used a WeiChat account (the Chinese version of Facebook) to communicate his view of the changes taking place. Fosun also pushed very hard for its leaders to adapt. Leaders who were unable to keep up with the company's changing business strategy and evolve their own competencies were quickly weeded out. To some people, the changing team may not have seemed that stable. However, it was the new way to achieve success at Fosun.

Fosun placed great emphasis on *learning on the march*, the ability to acquire diverse and cross-domain operational skills while in the process of doing day-to-day work. Learning agility was a key part of the hiring process. Starting in 2018, learning agility has been used in leadership development programs for high-potential leaders. Fosun employed Leader's Gene Consulting—a boutique leadership consulting firm located in Shanghai—to conduct the *TALENTx7*® online self-assessment of learning agility as part of that program. Based on the individual and group assessment results from the *TALENTx7*®, the company has conducted customized leadership development programs. Consultants from Leader's Gene facilitate workshops for participants to understand the findings from their assessment reports to enhance their self-awareness.

This approach was first initiated at the company's headquarters, then rolled out at Fosun subsidiaries in the healthcare industry as well as in the real estate industry. About 30 HR managers were certified on the *TALENTx7*® tool, and introductory sessions were facilitated for the selected high-potential talents to help them enhance self-awareness on their learning agility.

Outcomes

Since being listed on the Hong Kong Stock Exchange (00656.HK) in 2007, Fosun has been growing steadily each year. The company recorded revenues of RMB 109.4 billion (ca. US$16.5 billion) with total assets worth RMB 681.51 billion (ca. US$99.13 billion) as of June 2019 (Fosun International Limited, 2019). As a global corporate citizen, Fosun has been giving back to society by initiating programs such as (a) the "Rural Doctors Campaign" to alleviate poverty through healthcare and (b) colaunching a global youth accelerator program called "Protechting," which provides training to young entrepreneurs resulting in job creation worldwide. Most importantly, Fosun provides different services and products to countless families in need across the fields of health, happiness, and wealth.

Guangchang Guo, Fosun Chairman

_____

"There are plenty of reasons as to why Fosun is at where it is today, and among all of them I believe the company's willingness and ability to learn fast and adapt to the changing circumstances over time plays a critical role. Since its establishment, talents and teams have always been Fosun's most valued assets. Fosun aspires to be a platform for entrepreneurs and creates opportunities for those with ambitions and dreams. The entrepreneurial spirit means always being vigilant, venturing out of your comfort zone, and constantly improving yourself through learning. In a fast-changing world of rapid technological innovation, we must always maintain full energy, keep abreast of the times and forge ahead" (Fosun communication letter to shareholders, 2019).

Lessons Learned

From what Fosun has experienced in the last decade, we find it has done well in at least three aspects, which can be valuable lessons for other companies:

1. Fosun has a highly learning agile CEO. Based on his acute business instincts, he quickly captures changing business opportunities, adapts himself quickly, and also drives organizational change.
2. The pace of strategy and relative organization change is faster than in most other companies. This is especially critical for large organizations in the new decade.

3. It is important for the HR function to quickly equip themselves with the right tools to implement an agile talent strategy. Many business leaders are aware of the importance of learning agility, but many of them have vague or even contradictory understandings. Questions like, What does it really mean? How do we measure it? and How do we incorporate this concept into talent acquisition and development? must be answered by HR professionals. Therefore, interventions involving outside experts to certify or provide training adds significant value.

Reference

Fosun International Limited. (2019). *Interim 2019 shareholder report*. Shanghai, China

Case Study H

The Order of St. Francis Healthcare

Assessing and Developing Learning Agility to Build Transformational Leaders

David F. Hoff and Todd A. VanNest

In 2015, E·A·S·I–Consult® was contacted by the Order of Saint Francis (OSF) Healthcare regarding a program they wanted to create focused on transformational leadership for "high-potential" mission partners (i.e., employees). It eventually came to be known as the Transformational Leadership Program (TLP). The initial group consisted of 60 leaders, with program content focusing on leadership style, organizational climate, and transformational competencies. The program has been in place for more than 4 years and attended by more than 150 high-potential leaders. Although TLP was impactful and resulted in measurable individual and organizational change, there seemed to be a missing element.

What Was Done

The existing 3-day event was expanded to 4 days and became part of a larger 12-month experience. Program participants were brought together for follow-up sessions. The follow-up sessions were interspersed with time back on the job to apply learnings, resulting in even greater growth and change. The facilitators believed participants needed the opportunity to try out new skills and concepts in the learning environment in order to adjust them before applying them back in their job settings.

Incorporation of Learning Agility Assessment

The original TLP provided participants feedback through assessments on (a) organizational climate, (b) leadership style, and (c) transformational competencies. The TLP and subsequent updates were designed by E·A·S·I–Consult with input from OSF. During the pilot year of the TLP, E·A·S·I–Consult worked with Warner Burke, who had conducted research and developed a set of questions to measure learning agility. The *Burke Learning Agility Inventory*™ (LAI™) seemed like a critical addition to the TLP. It included assessment instruments, a platform to administer those assessments, and feedback reports. The Burke Learning Agility Inventory™ (Burke, 2019) consists of 38 questions measuring nine dimensions as described in Box H.1.

Box H.1 Dimensions of the Burke LAI™

1. **Flexibility**—Being open to new ideas and proposing new solutions.
2. **Speed**—Acting on ideas quickly so those not working are discarded and other possibilities are accelerated.
3. **Experimenting**—Trying out new behaviors (approaches, ideas) to determine what is effective.
4. **Performance Risk-Taking**—Seeking new activities (tasks, assignments, roles) that provide opportunities to be challenged.
5. **Interpersonal Risk-Taking**—Discussing differences with others in ways that lead to learning and change.
6. **Collaborating**—Finding ways to work with others that generate unique opportunities for learning.
7. **Information Gathering**—Using various methods to remain current in one's area of expertise.
8. **Feedback Seeking**—Asking others for feedback on one's ideas and overall performance.
9. **Reflecting**—Slowing down to evaluate one's own performance to be more effective.

Based on E·A·S·I–Consult's recommendation, both the Burke LAI™ and *Burke 360 Learning Agility Survey* (LAS) were incorporated into OSF's TLP. Participants received two different versions of the Burke during the 12-month TLP. The first time they received the Burke LAI™ results was at the beginning of the 12-month experience. During a 4-day Transformational Leadership (TL) Workshop, which occurred at the 6-month point in the

TLP, participants received the Burke 360 LAS. This 360 approach allowed for input from up to five perspectives, which typically consisted of self, boss, peers, and direct reports.

Each participant's feedback report was comprehensive and included the following five levels of ratings:

- Level 1—Overall (self-view vs. all others combined).
- Level 2—Dimension scores by perspective (self, boss, direct reports, etc.).
- Level 3—Aggregate scores (5 = highest, 1 = lowest; unrecognized strengths and blind spots).
- Level 4—By dimension by item by perspective.
- Level 5—Qualitative (open-ended) responses.

A graphic representation of the process is presented in Figure H.1.

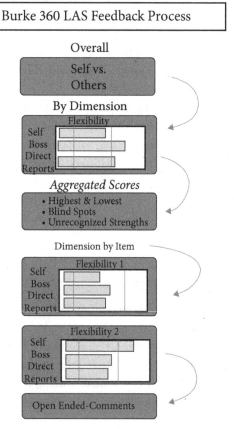

Figure H.1 Burke 360 Learning Agility Survey feedback process.

The *Burke 360 LAS* is the version of the Burke used in the 4-day TL Workshop that was part of the 12-month TLP. Box H.2 depicts a high-level overview of the 4-day TL Workshop and where the Burke 360 LAS fits.

Box H.2 Overview of Transformational Leadership Workshop

- **Day 1**. Burke 360 LAS
  - Organization Climate
  - Evening of Day 1: Write Learning Agility Critical Incidents
- **Day 2**. Learning Agility Critical Incidents Review in Small Groups
  - Leadership Styles
  - Transformational Competencies
- **Day 3**. Individual Integration Sessions
  - Decision Game Simulation
- **Day 4**. Individual Integration Session
  - Discuss Decision Game Results (Including Learning Agility)
  - Individual Goal Setting (Goals could include aspects of improving learning agility)

Workshop Day 1

Participants received their individual Burke 360 LAS results, consisting of the 23-page report. Participants received a learning journal or workbook designed to aid them with the process of capturing and distilling the data from their assessment. Two facilitators circulated among the 25 participants to answer questions. In many cases, the participant received information from others that was different from their self -perception. During the remaining 3 days of the program, participants had several opportunities to reconcile these differences and determine a plan forward.

On the evening of Day 1, following receipt of their feedback, participants were asked to write about four previous situations: (a) two examples of successfully dealing with an unfamiliar situation, not knowing what to do but figuring it out; and (b) two examples of unsuccessfully dealing with an unfamiliar situation and being unable to figure it out. In all four situations, they were asked to use the nine learning agility dimensions to help them reflect on those that had been used in the successful situations and could have been used in the unsuccessful situations.

Workshop Day 2

During Day 2 of the TLP workshop, participants worked in triads. First, one participant described his or her four situations and self-evaluation of the learning agility dimensions that were demonstrated or could have been demonstrated. The two other members of the triad were asked to listen and provide their evaluations of dimensions demonstrated or ones that could have been demonstrated. The purpose of this exercise was to give all participants further practice in recognizing when learning agility was being demonstrated in themselves and in others or when it could have been demonstrated and how.

At the end of Day 2, four to five participants volunteered to serve as team leaders for the following day's capstone simulation. The simulation guidelines also were explained to the team leaders: (a) The objective of the simulation was to make as much money as possible; (b) each team was expected to build and sell three different products across three rounds of the simulation; (c) there was a specific time period for building the products in each round of the simulation; (d) facilitators would only buy products that met the quality standards specified. After this briefing, leaders selected their teams one at a time using a draft system. Subsequently, they were free to do any preparation for the simulation that occurred on Day 3. Team leaders were encouraged to think about opportunities to use the nine dimensions of learning agility along with other concepts emphasized in the program (e.g., performance risk-taking, feedback seeking, or leadership style).

Workshop Day 3

On Day 3, the three rounds of the simulation were conducted. At the end of the simulation, team leaders were given a set of questions to evaluate their team's performance. Team members were also given a set of questions and asked to evaluate their leader based on the concepts of learning agility and other leadership focus areas. Evaluations were performed independently by leaders and team members. Next, the team leader and team members met, shared perspectives, and tried to reach consensus based on specific examples that led to their team's performance. Each of the teams then made a 5- to 10-minute presentation to the larger group on learning agility, other leadership focus areas, and how both impacted their team's performance positively and negatively. By the end of this large group discussion, participants could more clearly see how the use of learning agility can impact their performance, particularly in unfamiliar situations.

Workshop Day 4

During Day 4 (and end of Day 3), each participant was given the opportunity to meet individually with one of the facilitators for a 20-minute data integration session. The session was led by the participants and used to ask any questions about unresolved issues related to the assessment information they had received. From this discussion, it was hoped each of the participants would have identified one or two opportunities for their own improvement as a leader.

Finally, time was devoted to goal setting and the sharing of those goals. The expectation was that these were "on-the-job" changes the participant intended to make based on the information learned during the program. Participants were also given an overview of when they would be reconvening as a group going forward and what the focus of those follow-up sessions would be.

Postworkshop Sessions

Follow-up sessions occurred approximately every 2 months and were a half- to full-day sessions. Learning agility was the focus in each of the follow-up sessions. The purpose was to give participants time back at their job to try out the things they were trying to do differently to improve. The follow-up sessions were intended to "refresh" the content of learning agility and other leadership areas, as well as to discuss what was working and what was not working. Participants used their colleagues and the facilitators as resources to continue to improve their performance.

The Outcomes

Parallel Criterion Validity Research

Warner Burke and E·A·S·I–Consult have an ongoing commitment to conduct research related to the Burke assessments. OSF is also committed to research and volunteered the OSF TLP participants to be part of a criterion-related validation study using the Burke LAI™. In 2017, the Burke LAI™ was studied in relation to OSF leader performance measures. Data were collected as part of a leadership development program. The sample was comprised of midlevel and senior leaders at the organization, with data collected over a 5-month period (October 2016 to February 2017) and performance data collected from participants' supervisors in March 2017. This resulted in 74 participants with ratings on both the Burke LAI™ and supervisor ratings of performance.

Performance was measured using an eight-item survey completed by each participant's supervisor. The eight items were dimensions of performance, transformational leadership, results orientation, continuous learning, financial and operational performance, service orientation, service quality, and drives or enables growth and overall performance.

Correlations were computed to determine the relationship between the Burke LAI™ and the performance outcomes. We found that overall scores on the Burke LAI™ correlated significantly with the performance measure Results Orientation (driving aggressive goals to strategic targets) for midlevel and senior leaders ($r = 0.31, p < 0.01$). Similarly, the overall Burke LAI™ score correlated with Drives or Enables Growth ($r = 0.25, p < 0.05$). We observed that seven of the nine dimensions on the Burke LAI™ correlated with at least one of the eight leadership attributes used to evaluate leadership success (correlations ranged from $r = 0.23$ to $0.39; p < 0.05$ to $p < 0.01$). This led us to conclude that participants in this study who scored higher on the Burke LAI™ were better performers.

Other Outcomes

The following are other outcomes that resulted from the TLP:

Upon completion of the 4-day workshop, participants were thrust into the role of mentor, helping others in the organization interpret their own learning agility assessment data. This was based on the idea that the best way to learn something is to teach it to others.

- Participants who were seen by TLP facilitators as exemplars of learning agility were given the opportunity to teach others by sharing successes during leadership meetings or delivering a TED Talk type presentation in leadership forums.
- TLP participants were asked to facilitate a 40-member administrative group tasked with increasing productivity using learning agility dimensions.
- Project teams revised the structured interview questions used by the organization to select future team members to include questions assessing learning agility.
- TLP participants reported using learning agility items from the assessment to reframe questions to more effectively address problem-solving initiatives.

Lessons Learned

The following are some of the key lessons learned from developing and implementing the TLP at OSF Healthcare:

Assessment data (Burke 360 LAS) were critical to creating the dissonance needed for participants to change. Multirater (Burke 360 LAS) feedback was critical to participants' understanding how they were viewed differently by various stakeholders and that all perspectives were accurate. Moreover, when all multirater feedback ratings demonstrated agreement on a development area, it was harder for the participant to deny an issue existed. The qualitative data often provided "color commentary" supporting the quantitative data. The combination is much stronger than each piece individually.

It is important to acknowledge that real behavioral change takes time and requires ongoing reinforcement. Reinforcing approximations toward the desired behaviors increases the likelihood of eventual goal attainment. Having participants lead their own individual integration session on Day 3 and 4 of the TL Workshop required them to take ownership for their information and their own learning.

Reference

Burke, W. (2019). *Burke Learning Agility Inventory technical report*. St. Louis, MO: E·A·S·I–Consult.

Case Study I

Southeastern University, Free Methodist Church, and OneAccord

Learning Agility Starts at the Top

Robert B. McKenna, Daniel Hallak, Kent Ingle, Glen Prior, and Jeff Rogers

One of the most memorable conversations our WiLD Leaders team has ever had was with the CEO of a very large and well-known hospital. In the CEO's office, there was a floor–to-ceiling whiteboard listing the dozens of leadership development programs the hospital had put in place—the cost of which was in the millions of dollars. At some point, we asked the CEO if he used any of the programs on the whiteboard for himself. He quickly responded, "No." We then asked, "If you don't use them but you push them to other leaders, what are those programs to you?" He declared, "Noise." His response captured the critical reason why senior leaders investing in themselves is so important to the success of any effort designed to develop and to change other leaders.

Developing a learning agile culture takes guts because it means going be-yond the usual oversimplified and depersonalized solutions. A culture with learning agility requires truly pushing the limits. Becoming more learning agile as an organization is also anything but a short-term play. It is a long-term proposition requiring leaders who are willing, not only to press their people toward increased learning agility, but also to press themselves there. To the extent that learning agility is about learning to learn well and to the extent that learning is fundamentally about change, it requires us to step to-ward changes that some in organizations may not be willing to step toward.

As an organization deeply invested in developing whole leaders, we have seen the power of an intentional investment in developing a culture that supports learning agility. This case study is an overview of three separate organizations with whom WiLD Leaders has partnered. While the organizational contexts differ, the efforts in each of these organizations revolved around at least one common factor—a courageous leader at the top who was willing to ask the questions that are not typically asked. These are leaders who are not without flaws, but who brought a fundamental conviction about the importance of learning agility that has been critical in our work with their organizations.

Southeastern University—Learning Agility Is a Long-Play Proposition

Nearly a decade ago, we had the opportunity to work with the senior leadership team at Southeastern University (SEU) soon after the arrival of their new president, Dr. Kent Ingle. SEU was a university that had been on uncertain ground but now has a promising horizon. Prior to Kent taking the helm, the institution had been without a top leader for a prolonged period of time.

As with any organization, SEU experienced the challenge of developing leadership capacity for their next phase and in support of their strategic plan. A primary element of Kent's strategic vision was to build a football stadium—no small goal for a university of its size. Building a football stadium transcended athletics. Football represented a nexus of school pride; it was something for a community to rally around. The stadium and football team catalyzed a new vision that would forge a community identity, bringing together students, alumni, faculty, staff, parents, and donors. Actualizing the vision would cause systemic change and be met with a great deal of resistance, requiring learning agility—especially from the top leaders.

When Kent asked the WiLD Leaders team to come and work with his senior leadership, he asked an unforgettable question: "Can you make sure to push my senior leaders?" This question was energizing because we are at our best, and we know the opportunity is right, when we can push. Learning agility is about moving well; it takes practice and training to fine-tune agility in leaders. After several challenging multiday sessions with the leadership team, we did push. However, we were not very sure it went well. As members of the WiLD Leaders got on the plane to head back to Seattle after the last day with the Kent's leadership team, we were thinking, "We may have just broken their team. Did we do the job we were hired to do?"

Fast forward 8 years later. Two of the newer senior executives at SEU who were not on the team when we first engaged with the university came to Seattle to get a personalized tour of the system we had developed for building developmental capacity in leaders. At some point during their visit, it came up that I had worked with their team years before, and immediately one of them said, "We know about those meetings. Some of the things you prompted during your time with Dr. Ingle and the rest of the leadership team are still being talked about today."

More recently, our WiLD Leaders team returned to the SEU campus to work with other senior leaders and students across campus. Upon pulling up to the gate, we were immediately struck by the still new football stadium that now stands as a landmark at the university's entrance. In that moment, we were reminded that building a culture agile enough to do the impossible and navigate into large and seemingly unattainable goals requires people who are willing to change and leaders who are willing to ask the hard questions—and in this case, courageous enough to demand that everyone be pushed. This was not pushed with the intent of pushing them out, but pushed with the intent of becoming more willing to stretch into possibilities.

It was not only the football stadium that was an obvious indicator of the shift toward a more learning agile organization, but also the people and, more specifically, people willing to change and to learn and grow. SEU has a president who is willing to ask the hard questions and willing to stand strong in the space between knowing and learning—the place where questions may supersede the answers. As Dr. Ingle said, "Opposition is an opportunity to step up our leadership." He is a leader who lives by these words and is committed to being agile as he encourages it in others.

Reflections of Dr. Kent Ingle, Southeastern University President

"Developing learning agility starts with listening. Learning agility always starts with positioning yourself and organization to consistently solicit and focus on feedback of all types. Until we do our job as listeners, we cannot shape our roles as leaders. When we developed our football program, we took the time to listen to our constituents, which made our time pushing on our leadership team more impactful. Our team at the time needed to develop personal contextual awareness to recognize how important this change would be for our organization. This time with our team taught us the significant value of developing a learning agile culture. This culture has unlocked a world of possibilities for our organization."

Free Methodist Church—Learning Agility Requires Asking the Difficult Questions

Along with Charles Latchison and Fraser Ventner, Glen Prior is an entrepreneur, businessperson, and superintendent for a region of a denominational church known as the Free Methodist Church in Southern California. Before any of us minimize the organizational complexity of a denominational church, realize that Glen is leading one of the most organizationally complex environments imaginable. Maintaining the missional meaning of an ecosystem of dozens of independent yet aligned churches while also ensuring their economic viability is a huge task.

When Superintendent Prior first encountered the WiLD Leaders approach to developing whole leaders, he asked a loaded question: "If I use your system for developing whole leaders in my organization, will some of my people leave?" What a question! It was one of those situations where we knew the true answer and yet also knew the answer many leaders would expect. We chose to speak the truth: "Yes, some will leave. The wrong people will leave to the right places and the right people will stay with greater purpose." We recognized that we were the right consultants when he responded, "Good!"

While Glen's response could be seen as flippant and uncaring, as consultants we knew what he meant, and he knew what we were going to challenge in his leaders. If his leaders were not willing to ask the hard questions that are the roots of development, they would likely self-navigate out toward jobs and organizations that would make them more comfortable. You see, in our minds, building learning agility requires leaders who are willing to be invested in their own learning agility and who are developmentally ready to challenge themselves just as much as they challenge others.

We are not overemphasizing selection over development, but building a learning agile culture (especially one from scratch) requires leaders who are willing to stretch, to learn, and to change—even if it might hurt a little. Like Kent, Glen was fully aware that developing whole leaders and building a learning agile culture is a long play and may take some pruning on the part of the organization and the leaders who may or may not stay. It is not a callous way to think about people ready for development. Rather, it is a more honest way in seasons where learning agility is going to be the key.

Reflections of Glen Prior, Superintendent, Free Methodist Church

"Looking back over my experience pressing into learning agility, one thing stands out above the rest—the magic is in the process. There is no magic bullet. The leader must lead. There are many tools and plans on the market to help teams break through or move past a tipping point, or rally in some way for the purpose of achieving a preferred future. In my experience, the magic is in the process, not the tools. As a leader, there are some things I can accomplish by edict. For example, I can insist that people do a task, come to a meeting, or engage in a process. But unless I am fully engaged myself with the group in an open, honest, and vulnerable process, the results will only go as far as demand can dictate—and that is not far in an organization.

Having decided from the start to experience everything with our leaders together, I have seen dynamic results in individuals more than groups. When individuals awaken to their gifts and talents and are able to connect to a larger and more meaningful purpose, their influence is multiplied. Participating with them in the process of discovery has given me more opportunities to have clarifying conversations that allow me to move more quickly to adjust their roles and responsibilities, and even to counsel some of them toward other opportunities that would excite them or be a better fit. Being clear with the expectations up front, fully participating as the leader to both model and discover things I might not otherwise see, and quickly following up with individuals as they have moments of insight is creating a team with clarity of mission, purpose, and belonging".

OneAccord—Developing Agility Starts at the Very Top

Several years ago, our team met one of the most well-networked and humble business leaders imaginable. Jeff Rogers is the founder of OneAccord in

Seattle, Washington, with an investment arm known as Solomon's Fund. As a private equity firm, the vision is long term. OneAccord acquires and holds companies to grow them, with a focus on preserving and expanding the legacy of the previous owner(s) and bringing about strong returns for their investors over time.

One of the greatest tensions organizations face is the challenge of establishing systems to drive organizational effectiveness and efficiency while at the same time caring deeply about the people in the organization. As Jeff said, "We believe in absolute truth and absolute compassion." While those words could be written in any business journal as words of the day, the reality of doing business well and for the sake of the people is a very real challenge. The reality for Jeff and his firm is that acquiring successful legacy businesses is a complex leadership challenge, requiring leaders—indeed, teams of leaders—who are willing to change and shift their mindsets quickly. While learning agility in a complex multiorganizational reality is challenging, it is critical if organizations want to build sustainable and agile cultures for the future.

What was most interesting in our work with OneAccord as a business entity was that they were willing to put several CEOs through a systemic and long-term leader development process, including Jeff (the chairman) and Scott (the CEO of the fund). We also had an opportunity to work with the group of CEOs from Solomon's Fund, all of whom run businesses in the portfolio. In this case, the opportunity was to invest in the senior leaders first, living the reality that creating learning agile cultures must start at the top.

Jeff realized very quickly these senior leaders still needed his investment in them. Just because they had vast experience did not mean they did not need support. On the contrary, the greater the agility required in the role, the greater the support for learning that is necessary. If the most senior leaders are unwilling to invest in themselves, how can they invest in others? Having Jeff involved as a participant changed the tone of the development efforts as he was growing and learning right alongside his leaders. It moved him from looking *at* his people to looking *with* his people.

Reflections of Jeff Rogers, Founder, OneAccord

"If part of agility is a leader asking questions, then one of the questions that led OneAccord to leverage a whole approach focused on developing experienced leaders was this: Do seasoned, values-aligned, well trained leaders deserve continued investment? What causes someone to be attracted—and remain with—an organization? We found that more than any other attribute—more than compensation, advancement, or location—is personal growth.

For OneAccord, having a solid platform, built on time-tested values, with a program that works across multiple industries is key. With several different businesses, we are responsible to steward—for the good of the employees, our customers, and our investors—finding a solution that can be used by every leader, and in turn their management teams gives a competitive advantage.

Sharing a common language which provides the ability to cross-train amongst organizations was also important. Business is challenging and sometimes pretty messy, requiring us to pivot, and even pivot on the pivot, especially as it pertains to leadership. Decisiveness needs to be based on principles—not emotion; having leaders who make decisions aligned with values and competency doesn't happen without intentionality."

Lessons Learned

No matter the industry or business sector, a mission and a strategy do not advance without agile leaders. Every leader we speak with describes the environments in which they operate with words such as dynamic, fast paced, changing, uncertain, ambiguous, and volatile. For example, how many times have you heard or read that we live in a VUCA (volatile, uncertain, complex, and ambiguous) world? While the contexts differ, the need for learning agility has never been greater. In all three organizations described in this case study, the common factor is a leader at the top who is courageous enough to see learning agility as a long- term play that will shake up and disrupt leaders—sometimes to their very core.

Whether an organization is building a football stadium, investing deeply in leaders who may or may not stay, or responding to volatile conditions, it is critical for top leaders to consider their own willingness to develop learning agility in themselves alongside other leaders. There were three lessons we took away from these different situations: First, building a learning agile culture is a long play—requiring a perspective that may span several years (but starts in the present). Second, building learning agile cultures requires asking the harder questions, and harder questions will always be challenging for some. And finally, building learning agility within an organization is more than a momentary and comfortable process. It is about learning to learn along with a willingness to keep learning, which starts at the very top of the organization.

Case Study J

Johnson & Johnson

The 134–Year-Old Start-Up

Miriam Nelson, Sarah Brock, and Kevin Hedman

In 1886, many of the advances we take for granted today were beyond most people's imaginations. If people and organizations today are hindered by an ability to adapt to big data and artificial intelligence, back in the late nineteenth century our progress was threatened by even more fundamental and daunting obstacles. Back then, the transformative new ideas revolved around sterility and sepsis, and the innovators of the time were focused on protecting society against infection, bacteria, and unsanitary conditions.

Johnson & Johnson (J&J), of course, was instrumental in bringing Lister's and Pasteur's breakthroughs into countless operating rooms, doctors' offices, and homes. Since then, the company has grown into one of the world's largest corporations. It has a long history of success that today's Amazons and Googles can only dream of. As can be seen in Table 1.2 in Chapter 1, J&J is 1 of only 52 companies listed in *both* the 1955 and 2020 Fortune 500 rankings.

In a book about organizational *endurance*, J&J would also be a vital case study. The company has thrived over an extended period of time during which both the business world and the healthcare field have shifted profoundly. The company's credo has given it a "true north" that has helped it persevere with focus, clarity, and dedication in a constantly changing world. This credo includes the statement, "We must experiment with new ideas," suggesting the company has always understood that innovation will be a critical ingredient to its success. But what about agility? How does a company with a long history and a vast footprint learn to pivot quickly?

At J&J, cultivating learning agile leaders is a constant topic of conversation among talent management professionals and top executives. To a large extent, it has been provoked by the upheavals in the healthcare world. The company is faced with the complexities of global patient access, an intense competitive landscape, and an unprecedented proliferation of data. At the same time, new treatments promise to make a real impact in millions of people's lives, provided science remains at the center of organizational decision-making.

Much like antiseptic practices and equipment have made modern surgery possible, agility is seen as fundamental to navigating the current environment and unlocking future value. Within J&J, conversations are framed as the need to operate not as a venerable, long-standing, and massive corporation, but rather as a nimble, entrepreneurial enterprise. J&J aspires to be the rarest of companies—a 134–year-old start-up.

What Was Done

To this end, J&J continues to think deeply about how learning agility can be brought into the company, instilled at all levels, and enshrined in decision-making practices. This encompasses everyone from the newest employee (who has likely been hired for a combination of both expertise and agility in working across boundaries) to the most senior executives (who are charged with ensuring the creative abilities of teams can be channeled in the most promising directions). It also encompasses both simple decisions (like how many meetings to hold on a topic) and critically complex matters of strategy (e.g., which acquisitions to pursue). Thus, learning agility at J&J has individual, leadership, and company-wide components. In this case study, we consider some specific examples of agility in two main categories: (a) team/organizational and (b) individual/leadership.

Team and Organizational Agility

With many diverse businesses operating within each of its three major segments, J&J is characterized by an intricate matrix of product lines, functions, regions, and roles. This structure could easily lead to a culture where slow bureaucracy takes the place of nimble, decisive action. The company is sensitive to this challenge and has made it a priority to ensure a complex organization can also be an agile organization. To accomplish it, J&J has taken steps to ensure that learning agility is embedded as an actual management habit. The organization has found success at treating agile leadership as a core criteria, alongside other long-standing priorities ranging from patient safety to financial prudence. The idea is to move from studying agility to putting it into practice. It involves removing obstacles, streamlining decision-making protocols, and creating a culture where people can act without consensus or full certainty.

One way the company has unlocked agility is by studying how acquired companies do things. If a business has reached a point where J&J is considering acquisition, it has most likely already accomplished great things. If it has done great things, it probably has a culture that encourages experimentation and risk even when stakes are high and quality is king. J&J has made it a priority to study these cultures—the decision-making rights and the entrepreneurial methodologies—as part of its acquisition process. This approach helps to ensure the subsequent integration does not stifle what had made the acquisition so compelling in the first place. This ideally gives, i the new company reach and resources rather than adding additional layers of bureaucracy. It also helps give J&J ideas for how the agile learning, brainstorming, risk-taking, and innovation practices of successful smaller businesses can be adapted and unleashed within a massive global corporation.

Another way J&J has brought learning agility to the forefront of decision-making can be seen in its successful efforts to increase speed by placing the patient at the center of decision-making. Although it sounds simple, drug, device, and treatment development are anything but simple. Vast amounts of money must be spent. Pools of highly specialized talent must be deployed. High regulatory hurdles must be crossed. A thousand factors must be met at a level of precision that does not necessarily leave a lot of room for flexibility.

The company's entry into CAR-T cancer therapy provides an example of how learning agility can exist in harmony with exactitude. CAR-T refers to a promising new treatment in which patients' own cells are modified and reinfused, not only to fight existing cancer cells but also to help prevent their recurrence. Once J&J decided to invest in this area, a cross-functional team was quickly formed and empowered to make major decisions. Team members had the support of senior management and were given the opportunity to learn by taking risks and drawing on resources, provided the paramount considerations were patient safety and cost-efficient care. While the treatment itself is still in its early stages, J&J's strategy has already shown some impressive results. Four manufacturing facilities were set up in just 18 months, as opposed to the typical 2–3 years. Moreover, the team was able to drive down product costs per patient by nearly 50%—for therapies that currently cost many thousands of dollars, this reduction makes a huge difference.

For the consumer segment, similar changes are unfolding. In the United States, this division has adopted an agile operating model as part of its global transformation. Much of this effort involves recentering teams on what is most important—the customer. Teams closest to customers have been given the autonomy to make quick decisions, about both product innovation and business model changes. There is also a push to eliminate repetitive and less necessary tasks, enabling employees to focus on doing the things that will make a difference for the people J&J serves. It has led to more rapid execution as well as helped spur a culture of experimentation and learning, rather than one where certainty and consensus are prerequisites for action.

Individual and Leadership Agility

If J&J's efforts to become an agile organization are still in progress, that is in large part because it is still cultivating a learning agile workforce. This transition includes two dimensions, both seen as equally important. The first is the whole employee population; the second is those in the leadership ranks. Both need to be agile for the organization to have any chance of being so. It means learning agility needs to be at the center of the company's entire talent philosophy (i.e., from the first interview a promising college recruit has with the company to the selection of its most senior executives).

As learning agility becomes more central to the company, it is becoming increasingly important to new employees. Occupational expectations have changed for incoming generations. While in the past, job security or a reliable career path might have been top of mind, Millennials tend to crave diverse experiences and embrace varied responsibilities. J&J's internal surveys of millennial employees provides support for this view. A survey of 9,000 of them showed that prospects of career advancement and enrichment were a major motivation and retention factor. In essence, they believe their need for diverse experience would be met in a broadly based healthcare company with many different avenues available to them.

To retain, engage, and develop its newer employees, J&J has launched an "early-in-career" development agenda. The different components of this program are designed with the different dimensions of learning agility in mind. Participants gain access to different types of responsibilities and are given a chance to try new things. This approach builds breadth of perspective and stretches their skill set. At the same time, they are encouraged to reflect on their core purpose while working in "learning pods" that facilitate cross-functional interconnectedness. The aim is to stretch these new employees intellectually while enabling them to collaborate across boundaries, exercising the different "muscles" needed for them to emerge as fully learning agile leaders.

Feedback about this program has been positive. It receives very high scores from participants, with 87% of participants rating it as "extremely positive." The data indicate they enjoy the opportunity to work with leaders in different areas, as well as the chance to take on new experiences in a safe environment. Overall, 93% believe it contributed significantly to their development, and over 90% of their managers saw growth in those who participated in the program. While it is too soon to conclude whether these early developmental activities will correspond with heightened learning agility as these young participants reach the pinnacles of their careers, early indications are promising.

The "Talent Marketplace" is another idea J&J has launched to both fuel agility and enhance people's career development. This program was launched as part of the company's broader talent strategy in emerging markets and has initially encompassed a cohort of several hundred HR and consumer team members in China. These individuals access the Talent Marketplace to "bid" for a place on projects that are interesting to them and will provide opportunities for new learning experiences. The Talent Marketplace gives people the ability to own their development and contribute more widely, as well as an opportunity to learn from new experiences.

J&J has made strides in giving employees access to a wide variety of learning experiences, believing it is core to developing learning agility on both an individual and an organizational level. Likewise, the company has been assessing people through a framework that centers on learning agility, partnering with Korn Ferry to build a custom approach. For many years, the two organizations have worked together to ensure a robust exploration of participants' learning agility is a core component of assessments for succession, selection, and development.

J&J uses assessment for several different purposes (e.g., selecting senior leaders, developing high potentials). Consequently, it makes use of multiple methodologies and tools depending on the organization's need. For instance, some assessments involve custom simulation "day in the life of an executive" exercises, while others use a more streamlined approach that involves a behavioral interview and a battery of assessment tests. Regardless of the

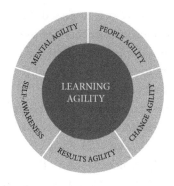

Mental agility – Ability to examine problems in new, unusual ways

People agility – Skilled communicator who can work with diverse types of people

Change agility – Likes to experiment and comfortable with change

Results agility – Delivers results in challenging, first-time situations

Situational self-awareness – Extent to which individuals know their impact on situations (as well as the impact situations are having on them).

Figure J.1 Learning agility model.

model used, all these assessments involve proprietary Korn Ferry tools that measure learning agility via psychometric tests based on the model depicted in Figure J.1.

Many thousands of these assessments have been taken, permitting Korn Ferry and J&J to investigate, understand, and act on robust data that indicate where leaders are most agile as well as what areas require further investment and development.

In the China cohort mentioned, these assessments have indicated most participants in the Talent Marketplace are quick to learn, adept at forming networks, and keen to engage others in their efforts. In terms of the learning agility model depicted in Figure J.1, they score well with respect to mental agility and people agility. In contrast, they may be more cautious about trying new ideas or embracing risky options. They tend to be less change agile in other words. With this insight in mind, J&J can pinpoint development programs accordingly. Appropriate development experiences provide opportunities to take risks as well as access to creative ideas. Creative mentors can be assigned and the appropriate training programs tailored to group needs. The learning agility assessment allows J&J to do a deep dive into the barriers to learning and innovation that exist among and across teams and determine how best to remove them. In a few years' time, we can reassess these individuals to determine whether their learning agility has grown along with their careers.

As the company examines, engages, and supports its new talent with the aim of helping them become more learning agile, J&J also has invested considerable energy measuring the agility of its senior leaders. In partnership with Korn Ferry, more than 800 senior leaders have been assessed through various means. Multiple forms of senior leader assessments are used by J&J (e.g., consultant-led competency interview, psychometric testing, simulations, and 360-degree surveys), depending on the purpose of the assessment. All of these assessments include a focus on learning agility.

Because learning agility is *reflected* in specific behaviors, psychometric testing using Korn Ferry tools was determined to be the best assessment approach to isolate learning agility. While 360-degree feedback data, for example, can give a good picture of how the person operates in their current role, it cannot fully capture the underlying agilities within their personality profile. However, other assessment elements can illuminate the context within which the individual does or does not show learning agility. For instance, if an assessment reveals high underlying learning agility, yet an analysis of their past experience suggests their prior roles have not yet involved a strong innovation component, this finding can help guide recommendations about the ideal future trajectory for this person.

The Outcomes

So far, the results have shown senior leaders are typically learning agile in some ways but have opportunities to improve in others. As a whole, these executives demonstrate high levels of mental agility. They also have the interpersonal and intercultural agility needed to operate effectively across global boundaries and win the trust of diverse teams. Interestingly, the assessments show they are similar to the early career talent, in that they are less change agile. They tend to be more cautious about taking risks, even though their agile thinking usually renders them quite deft at appreciating the benefits of innovation at a conceptual level.

These findings indicate the importance of building learning agility capabilities early, so that new talent can gain confidence and comfort with taking risks later in their careers. It also illustrates a need to think carefully about what must be done to build a risk-friendly and enterprising environment when many at the highest leadership levels may not be very comfortable with it. Talent conversations and executive discussions about agility at J&J often revolve around how to remove the barriers to being bold, stretching others' ability to act as change agents without compromising what is essential to the organization and its customers.

Hiring different types of talent, assessing for learning agility, incentivizing innovation, minimizing bureaucracy, diversifying people's experiences, establishing greater connectivity, and regularly measuring outcomes all are important pieces in the agility puzzle at J&J. The company's developmental efforts involve many different activities, but they typically have the concept of learning agility as a critical component. Coaches and mentors are enlisted to help leaders build the people agility needed to work across a daunting, complex matrix of reporting relationships, business lines, and functional groups. Next, career steps are tailored to help people stretch their results agility, such as placing a promising executive who has always delivered on clear mandates into a position where objectives are less well defined and the meaning of success is ambiguous.

In terms of selection and promotion, J&J talent and hiring managers consider the agility requirements of the role alongside its business demands. Does the position call for a change agent? A gifted diplomat? An intense driver? An inspirational visionary? Most leadership roles require someone who can be learning agile in multiple ways, and J&J can consider the ideal mix and tailor it to their assessment of candidates. Subsequently, this information can be used to give an edge to the candidate who has all the vital agilities, but lacks some of the expected experiences over another a candidate who might have all the requisite expertise but shows less of the needed agility.

Lessons Learned

J&J's efforts to embed learning agility into a large, complex, and global organization have been ongoing for years. The company has discovered ways to make the benefits of agility known to the wider organization and—ultimately—embraced by its business leaders. While it may not always be possible to quantify the importance of learning agility, it *is* necessary to translate it into the language of organizational stakeholders. If an executive needs to strategize an innovation agenda, how does having high mental agility equip him or her to do that? J&J's talent leadership wants to directly connect agility to the factors that matter to the organization, as well as the factors that matter to its people.

Concurrently, the talent management team has been learning how to scale new ideas to the scope required within a company of J&J's size and reach. The

Talent Marketplace discussed previously began as a small prototype launched with a focus on providing great learning experiences to its participants. As J&J considers how to build on its initial successes, it is learning the processes needed to turn a good idea into a versatile, repeatable one.

Accountability measures are an area where lessons and standards are important, but still emerging. If learning agility is a precious resource for an organization—and if it can be measured with reasonable accuracy—then it stands to reason that leaders can be accountable for instilling it in their talent and in their organizations. However, it is not yet apparent how best to approach this question. If viewed as similar to any personal attribute that might be viewed as desirable (e.g., intelligence, empathy, agreeableness, determination), learning agility encounters the same dilemma of all those characteristics. They can manifest themselves in wildly different ways depending on the individual and his or her context. A highly intelligent person can solve the company's most vexing problems or he or she could write inscrutable philosophical treatises on company time. An empathetic colleague could be a great source of support during tough times or he or she could avoid making the hard decisions that might upset others.

Likewise, a learning agile leader could be the bold, inspiring voice who guides the team through uncertain waters. He or she also could be the impossible dreamer who gets everyone excited about fuzzy new ideas that come to nothing. J&J has been active about ensuring learning agility is central to their assessments, but they also ensure each assessment takes into account multiple other elements that can be equally important. The company has a strong and consistent competency model that can be used to determine whether people's learning agility is manifesting itself in the right leadership behaviors. It also recognizes the paramount value of track record. While experience isn't everything, a demonstrable history of showing the necessary skills and delivering the strong results speaks for itself. In other words, J&J has learned that an integrated assessment and development approach is necessary; however, it is one that focuses on the whole person rather than tries to fit everyone into a single schema.

If J&J is successful at inculcating agility at all levels and in all segments, it will not necessarily be a huge departure for the company. Companies with endurance have always been agile. No business reaches its 134th birthday without being able to change with the times. It is why it is challenging to paint a precise picture of what a "more agile J&J" will look like. The nature of agility itself precludes it. Agility is not about having a firm, fully defined vision the company must reach regardless of upheavals in the market and radical transformations of the global healthcare industry. Rather, it is more about being resolute in purpose and adaptable about everything else.

Index